1986 YEARBOOK
EVENTS OF 1985

FUNK & WAGNALLS NEW ENCYCLOPEDIA 1986 YEARBOOK

LEON L. BRAM
Vice-President and
Editorial Director

NORMA H. DICKEY
Editor in Chief

Funk & Wagnalls, Inc.

Publishers since 1876

CONTENTS

MEMBERS OF THE STAFF

FOREWORD: THE EVENTS OF 1985

The year 1985 was marked by terrorism and tragedy. In the Mediterranean, particularly, militants connected with various Palestinian and fundamentalist factions in the Byzantine politics of the Mideast staged a series of terrorist incidents. A TWA jet was hijacked and eventually flown to Lebanon, where 39 Americans were held hostage. An Italian cruise ship was taken over by terrorists. Sixty people died in the hijacking of an Egyptian airliner. And terrorists launched bloody attacks at airports in Rome and Vienna, killing 16. Among serious natural disasters, there was a devastating earthquake in Mexico and a massive volcanic eruption in Colombia. In South Africa, another sort of tragedy was being played out, as racial strife intensified.

Despite the tragedy and unrest, there were signs of promise. The famine in Africa eased thanks to improving weather conditions and large-scale emergency food shipments; rock musicians staged spectacular fund-raising concerts in an effort to help. In the United States the economy was growing, though rather slowly, and inflation was under control, but the soaring budget and trade deficits caused serious concern. During November, President Ronald Reagan and Soviet leader Mikhail Gorbachev, who had come to power ear-lier in the year, met for talks in Geneva; though they reached little substantive agreement on arms control, they were hailed for having taken a step toward easing international tensions.

It was a year of anniversaries—among them the 40th anniversary of the end of World War II and the founding of the United Nations, the 50th anniversary of the U.S. social security system, and the 300th anniversary of the births of Bach, Handel, and Scarlatti.

It was also the year Coca-Cola changed its formula—but had to backtrack and reissue "Coca-Cola Classic"; Miami Vice took fire on TV; and Pete Rose broke Ty Cobb's record for most career hits.

A temporary breakdown in the St. Lawrence Seaway focused attention on the vast inland waterway shared by the United States and Canada; this gateway to the North American heartland is described in the first feature article, on the Great Lakes. A second article profiles those sporting daredevils who, for some reason, find fun in feats that would give other people nightmares. A third feature article, marking the 25th anniversary of the world's first weather satellite, explains how satellites and other high-tech innovations have made weather forecasting better than ever.   THE EDITORS

The Great Lakes

by JAMES L. KERWIN

James L. Kerwin is environment editor and feature writer for the Detroit News. He has received conservation awards from the U.S. Environmental Protection Agency and the Michigan Outdoor Writers Association.

As it slowly crunched and gouged its way down the continent, North America's last massive glacier created a chain of interconnected inland seas that were to play a key role in the development of a vast region rich in natural resources. The Great Lakes—and their link to the Atlantic Ocean, the St. Lawrence River—came to serve as the gateway to the North American heartland. This huge waterway, straddling the peaceful border between the United States and Canada, has been a vital transportation route for exploration and trade, a food pantry, a source of immeasurable pleasure, and a priceless reserve of fresh water.

Lifeblood to a Region

The Great Lakes watershed is home to 45 million residents and a variety of industries in parts of the Canadian province of Ontario and eight U.S. states—Minnesota, Wisconsin, Illinois, Indiana, Michigan, Ohio, Pennsylvania, and New York. The five lakes—Superior, Michigan, Huron, Erie, and Ontario—linked by rivers and canals and emptying through the St. Lawrence into the Atlantic, are the lifeblood of the region. They supply drinking water (at relatively cheap rates) to an estimated 26 million people and bring needed water to a proliferation of industrial plants. The lakes system also produces prodigious amounts of hydroelectric power for homes and industries, and scores of coal-burning or nuclear power plants draw their cooling water from the Great Lakes.

Canals at Sault Ste. Marie linking Lakes Superior and Huron.

8

The lakes play a key role in the climate of the region. They absorb heat in spring and summer and release it into the atmosphere in fall and winter, thus tempering extremes of the seasons. This warming "lake effect" has spawned several "fruit belts," where orchards and vineyards thrive.

Today, light industry is replacing some of the area's heavy manufacturing, which has been undercut by foreign imports. But new waterfront industrial developments have sprung up, taking advantage of renovated water supply systems, cheaper water rates, and savings in maintenance due to the low mineral content of lake water.

The inland waterway formed by the Great Lakes and the St. Lawrence River was largely responsible for the region's development as an industrial and agricultural center in the first place, and it continues to serve as an important artery for commerce and transportation. Over the years, the waterway itself has been gradually improved for navigation—especially by the building of canals and locks to bypass waterfalls and overcome a total drop of 600 feet from Lake Superior to the sea. In 1959 the United States and Canada completed the final link—a $446 million project clearing the way through 180 miles of rapids on the St. Lawrence to open the entire waterway to medium-sized oceangoing vessels. This stretch of water from Montréal upstream to Lake Ontario is known as the St. Lawrence Seaway. (Often

Vessels like the 1,000-foot ore carrier shown below transport iron ore from the western shores of Lake Superior to ports in the industrial Midwest.

The enormous inland waterway formed by the five Great Lakes and the St. Lawrence River is the lifeblood for some 45 million people and a vast array of industries.

the same term is used to designate a wider area, sometimes the whole continuous route from the western shores of Lake Superior to the mouth of the St. Lawrence.) The long, narrow Great Lakes ore boats known as lakers—or simply as "boats" in the parlance of the region—carry close to 200 million tons each year of grain, iron ore, coal, and other products between ports on the inland waterway. At the same time, "salties," as oceangoing vessels are called, carry the region's products to far-flung ports abroad.

Magnet for Tourism

Tourism is big business in the Great Lakes region, with expenditures of $8 billion to $15 billion a year attributed directly to activities along the coastline. Thousands of miles of sand beaches and summer cottages dot the shores. Succulent types of panfish, lake trout, implanted coho and chinook salmon, and the elusive muskellunge lure anglers to the lakes. Pleasure boats ranging from makeshift fishing rafts to opulent yachts and racing schooners ply the lakes and their tributaries. No other region in the North American continent provides such easy access to so many different waterways for so many people.

In addition to scenic coastlines, the lakes contain thousands of islands, so many that there never has been an accurate count. Some are merely rock outcroppings

or sandbars barely showing above the surface of the water. Others are more substantial. Manitoulin Island, in the wide waters of Georgian Bay in northern Lake Huron, is the world's largest island in fresh water; it is strewn with over 100 lakes filled with trout, pickerel, and many types of panfish.

A Profile of the Lakes

The Great Lakes system generally drains from west to east, emptying into the Atlantic. At 602 feet above sea level, the westernmost lake, Superior, is the highest in altitude. It is also the largest freshwater lake in the world. Superior's rocky, tree-lined shore was the setting for Longfellow's *Song of Hiawatha;* according to the poem, Indians called the lake "Gitchee Gumee," which means "Big Sea Water." The lake's deep, chilling waters have preserved fascinating shipwrecks from the late 19th and early 20th centuries; divers can investigate these wrecks today in Isle Royale National Park, just below the U.S.-Canadian border.

Water emptying from Lake Superior descends through the St. Marys River to Lake Huron, the second-biggest of the Great Lakes and the fifth-largest lake in the world. Much of its shoreline is dotted with summer homes, on both the U.S. and the Canadian sides. It is joined by the Straits of Mackinac to Lake Michigan, the

only Great Lake lying entirely in the United States. Ranked sixth among the world's lakes, Michigan is long, but relatively narrow, rather like a huge cul de sac, with water flowing in and out naturally only at the northern end. The Chicago Sanitary and Ship Canal, an artificial diversion completed in 1900, allows water from Lake Michigan to drain into the Mississippi (through the Illinois River); this drainage canal was built to combat pollution in the lake, which nevertheless remains a serious problem.

Lake Huron water flows into Lake Erie through the St. Clair River, Lake St. Clair, and the Detroit River. Erie ranks 12th in area among the world's lakes and is actually longer than Lake Huron, but it is only 50–60 feet deep over much of its western section. It drains through the Niagara River and world-famous Niagara Falls into Lake Ontario, smallest of the Great Lakes.

Floods and Storms

Normally, the lakes' water levels rise and fall in moderate cycles. But because of abnormal precipitation, levels rose sharply in the early 1970's and have climbed sharply again during the past several years. In 1973 the populous southeast coast of Michigan's Lower Peninsula suffered more than $24 million in damages when stiff east winds across Lakes

Pictured Rocks National Lakeshore, above, on Lake Superior's southern shore, and Indiana Dunes National Lakeshore, below, which stretches along Lake Michigan, are two of the region's most popular scenic and recreational spots.

13

Bountiful grape harvests in Canada's Niagara region are made possible by Great Lakes waters, which absorb heat in the spring and summer and release it into the atmosphere in winter, exercising a moderating effect on the climate.

Erie and St. Clair sent water surging as far as a mile inland. The U.S. Army Corps of Engineers subsequently erected more than 100 miles of protective dikes in an effort to prevent additional heavy damage. In 1985 water reached new record levels—nearly 3 feet above normal in some areas—raising fears of renewed flooding.

A key problem is that the largest lakes in the system (Superior, Huron, and Michigan) are at the top, the smallest at the bottom, with narrow channels connecting the lakes. Widening these channels to carry excess water and help prevent flooding has been suggested. But researchers for the Army Corps of Engineers say shorelines that would be affected are too built-up.

Another problem posed by nature involves the sporadic severe storms on the lakes, which have caused the loss of more than 1,500 vessels and thousands of crew and passengers over the years. Many of the disappearances are shrouded in mystery: the craft never reaches port, and no trace of the wreckage is found. The most notable gale occurred in November 1913, when ten lake vessels laden with ore, lumber, and grain sank with a loss of more than 200 lives.

Explorers and Trappers

In the 16th century the French were the first Europeans to explore and settle the Great Lakes and St. Lawrence region. Some of the earliest explorers were in search of a new route to the Orient—among them Jacques Cartier, who in 1535–1536 discovered the St. Lawrence River and navigated upstream as far as present-day Montréal.

It was primarily the prospect of a lucrative fur trade that attracted the later explorers. By around 1615 both Étienne Brulé and Samuel de Champlain had apparently explored the wilderness shoreline of Lakes Ontario and Huron. Missionaries such as Father Jacques Marquette later joined with the trappers and traders in exploring the entire region by canoe, while seeking to convert the Indians to Christianity.

The first large ship known to sail the Great Lakes, the *Griffon*, was built and launched above Niagara Falls in 1679 by the French explorer La Salle. Sailing across the Great Lakes and into Green Bay, on the western shore of Lake Michigan, he is said to have aroused fear in many of the local Indians, who saw the vessel as a sign of the white man's awesome power. After leaving the *Griffon* at Green Bay, loaded with furs, La Salle and a

This 1814 engraving depicts the
United States victory over
British forces in the historic
battle for control of Lake Erie
on September 10, 1813.

few companions went on a further journey by canoe;
the *Griffon* itself was never heard from again, and its
remains have never been found.

The fur trade was one of the colonial prizes fought
over by the British and the French during the French
and Indian War; by the war's end in 1763, Britain had
wrested control of the Great Lakes region and its
lucrative fur trade from France. The region was again a
battleground during the War of 1812. In a major naval
battle of that war, British forces attacked the American
fleet on Lake Erie in September 1813. The U.S.
commander, Oliver Hazard Perry, though his flagship
was nearly destroyed, took but 15 minutes to rout the
British and win control of the lake; he sent a famous,

*Mackinac Island, once an Indian
meeting ground and fur trading
post, is now a fashionable
resort. Motor vehicles are
banned on the island.*

Thunder Bay, Ont., site of the world's largest grain elevator (above), is the biggest wheat-shipping port in the world.

terse message to the commander of American land forces: "We have met the enemy and they are ours."

In the first half of the 19th century, the merchant and fur trader John Jacob Astor established a major fortress and trading center at Mackinac Island. Today one can view his home and the early trading post on this historic island, where motor vehicles are banned and transportation is still by carriage or by foot.

Shipping, Past and Present

During the 19th century, rich forests and fertile land attracted a growing population to the Great Lakes region. The lakes themselves had become a busy inland seaway even before the Civil War, with schooners carrying supplies of white pine from Michigan to Chicago and other burgeoning lakeshore communities. By midcentury agricultural products, too, were being moved by ship to towns that grew into major cities—including Duluth, Milwaukee, Detroit, Cleveland, Buffalo, and Toronto, as well as Chicago.

During the 20th century, the population of the Great Lakes region continued to expand as industry grew. Further improvements were made in the waterway to increase its potential for shipping. Among these was the completion in 1932 of the new Welland Ship Canal between Lake Ontario and Lake Erie. Completion of the St. Lawrence Seaway in 1959 opened the Great Lakes to significant international shipping. Duluth, at the western end of Lake Superior, was transformed into a virtual ocean port, though it lies nearly halfway across the continent. Thunder Bay, Ontario's major port on the same lake, became the largest wheat-shipping port in the world.

The role of shipping in the story of the region—past, present, and future—cannot be overestimated. In the mid-1980's, however, that role was being reassessed in the light of economic shifts as well as limitations in the waterway itself. Even with all the engineering projects, the waterway cannot accommodate the largest oceangoing ships. The shipping season is largely restricted to nine months of the year because of heavy winter ice, and tolls on canals and locks have been kept discouragingly high to help cover costs. Among unfavorable economic developments in the 1980's was the decline in U.S. steel production and in shipments of iron ore to steel mills. Poor grain harvests in Canada have also been a problem.

In mid-October a lock in the Welland Canal collapsed, choking off traffic between Lakes Ontario and Erie and leaving about 70 ships stranded for weeks, as repairs were made. The accident, which cost hundreds of thousands of dollars in lost revenues for each ship, also raised questions about the physical condition of the now-aging seaway system. Meanwhile, there has been a slack in shipping from northern Great Lakes ports, with seaway traffic now running at less than two-thirds of capacity. But ports on the lower lakes have experienced a growth, partly attributable to increasing foreign imports. Because of this trend and the overall economic importance of the seaway, many

Lakefront areas can experience flooding periodically; here a Michigan couple evacuate their home after waves crashed over breakwaters in western Lake Erie.

A damaged lock in Ontario's Welland Canal stranded dozens of ships in the upper Great Lakes and delayed others seeking entry in October and November. Here, a curving pipeline pours concrete into molds which will become the new walls of the lock.

The Chicago skyline provides a dramatic backdrop for a sailboating excursion on Lake Michigan. Racing schooners, yachts, and makeshift fishing rafts are some of the craft that ply Great Lakes waters.

observers are still clamoring for renovation and improvement of the seaway.

The Fish Population

Another haunting question at present is the future of commercial fishing on the Great Lakes. Fishing was a major industry during the 19th and early 20th centuries but has declined because of overfishing, the ravages of the sea lamprey, and pollution.

Scientists say there once were 200 species of fish in the Great Lakes, including huge sturgeon weighing several hundred pounds, so plentiful they were often dried and burned for fuel, like logs. Overfishing wiped out the sturgeon by the beginning of the 20th century, however, and the population of northern pike had dropped below commercial quantities by the mid-1920's. The sea lamprey, an intruder from the Atlantic Ocean, invaded the Great Lakes through shipping canals and by the early 1950's had nearly killed off many other species. Chemical treatment of streams where the sea lamprey spawn has since eliminated most of this threat.

The opening of the St. Lawrence Seaway made the lakes increasingly vulnerable to yet another marine pest: the alewife, a fish of little commercial value. These fish periodically died in large numbers, littering beaches in the late 1960's and making them unusable for recreation during peak summer months. This story also had a happy ending. Conservation officials introduced coho and chinook salmon from the Pacific Northwest; the salmon not only gobbled up the alewives but also gave lake sports enthusiasts a new kind of game fish to go after. Today, however, pollution in the lakes continues to be a key concern for the fishing industry, as well as for tourism.

Pollution Problems

As a major industrial and agricultural area, as well as a population center, the Great Lakes region has made the lakes (and rivers feeding into them) a repository for its wastes. Untreated or inadequately treated sewage from residential communities, organic and inorganic wastes from industry, and runoff from farmland (containing insecticides and fertilizers) all have contributed to pollution in the lakes. Decaying organic material, decomposed by bacteria that live on oxygen, has led to oxygen depletion, which, along with pollutants in the waters, kills off fish. Nitrogen and phosphorus contained in fertilizers and detergents have stimulated the growth of algae and other plant life, which also choke out fish and degrade the water quality.

Individual lakes and their tributaries have suffered in varying degrees from these problems. The Environmental Defense Fund recently rated Lake Ontario as the most severely polluted of the lakes. The group ranked Lake Michigan second, followed by Erie, Huron, and Superior.

Industrial pollution in the Great Lakes system appeared to reach its peak in the 1960's when two rivers—Cleveland's Cuyahoga and Detroit's Rouge—caught fire and had to be hosed down by local fire

Dead alewives wash up along the shores of Lake Michigan. Pollution in the lakes and their tributaries remains a serious threat to fishing and tourism.

French settlers once dominated the Great Lakes region. Fort Michilimackinac in Mackinaw City, Mich., one of their military and trading posts, is now a popular tourist attraction.

departments. At this time there were dire predictions that Lake Erie, a favorite dumping ground for industrial waste and for waste from Detroit's once faulty sewage-treatment plant, was suffering irreversible damage; by 1967 it was pronounced near death. But a crackdown on industrial polluters and an extensive upgrading of the Detroit sewage works helped to restore the lake to a large degree, and anglers now catch their daily limits of walleye and perch. In general, tighter federal regulations have helped limit the discharge of harmful wastes into Great Lakes waters. Occasional taste and odor problems in drinking water have largely disappeared (most water supplies, in any event, are drawn from a few miles offshore).

Among current concerns is the absorption by food fish of the toxic materials found in the lakes and their tributaries. These chemicals, researchers warn, may be cancer-causing agents when ingested by humans; pregnant women, nursing mothers, and young children are considered to be at greatest risk.

However, commercial use of many toxic chemicals, including PCB's, mirex, and dioxin, has now been banned or is being phased out. Programs to require more extensive pretreatment of harmful industrial wastes are being instituted throughout Ontario and hundreds of U.S. communities. The federal Environmental Protection Agency was planning an experimental cleanup project for Waukegan harbor, in northeastern Illinois on Lake Michigan, where PCB's have saturated the bottom sediments, though there were legal problems with the project. Cleanup plans that could serve as models for other highly polluted areas were being developed for the Grand Calumet River in western Indiana, currently devoid of aquatic life. There have also been major strides in controlling the phosphorus that caused the growth of algae scum on the lakes.

Looking to the Future

Cleanup and monitoring projects, and indeed the future of the lakes themselves, depend on energetic cooperation on the part of industry and governmental agencies. An important step in this direction was taken in 1972 when U.S. President Richard Nixon and Canadian Prime Minister Pierre Elliott Trudeau signed a pioneering Great Lakes water-quality and cleanup pact. It called for billions of dollars of spending by the U.S. and Canadian governments and by industry for such steps as construction of waste treatment facilities and establishment of controls on pesticide residues, storm-water discharges, and other possible threats to lake water and aquatic life. However, Canadian officials now complain that U.S. spending has been less than agreed upon.

A strong concern of government leaders in the Great Lakes region is the possible diversion of lake water to the arid Southwest, to alleviate shortages there caused by rapid population growth. There have been no specific proposals as yet to draw water away from the Great Lakes to the Sunbelt, but concern is growing. The lakes region has already lost labor and industry to the Sunbelt. Diverting or selling water, government officials contend, would weaken efforts to attract badly needed industry and diversify the lagging economy. Accordingly, officials from the eight lake states and the Canadian provinces of Ontario and Québec drew up a charter aimed at preventing any action that adversely affects water levels or harms the environment. The charter, signed in February 1985, sets up a system for registering withdrawals of more than 10,000 gallons a day and calls on the states and provinces in the region to pass laws regulating diversions of more than 2,000 gallons a day.

FINDING FUN IN DANGER

by JACK McCALLUM

Two days after Jean Boenish's parachutist husband was dashed against a Norwegian cliffside and killed, she herself jumped off a cliff near the site of the tragedy and parachuted safely to earth in the name of sport.

Jack McCallum is a staff writer for Sports Illustrated.

"I was up investigating the site, and I thought while I was up there I may as well make a jump myself," said Mrs. Boenish, who with the death of her husband became the director of the United States BASE Association (USBA), a group dedicted to parachuting off of things you'll find hard to believe. "Cliff sites are few and far between, and we had come all this way. Plus, I felt it would be good for the other jumpers, to show we had to keep things going. If someone else had done it, it might've been considered disrespectful."

Needless to say, the late Carl Boenish, who was 43 when he made his last jump off the 5,000-foot cliff in July 1984, would have wanted it that way. Boenish was not crazy, nor is his wife. She is intelligent, soft-spoken, and, she says, "everyone tells me I look like a librarian," which she does. But she, like thousands of others, feels something that most of us do not: the need/desire/compulsion—call it what you will—to put herself into a possibly life-threatening situation for the sake of fun.

Nobody knows exactly how many certified—some might say certifiable—weekend risk-takers are in our midst. But an increasing number are clawing their way up cliffs, gliding off mountains and bridges, scaling city buildings, and otherwise using their wits and skill to accomplish feats the rest of us get nervous even thinking about.

Clinging to the face of a Colorado precipice, climber Paul Sibley stretches for a fingertip hold.

23

Favorite Dangers

Climbing up a sheer canyon wall can be daunting enough even with the aid of pitons, the steel spikes that are hammered into the rock. The trend among climbers has been toward less rather than more. Some now scurry up rock faces using only their hands, feet, wits, and courage. One climber in particular, a Yosemite living legend named John Bachar, has set new standards for the sport by using only boots and gymnast's chalk, disdaining even a safety rope. Says Bachar, "You can't forget the fact that you're right next to the edge all the time. If you make any kind of mistake, you're going to die."

Go into the mountains around Albuquerque, N.M., on a Friday afternoon and you can see dozens of men and women leaping off the peaks like birds. Actually, they are harnessed to kitelike hang gliders. Hang gliding can be relatively safe and is, needless to say, altogether exhilarating, but many practitioners have given it up as too risky. "I saw too many people get killed," says Larry Newman, a world champion in

Daredevil Ben Colli gets ready to rappel down the side of Atlanta's 75-story Peachtree Plaza hotel with the aid of a mountaineering rope.

HOW MANY DANGER LOVERS?

Thousands of people are involved in sports that most of us might consider a little risky, although many of these sports have rigorous safety standards and very good safety records. Most of the numbers given below are speculative; one or two are no more than educated guesses.

Ballooning: By rough count there are about 5,000 active, certified balloon pilots flying the approximately 3,700 hot-air and gas balloons in the United States.

BASE jumping: The U.S. BASE Association reports a membership of 2,000 worldwide.

Climbing: Rock and ice climbers appear to be loners—there are no national organizations in North America that cater to or count them. Michael Kennedy, the editor of *Climbing* magazine, estimates that there are 40,000–50,000 fairly serious climbers in North America.

Hang gliding: Knowledgeable observers reckon that about 15,000 people are regular hang glider pilots in the United States.

Parachuting: About 70,000–80,000 people make a first parachute jump for the sake of sport each year in the United States. Most of them stop right there, and even more quit after a few jumps, but there are about 35,000 active and experienced sport parachutists in the United States. In Canada, 5,000–6,000 make a first jump each year, and some 2,500 people are involved over the long term.

Ultralight aircraft: Some 35,000–40,000 of these flying machines (lighter than 254 pounds) have been sold in North America. In addition, at least a few have been built in their pilots' garages.

1977. "My efforts to promote safety in the sport by and large fell on deaf ears."

Parachuting from an airplane has been practiced by weekend enthusiasts for so long that it can practically be removed from the category of dangerous pastimes. You may not agree with that, of course, if you know of someone killed by a fall when a parachute didn't open, but by and large improvements in equipment and stringent controls have legitimized sport parachuting as an avocation of the perfectly sane. So safe has it become that others feel a need to look for more adventuresome ways of jumping.

25

Consider, for example, one Ben Colli, who on New Year's Eve in 1976 took off his clothes, put on a baby diaper, and jumped from the top of the Atlanta Hyatt Regency's 22-story atrium holding a long mountaineering rope (he slowed himself down with rappelling equipment). By now, Colli's swoops down the outside of the 75-story Peachtree Plaza hotel in Atlanta have become an annual event. And let us not forget the bungee boys, those members of the Oxford Dangerous Sports Club who a few years ago stole some headlines by jumping off bridges in top hat and tails holding onto long rubber bungee cords, which bounced them back up before they came to harm.

The quintessence of this world of dangerous sport may well be BASE jumping. BASE is an acronym for *Building, Antenna, Span* (bridge), and *Earth* formation. To qualify as a BASE jumper, one must parachute off all four, which often requires jumps from heights as low as 170 feet. (Sport parachutists—who jump from planes—open their chutes at 2,000 feet or above to allow a safety margin for opening a reserve chute.) "You can make a chute open reliably at 75 feet," claims Phil Smith, a Houston trucking company employee who with over 135 BASE jumps off more than 30 different objects was recognized as BASE's ace. But, as Phil knows, that's only half the fun. If and when you land safely, you may well be arrested for trespassing. "I've been arrested three times—two bridges, one tower," says Smith, "and hassled a lot more times than that."

This survey is only a small patch on the crazy quilt of dangerous sports Americans are willing to try. Every such activity has an offshoot or two. Hang gliding enthusiasts, for example, may drift—literally—into flying ultralight aircraft, which in their susceptibility to the vagaries of the weather will never be mistaken for the swing on the back porch. Rock climbers often glide quite easily into the sport of ice climbing, which is as difficult as it sounds, though most ice climbers do deign to use pitons and crampons (spikes that can be strapped to boots). Look up on a pleasant Sunday afternoon and you may see a hot-air balloon or two. While you're looking, you might remember the words of editor and critic H. L. Mencken, who once said of balloonists, "They have an unsurpassed view of the scenery, but there is always the possibility that it may collide with them."

Even when all goes well, high-altitude balloonists are

Building

Antenna

In order to qualify as a BASE jumper, you must be ready, willing, and able to parachute off four different types of structures: a tall building, like the Los Angeles skyscraper above left; an antenna tower, like the one being scaled by Jean Boenish, above right; a span, such as the bridge at New River Gorge, Va., below left; and an earth formation, such as the Half Dome monolith at Yosemite, below right.

Span

Earth formation

always testing the limit of one's ability to survive in a low-oxygen environment. Restaurateur-adventurer Rocky Aoki recalls flying with balloonist Ben Abruzzo (who later died in a plane crash). "I saw castles in the air, and he saw a yellow kitten running around the gondola. We knew it was time to come down." Luckily, they could!

Who Are These People?

Do these aficionados of danger in sport, these "conquistadores of the useless," as mountaineer Lionel Terray wryly called people like himself, have common character traits? Are they of one political party or one socioeconomic group? Could you single them out at a cocktail party?

The quick answer is no. Ask a rock climber if he or she has the same personality as, say, a hang gliding devotee, and chances are you'll get a crinkling of the eyebrows and a contemptuous snort. "Are all writers the same?" one asked in response to the question. (Perhaps only in that, as a group, they tend not to jump off cliffs on a pogo stick, as Carl Boenish once did.) "We have housewives, doctors, lawyers, bums, and drug addicts in our group," observes BASE's Jean Boenish.

In many cases one can at least comprehend the wellspring of the daredevil's compulsion. Rock climbers are quite often former gymnasts looking for a new and perhaps more primal outlet for their talents. BASE jumpers are usually qualified sport parachutists who came to find jumping from a plane too routine. Hang gliding enthusiasts are frequently pilots who have branched out in search of a purer, less controlled aerial environment.

Progress and Its Discontents

There is the suspicion within most of us that we are not as brave, not as full, somehow, as our ancestors. Never mind parachuting off the local bank building—for real risks try taking the *Niña, Pinta,* and *Santa Maria* out on an uncharted sea. A contemporary sailor with even minimal navigational skill knows more than the explorers who set sail in the 15th and 16th centuries. This present-day advantage exists to varying degrees in most dangerous sports. So much has already been done, and there's so much better equipment to do it with.

"The new equipment is so good," says Yvon Chouinard, one of the grand old men of climbing who now specializes in what he calls "dead vertical ice"

(frozen waterfalls, for example), "that it's almost made it too easy. It has a way of overpowering the difficulty of the ice. The sport has sort of topped out." (The next time you're hammering a piton into a frozen waterfall 100 feet above a raging river, just remember how easy it's supposed to be.) Even BASE jumping has been made much safer and easier by technological improvements. Ten years ago parachutists wore paratrooper boots and lugged around 40-pound chutes, but now there are lightweight, steerable chutes and sport jumpers can wear jogging shoes—all the better for BASE jumpers, who often have to be up and running as soon as they land, to avoid the authorities. It takes a tragedy like the one that befell Carl Boenish (one of several BASE-jumping deaths acknowledged by the USBA) to remind experienced parachutists of the limits of technology.

Daredevils are constantly looking for a new way to do it, a way to circumvent this cursed reality of modernity. Since their sports are intensely individual and personal, only they can set the bounds, and many are continually adjusting the dangerous rules of their dangerous games. If a mountain climber does Everest, then he must do Everest a different, more treacherous way the next time. When you've fulfilled the impossible dream, you can't rest content; it's time to dream

Soaring into the blue strapped to a hang glider has become a popular sport in the United States, with about 15,000 devotees.

With only gymnast's chalk on his fingers and climbing boots to find toeholds—but no safety rope—John Bachar (facing page) free-solos up the sheer face of a cliff.

29

something still more impossible, and go out and do it. That is how dangerous sports can become fatal sports.

Putting Fear to Work

Most dangerholics dissociate themselves from death, preferring to focus on the skill and planning that go into their sports, rather than the risks. "People see me on the rock without any ropes and they think it's foolhardy," says Bachar. "Some think it's dangerous, that it's just an act. What they don't understand is how much ability you need to have and how much concentration it takes." And how much training you have to do. Bachar's workouts include one-arm pull-ups with weights ranging from 3 to 10 pounds in his free hand, two-arm pull-ups with as much as 135 pounds strapped to his body, and as many as 140 fingertip pull-ups.

BASE's Phil Smith says, "I get such a feeling of satisfaction from my jumps that people who think I'm just crazy don't realize. I work every jump like a problem. How do I get in? What's the wind? What about the chute? Where do I land?"

A formation of free-falling skydivers have spun off two links in their human chain—not surprising considering that the divers can reach speeds of up to 200 miles per hour.

But for all the levelheaded enjoyment these athletes claim, it is simply straining credulity not to think that, in the chest of each of them, there beats the heart of an adrenaline junkie. "I guess that's true," says Smith. "I am somewhat addicted to that feeling. I'm always real scared before I jump, no matter how experienced I get. And it's such a charge when I do it. It's hard to explain." Not for Bachar: "You can't forget the fact that you're right next to the edge all the time, and that you must be perfect."

"Without risk it wouldn't be the same," says John Lowe, another noted rock climber. "If you eliminate risk, you eliminate reality." Lowe doesn't just talk a good game. As a member of a climbing expedition that once scaled a challenging peak in the Himalayas, Lowe had felt strangely empty. So he stayed behind and took another route up the mountain all alone. "I'm not interested in just getting up the easy routes," he says. "The ultimate challenge is technical difficulty and high altitudes."

The significant point is how these athletes use their fear. Smith says it forces him to focus on the task at hand and make better plans. Fear, says Lowe, is necessary "to sharpen your perceptions. You've got to be aware of the abyss. You have to have the mental control—not to conquer fear, because if you lose some fear you can become a dangerous climber." In an intensely physical sport like climbing, that fear can take a quite palpable form, as it does when climbers are struck by "sewing-machine knee," a malady that makes one knee jerk uncontrollably up and down. It can be caused by a tired or overstretched leg, but it can also be brought on by pure and simple fright. Whatever the source, the only cure is to relax and talk yourself out of it—quite a lot easier said than done.

Bold or Foolhardy?

There are those on the sidelines who feel that the practitioners of dangerous sports aren't doing enough to act on their fear. "It is my personal opinion that someone who free-solos in rock climbing [climbs alone without a safety rope] on extreme terrain is being irresponsible with his own life," says Bill Wendt, who as the chief park ranger at Yosemite National Park had responsibility for investigating about 40 climbing fatalities.

It's not just the folks in the bleachers who complain about the irresponsibility. Larry Newman, the chief executive officer and major stockholder of American

A parachutist maneuvers down to earth with a square-shaped, steerable parachute that can be guided away from the various high elevations like cliffs and antenna towers that now attract the most adventurous chutists.

Two balloons drift silently over the countryside; since the balloons cannot be steered, the pilots depend on the wind to carry them to an open space for landing.

Aircraft in Albuquerque, simply could not abide the fearless mind-set that many hang glider pilots adopted as natural. And if they weren't fearless to begin with, says Newman, they made sure they became so before taking off. "I flew almost daily from 1974 to 1980," says Newman. "I loved the feeling, one of absolute peace. I did not do it for the thrill factor. But many hang gliders today are in what I might call the hippie category. It's, 'Hey, let's sit around, smoke some pot, drink some beer, and then go hang gliding.' That sort of mentality drove me away. The sport could be safe. But what you have is pilots forgetting to hook up their harness and taking off in adverse conditions. It's terrible."

The problem in hang gliding and in many other potentially dangerous sports is a dearth of regulation and a lack of appreciation of the need for proper training. "When you learn to pilot a Lear jet, all the training just squeezes out the recklessness," says

Newman, a qualified Lear pilot. "That's a good thing. But when there's no training, there's no respect for safety. Safety is not inbred." Therefore, a sport like hang gliding, which cannot be regulated short of stationing a police officer on every mountain peak, is intrinsically more dangerous than a sport in which airport clearance is necessary.

Proper training, intense or otherwise, seems to be available for most of the dangerous sports. Indeed, many rock climbers, skin divers, pilots, parachutists, and sailors scratch out a living by giving lessons. But there is the dilemma of emulation. It is one thing to listen carefully to John Bachar's rock-climbing instructions, another to watch him scramble off alone to challenge his private demons when lesson time is over, and quite another to think you can do the same thing when no one's around. This is true in all sports, of course, but throwing out an arm trying to duplicate Dwight Gooden's fastball is not the same as plunging 200 feet to your death down a sheer rock face.

The BASE Jumpers

No single group encapsulates the gloriously madcap cast of sporting daredevils better than the BASE jumpers. They are a mixed lot, and their activities may seem to verge on the ludicrous. Fly to Norway and jump off a cliff one weekend, jump from a midtown skyscraper in your hometown the next. Careful technique is essential to the jumps. Most BASE jumpers acquired their parachute training the old-fashioned way—by jumping out of planes—but there is quite often a point where technique becomes irrelevant and the gods decide whether or not to lower a safety net. Thus did Carl Boenish—a man generally considered safety conscious—plunge to his death. And though the sport has a veneer of officialdom—it has a newsletter, videocassettes for sale, an articulate spokeswoman in Jean Boenish, and an official philosophy that "does not advocate, recommend, or endorse anyone breaking the law"—it also has a touch of the outlaw about it, what with illegal trespass sometimes a necessity to accomplish a jump. All in all, it seems like a sport Butch Cassidy and the Sundance Kid would have appreciated.

BASE jumping had its origins in 1978, when Carl led the first expedition of parachutists using modern equipment to jump off El Capitan, a 3,600-foot sheer cliff in Yosemite. By September of 1980 there had been 479 recorded parachute jumps off El Cap, and

On display in San Francisco, the 77-foot-high "Rainbow Hotel" balloon easily suspends its pilot, Chuck Foster, one of the best balloonists in the United States, above earthbound spectators.

33

authorities put a halt to it. No matter; scores of parachutists, having discovered different and much, much lower horizons for their magnificent weekend obsession, began searching for other fixed objects from which to jump. A new slogan was born: "The ground's the limit!"

And so it was. "I came back from El Cap one weekend," said Smith, a former Marine Corps paratrooper, "and it was in my blood. All I wanted to do was jump off things." Particularly tempting Smith was the siren song of an industrial age—Houston's as-yet-unfinished 72-story Texas Commerce Tower, which would be the biggest building in Texas. "I just couldn't get it out of my mind, " said Smith. "Every day it was right there for me to look at."

Much of the fixed-object parachuting was being filmed by Carl Boenish, who became the group's unofficial guru. Widely recognized as the greatest free-fall photographer in the world, Boenish had an organizational sense to go with his offbeat sense of adventure. Boenish and some of the group began

Ice climbers make their way up the perilous surface of a frozen waterfall.

searching for an acronym that would accurately encompass all categories of fixed-object jumping. "We tried TBBE for a while," says Smith, "but it sounded a little strange. Finally, a group of us were together one night in Dallas and someone, I think it was Carl, came up with BASE. It was perfect. . . ."

It remained for someone to officially certify BASE jumping, to cut the ceremonial ribbon, as it were. Smith already had an A, an S, and an E to his credit, and he had his B in his sights. The historic jump was set for the morning of January 18, 1981. Smith, whose idea it was to parachute off the tempting Texas Commerce Tower, would go first, thus earning the title of Base Number One. He would be followed by jumping partner and close friend Phil Mayfield, who would be Base Number Two. Jean and Carl Boenish eventually became Three and Four. (Despite all that they had done for the sport, the Boenishes had declined the honor of being first and second, since they were not crazy about trespassing. And besides, their photographic talents would be needed on the ground, to record for future generations the first completion of the entire BASE cycle.)

Smith had done his homework. He had crept into the site and climbed up the building about a dozen times before the launch date, to check wind conditions and landing sites. That still did not make him feel exactly serene as he perched on the 72nd floor of the building, his baggy, high-drag jump suit flapping in the early morning wind. Mayfield, standing upwind, began the countdown. When he reached "go," Smith jumped, suppressing the urge to let loose with his customary blood-curdling yell, lest he attract attention to the bizarre activity not quite in keeping with downtown Houston's Sunday morning tranquillity. Then it was Mayfield. Seconds that seemed like hours for the jumpers passed before Smith landed on the grassy top of an underground parking garage and Mayfield reached terra firma in a parking lot across from Western Union—special delivery. The jumpers scurried into their getaway cars and sped off, with only a few dumbstruck passersby any the wiser.

What does it mean that Smith, Mayfield, the Boenishes, and about 100 others from all over the world have jumped off four different kinds of fixed objects? Was it worth the sacrifice of Carl Boenish? "I know what he'd say," declares Smith. "He'd say, 'Keep jumping.'"

PREDICTING THE WEATHER

by ALLAN CHEN

Allan Chen is a reporter for Discover magazine.

Thundering into the sky at the tip of a Thor-Able rocket 25 years ago was a satellite containing two cameras, data recorders, transmitters, and other assorted electronics. It was a humble machine compared to today's sophisticated satellites, with their integrated electronics and remote sensing devices, but it was a milestone all the same. The satellite, called Tiros 1, was the world's first weather satellite.

When Tiros 1 (for Television and Infrared Observation Satellite) lifted off from Cape Canaveral on April 1, 1960, no one could be sure that weather satellites would become the indispensable tool of the meteorologist that they are today. The images it sent back were fuzzy, and at first not all meteorologists took seriously the craft responsible for them. Nonetheless, those pictures heralded a new phase in weather forecasting. Meteorologists could now combine two different scales of observation into a single picture of the weather in flux: the detailed data from weather stations, balloons, ships, and airplanes reporting local weather conditions and the large-scale patterns of global weather reported, crudely at first, by the weather satellites.

Satellites have not been the only innovation over the past 25 years to give forecasters a real boost in range and accuracy. As computers grew more powerful, meteorologists were increasingly able to use their memory and processing power to design more accurate mathematical models of the weather—computer simulations that in essence turn the weather into complex equations with variables like temperature, pressure, and so on. The actual temperature and

pressure at evenly spaced points within the atmosphere and at regular time intervals are entered into the equations, which represent atmospheric processes mathematically—by no means perfectly, but with ever-increasing success.

Benefits of Better Forecasts

The improved forecasts that have grown out of these computer-generated models and an expanded observational network have led to some spectacular benefits. One example: the storm warnings that save lives when a hurricane is about to slam into a heavily populated area. In August 1985 weather satellites tracked Hurricane Elena as it unexpectedly changed course along the Gulf Coast time and again. In response to U.S. National Weather Service warnings, hundreds of thousands of people were evacuated. Although property damage was extensive, the death toll was held down to four.

Farmers use frost warnings to cushion the blow to their crops from freezing temperatures, by harvesting them before the frost comes or spraying them with cold water, which turns into insulating ice. City authorities use forecasts to determine whether to close schools because of heavy snowfall and when to mobilize snowplows and salt spreaders. A number of brokerage houses now employ a staff meteorologist because bad weather conditions could mean major price fluctuations on commodity markets in everything from orange juice to coffee beans. The aviation industry—

Forecasts continually prove their usefulness. Frost warnings alert citrus growers to spray their crops with water, which freezes into a protective shell (right). Especially valuable are warnings of approaching hurricanes; at left, South Carolina residents seek shelter from Hurricane Diana in 1984.

itself a major provider of weather data through aircraft and airport weather stations—is highly dependent on weather information to decide whether or not to send up a flight in bad weather or reroute it out of harm's way.

Mistakes Can Happen

Weather forecasts in the local paper or on the evening news will still let us down from time to time, as anyone who has ever been rained out of a picnic or baseball game knows. Incorrect forecasts can also lead to major disasters when, for example, an unexpected severe summer squall overturns boats or heavy rain causes a flash flood.

The case of the Georges Bank fishing vessels illustrates how shaky forecasting can still be—and how important. When the crews of two commercial boats set course for Georges Bank, off the coast of New England, to catch lobsters on November 21, 1980, the National Weather Service had forecast fair conditions. But the next day, 100 miles out at sea, the vessels encountered a severe storm, and four crew members died. The families of three of them filed suit against the U.S. government when they learned that the National Oceanic and Atmospheric Administration (NOAA), which oversees the National Weather Service, had failed to repair a weather buoy at Georges Bank. The families' lawyer argued that Weather Service forecasters needed data from the buoy to have predicted and followed the storm's course accurately. U.S. District

After a miscalculation led forecasters to predict only 4 to 8 inches of snow, New Yorkers were surprised in February 1983 by one of the worst storms of the century, with accumulations of about 20 inches. Here residents of the borough of Queens struggle to cope with the snow-covered streets.

Court Judge Joseph Tauro ruled in favor of the families, ordering the government to pay $1.25 million in damages. NOAA appealed the ruling.

Some forecasters have said that even with the buoy working properly, meteorologists would not necessarily have been able to issue an accurate forecast. Whatever the final outcome of the case, it is clear that the weather is still quirky, incompletely understood, and predictable only at times. The reasons for its unpredictability include equipment failure, but they are rooted in the sheer complexity of the weather machine.

A Giant Heat Engine

The weather is like a giant heat engine. It is powered by energy from the sun, which heats air, water, and land. If the earth's surface were completely smooth and uniform, with no mountains, seas, or patches of vegetation, and if the earth's axis of rotation were not tilted and the sun heated all parts of the globe evenly throughout the year, the weather would not change very much. But because water absorbs heat more slowly than land, because snow reflects most of the sun's radiant energy while lush forests absorb almost all of it, and because the equator gets more energy from the sun than do the poles, the unevenly distributed energy is constantly trying to rearrange itself over the earth's surface.

Wind is the earth's way of rearranging heat. Hot air from tropical latitudes rises and moves both north and south from the equator, and eventually it cools and falls. Where this cold, heavy air meets warm, light air, we often find stormy weather. Air currents form systems called cyclones and anticyclones. The latter, circulating clockwise in the northern hemisphere and counterclockwise in the southern hemisphere, bring high barometric pressure and fair weather. Cyclones, which revolve counterclockwise in the northern hemisphere and clockwise in the southern hemisphere, bring low barometric pressure and generate the storms we are most familiar with—hurricanes, snowstorms, and rainstorms.

Where Information Comes From

Forecasting the weather is an excercise combining intuition with science in the ingenious use of a limited number of weather observations from many different sources. The National Weather Service maintains hundreds of surface stations, many of them automated, throughout the United States and also exchanges data with the Canadian Atmospheric Environment Service. Twice a day, observers send up about 70 balloons carrying radiosondes—instrument packages that take readings as they travel up through the atmosphere. There are roughly 40 weather buoys in coastal zones.

Meteorologists at regional offices use computers to call up maps and other information for forecasts; the information is collected by the National Weather Service from sources such as satellites, weather buoys, surface stations, and instruments carried on airplanes and ships at sea.

Ships at sea help fill some of the gaps, and wide-body aircraft carry weather instruments, too.

The weather satellites operated by NOAA may be the most interesting of all the devices keeping an eye on the weather. Two polar orbiting satellites circle the globe in a north-south orbit. Each completely covers the turning earth twice a day, beaming back pictures of clouds and measurements (taken with sensors and instruments) of temperature and humidity at different atmospheric levels, sea-surface temperatures, and snow and ice cover. NOAA also operates Geostationary Operational Environmental Satellites (GOES), which are located 22,300 miles above the equator. Their velocity matches that of the turning earth, so that they always stay above the same spot on the ground. The satellites view the earth every half hour, night and day.

The immense mass of weather data collected goes to the National Weather Service's central computer facility in Suitland, Md., a suburb of Washington, D.C. There, Weather Service meteorologists put together maps showing warm and cold fronts, cyclones, winds, and precipitation, and they develop forecasts for the short, medium, and long term.

Folk Wisdom and Science

Today's forecasters are the heirs of a long tradition that has gradually evolved from folk wisdom and magic

into something more like science. There is an old saying, ''Red sky in morning, sailor take warning/Red sky at night, sailors' delight.'' In fact, the warnings come true when the morning sun is shining red against storm clouds bringing rain from the west—but other types of clouds can turn the sky red, too. Living creatures offer possibilities for prediction: ''Swallows fly high, clear blue sky/Swallows fly low, rain we shall know.'' Many birds do fly low before a storm because they are sensitive to changes in atmospheric pressure, which drops just before a storm. They will stay closer to the ground, where the pressure is highest. Other birds won't fly at all before a storm. Changes in the general behavior of animals can be noted, too. Some creatures may be restless before storms. Nevertheless, neither bird nor beast will give you as much warning as the 24-hour forecast.

Modern weather forecasting could not have begun without instruments capable of quantifying changes in the atmosphere. Evangelista Torricelli is thought to have invented the barometer in 1643 to demonstrate that air can become heavier or lighter. The first reliable thermometers were devised at around the same time. Ancient cultures had used wind direction meters and rain gauges, but the development of modern anemometers (which measure wind speed) and self-

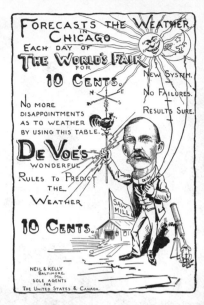

A weather manual printed in 1893 confidently promises to predict the weather during the Chicago World's Fair.

The tornado, which typically appears as a rotating funnel-shaped cloud (right), is the most dangerous of all storms. Learning more about tornadoes may help scientists predict them earlier and more accurately. ''Tornadochasers'' (left) place an instrument-packed canister in what they hope will be the path of a twister. Far left, a three-dimensional model of a massive tornado shows rain density at six different altitudes.

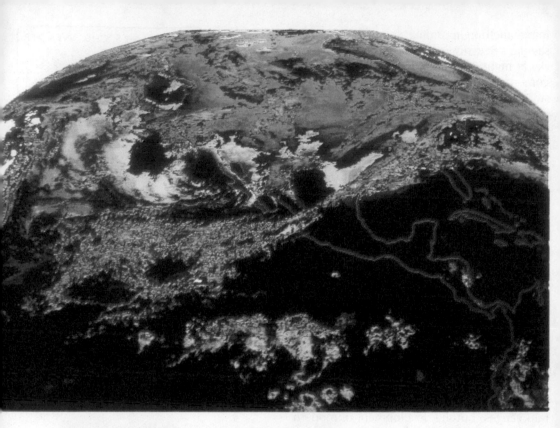

Orbiting satellites beam back pictures (above, a photograph of cloud cover) as well as measurements of temperature, humidity, and wind speed at different levels.

recording rain gauges also began in the 17th century. By the 18th century, amateur observers were keeping diaries of the weather with these instruments.

From Telegraph to Computer

With the invention of the telegraph in the mid-19th century, it no longer took weeks for measurements to arrive at a central location for analysis. In 1849, Joseph Henry, physicist and first secretary of the Smithsonian Institution, initiated the first centralized pool of weather data in the United States. Telegraph companies sent data gathered by volunteer observers to the Smithsonian, where the information was collected, studied, and then retransmitted by the telegraph services as weather summaries. The United States Weather Bureau began life as a division of the U.S. Army Signal Corps in 1870, and some 20 years later it became part of the Department of Agriculture. Its name was later changed to the National Weather Service, and it is now part of the National Oceanic and Atmospheric Administration (which is itself part of the Department of Commerce).

Even with instruments and telegraphs, 19th-century weather forecasters lacked some basic tools, notably a systematic understanding of how changes in the atmosphere cause different forms of weather. The field was waiting for breakthroughs, and it got them in the 1920's from the "Norwegian School," which developed the concepts of the polar front and the air mass, and from British physicist and mathematician Lewis Fry Richardson, who wrote *Weather Prediction by Numerical Process.*

During World War I, Norwegian forecasters were cut off from distant weather observations, so they had to find a way to compensate for the missing information. At the Norwegian Geophysical Institute, Vilhelm Bjerknes and his son Jacob began to work out equations relating weather's measurable elements. According to the polar front theory they developed, cyclonic storms are born when masses of cold polar air, which often move west in the northern hemisphere, meet masses of eastward-moving warm air. Borrowing war terminology, the Norwegians called the leading edges of these masses fronts. Cold air at the front would push warmer, moisture-laden air upward; the moisture would cool, condense, and fall to the ground as rain. Here was the cause of rainstorms. From these beginnings, other scientists refined the polar front theory and turned it into a legitimate tool of forecasting.

Richardson's book, published in 1922, envisioned the basic principles behind today's mathematical models of the weather. Richardson also imagined, in a wild postscript to a very technical work, a forecast factory where a team of human calculators would be arrayed at regularly spaced stations "in a large hall like a theatre, except that the circles and galleries go right round through the space usually occupied by the stage. The walls of this chamber are painted to form a map of the globe." Calculators would mathematically work out the weather for their areas, looking only at data from immediately adjoining stations. Unfortunately, they would not have been able to work fast enough to produce useful results.

Developing a machine that could make the necessary calculations to predict weather fast enough to be useful was an impetus behind the creation of the computer. Together with weather satellites and theoretical advances, computers brought weather forecasting into the modern age, and jumps in forecasting reliability are directly attributable to the introduction of more powerful computers and better computer models. In the late 1960's, 13 percent of the

The NOAA-B weather satellite is lifted into an acoustic vibration chamber to be tested before being launched into space. Once securely in orbit, satellites provide a wide range of data and images of the earth's weather and environment.

time, forecasters were making an average temperature error of 10°F in the next day's forecasts. Now the comparable error is only about 3.5°F. Today's four-day forecasts are as accurate as two-day forecasts were ten years ago.

What We Still Can't Do

These are impressive gains. Yet most of us may still be unimpressed by the performance of our local weather forecaster. In February 1983, for example, one of the worst snowstorms in recent memory hit the East Coast. Parts of New York City recorded 22 inches of snow, and Boston got 14 inches. The forecast from New York City's Weather Service office that morning was for only 4 to 8 inches, and only 3 to 6 inches were expected in Boston. What happened? A very small change in the path of the storm dumped more precipitation over the heavily populated Northeast region than forecasters had expected.

More recently, in September 1985, the National Weather Service warned that Hurricane Gloria would be one of the century's worst storms. Massive precautions were taken in the populous Northeast, and

the storm turned out to be not nearly so bad as expected. It had traveled more quickly than anticipated, and its winds had died down significantly.

Forecasting's greatest gains have come from the prediction of large-scale features such as pressure systems; on a smaller scale, problems remain. Part of the difficulty is that even within a very small geographic area, weather can vary from point to point. Incomplete data coverage also hinders accurate forecasting. The average distance between reporting stations in the United States is about 200 miles, and a lot of weather slips between the gaps of the network—for example, the sudden summer squall, which some forecasters say is one of the hardest weather forms to predict.

The quality of computer models, or simulations, also limits forecast reliability. The National Meteorological Center outside Washington, D.C., now uses a supercomputer that is as much as 50 times faster than its predecessor, as well as—beginning in 1985—a new, more sophisticated short-range forecasting model called the Regional Analysis and Forecast System. At the

Downed telephone poles and damaged houses are familiar sights after a hurricane. At left, a blocked highway on Long Island, N.Y., was one of the aftereffects of Hurricane Gloria, which swept along the eastern seaboard in late September. At right, residents of Indian Rocks Beach, Fla., view the damage done by Hurricane Elena, which ravaged the Gulf Coast in late summer.

Canadian Meteorological Center, located in Dorval, Québec, Canada's first supercomputer was installed in 1984. It performs some 50 million calculations per second. The CMC expects that the more detailed weather models made possible by the increased computer power will enable it to extend its forecasts from five days to seven or even ten.

Improved Technology—Better Forecasts

As these models continue to improve, will they ever be able to predict the weather with accuracy far into the future? The answer seems to be no—there is a limit to how far ahead we can know what the weather will do. Studies by scientists at the Massachusetts Institute of Technology and the Geophysical Fluid Dynamics Laboratory in Princeton, N.J., have established that the limit for accurate forecasts is about two weeks. By not trying for too much detail and by trying to predict, say, cyclones over a third of the United States instead of the conditions in one city, a forecaster might get accurate predictions of up to three weeks—possibly more, depending on how big a compromise is made.

Major improvements in weather station technology are not far off, however—as long as money is available. One promising start is a pilot program called Profs, the Program for Regional Observing and Forecasting Services, in Boulder, Colo. The goal of this NOAA effort is to improve forecasts for up to 12 hours in advance. Profs combines new weather observation technology with computers capable of processing data more efficiently to create a coherent picture of the weather. The observational technology includes Doppler radar, which is capable not only of sensing the presence of, say, a rainstorm, but also of measuring the speed and direction of wind in the storm by sensing the particles of dust it carries. Doppler radar can display hailstorms and wind shear, the deadly wind currents that cause some plane crashes, and it allows forecasters to predict tornadoes with as much as ten minutes' warning, compared with two or three at best for standard radar.

Engineers in the United States are at work on a new generation of weather satellites, including one in the GOES series with sensors able to pick out detail as fine as 1 kilometer in visible light and to measure temperature and humidity through the clouds. As with Tiros, no one can say how much all of this will improve weather forecasts. But then, skeptics laughed at Tiros, too.

Gathering weather data is made easier by such innovations as the environmental data buoy (above), which collects ocean data. Below, a radiosonde (carried by a balloon) sends back atmospheric readings.

1986 YEARBOOK
EVENTS OF 1985

CHRONOLOGY FOR 1985

January

8 • The White House announces that Treasury Secretary Donald Regan and White House Chief of Staff James Baker will exchange jobs.

14 • The Israeli cabinet approves a unilateral pull-out of Israeli troops from Lebanon.

20 • President Ronald Reagan takes the oath of office for his second term.

24 • A U.S. jury finds that *Time* magazine did not libel former Israeli Defense Minister Ariel Sharon.

February

4 • President Reagan sends Congress a $973.7 billion budget proposal, projecting a $180 billion deficit.

6 • Reagan's State of the Union message urges tax reform, smaller government, and a stronger military.

MARCH 17

7 • A Polish court finds four state security policemen guilty of the 1984 killing of a pro-Solidarity Roman Catholic priest.

11 • Jordan's King Hussein and Palestine Liberation Organization leader Yasir Arafat agree on a joint effort for peace in the Middle East.

12 • Canadian Defense Minister Robert Coates resigns in a scandal over his visit to a West German nightclub.

18 • General William C. Westmoreland drops his libel suit against CBS over allegations he had conspired to understate enemy troop strength.

23 • The U.S. Senate confirms Edwin Meese III as attorney general.

March

3 • British coal miners call off their year-long strike.

11 • A day after the death of Konstantin Chernenko, Mikhail Gorbachev is chosen to succeed him as leader of the Soviet Union.

15 • José Sarney is sworn in as Brazil's interim civilian leader because of the illness of President-elect Tancredo Neves.

• U.S. Labor Secretary Raymond Donovan resigns to face trial on fraud and larceny charges.

17 • President Reagan and Canadian Prime Minister Brian Mulroney meet in Québec City for two days of talks.

18 • ABC agrees to a takeover by Capital Cities Communications.

21 • At least 20 blacks are killed by police gunfire in Uitenhage, South Africa.

24 • A U.S. military liaison officer is shot and killed by a Soviet sentry in East Germany.

MAY 29

31 • President José Napoleón Duarte's Christian Democrats win a majority in legislative assembly elections in El Salvador.

April

6 • Sudanese President Jaafar al-Nimeiry is ousted in a military coup.

7 • Soviet leader Gorbachev declares a moratorium on the deployment of medium-range missiles in Europe.

14 • Moderate socialist Alan García Pérez takes first place in Peruvian presidential elections.

17 • The antidiscrimination section of the Canadian Charter of Rights and Freedoms takes effect.

21 • Brazilian President-elect Neves dies, and Sarney becomes president.

May

1 • The White House orders a trade embargo against Nicaragua.

5 • President Reagan makes a controversial visit to a German military cemetery at Bitburg, West Germany.

20 • Israel frees 1,150 prisoners, many of them terrorists, in exchange for 3 Palestinian-held POW's.

28 • President Reagan unveils a sweeping tax reform proposal.

29 • British soccer fans rampage at the European Cup championship game in Brussels, leaving 38 people dead.

June

12 • Spain and Portugal sign a treaty admitting them to the European Community as of January 1, 1986.

14 • A TWA jet en route from Athens is hijacked by Lebanese Shiite gunmen, who hold crew and passengers hostage.

19 • Salvadoran guerrillas kill 13 people, including 6 Americans, at a strip of sidewalk cafés in San Salvador.

JUNE 30

21 • A body exhumed from a Brazilian cemetery is identified by experts as that of Nazi war criminal Josef Mengele.

23 • An Air-India jet with 329 aboard crashes into the Atlantic, possibly destroyed by a terrorist bomb.

30 • The last of the surviving hostages from the TWA hijacking are freed, without public concessions on the part of the United States; during the hijacking an American marine was murdered.

July

2 • Andrei Gromyko is named Soviet chief of state; Eduard Shevardnadze replaces him as foreign minister.

10 • A ship belonging to the environmental group Greenpeace is sunk by mines in New Zealand waters.

13 • President Reagan undergoes surgery for colon cancer.

20 • South Africa declares an indefinite state of emergency in many areas, in an effort to curb social unrest.

28 • Ugandan President Milton Obote is ousted in a military coup.

August

1 • The U.S. House and Senate pass a budget resolution calling for $967.6 billion in spending for the 1986 fiscal year, with a $171.9 billion deficit.

15 • In a major speech, South African President P. W. Botha rejects foreign and domestic calls for major changes in apartheid.

20 • Moderate Sikh leader Harchand Singh Longowal is assassinated in Punjab, a month after having signed an accord with the Indian government.

27 • Nigerian leader Major General Mohammed Buhari is ousted in a military coup.

September

9 • President Reagan orders limited trade and financial sanctions against South Africa.

19 • Mexico is struck by a severe earthquake that devastates the capital city and leaves thousands dead.

20 • France's defense minister resigns and its intelligence chief is fired, over the role of French security agents in the mining of the Greenpeace ship.

22 • The United States and four other Western industrial nations announce an effort to drive down the value of the U.S. dollar, and thus possibly cut the U.S. trade deficit.

25 • Two days after Canadian Fisheries Minister John Fraser resigns in a tainted-tuna scandal, Communications Minister Marcel Masse resigns his post over alleged campaign irregularities.

October

1 • Israeli planes bomb PLO headquarters in Tunisia; about 70 people are killed.

2 • One of four Soviets kidnapped by terrorists in Beirut is found shot to death.

SEPT. 19

OCT. 24

9 • Palestinian hijackers relinquish control of the Italian cruise ship *Achille Lauro*, after holding passengers hostage and killing one American.

11 • A plane carrying the *Achille Lauro* hijackers under a safe-conduct from Egypt is forced by U.S. jet fighters to land in Italy.

15 • Nicaragua declares a state of emergency and suspends civil rights.

24 • Salvadoran guerrillas exchange President José Napoleón Duarte's daughter, kidnapped in September, and a number of captured mayors for political prisoners and safe-conduct for wounded rebels.

28 • John A. Walker, Jr., a key figure in a Soviet spy ring, pleads guilty to espionage charges.

November

3 • Philippine President Ferdinand Marcos calls for a presidential election in early 1986.

DEC. 11

4 • Alleged KGB defector Vitaly Yurchenko, claiming he was kidnapped and drugged by U.S. agents, announces he is returning to the Soviet Union.

• Two French agents plead guilty in New Zealand to reduced charges in the sinking of the Greenpeace ship.

5 • New Jersey Governor Thomas H. Kean (R) is reelected, while Gerald Baliles (D) wins the Virginia gubernatorial contest.

7 • After leftist rebels occupy the Palace of Justice in Bogotá, Colombia, holding hundreds of hostages, government troops retake the building by force; the incident leaves about 100 people dead.

13 • The Nevado del Ruiz volcano erupts in Colombia, setting off an avalanche of mud and rocks and killing about 25,000 people.

15 • British Prime Minister Margaret Thatcher and Irish Prime Minister Garret FitzGerald sign an accord on Northern Ireland.

19 • President Reagan and Soviet leader Gorbachev begin two days of summit talks in Geneva.

24 • An Egyptian airliner hijacked by terrorists after takeoff from Athens is stormed on the ground in Malta by Egyptian commandos; the incident causes 60 deaths.

December

2 • A three-judge court in Manila acquits General Fabian Ver and all 25 other defendants of involvement in the 1983 assassination of opposition leader Benigno Aquino.

• The Parti Québécois, under new leader Pierre Marc Johnson, is overwhelmingly defeated in Québec elections by Liberals under the leadership of former Premier Robert Bourassa.

8 • Pope John Paul II officially concludes a two-week extraordinary Synod of Bishops.

9 • Oil ministers of the Organization of Petroleum Exporting Countries end a three-day meeting agreeing to cut oil prices as needed to protect OPEC's "fair share" of the market.

• Five former Argentine military leaders are found guilty of crimes committed in the 1970's, when more than 9,000 people disappeared during a government campaign against leftist terrorists and dissidents.

11 • General Electric agrees to acquire RCA Corporation for more than $6 billion.

• Philippine opposition leaders agree on a unified ticket for scheduled 1986 elections, with Corazón C. Aquino as presidential candidate and her rival Salvador Laurel as running mate.

12 • President Reagan signs a major bill mandating deficit cuts over a five-year period and a balanced budget by 1991.

17 • The U.S. House approves a tax reform measure that differs significantly from President Reagan's original proposal.

27 • Terrorists armed with grenades and submachine guns launch nearly simultaneous attacks at Rome and Vienna airports, leaving 20 dead including 4 of the gunmen.

A

ACCIDENTS AND DISASTERS. The following were among the noteworthy accidents and disasters of 1985:

Jan. 13, Ethiopia: A train carrying 1,000 passengers plunged into a ravine 100 miles east of Addis Ababa, killing almost 400 people and injuring about 370 others, in what was described as the third-worst rail disaster in history.

Jan. 21, Nevada: A chartered Lockheed Electra turboprop plane crashed shortly after takeoff from Reno; 70 of the 71 people aboard lost their lives.

Feb. 1, Soviet Union: An Aeroflot TU-134 crashed near Minsk in what Soviet newspapers called a "catastrophe"; the plane was believed to be carrying about 80–90 passengers.

Feb. 7, Italy: A six-story apartment building in Castellaneta in southern Italy collapsed, leaving at least 34 people dead.

Feb. 13, Philippines: About 30 people perished when a fire raced through a Manila hotel; antigovernment guerrillas claimed responsibility.

Feb. 19, Spain: All 148 people aboard were killed when an Iberia Air Lines Boeing 727 crashed into a mountain while approaching Bilbao airport.

Feb. 23, India: Fire swept through a moving passenger train in the state of Madhya Pradesh, killing at least 34 people.

Mar. 3, Chile: A powerful earthquake measuring 7.8 on the Richter scale rocked central Chile, leaving at least 175 people dead, thousands injured, and as many as 1 million homeless.

Mar. 23, Bangladesh: Some 200 of the approximately 300 passengers aboard a river ferry drowned near Dacca when the boat capsized and sank in a storm.

Mar. 27, South Africa: A school bus plunged into a reservoir near Johannesburg, killing 41 high school students.

Apr. 20, China: An explosion at a fireworks factory in Taoyuan killed more than 80 people.

Cyclone survivors in Bangladesh await distribution of food by helicopter. More than 10,000 died and a quarter of a million were left homeless when a cyclone and tidal waves swept the coastal region and low-lying islands in the Bay of Bengal in May.

Apr. 21, Philippines: Forty-one people died and at least 50 others were injured in a movie-theater fire in Tabaco.

Apr. 26, Argentina: At least 79 people were killed and 250 injured when fire engulfed a mental home in Buenos Aires.

May 3, Soviet Union: About 80 people, some said to be prominent military officials, died when an Aeroflot airliner collided with a military plane at Lvov airport in the Ukraine.

May 11, England: A flash fire at a soccer match in the West Yorkshire city of Bradford consumed a packed wooden grandstand in 4 minutes; 58 people died.

May 17, Japan: A gas explosion deep in a coal mine on the Japanese island of Hokkaido killed 61 miners and injured 22.

May 24–25, Bangladesh: A cyclone rose from

55

ACCIDENTS AND DISASTERS

the Bay of Bengal with up to 100-mile-an-hour winds, driving waves over tiny islands and devastating 7 southern districts; it left over 10,000 dead and 250,000 injured.

May 26, Spain: Two tankers at a refinery on the Bay of Algeciras, near Gibraltar, exploded, killing more than 20 and injuring 36.

May 31, North America: Nearly 90 people lost their lives and 1,500 were injured when tornadoes hit Ontario, Ohio, Pennsylvania, and western New York State.

June 11, Israel: A train hit a school bus south of Haifa, leaving 4 adults and 17 children dead; 17 other children were hospitalized.

June 17, Egypt: At least 30 people perished in the collision of a passenger train and a freight train at Isna, in southern Egypt.

Troops gather around the remains of Japan Air Lines flight 123, which slammed into Mount Osutaka on August 12. With 520 dead, the crash was the worst single-plane accident on record.

June 23, Ireland: In the worst disaster at sea in aviation history, an Air-India Boeing 747 en route from Canada exploded and plummeted suddenly into the Atlantic southwest of Ireland, killing all 329 people aboard.

June 25, Oklahoma: Twenty-one workers were killed and five injured in an explosion at a fireworks factory near Hallett, west of Tulsa.

Late June, Philippines: About 130 people died when typhoons and monsoon rains hit the islands and set off the worst flooding in Manila in 13 years.

July 12, China: At least 56 workers lost their lives in a gas explosion at a coal mine in Guangdong Province, north of Hong Kong.

July 19, Italy: Over 230 people were killed in the northern mountains when an earthen dam burst, releasing a torrent of mud and water that destroyed the town of Stava.

July 24, Colombia: A Colombian DC-6 caught fire and crashed en route from Leticia to Bogotá, killing all 70–80 aboard.

Late July, China: Four weeks of torrential rains, hailstorms, and flooding killed more than 600 people and left hundreds of thousands homeless.

Aug. 1, Wyoming: A thunderstorm dropped a record 6 inches of rain and 6 inches of hail on Cheyenne in under 4 hours, killing 12 people.

Aug. 2, Texas: Attempting to land at Dallas-Fort Worth International Airport, a Delta Air Lines Lockheed L-1011 jet plunged toward the ground, hit cars on a highway, and burst into flame, killing 136 of the 161 people aboard and the driver of one car.

Aug. 3, France: Two trains traveling at about 60 miles an hour collided head-on in south-central France, killing 35 people.

Aug. 12, Japan: All but 4 of the 524 people aboard a Japan Air Lines Boeing 747 died when the plane went out of control and crashed into a mountain between Tokyo and Osaka; it was the worst single-plane disaster in history.

Aug. 13, India: About 50 people were killed when an overcrowded tenement in Bombay collapsed as its residents slept.

Aug. 18, China: At least 114 people died when a tourist ferry capsized in the Songhua River, near the northeastern city of Harbin.

Aug. 22, England: As a British Airtours Boeing 727 charter jet was taking off from Manchester Airport, an engine exploded; 55 of the 137 people aboard were killed.

Aug. 23, China: An earthquake of magnitude 7.5, centered 80 miles north of Kashi, killed 60 and left 16,000 homeless.

Sept. 6, Wisconsin: A Midwest Express Airlines DC-9 crashed after takeoff from Milwaukee, killing all 31 aboard.

Sept. 19–20, Mexico: Over 7,000 people were killed and thousands of buildings destroyed when two earthquakes measuring 8.1 and 7.5 on the Richter scale hit Mexico City and nearby states. Damage was estimated at $4 billion.

Sept. 26–27, United States: After showing winds of 150 miles an hour at sea, Hurricane Gloria moved up the eastern seaboard, causing massive power outages and eight deaths.

Oct. 7, Puerto Rico: Heavy rains brought on the worst mudslide in U.S. history, carrying Mameyes barrio in Ponce down a hillside, entombing at least 200 people; about 60 died elsewhere on the island.

Oct. 15–16, Vietnam: A typhoon hit the province of Binh Tri Thien, killing some 800 and demolishing hundreds of thousands of homes.

Oct. 21, 27, Philippines: Two separate landslides in the gold-mining towns of Monkayo and Diat killed up to 300 people.

Late Oct.–Nov. 6, United States: Hurricane Juan killed at least seven and caused an estimated $1 billion damage in Louisiana. Rains from the storm caused severe flooding in the Middle Atlantic states and Washington, D.C., leading to about 50 deaths.

Nov. 13, Colombia: Some 25,000 perished and nearly 4,000 were injured when the long-dormant volcano Nevado del Ruiz erupted, sending tons of mud and debris down its slopes.

Dec. 12, Canada: A chartered jetliner crashed on takeoff from Gander, Newfoundland, killing all 256 people aboard; 248 of the victims were U.S. soldiers returning to their base at Fort Campbell, Ky., from peacekeeping duty in the Sinai Peninsula.

Dec. 18, Philippines: A ferry capsized in the South China Sea between Manila and Palawan Island, leaving over 100 dead.

ADVERTISING. The McCann-Erickson advertising agency predicted that total U.S. advertising expenditures for 1985 would reach $96 billion, up 9 percent over 1984. Cable television, direct mail, and local retail advertising expenditures were expected to increase the most.

Advertisers. Major advertisers made significant changes in some long-standing traditions. Procter & Gamble, the leading U.S. advertiser, dropped from its products its 103-year-old logo featuring a man in the moon and 13 stars (representing the original 13 colonies). Since 1980 the symbol had been the target of persistent rumors linking it with devil worship and the Church of Satan. Also, Merrill Lynch decided to retire its bull, after having used the symbol for 15 years in connection with its "bullish on America" theme.

The Coca-Cola Company tampered with its 99-year-old formula for Coke, the world's most popular soft drink. After introducing New Coke in April, the company weathered almost three months of consumer indignation before reintroducing the original formula under the name Coca-Cola Classic. President Donald Keough admitted that the public's passion for original Coke had caught the company by surprise, despite intensive marketing research. With both types being sold, surveys showed the old Coke was outselling the new in most areas, often by wide margins. Meanwhile, the Coca-Cola Company and PepsiCo had both increased the ad budgets for all of their cola products.

Wendy's dropped Clara Peller, star of the hamburger chain's fabulously successful "Where's the beef?" commercials of 1984, after Peller began appearing in commercials for Prego Plus spaghetti sauce. In the TV spot for Prego, Peller exclaims, "I finally found it" (presumably the meat she hadn't seen at Wendy's competitors). The announcer confirms, "Real beef—it's in there."

Award-Winning Advertising. In Cannes, France, the International Advertising Film Festival gave its Grand Prize to Pepsi's "Archaeology" television spot. It showed a professor and a group of students at a future archaeological dig puzzled in an attempt to identify a Coke bottle. (They were drinking Pepsi.) The Clio Award for best TV campaign went to Anheuser-Busch's Bud Light 1984 Olympics spots. One called

A Coke-lover expresses her opinion of the soft drink's formula change; three months after the company introduced the new flavor, consumer protests and sluggish sales forced a decision to bring back the original formula, billed as "Coca-Cola Classic."

"Heartland" showed two farmers trekking to the roadside to see the Olympic torchbearer run by.

President Ronald Reagan was chosen as *Adweek's* "Marketer of the Year," chiefly on the basis of effective media use during his reelection campaign. Among the campaign's efforts was a commercial, called "The Bear," which depicted the Soviet Union as a menacing bear and called for the United States to become as strong.

Yuppies. "Yuppies," or young urban professionals, continued to be the most demographically desirable market to reach. Similar labels proliferated to describe comparable affluent groups—young upwardly mobile professionals in general (yumpies), those who were black (bumpies), and those who were mothers (yummies), as well as their children (puppies).

Media. *Good Housekeeping* magazine celebrated its 100th anniversary with its largest advertising issue ever. Only *Sports Illustrated's* 1984 Olympics special issue had more ad revenue. The companies earning the most from advertising in 1985 were, according to *Adver-*

tising Age, the American Broadcasting Companies, CBS Inc., Time Inc., RCA (owner of NBC), and the Times Mirror Company. During 1985, Capital Cities Communications took over ABC, further securing ABC's position among the media giants.

For the fall season the average price of a 30-second commercial on prime time network television was $118,840, or 14.2 percent more than the figure for the previous season. The most expensive series to advertise on was *The Cosby Show* ($270,000), followed by *Dynasty* ($230,000). As rates escalate, commercials are getting shorter. "Split 30's" in which two brands of the same advertiser split a 30-second spot, and stand-alone 15-second spots were expected to eventually replace 30-second commercials, much as the latter replaced minute-long spots in the 1960's.

Regulation. Groups combatting alcoholism and drunken driving sought to ban beer and wine advertising on TV and radio. (Little or no advertising for hard liquor appears on those media because of self-regulation by distillers.) The Federal Trade Commission did not respond to calls for such a ban. However, the FTC chairman did warn brewers that the commission's staff would monitor promotional and advertising practices directed at college students.   B.G.V.

AFGHANISTAN. The war in Afghanistan continued between the Marxist government of President Babrak Karmal and its Soviet supporters, on the one hand, and the Mujahedeen (holy warriors or freedom fighters) on the other.

War. Despite vast material advantages and signs of improvement in the Afghan Army's performance, Soviet occupation forces were still denied control of the countryside and most of the population. In May the Soviets launched a massive sweep against Mujahedeen forces besieging an Afghan Army post at Barikot, involving some 10,000 troops, 2,000 vehicles, and 150 aircraft. As the Soviets moved in, they decimated settlements on the way. Mujahedeen units were mauled and scattered, but the Soviets withdrew after mining the trail from Pakistan. In late September the Soviets reportedly concluded an unsuccessful month-long drive to cut off supply routes from Pakistan; casualties were said to be heavy on both sides. In late November there was heavy fighting around Herat.

Mujahedeen units increased their own assaults on convoys and garrisons, as well as on pipelines and power lines They held on to sections of the largest cities and in Kabul made hit-and-run attacks on government buildings, including the Soviet embassy. On September 4, guerrillas shot down a domestic Bakhtar Airlines plane as it took off from Kandahar airport, reportedly killing all 52 people aboard; the Mujahedeen said they had reports that the airliner was carrying Soviet advisers and Afghan secret police and military officials. In late October guerrillas reportedly fired two missiles into the main mosque in Herat, killing 14 people. A few weeks later, guerrillas destroyed 16 fuel trucks in an attack on a Soviet convoy; 15 civilians were killed in the incident, when a bus they were riding was caught in the cross fire.

A report by the UN Commission on Human Rights, released in December, concluded that the war had involved massive human rights violations, including bombings and killings of civilians. Meanwhile, talks under UN auspices aimed at ending the war were continuing.

Campaign for Support. The regime increased its efforts to win popular support by seeking to identify itself with Islam. It established a Ministry of Islamic Affairs and infused its official statements with phrases designed to evoke religious sentiments. The government also asked for and duly received the endorsement of a specially convened national assembly, which it had stacked with party loyalists. Such internal posturing was helped by Moscow's careful effort not to classify Afghanistan as a member of the Communist bloc. Meanwhile, the war's longevity created opportunities for the long-term indoctrination of some 15,000 Afghan orphans, as well as offspring of party members, sent to the Soviet Union for schooling.

The depopulation of the countryside, the destruction of agriculture, mass conscription, and disruption of transport—all resulting from the war—had drastically reduced food supplies. Conditions of near famine in rural areas forced the migration of many to the cities (as well as to neighboring Iran and Pakistan). Access to scarce goods was tied to affiliation, or at least collaboration, with the ruling party.

International Relations. Pakistan still played a pivotal role in the war. From the beginning of the fighting, it provided the Mujahedeen with arms and other supplies and also accepted about 3 million refugees. In the summer, two Soviet MI-24 helicopter crews defected by flying their craft to Pakistan; negotiations for the return of the crews and equipment produced no result. On October 31 a Soviet soldier sought refuge in the U.S embassy in Kabul, claiming he wanted to leave Afghanistan. Although the U.S. chargé d'affaires offered to try to secure asylum status for him, he decided to return to the Soviet Union after meetings with the Soviet ambassador and assurances he would not be prosecuted.

The United States reportedly spent over $250 million on military and humanitarian aid to the Mujahedeen in fiscal year 1985, and in October, Congress was said to have secretly approved another $250 million in military aid. Major assistance was also furnished by China and by Islamic nations.

See STATISTICS OF THE WORLD.   N.P.N.

Africa

Rains returned to much of Africa in 1985, but the famine was only partially alleviated. In South Africa, conflict between the white-minority regime and its opponents became more intense. Governments in several countries changed hands, with retirements in Tanzania and Sierra Leone and coups in Sudan, Uganda, and Nigeria.

At the beginning of the year, 21 African countries were listed by the Food and Agricultural Organization (FAO) as "severely affected" by food shortages. By year's end, according to the UN Office of Emergency Operations, some 19 million people were still at risk, and 3 million who had left home in search of food remained homeless. Concern over food shortages had eased in a number of countries because of substantial rainfall, but the situation was still serious in Angola, Botswana, Ethiopia, Mozambique, and Sudan. Graphic television coverage of the drought crisis sparked an outpouring of relief efforts. They included the single record "Do They Know It's Christmas?," produced by an all-star group called Band Aid in Britain in late 1984; the USA for Africa recording "We Are the World" in early 1985; and a Live Aid concert staged in London and Philadelphia in July. These efforts netted a combined total of more than $100 million. In March the U.S. Congress appropriated $800 million for African food aid. Relief officials warned, however, that recovery from famine would be difficult at best and that fading public attention could mean insufficient relief for those still starving, as well as inadequate funds for long-term development efforts.

Economic Developments. Despite scattered signs of improvement, such as in food production in Zimbabwe, most of the continent, in dire economic straits even before the drought of the 1980's, faced enormous obstacles on the road to recovery. Aid from industrial countries had fallen in real terms, and Africa's debt had mounted to a total of about $170 billion. Even excluding money owed to the International Monetary Fund (IMF), sub-Saharan Af-

rica's scheduled repayments were approximately $8 billion a year from 1985 to 1987, more than triple the annual payments between 1980 and 1982.

The World Bank's 1985 *World Development Report* noted that, for the 22 low-income African countries in particular, the ratio of debt to gross national product had risen from 17.5 percent in 1970 to 54.5 percent in 1984. The $27 billion debt of these countries was almost three times their total annual exports. For these same countries, growth in GNP per capita, which had been stagnant for the period from 1973 to 1980, was negative after that time.

In February the World Bank set up a new $1.1 billion loan facility for Africa, contingent on policies encouraging farming and private business. The United States decided not to contribute, agreeing with the World Bank's emphasis but preferring to concentrate on bilateral aid.

Organization of African Unity. Meeting in Addis Ababa in July, the 51-member Organization of African Unity adopted a declaration that most countries on the continent were near "economic collapse." African leaders and external critics generally recognized that much of the problem stemmed from policy errors of the last 20 years. The need for higher prices and more opportunity for agricultural producers was widely acknowledged. But without adequate resources from improved world prices, debt cancellation, and increased international aid, leaders argued, new policies might have no chance to succeed. The outgoing OAU chairman, President Julius Nyerere of Tanzania, expressed a common view when he asserted that IMF belt-tightening policies had made the situation worse. Forced to give priority to paying their foreign debts, many countries were being left virtually bankrupt, with little hope of economic recovery.

Niger's Foreign Minister Idé Oumarou, a man with a reputation as an efficient technocrat, was elected secretary-general of the organization. Senegal's President Abdou Diouf succeeded Nyerere as chairman. Political issues were less prominent than in previous summits, but Morocco and Zaire were still absent, after having walked out in 1984 in protest against the admission of Western Sahara.

Southern Africa. Escalating conflict in South Africa continued throughout 1985, despite a state of emergency declared in many parts of the country in July. On March 21, the 25th anniversary of the Sharpeville massacre of 69 black protesters, police killed at least 20 people at Uitenhage in the Eastern Cape region. Between September 1984 and December 1985 the recorded death toll in black townships was about 1,000; most were killed by police and some by blacks attacking government collaborators. The number detained had passed 4,500. Among those on trial were 16 key leaders of the largest antiapartheid coalition, the United Democratic Front. Late in the year, charges against 12 of these 16 defendants were dropped by the prosecution, in an important victory for antiapartheid forces.

The government of President Pieter W. Botha refused to consider significant reforms in the apartheid system of white-minority domination, despite mounting internal conflict and adverse international reaction on both political and economic fronts. In September, South Africa froze payments on much of its foreign debt for four months, after U.S. banks refused to roll over short-term loans coming due. Demonstrations and threatened congressional action led the Reagan administration to adopt limited sanctions in September, including banning Krugerrand sales and limiting new bank loans. Other Western countries, notably including France and Canada, took somewhat stronger measures.

In September a delegation of South African business leaders met in Zambia with leaders of the outlawed African National Congress, which

in January had called on South Africans to make the country "ungovernable." The Pretoria government condemned the encounter and continued to refuse to release the imprisoned ANC leader Nelson Mandela. An August Gallup survey reported that 49 percent of urban South African blacks favored Mandela for president, while 24 percent chose Nobel Peace Prize laureate Bishop Desmond Tutu; only 6 percent named Chief Gatsha Buthelezi, head

In the tragic exodus from Ethiopia to Sudan—a flight from the famine and fighting in the northern provinces—a starving woman is lifted onto a truck taking the refugees to another camp in Sudan where food and water may be more plentiful. Ethiopia and Sudan were both especially hard-hit by continuing famine in 1985.

Nigeria's new president, General Ibrahim Babangida, leaves a meeting of his Armed Forces Ruling Council, flanked by top army officers. Babangida seized power in a bloodless military coup in August.

of the Zulu homeland, who is seen by many blacks as a supporter of the white regime.

In the southern African region, Zimbabwean and Mozambican troops took the main base of South African-backed guerrillas in August, capturing documents that forced Pretoria to admit it had been violating the March 1984 Nkomati Accord, barring such intervention in Mozambique. In June, South African commandos seeking South African insurgents raided the Botswana capital of Gaborone and killed 16 people. Pretoria also stepped up support for Unita (National Union for the Total Independence of Angola) guerrillas in Angola, blocking an Angolan government offensive against Unita base areas in September. U.S.-backed negotiations over independence for South African-occupied Namibia and withdrawal of Cuban troops from Angola were at a standstill after the U.S. Congress in July repealed the Clark Amendment, which had barred U.S. aid to the Unita guerrillas in Angola. In November, President Ronald Reagan indicated that his administration now favored covert aid to the rebels; earlier, the U.S. State Department had publicly opposed such aid, on the grounds that a political settlement might be negotiated.

Other Regional Conflicts. In other African conflicts, the Moroccan Army expanded its control over more of the Western Sahara, a former Spanish colony that Polisario guerrillas were seeking to establish as an independent state. The army appeared to have completed construction of a wall 9 feet high and more than 1,500 miles long to protect the Western Sahara's major towns and phosphate deposits. Meanwhile, the Ethiopian Army was hard pressed in its efforts to put down guerrilla movements in Eritrea and Tigré. The rebel groups, pitted against the regime of Mengistu Haile Mariam, continued to hold large rural areas but were plagued by their need to get food during the continuing drought. In West Africa, border clashes broke out late in the year between Mali and Upper Volta (Burkina Faso).

Retirements and Coups. In November, Tanzania's President Nyerere retired, giving way to newly elected Ali Hassan Mwinyi as president. Nyerere had led his country since independence in 1961. In Sierra Leone, President Siaka Stevens retired after ruling the West African coastal nation for 17 years; he was succeeded in November by Major General Joseph Momoh. Elsewhere, several governments were ousted by coups. After a general strike early in the year, Sudan's President Jaafar al-Nimeiry was overthrown in April by the army; the new regime declared a policy of nonalignment and sought to negotiate a settlement with rebels in the south of the country. In July a coup in Uganda ousted President Milton Obote; the new government later reached a peace settlement with the opposition National Resistance Army, but the truce collapsed. In Nigeria a bloodless coup within the army replaced military leader Mohammed Buhari with Army Chief of Staff Ibrahim Babangida. The new government sought to restore civil liberties and revive the economy.

A coup attempt in Liberia against General Samuel Doe, after elections in which Doe's opponents charged fraud, was bloodily suppressed in November. In North Africa, Libya's controversial leader, Colonel Muammar al-Qaddafi, stayed in power, although he was reportedly threatened by internal discontent and by external threats, including a leaked CIA plan for a campaign against him.

Women's Conferences. Two of the most important events of the year in Africa were the conferences on women held in July in Nairobi, Kenya. One conference was sponsored by the United Nations, the other by about 150 non-governmental groups. These meetings drew some 15,000 women from all over the world. More than half were from Africa, many from rural areas in Kenya itself. The conferences focused new attention on the neglected role of African women in the struggles for national development.

See also separate articles on many of the individual countries mentioned. W.M.

AGRICULTURE AND FOOD SUPPLIES. World agriculture's food output increased by about 1 percent during 1985, rising above 1984 levels particularly in the United States, Canada, the Soviet Union, and India. But attention focused on sub-Saharan Africa, where prolonged drought had brought death to hundreds of thousands and political turmoil complicated food relief efforts.

World Output. World grain production in 1985 was expected to reach 1.67 billion metric tons, an increase of about 1 percent over 1984. The U.S. Department of Agriculture (USDA) estimated the world's coarse grain harvest at a record of nearly 840 million tons. However, wheat, at just over 500 million tons, was down slightly. Rice, on a milled basis, was projected at 320 million tons, a record by a narrow margin. Oilseed production, about half of it soybeans, came to more than 190 million tons, slightly above the 1984 figure.

Meat and poultry output rose slightly, to an estimated 123 million tons. Year-end beef stocks in the major producing countries were down. Egg production was projected at about 360 billion.

World sugar production was forecast at about the same level as the revised figure for 1984, or just under 100 million tons. Sugar consumption was expected to grow modestly in Eastern Europe and the Middle East, while leveling off in Western Europe, Japan, and the

United States, as substitute sweeteners became increasingly popular. Coffee output, projected at 99 million 60-kilogram bags, appeared to be up substantially from 1984, and cocoa bean production was also up greatly.

Cotton was projected to drop from 86 million bales in 1984 to under 80 million bales, mainly because of an anticipated large decline in China's harvest. Tobacco, at a little more than 6 million tons, was down slightly from 1984, and tobacco consumption in developed countries was declining.

United States. Despite a good crop year in 1985, the outlook for U.S. farm income declined, partly because ample supplies kept producer prices down. Reduced exports and falling land values also greatly hurt farmers. Many were deeply in debt, and loan foreclosures were rising. In March, President Ronald Reagan, in a cost-cutting move, vetoed a bill that would have provided interest subsidies and loan guarantees and speeded support payments to farmers. Later in the year, the Farm Credit System, a network of cooperative farm banks that held close to $80 billion in farm loans, appeared near collapse. Congress then passed, and the president signed, a measure to rescue the system, authorizing a new agency to take over delinquent loans; the agency would seek to renegotiate some loans, foreclosing on mortgaged farms where this was impossible. Reagan also reluctantly signed a major bill providing $52 billion to support commodity prices and farmers' incomes over three years. The measure also increased spending for food stamps and made homeless people and poor working families eligible for the program. Meanwhile, country singer Willie Nelson led some 50 performers in a 14-hour "Farm Aid" concert in September; the concert did not bring in as much revenue as had been hoped, but it was seen as increasing public awareness of farmers' economic troubles.

Net farm income for 1985 was forecast at $25 billion to $29 billion, down from the $35 billion reported for 1984. In the first nine months of 1985 farmers received prices averaging 13 percent lower than in the previous year. Exports were expected to hit a six-year low. Meanwhile, the general perception that agriculture's profitability had diminished was

Low agricultural prices and high debts have created an economic crisis for farmers. Above: a potent message mowed on a wheatfield by a frustrated Texas farmer. Right: a foreclosure auction of farm and equipment in Kentucky. Far right: movie star Jane Fonda listens as actress Jessica Lange testifies before the House Democratic Caucus Task Force on Agriculture about the suffering of farm families which she witnessed firsthand during the making of the film Country.

leading to the sharpest decline in farm land values since the 1930's.

Crops. Production of four feed grains (corn, sorghum, barley, and oats) was forecast at nearly 27 million tons, a record. However, production of food grains (wheat, rice, and rye) was estimated at 72 million tons, down almost 10 percent. The rye crop declined by a projected 40 percent. Oil crops were expected to increase almost 5 percent, with soybeans, at 56 million tons, up 11 percent.

Cotton production was forecast at nearly 14 million bales, up 5 percent, while tobacco production was down 12 percent. Apples and pears were down slightly, and peaches, reflecting freeze damage in the eastern states, were down 20 percent. Grape production was up, however, with wine varieties estimated at just over 2 million tons, an increase of close to 20 percent.

Livestock, Dairy, and Poultry Products. The number of cattle and calves on U.S. farms as of July 1 was 116.3 million, down 4 percent from a year earlier; producers continued to reduce inventories in response to record sup-

plies and low prices. Beef output was expected to drop 6 percent. Production costs for hog raisers were the lowest since early 1983, but returns at midyear were not far above the break-even point. In July the International Trade Commission, finding that imports were hurting U.S. producers, allowed duties to be levied on Canadian live hogs.

Poultry and milk production were both up, while egg output was down slightly. The USDA reduced milk price supports in April and again in July. In September stocks of dairy products held by the USDA were equivalent to 11 billion pounds of milk, despite government efforts to distribute the surplus to the armed forces, schools, the needy, and other outlets.

Canada. Canada had good grain crops in 1985. Wheat production was forecast at almost 24 million tons, up 8 percent from the final 1985 figures, while the coarse grain harvest of 23 million tons was up 3 percent. Oilseed output increased slightly. Beef production amounted to 1.0 million tons, about the same as in the previous two years. Pork production, at 900,000 tons, was also unchanged but would have been

higher had it not been for unusually heavy exports of live hogs to the United States. The flue-cured tobacco crop was down about 10 percent.

Latin America and Caribbean. Countries south of the United States enjoyed a generally good year, with production of coffee up 9 percent and cocoa beans up 23 percent. Grain crops were about equal to 1984, while sugar output declined. The green coffee crop was estimated at close to 67 million bags, up nearly 6 million, largely reflecting a heavy increase in Brazil's output. However, drought threatened to reduce Brazil's 1986 crop. Argentina's grain shipments reached record levels during the first four months of 1985, and Brazil's citrus crop was a record.

Western Europe. Wheat production was expected to be down about 8 percent from the revised record crop of 1984, but the projected coarse grain harvest of 101 million tons was close to 1984's large crop. The European Economic Community successfully reduced dry milk stocks by feeding them to pigs and poultry. In a so-called pasta war, the United States raised duties on pasta to compensate for high EEC duties on U.S. citrus; the EEC retaliated by increasing tariffs on U.S. walnuts and lemons. In mid-October the Reagan administration also charged that subsidized EEC wheat exports were depressing the world market and initiated proceedings against the EEC through the General Agreement on Tariffs and Trade.

Soviet Union and Eastern Europe. Total grain production in the Soviet Union was forecast at 190 million tons, up 12 percent from 1984. The total included 83 million tons of wheat and 95 million tons of coarse grains. Grain imports totaled 39 million tons from July 1984 to June 1985, down substantially from 1983–1984. Wheat and coarse grain harvests were expected to be down in most of Eastern Europe, but Poland expected a record grain crop.

Africa. Famine continued to take a heavy toll in Ethiopia, Sudan, and other sub-Saharan countries. As many as 150 million Africans were suffering from food shortages in some degree, according to delegates at the annual meeting of the Organization of African Unity in July. One estimate put deaths in Ethiopia alone at hundreds of thousands through mid-1985. U.S. food assistance in fiscal 1985 through mid-July totaled over 3 million metric tons; private donations over $120 million were also reported by midyear. Entertainers in Britain, Canada, and the United States donated their services, making records and appearing in rock extravaganzas in July that reached an estimated 1 billion viewers. However, much of the food and other supplies never reached the hungry; an estimated 60 percent of the food shipped to Ethiopia in fiscal 1985 sat undistributed, partly because of civil war in northern sections of the country. Although concern had eased in many areas by year's end, because of abundant rains, Ethiopia and four other countries—Sudan, Botswana, Angola, and Mozambique—remained in serious straits. Experts warned that the prognosis for Africa's agricultural future was still bleak.

Asia. Grain production in Asia continued to be adequate for needs. In China the grain crop was forecast at about 380 million tons, close to 30 million tons below the record figure for 1984. Weather conditions were blamed for the drop, which caused no hardship since grain stocks were abundant.

India's estimated grain harvest of 138 million tons was somewhat above 1983 and 1984 figures, providing enough for some exports. In June it was reported that India had stopped buying its own farmers' wheat, despite a mandate to purchase all offered for sale, because government warehouses were full.

Oceania. Australia's 1985–1986 wheat crop was forecast at 17 million tons, down almost 10 percent from 1984–1985. But beef production was up slightly, and sheep meat production was up nearly 20 percent. Near drought conditions in eastern New Zealand early in the year led to increased slaughter of meat animals; beef and veal production was expected to increase by over 11 percent, sheep meat by 6 percent.

Fisheries. Quota restrictions, management measures, and anticipated lower catches of small open-sea fish threatened to drop the 1985 world catch of fish and shellfish below the high 1984 levels. Fish meal production was expected to be down, and the supply of cod was expected to be on the low side.

On March 18, Canada and the United States signed a treaty in Québec regulating salmon fishing in the Pacific Northwest. Harvests were to be cut in 1985, initiating a 14-year stock rebuilding program.

In a victory for conservationists that threatened to complicate U.S. relations with Japan, a federal appeals court ruled that the United States must reduce the Japanese fishing quota in U.S. waters because Japan refused to abide by an international ban on whaling. The ruling was made despite a 1984 agreement with Japan to delay U.S. sanctions. An appeal of the ruling was filed.   H.W.H.

ALABAMA. See STATISTICS OF THE WORLD.

ALASKA. See STATISTICS OF THE WORLD.

ALBANIA. The death of Albanian party chief Enver Hoxha, on April 11, 1985, ended 41 years of Hoxha's personal brand of hard-line Stalinist rule but otherwise promised little immediate change. Hoxha had dealt ruthlessly with opponents, including possible supporters of former Prime Minister Mehmet Shehu, who died myteriously in 1981, and had built a new leadership structure around his own chosen successor, President Ramiz Alia.

The 59-year-old Alia, though a zealous leader of the Albanian Party of Labor (APL) and a veteran of the "People's Revolution" of 1944, had neither charisma nor his predecessor's prestige and authority. Instead, he faced factionalism, tribal differences, and desires to settle old scores. The army resented party interference, older leaders resented being shunted aside to make way for Alia and his supporters, and there was rumored restlessness and disaffection among Albanian youth.

Although Alia and other Albanian leaders reiterated the country's traditional isolationist policy, the easing of this stance that had already been in progress before Hoxha's death appeared likely to continue. France, Italy, and West Germany sent messages of condolence when Hoxha died, and Albanian propaganda against these countries eased. However, a Soviet message of condolence was rejected as "unacceptable." Closer ties with China seemed attainable, though a reversion to Albania's pre-1978 client status was considered unlikely. Relations with the United States remained poor. Traditional ethnic frictions with Yugoslavia persisted, although Yugoslav officials had attended January ceremonies marking completion of the Albanian section of a railway that was soon to link Albania to an international rail network.

In a major August speech, Alia revealed that Albania had begun talks with Britain regarding the return of $36 million in gold that formerly belonged to the royal house of King Zog and was being held in the Bank of England. Alia also commented that "obvious progress" had been made in cultural and economic relations with Greece and in trade, cultural, and technological exchanges with Italy. A high-level French delegation, headed by Secretary of State for Foreign Relations Jean-Michel Baylet, visited Albania in September and met with Prime Minister Adil Çarçani.

See STATISTICS OF THE WORLD.   R.A.P.

ALBERTA. See STATISTICS OF THE WORLD. See also CANADA.

ALGERIA. Speaking to a February 1985 conference of high-ranking government officials, President Chadli Benjedid startled his audience by calling for a review of the National Charter, which had defined Algerian ideology since 1976. The president said his goal was to "enrich" the charter, which proclaimed Algeria a one-party Islamic socialist state. The speech also was intended to respond to public criticism from different sources.

The government had to deal with various expressions of discontent. A number of Berber activists were arrested and then released in February when they organized a protest on cultural policy. In April police clashed with demonstrators in the Casbah, Algiers's oldest neighborhood, after a house collapsed, killing one person. During the same month, about 30 Muslim militants were sentenced to prison terms of 3 to 12 years for fomenting violence in late 1982 and early 1983. In July, for the second time in two years, the government detained dissident lawyer Ali Yahia, who had just established an Algerian Human Rights League. Finally, on December 16, former President Ahmed Ben Bella, who had been deposed in 1965 and then kept under house arrest for 15 years, announced in London the formation of a united front to oppose one-party rule in Algeria. Two days later, the Algerian government accused Ben Bella of having defrauded the state of $6 million while in office.

In response to grievances, the government increased expenditures for both housing and agriculture in its five-year plan for 1985–1989. Meanwhile, three new strikes in the Sahara increased the country's oil reserves, but poor market conditions remained a serious problem. The national company Sonatrach protected an important natural-gas market by renegotiating a long-term contract with Spain. The government announced in June that it would buy 1 million metric tons of U.S. wheat; the deal angered the European Economic Community, which had been Algeria's chief supplier.

The wheat deal came two months after Benjedid made an unprecedented six-day visit to the United States. Algeria had seen an opportunity to improve relations in the aftermath of Morocco's 1984 pact with Libya, a development troubling to the Reagan administration. During the April visit, an agreement was signed making Algeria eligible for the first time to purchase U.S. arms. Algeria reinforced its U.S. ties in June by helping to negotiate for the release of hostages aboard TWA Flight 847. The jet, hijacked by Lebanese Shiite terrorists while en route from Athens to Rome, followed an erratic course in which it landed twice at the Algiers airport, where scores of passengers were freed.

See STATISTICS OF THE WORLD.   R.A.M.

AMERICAN SAMOA. See STATISTICS OF THE WORLD. See also PACIFIC ISLANDS.

ANGOLA. President José Eduardo dos Santos was reelected to a second five-year term by Angola's ruling party in December 1985. At a party conference in Luanda, he stressed the country's links to Cuba and the Soviet Union and strongly denounced U.S. policy in southern Africa. Meanwhile, events in Angola continued to be dominated by the conflict with South Africa and the related insurgency of the National Union for the Total Independence of Angola (Unita), backed by South Africa.

The withdrawal of South African forces from southern Angola, mandated by a 1984 agreement that the United States had helped bring about, was completed in April 1985. The U.S. government continued to act as broker between Angola and South Africa, seeking an agreement on withdrawal of Cuban troops from Angola and on the independence of Namibia (South West Africa), the territory to the south of Angola occupied by South Africa in defiance of UN rulings. The United States reportedly offered a compromise plan, but South Africa rejected it and instead announced its own "interim" administration for Namibia.

In an incident on May 21 in the Angolan enclave of Cabinda, two South African commandos were killed and one was captured; the prisoner admitted that they were to attack Angolan oil-storage facilities. The U.S. diplomatic role was also impaired in July when Congress repealed the Clark Amendment, which had posed a barrier to U.S. support for Unita or other Angolan guerrilla groups. In response to Congress's move, Angola broke off talks over Namibia; these were resumed in late November. Late in the year, the Reagan administration was reportedly considering resumption of aid to Unita.

Meanwhile, Unita guerrillas continued to mount attacks in southern and eastern Angola. Unita had launched one of its biggest operations in December 29, 1984, against the diamond mining town of Kafunfo; that attack reportedly resulted in as many as 200 deaths. The guerrillas also destroyed a Transamerica Airways transport plane, killing the American copilot and kidnapping 27 hostages, who were released some ten weeks later after being marched 600 miles to Unita's headquarters in southeastern Angola.

In August, Angolan government troops launched a major offensive against Unita base areas around the headquarters. The attack came close to success but was repulsed with the aid of South African air strikes.

In September, South Africa announced a week-long raid into Angola, characterized as a preemptive strike against bases of Southwest Africa People's Organization (Swapo) guerrillas, who were fighting against South African occupation of Namibia. According to South African sources, 15 insurgents were killed. At the end of the month, a South African air raid in southeastern Angola reportedly killed over 65 people. And South Africa reported that its soldiers had launched a new raid in December, killing at least six guerrillas.

Oil production was projected to exceed 220,000 barrels per day by the end of 1985, but in other respects the Angolan economy appeared to be depressed. In April the government signed an agreement with the European Economic Community, thus becoming eligible for EEC trade preferences and aid.

See STATISTICS OF THE WORLD.   W.M.

ANTHROPOLOGY. In 1985 researchers analyzed fragments of a primate fossil believed to be over 40 million years old and reported on the excavation of what were said to be the world's oldest communal buildings. Linguistic anthropologists carried on efforts to save an Eskimo language from extinction.

New Primate Fossils. A report published in the August 23 issue of *Science* magazine contended that fragments of a primate jawbone found in southern Asia were those of an early species that lived between 40 million and 44 million years ago. Called *Amphipithecus mogaungensis* (after the nearby village of Mogaung in northwestern Burma), the mammal was said to represent a crucial link between lower primates and the higher primates, or anthropoids, that evolved into monkeys, apes, and humans.

From the size of its jaw and teeth, the authors conjectured that *Amphipithecus mogaungensis* was 2½–3 feet tall and weighed 15–20 pounds. Its exceptionally deep mandible and nearly square second molar were two chief characteristics linking it to the higher primates, although its identification as a direct ancestor of later anthropoid groups was uncertain. Predating all previously identified anthropoids by at least 5 million years, the animal is believed to have lived in trees and subsisted on fruit. The authors suggested that, in light of their findings, scientists might have to revise the generally accepted view that higher primates originated in Africa.

Ancient Village. Researchers from the United States, Turkey, and West Germany, who had been working for the previous 22 years on a site in southeastern Turkey known as Cayonu, announced the results of their fieldwork in June. Having excavated about 1 acre of an ancient 7-acre village, they discovered what they believed to be the world's oldest communal buildings. Robert Braidwood, of the

University of Chicago, said that the purpose of the buildings, which date back about 10,000 years, and the ethnic origin of the village's inhabitants were uncertain. The three structures contained pilasters (columnlike wall supports) and terrazzo (mosaic-type) floors with white marble chips used to form lines. One of the buildings also contained fragments of burned skulls, possibly indicating some kind of death rite. Remains of about two dozen homes were also uncovered, along with copper drills, hooks, and pins. These implements, said Braidwood, were the first solid evidence that people used copper at such an early period.

The researchers sought to establish a cultural link between the Cayonu site and other ancient sites in the Middle East, especially Catal Huyuk, also in Turkey. Catal Huyuk dates from approximately 8,500 years ago and covers 32 acres. That site yielded elaborate works of architecture, religious art, and, possibly, fertility cult shrines; it also offered evidence of efficient agricultural practices.

Eskimo-Language Rescue. Linguistic anthropologists were engaged in a project designed to save the native language of the approximately 3,000 Inuvialuit Eskimos of Canada's western Arctic. The language, known as Inuvialuktun, consists of three dialects and emphasizes precise descriptions of kinship ties and elements of the natural environment. Such linguistic characteristics are common to the kinds of small, cooperative hunting and gathering societies that the Eskimos lived in many years ago, before European political and economic domination forced them to change their way of life and also learn English.

The Inuvialuit had their first contacts with European whalers and traders in the 19th century. In the 1920's missionaries established schools for the Inuvialuit; they also punished Inuvialuit children who would not speak English. Later, government services and jobs also provided incentives to make English the priority language. According to a recent survey, fewer than 20 percent of the Inuvialuit could speak their native tongue with fluency by that time, although the vast majority thought it was highly desirable to be able to do so.

The federal government in Ottawa, in conjunction with the government of the Northwest Territories, was sponsoring the current project to revive Inuvialuktun as an important second language. Linguistic anthropologists were working with the most knowledgeable living speakers of Inuvialuktun (mostly elderly women) in order to compile basic dictionaries and grammars of the three dialects. They also combined formal language classes with two-week camps in the tundra so that Inuvialuit children could apply their language to nature, just as their ancestors once had done. The organizers of the project believe they are pioneering a model that could be used to rescue other native languages of North America.

P.J.M.

ANTIGUA AND BARBUDA. *See* STATISTICS OF THE WORLD.

ARAB LEAGUE. During its 40th anniversary year in 1985, the Arab League held two unusual meetings. The first, a special session of the league's council, was convened in Tunis on June 8 at the request of the Palestine Liberation Organization to "look into the aggressions against the Palestinian camps in Beirut" by Shiite Muslim militia forces. Lebanon boycotted the meeting because it considered the fighting an "internal" affair. The Council called on "all parties concerned" to "put an end to the siege of the Palestinian camps and to withdraw all the forces that have besieged the areas" nearby. The five-point resolution also asked for liberation of all detainees, facilitation of the work of Red Cross and Red Crescent rescue teams, and cooperation with an Arab League effort to ensure compliance with a cease-fire.

A second meeting was convened by Morocco's King Hassan at Casablanca during August to examine the Palestine problem and to resolve inter-Arab disputes. Hassan's apparent disregard of the implicit rule calling for consensus between "radical" and "conservative" regimes before convening a summit resulted in a boycott by 5 hard-line states among the league's 21 active members: Algeria, South Yemen, Libya, Syria, and Lebanon. After acrimonious debate, a final communiqué was issued that noted but failed to endorse the recent agreement between Jordan's King Hussein and PLO leader Yasir Arafat on an Arab peace plan. The members established two special commissions, one to

Jubilant treasure hunter Mel Fisher (standing, at left) lifts a champagne glass as his son hoists a crusty bar of silver—part of the immense treasure trove from the sunken Spanish galleon Nuestra Señora de Atocha *that Fisher's expedition found off the Florida keys in July, after a 17-year search.*

ARCHAEOLOGY

ARCHAEOLOGY. Shipwrecks dominated the archaeological news in 1985. In Turkey, a Bronze Age wreck, one of the earliest ever found, was being meticulously recovered in a four-year program of fieldwork. The wreck of a Spanish galleon, off Florida, promised to yield millions of dollars for a treasure-hunting company, and archaeologists identified the wreck of a pirate ship off Massachusetts.

Bronze Age Wreck. In the beginning of 1985, early findings from one of the most important discoveries of the century—a Bronze Age shipwreck, located near the village of Kaş, just off the southern coast of Turkey—were reported in the pages of *National Geographic*. Scientists from Texas A & M's Institute of Nautical Archaeology, including George Bass, Cemal M. Pulak, and Donald Frey, investigated the site.

An extensive collection of Bronze Age goods was aboard the unnamed cargo ship, which sank off the Cape of Ulu Burun sometime around 1400 B.C. Study of these items should shed light on trade patterns in the ancient Mediterranean and on important international ties between cultures in antiquity. Never before has a shipwreck provided so much primary evidence for the transport of raw materials in the Late Bronze Age. The cargo included 84 full-sized or half-sized "ox-hide" metal ingots, some still stacked as they had originally been stowed on the ship. Along with the copper and tin ingots, underwater archaeologists recovered raw glass ingots—the earliest ever found—as well as elephant and hippopotamus ivory, resin, glass beads, stacks of Cypriot pottery, and Syro-Palestinian lamps. The most significant find may be the traces of the ship's hull and planking, which were joined together by the mortise-and-tenon method. The earliest evidence for this type of ship construction had previously appeared in a shipwreck from 1,000 years later.

Treasure Ships. In July, some 40 miles west of Key West, Fla., divers uncovered the richest trove of sunken treasure ever found in U.S. waters. The fortune in gold, silver, and jewels had been the cargo of the royal Spanish galleon *Nuestra Señora de Atocha*, a 550-ton flagship known to have sunk in a 1622 hurricane. The discovery was made by Treasure Salvors, Inc.,

seek settlement of Jordan's and Iraq's disputes with Syria, a second to seek solution of Iraqi-Libyan and PLO differences; the league also called for stability in Lebanon and for cooperation between the PLO and the Lebanese government to protect Palestinian refugees. Iran's determination to continue the war against Iraq was denounced, and Iran was warned that the Arab nations would be forced to "reconsider their relations" with Iran if it prolonged the war.

Arabsat 1, a satellite of the Arab Space Communications Organization, was launched from French Guiana in February. Arabsat 1B was launched by the U.S. space shuttle *Discovery* in June.   D.P.

a Key West-based operation headed by veteran treasure hunter Mel Fisher. The company had been searching for the wreck's scattered remains since 1969, attracting investors along the way and locating other wrecks. Its first discovery of Atocha remains came in the early 1970's. The 1985 find was the company's largest haul ever: the total value of the Atocha's cargo has been estimated to be as much as $400 million.

Some archaeologists expressed fear that the galleon's remains, a major archaeological find, would not be excavated scientifically, although Fisher and Duncan Mathewson, a marine archaeologist associated with Treasure Salvors, announced that what was left of the ship would be properly handled and documented. The Atocha's remnants, which are remarkably well preserved, could shed much light on 17th-century ship life and trade.

Meanwhile, other salvage experts continued to hunt for lost treasure. In September, Barry Clifford claimed to have found the wreckage of the H.M.S. Hussar, a British frigate that sank in 1780 in New York's East River carrying gold now thought to be worth as much as $500 million. In November another Clifford find, off Wellfleet, Mass., was positively identified as the pirate galley Whydah, the subject of Cape Cod folklore since it sank in February 1717. Clifford planned to open a Boston museum housing artifacts from the ship, which experts said was the first pirate vessel ever recovered by archaeologists.

Peruvian Ruin. Considerable media attention was focused on Gran Pajaten, an isolated mountain ruin in Peru—especially on the claim that this "lost city" of an unknown pre-Inca civilization had been "rediscovered" by a University of Colorado archaeological team. It

Dedicated Custer buffs join archaeologists in the search for artifacts at the site of the Battle of Little Bighorn in Montana; by combing the area with metal detectors for bullets and spent shells and plotting battle lines, they hope to solve the mystery of what really happened at Custer's Last Stand.

turned out that the site had been investigated as early as 1963 by Douglas Eugene Savoy, an American explorer, and others. The new team, in any case, found 18 ancient buildings and a number of well-preserved 3-foot-high wood carvings of male figures on round burial towers built into the mountainside. The number of burial remains and other evidence suggest that the site was densely inhabited. It was tentatively dated somewhere between A.D. 500 and 1500.

Custer's Last Stand. Research at the Custer Battlefield National Monument reported in April provided a new look at one of the most dramatic days in American history. On June 25, 1876, the U.S. Cavalry officer George Armstrong Custer led a few hundred men into the Little Bighorn region of southeastern Montana, where they were killed by over 1,500 waiting Indians. History buffs have pored over the details of this battle for years, and the new archaeological evidence highlights aspects of the battle and verifies historical details.

Archaeologists Richard Fox and Doug Scott and a crew of volunteers carried out most of the fieldwork with the aid of metal detectors; each area was carefully coded and excavated. The researchers' report included information on the weapons used on both sides, the flow of the battle, and even what the soldiers may have eaten. An analysis of artifacts based on "artifact patterning"—the study of where and how artifacts are distributed—helped detail many of the day's events. Further excavations were planned.   B.R.

ARCHITECTURE. Among noteworthy developments in architecture, important new corporate headquarters were completed in 1985 in the United States, the United Kingdom, and Hong Kong.

New Buildings. By far the most significant work of architecture to be completed was the Hong Kong and Shanghai Banking Corporation headquarters in Hong Kong. Designed by British architect Norman Foster with engineers Ove Arup & Partners, the bank breaks new ground in every aspect of skyscraper design except height (less than 50 stories). Its sophisticated structural system, based upon the principle of suspension, resembles a ship's masts and spars. The interior plan is equally innovative—there are, in effect, three office towers within the main tower, with all three sections stacked atop a huge banking hall. The glass and aluminum tower, with its helipad cap, is a striking addition to the chaotic Hong Kong skyline. Built at a cost of $640 million, it is also an extravagant symbol of the bank's faith in Hong Kong, the British colony due for repossession by China in 1997.

The Hong Kong and Shanghai Bank and a

With its color-coded utilities (plumbing, heating, and ventilation) suspended over the roof on steel poles, the new PA Technology Laboratory in Hightstown, N.J., boasts a column-free interior that can be used to maximum effect. The building, designed by Richard Rogers, exemplifies the latest high-tech style.

second project, new headquarters for Lloyd's of London, designed by British architect Richard Rogers and scheduled to open in 1986, together set the high water mark of British high tech architecture. Characterized by exposed and often exaggerated structural and mechanical parts, the high tech style is exemplified by the 1977 Centre Pompidou in Paris, designed by Rogers and Renzo Piano. Rogers's headquarters for Lloyd's, while a smaller and less spectacular commission than Foster's Hong Kong bank, is nonetheless equal proof of the gradual acceptance by corporate clients in the Commonwealth, if not elsewhere, of the once radical high tech style.

The 1985 Gold Medal of the Royal Institute of British Architects, the United Kingdom's highest honor for architects, went to Richard Rogers. The year also marked the completion of Rogers's first commission in the United States, the small PA Technology facility in Hightstown, N.J. It is a "flexible shed." All mechanical services, such as the heating and electrical systems, are placed outside the building on huge A-frame steel poles that also support a suspended roof, providing a completely column-free interior for maximum flexibility in utilizing space.

The most significant commissions completed in the United States were, like the Hong Kong bank and Lloyd's, corporate headquarters; there, however, similarities end. The new Humana building in Louisville, Ky., headquarters for the private healthcare corporation, is an idiosyncratic, colorful, and highly ornamented tower— the largest building completed to date by postmodernist Michael Graves of Princeton, N.J. The new Procter & Gamble headquarters in downtown Cincinnati, designed by Kohn Pedersen Fox Associates of New York, recalls American skyscrapers of the 1920's and 1930's. It is an L-shaped complex with a generous public terrace. These two buildings and others under construction in many American cities evince a trend toward postmodern architecture with historical references and a frankly decorative style.

Neither the high tech Lloyd's building and Hong Kong bank nor the postmodern Humana and Procter & Gamble buildings are, strictly speaking, cutting-edge design. They document

Twin towers, with the sculpted shapes, pointed tops, and lively decoration of postmodern architecture, make Procter & Gamble's new headquarters in downtown Cincinnati by Kohn Pedersen Fox Associates a dramatic example of the shift in corporate architecture away from anonymous boxy buildings toward the latest in high-profile architectural design.

instead a period of consolidation in architecture. Similarly, the most notable public structure completed in 1985—Richard Meier's Museum of Decorative Arts in Frankfurt, West Germany—is a refinement of ideas that were explored by that architect over the course of two decades.

Urban Planning. After two years of debate, the city of San Francisco adopted a new zoning code that will drastically limit growth in the downtown area. This innovative code limits new office construction to about 50 percent of the square footage previously allowed. It also reduces the maximum height for new buildings from 700 feet, or 55 stories, to 550 feet, or 43 stories; aims to shift development from the downtown financial district to a nearby rundown area; establishes guidelines

for skyscraper silhouettes in an effort to break free of the "bland box syndrome" and vary the skyline; and provides protection for historic structures.

In New York City, a very large and important piece of land was put up for sale by the city and the Metropolitan Transit Authority, co-owners of the Columbus Circle Coliseum site. With the opening of a new convention center in 1986, the Coliseum will become redundant; its prominent site at the southwest corner of Central Park enticed 13 developers to bid for the right to build a mixed-use complex on the land. The lowest bidder offered a design by Canadian architect Moshe Safdie, whose two towers of faceted glass separated by a slender 30-foot slot struck many critics as out of keeping with other Manhattan architecture.

In September, New York barred new high-rise buildings on residential side streets of Manhattan's Upper East Side. The action was aimed at protecting the neighborhood's architectural character and encouraging six-story buildings matching in height the existing brownstones, town houses, and tenement buildings.

Preservation. The proper role of government in promoting and regulating historic preservation was a topic of paramount importance to architects and preservationists. The Reagan administration once again recommended no funding for the National Trust for Historic Preservation. (Previously, Congress appropriated operating funds for the organization despite administration recommendations against it.) In addition, the tax reform proposals set forth by President Ronald Reagan called for the elimination of tax credits for historic preservation.

Museums. Michael Graves's scheme, unveiled in May, for an addition to the Whitney Museum of American Art in New York City provoked widespread criticism. Graves designed a colorful and elaborate building that would rise beside and over the top of the original gray granite museum, designed by Marcel Breuer in 1966. An addition to Frank Lloyd Wright's Solomon R. Guggenheim Museum in New York was also in the works. Gwathmey Siegel & Associates designed an 11-story tower to replace an existing annex, which stands adjacent to the museum and was designed according to Wright's sketches by one of his associates.

A new Canadian Center for Architecture, founded by Seagrams heiress Phyllis Lambert, was being built in Montréal; the center will have an extensive collection of architectural photographs, prints, drawings, and models, as well as archives and a library.

Awards. Austrian architect Hans Hollein won the prestigious Pritzker Prize. The American Institute of Architects awarded its Gold Medal posthumously to William Caudill, a founding partner of CRS Associates in Houston. Eero Saarinen's General Motors Technical Center in Michigan received the Twenty-five Year Award for distinguished and enduring architectural design.   D.D.B.

ARGENTINA. The year 1985 marked a difficult passage for Argentina's new democracy. A severe economic crisis prompted the government of President Raúl Alfonsín to impose austerity measures, and, amid some unrest, the government declared a state of siege late in the year.

Economic "Shock Plan." Economic problems mounted in the first half of the year. Inflation was the most obvious critical issue: at 688 percent, 1984's rate was double that of 1983, and by mid-1985 inflation had doubled again. Gross domestic product was declining sharply, and projected automobile production for the year was at its lowest level in two decades. Official unemployment reached 6 percent in April, and unofficial estimates of unemployment were much higher.

Terming this situation the equivalent of a "war economy," President Alfonsín on June 14 announced a "shock plan" for the economy. It provided for an indefinite freeze on wages and prices at June 12 levels, promised deep cuts in the government deficit, and unveiled a new currency, the austral, equal to 1,000 old pesos and linked to the U.S. dollar. Interest rates were lowered to reduce inflation, and the printing of new currency was tied to actual reserves on hand to prevent devaluation—that is, the government pledged to cease paying its bills by simply printing money.

The first months of the new plan produced mixed economic results. Inflation fell to a monthly rate of 6.2 percent for July, from June's monthly rate of 30 percent; by September it was down to 2 percent a month. Bank deposits and the stock market were up, reflecting the initial optimism of business sectors. Labor leaders, however, claimed that 600,000 workers had been laid off since the plan began.

The International Monetary Fund responded favorably to the plan, as a previously suspended $1.4 billion standby loan was approved. Argentina made several payments of overdue interest on its more than $45 billion debt, making possible the rescheduling of the 1982–1985 debt due (some $16 billion) and final agreement on $4.2 billion in new loans from banks. The IMF agreement also helped make possible a series of new loans scheduled to reach Argentina through May 1986.

Trials of Military Leaders. Nine members of the military juntas that had ruled Argentina from 1976 to 1982 went on trial in April. The charges—stemming from the military's "dirty war" against dissidents and terrorists—included illegal deprivation of liberty, torture, homicide, theft, illegal entry, and forging of documents. In all, hundreds of witnesses testified at the eight-month trial. On December 9 a civilian court declared five of the defendants guilty, including General Jorge Videla, president of the first junta that came to power, and General Roberto Eduardo Viola, president of a subsequent junta. Viola received a 17-year prison term; Videla was sentenced for life. The other defendants were acquitted.

Meanwhile, a verdict was awaited in a separate closed-door trial of 16 officers by a military court. The court-martial, which began in 1983, accused members of the third junta and others of "negligence" in conducting the country's 1982 war with Great Britain over the Falkland Islands.

State of Siege. In the wake of an increase in bombings and bomb threats during the preceding months, the Alfonsín government declared a 60-day state of siege on October 25. According to official sources, the action was taken primarily to allow the government to detain six military officers and six civilians suspected of right-wing terrorism; a judge had earlier ruled that the suspects could not be arrested unless a state of siege was in effect. The government promised to maintain civil rights provided that they did not impede efforts against terrorism.

Elections. Midterm elections on November 3, the first such elections to be held in 20 years, allowed Alfonsín's Radical Party to maintain its majority in the lower house of Congress. The victory, however, was not of the magnitude the party had hoped for. The Radicals polled 43 percent of the vote and gained one seat, while the second-place Peronists, sharply divided into two warring factions, lost seven seats.

Foreign Affairs. The long-standing dispute with Chile over the Beagle Channel, at the southern tip of South America, was officially resolved in May, when a Vatican-mediated treaty was ratified by Argentina and Chile. In November the Argentine government arrested a former Gestapo leader, Walter Kutschmann, on a special extradition warrant from West Germany. Kutschmann, who had been living in Argentina under an assumed name since 1947, would be the first Nazi fugitive ever extradited by Argentina.

See STATISTICS OF THE WORLD. J.F., Jr.

ARIZONA. See STATISTICS OF THE WORLD.

ARKANSAS. See STATISTICS OF THE WORLD.

ART. Major art exhibitions in 1985 included several on the painting and sculpture of India. The auction houses Christie's and Sotheby's were both found to have engaged in questionable practices.

Festival of India. The Festival of India, a celebration in the United States of Indian arts, sciences, and crafts, got under way in May with "The Sculpture of India: 3000 B.C.–1300 A.D." at the National Gallery of Art in Washington, D.C. Simultaneously, "The Arts of South Asia" appeared at Washington's Freer Gallery of Art. September saw the gala opening of "India!" at the Metropolitan Museum of Art in New York City, offering 350 religious and secular works from the 14th through the 19th centuries. About 20 exhibitions covering Indian art from miniature painting to court costumes were to appear in 1985 and 1986 at other museums in cities across the country, including San Francisco, Cleveland, and Boston. The

Art Wacko

"Raindrops Keep Falling on My Shed," "Orange You Glad It's Framed," "Brown Bug in Drag"—these are among a collection of works of art in a class by themselves. Selected by experienced, discriminating art buyers who comb garage sales, church bazaars, and secondhand stores for paintings with that . . . certain something, they are the certified World's Worst oil paintings. Not every grossly inferior painting qualifies as a World's Worst. Norman Watt of the University of British Columbia and his friend William Goodacre favor paintings of impossible scenes (such as the sun setting in front of the mountains) or perhaps nudes with the hard-to-draw parts left out. Most of these master works are auctioned off to benefit the British Columbia Paraplegic Association, but some are offered to world-class museums in the hopes of obtaining valuable rejection slips. So far both the Prado in Madrid and the Hermitage in Leningrad have actually accepted donations.

festival was sponsored by the government of India and by government and private sources in the United States.

Other U.S. Exhibitions. The 1985 Biennial Exhibition at the Whitney Museum of American Art in New York City presented works created during the previous two years that were deemed

A pair of 18th-century Sèvres vases painted with Oriental scenes were among 700 objects in the lavish "Treasure Houses of Britain" exhibit at Washington's National Gallery. The exhibit—the largest in the gallery's history—displayed paintings, sculpture, furniture, and other works on loan from Britain's gracious country homes.

by the curators to represent the best new American art. This exhibition seemed to most critics to provide a relatively cohesive view of current art. A central thread running through work as diverse as that of Jasper Johns and Cindy Sherman was how commercial imagery—from advertising to computer terminals—dominates American life and consciousness. Photography assumed a more central place in this biennial than in any previous one. Moving up fast, however, was a new style of art originating in New York's East Village, represented in this show by the cartoon-like work of Rodney Alan Greenblat and David Wojnarowicz.

Retrospectives of contemporary artists included Leon Golub at New York's New Museum of Contemporary Art, Jonathan Borofsky at the Whitney, and Robert Motherwell at the Guggenheim. Works by Henri Rousseau and Kurt Schwitters were featured in major exhibitions at the Museum of Modern Art in New York. The Guggenheim presented "Kandinsky in Paris: 1933–44," the last part of its trilogy on the work of Wassily Kandinsky. "The Circle of Montparnasse: Jewish Artists in Paris 1905–1945," at New York's Jewish Museum, examined the time when Marc Chagall, Jacques Lipchitz, Amedeo Modigliani, and others were drawn to a single neighborhood where Jewish art flourished. Meanwhile, the Philadelphia Museum of Art hosted the only U.S. showing of "Chagall: A Retrospective," an acclaimed exhibition of 200 works by the Russian émigré painter, who died in March. The exhibition, organized by the Royal Academy of Arts in London, stressed Chagall's work from 1910 to 1920 and showed the impact of that work on modern art.

A show by Jennifer Bartlett at the Walker Art Center in Minneapolis occasioned a media blitz on this highly praised star. Other shows included "Degas: The Dancers" at the National Gallery of Art, "The New Path: Ruskin and the American Pre-Raphaelites" at the Brooklyn Museum, and "The Age of Caravaggio" at the Metropolitan Museum of Art. A major Renoir exhibition opened in October at the Boston Museum of Fine Arts. "Treasure Houses of Britain: Five Hundred Years of Private Patronage and Art Collecting," which opened at

Marc Chagall, who died at age 97 in France, was internationally renowned for his unconventional vision of the world, which he expressed in brightly colored paintings such as The Bride and Groom of the Eiffel Tower, *1938–1939.*

Washington, D.C.'s National Gallery of Art in November, included some 700 paintings, sculpture, pieces of furniture, and other works from Britain's remarkable country houses.

Museums. Established museums planned major expansions and new museums opened across the United States at an unprecedented rate. Both the Whitney and the Guggenheim announced plans for major expansions. The Whitney's controversial design called for a 10-story addition that would more than double its current space. The Guggenheim envisioned an 11-story addition for gallery, storage, and office space.

In September, Dartmouth College in New Hampshire opened the Hood Museum of Art, a $7 million facility containing ten galleries. The Museum of Art in Dallas opened its new 15,000-square-foot decorative arts wing in late November. The Virginia Museum of Fine Arts

The still dreamer and watchful lion of Henri Rousseau's Sleeping Gypsy *of 1900 formed the centerpiece of a retrospective of his works held at the Museum of Modern Art in New York City.*

in Richmond inaugurated a $22 million West Wing in December. Atlanta's High Museum of Art was to open a satellite facility in the city's downtown area early in 1986. The new Museum of Art in Fort Lauderdale, Fla., was expected to open in January 1986, in a three-story $7.5 million facility designed by Edward Larabee Barnes.

Events in Europe. The new Picasso Museum opened in Paris in September. Now housed in the 17th-century Hotel Sale was the world's largest collection of Picasso masterpieces, created from 1901 until the artist's death in 1973; also in the museum was Picasso's private collection of works by other artists, including Renoir, Cézanne, Degas, Rousseau, Matisse, and Miró. In an effort to reestablish itself as a leading center of contemporary art, the city of Paris in March introduced the "Nouvelle Biennale de Paris," an international exhibition of painting, sculpture, music, photographs, and video.

In Vienna a massive exhibition at the Kunstlerhaus, "Dream and Reality: Vienna 1870–1930," recapitulated achievements of the turn-of-the-century Viennese avant-garde. In Munich, "The German Romantics" revealed the achievements of German painting between 1800 and 1850, including work by Caspar David Friedrich and others. In London, Charles Saatchi's personal museum, housing his massive collection of contemporary art, opened to the public. The interior of the former factory building was converted into a large white space designed to present to best advantage the huge colorful canvases by leading artists of the 1970's and 1980's.

Nazi Art Loot. *Artnews* magazine in December 1984 published a story noting that thousands of works of art seized by the Nazis in World War II had been held for decades by the Austrian government, which had done little to publicize its holdings or facilitate efforts of owners and heirs to recover their property. In response, the Austrian government at first announced it would auction the works—including paintings, sculptures, and objets d'art—and give the proceeds to an appropriate charity; Austrian officials also said the auction probably would not include several hundred works of art that had been quietly placed in Austrian museums and government offices. *Artnews* publisher Milton Esterow and Jewish leaders pressed for full disclosure of the works' identities and a publicity campaign to encourage rightful owners or heirs to make their claims. In December 1985 the government published a list of over 8,000 works of art, books, coins, and other confiscated objects now in government possession; claimants were to be given until September 30, 1986, to come forward. After that period, all unclaimed works would be auctioned, with the proceeds distributed to organizations to aid Holocaust victims.

Tilted Arc. Controversy surrounded *Tilted Arc,* a 12-foot-high, 120-foot-long curved piece of rusted steel executed by Richard Serra and displayed since 1981 on the plaza of a federal office building complex in Manhattan. General Services Administration hearings in March occasioned a bitter confrontation between the art world and the public. Detractors denounced the sculpture as a target for graffiti and as an ugly wall that prevented use of the plaza for public events, while defenders called it a challenging work of art that added aesthetic energy to a poorly designed space. In May the GSA announced that another site would be considered.

Auction House Scandals. David Bathurst resigned as chairman of Christie's in Britain and the United States, after admitting in a court deposition that he had lied about the sale of two paintings in a 1981 auction. Bathurst had announced that a Van Gogh and a Gauguin had sold for a total of $3.4 million when in fact neither had sold; bidding had stopped short of the owner's lowest acceptable selling price. Bathurst defended his action as an effort to "maintain stability in the art market" and protect the paintings' value. He was fined $80,000 and lost his New York auctioneer's license for two years, while Christie's New York president, Christopher Burge, lost his license for four months.

Sotheby's agreed to an out-of-court settlement in a case involving a 1984 auction of Hebrew books and manuscripts. Alexander Guttmann, who had smuggled the works out of Nazi Germany, had consigned them to Sotheby's. The New York State attorney general had charged that Sotheby's knew Guttmann did not have proper title and withheld key information from the public. Sotheby's claimed it had gone to great lengths to determine if Guttmann had title. The settlement did not resolve questions of possible wrongdoing but did require that most of the works sold at the auction be recalled from buyers and redistributed to institutions. Sotheby's also relinquished commissions from the $2.2 million sale.

Major Sales. In April, Sotheby's New York sold old master and impressionist paintings from the estate of Florence Gould for some $34 million, the highest total ever for a single art collection.

A problem plaguing major sales was the insistence by sellers on very high reserve prices. At a sale of impressionists and modern masters at Sotheby's London on March 26, 46 percent of the paintings failed to sell. An even bigger failure was the sale in May of the Samuel T. Fee collection of old masters, at Christie's New York. The collection, scorned by the art com-

Richard Serra's Tilted Arc, *a huge curve of rusted steel commissioned by the General Services Administration for Federal Plaza in downtown Manhattan, was the focus of hearings to decide its fate. Pitted against a highly vocal, Arc-hating general public were the sculptor and his advocates in the art world.*

As Halley's celebrated comet streaked across the sky beginning in late 1985, it was accompanied by both scientific probes and an intensive media blitz. At left, entrepreneur Owen Ryan is surrounded by his "official" Halley's comet logo paraphernalia. Above, the sky wanderer as seen during its last swing near the earth in 1910. Astronomers study comets to learn about the raw material of the solar system.

munity, had been formed for investment purposes over a period of only a few years. Two-thirds of the works failed to sell.

Nonetheless, the few truly important old masters to appear on the block attracted record bidding. In April the J. Paul Getty Museum paid £7.5 million for Andrea Mantegna's *Adoration of the Magi* at Christie's London. At Sotheby's London an English collector paid £2 million for Guido Reni's *David With the Head of Goliath,* a record price for the artist. At the Christie's Fee sale, one of the seven works that did sell—Jan van de Cappelle's *Visit of the Stadtholder, Prince Frederick Hendrick, to the Fleet of the States General at Dordrecht*—fetched $1.65 million from an anonymous American collector. That was the highest price paid for an old master at an American auction since Rembrandt's *Aristotle Contemplating the Bust of Homer* was sold to the Metropolitan in 1961.

Art Thefts. Nine impressionist paintings, including five by Monet and two by Renoir, were stolen at gunpoint from the Marmottan Museum in Paris one morning in October. The paintings, valued at a minimum of $12.5 million, included Monet's *Impression, Sunrise,* which gave its name to the impressionist movement in art. Some 140 highly valuable pre-Columbian artifacts created by Mayas, Aztecs, Mixtecs, and Zapotecs from gold, jade, obsidian, and turquoise were stolen from the National Museum of Anthropology in Mexico City in December.   B.B.S.

ASTRONOMY. Several major telescopes were authorized, under construction, or moving toward completion in 1985. Both astronomers and the general public eagerly awaited the approach of Halley's Comet. Soviet researchers revealed data about the planet Venus, and astronomers continued to debate the nature of the "hidden" mass in the universe.

New Telescopes. Radio astronomers in the United States and Australia received go-aheads to build the largest instruments ever constructed for radio wave observations. The American project, called the Very-Long-Baseline Array, was intended to combine the signals from ten antennas, each 25 meters (82 feet) in diameter, scattered across the continental United States, Puerto Rico, and Hawaii. With an effective diameter of 8,000 kilometers, or 5,000 miles, this instrument would permit the detection of extremely tiny and distant celestial sources, ones that may be the oldest objects in the universe. The Australia Telescope, scheduled to become operational in late 1988, was to be much more compact; its eight antennas in New South Wales will have a maximum separation of only 320 km.

Steadily moving toward completion was the Hubble Space Telescope (HST), an instrument that should revolutionize optical astronomy. In 1984 its five principal scientific instruments passed acceptance tests, and in 1985 they were joined to the other major parts of this billion-dollar spacecraft. Scheduled for deployment by the space shuttle in the second half of 1986, HST should detect celestial objects seven times fainter than previously possible. Its images should also reveal details more than five times smaller than earth-based telescopes can record.

Also moving ahead was construction of a giant telescope sponsored by the University of California and the California Institute of Technology. A ground-breaking ceremony was held in September atop the 13,800-foot dormant Hawaiian volcano Mauna Kea, with completion expected in 1991. The telescope was to have a mosaic of 36 mirrors with a combined diameter of 10 meters.

Halley's Comet. As its elongated orbit around the sun brought it near the earth for the first time in three-quarters of a century, Halley's Comet provoked an unprecedented media blitz. With the celebrated solar system wanderer expected to become visible through binoculars and small telescopes beginning late in 1985, many enthusiasts were prompted to buy optical equipment. Some manufacturers could not keep up with the demand for telescopes and accessories. Halley-related memorabilia took

every imaginable form—from T-shirts to cocktail glasses—and thousands booked trips to the southern hemisphere, where the comet would be best seen in April 1986. The craze was ironic because, according to some predictions, Halley's Comet was expected to make one of its poorest showings in the 2,000 years it has been observed.

The launch of three spacecraft, one by the European Space Agency and two by Japan, brought to five the number of probes scheduled to rendezvous with Halley's Comet in March 1986. (Two Soviet spacecraft had been launched in December 1984; they flew by Venus in June 1985.) They would not be the first to intercept a comet, however; the U.S. International Cometary Explorer flew through the tail of Comet Giacobini-Zinner on September 11. Findings from that mission, in which the Explorer passed within 4,900 miles of the comet's nucleus, confirmed that comets are celestial "dirty snowballs." Water molecules were detected in abundance, but dust particles were fewer than had been expected. The latter finding was good news for the Halley probes, since impacting dust particles can destroy a spacecraft.

Venus. At a conference held in March, Soviet planetologists described to Western scientists the results from their Venus probes Venera 15 and 16, which began orbiting the planet in October 1983. For eight months the Veneras collected radar data for mapping purposes. The spacecraft were able to isolate features as small as 1 to 2 km across on Venus's cloud-shrouded surface while measuring mountain heights to an accuracy of 50 m. The Veneras found that the planet's skin had been molded by volcanic activity, movements of its crust, the impact of meteorites, and other processes not yet understood. Soviet scientists concluded that Venus's surface has evolved less rapidly than that of our planet and that the observed surface is 500 million to 1 billion years old. Geologically, this means that Venus is a more dynamic body than Mars but less dynamic than the earth.

Galaxies. Largely through recent observations at infrared wavelengths, astronomers have come to believe that many galaxies undergo relatively brief though widespread episodes of star formation sometime during their lives. When this happens, the infrared luminosity of a "star-burst" galaxy increases enormously. Often this extreme luminosity is accompanied by maser emission (microwave output, analogous to the light from an optical laser) from the hydroxyl radical (a combination of one atom of hydrogen and one of oxygen), which is also regarded as indicative of stellar birth.

For the most luminous infrared galaxies, up to 100 billion newborn stars would be needed to produce the observed emission. But what could trigger such a massive spawning? In 1984 and 1985, a growing consensus developed holding that collisions between galaxies are responsible. During such an event the gases from both galaxies merge and become compressed, encouraging the formation of particularly dense pockets, which later collapse gravitationally under their own weight to produce the new stars.

"How much invisible matter is there in the universe?" This is currently one of the most debated questions in astronomy. Some researchers believe this "hidden" mass outweighs that which we can see by 10 to 100 times.

Obvious candidates for this missing stuff include rocks, comets, and planets, as well as "dead" and brown dwarf stars; microscopic particles such as protons and neutrons qualify too. But equally interesting are the so-called nonbaryonic particles such as photons and neutrinos. Exotic brands of this kind of matter would include photinos, axions, and primordial black holes—none of which has been proved to exist.

Nevertheless, the potential presence of exotic particles, coupled with the fact that 90 percent or more of the matter in the universe is invisible, has led to the most comprehensive theory yet describing how galaxies form. It envisions "cold, dark matter," consisting of nonbaryonic particles, and was set forth in late 1984 by researchers at the University of California and at Cambridge University in England.

Meteorites. Chondrites are the most common kind of meteorite to strike the earth, but the source of these stony bodies has remained a mystery. Recently, however, a computer simulation demonstrated that asteroids of similar composition, located some 400 million km

from the sun between Jupiter and Mars, can be abruptly thrown earthward by the gravitational influence of Jupiter. L.J.R.

AUSTRALIA. An abrupt decline in the value of the Australian dollar and disputes over taxes and wages temporarily placed an "accord" between the Australian Labor Party (ALP) government and the trade unions at risk in 1985. These developments were closely linked to foreign policy issues, especially the Anzus military alliance (involving Australia, New Zealand, and the United States), and to the government's stance on nuclear disarmament.

Foreign Affairs. The New Zealand Labor government's refusal to permit nuclear-armed or nuclear-powered U.S. ships to enter its ports was supported by elements of the ALP, but not by Prime Minister Robert Hawke. In a February letter to New Zealand Prime Minister David Lange, Hawke appeared to be pressuring the New Zealanders to fall into line with U.S. requirements. While Hawke was in Brussels the same month, a furor erupted with the discovery that in 1983 he, Foreign Minister William Hayden, and then-Defense Minister Gordon Scholes had agreed that the United States should be allowed to test-fire the MX missile into the sea off Tasmania. Denunciation of this agreement by some ALP members prompted Hawke to abandon it. He also revealed that planned Anzus "Sea Eagle" exercises had been canceled, but he said Australia would conduct military exercises separately with the United States and with New Zealand.

After traveling from Brussels to Washington, Hawke was helped by a State Department announcement that the United States did not need Australian assistance with the MX tests. But a joint communiqué in which Hawke approved of the U.S. "strategic modernization program" caused another furor among ALP members and others who opposed Washington's Strategic Defense Initiative ("Star Wars"). The Labor government continued to tread an uneasy path between support for the United States and advocacy of nuclear disarmament. When the United States declined to attend Anzus ministerial talks with New Zealand, the Australian government canceled them and conducted bilateral talks with U.S. representatives in Canberra. Australia declined, despite

U.S. overtures, to join in research for the Strategic Defense Initiative.

In August, Hawke persuaded heads of government of the Pacific Forum, meeting in Rarotonga, in the Cook Islands, to endorse a treaty declaring the South Pacific a nuclear-free zone. The treaty did, however, limit the rights of signatories to admit, or restrict, vessels carrying weapons in their waters. Australian Defense Minister Kim Beazley, visiting Washington in August, argued that the treaty was directed mainly against French nuclear tests in the region and against the proposed dumping of nuclear wastes by Japan.

Economic Developments. The value of the Australian dollar plummeted during the year, in what was widely interpreted as an anxious reaction to the prime minister's perceived vulnerability to party factionalism. The currency had remained relatively stable in 1984, hitting a high of 96.55 U.S. cents, but by April 1985 it had plunged to 62.8 U.S. cents. (By year's end it stood at about 68 U.S. cents.) Meanwhile, a record trade deficit was being posted.

In June the government published a report on tax reform for consideration by a promised "taxation summit." Key proposals included a new capital gains tax and a shift from dependence on direct income taxes to a broad-based consumption tax of 12.5 percent on most goods and services. Pensioners and other disadvantaged groups were to be compensated through the social security system. The consumption tax was supported by major business organizations but not by retailers or labor unions, and some welfare groups opposed a tax on foodstuffs and other goods. The July "summit" became a rout for the government when major business organizations rejected capital gains taxes demanded by unions and others in return for accepting a consumption tax. The prime minister, in negotiation with the trade unions, dropped the idea of a consumption tax in favor of a broadened sales tax at the wholesale level, but this measure also was finally abandoned. Some tax revisions were adopted later in the year.

Economic policy continued on the path of deregulation and encouragement of the private sector. In February, Treasurer Paul Keating approved the issuance of licenses to 16 foreign banks, some of which planned to collaborate with local interests. In August he projected a reduced deficit for 1985–1986. Apart from initiatives directed at reducing youth unemployment, the budget contained few new commitments, conforming comfortably with Hawke's promise to hold the line.

In September the Hawke government secured a two-year extension of the 1983 wage stabilization accord between the government and unions, which provided for centralized wage-setting tied to the consumer price index. Keating had proposed that the national wage

AUSTRALIA

increase currently due be "discounted" below the inflation rate; a compromise agreement reached in September provided for a discounted increase for the next wage settlement, in April 1986, with a compensating tax cut to be enacted effective in September 1986. Meanwhile, inflation in fiscal year 1985–1986 was expected to be about 8 percent, as against 5.6 percent in the previous fiscal year.

Politics and Government. A factional dispute within the opposition Liberal Party culminated in September when party leader Andrew Peacock failed in an attempt to have John Howard, the party's deputy parliamentary leader, dismissed from that post. Peacock thereupon resigned as party leader, and Howard was elected to succeed him.

Court action continued in the case of High Court Justice Lionel Murphy. He had been accused by the chief magistrate of New South Wales of having attempted to intervene in the trial of a lawyer accused of corruption. Murphy, on leave from the court, went on trial before the state Supreme Court, and on July 5 a jury found him guilty on one of two counts of attempting to pervert the course of justice.

However, jurors subsequently claimed they had been misled by the trial judge and court officials. Murphy appealed and won a retrial.

State Developments. Labor retained power by a reduced margin in the Victoria state election in March; in October the state's incumbent governor, Brian Murray, was forced to resign because of a scandal involving acceptance of free air fare. In Western Australia, Premier Brian Burke fought federal government plans to introduce national land-rights legislation for aborigines that would have entailed a right to veto mining operations on their land; the federal government ultimately acceded and dropped the plan. The Queensland state government was embarrassed when police raided fertility control clinics and seized extensive files, which revealed that some National Party members had undergone illegal vasectomies. In South Australia, Labor Premier John Bannon was returned to power with a clear majority after December 7 elections. The outcome was taken as a setback for the new national Liberal leader, who had campaigned vigorously for the state's Liberal leader.

See STATISTICS OF THE WORLD.   B.J.

Ayers Rock, the massive national landmark in the Northern Territory, was restored to Australia's aboriginal people. They received legal title to the huge monolith and the surrounding national park, which includes several sites sacred to the aborigines.

AUSTRIA. Austria's two-year-old coalition government, composed of the senior-member Socialist Party and the right-wing Freedom Party, weathered a major political storm and other incidents in 1985. The storm erupted in late January over the decision by Defense Minister Friedhelm Frischenschlager to receive personally, at a military airfield in Graz, former SS Major Walter Reder, an aging Nazi war criminal returning to Austria after his release for health reasons from prison in Italy. Frischenschlager's action was unanimously condemned by the country's political parties. The conservative daily *Kurier,* voicing the opinion of many who saw published photographs of the minister greeting the former Nazi, said it had brought disgrace upon Austria. In Parliament the opposition People's Party called for a vote of no confidence, which the government survived, 98-80, on February 1. Frischenschlager apologized for his action, which he said had been meant as a humanitarian gesture.

On December 27, minutes after a similar attack in Rome, Palestinian terrorists fired submachine guns and rolled out grenades in a check-in lounge for El Al Airlines at the Vienna airport. Four people were killed, including one terrorist, and nearly 50 wounded. Two surviving gunmen were to be tried for murder. The event was a particular embarrassment to the government because of its pro-Arab policies.

Another issue that plagued the government was the planned construction of a hydroelectric plant at Hainburg, on the Danube River. After meeting with extensive resistance from conservation groups and the general public, the government instituted an ecological commission to look into the project and possible alternatives. Plans to build the plant at Hainburg were shelved, although other sites were under consideration.

The Austrian wine industry suffered a blow in midsummer when the toxic chemical diethylene glycol, used in antifreeze, was found in a number of domestic and exported Austrian wine brands. The chemical, which can cause brain and kidney damage, had been added as a sweetening agent. Over 50 farmers, wine dealers, and chemists were arrested in the wake of the scandal, which resulted in widespread confiscations and embargoes of Austrian wines. In October Parliament gave final approval to a strict law reducing permissible levels of sugar and other additives in Austrian wines and establishing a system of inspections.

See Statistics of the World. R.S.

AUTOMOBILE INDUSTRY. Record sales, state-mandated seat-belt legislation, diversification by the Big Three automakers, and a rollback of the federal fuel economy standard highlighted the year 1985 for the U.S. auto industry.
Sales. Automakers sold a record 15.6 million domestic and imported cars and trucks in the United States during the 1985 model year. Although car sales of 11.1 million fell slightly short of the 1973 record of 11.7 million, deliveries of 4.6 million trucks surpassed the 1978 record of 4.2 million. The sales boom was kindled by cheaper gasoline, moderate financing costs, generally good economic times, an array of aerodynamically styled, electronically advanced cars, and increasingly popular minivans and small pickups.

U.S. manufacturers sold 8,389,649 cars, good for 76 percent of the market and their best showing since 1979, when 8.62 million autos were delivered. Imports enjoyed record sales of 2,681,635 cars. General Motors, responsible for 41 percent of all vehicles sold, delivered 4,694,979 cars and 1,607,212 trucks, its best year since 1979. Ford sold 2,170,410 cars and 1,249,958 trucks, good for 21 percent of the market and also its best performance since 1979. Chrysler also did well.

After the Reagan administration declined in March to ask Japan to extend its "voluntary" auto export control program, the Japanese government raised shipments to the United States from 1.85 to 2.3 million cars annually.
Profits. Despite a rise in actual sales, profits by the Big Three automakers dropped. Analysts attributed this to the cost of financing sales incentive programs and to increased competition from foreign automakers. GM netted $2.8 billion during the first nine months of 1985, compared with $3.6 billion in the first three quarters of the previous year. Ford reported profits of $1.8 billion for the first nine months, down from $2.2 billion for that period the year before. Chrysler made $1.4 billion through the end of September, a decrease from $1.8 billion during the first nine months of 1984.

New Models. General Motors in June launched the new Chevrolet Nova, the front-wheel-drive subcompact being assembled in California by New United Motor Manufacturing Inc., a joint-venture company owned by GM and Toyota. The vehicle, 70 percent of whose parts are Japanese-made, is derived from the Japanese Sprinter, which is mechanically identical to the car sold in the United States as the Corolla. GM replaced its aging rear-wheel-drive Oldsmobile Delta 88 and Buick LaSabre with shorter, lighter front-wheel-drive vehicles. Meanwhile, it discontinued the Chevrolet Citation and Buick Skylark, the last of its front-wheel-drive X-body compacts. The cars were phased out a year earlier than originally planned, because of negative publicity and declining sales arising from 16 safety-related recalls and a government lawsuit demanding recall of more than a million vehicles for alleged brake defects.

Ford's Lincoln-Mercury Division launched its West German-built high-performance sedan, Merkur, in January, and the company's Ford Division introduced its Aerostar minivan in July. The firm unveiled its front-wheel-drive Ford Taurus and Mercury Sable in December. About a foot longer than the firm's compact Tempo/Topaz, and aimed at middle-of-the-market "yuppies," the Taurus and Sable represented a $3 billion investment, Ford's biggest ever in a new product.

Perhaps the most widely discussed new import was the minicompact Yugo, dubbed the "throwaway car" by some pundits. The Yugoslav-built Yugo, priced at $3,990, was selling for about $1,000 less than the next lowest priced cars, the Japanese-built Subaru and Chevrolet Sprint.

Prices. Automakers tended to raise prices more on their larger, more profitable, less fuel efficient cars than on highly competitive small vehicles. In a period of mild inflation, price hikes on 1986 models were generally small. GM, after raising prices on 1985 models in late 1984, had an average per-car price of $13,227, highest of any domestic automaker. The average price of all domestic and imported cars sold almost doubled from $6,861 for 1979 models to nearly $12,000 for 1986's.

Fuel Economy. The Department of Transportation reduced the federal fuel economy standard for 1986 cars from 27.5 to 26 miles per gallon, saying the rollback was necessary to protect jobs in the domestic auto industry. GM and Ford had sought the lower standard because of increased demand for their larger, less fuel efficient cars. These firms otherwise would have had to pay huge fines or restrict production of larger cars and cut back on employment. Chrysler, whose cars met the original standard, was angered by the rollback, which, late in the year, was challenged in court suits by four big cities, the state of California, and a coalition of consumer groups. Meanwhile, a car manufacturer which had not followed the regulations for 1983 and 1984 was heavily penalized. In early December, the National Highway Traffic Safety Administration fined Jaguar Cars Inc. $6 million, claiming the company had sold cars that did not meet fuel economy standards.

Safety. A number of states, led by New York and New Jersey, passed seat belt legislation requiring front-seat car occupants to be buckled up or face fines. If states containing two-thirds of the U.S. population enact such laws by April 1989, the Department of Transportation will revoke a ruling requiring automakers to equip cars with automatic occupant restraint systems such as air bags. Auto manufacturers are urging the states to pass seat belt laws.

Saturn at Spring Hill. In January, GM announced the creation of a wholly owned subsidiary, the Saturn Corporation, intended to manufacture subcompact cars at a cost that would allow GM to compete effectively with Japanese imports. In late July, GM reached agreement with the United Auto Workers on an innovative contract for the 6,000 workers to be hired by Saturn. They would be paid a salary rather than an hourly wage and work in production teams, each responsible for a certain area of the plant. Saturn workers would receive base pay of about 80 percent of what auto workers in existing plants make but would be protected against layoffs, unless there were "unforeseen or catastrophic events." A few days later, GM announced that Saturn's manufacturing plant would be built in Spring Hill, Tenn. Saturn's headquarters and engineering department, however, were to be near Detroit.

Chrysler Strike. With contract talks at an impasse, Chrysler workers in the United States and Canada walked off their jobs on October 16. After having made concessions to help the company weather its 1979–1982 financial crisis, the workers now wanted "something extra." For the Canadians, the strike lasted only four days, and a U.S. agreement was announced October 23. In both cases Chrysler agreed to raise wages and benefits to the levels at Ford and GM.   D.L.L.

B

BAHAMAS. See STATISTICS OF THE WORLD. See also CARIBBEAN BASIN.

BAHRAIN. See STATISTICS OF THE WORLD. See also PERSIAN GULF STATES.

BANGLADESH. Progress toward national democratic reforms faltered under the martial-law regime of Lieutenant General H. M. Ershad in 1985, with Ershad and opposition leaders apparently unable to agree on a framework for elections. On March 1, in reaction to a decision by the two main opposition parties to boycott parliamentary elections scheduled for April 6, Ershad announced a return to strict enforcement of martial law and a ban on all political activity. The parliamentary elections were canceled, and a national referendum on Ershad's conduct in office was scheduled for March 21.

According to official results, the March referendum was a great success. Ershad secured the approval of a 94 percent majority among 34.6 million valid votes—a record turnout of 72 percent. However, opposition leaders contended that the results had been rigged, and foreign observers noted that the numbers of voters at polling places did not appear large.

Early in June, General Ershad promulgated a martial law order that dissolved and banned student unions in all Bangladesh colleges, residence halls, and universities. In the autumn, however, his government began permitting "indoor political activity"—but not public meetings—under martial law. And in December, Ershad entirely removed the ban on political activity and indicated intentions to hold elections as early as possible in 1986.

On May 24 and 25 a tropical cyclone with winds up to 100 miles per hour drove waves 10 to 15 feet high across many low-lying islands in the Bay of Bengal, killing over 10,000 people and leaving some 250,000 homeless. It was the same area in which a 1970 cyclone had killed at least 300,000. Emergency relief supplies from the central government and foreign donors, including India, helped survivors rebuild their livelihoods—only to face the next cyclone when it comes.

Gross domestic product increased by 4.5 percent during fiscal year 1984–1985, while production of food grains rose to 15.5 million long tons. There was also an increase in the value of exports, especially in certain nontraditional exports such as ready-made garments.

The conclusion of an agreement between the Indian government and antiimmigrant agitators in the state of Assam, directly north of Bangladesh, raised potential difficulties in India-Bangladesh relations. The pact called for the deportation from Assam of some 2.6 million post-1971 immigrants, who were believed to have slipped into relatively uncrowded Assam from Bangladesh. It also called for resumption of construction on a border fence, which had been temporarily halted. The Bangladesh government maintained that there were no immigrants from Bangladesh in Assam, and therefore refused to accept any who were deported. Despite the pact, Bangladeshi officials said they foresaw no deterioration in relations.

See STATISTICS OF THE WORLD.   R.C.

BANKING AND FINANCE. Rising interest rates in the United States and a soaring U.S. dollar caused concern early in 1985, but before long these trends had begun to reverse. The sliding interest rates and declining dollar brought cheer to financial markets. The U.S. stock market welcomed the trends and hit new highs, and U.S. banks were glad to have a chance to reduce the interest rates offered to depositors. Outside the United States, despite improvement in the world economy, the rescheduling of debts of developing countries remained a vexing and dangerous problem.

Stock Market. The U.S. stock market took off early in the year, marked time for several months, and came on strong again toward the end of the year. The 1,300 barrier on the Dow

Jones average of 30 industrial stocks fell for the first time in May. The renewed rise, starting in September, was at least partly in response to an agreement by the five leading industrial nations to try to lower the value of the dollar. The average broke through 1,400 on November 6, and on December 11 it closed above 1,500 for the first time ever in its history. Indexes measuring broader market activity also posted all-time highs.

Interest Rates. A rise in interest rates early in the year was worrisome to investors. Between the beginning of the year and mid-March, three-month Treasury bills climbed from 7.9 percent to 8.7 percent, and 30-year Treasury bonds edged upward from 11.5 percent to 11.9 percent. The rises reinforced fears that a clash between big government budget deficits and the credit demands of a growing economy would keep pushing rates up until a serious recession set in.

The real trend for 1985, however, proved to be downward. The economy turned out to be weaker than at first thought, showing only scant growth. The combination of a stagnant economy and an easier credit policy by the Federal Reserve sent rates tumbling. By mid-June, three-month Treasury bills had hit a seven-year low of 6.7 percent, and they rebounded by only about half a point by December. The 30-year Treasury bonds fell to 10.4 percent in June and edged downward to about 10 percent in November. The prime rate, which banks use as the base rate for lending to corporate customers, started the year at 10.75, then tumbled, falling below 10 percent for the first time since 1978; it stayed at around 9.5 percent between June and December.

Bank Profits—and Losses. U.S. financial institutions welcomed the lower interest rates. Savings and loan associations (or thrift institutions) had much of their money invested in home mortgages taken out before interest rates soared in the early 1980's. Because the S&L's had to offer high-interest accounts to attract depositors, they were paying more interest on deposits than they earned on loans. But falling interest rates reversed this situation, and 1985 shaped up as the best year ever for the thrift industry. Profits at commercial banks were up sharply during the first half of 1985, and—

pressured by their regulatory agencies—banks put much of their profits into capital reserves as a buffer against losses on bad loans.

The reserves were sorely needed. Despite the continued growth of the economy, which usually provides borrowers with increasing income, loan losses at financial institutions were heavy. Losses were especially heavy on farm and real estate loans and on loans to oil and shipping companies. Thus, while some banks prospered others were failing at a record rate. The comptroller of the currency warned in November that many banks were paying too much in dividends to keep sufficient reserves in case of bad loans.

Overaggressive lending and investment policies got several institutions into trouble, especially S&L's. In Cincinnati, the Home State Savings Bank suffered heavy losses on investments placed through a small government securities dealer. Home State deposits were insured by a private insurance fund rather than by a federal government agency. When depositors saw that Home State's losses might exceed the amount of money in the insurance fund, many withdrew their money. The panic spread to other institutions insured by the private Ohio Deposit Guarantee Fund. In March, Ohio Governor Richard Celeste closed all 71 privately insured thrifts. All except Home State

reopened within ten days, some with limits on withdrawals, but no runs on deposits occurred.

In Maryland, depositors lined up outside Baltimore's Old Court Savings & Loan in May, after officials of the thrift's private insurance fund forced a management shakeup. They acted after discovering heavy losses on real estate and construction ventures. As the run on deposits spread to other privately insured institutions, Governor Harry Hughes limited monthly withdrawals from all such institutions to $1,000. Restrictions were soon dropped or relaxed on all but the most troubled thrifts, and the state insured deposits in many thrifts while they applied for federal deposit insurance.

These events were symptomatic of deep-rooted problems. After bank deregulation, thrift institutions that had essentially been limited to home mortgages had sought varied investments, notably in real estate but also including such high-return possibilities as racehorses and oil wells—in order to make money on the high-rate deposits they were collecting. But, of course, investments with high returns also carry high risks. Investment mistakes affected not only the small, private insurers: the Federal Savings and Loan Insurance Corporation, insurer for most thrifts, had liquid assets so small that they could theoretically have been wiped out by the failure of one large thrift. In March

The strong dollar was a problem to the U.S. economy but a windfall for tourists abroad.

89

the Federal Home Loan Bank Board, the FSLIC's overseer, began assessing an extra fee of one-eighth of 1 percent of thrifts' deposits in order to rebuild FSLIC assets. In November the board approved a new entity, the Asset Liquidation Association, to take over $3 billion in problem assets—such as real estate foreclosed on by a failed thrift—from the FSLIC. In exchange, the FSLIC would receive securities or possibly cash.

Crackdowns by the Feds. The travails of the thrifts were at least partly responsible for U.S. government actions against some small dealers in Treasury debt and other government securities. Home State Savings Bank, several other thrifts, and some Florida municipal finance agencies were heavy losers when on March 4 the U.S. Securities and Exchange Commission shut down E.S.M. Government Securities Inc. in Fort Lauderdale, Fla. The SEC accused the company of fraud and said it was unable to meet up to $300 million in obligations to its customers. In April the SEC closed several government securities dealers associated with the Bevill, Bresler & Schulman securities group in Livingston, N.J., when they informed the SEC they could not meet obligations.

Government agencies pursuing drug cases enforced regulations requiring banks and other institutions to report possible instances of "money laundering"—efforts of organized crime to disguise the source of illegal profits. Crocker National Bank of San Francisco paid a $2.25 million fine in August for failing to report large cash transactions, as required by law. Several other banks, including First National Bank of Boston, paid smaller fines.

Interstate Banking. The U.S. Supreme Court held June 10 that states can create regional banking compacts, under which banks can operate across state lines; regions were allowed to keep out big banks from New York and other money centers. The subsequent avalanche of interstate banking mergers augured a major consolidation of the nation's banks. In September the Federal Deposit Insurance Corporation proposed to preserve competition through more stringent restrictions on takeovers by big banks

Bank panics created the ultimate in long bank lines as depositors lost confidence in privately insured savings and loan associations. Below, a rush of withdrawals in Maryland. At left, depositors in Ohio demand their savings after the governor closed the banks for a "holiday" in order to prevent their complete collapse.

entering new markets than on mergers by small banks.

A U.S. appeals court decision in May threw into question one path the big banks had used to operate outside their home states. The court ruled that bank holding companies could not operate "nonbank banks"—those offering limited services (loans or deposits but not both). The decision was appealed.

Ten Largest Banks. As of midyear, the biggest U.S. bank holding companies, ranked by assets, were the following: Citicorp, $159.6 billion; BankAmerica, $120.3 billion; Chase Manhattan, $86.3 billion; Manufacturers Hanover, $75.9 billion; J. P. Morgan, $63.8 billion; Chemical New York, $57.3 billion; Security Pacific, $47.9 billion; First Interstate, $46.8 billion; Bankers Trust New York, $43.9 billion; First Chicago, $39.9 billion.

The Mighty Dollar. The United States headed for a record $150 billion trade deficit in 1985, as Americans took advantage of a relatively strong dollar to buy foreign imports. (The high value of the dollar in relation to other currencies made imports relatively cheap.)

The dollar, which had been up sharply in 1984, had continued to rise early in 1985. Several factors pushed it up. The swift U.S. recovery from the worldwide recession attracted foreign investment. U.S. interest rates forced up by big federal budget deficits sparked demands for dollars by foreigners putting their money into U.S. banks, notes, and bonds. Foreign governments, fearing that their currencies might weaken further, kept their own interest rates up to remain competitive, foreclosing a strong recovery in their economies and perpetuating a vicious cycle. The strong dollar made it difficult for foreign governments to fight inflation, because prices of many of their imports were denominated in dollars.

U.S. trading partners complained about the strong dollar, but political gridlock in Washington prevented significant cuts in the budget deficits. Another approach favored by foreign governments, that of intervention in the currency markets, ran up against the Reagan administration's free-market philosophy. Nevertheless, the West German government began to sell dollars in February, and the United States intervened quietly, in modest amounts.

On February 26 the British pound hit an all-time low of 1.04 to the dollar, but then the dollar began to weaken for a time. It recovered, but a decline in U.S. interest rates in mid-March led to a longer-term decline in the dollar. By midyear the pound was worth $1.35.

Concerned that the dollar was nevertheless still too strong to permit U.S. manufacturers to compete with foreign firms, the U.S. government acted boldly in September. Treasury Secretary James Baker and Federal Reserve Chairman Paul Volcker met with their counterparts from Britain, France, West Germany, and Japan. A statement that the five nations were "ready to cooperate more closely" to drive down the dollar triggered the largest one-day drop in the dollar's value in 12 years. The dollar continued to trend lower after that time; by year's end it was at its lowest point since May 1983.

Third World Debt. The strong dollar exacted an awful price from developing nations struggling under their dollar-denominated debt burdens. Although interest rates were falling somewhat, the strong dollar made many imports expensive and raised the local cost of debt service. At the International Monetary Fund meeting in South Korea in October, U.S. Treasury Secretary Baker called on developing nations to develop sound, growth-promoting economic policies. If they did so, additional funds would be provided: commercial banks would lend large debtors who no longer had access to regular commercial credit an additional $20 billion over three years; another $9 billion (a 50 percent increase) would be disbursed by the World Bank and the Inter-American Development Bank; finally, the IMF would reserve $2.7 billion in scheduled repayments from its debtors to aid the poorest countries. The nearly 10,000 bank and government officials in Seoul greeted this proposal with cautious approval, and in mid-December the IMF and the World Bank announced that commercial banks holding 90 percent of the loans to developing nations had thrown their support behind the plan. Latin America's debtor nations, meeting in Cartagena, Colombia, called the plan a "positive step" but still "insufficient."

The IMF suspended a $1.4 billion loan to Argentina before the first disbursement in February because, despite the imposition of austerity measures as a condition for the money, Argentina's inflation rate continued to soar. President Raúl Alfonsín announced a new program in June. He declared a three-day bank holiday to permit a fundamental recalibration of the currency into a new unit, the austral; each austral would be worth 1,000 pesos. Argentina was then allowed to draw on its line of credit, and it signed a new loan agreement with its foreign creditor banks in August; it was required to catch up on its interest payments in return for stretched-out payments on existing loans and $4.2 billion in new money.

An improvement in its trade balance helped Brazil stay current on its debt payments, but in September, President José Sarney rejected austerity programs advocated by the IMF. The IMF then withheld $1.5 billion available to Brazil under a 1983 agreement. In November, in a challenge to the IMF, Brazil said it would try to renegotiate some of its foreign bank debt before reaching an agreement with the IMF. Mexico devalued its peso by a substantial degree in July; the final portion of a $48.7 billion debt rescheduling agreement was signed with 600 foreign banks in August. In July, Cuban President Fidel Castro urged debtor nations to repudiate their loans. Peru's president, Alan García Pérez, said his nation would devote no more than 10 percent of its annual export earnings to servicing its debt, and he hinted Peru might pull out of the IMF if it did not ease the repayment burdens on the Third World.

South Africa suspended payments on its international debt after persistent domestic unrest eroded investor confidence. When Pretoria declared a partial state of emergency in July, many international lenders refused to renew loans or issue new ones. Capital fled the country, and in September, South Africa suspended principal payments on its debt for the rest of the year.

Other Financial Woes. On July 19 the Italian lira fell 20 percent against the dollar in a few minutes of heavy selling triggered by a large order for dollars by the national oil company. The next day, a formal devaluation of the lira within the European Monetary System was agreed on. In Japan, on August 13, Sanko Steamship Company became the largest firm in the nation ever to file for bankruptcy. In Canada, two Alberta banks, done in by bad real-estate and oil-industry loans, were closed by the Canadian government in August; they were the first banks to fail in Canada since 1923. G.D.W.

BARBADOS. See STATISTICS OF THE WORLD. See also CARIBBEAN BASIN.

BEHAVIORAL SCIENCES. Research reported in 1985 challenged long-held beliefs as to the likelihood of recovering from schizophrenia and examined possible links between such characteristics as severe depression and immune disorders.

Recovering From Schizophrenia. People who suffer from repeated bouts of schizophrenia are likely to get worse and rarely recover, according to many psychiatrists, but Yale University researchers challenged that conclusion. They found that a majority of "hard-core" schizophrenics released from a Vermont state mental hospital in the mid-1950's had significantly improved and were living in the community by the early 1980's.

Schizophrenia encompasses a range of severe mental symptoms that often include social withdrawal, inappropriate emotions, hallucinations, and delusions. About 1 percent of the U.S. population has some form of schizophrenia. Yale psychiatrist Courtenay M. Harding and coworkers found that even the worst cases of schizophrenia may turn around over 10 to 20 years, although it is difficult to predict which patients will eventually improve. In the course of following a group of patients over about 30 years, they rediagnosed patients at a Vermont mental hospital according to modern guidelines and then tracked down schizophrenic patients and their families. One-half to two-thirds of the 118 patients classified as schizophrenics under the new guidelines displayed few or no psychiatric symptoms, required little or no help meeting basic needs, and led relatively full lives. Schizophrenia, however, remains a perplexing set of disorders. It is not clear, for example, whether the Vermont patients would have shown the same improvement if they had not participated in psychological rehabilitation and job programs on release from the hospital. There is a great variation in the outlook for individual schizophrenia patients, and any attempt to predict an outcome should be made in consultation with the psychiatrist and other treating professionals who know the patient well.

Side Effects of Depression. Researchers at Mount Sinai School of Medicine in New York City found that a weakening of the body's immune system is associated with severe depression that requires hospitalization, but not with certain other psychiatric disorders or with being hospitalized as such. In 1984, Steven J. Schleifer and coworkers had reported that lymphocytes, the cells most involved in protecting against disease, proliferate far less than normal in hospitalized patients who are severely depressed. In 1985, on the other hand, they observed that hospitalized schizophrenics, hospitalized surgical patients, and depressed patients not requiring hospitalization respond normally to lymphocyte stimulation. These three groups had total numbers of lymphocytes that compared favorably with healthy subjects—suggesting that the weakening of the

immune system may be specifically related to severe depression. The steep drop in immune activity during severe depression may be fostered by the weight loss and sleep disturbance that characterize this particular mental disorder, Schleifer observed.

Depression of a milder sort may be related to a substantial number of childhood learning disabilities, according to psychologist David Goldstein of Temple University in Philadelphia. These learning disabilities occur among children of normal or near-normal intelligence and often involve hyperactivity and an inability to read or understand arithmetic. In a five-year study of schoolchildren, Goldstein and coworkers found that depression appeared to lead to academic failure among one-third of a group of 159 learning-disabled students. For the rest, said Goldstein, depression may well have been the consequence of learning failures caused by neurological problems. The youngsters with depression-caused learning problems showed evidence of poor relationships with others, inappropriate behavior, pervasive unhappi-

Calling Dr. Ruth . . .
Ruth Westheimer, a diminutive 57-year-old German-American wife and mother, is also a television and radio superstar, a best-selling author, and more. The former Holocaust refugee, who received a doctorate in education from Columbia University in 1970, caught on with the public when she started a phone-in radio program offering advice on sexual problems. By 1985 her radio program, now called *Sexually Speaking*, was broadcast on about 80 stations around the United States, and the *Dr. Ruth Show* was being seen in some 24 million cable TV homes. Dr. Ruth's lively, candid advice on sex, oddly enough, offends few people, and has kept her busier than one could imagine. By late in the year her first book, *Dr. Ruth's Guide to Good Sex*, had sold 100,000 copies and another volume, *First Love*, had appeared (though copies had to be recalled because of an embarrassing typo, calling the time near ovulation "safe," rather than "unsafe," for the rhythm method of birth control). She even had a board game out entitled "Dr. Ruth's Game of Good Sex," and was soon to appear in a movie.

Ruth Westheimer

ness, and psychosomatic complaints. Their school performance improved markedly after they received special instruction in small classes and two hours of individual therapy per week.

Traits That Go With Intelligence. Research at Johns Hopkins University in Baltimore found that children with extremely high levels of mathematical or verbal ability are far more likely than children of normal ability to be left-handed, nearsighted, or afflicted by asthma or other allergies. These three biological factors therefore appear to be associated with higher intelligence although, as psychologist and study director Camilla Benbow notes, they have not been shown to cause it. In a national sample of over 100,000 children between 12 and 13 years of age, Benbow found 292 youngsters who had scored at least 700 out of 800 on the mathematical section of the Scholastic Aptitude Test and 165 who had scored at least 630 out of 800 on the verbal section (there was some overlap between the two groups). Both sections are designed to be taken at a later age, by high school seniors. Over 20 percent of the children with these top scores were found to be left-handed or ambidextrous, twice the rate observed among the general population. These youngsters were also twice as likely to have allergies and four times as likely to be nearsighted. The study found that 80 percent of the high-scorers had at least one of these three characteristics.

The Hopkins research was based in part on a theory proposed by the late Harvard University neurologist Norman Geschwind. He believed left-handedness, immune disorders including allergies, and learning disabilities were all linked to a variation in the development of the brain before birth.   B.B.

BELGIUM. In parliamentary elections on October 13, 1985, the governing coalition headed by Prime Minister Wilfried Martens increased its majority by 2 seats. The four-party coalition won 115 seats in the 212-member Chamber of Representatives, and a mostly unchanged cabinet was installed on November 28.

The Martens government—Belgium's longest-lasting in 20 years—had resigned in July following a dispute over responsibility for security measures at the European Cup soccer championship game in Brussels in May. Vio-

lence broke out before that game, to be played between British and Italian teams, and 38 people died. A Belgian parliamentary commission blamed British fans but also criticized the security at the stadium. The ensuing election campaign was fought primarily on economic issues, however. Martens characterized the results as an endorsement of the stringent economic policies the government, and other European governments, had followed. "For the first time in Europe," he said, "the population approved our austerity policy. It's a historic event."

Economic trends were generally favorable, continuing the recovery begun in 1984. Industrial output was forecast to grow by 3 percent and exports of goods and services by 4.5 percent. The balance on current account continued to improve, with a surplus likely for the year. Consumer prices, moderated by a freeze on real wage increases, rose 4.6 percent over the 12 months ending in September 1985. The unemployment rate fell from 12.9 percent at the beginning of the year to 12.1 percent in September, still one of the highest rates in Western Europe.

In March the government announced its decision to accept deployment of 16 U.S. cruise missiles at an air base near Florennes in southern Belgium. The 16 missiles, which became operational shortly after the announcement, were to be followed by another 32 cruise missiles in 1987. The missile issue was highly controversial in Belgium, where a poll in January showed that 64 percent of the people preferred to postpone deployment for at least a year. In October tens of thousands demonstrated in Brussels against deployment. Belgium's defense minister said in September that the country over the long term would be repatriating as many Belgian troops as possible from West Germany and cutting Belgium's warplane commitment to NATO.

In late 1984 and 1985, radical leftist groups carried out bombing attacks against NATO facilities, U.S. and West German defense firms, the Brussels gas and electric company, and other targets. Damage was done to parts of the NATO fuel pipeline running through Belgium, facilities of NATO headquarters and the North Atlantic Assembly in Brussels, offices of two

The broken bodies of spectators, most of them Italian, litter Heysel Stadium in Brussels after English soccer fans attacked Italians in the stands at the European Cup final. A masonry wall collapsed on the fleeing Italians, adding to the toll of hundreds of injured, in addition to the 38 suffocated or crushed to death.

political parties and a Belgian court building (where one person was killed). Four suspects in these attacks were arrested in December. Violence of another kind erupted on November 9, when gunmen killed 8 people while robbing a supermarket. It was the latest in a chain of robberies by a gang that had killed 27 people since 1982.

See STATISTICS OF THE WORLD.　　W.C.C.

BELIZE. See STATISTICS OF THE WORLD.

BENIN. See STATISTICS OF THE WORLD.

BHUTAN. See STATISTICS OF THE WORLD.

BLACKS IN THE UNITED STATES. The use of racial quotas in hiring continued to be a center of controversy in 1985. Meanwhile, statistical studies issued during the year showed that blacks in the United States remained economically disadvantaged and had significantly poorer health than non-Hispanic whites.

Racial Issues. In January the chairman of the United States Commission on Civil Rights, Clarence M. Pendleton, Jr., called quotas in hiring a "dead issue" because of a June 1984 Supreme Court ruling that valid seniority systems take precedence over the protection of jobs held by minorities. In March major civil rights groups boycotted commission hearings on the quota question, saying that Pendleton's

attacks on quotas made the meetings useless. Pendleton, a black, supported President Ronald Reagan's claim that black leaders were distorting the administration's record on civil rights so as to maintain their own leadership positions.

In April the Justice Department said it would seek to overturn quotas imposed by judges as a result of Justice Department suits brought in support of such quotas prior to the Reagan presidency. It said the 1984 Court ruling had removed the legal underpinning for any earlier rulings. More than 50 local government units were asked to eliminate or modify their racial hiring quotas, and the department sued the city of Indianapolis to end recruitment by quota of blacks and women for its police and fire departments. The National Association for the Advancement of Colored People, in turn, sued to prevent the department from taking further action against the quota system, but the suit was dismissed.

In a letter to Senator Edward Kennedy (D, Mass.) made public in August, William Bradford Reynolds, assistant attorney general for civil rights, wrote that he measured the success of affirmative action by the "number of persons recruited to apply" for jobs, not the number

A commemorative stamp for Mary McLeod Bethune, a pioneer in the fight for educational opportunities for blacks, was unveiled by her son, Albert Bethune, and Assistant Postmaster General Mary Layton.

actually hired. Affirmative action's purpose, he said, is to correct the tendency for women and minorities not to apply for some jobs because of prior discrimination. Earlier, in June, Reynolds was denied a promotion to associate attorney general when the Senate Judiciary Committee refused to report his nomination to the full Senate. Civil rights groups contended that Reynolds had failed to enforce civil rights laws and had misapplied court decisions. Stormy nomination hearings before the committee found Reynolds frequently trapped by conflicting or misleading testimony; an angry President Reagan called the hearings an ideological assault on Reynolds. Reynolds continued in his current post.

Marianne Mele Hall, chairman of the federal Copyright Royalty Tribunal, resigned in May after it became known that she was listed as coauthor of a book that ascribed to blacks a taste for "jungle freedoms" and avoidance of work and personal responsibility.

Troubling Statistics. Data issued in 1985 underscored gaps that still existed between blacks and whites. The U.S. Census Bureau reported in May that, in 1984, 59 percent of all black families with children were headed by one parent; the figure for whites was 20 percent. The Census Bureau later reported that some 34 percent of all blacks were in poverty, compared with 12 percent of whites.

The unemployment rate for blacks stood at 15.9 percent in November 1985, more than double the rate for whites. In June the Children's Defense Fund issued findings showing that only 67 percent of black children had a parent with a job; the figure for whites was 86 percent. The same study noted that in 1982 more than 55 percent of all black children were born to unmarried women, a figure it said "essentially guarantee(s) the poverty of black children for the foreseeable future."

The Alan Guttmacher Institute reported in March that the pregnancy rate among black teenagers (163 per 1,000) was twice as great as that among whites (83 per 1,000). The National Center for Health Statistics estimated early in the year that a white baby born in 1982 could expect to outlive a black baby by about six years. In October the U.S. Department of Health and Human Services issued a report noting that blacks and other minorities were generally less healthy and died younger than non-Hispanic whites. The report said that 60,000 deaths could be avoided each year if death rates of minorities were as low as those of non-Hispanic whites, especially for heart attacks and strokes, homicides and accidents, cancer, and infant mortality.

Farrakhan Controversy. The Reverend Louis Farrakhan, charismatic leader of the Nation of Islam, a black religious group, drew large crowds during a 14-city nationwide speaking tour. Farrakhan's message to his largely black audiences embodied a positive call for black self-reliance and economic independence, coupled with a plea for spiritual renewal. But it also included severe rebukes to his critics, with elements of anti-Semitism. For example, during a speech in Washington in July, he referred to the "wickedness" of Jews, adding that "black people will not be controlled by Jews." In his final speech of the tour, before an enthusiastic crowd of 25,000 in New York City, Farrakhan said that "ugly names" he had been called "only serve as fuel to the fire in me to make me fight harder." Other black political and religious leaders found themselves divided in their reaction to Farrakhan.

Elections. On November 5, L. Douglas Wilder, a black state senator whose nomination had initially been considered a problem for the

Democratic state ticket, was elected lieutenant governor of Virginia by a comfortable margin. Wilder, a veteran of the Korean war, who studied law at Howard University in Washington and became a state senator in 1969, was the first black ever nominated for statewide office in Virginia. Becoming lieutenant governor would make him the highest-ranking black state official in the United States.

The year also saw the reelection of prominent black mayors in Atlanta, Detroit, and Los Angeles (see ELECTIONS IN THE UNITED STATES and PEOPLE IN THE NEWS: Tom Bradley).

M.Gr. & D.Y.

BOLIVIA. Racked by hyperinflation estimated at more than 8,000 percent a year and torn by labor unrest that led to repeated general strikes, Bolivia installed a new president in 1985.

Eighteen candidates ran for president in the July 14 election. Former President Hugo Banzer Suárez, 59, who had been in power from 1971 to 1978, received 28.6 percent of the popular vote, and his party gained 51 seats in Congress. Three-time President Víctor Paz Estenssoro, 77, of the Nationalist Revolutionary Movement, won 26.4 percent and a bloc of 59 seats. Jaime Paz Zamora, 43, a nephew of Paz Estenssoro, claimed 8.9 percent of the popular vote and the support of 16 in Congress. Since no candidate received half the vote, Congress had to decide among the three highest vote-getters. After Paz Zamora was eliminated on the first ballot, all the parties represented in Congress except Banzer Suárez's National Democratic Alliance voted for Paz Estenssoro. He took office on August 6 for his fourth term as Bolivia's president.

President Paz Estenssoro promised to cut the bloated public sector, end subsidies to the inefficient state mining companies, and encourage joint ventures of foreign and domestic capital. On August 29 the peso was devalued by 95 percent; the devaluation eliminated a great disparity between official and black market rates. The new exchange rate, to be adjusted twice weekly, was intended to reactivate legitimate trade and reduce smuggling. The government also decentralized the petroleum and tin monopolies and allowed the companies to dismiss workers, froze wages and prices, and removed subsidies on foodstuffs.

In response, the Bolivian Workers Central (COB), the country's powerful labor confederation, called a general strike that began on September 3. Paz Estenssoro ordered strict compliance with labor laws and activated laws under which strike organizers could be imprisoned and workers dismissed. Troops were ordered to protect the state petroleum enterprise, airports, railroads, and telephone and electrical installations from sabotage and terrorism. Although some strikers began returning to work, tens of thousands were still on strike when, on September 19, the government declared a 90-day state of siege. Prostrike labor leaders were arrested, including the executive committee of the COB. The walkout was ended in early October in return for a release of union leaders from detention.

In Bolivia, as in several other Latin American countries, astronomical inflation was thwarting attempts to repay huge foreign debts and meet IMF conditions for new loans. The Bolivian peso had lost so much of its value that taking money to the bank was a feat of physical strength.

Amid reports that Bolivian coca leaf production was on the increase, the U.S. Congress passed legislation, signed by President Ronald Reagan in August, providing that U.S. foreign aid to Bolivia would be substantially reduced, unless Bolivia met certain specified goals in the control of cocaine production.

See STATISTICS OF THE WORLD.   L.L.P.

BOTSWANA. *See* STATISTICS OF THE WORLD.

BRAZIL. Brazil was returned to civilian rule in 1985, but the newly elected leader, Tancredo de Almeida Neves, was prevented by serious illness from ever succeeding to office, and the leadership of the country fell to the man elected as vice-president.

Return to Civilian Rule. On January 15 an electoral college chose 74-year-old Tancredo Neves, former governor of Minas Gerais and an opponent of five successive military governments, as Brazil's first civilian president since 1964. Brazilians danced in the streets to celebrate the event, but their joy turned to anxiety as Neves, the candidate of the broad-based Democratic Alliance, underwent emergency abdominal surgery on March 14, a day before his scheduled inauguration. Vice-President-elect José Sarney was sworn in as acting president the following day. He exercised the formalities of the office in a period of governmental near-paralysis for nearly five weeks; meanwhile, a series of seven operations had failed to correct Neves's worsening abdominal condition, and he died in a São Paulo hospital on April 21.

The mild-mannered José Sarney, former governor of Maranhão and federal senator, automatically became president upon Neves's death. One of Sarney's earliest decisions, complying with Neves's electoral promises, was to call mayoral elections for November 15 in the 23 state capitals and other municipalities whose mayors had been appointed under the military. The elections gave nearly 30 million voters— half of the electorate—an opportunity to pass indirectly on the stewardship of the Democratic Alliance and its dominant party, the Brazilian Democratic Movement, which indeed took most of the mayoralties. However, one of the major winners was former President Jânio Quadros, a strongly anti-Communist conservative who was elected mayor of São Paulo.

Quadros had been supported by the Liberal Front, the other party in the governing coalition; his campaign and victory severely ruptured the alliance. The Democratic Movement also suffered a key defeat in Rio de Janeiro, where Socialist Leonel Brizola won easily.

In another major action that fulfilled a promise by Neves, Congress on May 8 approved a government-backed bill for congressional elections and the selection of a constituent assembly in November 1986. The assembly would meet in early 1987 to adopt a new constitution. Sarney, who enjoyed a six-year mandate, also sent a message to Congress on May 7 proposing abolition of the electoral college, direct elections for president, and adoption of a four-year presidential term.

Economic Affairs. The government made several key decisions pertaining to Brazil's public finances. Sarney ordered a cut in state enterprise investments and a $2.5 billion increase in taxes. The package was supposed to reduce the current budget deficit by about $8 billion, considerably less than the reductions proposed by the International Monetary Fund as a condition for refinancing foreign debts due between 1985 and 1991. Earlier, in April, Finance Minister Fernando Dornelles—Neves's nephew and a former head of Brazil's tax office—had cut federal spending by 10 percent, imposed a hiring freeze, closed down an important investment bank, and imposed selective price controls. Dornelles resigned in August, when Sarney refused to accept still deeper spending cuts. Late in the year, Brazil, the IMF, and foreign banks were engaged in negotiations on the approximately $104 billion in debt owed by Brazil. Brazil indicated it would seek to renegotiate some of its debt with the banks before reaching an accord with the IMF.

On April 30, Sarney signed an executive decree doubling the minimum monthly wage to nearly $60. Shortly before that time, Labor Minister Almir Pazzianotto repealed several of the previous military regime's regulations hampering union activity.

Agrarian Reform. After coming to office, the Sarney government announced it was going ahead with plans to implement the Land Statute of 1964, using mainly public property in an endeavor to provide peasants with plots of land

by 1990. After some 3,500 large-estate holders (*fazendeiros*) descended on Brasília to lobby in Congress against the appropriation of funds for the program, the Ministry of Agrarian Reform and Development announced that major landowners owed nearly $1 billion in unpaid land taxes, which would be collected to finance the program. Sarney, in a nationwide address, decried Brazil's imbalance in land proprietorship, pointing out that "45 percent of our rural land is owned by 1 percent of the population." In October a law was passed providing for the distribution of 106.5 million acres of state-owned and unfarmed private land to 1.4 million peasant families over a four-year period.

The concentration of land in the hands of a few had led to violence, as peasant squatters or renters evicted from their farms clashed with gunmen (*grileiros*) hired by landowners. Close to 200 deaths had been reported in such conflicts since early 1984.

Foreign Affairs. Brazilian diplomatic efforts concentrated on increasing trade with the rest of Latin America and with the black states of southern Africa, as an alternative to U.S. markets in the face of growing U.S. protectionist sentiment.

Brazil announced in July that it would join Argentina, Peru, and Uruguay in support of

Crowds of Brazilians join the funeral procession of President-elect Tancredo Neves as his body is taken to lie in state in Brasília. Although he had died before taking office, the people turned out to honor the first civilian president to be chosen after 21 years of military rule. Neves's vice-president, José Sarney (right), succeeded him.

the so-called Contadora process, without actually joining the "Contadora group." (The Contadora group of nations, which has sought a negotiated settlement of regional issues in Central America, consists of Colombia, Mexico, Panama, and Venezuela.) The government also said that Brazil did not support U.S. economic sanctions against Nicaragua. The Sarney government did impose trade sanctions on South Africa, including a ban on the export of arms, fuel, and electronic equipment.

See STATISTICS OF THE WORLD.   N.J.P.

99

BRITISH COLUMBIA. *See* STATISTICS OF THE WORLD. *See also* CANADA.

BRUNEI. *See* STATISTICS OF THE WORLD.

BULGARIA. In pursuit of its policy of ethnic homogeneity, the Bulgarian government in 1985 continued to put pressure on members of the country's Turkish minority to adopt Slavic surnames and to refrain from the use of the Turkish language in public. Early in the year, reports from diplomatic and other sources indicated that as many as several hundred people had died in clashes protesting these policies. In January, Turkish President Kenan Evren expressed his nation's concern to Bulgarian leader Todor Zhivkov, and the following month, Turkey offered to accept at least 500,000 ethnic Turkish immigrants from Bulgaria. But the Bulgarian government denied the existence of any problem and did not comply.

Faced with unusually low temperatures, which caused an energy crisis throughout Eastern Europe, the government introduced strict electricity rationing measures. Streetlights were turned off in all cities and towns except Sofia, and electrical heating of industrial and public buildings was prohibited.

The trial of three Bulgarians and several Turks, including Mehmet Ali Agca, accused of plotting to assassinate Pope John Paul II in 1981, opened on May 27 in Rome. The defendants had been indicted on the strength of testimony provided by Agca, the Turk already convicted of attempting to kill the pope. Of the Bulgarian defendants, only Sergei I. Antonov, the former head of the Bulgarian airline office in Rome, was present; the other two, Zhelyo K. Vasilev and Todor S. Aivasov, both attached to the Bulgarian embassy in Rome at the time of the assassination attempt, were in Bulgaria and were being tried in absentia. (They testified at a special session convened in Sofia in December.) The Bulgarians consistently denied any involvement in the plot, which Agca had claimed was organized by the Bulgarian and Soviet secret services and a Turkish right-wing group.

Bulgaria observed the 1,100th anniversary of the death of St. Methodius, who, together with his brother, St. Cyril, had played a major role in the conversion to Christianity and cultural development of the Slavs. There were conferences, lectures, and concerts, all stressing Methodius's historical contribution to the development of Slavonic literature and culture. *See* STATISTICS OF THE WORLD.   R.A.P.

BURKINA FASO. *See* STATISTICS OF THE WORLD: Upper Volta.

BURMA. In August 1985, San Yu, who had succeeded military strongman Ne Win as Burma's largely ceremonial president in 1981, was named to the newly created position of vice-chairman of the country's single political party, the Burma Socialist Program Party (BSPP), at the organization's fifth national congress. Ne Win himself was elected to another four-year term as chairman of the party, which is inseparable from Burma's government, indicating that he was not yet ready to give up leadership of the country. Ne Win did, however, appear to be putting San Yu in an important position as a possible successor.

Most important of Burma's several continuing insurgencies was that of the Karen National Union, which continued its 37-year fight for an independent state for the Karen ethnic minority, about 10 percent of the population. Since November 1984, Burma's army has sought to systematically destroy the villages in which Karen rebels' families and supporters live and to block the smuggling trade on which the Karens depend financially. However, smuggling is the main source of many imported goods in Burma, and as a result of the army's campaign, medicines and electrical goods were in especially short supply in 1985.

Burma's economy was adversely influenced by the drop in the world rice price, which amounted to about 40 percent since 1981. The government increased emphasis on other crops, such as tobacco, coffee, jute, and cotton.

In March, President Li Xiannian became the first Chinese head of state to visit the country since 1966. The Chinese leader met with President San Yu and BSPP Chairman Ne Win to discuss increased trade and the effects on the region of the continuing war in Cambodia. Burma also sought improved ties with a major neighbor to its west, Bangladesh, and the two governments agreed to new maps demarcating their common border.

See STATISTICS OF THE WORLD.   R.L.B.

BURUNDI. *See* STATISTICS OF THE WORLD.

C

CABINET, UNITED STATES. *See* PRESIDENT OF THE UNITED STATES.

CALIFORNIA. *See* STATISTICS OF THE WORLD.

CAMBODIA. In March 1985 the Vietnamese occupation army, which had taken control of Cambodia in early 1979, concluded its biggest dry-season offensive yet, against base camps of the non-Communist Khmer People's National Liberation Front (KPNLF), the Communist Khmer Rouge, and non-Communist forces loyal to Prince Norodom Sihanouk. Willing to absorb very high casualty rates and frequently crossing the nearby border into Thailand, on the ground that the Thais were sheltering resistance fighters, Vietnamese troops overpowered the outnumbered resistance forces, compelling them to adopt a complete guerrilla strategy and infiltrate deep inside Cambodia. The offensive drove more than 200,000 Cambodians to flee the base camps into Thailand.

Prince Sihanouk, head of the coalition government of the resistance, threatened to resign after discovering that Khmer Rouge troops had murdered soldiers from his forces. But political considerations appeared to keep him from resigning and the coalition from falling apart. Late in the year, a dissident movement within the KPNLF was challenging KPNLF leader Sonn Sann.

In September the Khmer Rouge announced the official retirement of Pol Pot as commander-in-chief of the Khmer Rouge forces. The Vietnamese had demanded that Pol Pot—head of the brutal former Khmer Rouge regime—be "eliminated" before any settlement of the war could be negotiated. However, Hanoi dismissed the report of his retirement as a cosmetic to improve the image of the resistance movement. Pol Pot was to remain with the Khmer Rouge as head of a defense institute.

Within the Vietnamese-backed Phnom-Penh government, Foreign Minister Hun Sen was named prime minister succeeding Chan Si, who had died at the end of 1984. A program

Carrying their meager possessions, Cambodian civilians flee toward refuge in Thailand, shortly before a massive Vietnamese assault in January on the guerrilla base camp of Ampil. Vietnamese troop offensives swelled the population of Thailand's refugee camps with over 200,000 new arrivals.

of "Cambodianization," under which civilians were drafted into labor brigades to build up "national defenses" against the resistance, continued during the year, and a civilian People's Defense Force was formed to guard roads and patrol streets in the capital.

In late January and early February, UN Secretary-General Javier Pérez de Cuéllar visited Southeast Asia, including Vietnam, on a peace mission. He was followed, in March, by Australia's foreign minister, William Hayden. Both failed to find an acceptable formula to bring the warring parties to a negotiation session. A proposal put forth by the Association of Southeast Asian Nations in July for indirect talks involving the Phnom Penh government, the Vietnamese, and the three resistance groups was rejected by Hanoi. Also rejected, by China, was a call by Sihanouk for an international conference including the United States and the Soviet Union.

See STATISTICS OF THE WORLD.   E.H.B.

CAMEROON. See STATISTICS OF THE WORLD. See also AFRICA.

CANADA. In 1985 the Progressive Conservative cabinet of Prime Minister Brian Mulroney (see biography in PEOPLE IN THE NEWS) was still adjusting—sometimes uneasily—to the powers and tribulations of office. The Conservatives' hesitation in bringing forth a distinctive legislative agenda or economic program since their return to power in 1984 left them vulnerable to attacks by the opposition Liberals and New Democrats. There were important political changes in the provinces—including Ontario, where long-dominant Tories were ousted from power, and Québec, where Liberals regained power from the Parti Québécois.

Mulroney's Course. The Mulroney government, with 211 seats in the 282-member House of Commons, took its methodical and deliberate time setting its course. On May 23, fully eight months after taking office, the government proposed its first budget. By cutting $1.8 billion in outlays and increasing taxes by $200 million, Finance Minister Michael Wilson proposed to trim the federal deficit by $2 billion—to $33.8 billion in the 1985–1986 fiscal year. (References are to Canadian dollars throughout.) Wilson imposed a surtax on those with middle incomes and above, cut job creation programs,

and scheduled gradual reductions in the size of the federal public service. To promote private investment—especially in small businesses and the stock market—he declared a lifetime tax holiday for every Canadian for up to $500,000 worth of capital gains.

The most politically damaging item in the budget turned out to be Wilson's plan to partly "deindex" old-age security pensions, which for years had escalated automatically with the Consumer Price Index. The finance minister said the measure would save the treasury $1.6 billion a year by 1990. But it caused a flurry of opposition and forged the nation's normally quiescent and politically unorganized elderly into a powerful pressure group. After weeks of defending deindexing, Wilson announced that he was backing off. To recoup the expense, he extended a surtax on large corporations and increased fuel taxes.

The Conservatives had other political difficulties in their first year. Opposition MP's and editorial writers harassed ministers about the hundreds of patronage appointments that occurred as the new regime set about installing friendly figures in government agencies, crown corporations, and ambassadorial posts. Roy McMurtry, for example, had been a minister in the Conservative government of Ontario before being dispatched by Mulroney as high commissioner (ambassador) to Great Britain. Stanley Hartt, Mulroney's friend and fellow-lawyer from Montréal, suddenly vaulted to the powerful position of deputy minister of finance.

Mulroney's first defense minister, Robert Coates, resigned in another sort of scandal in February when a newspaper reported that he and two staffers had been drinking in a strip club frequented by prostitutes, near the Canadian Armed Forces base at Lahr, West Germany. Coates said his behavior was no threat to national security, and he sued the newspaper for libel. In late September two other cabinet ministers resigned. Fisheries Minister John Fraser quit after the disclosure that he had ordered more than a million cans of tuna onto the market even though his own inspectors had judged it unfit for human consumption; Fraser had wanted to protect about 400 fish-plant jobs that would have been threatened. Then, Communications Minister Marcel Masse quit amid

Stanley Hartt (right), a Montréal lawyer selected for the powerful position of deputy finance minister by Prime Minister Brian Mulroney, gets some pointers from the P.M. Although labeled a patronage appointment by some, Hartt had proven himself to Mulroney by helping to avert a postal strike as a conciliator during contract negotiations and by organizing a national economic conference.

a police investigation of alleged overspending in his 1984 campaign. (He was reinstated after the probe found no wrongdoing.) In December another cabinet member, Transportation Minister Suzanne Blais-Grenier, resigned in a policy dispute.

Aside from the budget, there were three principal elements of government economic policy. For one thing, the Foreign Investment Review Agency (Fira) was transformed by legislation into Investment Canada as of July 1. Instead of reviewing prospective foreign investments to ensure that they were of "significant benefit" to Canada, the new body's mandate was to encourage foreign investment. Second, the National Energy Program—the previous Liberal government's policy that favored the domestic petroleum industry as against big foreign companies while limiting price increases desired by oil-producing provinces—was finally dismantled by the Tories, following agreement with oil-producing western provinces at the end of March. Energy Minister Pat Carney rescinded some half-dozen different taxes, along with an exploration grant scheme tied to the level of the recipients' Canadian ownership. The government also deregulated oil and natural gas prices, permitting them to rise (or fall) with the international market. Finally, it abolished the NEP's "back-in" rule, which empowered crown-owned Petro-Canada to take a share in any other company's Arctic or offshore discovery.

The third element of economy policy emerged in white papers, as proposals to allow insurance and other financial companies to enter the banking business and to deregulate the transportation industry—including airlines, rail freight, shipping, and trucking.

Economy and Business. The Canadian economy gave every sign of robust growth in 1985—continuing the postrecession recovery begun in 1983. In 1984 the chief stimulants to growth had been exports and consumer spending; in 1985 investment by business and government led the way. Encouraged by lower interest rates, the growth rate in private and public investment was expected to reach 9 percent or more in 1985. Discounting an inflation rate of about 4 percent, that represented real investment growth of 5 percent—the first real growth in investment since the start of the 1981 recession. By November, analysts were expecting the gross national product to show a healthy growth of 3–4 percent for 1985.

Despite the promising growth, however, unemployment remained stubbornly high. After averaging 11.3 percent in 1984, the rate subsided only slightly to a little above 10 percent in late 1985. Moreover, the Canadian dollar took rough treatment on the exchange markets, falling to just over 71 U.S. cents in March. The low dollar kept Canadian exports competitive in foreign markets, but it also placed extra inflationary pressure on the economy by raising the price of imports.

In a controversial move, the government agreed in principle to sell de Haviland Aircraft of Canada Ltd. to a U.S. company—Boeing Aerospace—for Can$155 million.

A group of Toronto's older citizens confront their parliamentary representative with a petition against a government proposal to reduce old-age security pension increases.

Civil Rights and the Law. No aspect of Canadian life underwent more important change in 1985 than the nation's legal system. Section 15 of the Charter of Rights and Freedoms—the so-called equality section—took effect on April 17, three years to the day after Queen Elizabeth proclaimed the charter into law as part of Canada's new constitution. The section declares that "every individual is equal before and under the law and has the right to the equal protection and equal benefit of the law without discrimination." Parliament and the provinces had delayed application of the section so that they would have time to amend existing federal and provincial laws that appeared to violate the guarantee of equality. However, the courts will ultimately have to decide what Section 15 means in particular cases.

The flow of historic judgments on the charter from the Supreme Court of Canada continued during the year, as other parts of the 34-section charter were tested in the courts. In a key criminal-law case decided in May, the Supreme Court ruled that everyone has the right to call a lawyer when detained by police or other authorities, even if not formally arrested. In a civil-law case decided in late April, it struck down the federal Lord's Day Act, which restricted Sunday shopping, as an unconstitutional breach of religious freedom. The high

court ruled earlier that persons applying to stay in Canada as refugees cannot be deported without a hearing.

Foreign Affairs. Canada, together with other North Atlantic Treaty Organization countries, was invited by U.S. President Ronald Reagan to take part in his proposed Strategic Defense Initiative. The SDI ("Star Wars") notion of creating a high-tech shield against attacking missiles provoked intense controversy in Canada. Mulroney and External Affairs Minister Joe Clark showed no enthusiasm for formal Canadian participation but avoided making a policy statement at first. Finally, in September, Mulroney announced that his government, while not opposed to the SDI program, would not take part in it; Canadian companies, however, would be free to bid for contracts.

Meanwhile, the Conservatives were attempting in other ways to improve U.S.-Canadian relations, which had suffered periodic strains during the years of Liberal Prime Minister Pierre Elliott Trudeau. The symbol of their efforts was a "blarney summit" between Mulroney and Reagan that began on St. Patrick's Day in Québec City. The conference was staged as a neighborly meeting of two congenial political leaders delighted by their common Irish roots. Acid rain, an issue of real disagreement between Ottawa and Washington, was handled by appointing a two-member panel to seek a compromise. On trade, the two agreed to strive not to erect barriers between their two countries.

As a rule, Canada's resource-exporting regions support the opening of expanded U.S. markets and would welcome cheap U.S. imports in return, but manufacturing areas in central Canada worry about U.S. competition. Mulroney, therefore, began cautiously by tempering the issue with a euphemism—referring not to free trade but to "trade enhancement." However, as the year progressed, there seemed more public support for free trade with the United States. The idea was backed by a joint committee of the Senate and House of Commons. And in September a royal commission studying the Canadian economy offered a strong recommendation in favor of free trade with the United States, which Mulroney followed up by asking for new bilateral negotiations on the matter.

Another area that attracted the government's attention was the deteriorating situation in South Africa. As the U.S. Congress began debating tougher sanctions, External Affairs Minister Clark announced a series of measures intended to put more pressure on the apartheid regime. He canceled a double taxation agreement with South Africa, sought to discourage Canadian banks from selling Krugerrands (South African gold coins), and stopped the supply of government-backed export insurance. In September banks were asked to ban loans to the Pretoria government, and direct transport of both freight and passengers between Canada and South Africa was embargoed.

Regional Review. As Canadians became accustomed to the new Conservative face of government in Ottawa, political changes were taking place in some provinces. In Ontario, William Davis resigned as premier and was succeeded in early February by veteran Tory politician Frank Miller. Miller called an election to secure a mandate for himself, but the Conservatives, who had ruled Canada's most populous province for 42 years, won just 52 seats in the May 2 election, compared with 48 for the Liberals and 25 for the New Democratic Party. The Liberals and the NDP agreed to bring down the Tories in a no-confidence vote in the legislature and then to cooperate

with a Liberal cabinet for at least two years. As a consequence, Liberal leader David Peterson became premier (see biography in PEOPLE IN THE NEWS). Miller announced his resignation as Conservative leader in August; he was replaced by Larry Grossman, a former provincial minister, in November.

In Québec, Premier René Lévesque announced his retirement in June, nearly nine yeas after his Parti Québécois had come to power on a platform that included separation from the rest of Canada. Lévesque had been harried by cabinet resignations and seemingly exhausted by the failed struggle for the special status within Canada the party had called sovereignty-association. His successor, chosen by PQ members in September, was lawyer-physician Pierre Marc Johnson, the son of a former Québec premier. On December 2, the PQ suffered a crushing electoral defeat at the hands of the Liberals under former Premier

The newly instituted Section 15 of Canada's Charter of Rights and Freedoms guarantees equal rights for all; to implement it, members of LEAF (the Legal Education and Action Fund) were initiating test cases on such women's rights issues as equal pension benefits and support for single mothers.

Robert Bourassa, who took 98 of the 122 legislative seats.

In Alberta, Premier Peter Lougheed announced in June that he would step down in the fall after 14 years in office. Lougheed had led his Conservative party out of oblivion in the 1960's and had become premier in time to preside over the province's great oil boom of the 1970's—as well as the bust that followed. The provincial Tories met in October and chose Richard Getty, a businessman and former provincial cabinet minister, to succeed Lougheed.

In the Yukon Territory an upset occurred in May when the Conservatives, in power since party politics were introduced there in 1978, lost their hold on the 16-member Legislative Assembly to the NDP, which won 8 seats. NDP leader Tony Penikett became premier, with Liberal support.

In New Brunswick, Conservative Premier Richard Hatfield was acquitted early in the year of drug possession charges. (The case stemmed from the discovery of marijuana in his briefcase in September 1984 as Hatfield boarded a plane to accompany Queen Elizabeth II on a tour marking New Brunswick's bicentennial.) Nevertheless, the trial caused Hatfield considerable political embarrassment and contributed to the defeat of Conservative candidates in two by-elections. Conservatives also lost some support in elections in Newfoundland and Labrador on April 2, dropping from 44 to 36 seats in the 52-member House of Assembly.

Economic concerns accounted for some of the political changes but not all. Unemployment rates late in the year remained above 10 percent in six of the provinces—reaching close to 20 percent in Newfoundland and Labrador. The economies of most provinces were also burdened by large budget deficits, requiring tax hikes or spending cuts.

In other developments around the country, the Supreme Court in June ruled that most of Manitoba's laws, those passed in English only, are invalid unless they are translated into French, in accordance with an agreement made in 1870 when the province joined the Confed-

A Run for the Money
In May, Steve Fonyo, 19, who had lost his left leg to cancer at age 12, completed a remarkable, 4,924-mile, 14-month marathon across Canada, using an artificial leg and a gait adapted to his condition. Having survived a bitter winter, he reached the Pacific coast off British Columbia in a rainstorm, to the applause of 6,000 well-wishers. Terry Fox, another youth who lost a leg to cancer, had been forced by illness to abandon a similar effort in 1980, and the Canadian Cancer Society was reluctant to sponsor Fonyo's try. His early backing came mostly from controversial oil millionaire J. Robert Carter, who had once pleaded guilty to sexual offenses. But no one could dispute Fonyo's achievement. The son of Hungarian immigrants, Fonyo grew up mostly in British Columbia, where his family opened a restaurant. After his leg was amputated, Steve became depressed, but he overcame his insecurity—and raised Can$11 million for cancer care and prevention.

Steve Fonyo

eration. In Alberta and Saskatchewan drought continued to affect grain production, and low prices further reduced farm incomes.

See STATISTICS OF THE WORLD.   J.H.

CAPE VERDE. See STATISTICS OF THE WORLD.

CARIBBEAN BASIN. The Caribbean was the scene of joint military exercises in 1985. There were economic problems in many countries, and Haiti experienced continuing repression.

Military Affairs. A joint military exercise on St. Lucia in September, code-named Exotic Palm, involved personnel from the United States, Great Britain, and seven Caribbean island nations, six of them members of a Regional Security System formed in 1982. Jamaica, though not an RSS member, joined the exercise. St. Vincent, though a member, declined to participate. Exotic Palm involved members of the U.S.-trained special services units of Dominica, Grenada, St. Lucia, and St. Kitts-Nevis (none of which have armies), plus army contingents from Antigua and Barbuda, Barbados, and Jamaica. Grenada, under a new coalition government headed by Prime Minister Herbert Blaize, had joined the RSS earlier in the year. On June 11, U.S. military intervention had ended in Grenada when the last of 67 regular U.S. troops departed; 25 other U.S. Special Forces soldiers stayed on to provide counterinsurgency training for police.

Caricom Summit. Dwindling intraregional trade was the main focus of the sixth annual summit meeting of the 13 Caribbean Community (Caricom) nations, held on Barbados in July. No progress was reported in solving the problem. The Caribbean Association of Trade and Industry later stated that "a major relaxation of most of the current nontariff barriers in intraregional trade" was needed to avert "a serious worsening of an already bad economic situation."

Caribbean Basin Initiative. Eleven of the Caricom nations' leaders, in a letter to U.S. President Ronald Reagan, criticized implementation of his much-publicized Caribbean Basin Initiative (CBI), a program of trade, aid, and investment incentives launched in January 1984. The letter said confidence in the CBI "could be gravely eroded" unless more products from the region were given duty-free access to U.S. markets.

Drugs. Many of the Caribbean islands have long been used as major transshipment points for smuggling drugs from South America to the United States, and it is estimated that 13 percent of the marijuana imported into the United States is grown in Jamaica. During 1985, awareness of the dimensions of domestic drug use increased in the region, while the governments of both the Bahamas and the Turks and Caicos Islands were directly affected by drug-smuggling charges. Bahamas Prime Minister Lynden Pindling weathered a scandal that threatened to topple his government, when Parliament merely issued a resolution condemning the involvement of government officials in drug trafficking but took no further action. In contrast, Turks and Caicos Prime Minister Norman Saunders resigned after his arrest in Miami on drug-smuggling charges (to be replaced by veteran politician Nathaniel Francis). He was later convicted on lesser charges and fined, as well as being sentenced to eight years in prison. Stafford Missick, the islands' former commerce and development minister, who was convicted in Miami on similar charges as well as on conspiracy charges, was sentenced to ten years in prison.

Leadership Changes. Prime Minister Tom Adams of Barbados and President Forbes Burnham of Guyana both died of natural causes during the year. Adams was replaced by Deputy Prime Minister H. Bernard St. John, with general elections scheduled for 1986. Burnham was replaced by Prime Minister Desmond Hoyte, who was confirmed in the post on the basis of December 9 elections and inaugurated three days later. Opposition leaders claimed that the elections had been marred by widespread irregularities, and the leading opposition leader, Cheddi Jagan, charged that he had been roughed up at a polling place. Hoyte was expected to be more pragmatic and more sympathetic to the United States than his predecessor.

Dominica. Prime Minister Mary Eugenia Charles won a second five-year term when her Dominica Freedom Party took 15 of the 21 House of Assembly seats up for election on July 1. Among opposition winners of legislative seats was former Prime Minister Patrick John. John was subsequently retried on charges of having conspired to overthrow the Charles government in 1981. He was convicted in October and sentenced to 12 years in prison.

Guadeloupe. In April separatist leaders from all French overseas departments met on Guadeloupe and pledged to seek independence from France for their homelands. Later, six days of demonstrations that nearly paralyzed Guadeloupe ended on July 29, when Georges Faisans, a proindependence activist, was released from a Paris jail. He had been sentenced to three years' imprisonment for attacking a white teacher who had kicked a black student on Guadeloupe. Earlier in the year, three people were killed in a bomb blast attributed to militant separatists.

Haiti. In the absence of democratic safeguards and media access, opponents of Haitian President Jean-Claude Duvalier boycotted a July 22 constitutional referendum, in which voters were asked to ratify the legislature's approval of constitutional changes. These included the official confirmation of Duvalier as president for life, empowering him to name his successor and giving him the right to appoint prime ministers as well as to remove elected mayors from office. The government reported that 99.9 percent of the voters had supported the changes; domestic critics and foreign observers charged that the election had been characterized by massive fraud. Continuing repression of all political opposition marked a year that included major protests led by Roman Catholic clergy and by students. During one protest late in the year, police shot or beat to death four students; the government also jailed a key opposition leader and shut down a major radio station operated by the church. On December 31, Duvalier reorganized his cabinet.

Jamaica. Demonstrations over gasoline price increases paralyzed the island for two days in January, and there was a week-long general strike by public employees in June protesting austerity measures, imposed to deal with Jamaica's economic problems. Conservative Prime Minister Edward Seaga's Jamaica Labor Party continued to hold all 60 seats in Parliament, after an opposition boycott of the December 1983 elections.

Dominican Republic. The government of President Salvador Jorge Blanco sought to comply in some degree with demands of the International Monetary Fund for austerity measures, while at the same time keeping a lid on popular discontent. In April the IMF approved a $78.5 million standby loan, and foreign creditors subsequently rescheduled part of the payments due on the country's massive $2.9 billion foreign debt. But the government had already modified its austerity program after riots in which four persons were killed, and a further modification was agreed to in July to avert a threatened general strike. Future prospects for coping with the country's financial problems while avoiding social conflict appeared bleak.

See also STATISTICS OF THE WORLD; CUBA; PUERTO RICO.   D.B.

CENTRAL AFRICAN REPUBLIC. *See* STATISTICS OF THE WORLD.

CEYLON. *See* SRI LANKA.

CHAD. During 1985, civil war continued in Chad between forces loyal to President Hissène Habré and antigovernment rebels led by former President Goukouni Oueddei. French troops, which had supported the government side, were removed from Chad in late 1984, in accordance with a mutual withdrawal agreement reached with Libya, which backed the rebels. Despite the agreement, Libyan troops reportedly remained both in the disputed Aouzou strip region of Chad and in other parts of the north. French troops were stationed in the Central African Republic (CAR) and other nearby Francophone African countries. Habré appeared to be conceding the northern third of the country to rebel forces, while becoming more firmly entrenched in Chad's capital, N'Djamena, and in the southwest.

In January southern commando groups ("codos") united and joined forces with the southern wing of Goukouni's GUNT (Transitional Government of National Unity) forces. Bitter fighting between the codos and Habré's FANT (Chad National Armed Forces) caused thousands of southern refugees to flee to the CAR and Sudan throughout the year, as much to escape FANT brutality as to avoid the fighting. Some armed rebels also fled to CAR refugee camps, which led to armed incursions by Habré's forces into the CAR. Habré made a conciliatory tour of southern cities in March and had some success in inducing codos to join his army. April saw a combined CAR-

Chad military operation to clear out rebels from both sides of the border. However, neither a military nor a diplomatic end to the war seemed likely, despite mediation efforts by Mali and other countries.

A nearly 50 percent decline in food production and a one-third drop in the cotton crop (with which food exports are purchased) led to starvation conditions in Chad's southern breadbasket by mid-March. In addition, Nigeria closed its borders, cutting off a major supply of food that Chad buys with livestock exports, and expelled aliens from Chad and other countries. Emergency food relief was sent to Chad from abroad, but political and transportation problems severely limited its distribution.

See STATISTICS OF THE WORLD.   G.L.

CHEMISTRY. Several food additives were under fire in 1985 because of possible health hazards. A new, cheaper method of enriching uranium was seen in the offing. Chemists reported advances in enzyme research.

Food Additives. Salts of metabisulfite, bisulfite, and sulfite are commonly used as antioxidants to preserve fresh fruits and vegetables in supermarkets and restaurants, as well as in certain medications, canned foods, and beverages. The sulfites are generally harmless, but as many as 1 million people in the United States may have mild to severe allergic reactions to them. Since 1983 the U.S. Food and Drug Administration has received reports of more than 500 severe reactions linked to sulfites, including several deaths. In August, after three years of prodding by consumer groups, the FDA announced it would seek to ban the use of six kinds of sulfites in fresh fruits and vegetables.

Several artificial colorings commonly put into food, drugs, and cosmetics have been found to cause cancer when consumed in large quantities by laboratory animals. Early in 1985 a Washington, D.C.-based consumer organization called Public Citizen sued the U.S. Department of Health and Human Services (of which the FDA is a part) seeking to have the dyes removed from the market. The most widely used is Red No. 3, an ingredient in about 2,000 different foods. In May the FDA convened a scientific panel to examine the safety of Red No. 3 and five dyes used only for drugs and cosmetics.

Risk-free salads may soon be possible since the government is trying to ban the use of sulfites to preserve the fresh appearance of fruits, greens, and vegetables. Sulfites have been found to cause allergic reactions in many people.

Aspartame, a low-calorie sugar substitute better known under the brand names Nutra-Sweet and Equal, has quickly become the most popular artificial sweetener available. The FDA has received several hundred complaints about side effects ranging from dizziness to brain damage, but most of the reports are anecdotal in nature. One scientific study reported in July found that offspring of pregnant mice who received aspartame took longer after birth to focus their eyes. Some scientists now believe aspartame use should be minimized by pregnant women and by infants under six months, as well as by people carrying the gene for phenylketonuria. However, the American Medical Association's Council on Scientific Affairs found aspartame safe except for those carrying this gene. Phenylketonuria is an inability to metabolize the amino acid phenylalanine, a component of aspartame; individuals with the disorder who do not control their consumption of phenylalanine could develop mental retardation.

Uranium Enrichment. Faced with a declining world market for enriched uranium, the U.S. Department of Energy announced in June that it was shutting down one of its three enrichment plants—a facility at Oak Ridge, Tenn.—and halting construction of an enrichment facility near Portsmouth, Ohio, that had already cost $2.6 billion. The department said it would focus its research and development efforts on a new laser technique.

Uranium occurs most commonly as two isotopes (forms of the element having different numbers of neutrons in their atomic nuclei): uranium 238, which is effectively inert, and uranium 235, which can support a nuclear reaction in a power plant or bomb. Naturally occurring uranium contains only about 1 percent uranium 235; that proportion must be increased to about 4 percent for the uranium to be used in a power plant.

The plant that was shut down enriched uranium by a process called gaseous diffusion; the facility where construction was halted was a gas centrifuge plant. Both processes require tremendous amounts of energy and huge facilities. The laser technique is simpler and cheaper, needs less space, and may use less energy; it was expected to be widely used as well for the isolation of rare isotopes for scientific and medical research.

Designer Enzymes. Enzymes are naturally occurring proteins that can catalyze—speed up—chemical reactions with high specificity; chemists have used them to carry out reactions difficult to achieve by conventional techniques. Since the range of enzymes is limited, scientists have sought to modify enzymes so that they can catalyze reactions other than those they catalyze in nature. In April a team of scientists from the University of California at San Francisco reported that they had altered the enzyme trypsin by changing one of its component amino acids. Trypsin is an enzyme that breaks down proteins through the cleavage of bonds linking specific amino acids. Normally, trypsin isolated from rat pancreases breaks bonds involving the amino acid arginine about 12 times as fast as those involving the amino acid lysine. The team changed one amino acid in the part of the trypsin molecule that binds to the protein to be broken apart; they then found that the altered enzyme broke bonds involving lysine about twice as fast as those involving arginine. It may eventually be possible to design enzymes in this manner to carry out any reaction desired.

Plastic Bats. Plastic baseball bats have been made in the past, but they have not been durable enough to withstand repeated contacts involving speeds of 180 miles per hour or more (a bat moving at, say, 90 mph meeting a ball pitched at 90 mph). This problem has apparently been solved in a new bat introduced in July by the Worth Bat Company of Tullahoma, Tenn. The polycarbonate/polybutylene terephthalate plastic shell is reinforced with graphite fibers for added strength, much like graphite-reinforced tennis rackets. The bats do not produced the annoying "pinging" sound of aluminum bats and are expected to last five to ten times as long as wood bats.   T.H.M.

CHESS. A tumultuous year in chess reached its climax on November 9, 1985, when Gary Kasparov captured the world title by defeating Anatoly Karpov in the final game of a 24-game championship series. In winning the match, played in Moscow between two citizens of the Soviet Union, Kasparov became, at age 22, the youngest champion in chess history.

Altogether, the two men had played 72 times in two title matches spread over 14 months. Their first match began in September 1984. The winner was to be the first to win six games, with draws having no effect on the outcome of the match. Karpov, the champion since 1975, took a 4-0 lead after nine games, but then Kasparov shifted from an aggressive to a more defensive style and began to wear down the champion. After a record 17 consecutive draws, Karpov won game 27. Kasparov took game 32 and, after many more draws, smashed through to win games 47 and 48.

With Karpov still leading 5-3 but near exhaustion, International Chess Federation (FIDE) President Florencio Campomanes of the Philippines terminated the match on February 15. He cited the strain of the 159-day event on players and organizers. The outspoken Kasparov denounced the decision, and many suspected that Campomanes had acted to save Karpov, who also happened to be the favorite of the Soviet chess establishment.

Gary Kasparov (right) dethroned fellow Russian Anatoly Karpov in November to become, at 22, the youngest world chess champion in history. The challenger's stunning strategy in the 24th and final game clinched a 13-11 victory in the match.

The second match began in September under new FIDE rules. It was to be limited to 24 games, and the first player to score 6 victories or 12½ points (a win would count for 1 point, a draw for ½ point) would be declared the champion. In the event of a 12-12 tie, Karpov would keep his title. The rivals differed in style and personality. Karpov, 34, was a master strategist but colorless in execution; he also held political views that conformed well with those of the Soviet Communist Party. Kasparov, in contrast, played boldly and was quick to sacrifice pieces in his relentless pursuit of his opponent's king. He was similarly bold in his political views.

The match was close throughout. Game 16, in which Kasparov sacrificed a pawn to win, was seen as the turning point and as the most brilliant game of the match. Trailing 12-11 and anxious to win the 24th and final game, Karpov played aggressively. So did Kasparov, who had the black pieces; he sacrificed two pawns in order to expose the white king to an inescapable trap. Karpov resigned and Kasparov had won the match 13-11, capping a meteoric rise. He had begun to play chess at age 6, had won a major international tournament at 16, and had become an international grand master at 17.

After the first Karpov-Kasparov match was ended, FIDE ruled that if Karpov lost the championship in the upcoming match he was entitled to a rematch within six months. If there is a rematch, the loser would have to play the winner of a new round of eliminations already under way in 1985; the winner in that match would then play the world champion. J.T.S.

CHILE. In June 1985 the government of General Augusto Pinochet Ugarte reduced its declared "state of siege" to a "state of emergency," but the change was of modest significance. Under the original state of siege, imposed in November 1984 following a widely observed strike, six opposition magazines were closed down and the government had the right to wiretap, open mail, and hold dissidents indefinitely without charges. In four months' time, the Chilean Commission on Human Rights reported 12 killings by security and 31,777 mass detentions, among other alleged abuses.

On June 16 the state of siege was downgraded to a state of emergency, after the cabinet argued that Chile's international image was suffering. Earlier in June, however, the government had modified the constitution so that presidential powers during a state of emergency were roughly the same as those during a state of siege. The real impact of the change was the reappearance of the six banned publications.

Despite a tradition of international fractiousness, Chile's political parties—still technically illegal—made an effort to band together in the face of events. At the end of August, 11 opposition parties signed an accord outlining a plan to restore democracy and, a week later, organized the largest antigovernment protest in nearly a year. Thousands of Chileans also signed the accord and protested peacefully by remaining in their homes on the afternoon of September 4. Concurrent demonstrations, led by a separate Marxist coalition, resulted in the reported deaths of ten people. Several days later, the government announced an extension of the state of emergency and renewed press restrictions. Unions and leftist parties staged mass protests later in the year. Demonstrations were also held by university students; more than 400 were arrested at one such protest.

The government was shaken up at high levels by an investigation into the abduction and brutal murders of three prominent Communist Party members. Relatives went on a hunger strike but called it off in mid-May when magistrate José Cánovas Robles initiated a full inquiry. On August 1, 14 police officers were charged with involvement in the murders, and a day later General César Mendoza Durán resigned from the junta and as chief of the carabineros (police). A number of high-level carabineros were subsequently retired.

The first half of the year brought a trade surplus of more than $400 million. The peso was devalued nearly 9 percent in February and another 7.8 percent in June, while tariffs were lowered from 35 percent to 20 percent. In return for a $750 million IMF loan, Chile agreed to maintain a realistic exchange rate. International bankers agreed to refinance $5 billion in loans over 12 years, with a 6-year grace period.

A March 3 earthquake in central Chile killed over 175 people and left as many as 1 million homeless. Initial government estimates pegged the total damage at the staggering figure of

A massive earthquake devastated the cities of Chile's central region on March 3. The façade of this Santiago building was torn away, with only some door frames remaining intact.

nearly $2 billion, making the quake perhaps the most expensive in Chile's tremor-ridden history.

Chile's long-standing dispute with Argentina over the Beagle Channel drew to a formal close in April, when the junta ratified a 1984 treaty mediated by the Vatican.

See STATISTICS OF THE WORLD.   J.F., Jr.

CHINA, PEOPLE'S REPUBLIC OF. In 1985, China was in transition: in politics, from pragmatic strongman Deng Xiaoping, who was in his 80's and indicated plans to retire, to successors who might not carry on his policies; in government, from cumbersome economic and military systems to more modern and efficient ones; and in foreign affairs, probably, toward greater international influence.

Changing Leadership. In response to pressure from Deng in behalf of younger people, retirements were announced in September at a meeting of the Communist Party Central Committee. Ten of 24 Politburo members and 64 of 340 members of the Central Committee resigned, including many military figures opposed to Deng's policies. Among those leaving the Politburo were Marshal Ye Jianying, 88, a powerful former military commander, and Deng Yingchao, 81, widow of former Premier Zhou Enlai. Zhou's foster son, Deputy Minister Li Peng, 57, was one of several newcomers named to the Politburo. The defense and culture ministers were among those leaving the Central Committee, but Hua Guofeng, 64, former prime minister and party chairman and a Mao Zedong loyalist, was not retired. The new Politburo and Central Committee appointees were generally much younger than their predecessors, as were several recently appointed government ministers.

Deng was seeking to streamline the Communist Party, whose membership had reached 40 million, into a mechanism able to rule the country efficiently. His personnel changes reached all levels of the party and were aimed in large part at eliminating official corruption, which had proliferated as central political and economic controls had been relaxed. More than a million civil servants, thousands of military officers, and countless managers had retired in the past two years, and retirements were continuing.

Politics and Society. Chinese Catholics won some concessions, including the reopening of a few churches and visits by Mother Teresa of Calcutta and Jaime Cardinal Sin of Manila. Ignatius Kung, former bishop of Shanghai, was freed after 25 years in prison; he was said to have "repented" of "unpatriotic ways." But Peking rebuffed a friendly statement by the pope, and Catholics still did not have ties with Rome.

The Communist Party made changes in education to stress greater autonomy for individual institutions and higher academic standards. Private schools were to be permitted. A requirement for nine years of education was to be introduced gradually. A congress of Chinese writers received vague assurances of greater creative freedom. Amnesty International remained critical of China for the frequency of its executions and its large number of political prisoners.

Economy. Although moving toward "market socialism," the Deng leadership evidently did not want to go the whole way, still less to adopt capitalism. What it did want was to retain a basically "socialist" (Communist) system while grafting onto it certain features of capitalism thought to be conducive to efficiency. What it tended to get was a mishmash of the good and bad features of both. A relaxation of central controls in late 1984 led to a large increase in circulating money, wage and price increases, and a surge in profiteering, black market activity, and smuggling. The official response, announced March 27 by Premier Zhao Ziyang, was swift: strict central control was reinstituted over investment and wage funds, cash in circulation, credit, and administrative budgets.

Exploration for offshore oil, carried on by foreign companies under contract with Peking in the South China Sea for several years, continued to show disappointing results, and in the spring of 1985 the companies were invited to begin prospecting onshore.

Foreign firms found the generally more relaxed and decentralized economic system rather confusing. They were now expected to deal with individual firms, not solely with the government, but these firms were often hard to do business with and sometimes even hard to find.

Shenzhen, the most important of the four Special Economic Zones set up in 1979 to attract foreign capital and technology and generate hard-currency export earnings, was found wanting. Its enterprises were not high tech enough to produce exportable goods in significant quantities; foreign capital, furthermore, was not flowing in at the desired rate. In midyear, Peking decided on less ambitious growth targets for the special zones and for 10 of 14 other ports opened to foreign investment in 1984. A new five-year economic plan, announced in September for 1986 to 1990, envisaged a continued commitment to liberalization of the economy and an "open" relationship with the outside world.

Imports were heavy during the year and it was predicted that the trade deficit would be greater than in 1984. In keeping with a moderate warming trend in Sino-Soviet relations, China signed a five-year trade agreement in Moscow in July, with a total price tag of $14 billion. The Soviet Union was to build 7 new plants and modernize 14 old ones for the Chinese. Also in July, China and Indonesia agreed to resume direct trade for the first time since 1967.

The Unification Question. On May 27, when the 1984 Sino-British "Joint declaration" on Hong Kong came into force, Hong Kong officially entered a 12-year transition period leading to Chinese rule. In June, China's National People's Congress established a Basic Law Drafting Committee to design Hong Kong's political structure after 1997.

Deng Xiaoping and his colleagues hoped that the Hong Kong arrangement would be a model for an accommodation with Taiwan; Deng sought to generalize the applicability of the arrangement by enunciating a doctrine of "one country, two systems," the socialist and the capitalist. All this had little observable effect on Taiwan, where no one was known to favor unification on Peking's terms ("autonomy" for Taiwan). Negotiations were reportedly under way to replace the Portuguese administration of Macao, near Canton, with a Chinese administration beginning in 1986.

Foreign Affairs. Peking was determined to maintain a viable relationship with the United States as being vital both to its security and to its modernization, but also to improve its difficult relations with the Soviet Union in order to reduce the danger from that direction and avoid undue dependence on the United States. Semiannual talks with Moscow at the deputy foreign minister level continued, though apparently without resolving any fundamental issues. Peking demanded that Moscow drastically reduce its powerful forces near the Sino-Soviet border and withdraw from Mongolia, Afghanistan, and Indochina; the Soviets gave no clear sign that they intended to do any of these things. However, for its part, Peking showed little negative reaction to the 1984–1985 dry season offensive by Soviet-backed Vietnamese forces against Cambodian guerrillas the Chinese supported. In July a Sino-Soviet trade agreement was signed. In December, Moscow and Peking agreed to exchange visits by foreign ministers in 1986.

Despite a number of irritants, of which arms sales to Taiwan were probably the most serious, the developing relationship with the United States was still the de facto centerpiece of Chinese foreign policy. The Sino-American relationship had evolved into two main aspects: defense cooperation (as it is called in the Pentagon) and economic cooperation (especially the transfer to China of high technology). The United States had grown more willing since 1983 to sell "dual use" technology (having military as well as civilian applications) to China. Still, serious bureaucratic obstacles occurred in Washington and in Paris, where U.S. allies in the Coordinating Committee for Multilateral Export Controls often delayed U.S. applications for sales to China, for the sake of competitive advantage. By 1985, the United States was beginning to consider the sale of strictly defensive arms, such as antitank weapons, to China.

After General Secretary Hu Yaobang visited Australia and New Zealand in April, Peking began to follow New Zealand's example by insisting that port calls by U.S. naval vessels be by nonnuclear ships only; because the United States, as a matter of policy, refused to say if any given ship carried nuclear arms, U.S. naval port calls were in effect barred.

During President Ronald Reagan's visit to China in 1984 an agreement on nuclear power cooperation had been initialed.The U.S. nuclear power industry strongly favored the agreement, but implementation had been stalled by suspicions, notably in the U.S. Senate, that China, which was believed to have aided the Pakistani nuclear weapons program, might divert materials and/or technology acquired from the United States to its own military use or those of others. China sought to counter such suspicions and, in September, also announced that some of its civilian nuclear plants would be opened to international inspection and safeguards. President Li Xiannian visited the United States in July; the nuclear power cooperation agreement was signed and submitted to Congress soon thereafter. It went into effect after the Senate finally approved it late in the year and the House took no action against it. U.S. Vice-President George Bush visited China in October; he announced that

the Coordinating Committee nations would relax their rules governing nonmilitary high-technology exports to China.

In December, China agreed in principle to buy over $1.5 billion worth of nuclear-generating equipment from France and Great Britain. Meanwhile, Japan and China signed a nuclear power cooperation agreement in the summer. China also began to quietly develop significant commercial relations with Israel, which it had

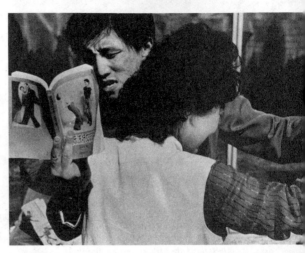

A new kind of cultural revolution is sweeping China. At right, a couple follows a step-by-step manual at a lunch-hour dance lesson; old-fashioned steps are especially popular. Below, the owner of a new Japanese refrigerator carts it home on a bicycle, with a young family member riding shotgun.

The 20th anniversary of the Selma-to-Montgomery voting-rights march was commemorated by more than 2,500 participants, including (from left) the Reverend Jesse Jackson; the Reverend Joseph Lowery, president of the Southern Christian Leadership Conference; Evelyn Lowery; and Coretta Scott King. They are shown crossing the Edmund Pettus Bridge, where Alabama state troopers and sheriff's deputies attacked marchers in 1965.

tended to hold at arm's length out of concern for Arab feelings.

See STATISTICS OF THE WORLD.   H.C.H.

CHINA, REPUBLIC OF. *See* TAIWAN.

CIVIL LIBERTIES AND CIVIL RIGHTS. While the Reagan administration continued its conservative approach to civil liberties, the Supreme Court's rightward turn in 1984 was less in evidence in 1985. The Court reaffirmed support for church-state separation and generally backed individual claims in free speech, discrimination, and criminal procedure cases. (*See also* BLACKS IN THE UNITED STATES; SUPREME COURT OF THE UNITED STATES; WOMEN.) The AIDS epidemic raised controversial civil rights issues during the year.

Church-State Issues. In several cases involving the separation of church and state, the Supreme Court dealt a major setback to the Reagan administration, which had entered the cases seeking a "special status" for and "accommodation" to religious interests. In his State of

the Union message in February, President Ronald Reagan reaffirmed his support for voluntary prayer in the public schools. But the Court held in *Wallace* v. *Jaffree* that an Alabama law authorizing a one-minute period of silence in public schools for "meditation or voluntary prayer" was unconstitutional. The Court said the law constituted an endorsement of prayer, which violated the requirement of state neutrality in religious matters. However, the Court did suggest that a moment-of-silence rule that did not specifically mention prayer would stand.

In *School District of the City of Grand Rapids* v. *Ball* and *Aguilar* v. *Felton*, the Court held unconstitutional the sending of publicly paid schoolteachers into parochial schools to teach classes on secular subjects, including remedial classes. The Grand Rapids programs were found to involve a "symbolic union" of church and state and to constitute a financial subsidy to parochial schools. The *Aguilar* case involved the use of federal funds by New York City under the Elementary and Secondary Education Act of 1965, which calculates such aid in terms of the numbers of poor children. The New York program was said to lead to "excessive entanglement" of church and state because it involved monitoring by city authorities to ensure that participating teachers and counselors were not involved in religious activities.

In a speech in August, Education Secretary William Bennett complained of "four decades of misguided court decisions" which had put religion out of the public schools. He said that the U.S. political system and the Judeo-Christian tradition were "welded together." Later, Bennett pledged support to school systems seeking to delay compliance with the Court's school aid decisions.

In *Estate of Thornton* v. *Caldor, Inc.*, it was decided that a state may not require an employer to give workers a day off on their chosen sabbath; the Supreme Court concluded that such a law would advance a particular religious practice. In *Board of Trustees of the Village of Scarsdale* v. *McCreary*, which was decided while Justice Lewis Powell was ill, the Court deadlocked 4-4 and thus let stand a lower court ruling that the First Amendment does not bar the placement of a Nativity scene by a church group on public property.

The Reverend Sun Myung Moon, founder of the Unification Church, was freed from prison in August after serving 13 months for evading taxes on funds that he claimed belonged to the church and not to him personally. Numerous religious and civil liberties groups concerned with the church-state implications of the case had criticized his conviction.

Speech and Press. Attorney General Edwin Meese III announced in May the formation of a commission to study pornography and named Henry Hudson of Arlington County, Va., as its chairman. Hudson, as county prosecutor, had eliminated adult bookstores and massage parlors from the county. Meese said the study was warranted by the greater ease of securing pornography and by the heightened realism and violence of such materials. In *Brockett* v. *Spokane Arcades*, the Supreme Court struck down a state law banning material that incites

"lust"; material that arouses sexual response is not necessarily obscene, said the Court.

In *Federal Election Commission* v. *National Conservative Political Action Committee*, the Court supported the view that a campaign donation is a form of speech. It struck down the section of the Presidential Election Campaign Fund Act that set a $1,000 spending limit for a political action committee on behalf of publicly funded presidential candidates.

Criminal Procedure. In *Tennessee* v. *Garner*, a case involving the fatal shooting of an unarmed 15-year-old youth fleeing police after a burglary, the Court held that police may not use deadly force where there is no threat of immediate harm to police or others. In *United States* v. *Sharpe*, the Court ruled that an individual may be detained for 20 minutes while law enforcement officers conduct a limited investigation of suspected criminal activity. But in *Hayes* v. *Florida*, the Court disapproved of police taking a suspect to the police station and fingerprinting him without having gotten a warrant.

The Court held in *New Jersey* v. *T.L.O.* that school officials do not need a warrant in order to search public school students. The case involved the search of a 14-year-old's purse after she was caught smoking; the contents revealed evidence of drug dealing. The Court declared that school officials need only "reasonable grounds" to search—not the usual court criterion of "probable cause"—if it is thought a violation of the law or of school rules has occurred. In *United States* v. *Montoya De Hernandez*, the Court upheld detention of a suspected "alimentary canal smuggler" for 16 hours until a monitored bowel movement took place. In that case, the suspect delivered 88 cocaine-filled balloons in four days, after "heroic efforts to resist the usual calls of nature."

Age Discrimination. The scope of the Age Discrimination in Employment Act of 1967 and its 1978 amendment to ban mandatory retirement before age 70 was tested in three cases before the Supreme Court. The law bans age-based discrimination or forced retirement below age 70 except "where age is a bona fide occupational qualification." In *Trans World Airlines, Inc.* v. *Thurston*, the Court held that

Indianapolis Mayor William Hudnut greets firefighters; the city was opposing efforts by the Justice Department to overturn an affirmative action plan providing for the hiring and promotion of blacks and women in the Indianapolis police and fire departments.

TWA had violated the act by compelling 60-year-old pilots to retire from the airline rather than transferring them to a flight engineer's position. The Court found this treatment discriminatory, since such transfers were granted to younger pilots disqualified for reasons other than age. In *Western Air Lines* v. *Criswell*, the Court held that the airline could not require all flight engineers to retire from the cockpit at age 60, because Western had failed to show that such an age limit was a bona fide occupational qualification (BFOQ). To prove that the limit is a BFOQ, said the Court, the employer must show that it is "reasonably necessary to the normal operation of the particular business" and that there is a basis for believing that all or substantially all persons over this age cannot perform the job. Failing that, the employer must show it would be "highly impractical" to test employees individually. In a third case, *Johnson* v. *Mayor and City Council of Baltimore*, the Court refused to permit Baltimore to require its firefighters to

retire at age 55, despite the fact that a similar rule for federal firefighters had been enacted by Congress.

Rights of the Handicapped. Section 504 of the Rehabilitation Act of 1973 provides that no person may be subjected to discrimination by reason of a handicap under any program or activity receiving federal aid. The Supreme Court held in *Alexander* v. *Choate* that it is not necessary to prove intent to discriminate in order to find a violation under Section 504.

Quotas. The Reagan administration continued to oppose the use of racial quotas in hiring, stating that a 1984 U.S. Supreme Court ruling had removed the legal underpinning for such a policy. The Justice Department asked many local government units to modify their use of quotas and filed suit against the city of Indianapolis in an effort to change its use of quotas for blacks and women in hiring police officers and firefighters (*see also* BLACKS IN THE UNITED STATES).

AIDS. The spread of the deadly disease called AIDS (acquired immune deficiency syndrome) raised important civil rights issues. Homosexuals, especially, have faced a new wave of prejudice, because they are a major risk group for AIDS. Individuals with AIDS or suspected of having AIDS have lost their jobs or their apartments or have received erratic medical treatment. Children with AIDS have been kept out of school or, if permitted to attend, have been isolated.

The development of a blood test for exposure to the AIDS virus sparked controversies. A negative result is considered a reliable indication that the subject is not an AIDS carrier, but many positive results are false and do not mean that the person has the AIDS virus. A few states mandated the test's confidentiality and barred insurers or employers from requiring that it be taken. Colorado, however, required that positive test results be reported to state health officials. The Pentagon decided to test all personnel and recruits for signs of exposure, in order to reject recruits with positive results and give medical discharges to personnel actually having the disease.

Gay Rights. In *Board of Education of the City of Oklahoma City* v. *National Gay Task Force* the Supreme Court divided evenly and thus let stand an appeals court ruling that a school board may fire or refuse to hire a teacher because of indiscreet sexual conduct, but not because the individual has spoken out in favor of homosexuality.

Draft. In *Wayte* v. *United States,* the Court upheld prosecutions under the draft registration law directed exclusively against those who publicize their defiance of the law. The Court said the policy did not amount to selective prosecution, which would have violated the equal protection provision of the Constitution. The U.S. Education Department dropped a pending rule that would have required colleges to verify whether male applicants for federal aid have registered for the draft. The Education Department said the rule was unnecessary because 98 percent of all young men were already registered with Selective Service.

M.Gr.

COINS AND COIN COLLECTING. The year began with an announcement by the U.S. Treasury Department that over $70 million had been turned over to the U.S. Olympic Committee and the Los Angeles Olympic Organizing Committee. The windfall was realized through the sale of three commemorative coins—two silver dollars and a $10 gold piece—produced by the U.S. Mint for the 1984 Olympics in Los Angeles.

The announcement of the success of the U.S. Olympic coin program was followed by news of another project—a three-coin commemorative set to be issued to help raise funds for the renovation of the Statue of Liberty in time for its centennial observance in 1986. Congressional authorizing legislation mandated that three coins be struck: a half-dollar marking the contributions of immigrants to the development of America, a silver dollar featuring the role played by Ellis Island as the gateway to the United States for millions of immigrants, and a $5 gold piece depicting the Statue of Liberty. Recalling the early criticisms of the designs of the Olympic coins prior to their release, the Mint placed an embargo on illustrations of the three new designs until the coins were actually struck. The striking ceremony for the first of the three coins, the $5 piece, was held in October.

President Ronald Reagan in September issued an executive order whose provisions included a halt to the importation of South African gold Krugerrands. Up to 1985, Krugerrands were the world's largest selling bullion coins. Late in the year, Reagan signed a bill providing for the minting and sale of general-circulation gold coins for the first time in over 50 years; they were to be issued in nominal denominations of $5, $10, $25, and $50, with actual values tied to the gold market.

In late July treasure hunter Mel Fisher found the prize of a lifetime of dreaming and searching. Divers for his Treasure Salvors, Inc., discovered the bulk of the rich treasure carried by the Spanish ship *Nuestra Señora de Atocha* when it went down off the Florida coast west of Key West in a hurricane in 1622. When the storm struck, the *Atocha's* cargo included more than 1,000 silver bars, as well as pieces of gold bullion and treasure chests estimated to contain more than a quarter million coins—with a total value believed to be as high as $400 million.

E.C.R.

COLOMBIA. In August 1985, President Belisario Betancur Cuartas began the fourth and final year of his term of office. The government was beleaguered by two major catastrophes: a deadly shootout between guerrillas and government troops in Bogotá and a volcanic eruption that ravaged numerous towns in northern Colombia.

A truce that President Betancur had negotiated in 1984 with Colombia's main rebel groups began unraveling late that year, with the outbreak of clashes near Corinto between government forces and the April 19 movement (M-19). A cease-fire was negotiated in January 1985, but in June, claiming the government had not lived up to its promise of political and social reforms, the movement stated that it was returning to armed struggle. Subsequent clashes resulted in more than 100 deaths, and then, on November 6, dozens of M-19 guerrillas shot their way into the Palace of Justice in Bogotá, where Colombia's two highest courts have their offices. The gunmen took at least 300 hostages. President Betancur repeatedly refused any negotiation with the rebels. Government troops counterattacked within a few hours and freed many captives from the building's lower floors, but the guerrillas continued to hold out, with

119

Colombian armed forces begin their assault on Bogotá's Palace of Justice, invaded by M-19 terrorists on November 6. By the end of the siege, about 100 people had been killed, including 11 Supreme Court judges.

other hostages, on the upper floors. A fire broke out during a later attack by soldiers and burned through much of the building for several hours. The next morning, before a final, decisive assault by government forces, the guerrillas reportedly shot and killed some judges and other hostages, including the chief justice of the Supreme Court. Most of the rebels were themselves apparently killed during the fighting. The death toll in the siege was around 100, including 11 judges (a 12th later died of a heart attack in the hospital). Some hostages were killed in cross fires during the government assault.

Later in the year, among other incidents, street fighting in Cali between police and M-19 guerrillas led to 26 deaths.

On the night of November 13 the long-dormant volcano Nevado del Ruiz in northern Colombia erupted, spewing forth flames and ash. The intense heat melted a glacier atop the volcano's peak, which poured tons of mud and rock into nearby rivers, causing them to overflow and engulf the city of Armero. The city—with a population of 25,000—was virtually destroyed, and most of its residents were entombed in mud that hardened, making it impossible to rescue them. A total of 14 towns and cities around the volcano were devastated. It was estimated that 23,000 people in Armero and 2,000 elsewhere were dead or missing, and around 4,000 injured, with thousands left homeless.

In other news, four of the more than 80 Colombians sought by U.S. authorities on drug charges were extradited to the United States in January. Drug traffickers countered with threats against the lives of public officials. In February, a jumbo jet of Avianca, the state-supported Colombian national airline, was impounded in Miami after the discovery on board of cocaine valued at $600 million.

To reduce Colombia's large budget deficit, the Colombian Congress authorized higher prices and new taxes on food, and a stiff austerity plan was introduced. Export bans on some 200 products were removed, and the peso was devalued.

Betancur met with President Ronald Reagan on April 4 in Washington, D.C. Topics of discussion ranged from peace in Central America to the war on drug trafficking. The Colombian president subsequently met with President Daniel Ortega Saavedra in Nicaragua.

See STATISTICS OF THE WORLD.   L.L.P

COLORADO. See STATISTICS OF THE WORLD.

COMMONWEALTH OF NATIONS. In October 1985, representatives of 46 of the 49 member states of the Commonwealth of Nations attended the Commonwealth's biennial meeting, in the Bahamas. Forty-one heads of government were among those present. The most vexing question that confronted the delegates was whether they could reach a consensus on actions to pressure the South African government into ending apartheid. (South Africa had withdrawn from the organization 24 years earlier, under criticism from other member nations.) The members dispatched a plea to South African leaders to stay the execution of

Benjamin Moloise, a black poet convicted of the murder of a black policeman, but Moloise was executed the next day. Beyond the futile clemency plea, conference delegates could reach little consensus on what should be done.

Many favored mandatory comprehensive economic sanctions against the Pretoria government, but British Prime Minister Margaret Thatcher, mindful of the importance of Great Britain's trade with South Africa, withheld her country's support. The leaders then withdrew to a private resort and endorsed a list of limited economic measures that had already been adopted individually by many member nations. These included banning imports of Krugerrands and no longer financing trade fairs in South Africa. The group also agreed to establish a "small group of eminent Commonwealth persons" to try to encourage the government to begin discussions with black leaders on ending apartheid. There was no doubt that the delegates were anxious and irritated by the divisiveness caused by the South African problem. Malaysian Prime Minister Mahathir bin Mohamad, a frequent critic of the Commonwealth, asserted that "if the Commonwealth refuses to do something definite, then the club should admit that it really cannot contribute towards solving the problems faced by its neighbors."

The final communiqué addressed several other issues. Commonwealth leaders called for international cooperation in fighting drug trafficking and terrorism and urged a ban on nuclear testing and on all types of chemical weapons.

Earlier in the year, Thatcher paid an April visit to Asian members of the Commonwealth. The trip was designed to improve trade relations between Britain and other Commonwealth countries. As would be the case later in the year, Malaysia's prime minister had sharp words for Britain and for the Commonwealth, commenting that his former belief that a commonwealth implied "a certain sharing of wealth" among its members was clearly erroneous. Thatcher had a more pleasant task as she flew next to Sri Lanka to inaugurate the Victoria Dam and hydroelectric plant near Kandy, Britain's largest completed overseas aid project.

J.O.S.

COMMUNIST WORLD. Serious problems continued to divide the Communist movement in 1985. The new Soviet leadership under Mikhail S. Gorbachev appeared anxious to resolve at least some of the strains, while improving relations with the West.

Soviet Transition. For the third time since the death of longtime Soviet leader Leonid Brezh-

The death of Communist leader Enver Hoxha (shown here, left, with Ramiz Alia, who became his successor in April) led to the first change of power in Albania in 41 years. Alia was expected to continue Hoxha's basic policies.

nev in November 1982, the Soviet Union chose a new leader. The death of Konstantin U. Chernenko in March, after only 13 months at the helm of the Communist Party of the Soviet Union, cleared the way for Gorbachev, at age 54 representing a new generation of Soviet leaders, to take his place as CPSU general secretary. Gorbachev moved immediately to consolidate his power. By the end of the summer he had not only removed his major competitor from membership in the politburo but had also replaced many of the top party and government officials remaining from the Brezhnev era with his own supporters and allies.

Domestically, Gorbachev focused on the critical need to rejuvenate the Soviet economy; analysts, however, believed major changes would be needed in the traditional Soviet economic incentive system in order to register significant progress. Gorbachev's foreign policy attempted to project an image of a dynamic Soviet Union committed to world peace (while, at the same time, refusing to give up any of its military or political advantages). Renewed arms negotiations with the United States and a November summit meeting with President Ronald Reagan in Geneva were seen as attempts by the Soviet leader to improve his country's international standing and, in part, to deflect U.S. criticism of Soviet support for Communist movements abroad (such as the Sandinista regime in Nicaragua).

Eastern Europe. Economic problems throughout most of Eastern Europe, but especially in Romania and Poland, remained acute. In Poland, there was growing confrontation between the Communist regime and the Roman Catholic Church. Late in the year, General Wojciech Jaruzelski stepped down from his post as prime minister, but he remained as head of state and retained the important post of party leader; observers believed he wished to concentrate on rebuilding the party organization. In Albania, Enver Hoxha, the country's party chief and Stalinist leader for the past 41 years, died on April 11. Some easing of Albania's hardline policies—particularly its isolationism—had begun before Hoxha's death and was expected to continue under the new regime of President Ramiz Alia.

Soviet attempts to control the contacts its Eastern European allies had with the West continued to meet resistance. East Germany and Hungary, in particular, sought to express, albeit in muted form, their feeling that relations with the West should be widened. In early August, East Germany's Communist Party daily reprinted an article from the official Hungarian party paper that had praised East German foreign policy, especially its relations with the West. Both countries were said to have been more optimistic than other Eastern European nations in their assessment of the November summit talks. For its part, the Soviet Union took fairly divergent positions on Eastern European ties to the West. In June the Communist Party newspaper *Pravda* warned the Soviet Union's allies against allowing national interests to take precedence over the "internationalist" interests of the socialist bloc as a whole. But the following month, a much more conciliatory article appeared in *Kommunist* that stressed the diversity among socialist states and advocated respect for their specific national interests.

Late in the year, after the Geneva summit, U.S. Secretary of State George Shultz visited Hungary, Romania, and Yugoslavia; his visits to the last two countries were marked by some contentiousness, but he noted "potential" for change among countries in the area.

Comecon. The Eastern bloc's Council for Mutual Economic Assistance, or Comecon, was another arena in which the Soviets exercised control. At a Comecon summit meeting held in Warsaw in late June, members of the Soviet delegation reportedly informed their Eastern European colleagues that, after years of "subsidizing" Eastern European economies with relatively cheap oil in exchange for poor quality goods, the Soviet Union was demanding larger amounts of higher-quality goods, processed food, and advanced technology—in return for reduced deliveries of oil. Simultaneously, Soviet leader Gorbachev made clear that Eastern European attempts to gain a degree of autonomy in their relations with the West would be tightly controlled. Furthermore, the draft of the new CPSU party program, published on October 26, emphasized a need for tighter economic discipline within Comecon.

Warsaw Pact. In April the 1955 treaty that created the Warsaw Treaty Organization was renewed for 20 years. Despite the agreement, differing priorities among member countries caused strains within the alliance. In an article published shortly before the ceremony marking the pact's renewal, Soviet General and Warsaw Pact Joint Armed Forces Chief of Staff Anatoly Gribkov called for greater commitment to cooperation among members in joint military exercises and training, as well as in the coordination of military doctrine. However, a Hungarian military commentator argued against the need for quantitative increases in armaments within the pact. Hungarian political leaders argued that economic problems limited their ability to commit greater resources to joint military efforts—a problem no doubt felt elsewhere in Eastern Europe.

Asia. Chinese leaders continued to push forward far-reaching economic reforms, including the introduction of free enterprise into both agricultural and industrial production. Chinese officials were closely monitoring these "experiments" in economic decentralization; many were said to feel that its very success could also spark social and political problems, as the gap between the haves and have-nots in the countryside began to expand. Sino-Soviet relations continued to improve, although the two countries made little progress toward resolving their major differences concerning soviet military intervention in Afghanistan, Soviet support for the Vietnamese occupation of Cambodia (Kampuchea), and the extensive Soviet military buildup along the Chinese border. In December it was announced that Chinese and Soviet foreign ministers would exchange visits in 1986, for the first time in over 20 years.

In Afghanistan the stalemate between Soviet forces (and those of the Soviet-backed regime in Kabul) and the Afghan resistance continued. Despite Soviet tactics aimed at destroying the rural sources of support for the resistance, Afghan freedom fighters still were able to deny control of most of the countryside to the Soviets and the Afghan government. The regime made efforts to win popular support by stressing Islamic sentiments in its rhetoric and downplaying socialism and its ties to Moscow; and a Ministry of Islamic Affairs was established.

In Southeast Asia, the Soviets completed the transformation of the former U.S. military facilities at Cam Ranh Bay, Vietnam, into their largest military base outside Warsaw Pact territory. Meanwhile, the Soviet-backed Vietnamese occupation army conducted its biggest dry-season offensive yet against Cambodian resistance forces, during the four-month period that ended in March; the rebels' base camps were overrun, forcing them to disperse and adopt guerrilla tactics against the enemy.

Nonruling Parties. Among the more interesting developments involving nonruling European Communist parties was the apparent recognition by the Soviets of the dissident Spanish Communist Ignacio Gallego as "secretary-general of the Communist Party of Spain." In fact, Gallego was the head of a breakaway party formed in early 1984 from pro-Soviet elements within the Spanish Communist movement. The official Communist Party, which has often been at odds with the Soviets over major issues of policy, was still headed by Gerardo Iglesias. The ranks of Spanish Communists were further riven when Santiago Carrillo Solares, longtime leader of the Spanish Communist Party, and a number of his supporters were removed from the central and executive committees following a dispute with Iglesias over the direction of the party. Carrillo later announced the creation of yet another Communist party. Carrillo was often at odds with the Soviets because of his advocacy of a Spanish approach to Communism.

See also articles on individual countries.

R.E.K.

COMOROS. *See* STATISTICS OF THE WORLD.

COMPUTERS. For the computer industry, 1985 was a tumultuous year. Sales slumped badly in many sectors of the business. Minicomputer manufacturers encountered the sharpest declines in their history, and sales of personal computers fell far short of expectations.

Hardware. In the business-computer world, IBM, which has the lion's share of the market for large computers, launched its 3090 "Sierra" series of mainframe computers. The first version, Model 200, was IBM's most powerful mainframe. In the race to create the world's most powerful computers, however, a small company, Cray Research, of Minneapolis, was

Auctioneer Ross Dove displays some of the thousands of surplus and discontinued items being unloaded by computer manufacturers in California's Silicon Valley, during an unprecedented downturn in the personal computer market.

king. Cray unveiled its newest, fastest super-computer, the Cray 2, a machine with a peak performance of 1.2 gigaflops, or 1.2 billion floating point operations per second. The su-percomputers are used by U.S. defense and intelligence agencies and by companies that need very high performance computing. The oil industry uses supercomputers for geological analysis in oil exploration, and the aerospace industry puts them to work in aircraft design.

The personal computer market was still dom-inated by IBM. Its top personal computer, the PC AT, attracted imitators, machines built by companies using the same standards. Some like Compaq's Deskpro 286, offered more features and better performance; others were more nearly clones. A few companies took a riskier approach: Commodore International and Atari Corporation, once the kings of the low-cost home computer market, brought out higher-priced personal computers. Priced at $1,295, Commodore's Amiga featured dazzling color graphics and sound, and it offered much more power than the low-cost home computers. Atari brought out the 520 ST, a similar color

computer based on the Motorola 68000 chip and priced lower than the Amiga or Apple Computer's Macintosh. Yet both Commodore and Atari faced heavy odds: the home market was a treacherous one and even IBM pulled back, suspending production of the PCjr.

Jobs Versus Apple. Steven Jobs, chairman and cofounder of Apple Computer and a leading industry pioneer, was ousted in May from day-to-day management of the company after a battle with president John Scully, whom Jobs had recruited for the post. Apple had been buffeted by disappointing sales. Jobs stayed on as chairman for a time, but in September he announced he would form a new company and hired away some Apple employees. He then resigned the chairmanship under pressure, and Apple filed suit against Job and a former Apple employee, charging misappropriation of company secrets and breach of contract and fiduciary responsibility.

Software. In the fast-moving area of software for personal computers, the year brought a range of new software designed for the Macin-tosh, primarily for the enhanced version with

124

512 kilobytes of random-access memory. Lotus Development Corporation of Cambridge, Mass., introduced Jazz, an integrated software program that combined a word processor, a spreadsheet, communications capability, and other features, while rival Microsoft Corporation of Bellevue, Wash., brought out Excel, a full-featured electronic spreadsheet. In the market for database software, Ansa Corporation of Belmont, Calif., introduced Paradox, a database program that can address several different files simultaneously, and Symantec Corporation unveiled a combined word-processing and database program, called Q&A, with a "natural language front-end." Q&A lets users retrieve information from the database by asking questions in conversational English.

Supercomputers. One of the most significant developments in education was the beginning of a major supercomputer program. With corporate and government money, the National Science Foundation established supercomputer research centers at Cornell University, the University of Illinois, the University of California at San Diego, and Princeton University. The NSF also donated an older Cray 1 supercomputer to a Pittsburgh consortium formed by Carnegie-Mellon University, the University of Pittsburgh, and Westinghouse Corporation. The supercomputer centers were created to permit researchers in physics, meteorology, mathematics, chemistry, biology, and other disciplines to use machines a thousand times more powerful than the minicomputers that are generally available for research. Eventually, as the $400 million NSF program expands, researchers across the United States will be able to access the supercomputer centers through high-speed data links. W.D.M.

CONGO. *See* STATISTICS OF THE WORLD.

CONGRESS OF THE UNITED STATES. The first session of the 99th Congress opened without the bold legislative agenda offered by President Ronald Reagan during his first year in office, four years earlier. His chief legislative priority was an overhaul of the federal income tax system, but many members of Congress lacked Reagan's enthusiasm for the task. Instead, members had other key concerns—including, in many cases, the swollen budget deficit. With new leaders in the Republican-

controlled Senate who were more confrontational with the White House, the Senate tangled with Reagan more often than it had during his first term. The Democratic-dominated House continued to oppose Reagan's requests for higher defense spending and cuts in domestic programs, but supported the president on aid to antigovernment rebels in Nicaragua and on funding for additional MX missiles. On the issue of sanctions against South Africa, an assertive Congress induced Reagan to modify long-standing policy positions. In December, Reagan vetoed legislation that sought to protect certain U.S. industries from foreign competition (*see* MANUFACTURING INDUSTRIES). Congress and the White House also were at odds over aid to America's beleaguered farmers, but important legislation was passed in this area (*see* AGRICULTURE *and* UNITED STATES).

Budget. On February 4, President Reagan proposed his budget for the 1986 fiscal year (beginning October 1, 1985), calling for another year of substantially higher defense spending and elimination of two dozen domestic programs, with deep cuts to be made in others, and no new taxes. The budget projected $973.7 billion in expenditures and $793.7 billion in revenues, leaving a $180 billion deficit. Republican Senate leaders, arguing that the president's budget did little to relieve the massive federal deficit, wrote their own version. It included a politically risky one-year freeze on social security benefits (no adjustment for inflation), termination of 13 domestic programs, and a defense spending increase only equal to the inflation rate. With Reagan's reluctant support, the Senate approved this resolution May 10; two weeks later the House passed its version, which froze defense spending but allowed a social security cost-of-living increase. While both measures cut the fiscal 1986 deficit by $56 billion, the House's three-year savings projection was far below the Senate's three-year cut.

Conference committee negotiations dragged on for weeks, until Reagan and House Speaker Thomas P. ("Tip") O'Neill, Jr. (D, Mass.), agreed to a compromise; it allowed the 1986 social security cost-of-living hike and gave the Pentagon a spending increase equal to the inflation rate. Senate Republicans felt betrayed by Reagan because he had moved over to side with them on the social security freeze in May and now was leaving them to suffer the political damage alone for this controversial stand. Nevertheless, most Republican senators went along with the Reagan-O'Neill plan, and both houses passes a budget resolution on August 1. It called for $967.6 billion in spending and $795.7 billion in revenues, leaving a deficit of $171.9 billion.

While the final agreement sharply scaled back domestic spending, the only major program abolished was general revenue sharing. Although the budget gave more to domestic programs and less to defense than Reagan wanted, it held to his original plan by avoiding new taxes and any cuts in social security cost-of-living increases.

Because of the budget delay, Congress was late in passing the appropriations bills needed to fund government agencies in fiscal 1986. By the end of the fiscal year on September 30, none of the 13 regular spending measures had made it to the president's desk, and emergency bills were passed to temporarily continue funding for most operations at fiscal 1985 levels. Ultimately, only 6 of 13 appropriations bills were passed, and Congress then approved a catchall spending bill for the remaining federal departments.

Concerns about the deficit surfaced in October, when the Senate faced a vote to raise the national debt ceiling above the $2 trillion mark. The bill was needed so that the government's borrowing authority would not expire, but three senators attached an amendment that would require a balanced federal budget by 1991. Under the plan, a reduction in the deficit would be mandated every year until the deficit was eliminated. If the president and Congress could not agree on a budget that met each year's target, the president would have the power to reduce spending almost across the board by equal percentages, with some areas, including social security and interest payments on the national debt, to be left untouched. The administration, which gave cautious approval to the plan, was concerned that by 1987 President Reagan might have to agree to cuts in military spending or to a tax increase, both of which he opposed. The Senate approved the increase in the debt ceiling with the amendment attached. Meanwhile, the Treasury Department resorted to extraordinary measures to keep federal borrowing below the debt ceiling. The House, splitting virtually along party lines, passed its own plan, as part of a bill to raise the debt ceiling.

With the government facing default on November 15, Congress passed at the last minute a measure raising the federal debt ceiling to $1.904 trillion. In December, Senate and House conferees agreed on a budget-balancing bill, which both chambers then approved by large majorities. The measure, which Reagan signed without fanfare, did not exempt defense spending from automatic cuts, as Reagan wanted, but provided for defense and nondefense items to be cut equally. Known as Gramm-Rudman after two Senate sponsors, Phil Gramm (R, Texas) and Warren Rudman (R, N.H.), the law was promptly challenged as unconstitutional in a suit filed by some members of Congress.

Tax Reform. Reagan on May 28 proposed a major overhaul of the federal income tax system. His plan lowered tax rates for individuals and corporations and increased the personal exemption, while eliminating numerous deductions. The proposal was intended to raise the same amount of total net revenue as the existing tax code, although some studies showed tax revenues would be reduced by the changes. It was estimated that, overall, individuals would pay less tax, while corporations would pay more. Despite controversy over important details, most members of Congress backed the idea of tax reform; in fact, several congressional reform plans had been developed before Reagan's. Representative Dan Rostenkowski (D, Ill.), chairman of the House Ways and Means Committee, supported tax reform, and in the fall his committee approved a tax bill that differed in significant ways from the president's plan. Reagan was unhappy with the House bill, and most House Republicans opposed it outright. It appeared that the House would reject the bill and thus in effect kill the tax-reform process, but Reagan brought strong pressure on GOP members, enough of whom finally shifted position to permit the bill to pass. The president hoped to get a bill more to his liking from the Senate in 1986.

A Republican walkout was the climax of a heated debate in the U.S. House of Representatives over Indiana's disputed 8th Congressional District seat. After months of argument and an official vote recount, the largely Democratic House resolved the issue by voting in Democrat Francis X. McCloskey. In protest, the Republicans marched out of the House chamber, held an outdoor news conference, and returned to a standing ovation from the Democrats.

Defense Spending. In the budget he submitted, Reagan sought $322 billion for the military, a boost of 5.9 percent after inflation. But the Senate's budget allowed just enough of an increase to cover inflation, while the House was even more stringent. The August budget resolution took the Senate's figure of $302 billion. But the House still sought to hold defense spending to the $292 billion level, approving a $276 billion military appropriations bill on October 30. (The remainder of the $292 billion would come from other bills.) In December the Senate and House compromised on a small increase in defense spending, below the rate of inflation.

Reagan won an important battle in March, when Congress approved $1.5 billion to buy 21 MX missiles in fiscal 1985 in addition to 21 authorized previously. The president convinced lawmakers that he needed the MX to demonstrate resolve in U.S.-Soviet arms control talks. But some Democrats who had helped save the MX announced they would try to cap MX deployment at 40 missiles. As part of the fiscal 1986 defense authorization bill, the House and Senate compromised on a 50-missile lid on deployment in existing silos. The agreement also authorized the purchase of additional MX missiles for testing and spare parts, and Congress approved funding for 12 missiles in fiscal 1986, beyond the 42 authorized previously.

Nicaraguan Contras. In June, Congress agreed on $27 million for nonmilitary aid to antigovernment rebels in Nicaragua—the first time since 1983 that the House had helped the guerrillas, and the first time Congress had approved open aid to them. The administration victory came only two months after the House had refused to resume U.S. aid. Many House members who had voted in April against aid to the contras changed their minds when Nicaragua's president traveled to the Soviet Union to seek assistance; also helping to alter the climate was a White House emphasis on "humanitarian" assistance. Reagan's achievement was tempered by the legislation's ban on CIA or Defense Department administration of the aid.

South Africa Sanctions. The House and Senate voted separately to impose sanctions against South Africa. A compromise measure approved by a conference committee and then by the U.S. House banned bank loans and computer sales to South African agencies that enforce apartheid, prohibited importation of South Africa's gold coins, and imposed a possible ban on new investment by U.S. firms in South Africa.The legislation went against the administration's policy of quiet diplomacy to promote change in South Africa; to avert Senate approval, Reagan issued an executive order implementing some of the proposed sanctions, and the Senate Republican leadership blocked consideration of the report.

Election Dispute. The November 1984 election in Indiana's 8th Congressional District was not settled until May 1, when—based on a House-sponsored recount—the House voted to seat Democratic incumbent Frank McCloskey over Republican challenger Richard D. McIntyre. Angry Republicans left the House chamber in protest the day McCloskey was sworn in. They argued that McIntyre should have been installed because the Indiana secretary of state had certified him the winner by 34 votes. Democrats claimed there were irregularities in the Indiana ballot count and insisted on a recount supervised by the House Administration Committee. The Democratic-controlled committee declared McCloskey the winner by four votes.

House Committee Leaders. House Democrats on January 4 ousted ailing Representative Melvin Price (D, Ill.) from the chairmanship of the Armed Services Committee and gave the job to Les Aspin (D, Wis.), the panel's seventh-ranking Democrat. The selection of Aspin, 46, to succeed the 80-year-old Price marked the first time House members had bypassed so many senior members in replacing a committee chairman. House Democrats chose Representative William H. Gray III (D, Pa.) as Budget Committee chairman; he succeeded James R. Jones (D, Okla.). D.G.

The protracted budget dispute ended on August 1, when Congress passed a resolution hammered out by a House-Senate conference committee (shown here at the end of the talks) calling for cutbacks in domestic spending, no new taxes, no cuts in social security cost-of-living increases, and no increase in defense spending beyond the inflation rate.

MEMBERSHIP OF THE 99TH CONGRESS IN 1985

Senators	Term Expires

ALABAMA
Howell T. Heflin (D) 1991
Jeremiah A. Denton, Jr. (R) 1987
ALASKA
Ted Stevens (R) 1991
Frank H. Murkowski (R) 1987
ARIZONA
Barry M. Goldwater (R) 1987
Dennis DeConcini (D) 1989
ARKANSAS
Dale Bumpers (D) 1987
David H. Pryor (D) 1991
CALIFORNIA
Alan Cranston (D) 1987
Pete Wilson (R) 1989
COLORADO
Gary Hart (D) 1987
William L. Armstrong (R) 1991
CONNECTICUT
Lowell P. Weicker, Jr. (R) 1989
Christopher J. Dodd (D) 1987
DELAWARE
William V. Roth, Jr. (R) 1989
Joseph R. Biden, Jr. (D) 1991
FLORIDA
Lawton M. Chiles, Jr. (D) 1989
Paula Hawkins (R) 1987
GEORGIA
Sam Nunn (D) 1991
Mack Mattingly (R) 1987
HAWAII
Daniel K. Inouye (D) 1987
Spark M. Matsunaga (D) 1989
IDAHO
James A. McClure (R) 1991
Steven D. Symms (R) 1987
ILLINOIS
Alan J. Dixon (D) 1987
Paul Simon (D) 1991
INDIANA
Richard G. Lugar (R) 1989
Dan Quayle (R) 1987
IOWA
Charles E. Grassley (R) 1987
Tom Harkin (D) 1991
KANSAS
Robert Dole (R) 1987
Nancy Landon Kassebaum (R) 1991
KENTUCKY
Wendell H. Ford (D) 1987
Mitch McConnell (R) 1991
LOUISIANA
Russell B. Long (D) 1987
J. Bennett Johnston (D) 1991
MAINE
William S. Cohen (R) 1991
George J. Mitchell (D) 1989
MARYLAND
Charles McC. Mathias, Jr. (R) . . 1987
Paul S. Sarbanes (D) 1989
MASSACHUSETTS
Edward M. Kennedy (D) 1989
John F. Kerry (D) 1991
MICHIGAN
Donald W. Riegle, Jr. (D) 1989
Carl Levin (D) 1991
MINNESOTA
David F. Durenberger (R) 1989
Rudy Boschwitz (R) 1991

MISSISSIPPI
John C. Stennis (D) 1989
Thad Cochran (R) 1991
MISSOURI
Thomas F. Eagleton (D) 1987
John C. Danforth (R) 1989
MONTANA
John Melcher (D) 1989
Max Baucus (D) 1991
NEBRASKA
Edward Zorinsky (D) 1989
John James Exon, Jr. (D) 1991
NEVADA
Paul Laxalt (R) 1987
Chic Hecht (R) 1989
NEW HAMPSHIRE
Gordon J. Humphrey (R) 1991
Warren B. Rudman (R) 1987
NEW JERSEY
Bill Bradley (D) 1991
Frank R. Lautenberg (D) 1989
NEW MEXICO
Peter V. Domenici (R) 1991
Jeff Bingaman (D) 1989
NEW YORK
Daniel P. Moynihan (D) 1989
Alfonse M. D'Amato (R) 1987
NORTH CAROLINA
Jesse Helms (R) 1991
John P. East (R) 1987
NORTH DAKOTA
Quentin N. Burdick (D) 1989
Mark Andrews (R) 1987
OHIO
John H. Glenn, Jr. (D) 1987
Howard M. Metzenbaum (D) . . . 1989
OKLAHOMA
David L. Boren (D) 1991
Donald L. Nickles (R) 1987
OREGON
Mark O. Hatfield (R) 1991
Robert W. Packwood (R) 1987
PENNSYLVANIA
H. John Heinz 3rd (R) 1989
Arlen Specter (R) 1987
RHODE ISLAND
Claiborne Pell (D) 1991
John H. Chafee (R) 1989
SOUTH CAROLINA
Strom Thurmond (R) 1991
Ernest F. Hollings (D) 1987
SOUTH DAKOTA
Larry Pressler (R) 1991
James Abdnor (R) 1987
TENNESSEE
James R. Sasser (D) 1989
Albert Gore, Jr. (D) 1991
TEXAS
Lloyd Bentsen (D) 1989
Phil Gramm (R) 1991
UTAH
Edwin J. "Jake" Garn (R) 1987
Orrin G. Hatch (R) 1989
VERMONT
Robert T. Stafford (R) 1989
Patrick J. Leahy (D) 1987
VIRGINIA
John W. Warner (R) 1991
Paul S. Trible, Jr. (R) 1989

WASHINGTON
Slade Gorton (R) 1987
Daniel J. Evans (R) 1989
WEST VIRGINIA
Robert C. Byrd (D) 1989
John D. Rockefeller IV (D) 1991
WISCONSIN
William Proxmire (D) 1989
Robert W. Kasten, Jr. (R) 1987
WYOMING
Malcolm Wallop (R) 1989
Alan K. Simpson (R) 1991

Representatives
ALABAMA
1. Sonny Callahan (R)
2. William L. Dickinson (R)
3. William Nichols (D)
4. Tom Bevill (D)
5. Ronnie G. Flippo (D)
6. Ben Erdreich (D)
7. Richard C. Shelby (D)
ALASKA
At large: Donald E. Young (R)
ARIZONA
1. John McCain (R)
2. Morris K. Udall (D)
3. Bob Stump (R)
4. Eldon D. Rudd (R)
5. Jim Kolbe (R)
ARKANSAS
1. Wiliam V. "Bill" Alexander, Jr. (D)
2. Tommy F. Robinson (D)
3. John P. Hammerschmidt (R)
4. Beryl F. Anthony, Jr. (D)
CALIFORNIA
1. Douglas H. Bosco (D)
2. Eugene A. Chappie (R)
3. Robert T. Matsui (D)
4. Vic Fazio (D)
5. Sala Burton (D)
6. Barbara Boxer (D)
7. George Miller (D)
8. Ronald V. Dellums (D)
9. Fortney (Pete) Stark (D)
10. Don Edwards (D)
11. Tom Lantos (D)
12. Ed Zschau (R)
13. Norman Y. Mineta (D)
14. Norman D. Shumway (R)
15. Tony Coelho (D)
16. Leon E. Panetta (D)
17. Charles Pashayan, Jr. (R)
18. Richard H. Lehman (D)
19. Robert J. Lagomarsino (R)
20. William M. Thomas (R)
21. Bobbi Fiedler (R)
22. Carlos J. Moorhead (R)
23. Anthony C. Beilenson (D)
24. Henry A. Waxman (D)
25. Edward R. Roybal (D)
26. Howard L. Berman (D)
27. Mel Levine (D)
28. Julian C. Dixon (D)
29. Augustus F. Hawkins (D)
30. Matthew G. Martinez (D)
31. Mervyn M. Dymally (D)
32. Glenn M. Anderson (D)
33. David Dreier (R)

34. Esteban Edward Torres (D)
35. Jerry Lewis (R)
36. George E. Brown, Jr. (D)
37. Alfred A. McCandless (R)
38. Robert K. Dornan (R)
39. William E. Dannemeyer (R)
40. Robert E. Badham (R)
41. Bill Lowery (R)
42. Dan Lundgren (R)
43. Ron Packard (R)
44. Jim Bates (D)
45. Duncan Hunter (R)

COLORADO
1. Patricia Schroeder (D)
2. Timothy E. Wirth (D)
3. Michael L. Strang (R)
4. Hank Brown (R)
5. Ken Kramer (R)
6. Dan Schaefer (R)

CONNECTICUT
1. Barbara B. Kennelly (D)
2. Samuel Gejdenson (D)
3. Bruce A. Morrison (D)
4. Stewart B. McKinney (R)
5. John G. Rowland (R)
6. Nancy L. Johnson (R)

DELAWARE
At large: Thomas R. Carper (D)

FLORIDA
1. Earl Hutto (D)
2. Don Fuqua (D)
3. Charles E. Bennett (D)
4. Bill Chappell, Jr. (D)
5. Bill McCollum (R)
6. Buddy MacKay (D)
7. Sam Gibbons (D)
8. C. W. Bill Young (R)
9. Michael Bilirakis (R)
10. Andy Ireland (R)
11. Bill Nelson (D)
12. Tom Lewis (R)
13. Connie Mack (R)
14. Dan Mica (D)
15. E. Clay Shaw, Jr. (R)
16. Lawrence J. Smith (D)
17. William Lehman (D)
18. Claude Pepper (D)
19. Dante B. Fascell (D)

GEORGIA
1. Robert Lindsay Thomas (D)
2. Charles Hatcher (D)
3. Richard Ray (D)
4. Patrick L. Swindall (R)
5. Wyche Fowler, Jr. (D)
6. Newt Gingrich (R)
7. George Darden (D)
8. J. Roy Rowland (D)
9. Ed Jenkins (D)
10. Doug Barnard, Jr. (D)

HAWAII
1. Cecil L. Heftel (D)
2. Daniel K. Akaka (D)

IDAHO
1. Larry E. Craig (R)
2. Richard H. Stallings (D)

ILLINOIS
1. Charles A. Hayes (D)
2. Gus Savage (D)
3. Martin A. Russo (D)
4. George M. O'Brien (R)
5. Wiliam O. Lipinski (D)
6. Henry J. Hyde (R)
7. Cardiss Collins (D)
8. Daniel Rostenkowski (D)
9. Sidney R. Yates (D)

10. John Edward Porter (R)
11. Frank Annunzio (D)
12. Philip M. Crane (R)
13. Harris W. Fawell (R)
14. John E. Grotberg (R)
15. Edward R. Madigan (R)
16. Lynn Martin (R)
17. Lane Evans (D)
18. Robert H. Michel (R)
19. Terry L. Bruce (D)
20. Richard J. Durbin (D)
21. Melvin Price (D)
22. Kenneth J. Gray (D)

INDIANA
1. Peter J. Visclosky (D)
2. Philip R. Sharp (D)
3. John P. Hiler (R)
4. Dan Coats (R)
5. Elwood Hillis (R)
6. Dan Burton (R)
7. John T. Myers (R)
8. Frank McCloskey (D)[1]
9. Lee H. Hamilton (D)
10. Andrew Jacobs, Jr. (D)

IOWA
1. James A. S. Leach (R)
2. Thomas J. Tauke (R)
3. Cooper Evans (R)
4. Neal Smith (D)
5. Jim Lightfoot (R)
6. Berkley Bedell (D)

KANSAS
1. Pat Roberts (R)
2. Jim Slattery (D)
3. Jan Meyers (R)
4. Dan Glickman (D)
5. Robert Whittaker (R)

KENTUCKY
1. Carroll Hubbard, Jr. (D)
2. William H. Natcher (D)
3. Romano L. Mazzoli (D)
4. Gene Snyder (R)
5. Harold Rogers (R)
6. Larry J. Hopkins (R)
7. Carl D. Perkins (D)

LOUISIANA
1. Bob Livingston (R)
2. Lindy Boggs (D)
3. W. J. Tauzin (D)
4. Charles Roemer III (D)
5. Jerry Huckaby (D)
6. W. Henson Moore (R)
7. John B. Breaux (D)
8. Cathy Long (D)[2]

MAINE
1. John R. McKernan, Jr. (R)
2. Olympia J. Snowe (R)

MARYLAND
1. Royden Dyson (D)
2. Helen Delich Bentley (R)
3. Barbara A. Mikulski (D)
4. Marjorie S. Holt (R)
5. Steny H. Hoyer (D)
6. Beverly B. Byron (D)
7. Parren J. Mitchell (D)
8. Michael D. Barnes (D)

MASSACHUSETTS
1. Silvio O. Conte (R)
2. Edward P. Boland (D)
3. Joseph D. Early (D)
4. Barney Frank (D)
5. Chester G. Atkins (D)
6. Nicholas Mavroules (D)
7. Edward J. Markey (D)
8. Thomas P. O'Neill, Jr. (D)

9. Joe Moakley (D)
10. Gerry E. Studds (D)
11. Brian J. Donnelly (D)

MICHIGAN
1. John Conyers, Jr. (D)
2. Carl D. Pursell (R)
3. Howard Wolpe (D)
4. Mark D. Siljander (R)
5. Paul B. Henry (R)
6. Bob Carr (D)
7. Dale E. Kildee (D)
8. Bob Traxler (D)
9. Guy Vander Jagt (R)
10. Bill Schuette (R)
11. Robert W. Davis (R)
12. David E. Bonior (D)
13. George W. Crockett, Jr. (D)
14. Dennis M. Hertel (D)
15. William D. Ford (D)
16. John D. Dingell (D)
17. Sander M. Levin (D)
18. William S. Broomfield (R)

MINNESOTA
1. Timothy J. Penny (D)
2. Vin Weber (R)
3. Bill Frenzel (R)
4. Bruce F. Vento (D)
5. Martin Olav Sabo (D)
6. Gerry Sikorski (D)
7. Arlan Stangeland (R)
8. James L. Oberstar (D)

MISSISSIPPI
1. Jamie L. Whitten (D)
2. Webb Franklin (R)
3. G. V. Montgomery (D)
4. Wayne Dowdy (D)
5. Trent Lott (R)

MISSOURI
1. William Clay (D)
2. Robert A. Young (D)
3. Richard A. Gephardt (D)
4. Ike Skelton (D)
5. Alan Wheat (D)
6. E. Thomas Coleman (R)
7. Gene Taylor (R)
8. Bill Emerson (R)
9. Harold L. Volkmer (D)

MONTANA
1. Pat Williams (D)
2. Ron Marlenee (R)

NEBRASKA
1. Douglas K. Bereuter (R)
2. Hal Daub (R)
3. Virginia Smith (R)

NEVADA
1. Harry M. Reid (D)
2. Barbara F. Vucanovich (R)

NEW HAMPSHIRE
1. Robert C. Smith (R)
2. Judd Gregg (R)

NEW JERSEY
1. James J. Florio (D)
2. William J. Hughes (D)
3. James J. Howard (D)
4. Christopher H. Smith (R)
5. Marge Roukema (R)
6. Bernard J. Dwyer (D)
7. Matthew J. Rinaldo (R)
8. Robert A. Roe (D)
9. Robert G. Torricelli (D)
10. Peter W. Rodino, Jr. (D)
11. Dean A. Gallo (R)
12. Jim Courter (R)
13. Jim Saxton (R)
14. Frank J. Guarini (D)

NEW MEXICO
1. Manuel Lujan, Jr. (R)
2. Joe Skeen (R)
3. Bill Richardson (D)

NEW YORK
1. William Carney (R)
2. Thomas J. Downey (D)
3. Robert J. Mrazek (D)
4. Norman F. Lent (R)
5. Raymond J. McGrath (R)
6. Joseph P. Addabbo (D)
7. Gary L. Ackerman (D)
8. James H. Scheuer (D)
9. Thomas J. Manton (D)
10. Charles E. Schumer (D)
11. Edolphus Towns (D)
12. Major R. Owens (D)
13. Stephen J. Solarz (D)
14. Guy V. Molinari (R)
15. Bill Green (R)
16. Charles B. Rangel (D)
17. Ted Weiss (D)
18. Robert Garcia (D)
19. Mario Biaggi (D)
20. Joseph J. DioGuardi (R)
21. Hamilton Fish, Jr. (R)
22. Benjamin A. Gilman (R)
23. Samuel S. Stratton (D)
24. Gerald B. H. Solomon (R)
25. Sherwood L. Boehlert (R)
26. David O'B. Martin (R)
27. George C. Wortley (R)
28. Matthew F. McHugh (D)
29. Frank Horton (R)
30. Fred J. Eckert (R)
31. Jack F. Kemp (R)
32. John J. LaFalce (D)
33. Henry J. Nowak (D)
34. Stan Lundine (D)

NORTH CAROLINA
1. Walter B. Jones (D)
2. Tim Valentine (D)
3. Charles Whitley (D)
4. William W. Cobey, Jr. (R)
5. Stephen L. Neal (D)
6. Howard Coble (R)
7. Charles Rose (D)
8. W. G. Hefner (D)
9. J. Alex McMillan (R)
10. James T. Broyhill (R)
11. Bill Hendon (R)

NORTH DAKOTA
At large: Byron L. Dorgan (D)

OHIO
1. Thomas A. Luken (D)
2. Willis B. Gradison, Jr. (R)
3. Tony P. Hall (D)
4. Michael G. Oxley (R)
5. Delbert L. Latta (R)
6. Bob McEwen (R)
7. Michael DeWine (R)
8. Thomas N. Kindness (R)
9. Marcy Kaptur (D)
10. Clarence E. Miller (R)
11. Dennis E. Eckart (D)
12. John R. Kasich (R)
13. Donald J. Pease (D)
14. John F. Seiberling (D)
15. Chalmers P. Wylie (R)

16. Ralph S. Regula (R)
17. James A. Traficant, Jr. (D)
18. Douglas Applegate (D)
19. Edward F. Feighan (D)
20. Mary Rose Oakar (D)
21. Louis Stokes (D)

OKLAHOMA
1. James R. Jones (D)
2. Michael Lynn Synar (D)
3. Wes Watkins (D)
4. Dave McCurdy (D)
5. Mickey Edwards (R)
6. Glenn English (D)

OREGON
1. Les AuCoin (D)
2. Robert F. Smith (R)
3. Ron Wyden (D)
4. James Weaver (D)
5. Denny Smith (R)

PENNSYLVANIA
1. Thomas M. Foglietta (D)
2. William H. Gray III (D)
3. Robert A. Borski (D)
4. Joe Kolter (D)
5. Richard T. Schulze (R)
6. Gus Yatron (D)
7. Robert W. Edgar (D)
8. Peter H. Kostmayer (D)
9. Bud Shuster (R)
10. Joseph M. McDade (R)
11. Paul E. Kanjorski (D)
12. John P. Murtha (D)
13. Lawrence Coughlin (R)
14. William Coyne (D)
15. Don Ritter (R)
16. Robert S. Walker (R)
17. George W. Gekas (R)
18. Douglas Walgren (D)
19. William F. Goodling (R)
20. Joseph M. Gaydos (D)
21. Thomas J. Ridge (R)
22. Austin J. Murphy (D)
23. William F. Clinger, Jr. (R)

RHODE ISLAND
1. Fernand J. St Germain (D)
2. Claudine Schneider (R)

SOUTH CAROLINA
1. Thomas F. Hartnett (R)
2. Floyd Spence (R)
3. Butler Derrick (D)
4. Carroll A. Campbell (R)
5. John M. Spratt, Jr. (D)
6. Robin Tallon (D)

SOUTH DAKOTA
At large: Thomas A. Daschle (D)

TENNESSEE
1. James H. Quillen (R)
2. John J. Duncan (R)
3. Marilyn Lloyd (D)
4. Jim Cooper (D)
5. William Hill Boner (D)
6. Bart Gordon (D)
7. Don Sundquist (R)
8. Ed Jones (D)
9. Harold E. Ford (D)

TEXAS
1. Jim Chapman (D)[3]
2. Charles Wilson (D)
3. Steve Bartlett (R)

4. Ralph Hall (D)
5. John Bryant (D)
6. Joe Barton (R)
7. Bill Archer (R)
8. Jack Fields (R)
9. Jack Brooks (D)
10. J. J. Pickle (D)
11. Marvin Leath (D)
12. Jim Wright (D)
13. Beau Boulter (R)
14. Mac Sweeney (R)
15. E. de la Garza (D)
16. Ronald D. Coleman (D)
17. Charles W. Stenholm (D)
18. Mickey Leland (D)
19. Larry Combest (R)
20. Henry B. Gonzalez (D)
21. Tom Loeffler (R)
22. Tom DeLay (R)
23. Albert G. Bustamante (D)
24. Martin Frost (D)
25. Michael A. Andrews (D)
26. Richard K. Armey (R)
27. Solomon P. Ortiz (D)

UTAH
1. James V. Hansen (R)
2. David S. Monson (R)
3. Howard C. Nielson (R)

VERMONT
At large: James M. Jeffords (R)

VIRGINIA
1. Herbert H. Bateman (R)
2. G. William Whitehurst (R)
3. Thomas J. Bliley, Jr. (R)
4. Norman Sisisky (D)
5. Dan Daniel (D)
6. James R. Olin (D)
7. D. French Slaughter, Jr. (R)
8. Stanford Parris (R)
9. Frederick C. Boucher (D)
10. Frank R. Wolf (R)

WASHINGTON
1. John R. Miller (R)
2. Al Swift (D)
3. Don Bonker (D)
4. Sid Morrison (R)
5. Thomas S. Foley (D)
6. Norman D. Dicks (D)
7. Mike Lowry (D)
8. Rod Chandler (R)

WEST VIRGINIA
1. Alan B. Mollohan (D)
2. Harley O. Staggers, Jr. (D)
3. Robert E. Wise, Jr. (D)
4. Nick Joe Rahall II (D)

WISCONSIN
1. Les Aspin (D)
2. Robert W. Kastenmeier (D)
3. Steve Gunderson (R)
4. Gerald D. Kleczka (D)
5. Jim Moody (D)
6. Thomas E. Petri (R)
7. David R. Obey (D)
8. Toby Roth (R)
9. F. James Sensenbrenner, Jr. (R)

WYOMING
At large: Richard Bruce Cheney (R)

---

[1] Seated by vote of the House May 1, 1985, in settlement of disputed November 1984 election result.
[2] Elected March 30, 1985, to fill vacancy due to the death of Gillis W. Long.
[3] Elected August 3, 1985, to fill vacancy due to the resignation of Sam B. Hall, Jr.

CONNECTICUT. *See* STATISTICS OF THE WORLD.

CONSTRUCTION. *See* HOUSING AND CONSTRUCTION.

COSTA RICA. President Luis Alberto Monge Alvarez—buoyed by his country's second straight year of positive growth—declared victory in 1985 over Costa Rica's worst economic crisis in modern times. The U.S. Agency for International Development continued to underwrite the recovery effort; in fiscal year 1985, AID money amounted to $202 million. A major problem was the decision by United Brands, in the wake of strike troubles and increased regional competition, to pull out of its banana operations in southern Costa Rica; Standard Fruit threatened to close its operations as well. With bananas accounting for 20 to 25 percent of Costa Rica's exports, such cutbacks would be severely damaging.

A key topic in the campaign for the scheduled February 1986 presidential election concerned how Costa Rica should deal with Nicaragua and the United States. The major party candidates—Oscar Arias of the ruling National Liberation Party (chosen in the first real party primary ever held in Costa Rica), and Rafael Angel Calderón of the opposition Social Christian Unity coalition—both proclaimed their faith in "Western democracy" and denounced Sandinista "totalitarianism" in Nicaragua. The mass media, meanwhile, waged a persistent campaign against the Nicaraguan regime.

As relations with Nicaragua worsened, border clashes between the Nicaraguan Army, contra forces opposing the Sandinista regime, and Costa Rican guardsmen generated strong reactions, especially after a late May incident in which two guardsmen were killed. Major national figures, including the candidates, wanted to invoke the Río Treaty (a mutual security arrangement) and enlist armed support from the United States. President Monge had already allowed 20 U.S. Army Special Forces advisers to begin training 750 civil guardsmen, shortly after two U.S. warships paid a controversial visit to the Atlantic port of Limón. The government also allowed the installation of a Voice of America transmitter, circumventing laws requiring ownership of all mass media by Costa Ricans.

See STATISTICS OF THE WORLD.   L.W.G.

CRIME AND LAW ENFORCEMENT. Espionage, white-collar crime, and Bernhard Goetz—the "subway vigilante"—dominated the U.S. crime scene in 1985.

Espionage. In what was termed one of the most serious breaches of national security in U.S. naval history, four persons were arrested as part of a spy ring that allegedly passed secret naval documents to the Soviet Union. One of the four, Arthur James Walker, a retired naval officer, was convicted in August on seven espionage charges; he was sentenced in November to life imprisonment. In October, Arthur's brother John, a retired Navy enlisted man, and John's son Michael, a Navy yeoman third class, pleaded guilty to all charges against them in return for a reduced, 25-year prison term for Michael. John Walker, who accepted a life sentence as part of the plea agreement, agreed to testify against his friend Jerry A. Whitworth, the alleged fourth member of the ring, who had pleaded not guilty to espionage charges in July and to a new indictment in December. John Walker said he had been channeling classified documents to Soviet agents for 17 years. Federal officials said money, not ideology, had motivated the accused.

In late November four other suspects were arrested on charges related to espionage—for three different countries. Ronald Pelton, a 14-year veteran of the U.S. National Security Agency, allegedly sold secrets to the Soviet Union for an estimated $25,000. Larry Wu-Tai Chin allegedly confessed that he had been passing information to China during his entire 33-year career as an analyst and translator for the CIA. Jonathan Jay Pollard, a Navy counterintelligence analyst, was charged with giving Israel scores of military documents; his wife, Anne Henderson-Pollard, was accused of assisting him.

Another major spy case was concluded when Svetlana and Nikolay Ogorodnikov pleaded guilty to having conspired with an FBI agent to pass secret documents to the Soviet Union. Svetlana Ogorodnikov received an 18-year prison sentence and her husband an 8-year term, under a plea bargain agreement. The trial of the FBI agent, Richard W. Miller, ended in a mistrial in November; a new trial was scheduled.

132

The Walker family spy ring has been called a new breed of spies, motivated less by ideology than by greed. At left is Arthur Walker, a retired naval officer; at right his brother John Walker, Jr., whose son Michael was also involved.

Samuel Loring Morison, a former analyst with the Naval Intelligence Support Center in Suitland, Md., was found guilty in October of giving classified photos to the British military journal Jane's Defence Weekly and of keeping other secret information at his home. He received a two-year prison term. Edward L. Howard, a former CIA agent who was working for the New Mexico legislature, apparently fled the country after learning he was under FBI surveillance; government officials said he had been identified as a spy for the Soviet Union.

White-Collar Crime. The year's most controversial case in white-collar crime involved E. F. Hutton, the fifth-largest U.S. brokerage firm, which pleaded guilty in May to an elaborate fraud scheme by which it had used as much as $250 million a day in bank funds without paying interest. Hutton was said to have bilked 400 banks out of at least $8 million between 1980 and 1982. Under a settlement with the government, the firm agreed to pay a fine and court costs totaling $2.75 million and to repay banks the money they had lost. The Justice Department brought no charges against any Hutton employees; in September the Senate Judiciary Committee announced plans to hold

hearings on the Justice Department's handling of a variety of cases, possibly including that of E. F. Hutton. The controversy also moved Hutton chairman Robert M. Foman to ask former Attorney General Griffin B. Bell to investigate the scandal. Bell's report led to the resignation of two high-level officials deemed responsible for failing to monitor the company's cash management system, but the report exonerated Foman.

Another case involved Paul Thayer, who, while chairman of LTV Corporation and member of the boards of Anheuser-Busch Inc. and Allied Corporation, had given friends information about acquisitions those companies planned to make. He later lied to the Securities and Exchange Commission about his actions. In May, Thayer received a four-year prison term and a $5,000 fine after pleading guilty to obstructing justice.

Also in May, General Electric pleaded guilty to having defrauded the U.S. Air Force of $800,000 in 1980 on a Minuteman missile project. GE was fined $1.04 million and agreed to repay the Air Force. Rockwell International Corporation pleaded guilty to similar charges in October and agreed to pay $1.5 million.

CRIME AND LAW ENFORCEMENT

In June three executives with Film Recovery Systems, a now-defunct silver reclamation plant in Chicago, were found guilty of murder in the death of employee Stefan Golab, a 59-year-old illegal immigrant from Poland. In 1983, while working at the plant, Golab became sick from inhaling cyanide and later died. The executives, who were charged with maintaining unsafe working conditions and failing to warn employees about hazardous chemicals, were sentenced to 25-year prison terms but were freed pending an appeal.

In August, Eli Lilly and Company, a pharmaceutical firm, pleaded guilty to charges that it had failed to inform the government about four known deaths and six illnesses related to its arthritis drug, Oraflex, while seeking approval to sell the drug. Oraflex has now been linked to over 100 deaths; it was withdrawn from the market in August 1982. Under a plea bargain, the company's chief medical officer pleaded no contest to a misdemeanor charge and was fined $15,000. The company was fined $25,000.

Automaker John Z. DeLorean was charged by a grand jury with defrauding investors in his failed car company of $12.5 million. He pleaded not guilty in September; the trial was scheduled for 1986.

Goetz Case. On December 22, 1984, Bernhard Goetz shot four youths who allegedly had been harassing him on a New York City subway car. After fleeing to New Hampshire, he surrendered to police in Concord on December 31, giving them a detailed confession. In January a grand jury indicted him only on charges of illegal possession of guns—an action that many decried as too lenient. But a second grand jury, convened after the Manhattan district attorney said there was new evidence, returned indictments against Goetz in March for attempted murder, assault, reckless endangerment, and criminal possession of a weapon. Goetz's attorneys moved to have the charges dismissed; a ruling on the motion was scheduled for January 1986. The case ignited bitter public debate as to whether the shootings were justified and brought to the forefront the public's simmering fear of crime in the city's streets and subways.

Mass Murders. A routine shoplifting arrest in South San Francisco on June 2 led law enforce-

Criminal—or Hero?
Bernhard Hugo Goetz was catapulted to national attention as a symbol of the public's exasperation with crime. On December 22, 1984, the self-employed electronics engineer pulled a .38-caliber revolver and shot four black youths who had allegedly accosted him on a Manhattan subway car and asked him for money. He fled, leaving one of the four paralyzed from the waist down. A few days later, Goetz, 37, surrendered to authorities in Concord, N.H., and confessed to his actions; by then, he had become a virtual folk hero, and a grand jury indicted him only for illegal handgun possession. When additional apparent evidence came to light—including Goetz's reported admission that he had fired a second shot into one of the youths—support for the "subway vigilante" declined. A second grand jury was convened, and Goetz was charged with more serious offenses, including attempted murder. He pleaded not guilty; a ruling on a motion to dismiss these charges was pending at the end of 1985.

Bernhard Goetz

ment officials to a grisly sex-and-torture chamber and mass burial ground on the outskirts of Wilseyville, southeast of Sacramento, Calif. The man who was arrested, Leonard Lake, committed suicide while in custody, by swallowing a cyanide pill. But evidence found in a stolen car Lake was driving led investigators to a tree-shrouded cabin, where they uncovered the charred and hacked remains of 11 bodies. Lake was subsequently linked to the disappearances of as many as 25 people. An alleged accomplice of Lake, 24-year-old Charles Chitat Ng, was captured in early July in Calgary, Alberta. In December he was convicted there on robbery and assault charges and given a 4½-year prison sentence; U.S. officials were seeking his extradition.

On August 31 in East Los Angeles, a man allegedly trying to steal a car was chased and caught by a crowd. Richard Ramirez, a 25-year-old drifter, was then held by police on suspicion of being the "Night Stalker" who for months had been sneaking into California homes at night and brutally assaulting and murdering his victims. At his arraignment on September 27, Ramirez was charged with 68 crimes, among them 14 killings and 22 sexual assaults.

Reversals. On June 10 a Rhode Island jury acquitted Claus von Bülow of twice trying to kill his wealthy wife, Martha, with injections of insulin. The Danish-born socialite was convicted of the same charges in 1982, but the Rhode Island Supreme Court subsequently overturned the verdict on a technicality. Both trials attracted wide media attention. Martha von Bülow remained in an apparently irreversible coma.

A month before von Bülow's acquittal, Illinois Governor James R. Thompson commuted the sentence of a man convicted in 1979 of raping a 16-year-old girl. Gary E. Dotson's term of 25 to 50 years was reduced to the 6 years he had already served, after his former accuser, Cathleen Crowell Webb, recanted her testimony in March. In commuting the sentence, Thompson cited Dotson's good prison record and length of time served, but he said he did not believe the recantation.

Extremists. James D. Ellison, founder and spiritual leader of the Covenant, the Sword and the Arm of the Lord, a white supremacist group,

Cathleen Crowell Webb poses on television with her accused rapist Gary Dotson after she claimed that she had lied at Dotson's trial in 1979. Dotson, sentenced to 25–50 years, had his term commuted to the 6 years already served in an Illinois prison. The disturbing case left many speculating as to whether Webb had lied at the 1979 trial or in 1985—and why.

was sentenced in September to 20 years in prison on charges relating to fires at a Jewish center and a homosexual church and the bombing of a natural gas pipeline. In April more than 20 members of the Order, a neo-Nazi group, were indicted for participation in a crime wave that included robbery, arson, and murder. Ten members were convicted on racketeering charges in December.

Four people were convicted in April of involvement in the Christmas 1984 bombings of three Pensacola, Fla., medical facilities where abortions were performed. Matthew Goldsby and James Simmons were sentenced to 60 years in prison and ordered to pay $353,074 each. Goldsby's fiancée and Simmons's wife were given five years' probation and fined $2,000 apiece.

Philadelphia Bombing. A violent confrontation in May between Philadelphia police and a radical back-to-nature group called MOVE devastated one of the city's neighborhoods. The intention was to evict the unruly group from its West Philadelphia home, where it was reportedly stockpiling weapons; however, po-

CRIME AND LAW ENFORCEMENT

lice were repulsed by gunfire when they sought to serve an eviction notice. Finally, police dropped a bomb on the residence, hoping to destroy a rooftop bunker and to blast a hole in the roof through which tear gas could be pumped. But a fire broke out that spread quickly, killing 11 MOVE members and destroying more than 60 homes.

Controversy erupted in the wake of the incident, when a report indicated that the bomb had contained C-4, a highly powerful military explosive that police had earlier denied was part of the device. District Attorney Edward G. Rendell announced a preliminary investigation into possible criminal violations by police; and, during the fall, a commission appointed by Mayor W. Wilson Goode to look into the disaster held 18 days of public hearings. At the hearings, the mayor, the city's former managing director, and the police and fire commissioners repeatedly contradicted one another's testimony about what they had known and told each other before and during the assault. On November 13, Police Commissioner Gregore J. Sambor announced his resignation.

Organized Crime. A series of trials involving alleged organized crime figures in New York City began in the fall in Manhattan federal court. More than 20 reputed members of the Bonanno crime group were put on trial on narcotics trafficking charges, in a case known as the "pizza connection" because pizza parlors were said to have been used as fronts for the drug deals. Carmine Persico, described by federal officials as boss of the Columbo crime family, went on trial with several others on racketeering charges. Also, Paul Castellano, reputed head of the powerful Gambino crime family, went on trial with nine others on a variety of charges including auto theft, drug trafficking, and murder. However, Castellano, along with a key associate, was shot to death in December after stepping out of his limousine on a busy Manhattan street. The killings were said to have been part of a power struggle within the Gambino family and may have been sanctioned by heads of the other four reputed New York crime families. The five alleged family leaders and four others were indicted in February and accused of participating in a crime "commission" that governed organized crime in the city. This trial, the most significant of the group, was scheduled to open during early 1986.

Executions and Prisons. Executions around the United States continued at about the same pace as in 1984. By the end of the year, 18 men had been executed, while over 1,500 other inmates waited on death rows. In 1984 there were 21 executions.

Local governments were turning increasingly toward placing correctional facilities under private control; about two dozen facilities had been handed over to private entrepreneurs by midyear. The Corrections Corporation of America made an offer in September to lease and operate the entire Tennessee state prison system; the state legislature was to consider the offer.   L.S.G.

CUBA. During 1985 the Cuban government made personnel changes, struggled with debt problems, and continued to have poor relations with the United States.

Political Changes. After a decade of stable leadership under President Fidel Castro, 1985 was a year of shifts possibly heralding a more far-reaching political reorganization. In February old-guard Communists heading the media and political education were purged from party posts and replaced by prominent Castro loyalists; subsequent shifts of junior government ministers and officials brought younger, better-educated cadres to other positions. Castro said the changes would free veteran leaders to concentrate on larger policy concerns. The president's brother, Armed Forces Minister General Raúl Castro, was given a refurbished civilian image and responsibility for overseeing daily operations; there was speculation that he was being groomed to become prime minister.

Economic Developments. Cuba's estimated $7.5 billion Soviet debt was rescheduled, with repayments now due to begin in 1991 instead of 1986. In September, Cuba renegotiated $90 million in Western debt payments and gained an extension of $375 million of short-term credit lines. Nevertheless, with commodity prices low, payments on the total $3.5 billion hard-currency debt posed a heavy burden. Cuba sought to increase exports to, and tourism from, the West. One exception to a general climate of lower expectations was a new law making most Cubans homeowners, by converting their rents to the state into mortgage payments.

Foreign Affairs. The year began with expectations of better U.S.-Cuban relations. In the wake of a December 1984 accord, providing for new emigration to the United States and repatriation of "undesirables" among those who had come to the United States in the 1980 Mariel boatlift, Castro hosted U.S. congressmen and clergy, gave interviews to American journalists and scholars, and stressed his desire for improved relations. In May, Cuba withdrew 100 military advisers from Nicaragua; the action followed a three-day visit by Castro to Nicaragua in January.

However, the Reagan administration's decision to go ahead with Radio Martí—programming about Cuba by anti-Castro exiles, beamed to the island on the Voice of America—spurred a sharp deterioration in relations. In response, Havana suspended both the immigration agreement and visits by Cuban exiles, said it was reconsidering its cooperation on prosecuting airline hijackers, and jammed the broadcasting, which it termed a "barefaced provocation." The war of words escalated during the months that followed, with Reagan calling Cuba "a terrorist state" and Castro calling Reagan "a madman, an imbecile, and a bum." In October, in a move seen as retaliation for Cuba's suspension of the December agreement, Reagan ordered restrictions on the entry of Cuban officials into the United States.

Meanwhile, Castro addressed his attention to Latin America's $360 billion foreign debt,

With the words "Buenas días, Cuba," Radio Martí, the U.S. government station, began its first broadcast to Cuba on May 20 as part of the Voice of America. President Fidel Castro's immediate response was to suspend a December 1984 agreement that would have allowed 20,000 Cubans to emigrate to the United States each year and let up to 3,000 political prisoners enter the United States in 1985.

which he declared was unpayable and ought to be canceled. His campaign culminated in a midsummer Havana debt conference attended by delegates from 21 countries, although by few official representatives. The conference endorsed Castro's ideas, but Latin American governments remained aloof.

See STATISTICS OF THE WORLD.   P.W.

CYPRUS. Greek Cypriot President Spyros Kyprianou and Turkish Cypriot leader Rauf Denktash met at the United Nations in January 1985 but failed to agree on a plan to reunify Cyprus's two ethnic communities. UN Secretary-General Javier Pérez de Cuéllar had arranged the meeting and prepared a reunification document based on talks he had had with the two leaders late in 1984. It reportedly called for a two-state federation, with the Turkish zone constituting 29 percent of the island. There would be a Greek Cypriot president, a Turkish Cypriot vice-president, and ten ministers of whom seven would be Greek Cypriots; the two groups would be equally represented in the upper house of the legislature, while the Greek Cypriots would have a seven-to-three majority in the lower house. Denktash said he was willing to sign the document, but Kyprianou expressed reservations on almost every major point and called for more negotiations.

Before the summit, Kyprianou had terminated the cooperation between his centrist Democratic Party and the Progressive (Communist) Party of the Working People (AKEL). After the summit, both AKEL and the pro-Western Democratic Rally party accused Kyprianou of deliberate obstruction at the UN meeting. Motions of censure carried in Parliament, but Kyprianou ignored them. In April, he told the UN he would accept a nominally revised document, but now Denktash refused to sign until new elections were held in Turkish Cyprus.

In November, after a bitter debate over Kyprianou's leadership, the Greek Cypriot Parliament dissolved itself and new elections were called for December 8. AKEL and the Democratic Rally, joined together in an unusual alliance, hoped to gain a combined two-thirds majority in the new Parliament so as to make constitutional changes that would require Kyprianou to resign if he did not abide by the wishes of Parliament in negotiations to reunify Cyprus. However, Kyprianou's Democratic Party increased its strength, winning 16 of the 56 seats in the expanded Parliament. The Communists won 15 seats (losing ground) and the Democratic Rally 19, not enough for a combined two-thirds majority. The Socialists took the remaining 6 seats.

In May voters in the self-proclaimed Turkish Republic of Northern Cyprus approved a new constitution that proclaimed the TRNC a secular, democratic republic and provided for joint defense and cooperation between the TRNC and Turkey. The constituent assembly declared that the document's ratification would not prevent establishment of a federation between Greek and Turkish Cypriots. In June, Denktash was elected president of the TRNC, with 71 percent of the vote. The National Union Party won 24 of 50 parliamentary seats and formed a coalition government with the Communal Liberation Party; NUP leader Dervis Eroglu became prime minister. Greece and Greek Cyprus condemned the whole process.

The Greek Cypriot economy continued to outperform the economy in Turkish Cyprus, which was hindered in its external trade by a lack of international recognition.

See STATISTICS OF THE WORLD.   P.J.M.

CZECHOSLOVAKIA. Contention and strain marked Czechoslovakia's relations with several nations, including the United States, in 1985. On September 28 a U.S. Army helicopter on a routine reconnaissance flight along West Germany's southeastern border with Czechoslovakia was fired upon by a Czechoslovak fighter plane, according to the U.S. Defense Department. The plane fired "two to four rockets" without hitting the helicopter. Prague rejected Washington's protest, maintaining that the Czechoslovak pilot had merely tried to warn the U.S. aircraft that it was "in danger of entering Czechoslovak airspace."

Closer to home, water projects and environmental issues ruffled relations. Austria's plans to construct a large hydroelectric plant on the Danube River, near the Czechoslovak border, were greeted with Prague's demand that it receive a lion's share of the waterway's utilization. Austria refused but decided to consider other sites for the project after pressure from environmentalists who opposed it. Meanwhile, Czechoslovakia urged that work be sped up on the Gabčikovo-Nagymarus dam, located on its border with Hungary. The Hungarians, however, wanted additional time to consider the dam's environmental impact and put off construction on their side of the project. Environmental issues were also raised when Czechoslovakia blamed the Western European countries for an increase in acid rain over the region. West Germany and Hungary, conversely, ascribed much of the problem to Czechoslovakia. When Czechoslovakia was asked, at an environmental conference in Munich, to reduce its sulfur dioxide emissions by 30 percent, it refused.

The Prague media, in an escalating campaign against the Roman Catholic Church, criticized the Vatican's foreign policy, de-nounced priests engaged in politics (which the Vatican itself opposes), and noted unfavorably the church's activities commemorating the 1,100th anniversary of the death of St. Methodius. In February the pro-regime association of Catholic clergy, Pacem in Terris, had its third congress in Prague.

Statistics indicated a modest growth for the country's economy, but it appeared that overall growth would fall well behind the targets set for the five-year period 1981–1985. Nonetheless, the 1985 budget called for an increase of 4.5 percent in defense spending. A drive for "electronization" for the period up to 1995 resembled fruitless campaigns of the past for "robotization" and "computerization"; it was accompanied by repeated calls for the intensification of production in general.

See STATISTICS OF THE WORLD.　　　R.A.P.

D

DAHOMEY. *See* STATISTICS OF THE WORLD.

DANCE. Productions of *Romeo and Juliet* dominated the dance scene in 1985, a year which also saw the revival of a ballet not seen for more than a century.

Romeo and Juliet. As the centerpiece of their 1985 seasons, both American Ballet Theatre and Joffrey Ballet (the second-largest and third-largest classical companies, respectively, in the United States) staged elaborate renditions of Shakespeare's *Romeo and Juliet*. ABT chose to perform the version created by Kenneth MacMillan for the Royal Ballet, while the Joffrey put on the Stuttgart Ballet's version by John Cranko.

Across the Atlantic, London Festival Ballet's artistic director Peter Schaufuss realized his long-held ambition to revive Frederick Ashton's 1955 version, originally mounted for the Royal Danish Ballet. Ashton's *Romeo and Juliet* is a work of intimate proportions that asserts the primacy of dance. Last performed by the Royal Danish Ballet in New York in 1965, it was thought to have been irretrievably lost. However, the Danish-born Schaufuss, armed with detailed notes by Niels Bjørn Larsen, one of the original Tybalts, and Larsen's 16mm amateur film of portions of the ballet, induced Ashton to supervise the revival.

Other Revivals. August Bournonville's *Abdallah* was given its first performance in more than 125 years by Utah's Ballet West, first in Salt Lake City in February, then at Washington's Kennedy Center in May. Two former Royal Danish Ballet dancers, Bruce Marks (Ballet West's director until mid-1985) and Toni Lander (the company's principal teacher), were the driving forces behind this venture, which attracted international attention. On the basis of the original scenario, discovered in 1971, and Holger Simon Paulli's score, discovered in 1981 and partially annotated by Bournonville himself, they were able to mount the ballet. (Lander died shortly thereafter.) *Abdallah,* with its exotic Arabian Nights plot, offered a number of charming classical dance episodes, interspersed with character dances, mime sequences, and magical stage effects. The cos-

Robert La Fosse and Leslie Browne were among the pairs of dancers who interpreted the poignant story of Romeo and Juliet in the American Ballet Theatre's first production of the work, choreographed by Kenneth MacMillan to the music by Prokofiev.

tumes by Jens-Jacobs Worsaae looked handsome, as did his sets, which made skillful use of modern devices to effect the ballet's numerous mechanical transformations.

Other revivals included Bronislava Nijinska's seldom seen 1923 masterpiece *Les Noces*, performed by the Feld Ballet and also by Pittsburgh Ballet Theater. The Oakland Ballet brought back its 1981 revival of Massine's *La Boutique Fantasque* for its 1985–1986 20th-anniversary season. The Joffrey revived Massine's delightful *Le Beau Danube*, and the Tulsa Ballet Theater, run by former Ballet Russe dancers Roman Jasinski and Moscelyne Larkin, put on Jasinski's adaptation of David Lichine's version of *The Prodigal Son*.

George Balanchine's fondly remembered 1947 *Divertimento*, to music by Alexei Haieff, was brought back in May, after a lapse of 33 years, by the Kansas City Ballet. Francisco Moncion, who danced in the first production, reconstructed it from his own memories and those of two other original cast members: Todd Bolender and Tanaquil LeClerq.

New York City Ballet. Reconstruction fever also struck New York City Ballet, which brought back Balanchine's 1958 *Gounod Symphony* for its 1985 season. NYCB had not performed *Gounod* for 20 years, and even Balanchine had deemed it lost. But Vida Brown Olinick, the company's ballet mistress in the 1950's, was able to restage the ballet from notes she had made when it was first choreographed and from films made when she was teaching the work to the Paris Opera Ballet in 1959. *Gounod* turned out to be a substantial addition to the repertory, unlike the new works by NYCB's two ballet masters-in-chief, Peter Martins and Jerome Robbins. Martins's small-scale works, whether would-be comic (*Eight More* and *Eight Miniatures*) or would-be dramatic (*Poulenc Sonata* and *Valse Triste*), made a negligible impact. Robbins's postmodern *Eight Lines* and his *In Memory of . . .*, to Alban Berg's *Violin Concerto,* were more ambitious but ultimately unsatisfying.

American Ballet Theatre. ABT had better luck with its chief novelty, *Field, Chair and Moun-*

140

tain, by postmodern choreographer David Gordon. His work—whose title refers to the music (by the 19th-century Irish composer John Field), the props, and Santo Loquasto's scenery—builds to a witty finale, in which the dancers perform with folding chairs. However, ABT star Fernando Bujones's first choreographic attempt, the plotless pastiche *Grand Pas Romantique,* to music by Adolphe Adam, offered little that was original. The company's production of Balanchine's *Donizetti Variations* proved the most substantial of its revivals aside from *Romeo and Juliet.*

Choreographers and Companies. After completing *Field, Chair and Mountain* for ABT, Gordon created new works for the Paris Opera's modern dance wing, the Groupe de Recherche Chorégraphique, as well as for the Dance Theatre of Harlem and his own Pick Up Co. For DTH's debut engagement at New York's Metropolitan Opera House in June, he created *Piano Movers,* to a Thelonious Monk jazz score.

Merce Cunningham created *Arcade* for the Pennsylvania Ballet. Premiering in September, it marked the first time in ten years that Cunningham choreographed a piece for a company other than his own. Paul Taylor, another grand master of modern dance, staged a number of his works for ballet companies. In September the Joffrey became the second classical troupe to mount his *Arden Court;* earlier, the Joffrey put on his *Cloven Kingdom.* For his own dancers Taylor created the romantic *Roses* and the disturbing *Last Look,* a paean to violence, anger, discontent, and obsession. The ever-creative Martha Graham, in her 90's, offered a new work, *Song,* during her company's second annual season at Lincoln Center.

Among the foreign companies that visited the United States, Belgium's Royal Ballet of Flanders, under Soviet émigré Valery Panov's direction, offered several of his fatuous works, including the evening-long *Three Sisters,* based on Chekhov's play. The Basel Ballet presented works by its director, Heinz Spoerli, including an idiosyncratic though handsomely designed *Coppélia.* The Hamburg Ballet suffered under the weight of the bloated Mahler ballets of its artistic director, John Neumeier, while the Sydney Dance Company traded heavily on the soft-core titillation of the ballets created for it by its director, Graeme Murphy. The Berlin Ballet came with Roland Petit's flimsy *The Blue Angel,* a vehicle designed for himself and Natalia Makarova. In November, Belgium's Ballet of the Twentieth Century brought a new ballet by its director, Maurice Béjart, a contemporary murder mystery entitled *Le Concours* (The Competition). A particularly notable import was *Tango Argentino,* a smartly paced revue that provided a captivating reprise of the sensuous dance from South America. It settled in for a long run in New York in the fall.

Transition. Royal Ballet artistic director Norman Morrice, under criticism in the London

A surprise hit of the New York dance season was Tango Argentino, *presenting a troupe of South American dancers and musicians in variations on a beloved and versatile dance form.*

press for the company's productions and standards, announced that he would resign at the close of the 1985–1986 season; he was to be succeeded by the company's popular male star Anthony Dowell. Henning Kronstam was succeeded as Royal Danish Ballet director by Frank Andersen, a company principal dancer. Helgi Tomasson, who in January retired from performing with NYCB, was chosen to replace Michael Smuin as artistic director of the San Francisco Ballet, and Bruce Marks left Ballet West to take up the reins of the Boston Ballet.   K.F.R.

DELAWARE. See STATISTICS OF THE WORLD.

DEMOCRATIC PARTY. The Democrats named a new national chairman in 1985 but made little headway in resolving ideological differences. A possible leading contender for the 1988 presidential nomination, Senator Edward Kennedy (D, Mass.), bowed out.

New Chairman. On February 1 the Democratic National Committee (DNC) elected as its chairman Paul G. Kirk, Jr., a former legal and political adviser to Kennedy. Kirk's victory over former North Carolina Governor Terry Sanford was generally interpreted as a victory for the party's liberals, although Kirk sought to play down the Kennedy connection by sponsoring a resolution requiring the party chairman to remain neutral during the campaign for the 1988 presidential nomination.

The new chairman's first task was to reassure Democratic leaders in the Sunbelt that the national party, without sacrificing its commitment to diversity, would appeal more consistently to "what is on the minds of average Americans." Unconvinced, a group of Democratic officeholders, mostly from the South and West and including Senator Sam Nunn (Ga.) and Governor Charles Robb (Va.), formed a Democratic Leadership Council in February, in an attempt to push the national party in a more conservative direction on both rules and issues. Meanwhile, 1984 presidential candidate Walter Mondale, his running mate Geraldine Ferraro, and others expressed concern that the party should not stray from its traditional loyalties.

Among defections from Democratic ranks, none was more embarrassing than that of John W. Scott, a Louisiana state representative and a member of the DNC. On June 24, as the DNC was about to meet, Scott announced his switch to the Republican Party in a letter to Kirk. Scott claimed the Democratic Party had "drifted far to the left of the mainstream."

Elections. Whatever their problems at the national level, the Democrats showed their muscle in local elections. Among the Democratic big-city mayors to be reelected were Ed Koch of New York, Tom Bradley of Los Angeles, Henry Cisneros of San Antonio, and Don Fraser of Minneapolis. A Democrat also won the governorship of Virginia.

Looking Toward 1988. Behind the scenes, maneuvering was under way for the 1988 presidential nomination. The big news of the year was Kennedy's announcement in December that he would not be a candidate. The senator, whose quest for the nomination in 1980 was hampered by questions about involvement in an automobile accident in Chappaquiddick, Mass., in which a woman died, said he wanted to put aside speculation about his intentions and focus on his Senate career. He also cited family reasons as a factor. Kennedy's announcement left the field clear for other possible contenders, including Senators Gary Hart (Colo.), Bill Bradley (N.J.), and Joseph Biden (Del.) and Governors Robb, Mario Cuomo (N.Y.), and Bruce Babbitt (Ariz.).

The party's 1988 presidential standard-bearer will in all likelihood be nominated by a convention in which Democratic officeholders play a somewhat larger role, and special-interest caucuses a somewhat smaller part, than in 1984. In May the party executive committee withdrew official recognition from several caucuses, including one representing homosexuals. In October the party's Fairness Commission proposed the addition of more than 200 seats at the 1988 convention, for a total of 4,133. The commission also moved that all Democratic governors and all members of the DNC automatically be made delegates, along with 80 percent of Democratic members of Congress, up from 60 percent under the old rules. These changes required the approval of the DNC.

See ELECTIONS IN THE UNITED STATES; REPUBLICAN PARTY. See also biography of Tom Bradley in PEOPLE IN THE NEWS.   G.M.H.

DENMARK. Approximately 300,000 private-sector workers went on strike in March 1985, in Denmark's most serious labor dispute since 1973. Talks between labor leaders, employers, and government officials broke down over terms for a two-year wage settlement. Union leaders wanted an annual pay increase of 4 percent and a reduction in the 40-hour work week. Government officials insisted on a maximum 2 percent wage hike.

Underlying the conflict was the Danish cabinet's resolve to maintain economic growth under conditions of fiscal and monetary restraint. Objectives of the policy included a reduction in the public deficit to 4.75 percent of the gross domestic product, measures to encourage both increased exports and investment in new production and services, and a decrease in private consumption. A 3.5 percent growth rate was expected for 1985, compared with the 4.5 percent rate in 1984.

When the nationwide strike began on March 24, cabinet officials immediately initiated talks with party leaders in the Folketing (Parliament) on possible emergency economic legislation. The upshot was an agreement between the four-party coalition (comprising the Conservatives, the Liberals, the Center Democrats, and the Christian People's Party) and the opposition Radical Liberals on a bill stipulating minimum pay increases of 2 percent in 1985 and 1.5 percent in 1986, plus a one-hour reduction in the work week. In the face of strenuous opposition from the Social Democrats and other parties on the left, the bill was passed by an 85-80 margin on March 30. Workers responded to the mandated settlement with continued strike activity. Twice during the first week in April, some 100,000 persons demonstrated outside the parliamentary building. Public-sector workers walked off the job in support, affecting transportation, hospitals, mail delivery, and garbage collection.

In partial response to the protracted labor dispute, the opposition Social Democrats adopted a four-year policy program in September, calling for an extension of worker influence in company decisions and improvements in social services. The Social Democrats ran on that program in local elections during late November; they held their own, while the ruling coalition lost ground and the left-wing Socialist People's Party made big gains.

In March the Folketing passed a resolution barring Denmark's participation in research involving the U.S.-sponsored Strategic Defense Initiative.

See STATISTICS OF THE WORLD.   M.D.H.

DISTRICT OF COLUMBIA. See STATISTICS OF THE WORLD.

DJIBOUTI. See STATISTICS OF THE WORLD.

DOMINICA. See STATISTICS OF THE WORLD.

DOMINICAN REPUBLIC. See STATISTICS OF THE WORLD. See also CARIBBEAN BASIN.

E

EARTH SCIENCES. During 1985 a powerful earthquake devastated Mexico City, while parts of northern Colombia were overwhelmed by a deadly volcanic eruption. North America was unsettled by temperature extremes, and climate was found to play a role in an oxygen shortage in the waters of Chesapeake Bay.

CLIMATOLOGY

Extremes of weather set records, destroyed crops and property, and took lives in North America during 1985.

Freeze and Thaw. Unusually cold weather spread across the United States in mid-January. The cold wave set more than 200 new daily temperature records and was blamed for at least 126 deaths nationwide. A combination of wind and cold equivalent to a still-air temperature of $-50°$ Fahrenheit moved the January 21 presidential inauguration ceremony indoors and caused most outdoor inaugural activities to be canceled. In Florida, damage to citrus and vegetable crops was in excess of

$1 billion. Markedly cold weather continued into February, leading at one point to the lowest temperature thus far recorded in the contiguous 48 states, a reading of −69.9°F in Peter's Sink, Utah.

Then in late February and early March, record high temperatures and heavy rains in Illinois, Indiana, and western New York melted snow cover and brought extensive flooding. A major tornado on May 31 took about 90 lives

Washington, D.C., fell victim to the weather in early November when heavy rains, associated with remnants of Hurricane Juan, caused the Potomac River to flood its banks. Several historic sites, including the Washington Monument (seen in the background), were closed to the public during the flood.

and caused hundreds of millions of dollars damage to property and crops in Ohio, Pennsylvania, western New York, and the province of Ontario. Spring also brought very hot and dry weather to southeastern United States, triggering fires that in Florida alone damaged or destroyed 200,000 acres and hundreds of homes. More than a thousand brushfires burned in 14 western states and parts of western Canada in June and July, the result of hot, dry, and windy weather. Continuing low precipitation in the eastern United States brought water levels in many reservoirs 30–50 percent below normal, necessitating water-use restrictions in some states.

Hurricanes. Several hurricanes struck the Gulf Coast and eastern seaboard in late summer and fall. Hurricane Elena, passing through the Gulf of Mexico toward Louisiana, veered suddenly toward Florida's Gulf Coast, then unexpectedly turned westward, passing inland at Biloxi, Miss. Before dissipating in early September, the storm left several people dead and well over $500 million in damage in four states. Later in September, Hurricane Gloria wound its way up the East Coast, alarming seaboard residents from North Carolina to New England. Although it did not turn into the "storm of the century" predicted by some, Gloria claimed several lives and caused massive power outages. Hurricane Juan battered the Gulf Coast in late October, leaving in its wake $1 billion in damage and at least seven deaths. Associated early November rains and flooding in the Middle Atlantic states killed about 50 people.

Wind and Air Safety. High local winds and downdrafts associated with a thunderstorm—conditions known as microbursts—were found to have been a factor in an August plane crash at Dallas-Fort Worth International Airport that killed 137 people. Microbursts are thought to have been responsible for crashes causing more than 600 deaths in all over the past 20 years; they occur suddenly in the middle atmospheric layers and are difficult to observe. Use at airports of a ground-based radar system developed by the U.S. National Oceanic and Atmospheric Administration was being considered in an effort to detect them, and installation of a $1 billion NOAA network of sophisticated radar, called Nexrad, was planned.

One of the most destructive volcanic eruptions in history occurred in Colombia on November 13, when the long-dormant Nevado del Ruiz blew its top. Shown here is what was once the town of Armero, now buried with most of its inhabitants under a mass of mud, volcanic ash, and sand.

Greenhouse Effect. It has long been widely believed that carbon dioxide accumulating in the atmosphere from the burning of fossil fuels has, like a greenhouse, a warming effect. Findings reported at the U.S. National Center for Atmospheric Research indicated that more than 30 other gases present in the atmosphere in very small, or "trace," quantities have an even greater potential to warm the atmosphere during the next 50 years. Among these are methane, formed from natural gas and the decay of organic matter, and nitrous oxide, produced from coal burning and from nitrogen fertilizers. N.M.R.

GEOLOGY

The Mexican earthquake of September, followed by the eruption of a Colombian volcano in November, dominated geological events in 1985.

Mexican Earthquake. On September 19 an earthquake registering 8.1 on the Richter scale, one of the most powerful in recent years, struck near the Mexican coast; together with its aftershocks it caused over 7,000 deaths and immeasurable damage. The quake was cen-

tered about 200 miles southwest of Mexico City, near the end of the Middle America Trench, which is located off the west coast of Mexico and Central America. Frequent earthquake activity occurs in this zone because the Cocos oceanic plate, a section of Pacific Ocean floor, is being thrust down, or subducted, underneath the coastal part of the North American plate upon which Mexico sits. Tremendous pressures, built up because one segment of the plate had not moved for some 75 years, were apparently released in the September event, which actually consisted of two ruptures 26 seconds and 60 miles apart, followed by dozens of aftershocks. Although a major earthquake had been expected in the vicinity, its timing was a surprise, since there were no recorded advance signals.

Mexico City itself suffered the bulk of the damage because it sits on an old lake bed of layered gravel, sand, and soft clay that amplifies seismic motions. Scientists speculate that long and powerful seismic waves, arriving at two-second intervals in the lake bed, interacted disastrously with the various layers and with

145

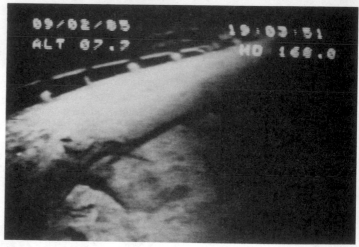

Seventy-three years after the "unsinkable" luxury liner Titanic *struck an iceberg and sank on April 15, 1912, oceanographers tracked down the wreckage 400 miles south of Newfoundland; it was upright on the ocean floor and extremely well preserved. Above, a contemporary painting of the tragedy in which 1,513 people died. Right, one of the first videotaped images of the* Titanic, *taken by the submersible Argo, a new deep-sea research device.*

the varying construction design of the buildings above, subjecting the buildings to intense sideways acceleration.

Colombian Volcano. Plate movement similar to that in Mexico was responsible for a devastating volcanic blast in northern Colombia. On November 13 a long-dormant volcano called Nevado del Ruiz suddenly erupted, spitting fire and ash into the night sky. Heat from the eruption melted ice and snow on the

peak's uppermost slopes, sending a dark avalanche of mud, rocks, and debris into rivers close by. Flooded with this material, the town of Armero soon became a viscid tomb for many of its inhabitants; 13 other towns and cities in the region were also ravaged. An estimated 25,000 people were found dead or reported missing, and thousands were left homeless.

Prediction. Based on predictions supplied by volcanologists, the Colombian government had apparently begun preparing for a possible disaster shortly before Nevado del Ruiz erupted. Although such predictions are still far from an exact science, researchers have been able to monitor many potential trouble spots. Much of the work done in earthquake prediction, for example, centers on California, a region with a particularly active geologic past. It is known that sections of California's San Andreas fault tend to rupture in repeat earthquakes that possess the same faulting mechanism, magnitude, rupture length, location, and sometimes the same epicenter and direction of rupture failure as earlier ones. Since 1857, five similar earthquakes of magnitude 5.5 to 6 have occurred on the fault in sparsely populated cattle country near Parkfield, Calif., at intervals of about 22 years. In April the U.S. Geological Survey announced that its own National Earthquake Prediction Evaluation Council (NEPEC) and the California Earthquake Prediction Council had both endorsed studies indicating that the next characteristic Parkfield earthquake should occur within several years of 1988.

Earlier in 1985, NEPEC endorsed predictions that southern California could expect another great earthquake similar to the 1857 rupture of about 200 miles of the San Andreas fault near Los Angeles. According to NEPEC, there is a moderate to high probability that "a large to great (magnitude 7.5 to 8) earthquake will occur in southern California during the next 30 years."

Dinosaur Extinction. The theory that a meteor hitting the earth 65 million years ago was responsible for the sudden extinction of dinosaurs and other life forms continued to enjoy widespread media attention, but it was met with skepticism or outright rejection from many scientists. According to the meteor theory, dust generated by the impact blocked sunlight and caused a catastrophic global cooldown. But many paleontologists—geologists who study the fossil record and who are the leading specialists on dinosaurs—still insist that the disappearance of dinosaurs occurred over millions of years and probably stemmed from a complex set of causes, including temperature and sea level changes and the spread of diseases by animal migration. Moreover, new evidence suggests that dinosaurs did indeed survive long periods of darkness, for example in high-latitude regions where the sun disappears for months.   R.L.K. & C.F.

OCEANOGRAPHY
Insight was gained in 1985 into the causes of oxygen losses in coastal waters. A robot research vessel made news when it found the wreckage of the *Titanic*.

Oxygen Depletion. Researchers from the Johns Hopkins University reported in April that climatic factors played a major role in a severe episode of anoxia (a shortage of the oxygen dissolved in water) at deep levels of Chesapeake Bay in 1984. Through a complex series of interactions between plants, certain bacteria, and decaying organic matter, anoxia usually kills marine organisms that need oxygen to survive. The investigators found that late snowmelt and heavy rains in the Susquehanna River basin (which empties into the bay), weather patterns forcing salty water into the bay, and fewer-than-usual summer storms that produce high winds all contributed to the anoxic episode. The U.S. Environmental Protection Agency and the states of Maryland and Virginia were studying how human activities like discharging sewage into the bay also contribute to the problem.

Titanic Find. The luxury liner *Titanic* sank in April 1912 in the North Atlantic, with a loss of more than 1,500 lives. In September 1985 the wreck was finally found, by a joint U.S.-French expedition engaged in testing the new submersible robot research vessel *Argo*. Twelve feet long and equipped with cameras, sonar equipment, and strobe lights, the *Argo* is towed by its mother ship near the ocean bottom, where it can work for weeks at a time, at depths as great as 20,000 feet. The *Titanic* was found lying upright at 13,000 feet, with its stern broken off and debris spread about the area.   M.G.G.

ECONOMY AND BUSINESS. U.S. economic growth slowed in 1985 after the boom year of 1984. American consumers spent heavily, but much of their money went for goods from other countries, contributing to a record trade deficit; the federal government also continued to cope with record budget deficits. Inflation was low, unemployment showed little change, and corporate mergers and acquisitions hit a record

Corporate Raider

One of the highest-paid corporate executives in history and possibly the most feared shark among corporate raiders, T. Boone Pickens, chairman of Mesa Petroleum, charges that most other executives "have no more feeling for the average stockholder than they do for baboons in Africa." Pickens says he is really saving companies from inept management by taking them over; critics, for their part, denounce him and his allies as money-hungry pirates. In May, Pickens lost a battle for Unocal (formerly Union Oil of California), but successful targets of his takeover bids have included Cities Service and General American Oil. Even when he failed in a 1984 effort to take over Gulf Oil, he and his friends pocketed $760 million, as stock soared during the fight for control. Born in 1928, Pickens grew up among the oil wells of Oklahoma and Texas—his father bought and sold leases—and, after working for Phillips Petroleum, he founded Mesa. He and his second wife live near Mesa headquarters in Amarillo, Texas.

T. Boone Pickens

pace. Around the world, developing countries remained saddled with enormous debts (see BANKING AND FINANCE), but economies of major industrial nations expanded modestly.

Economic Trends. U.S. economic growth slowed down in 1985, raising fears that the recovery from the 1981–1982 recession might be ending; the economy grew by 2.3 percent, the lowest rate since 1982. Growth fluctuated during the year, from a 1.1 percent annual rate in the second quarter to 3 percent in the third and a revised rate of 2.4 percent in the fourth quarter. Inflation, as measured by the consumer price index, was 3.8 percent for all of 1985—similar to the levels of the previous few years. The stock market took off early in the year, marked time, rose again, and settled down. Late in the year, a new rising trend brought the Dow Jones industrials average over 1,500 for the first time.

Projections for the U.S. economy were hazardous as it moved through uncharted territory: annual federal budget deficits approaching $200 billion and an unprecedented flood of imports, which were cutting deeply into growth. But some economists believed that the econ-

omy, instead of moving toward recession, was settling down in a so-called soft landing, that is, a period of slow growth followed by resumption of more rapid growth.

Consumers had sparked the sharp economic rebound in 1984, and they also spent heavily in 1985, although increasing debt burdens on households appeared likely to force some retrenchment. The personal savings rate as a percentage of disposable personal income fell during the year. Businesses, anticipating lower consumer spending, cut back on their inventories. Automobile manufacturers dropped interest rates to as low as 7.5 percent. Lower interest rates helped account for the increased third-quarter growth rate, but analysts feared that customers were merely moving up purchases they would have made later on. Retail sales, as a whole, were choppy, rising one month and falling the next. For much of the year, corporate profits declined under the weight of foreign competition and the overall slowdown in the economy. However, in the third quarter of 1985, after-tax profits rose about 5 percent, one of a number of positive signs late in the year.

Budget Battle. In the 1985 fiscal year, which ended September 30, the federal government took in $734 billion and spent $946 billion, or a deficit of $212 billion. In February, President Ronald Reagan submitted to Congress a budget for fiscal 1986 that included a deficit of $180 billion, even though he proposed to eliminate or cut back a number of programs to save over $50 billion. He rejected any tax increases to close the deficit gap. Reagan had also said he would never agree to any cutbacks in social security benefits, but for a time in 1985 he seemed ready to do so. Republicans in the Senate agreed to a budget plan that included a "compromise" on social security, and were outraged when Reagan pulled out of the agreement. Eventually both houses of Congress agreed to a budget resolution they said would cut the deficit by $56 billion in fiscal 1986 and by $276 billion over three years. However, projections by the Congressional Budget Office indicated that savings would be far less. The budget resolution preserved most programs Reagan had planned to kill, although freezes were imposed on some.

Late in the year, Senate and House conferees wrestled with a plan designed to eliminate budget deficits within five years. Outlays would be cut each year almost across the board, if Congress and the president failed to agree on how to close the gap to each year's target figure; certain expenditures would be exempt. Congress passed the so-called Gramm-Rudman bill in December, and Reagan signed it despite reservations.

The Deficit, the Debt, and the Dollar. Many economists blamed soaring budget deficits for the unbalanced recovery: the treasury's need to borrow was driving up interest rates; in turn, relatively high interest rates attracted foreign investments, which made for a strong dollar; the high value of the dollar hurt exports, attracted imports, and caused Americans to lose jobs. Also, the huge national debt was forcing more of the nation's tax dollars to be used to pay interest on the debt. In the early 1970's the government was spending 1.3 percent of gross national product on interest; in fiscal 1985 it spent about 3.3 percent for that purpose. During Reagan's first five years in office, the public debt doubled to $2 trillion.

The U.S. trade deficit, fueled in large part by a strong dollar, worsened in 1985, with imports expected to exceed exports by nearly $150 billion. The trade deficit accounted for a deficit of about $135 billion in the balance of payments on current account, a broader measure that includes trade in services and travel and transport expenditures. The current account deficit turned the United States into a net debtor nation, owing more to foreigners than foreigners owed the United States, for the first time since 1914.

The dollar peaked against other currencies early in the year, and the United States sold dollars in order to drive down the currency's value. As protectionist sentiment rose in the U.S. Congress, financial officials from the United States, Japan, West Germany, France, and Great Britain agreed in September on a plan to bring the dollar's value down, indicating

President Reagan made frequent trips this year to campaign for his tax reform plan; here, a September stop in Independence, Mo. The president called his proposal for sweeping changes in the tax code a "second American Revolution."

they would intervene in the currency markets if necessary. The mere threat of intervention sent the dollar tumbling, although there was no immediate strong effect on the balance of trade.

U.S. Employment. The civilian unemployment rate remained stuck at 7.3 percent until August, when it declined to 7 percent; it remained close to 7 percent, dipping to 6.9 percent by December. The jobless rate had been 7.4 percent when Reagan took office in 1981. However, the number of jobs was increasing; from the beginning of the latest business expansion in December 1982 to late 1985, more than 10 million jobs were created. Most of the new growth was in the services sector, while the manufacturing sector remained weak.

U.S. Monetary Policy. The Federal Reserve Board made it clear that it would not let the economy slip into a recession, even if avoiding recession meant abandoning the monetary targets used by the Fed to determine how much money it creates for the economy. As the economy demonstrated weakness, the Fed kept the money supply expanding well beyond its targets. In May the Fed lowered its discount rate, the rate it charges member banks for borrowing, from 8 percent to 7.5 percent. It brought short-term interest rates down (although real rates, after inflation, were still high) perhaps preventing a recession.

Tax Reform. In May, President Reagan unveiled a tax reform and tax simplification package that would reduce the number of tax brackets

The free trade vs. protectionism debate heated up, as many members of Congress demanded more U.S. trade barriers. Below, a Japanese-made Honda automobile rolls off a ship in Baltimore. Right, a lobbyist for the U.S. shoe industry, seriously damaged by foreign imports.

from 14 to 3, cut the top tax rate for individuals from 50 percent to 35 percent, and reduce the top corporate rate from 46 percent to 33 percent. The plan would end a number of tax preferences long enjoyed by individuals and corporations; perhaps its most controversial provision was the elimination of the federal deduction for state and local taxes. In early December the House Ways and Means Committee approved a comprehensive tax reform measure of its own. This measure altered Reagan's plan in significant ways, permitting the deduction for state and local taxes and providing top tax rates of 38 percent for individuals and 36 percent for corporations. Reagan urged passage of the bill to keep it alive in Congress. The bill finally passed the House with the reluctant support of some Republicans.

Mergers and Acquisitions. Merger mania among U.S. corporations continued at a feverish pace, in a wide range of industries, including broadcasting, airlines, and banking. Two tobacco companies, eager to diversify in order to absorb better the potential shocks from product-liability lawsuits, turned to food companies. Philip Morris agreed to buy General Foods for $5.8 billion, thereby creating the largest U.S. consumer product company. R. J. Reynolds agreed to acquire Nabisco Brands for $4.9 billion.

These acquired companies were attractive targets because they sold well-known brand-name products that had long enjoyed loyal support from consumers. Given the enormous start-up costs for a new product, it became easier for a company to break into a market by buying other companies. The appeal of brand names (Samsonite luggage, Hunt's ketchup, Tropicana orange juice) led to the takeover, subject to stockholders' approval, of the Beatrice Companies by Kohlberg, Kravis, Roberts & Company, the nation's top organizer of management buyouts, for $6.2 billion—the world's biggest merger up to that time, outside the oil industry. Then, in December, General Electric agreed to acquire the RCA Corporation, owner of the NBC television network, for $6.3 billion in a cash deal. Earlier, American Broadcasting Companies was acquired by Capital Cities Communications, Inc., for close to $3.5 billion.

In other major transactions, Allied Corporation agreed to acquire Signal Companies for nearly $5 billion, creating the prospect of a huge complex of aerospace and high technology, and Pantry Pride won its fight to take over Revlon, after a court rejected evasive action taken by Revlon. General Motors continued to diversify by agreeing to buy Hughes Aircraft for more than $5 billion. In another move toward diversification, one compelled by weakness in its basic industry, United States Steel agreed to acquire Texas Oil and Gas for $3.6 billion. Carl Icahn, one of the new breed of "corporate raiders," won a fight to take over Trans World Airlines after accumulating more than 50 percent of its shares and getting a competing suitor to withdraw his bid. But the final agreement left him with heavy paper losses, and he was barred from withdrawing the $320 million he invested in the airline.

The 1984 acquisition of Getty Oil Company by Texaco had a stunning postscript in November 1985 when a jury in Houston ordered Texaco to pay Pennzoil Company $11.1 billion, including interest, for interfering with Pennzoil's agreement to buy Getty. A Texas state judge upheld the award, by far the largest in the history of the U.S. civil justice system. Pennzoil argued that it had agreed to buy 40.2 percent of Getty in January 1984 but that the deal was improperly voided three days later when Getty accepted a larger offer from Texaco. Texaco appealed for a new trial.

World Economy. The economies of the world's other major industrial countries generally improved in 1984 and 1985, but the advance was uneven. The Organization for Economic Cooperation and Development—representing the world's major industrial nations—estimated that growth in its European members would be about 2.25 percent (after inflation) in 1985 and 1986; growth in Japan was forecast at 4.5 percent for 1985 and 3.75 percent for 1986. Much of the growth in 1984 in Western Europe and Japan was tied to the rapidly growing U.S. demand for imports. Exports from all countries rose 6 percent in 1984, while those to the United States alone soared by 26 percent. Countries seeking a place to invest their export earnings had an obvious choice—the United States, where interest rates remained high in relation to inflationary levels. The rush into dollars pushed the U.S. currency even higher, contributing further to the increase in U.S. imports.

By the end of 1985, however, some major shifts appeared to be taking place. The huge U.S. budget and trade deficits appeared to have peaked or leveled off, and intervention, both real and threatened, by the U.S. and other governments sent the dollar on a skid. Between late February and mid-December, the British pound rose by about 40 percent against the dollar, the West German mark rose by about 33 percent, and the Japanese yen by about 25 percent. A likely result: greater investments at home by the European countries and Japan. However, any decline in the U.S. appetite for imports would pose a special problem for developing countries, who would need to expand other markets or face greater difficulty in paying external debts.

Inflation was not a serious problem in the industrial countries; consumer price increases were projected at even less than in 1982, a recession year. Inflation was running below 3 percent in Japan and West Germany, and around 4 percent in Canada; a 6 percent rate in France was only half of its 1982 rate. The employment picture, however, was not bright. Although the total number of persons employed in Western Europe rose in 1984 for the first time in five years, the percentage of those unemployed edged upward to 50-year highs in some major countries. The OECD projected that in Western Europe the unemployment rate would reach 11 percent for all of 1985 and rise further in 1986. Great Britain, which was set back by a coal miners' strike that lasted almost a year, suffered from jobless rates exceeding 12 percent between 1983 and 1985. Canadian unemployment was still around 10 percent. Japan's rate, however, remained at under 3 percent.

International Trade. The U.S. merchandise trade deficit, after soaring from $69 billion in 1983 to $123 billion in 1984, appeared to be topping out at just under $150 billion in 1985. The aggregate trade surplus of the ten members of the European Economic Community (EEC) was expected to exceed $15 billion in 1985. The total volume of world trade was projected to increase only modestly, by about 3 percent.

Japan's 1985 trade surplus was expected to exceed 1984's $45 billion bulge. This success brought criticism from across the world, with demands for more open Japanese markets and less aggressive Japanese exports policies. Prime Minister Yasuhiro Nakasone appealed to his people to buy more foreign goods, and he promised various measures to reduce trade barriers and stimulate greater consumption from the savings-oriented Japanese. The newly industrializing Asian nations, including South Korea, Taiwan, Indonesia, Singapore, Hong Kong, and Thailand, prospered in both sales and services during the year, and China, India, and Turkey moved toward a more free-market orientation.

Members of the U.S. Congress, responding to complaints from import-ravaged industries, introduced more than 300 pieces of protectionist legislation. Some bills sought to restrict imports of certain goods from particular countries; others would impose import surcharges. One major bill that passed in December would have reduced imports of footwear, copper, textiles, and apparel by up to 30 percent, but President Reagan vetoed it. The administration opposed all such legislation, arguing that other countries would retaliate and further diminish U.S. exports. The administration, for its part, announced proceedings against Japan, Brazil, South Korea, and the EEC for restrictions and subsidies in various industries. The administration also initiated bilateral trade talks.

Leaders of the world's seven leading non-Communist trading nations met in Bonn, West Germany, in May at their annual summit. Their final communiqué was mostly vague and general, but the countries did agree to convene a new round of multilateral trade liberalization talks in 1986. In November 1985 the General Agreement on Tariffs and Trade (GATT) approved the talks, scheduling them to begin in the autumn of 1986. At the urging of the United States, the talks would be the first to place special emphasis on liberalizing international trade in services and high-technology goods. This would facilitate international operations by banks, insurance companies, and the telecommunications industry.

See also separate articles on individual countries. W.N.

ECUADOR. In August 1985, León Febres Cordero began his second year as Ecuador's president, with majority support in Congress as a result of party switches by members. During Febres's first 12 months in office, partisan conflict had often delayed important legislation and appointments.

A two-day general strike was called by the United Workers' Front (FUT) in January, after the government announced price hikes. Widespread violence was reported in Quito, and seven demonstrators were killed. FUT called workers out again in March to protest a 1985 minimum monthly wage of around $125; FUT demanded a minimum monthly wage of more than $200.

Oil exploration contracts were signed with subsidiaries of the Occidental Petroleum and Exxon corporations. By June, 23 companies had indicated an interest in further exploration. Petroleum production and investment plans had to be cut back, however, because of opposition from the Organization of Petroleum Exporting Countries. Dissatisfied with its quota of 183,000 barrels per day, Ecuador threatened to withdraw from OPEC.

Trade policies of the Febres government enabled Ecuador to regain lost export markets and increase shipments of traditional products, including cacao and shrimp. Export-sector growth was promoted in products with a high component of local raw materials. Tariffs were reduced and bans removed on imports of most finished goods. In March, Ecuador was granted a $110 million stand-by loan by the IMF, clearing the way for refinancing of $4.6 billion in debt. Febres returned from an official visit to Cuba in April with new trade and credit arrangements.

After Febres stated in early October that peace would not come to Central America until Nicaragua had a "legitimate popular election," Nicaraguan President Daniel Ortega Saavedra accused Febres of being "an instrument of the United States," which, Ortega said, was trying to use Ecuador to undermine the peace efforts of the Contadora group (Mexico, Venezuela, Panama, and Colombia). Ecuador quickly broke relations with Nicaragua in response.

See STATISTICS OF THE WORLD.　　L.L.P.

EDUCATION. In 1985, a new U.S. secretary of education aggressively advocated policies favored by conservatives. The proper role of religion in education was debated again. Teachers' unions backtracked on their opposition to testing teachers. The California Board of Education demanded that textbook publishers strengthen the presentation of evolution.

New Education Secretary. In January, President Ronald Reagan named William J. Bennett, a former university professor and chairman of the National Endowment of the Humanities, to succeed Terrel Bell as secretary of education. Bell had resigned in December. In his first press conference, the combative Bennett defended the administration's effort to cut grants and loans to college students, adding that the policy might force some students to engage in "divestiture" of their cars, stereos, and beach vacations. Bennett endorsed voluntary prayer in public schools, tuition tax credits, or "vouchers," to aid students in private schools, and a cut in federal aid to higher education.

Supreme Court Action. In June the U.S. Supreme Court, voting 6-3, rejected an Alabama law that permitted teachers to start the day's classes with a moment of silence, "for meditation or voluntary prayer." Justice John Paul Stevens's majority opinion held that the 1982 law was enacted "for the sole purpose of expressing the state's endorsement of prayer activities."

A few weeks later, the Court struck down a federal program providing remedial or enrichment instruction for needy children in parochial schools—an arrangement that had operated with little contention for nearly 20 years. President Lyndon Johnson had won enactment of a broad program of federal aid to poor children and, in a compromise, had agreed that all federal money would go to public school officials, who would be responsible for providing an equal amount of tutoring for needy children at private or parochial schools. The Court, 5-4, declared this arrangement unconstitutional. The U.S. Department of Education told public school districts they were still responsible for tutoring the children but must do so outside private school buildings. Bennett denounced the ruling.

In a decision that the administration ap-

Boston Latin School celebrated its 350th anniversary in 1985. The stiff collars and ties of an earlier era (above) are gone today; the student body is racially and ethnically diverse, and half the students are girls. But whatever the changes, academic standards remain as tough as ever.

said, would be a "first step" toward giving teachers the prestige of other professions, and he added that the current state teachers' exams set standards so low as to be embarrassing. Then, in midyear, the National Education Association reversed its long-standing opposition to teacher testing. At the urging of President Mary Hatwood Futrell, the NEA approved a resolution calling for "rigorous state standards for entry into the teaching profession." Previously, the association had opposed all such tests on the ground that they were unfair to minorities.

Both unions continued to oppose the testing of current teachers or the dismissal of licensed teachers on the basis of such tests. In the spring, Arkansas became the first state to adopt such a practice. More than 27,000 Arkansas teachers were tested in reading, writing, and mathematics, and about 10 percent failed one or more parts. Those who failed had to pass a retest by June 1987 or be dismissed. NEA officials called the test an embarrassing trial for experienced teachers. The NEA said it was challenging the tests in court and would sue the state on behalf of any teacher who lost a job because of the exam.

Teacher Astronaut. Sharon Christa McAuliffe of Concord, N.H., was selected from more than 11,000 teachers to be the first private citizen from the United States to travel in space. Tragically, she and six other astronauts were killed in the explosion of the space shuttle *Challenger,* just after its launching on January 28, 1986.

The Reform Issue. A survey showed that every state had adopted some key recommendations made in *A Nation At Risk,* issued by the president's National Commission on Excellence in Education in 1983. These included more stringent high school graduation standards, expanded testing of students, tougher certification standards for new teachers, and higher salaries to attract better teachers. California found a direct way to reward schools that were gaining better scores on state tests: it paid them. In May, 548 high schools, about half the state's total, won shares of a $14.4 million "incentive" fund because their seniors scored higher on the state basic skills test in 1985 than in the preceding year.

plauded, the Court in January held, 6-3, that teachers and school officials may search a student when "there are reasonable grounds for suspecting the search will turn up evidence that the student has violated . . . the law or the rules of the schools."

Bilingual Education. In September, Bennett attacked existing programs for students whose native language is not English. Criticizing the practice of giving such students schoolwork in their own language, he contended that, as a result, many never attain the fluency in English that, he argued, should be the primary goal of bilingual education. He branded the federal government's bilingual learning programs, which had cost $1.7 billion over 17 years, "a failed path" and called for local districts to be granted more flexibility.

Tests for Teachers. Calls for teacher-testing programs found support from an unexpected source: the teachers' unions. In January, Albert Shanker, president of the American Federation of Teachers, endorsed the creation of a national examination for new teachers. Such a test, he

A backlash against the reform movement was seen in 1985 when a group issued another report, *Barriers to Excellence: Our Children at Risk.* It contended that the poor, nonwhite, and handicapped were being ignored by a focus on educational excellence and the college-bound student. The report charged that progress had virtually halted in such areas as school desegregation, equalizing the financing of school districts, and lowering the dropout rate. Meanwhile, the U.S. Justice Department said in September that for years it had been investigating whether public schools were discriminating against minority students by lowering standards so it would be easier for them to graduate. The department said it hoped to identify schools guilty of such discrimination and seek corrective action through negotiation.

Rejected Textbooks. In September the California Board of Education rejected science textbooks submitted by a dozen publishers for use in junior high school classes. It complained that the books "systematically omitted" thorough discussions of evolution and said that

Parents and children in New York City join forces (above) to fight a decision allowing children with AIDS to attend public schools. In Indiana, Ryan White (below), a hemophiliac with AIDS who was barred from classes, listens to teachers over a telephone hookup while his mother supervises.

human reproduction and ethics were also inadequately treated. Schoolbook publishers were accused of watering down the treatment of evolution because of pressure from religious fundamentalists. In December the board adopted revised versions submitted by six publishers.

AIDS Controversy. The question of whether children afflicted with acquired immune deficiency syndrome (AIDS) should be allowed to attend classes with other children became a widely debated, emotional issue, although the actual number of AIDS children seeking admission to schools around the United States was small. Scientific evidence indicated that the disorder is contracted only through sexual contact, through contaminated hypodermic needles or blood transfusions, or to infants born to an infected mother; however, some parents and teachers were concerned that the disease could turn out to be spread in some instances by everyday contact in a classroom setting. Federal authorities recommended in August that children with AIDS be allowed in school on a case-by-case basis, after an evaluation of the medical risks involved; the American Academy of Pediatrics also endorsed this approach. School systems responded in different ways to the medical and ethical problems posed by children with AIDS. In Indiana, a hemophiliac who had contracted AIDS from a contaminated blood-clotting agent was barred from classes in a local public school, starting in December 1984. Late in 1985, a state hearing officer ruled he could return to class, but he remained barred pending an appeal by the school board. New York City health and education officials in September 1985 did permit an unidentified second grader believed to have AIDS to attend school; the policy was to make such decisions on an individual basis after review of each case by a special committee. The New York City policy was challenged by lawsuits and school boycotts.

College Trends. The cost of going to the average college rose 7 percent in the 1985–1986 academic year, according to estimates by the College Board. Total costs for tuition, fees, books, and room and board were put at $5,314 for public four-year institutions and at $9,659 for private four-year institutions.

On many campuses students demonstrated against South Africa's racial policies, demanding that their schools divest themselves of any stocks or bonds of corporations that do business in South Africa. Most institutions refused to take such a step, preferring selective divestiture and stricter review of racial-equality policies in U.S. firms in South Africa. An exception was Columbia University, which in October opted for divestment of nearly all its South Africa-linked stock. D.G.S.

EGYPT. Terrorist incidents dealt a blow to Egypt's standing in the Arab world, while President Hosni Mubarak withstood increased pressures from religious extremists at home.

Terrorism. While Mubarak promoted the peace initiative taken by Jordan's King Hussein and Palestine Liberation Organization chief Yasir Arafat, Egypt's standing in the Arab world—and its participation in the peace process—suffered a setback in October when four Palestinians hijacked the Italian cruise ship *Achille Lauro* shortly after it left the Egyptian port of Alexandria. When the ship anchored near Port Said, Egypt conducted negotiations between the hijackers and Italian and PLO officials, including Muhammad Abbas, the plot's alleged mastermind. After holding the ship for two days, the gunmen surrendered to Egyptian authorities, who promised them safe passage out of Egypt. The terms angered the United States, especially when it was learned that an elderly American Jewish hostage, Leon Klinghoffer, had been killed.

The following day an Egyptian airliner carrying the four Palestinians and Abbas left Egypt but was intercepted by U.S. Navy jet fighters and forced to land in Sicily. Italy arrested the hijackers but allowed Abbas to leave the country; the gunmen were convicted on weapons charges and awaited trial for hijacking and murder. Mubarak denounced the U.S. action as "piracy"—the incident had sparked protests in Egypt against Mubarak's ties with the United States and Israel—but relations were soon smoothed over somewhat.

In November an Egyptian airliner was hijacked by Arab gunmen who forced the plane to land in Malta and shot eight passengers, killing two (an American and an Israeli). Hours later an Egyptian commando team stormed the plane in a rescue attempt; 58 people were killed, and Egypt was criticized for its handling of the affair. Egypt said the hijackers, one of whom survived, were anti-Arafat Palestinians. Mubarak also accused Libya of complicity.

Copts and Muslim Fundamentalists. Mubarak allowed Pope Shenouda III, elected leader of the Coptic Christian community, to resume his papal duties after more than three years of forced internal exile. Shenouda was among those accused by Mubarak's predecessor, Anwar al-Sadat, of having fomented unrest.

In the spring, a liberal decree enhancing women's rights in divorce and other "personal status" matters was repealed by the People's Assembly under Muslim fundamentalist pressure. Around the same time, the government ordered the destruction of 3,000 copies of the classic Arabian story collection *A Thousand and One Nights,* on the grounds that its contents were morally corrupting.

The sheikh of Noor Mosque, Hafez Salama, intensified his demands for the government to adopt Islamic law (sharia). In July, Salama called upon the faithful to march on the presidential palace in support of his program. But Mubarak banned the march and also deployed more than 1,000 riot policemen to quash any attempt by the fundamentalists to defy the ban. Salama and many others were later arrested; Salama was released in August.

In late June Mubarak had launched a verbal assault on "religious fanatics," accusing them of threatening national unity and collaborating with an unnamed foreign power. On July 1 he backed the People's Assembly when it voted nearly unanimously to restore the earlier, more liberal "personal status" laws repealed in the spring. Two days later, the government announced that is was assuming control of all mosques in Egypt, in a move designed to undercut fundamentalist opposition.

In August, an Israeli diplomat was assassinated in Cairo; several Islamic groups claimed responsibility.

Sinai Incident. An Egyptian police officer who killed seven Israeli tourists after apparently going berserk at his guard post in the Sinai was sentenced in December to life in prison after a closed military trial in Cairo. Some Egyptians hailed the officer as a hero, and there were large demonstrations on his behalf.

In November, after an Egyptian airliner was hijacked by Arab gunmen who killed two passengers and forced the plane to land in Malta, Egyptian commandos mounted a rescue attempt during which 58 people died or were fatally injured. The commandos entered the plane by blasting their way through the cargo hold, seen here being examined by Maltese policemen the day after the operation.

Economy. On January 5, Minister of the Economy Mustafa Said introduced new measures aimed at clamping down on the black market in foreign currencies and at restricting Egypt's soaring imports. Political controversy over enforcement of the measures and opposition from some business leaders, however, resulted in Said's resignation in March and the restoration of the status quo. The growing import bill helped to force an official devaluation of the Egyptian pound (also introduced on January 5), even greater drops in the black-market, and unofficial open-market rates during the year. Egypt continued to rely heavily on aid from the United States, which in March promised $500 million in emergency aid for 1986 in addition to the $2.3 billion already scheduled. In September, Prime Minister Kamal Hassan Ali resigned and was succeeded by Ali Lofti, an economist who had been a finance minister under Sadat.

Relations with Libya. Tension between Libya and Egypt also mounted in conjunction with the expulsion of some 10,000 Egyptians working in Libya and the April coup in Sudan which ousted President Jaafar al-Nimeiry, a longtime Egyptian ally. During Mubarak's visit to Sudan in June, the new Sudanese leaders had reaffirmed their friendship for Egypt. However, in July Libya and Sudan signed a mutual defense pact.

See STATISTICS OF THE WORLD. K.J.B.

ELECTIONS IN THE UNITED STATES. Voters in major U.S. cities in 1985 returned incumbents to office for second, third, and even fourth terms. On the statewide level, Democrats in Virginia and Republicans in New Jersey enjoyed strong victories in which they attracted a broad spectrum of support.

Municipal Elections. On April 6, Dallas Mayor A. Starke Taylor won a second term in an extremely close race. A recount requested by his opponent, City Council member Max Rosenblatt, confirmed that Taylor had gained a less-than-500-vote margin, with 50.6 percent of the vote, thus avoiding a runoff. In contrast, most of the year's other major mayoral races were not very close. San Antonio's popular mayor, Henry Cisneros, won reelection with 73 percent of the vote, also on April 6. Three days later, Los Angeles Mayor Tom Bradley (see biography in PEOPLE IN THE NEWS) won a fourth term, easily outdistancing his chief challenger, longtime City Council member John Ferraro, by capturing more than two-thirds of the vote.

With a substantial 62 percent of the vote, Detroit's Coleman A. Young won a September 10 nonpartisan primary; he went on to win reelection easily in November. In New York, Edward I. Koch received more than 75 percent of the votes cast September 10 in the Democratic primary, easily defeating his nearest rival, City Council President Carol Bellamy. On November 5, Koch won his third term as mayor of the nation's most populous city with 78 percent of the vote, swamping Republican candidate Diane McGrath and Carol Bellamy, who ran on the Liberal line.

Incumbent George V. Voinovich was the leading vote-getter in the nonpartisan Cleveland primary on October 1. He went on to capture more than 70 percent of the vote in the November election, beating City Council member Gary Kucinich, brother of former Cleveland Mayor Dennis Kucinich. In an October 8 nonpartisan primary, Atlanta's Mayor Andrew Young won a second term with 81 percent of the vote, campaigning on his record of achievement in revitalizing the city with new businesses, including many foreign-owned corporations.

Houston Mayor Kathy Whitmire, who had supported a measure banning job discrimination against homosexuals that was repealed after a campaign led by her opponent, won a third term on November 5, with nearly 60 percent of the vote; she defeated Louie Welch, a former five-term Houston mayor. In Phoenix, on November 5, Terry Goddard won a second term as mayor with 86 percent of the vote.

Puerto Rican-born Mayor Maurice Ferre, of Miami, lost a bid for a seventh two-year term when he ran third in nonpartisan elections on November 5, behind two Cuban-born candidates. In the runoff on November 12, 36-year-old lawyer Xavier Suarez was the winner, defeating banker Raul Masvidal by a comfortable margin. The city's population is about 40 percent Cuban, but Suarez was the first Cuban-American to win the mayoralty.

State Elections. New Jersey's Governor Thomas Kean (R) defeated young Democratic challenger Peter Shapiro in a landslide victory on November 5, winning in each of the state's 21 counties, with support crossing racial, ethnic, and economic lines. Kean, who had won his first term by a narrow margin, ran with broad support in 1985, picking up endorsements from civil rights leader Coretta Scott King and from the state's AFL-CIO, as well as from more traditional GOP sources. His coattails apparently helped the GOP win control of the state assembly for the first time in 12 years.

In traditionally conservative Virginia, on the other hand, the Democrats were triumphant. Gerald Baliles, a former state senator and attorney general, won the governorship of Virginia, defeating Republican Wyatt B. Durrette, with 55 percent of the vote. Democrats also took the lieutenant governorship (L. Douglas Wilder, the first black state senator elected since Reconstruction) and the attorney general's post (Mary Sue Terry, the first woman ever elected to statewide office in Virginia).

Congressional Elections. Cathy Long, widow of the late U.S. Representative Gillis Long (D) of Louisiana, who died in January, won 52 percent of the vote on March 30 in a five-way race to fill the vacant congressional seat. In Texas, conservative Democrat Jim Chapman narrowly defeated Republican Edd Hargett in an August 3 runoff, to win the U.S. House seat vacated by Sam Hall (D).

Referenda. In Boulder, Colo., and Oberlin, Ohio, voters approved proposals urging their city governments to keep all nuclear weapons out of their cities. In New York City, however, a planned referendum on the use of New York Harbor as home port for ships expected to carry nuclear missiles was thrown off the ballot by a federal judge, on the grounds that it was unconstitutional for local voters to decide whether to accept federal military projects.

Voters in Oak Park, Ill., a Chicago suburb, upheld its status as one of the few localities with a ban on possession of pistols. The majority of voters in three New England towns declined to express disagreement with the U.S. Supreme Court's decision upholding the legality of abortion. Tucson, Ariz., voters approved controls on smoking in workplaces.   K.C.

ELECTRONICS. Video mania ruled the U.S. consumer electronics world in 1985. By late in the year, videocassette recorder (VCR) sales alone were racing 55 percent ahead of the figure for the first ten months of 1984, which was a record year. The VCR market continued to be dominated by the half-inch tape formats of VHS and Beta, with VHS generating by far the larger sales. In both formats hi-fi stereo VCR's, which had been introduced earlier, proved a strong new entry in the market, as they brought vastly improved sound quality to prerecorded video.

There were also new video products with the 8-millimeter tape format, which may eventually threaten the hegemony of the larger half-inch VCR format. The size of the 8-mm videocassettes, about as big as a conventional audio cassette, permitted further miniaturization of VCR's and other video products.

Continuing its commitment to the video market, Kodak in September introduced a series of electronic imaging products, including a video imager that produces photographs of the images on a television or computer screen in minutes. Another Kodak component used a compact floppy disk that, when processed by a Kodak lab, could store up to 50 35-mm film images; users could then display the photographs on a television or computer screen.

In the audio world, compact disk players continued to have a growing impact, with very strong sales and an ever-increasing library of disks. The market for small, portable CD players drew new entries, and manufacturers also brought out rugged CD players for automobiles. And in the market for Walkman-sized personal stereo players, Sony and Panasonic introduced models that had two cassette mechanisms, making it possible to either play two tapes in succession or record from one tape to the other.

For the electronic components industry, 1985 was a grim year. The manufacturers of semiconductor chips, the underlying technology vital to computers, consumer electronics, and other applications, suffered a steep decline, forcing them to lay off workers, cut salaries,

Here, Kitty

What soft furry creature wakes up when you clap your hands, purrs when you pat it on the back, comes at your command, plays freeze tag with your children, and never makes a mess on the floor? The answer: a stuffed animal with an electronic "brain" inside. A creation of Axlon Inc., of Sunnyvale, Calif., this "Petster" was selling for up to $100 or so (depending on the model) and was one of several plush electronic pets on the market. Axlon was also peddling A. G. Bear, a furry friend whose circuitry enables it to mimic its master's voice, while Worlds of Wonder Inc., in Fremont, Calif., offered Teddy Ruxpin, a lovable talking teddy bear whose mouth, nose, and eye movements are synchronized with his voice by means by special audio cassettes. Teddy, whose stories take children to a fantasy land and are said to impart "wisdom and timeless values," was available for around $60–$70, with a cassette/booklet package included.

U.S. marines at a sidewalk café were the target of an attack by urban guerrillas in San Salvador. In the shooting, which occurred on June 19, four off-duty marines and two American businessmen were killed, as well as seven other patrons of the restaurant. A branch of the Central American Revolutionary Workers' Party claimed responsibility.

and reduce production capacity. Nevertheless, the race to stay on the leading edge of the technology continued to bring advances. Leading U.S. and Japanese firms, for instance, brought out new 1-megabit random-access memory (RAM) chips, capable of storing a million bits of information, a four-fold advance over the 256K RAM chips widely used in computers and other electronic devices.

W.D.M.

EL SALVADOR. President José Napoleón Duarte consolidated his political position by winning control of El Salvador's national legislature in March elections. Government forces appeared to be increasing their strength, while left-wing rebels moved increasingly toward terrorist actions, among them a massacre at a strip of sidewalk cafés in San Salvador and the kid-

nappings of mayors and of President Duarte's daughter. A raid late in the year on an army basic training school, however, showed that the rebels could still execute well-planned hit-and-run attacks.

Politics. On March 31 about a million voters participated in elections for 60 legislators and 262 mayors. President Duarte's moderate Christian Democrats won 200 mayoralties and a majority (32 seats) in the national assembly, taking control from the extreme right. The far right Nationalist Republican Alliance (Arena) party, led by former Major Roberto d'Aubuisson, won 13 seats; the far right National Conciliation Party (PCN) also won 13. In September, d'Aubuisson resigned as Arena's head. The new legislative majority passed a judicial reform bill on July 4, which authorized a U.S.-trained investigative unit to pursue special cases, such as political murders. A new attorney general also was appointed.

Guerrilla War. With an increase in size to more than 40,000 men and its U.S.-supplied capacity for aerial reconnaissance, bombing, and strafing, the Salvadoran Army was able to expand its offensive operations greatly. However, the rebels of the Farabundo Martí National Liberation Front (FMLN) controlled about 30 percent of the country and were able to strike effectively within the capital, San Salvador. They also briefly held Santa Ana, the country's second-largest city, on June 7. Government efforts to repopulate areas recaptured from guerrillas had very limited success. In July rebels successfully attacked a large prison and freed 149 inmates, most of them common criminals.

On June 19, urban guerrillas gunned down 13 people at three adjacent sidewalk cafés in San Salvador. A group within the Central American Revolutionary Workers' Party claimed responsibility and stated that four off-duty U.S. marines, among those killed in the attack, had been the specific targets of the raid. It was claimed that the other nine people who were killed, including two U.S. businessmen, were shot because some restaurant patrons returned fire from the guerrillas. President Ronald Reagan vowed retaliation for the killings, and the U.S. government offered a $100,000 reward for information leading to the arrest and conviction of those responsible. The guerrilla group apparently involved was hit hard by Salvadoran forces in succeeding weeks. Three suspects were arrested in August, and legal action was pending late in the year.

On October 10 the rebels killed at least 40 soldiers and wounded 70 in a predawn raid on the army's main training base. Five U.S. advisers were in the compound at the time; the guerrillas stated that capturing or killing them had been their chief objective.

Several guerrilla commanders, including two women, were captured by the army during the year. In April an important rebel leader defected; he claimed to authorities that the insurgents received most of their arms from Nicaragua.

Kidnappings. On September 10, several armed men kidnapped President Duarte's 35-year-old daughter, Inés Guadalupe Duarte Durán, as she left the university where she was studying advertising and public relations. One of her bodyguards was killed in the abduction. The FMLN eventually took responsibility. After a series of demands and complex negotiations, she and a female companion were freed on October 24, along with more than 20 abducted mayors, in return for the government's release of 22 political prisoners (including Nidia Diaz, one of the woman rebels captured earlier in the year), and provision of safe passage for 96 wounded rebels. The rebels also reportedly pledged not to kidnap relatives of political and military leaders.

The Economy. The economy, reportedly in a shambles, was heavily dependent on U.S. aid. Budget deficits mounted, and unemployment was estimated at about 40 percent. U.S. aid came to more than $450 million in fiscal 1985; planned assistance for fiscal 1986 exceeded $480 million, of which about $350 million was economic aid. The land redistribution program was beset with problems, and 20,000 peasants demonstrated in January for further allocations.

Foreign Relations. In May, President Duarte met with President Reagan in Washington and appeared before both houses of Congress. In June, President Reagan nominated Edwin Corr to replace Thomas Pickering as ambassador to El Salvador; Corr was sworn in and assumed his post in August. President Duarte visited Honduras in July to discuss with President Roberto Suazo Córdova the relocation of the hundreds of thousands of Salvadoran refugees within Honduras, incursions into El Salvador by Honduran troops, and a border dispute between the two countries. Mexico named an ambassador to El Salvador on August 28, after a five-year vacancy in the post.

See STATISTICS OF THE WORLD. L.L.P.

ENERGY. Prices for oil and natural gas slid downward in 1985, eroding support for synthetic fuel programs in the United States. Meanwhile, nuclear power plants continued to generate controversy.

Oil. Slack demand and production exceeding their quotas by some member countries continued to bedevil the Organization of Petroleum Exporting Countries. Saudi Arabia, which had cut its production drastically in response to falling demand and was the last of the OPEC members to stick to official prices, began offering discounts on October 1 in order to boost production by about 1.5 million barrels per day (b/d). Meeting in December, the oil ministers of the 13 OPEC nations finally decided to stop trying to defend the cartel's $28-a-barrel oil price by cutting output. Instead, they adopted a strategy of cutting prices, as necessary, to protect a fixed share of the world oil market. Within a few days the spot price of oil plunged more than $3 to about $25 a barrel, and a full-fledged price war that could be ruinous to oil-producing nations seemed possible. (See also ORGANIZATION OF PETROLEUM EXPORTING COUNTRIES; SAUDI ARABIA.)

Substantially lower oil prices would be welcome news in many industrialized and Third World countries that are net oil importers, especially debtor countries such as Brazil and Argentina. But lower oil prices would also mean serious difficulties for major sectors of the U.S. oil industry, such as drilling contractors, the oil field service industry, and the small independent producers, all of which were already reeling from three consecutive years of declining oil prices. Third World oil producers such as Nigeria, Venezuela, and Mexico, which are heavily dependent on oil revenues to repay foreign debts, would also face new problems.

Antinuclear activists gather before the cooling towers of the Three Mile Island nuclear power plant in Pennsylvania to protest the restart of the undamaged Unit 1, which had been shut down in 1979 when its twin, Unit 2, was severely damaged in the worst accident ever in the U.S. nuclear power industry. The U.S. Supreme Court refused to postpone the restart of Unit 1.

U.S. Energy Secretary John Herrington said in September that the United States should take no action if oil prices tumble other than to add more oil to the Strategic Petroleum Reserve, the government stockpile held for use in emergencies. There was mounting evidence, however, that a return to lower cost energy could pose serious long-term difficulties for the United States. Proved U.S. reserves of crude oil increased 2.6 percent during 1984 to 28.5 billion barrels, but most of the gain was due to enhanced recovery techniques. Such methods are expensive, and if oil prices declined greatly, much of this oil would not be economically recoverable.

Falling oil prices appeared to be at least partly responsible for an increase in U.S. consumption of petroleum during 1984. However, preliminary data indicated that domestic petroleum consumption in the first half of 1985 was about 1.5 percent lower than during the same period in 1984, primarily because of a sharp 18 percent drop in demand for residual fuel oil (a heavy fuel oil used as boiler fuel by utilities and industry). Domestic production of crude oil during the first half of 1985 was about 1 percent higher than during the same period in 1984 and net imports fell about 15 percent.

U.S. Energy Consumption. Declining world oil prices, while temporarily benefiting consumers, may also reduce the incentive to conserve energy and thereby render energy-importing countries more vulnerable to the effects of future price increases or supply disruptions. There was already some evidence that this was occurring. In the United States, after four consecutive years in which total energy consumption declined, consumption rose 5 percent in 1984. Preliminary data indicated that U.S. gasoline consumption rose 1.7 percent in 1985, although total energy consumption was down slightly.

Natural Gas. U.S. natural gas markets entered an era of uncertainty on January 1, 1985, in the wake of partial decontrol of U.S. wellhead gas prices. The Natural Gas Policy Act, passed by Congress in 1978, provided for decontrol of prices for certain categories of natural gas on January 1: specifically, gas from new offshore leases made after April 20, 1977, new onshore reservoirs, new onshore production wells more than 5,000 feet deep, and some gas sold under prior intrastate contracts. Gas from these sources amounted to about 30 percent of field sources of gas flowing to interstate pipelines. Imports provide about 4 percent of the existing supply to interstate pipelines, gas that had been decontrolled earlier furnishes about 8 percent, and gas that under the Natural Gas Policy Act remains indefinitely subject to price controls accounts for about 58 percent.

Some energy analysts were concerned about the possibility of a sharp jump in gas costs to consumers following partial decontrol. Their concern stemmed from the fact that many contracts between producers and pipeline companies, signed at an earlier time when natural gas was in short supply, contain pricing provisions that index the price of gas to No. 2 fuel oil. Rigorous enforcement of those pricing provisions would result in prices for newly deregulated gas on the order of $5.75 to $7.50 per million British thermal units (BTU). However, because of a gas surplus and lower crude oil prices, such a jump did not occur. Furthermore, the average purchase prices of most categories of gas still subject to price regulation were below the ceiling prices set for them under the Natural Gas Policy Act.

Coal. Electric utilities and other major coal users started building stocks in 1984 in anticipation of a strike by the United Mine Workers in 1985. Instead of engaging in an industry-wide strike, however, as had been its practice in the past, the UMW elected to conduct selective strikes, which were directed primarily at three major anthracite producers. Since total U.S. anthracite production is only about 4 million tons annually, the strikes had little direct effect on coal output. Nevertheless, production of bituminous coal and lignite during the first half of 1985 was lower than in the first half of 1984 because of the extraordinarily high stocks that other large coal consumers had on hand at the beginning of the year.

Synthetic Fuels. Falling oil and natural gas prices have substantially altered the economics of U.S. synthetic fuels projects and eroded support for such projects in Congress. The Great Plains coal gasification plant at Beulah, N.D., which began producing in 1984, was the nation's first commercial-scale coal gasification plant and the major project of the U.S. Synthetic Fuels Corporation (SFC). The Department of Energy had awarded the project about $1.5 billion in federal loan guarantees, but its five sponsors (American Natural Resources Company, Tenneco, Inc., Transco Energy Company, MidCon Corporation, and Pacific Lighting Corporation) threatened to

abandon the plant unless the SFC approved a package of price guarantees for the gas produced.

In July 1985 the board of directors of the SFC approved a $720 million package of price guarantees for the Great Plains plant. The SFC agreed to guarantee that the Great Plains project would receive at least $6.75 per million BTU for its synthetic natural gas through 1988 and at least $5 per million BTU thereafter, until the entire $720 million was used. The agreement was contingent, however, upon a restructuring of the sponsors' government debts—an action rejected by Energy Secretary Herrington. On August 1 the plant owners defaulted on their federal loan, and the Department of Energy assumed control. The Energy Department said it would keep the plant in service until the spring of 1986, and filed a lawsuit in an attempt to force four of the former partners to continue buying the plant's production at the prices provided for in previous agreements.

The SFC itself became a casualty of the federal budget battles in 1985. The House of Representatives voted to rescind much of its funding and then passed legislation to abolish the corporation. Although the Senate voted to continue the SFC with reduced outlays, all funding was eliminated in December by Senate-House conferees considering an appropriations bill for the rest of the 1986 fiscal year. The corporation was to expire within four months of the enactment of the bill. The SFC was established in 1980 to promote efforts to make the United States less dependent on foreign oil.

Electrical Energy. During 1984 there was an increase in the use of coal, natural gas, nuclear power, and especially nontraditional sources such as wind and solar power to generate electrical energy. These trends seemed to continue through the first half of 1985. Total electrical energy production was about 2 percent higher than in the first half of 1984. Generation from miscellaneous sources rose almost 30 percent; generation from petroleum dropped 22 percent.

Nuclear Power. The efforts of Pennsylvania's General Public Utilities Nuclear Corporation to resume operation of the undamaged Unit 1 reactor at Three Mile Island were the focus of court battles during the year. Unit 2 at Three Mile Island had been the site of the nation's worst nuclear plant accident, in 1979; Unit 1 had been closed for refueling at the time and had remained so since. In May the U.S. Nuclear Regulatory Commission gave permission for a restart of the reactor, but the state of Pennsylvania and some private groups asked a federal appeals court to block it. The court upheld the NRC's ruling in August, and opponents of the plant's operation appealed to the U.S. Supreme Court. Justice William J. Brennan, Jr., temporarily halted operation of the plant, but the Court refused to hear the appeal of the NRC's ruling, and operation resumed in early October.

In December the NRC fined a Toledo, Ohio, utility $900,000 for violations that had led on June 9 to one of the most serious incidents since the Three Mile Island accident. In the June 9 incident, the Davis-Besse nuclear power plant lost its main and backup supplies of cooling water, experiencing, in all, 12 malfunctions of safety-related components. Mechanical failure and human error were blamed. Fortunately, damage to the plant was minor,

and no radiation was released. The fine was the highest ever assessed by the commission.

The Pacific Gas and Electric Company's Diablo Canyon plant near San Luis Obispo, Calif., the subject of much controversy, finally went into operation in 1985. Unit 1 began full-power operation in May, and Unit 2 followed in October. Original estimates had put construction costs at $430 million when construction was started in 1968; the plant ended up costing some $5.6 billion.

Utilities that succeeded in getting their plants into commercial operation were facing another problem: authorities in some states were refusing to grant them rate increases sufficient to recoup their investments in the plants. Pennsylvania Power & Light was allowed to recover only taxes, depreciation, and operating costs on its Susquehanna Unit 2 plant, opened in February, because the Pennsylvania Public Utility Commission ruled that it represented excess capacity. The Missouri Public Service Commission barred Union Electric Company from including $384 million of the cost of the $3 billion Callaway plant in its rate base, citing unjustified costs in construction.   D.F.A.

Acres of solar collectors in California's Mojave Desert gather power for the world's largest solar electricity generating plant, which was dedicated in February.

ENVIRONMENT. New concerns were raised in 1985 over such familiar environmental villains as dioxins and toxic pesticides, as well as over pollution in indoor air. Acid rain remained a topic of wide concern.

Dioxin. U.S. and Canadian researchers reported in May that a low level of the poisonous pollutants known as dioxins and their toxic-chemical cousins called furans probably could be found in the fat tissues of all North Americans. Though the levels they measured were 100 to 1,000 times lower than those known to cause acute effects in humans, the scientists expressed concern over possible long-term effects of these residues. Meanwhile, a Swedish cancer researcher reported that forestry workers who had used dioxin-contaminated herbicides were more likely to develop soft-tissue sarcomas—a rare cancer. Researchers from the U.S. Food and Drug Administration found dioxin residues in fish—contamination that they suspected resulted from pentachlorophenol (a wood preservative and fungicide) and dioxin-contaminated herbicide wastes emitted as water pollutants from production facilities. Dioxins also turned up in eggs, bacon, chicken, pork chops, and beef liver, possibly from agricultural use of pentachlorophenol.

Chemical Cleanup. The Environmental Protection Agency has responsibility for identifying hazardous-waste sites and seeing that the most dangerous are cleaned up. Although the EPA has learned of more than 20,000 such sites, the General Accounting Office reported in March that the EPA still lacked a comprehensive list of sites five years after being asked to inventory them. Looking in just seven states, the GAO found 489 sites that failed to make the registry. The GAO pointed out that without a comprehensive list, the EPA could not pinpoint "national priority" sites eligible for clean up. New additions in September increased the EPA's priority list to 850 sites.

The EPA required that, by November 8, operators of toxic waste landfills have adequate insurance coverage and also have wells in place for monitoring possible contamination of groundwater. In early December, it was announced that fewer than one-third of almost 1,600 such landfills met the requirements and that the remaining landfills would have to close.

The "Superfund" created by the federal government in 1980 to clean up toxic waste sites was scheduled to expire in 1985, and both houses of Congress approved bills to fund it for five more years at much higher levels than the $5.3 billion program the Reagan administration desired. The Senate approved a $7.5 billion program to be financed by a broad-based tax on manufactured goods. Subsequently, the House approved a $10 billion program, with financing largely by a sharp increase in taxes on petroleum and chemical companies. Congress adjourned without reaching a compromise on the issue.

Pesticides and the Like. Ethylene dibromide (EDB), a cancer-causing pesticide banned from most agricultural uses in 1984, turned up in 1985 in groundwater throughout Florida; the chemical had been used extensively in citrus groves there for 40 years. Research by the University of Florida's pesticide research laboratory showed that the rate at which EDB breaks down in water depends primarily on temperature. At the 72° Fahrenheit typical of Florida's groundwater, it takes between one and two years—a long time—for half the chemical to break down. Moreover, ethylene glycol, one of the pesticide's breakdown products, may degrade further to form formaldehyde, itself a toxic chemical.

In September the EPA said it was taking off the market three fumigants used as substitutes for EDB. Sale and distribution of the three—carbon tetrachloride, carbon disulfide, and ethylene dichloride—were to cease as of December 31; farmers and grain elevator operators were to be allowed to use their existing stocks of the pesticides through June 1986. The agency said it took the action because of the chemicals' potential for causing cancer.

In December 1984 highly toxic gas had leaked from a storage tank at a Union Carbide pesticide plant in Bhopal, India; the accident killed over 2,000 people, and survivors exposed to the gas suffered respiratory and other disorders. Long-term damage to the immune system and to chromosomes also was found. The gas, methyl isocyanate (MIC), was also being produced at Union Carbide's plant in

Institute, W. Va., and the company hastened to reassure its U.S. employees and neighboring communities that a similar leak could not occur there. But on August 11 there was a serious gas leak at Institute, involving aldicarb oxime dissolved in methylene chloride. Aldicarb oxime, together with MIC, is used to make aldicarb—the active ingredient in the pesticide Temik. Although no one died, 6 employees and some 135 area residents required treatment for eye, throat, and lung irritation.

About 140 pesticides or pesticide compounds were included in a list of more than 400 highly toxic chemicals prepared by the EPA and released in December. The EPA also provided data to help local communities estimate the degree of risk involved in certain quantities of each chemical, so as to determine whether emergency planning or preventive measures should be taken to minimize the prospect of accidental releases from an industrial plant.

Chemicals in Indoor Air. Results of a new EPA study released in September showed that toxic chemicals are typically present in the air at much higher levels indoors than outdoors. It makes no difference whether one's home is next to a factory or by a country field; chances are that chemicals like benzene and tetrachloroethylene will be found in the air. If standard EPA methods of figuring risk are applied, the data suggest that each year at least several hundred Americans may die from air pollution in their homes. Researchers studied some 350 homes in Bayonne and Elizabeth, two New Jersey cities with high concentrations of industry. They found that, for all the chemicals measured, indoor levels were much higher—sometimes 100 times greater—than outdoor levels. Comparison studies in rural and less industrialized towns—Greensboro, N.C., and Devils Lake, N.D.—showed about the same concentrations of organic chemicals indoors as in New Jersey.

The researchers did not determine what the indoor sources of pollution were, but one of them speculated that the sources might be certain consumer products—for example, paints, cleaners, plastics, and cosmetics—and building materials like adhesives and insulation.

Members of the United States Forest Service, their equipment loaded onto llamas, set out to test the effects of acid rain pollution in remote areas of Colorado.

Acid Rain. New developments enlivened the continuing controversy over the potential harmful effects of acid rain—abnormally acidic precipitation. Smoke from such facilities as ironworks, chemical factories, and nonnuclear power plants often contain large amounts of pollutants—especially oxides of sulfur and nitrogen. When these pollutants react with water vapor in the atmosphere, they become acids; there is evidence that, on falling to earth, they can seriously damage the natural environment by defoliating trees and harming aquatic life.

In June scientists from the Freshwater Institute of the Canadian Department of Fisheries and Oceans in Winnipeg published the results of a unique eight-year experiment in which they steadily added sulfuric acid to a small lake. By the end of the experiment populations of crayfish, sculpin, and minnows had been devastated, and symptoms of disease had appeared in the remaining fish. Further, a study of lake acidification in Scotland that was reported in March found a clear relationship between acid levels and the growth of industry. The study examined pollen grains and planktonic algae in the datable sediment layers of an acid lake. It was found that acidification had started around 1840, as industry began to grow and farming declined.

Conclusive evidence that sulfur dioxide emissions from industrial plants can cause acid rainfall at distant locations came in a report published in August. Researchers with the Environmental Defense Fund tracked the relationship between activity at metal smelters in New Mexico, Arizona, Nevada, and Utah and acid precipitation several hundred miles downwind. The smelters altered their output—and pollution emissions—frequently between 1980 and 1983, responding to changes in copper prices and economic conditions. Meanwhile, federal acid-rain monitoring stations in Colorado, Wyoming, and Idaho found that levels of sulfur dioxide in rain and snow rose and fell in direct proportion to the changes in smelter emissions.

In a court decision in July that surprised many observers, a federal district court judge ordered the EPA to reduce within nine months the level of sulfur dioxide that may be emitted by electric utilities. These emissions, linked to acid rain in Canada, have been the subject of unsuccessful negotiations between the U.S. and Canadian governments for several years. The ruling, in response to a petition by seven northeastern states, invoked a never-before-used section of the Clean Air Act requiring the EPA to cut air pollution when it can be shown to affect another nation. The ruling was appealed late in the year. Meanwhile, in Canada, the federal government and seven eastern provinces agreed in February to cut sulfur dioxide emissions by one half over nine years and share acid rain cleanup costs.

In June the EPA modified rules that had permitted companies to meet air quality standards by dispersing pollutants over a wide area through tall smokestacks, rather than by decreasing their emission. Critics charged that such dispersion increased the problem of acid rain. The modified rules allowed credit to be given to plants for reducing air pollution only if their stacks were no higher than necessary to keep smoke plumes from being carried to the ground by downdrafts.

In August the EPA released the first findings from its National Surface Water Study, a $6 million project initiated by former EPA head William Ruckelshaus. (Ruckelshaus resigned in January; his replacement was Lee M. Thomas.) The agency reported that 9 percent of the Northeast's lakes and 20 percent of Florida's were so acidic that biological changes were noticeable. EPA officials cautioned that the data did not indicate what caused the acidity, but there were signs of growing concern in the Reagan administration over possible industrial causes.

Leaded Gasoline. The EPA issued new rules in March that would reduce by 90 percent the amount of lead that could be added to gasoline after January 1, 1986. Lead, added to gas to increase its octane level, enters the atmosphere in motor vehicle exhaust fumes. It has been linked to such medical problems as abnormalities in newborn infants. The EPA also proposed to advance from 1995 to 1988 the deadline for the elimination of all lead in gas. This proposal was open to a period of public comment.

Asbestos. The Manville Corporation in August approved the creation of a $3 billion trust fund to compensate victims of diseases caused by asbestos. A fiber once widely used in insulation materials, asbestos is now known to cause asbestosis, which cuts breathing capacity, and mesothelioma, an abdominal cancer; both diseases are often fatal. When the danger posed by products Manville once manufactured became apparent, the company was confronted with thousands of lawsuits. In 1982 it filed for bankruptcy. The trust fund, which was subject to approval by a committee of creditors and by a bankruptcy judge, would compensate thousands of victims of asbestos poisoning over the next 25 years. In November, Eagle-Pitcher Industries of Cincinnati announced a $400 million plan to cover the cost of claims filed by workers who said they suffered health problems as a result of asbestos exposure.

PCB's. The EPA took new action against polychlorinated biphenyl (PCB) compounds. PCB fluids were used for many years to insulate electrical transformers in commercial buildings. In a fire, PCB's release smoke containing dioxin. The EPA in 1977 had banned the manufacture of PCB fluids. In July 1985 the EPA ordered all PCB compounds—or the transformers containing them—removed from commercial buildings within five years. The cost of doing so was put at $400 million. Within weeks after the EPA had issued its regulations, PCB leaks were found in transformers in the Smithsonian Institution in Washington, D.C., and in the White House.   J.R. & S.M.H.

EQUATORIAL GUINEA. *See* STATISTICS OF THE WORLD.

ETHIOPIA. As a result of an ongoing, devastating drought, as many as 1 million Ethiopians were estimated to have died of famine by mid-1985. Large amounts of aid were received from abroad, although much of it was not distributed, apparently because of logistical and political problems.

Famine. The inadequacy of land transportation to distribute food aid was underscored by reports that more than 200,000 tons of grain were backed up at Ethiopia's Red Sea ports by July, because of the condition of roads in the interior and a shortage of trucks. The shortage was exacerbated by the government's policy, possibly politically motivated, of transporting Ethiopians from northern areas wracked by

civil war and drought to the less affected southern region of the country. The government also appeared to be applying political criteria to food distribution by drastically cutting back or denying food aid to areas where rebels were active.

There were reports of mass ejections of starving people from refugee camps. In late April, about 50,000 people were apparently removed from a camp at Ibnet, in the north, which was then burned down by soldiers and members of the Worker's (Communist) Party of Ethiopia, the sole political party. After refugees returned, that camp was reportedly again evacuated in July. Apparently, many people were given seeds and returned home willingly to plant crops by late summer. However, some seemed too weak to survive the journey, and the return of rain in the spring, which had encouraged the seed distribution program, ironically increased the difficulty of transporting food assistance overland. According to one report at least 50,000 refugees died in the course of being resettled to the southern area of the country at gunpoint.

Many observers attacked the Marxist regime, under leader Mengistu Haile Mariam, for its handling of the famine crisis and for its expensive and inefficient efforts to create state farms. The government continued to maintain low producer prices—thus discouraging surplus food production while keeping down prices for politically influential urbanites. Efforts also continued to encourage the cultivation of coffee for export earnings.

Foreign Relations. Despite the regime's deep-seated antipathy toward the West, the famine inevitably increased dialogue on issues of food relief and development assistance. In fiscal year 1985 the U.S. Agency for International Development supplied over $270 million in relief assistance—about a third of the total aid from governments and charitable organizations. Soviet aid to Ethiopia continued to be mainly in the form of heavy military assistance.

Ethiopia's ties with Sudan were complicated by several developments, including the huge wave of Ethiopian refugees fleeing across the border into camps in Sudan and the shipments of relief materials through Sudan to Ethiopia's rebel-held areas in Eritrea and Tigré. Another

A devastating drought and the resulting famine caused large numbers of Ethiopians to flee to shelters such as the Kwiha refugee camp near Mekele.

source of friction was the airlift to Israel, during several months, of Ethiopian Jews, who had crossed into Sudan on their own. The operation, carried out by the Israelis, was canceled in January after it was publicly disclosed and the Ethiopian government vehemently objected. (The remaining Ethiopian Jews in Sudan were flown to Israel in March, in an operation run by the CIA.) After a military coup in Sudan in April, relations with the Sudan improved markedly, and diplomatic relations between the two countries were reestablished in June.

Ties with Libya weakened when Libyan leader Muammar al-Qaddafi ended his support of the Western Sahara Polisario group, which Mengistu supported strongly. Other African countries appeared increasingly restive about Ethiopia's establishment of a Marxist state. Nonetheless, an agreement was signed in March with Kenya for joint consultations on border problems.

Civil War. Armed secessionists in Eritrea continued to hold the countryside and to do intermittent battle with the Ethiopian Army, at great cost to the latter. In April an Eritrean rebel group revealed that secret peace talks had been held with government, representa-tives, but with inconclusive results. The secessionist movement in Tigré, just south of Eritrea, was somewhat quieter during the year because of the overwhelming influence of the famine.

See STATISTICS OF THE WORLD. R.E.B.

EUROPEAN COMMUNITIES, a supranational organization comprising the European Economic Community (EEC), the European Atomic Energy Community, and the European Coal and Steel Community. These may be referred to jointly as the European Community (EC), or Common Market. In 1985 the ten members were Belgium, Denmark, France, Great Britain, Greece, Ireland, Italy, Luxembourg, the Netherlands, and West Germany.

New Members. On June 12, Spain and Portugal signed a treaty of accession making them (after ratification by their own parliaments and those of the ten EC nations) official members of the EC as of January 1, 1986. The signing followed years of difficult negotiations and came about only when the last remaining opponent, Greece, withdrew its veto. Greece had feared competition for its wine and other agricultural products, but was mollified when the EC agreed to offer $1.5 billion in aid grants to Greece over a seven year period.

Milan Summit. This latest expansion of the EC came at a difficult time for the organization. At the Milan summit of EC leaders in June, there were evident profound divisions within the body. One faction, led by West Germany and France, fearing that the Community would be overrun economically by the United States and Japan, especially in the field of high technology, wanted to expand the EC and move quickly toward closer economic and political unity. This faction wished to amend the founding Treaty of Rome (1957), doing away with the single-nation veto, instituting majority rule, and eventually moving toward common foreign and defense policies. Another group, however, led by Britain and including Denmark and Greece, wanted to slow the integration process and retain the veto. The latter countries refused, for example, either to link the pound sterling with the European Monetary System or to abolish frontier formalities, as most of the other Community members had done.

Despite the sour mood overlying the Milan meeting, the EC leaders did reach agreement on several proposals. To begin with, they approved a general schedule leading to complete economic unity by 1992 (a pipedream, many analysts thought). They passed a package of measures, designed to benefit citizens of the Community, that provided for a common driver's license, shared television programs, and educational exchanges. The leaders also urged Japan to reduce its trade surplus by purchasing more goods from the EC; to impress the Japanese with their seriousness, they imposed anti-dumping duties of 45 percent on Japanese ball bearings. Perhaps most significantly, the ten made arrangements for a special conference in Paris in July, at which the European Research Agency was created. "Eureka," as it was promptly dubbed, was intended to move the Community into a position where it could play a role in high-technology production for the U.S. Strategic Defense Initiative, better known as "Star Wars."

Luxembourg Summit. At a two-day meeting in Luxembourg in early December, the ten EC leaders sought to narrow their differences over reorganization of the Community's structure. The result was a compromise agreement providing modest changes to strengthen the EC. The measures adopted, embodying the first changes ever in the organization's founding charter, provided for speedier elimination of remaining trade barriers among members by allowing more decisions to be made by a majority, rather than by a unanimous, vote. The agreement also called for closer coordination of foreign policies among member nations and committed members to the general goal of monetary unification. It did not, however, provide for a substantial increase in the decision-making powers of the European Parliament and fell short of the calls of some members for a major surrender of individual authority to Community decisions.

South Africa. In September, the ten EC nations, decrying South Africa's apartheid policy, imposed certain sanctions against the Pretoria government; they included curbs on exports of arms or sensitive materials and an end to all military or nuclear cooperation. A month before, EC members had recalled their ambassadors to South Africa in protest against the state of emergency declared in that country.

See also articles on individual countries mentioned. J.O.S.

F

FASHION. After a fall and winter characterized by the masculine approach to women's clothes, spring 1985 ushered in a bumper crop of gentler, more feminine fashions. By fall, women's designers were firmly committed to the return of the female form. Spring and summer menswear was generally conservative; fall menswear was dressier and more "upscale."

Femininity and Color. Color—bright, hot, and often paired in eye-popping combinations—

A luxurious curve-revealing gown, touched with ruffles at the hem and dramatically highlighted with contrasting black, was featured in Diane Von Furstenberg's first couture collection. The designer, staging a comeback, was noted for her enormously popular printed jersey wrap dresses in the 1970's.

was a striking part of the spring and summer clothes offered by many of America's and Europe's trendiest designers. Bright yellow and hot red were popular. Color extended from head to toe, with a proliferation of colored, textured, and patterned hosiery over shoes that combined vibrantly hued leather.

Prints, also in assertive colorations, were plentiful in the spring and summer, ranging from luscious chintz florals, cabbage roses, and hand-painted or batik florals to pulsating jungle prints, especially effective in the new sarong-wrapped skirts and shorts. For evening, black-and-white prints lent drama to some designs, but color also was popular.

Silhouettes moved in two directions at once. While many designers cut close to the body in skimming, curve-revealing lines for both day and night, two other trends—the big shirt and the flowing pajama pant—were also popular favorites. The pajama look ranged from folkloric to urbane and sophisticated. Meanwhile, oversized shirts, paired with narrow pants or short fitted skirts, were suitably relaxed for summer in the collections of many designers. A related look, which teamed an oversized, shoulder-accented jacket with shorts, skirts, or cropped pants, was eventually translated into the big look for fall apparel.

The Female Form Returns. By fall, curves and stylish, clean-cut lines defined the feminine body without confining or restricting it. The general consensus was that shoulders ought to

be big, bold, but softly rounded, while everything below them should taper sensuously. With more than a passing glance at the 1950's, designers created clothing with whittled waists,

Fashion Gone to Seed

One way to get back to nature is to wear nature on your back—in the form of a living grass suit created by artist Bill Harding. The enterprising Ohioan creates costumes for outdoor "performance" projects; besides attracting attention, he says, they give the wearer a "warm, womblike feeling" and express "the stubbornness of nature—that grass will grow anywhere." Making these grass garments is simple: just spray ordinary clothing with high-tack adhesive, sprinkle it with rye seeds, wrap it in plastic, and water it twice a day for around 12 days. Harding has sown outfits for the *Tonight Show* and for a Japanese talk show, as well as for events in Kansas City, Los Angeles, and elsewhere. He recently obtained a grant from the Illinois Arts Council to fund a "suit-in" in which 30 performers paraded through downtown Chicago. Jumpsuits, form-fitting dresses, hats, shoes, even a baby's outfit were transformed by the artist's green thumb into fashions requiring mowing rather than ironing. A conventionally dressed viewer could well be jealous; after all, the grass always looks greener on the other guy's suit.

curvaceous hips, and a sophisticated softness often achieved by the use of jersey or crepe. Women's suits and jackets lost all hint of masculinity.

Big sweaters with padded shoulders prevailed as the most popular toppers for the season's shapely skirts and pants. A virtual unknown on the fashion scene last year, stirrup-footed stretch pants—straight off the ski slopes of the 1950's—were seen everywhere, day and night, and provided the perfect foil for the season's big-yet-body-conscious tops. Softly pleated pants that tapered to the ankle were an easier-to-wear alternative. Brooches, belts, earrings, bracelets, and other striking accessories were also important to fall and winter fashions, as long as they were big, bold, and most often, gold. Ornamentation reached its peak in the season's evening wear, which comprised some of the most sumptuous, extravagant styles yet shown.

Conservative Menswear. Spring and summer menswear tended to be crisp, comfortable, and conservatively "correct" in its styling. Suits assumed a traditional guise with peaked or notched lapels, quietly defined shoulders, and narrow but barely suppressed waists. Banker's gray and navy predominated, with pinstripes, pindots, and subtle houndstooth patternings, although pale brown and even black both made surprise appearances. Bold, vigorous stripes were the leading pattern for shirts, which often sported contrasting collars.

Men's suits remained conservative but became dressier for the fall—modern, yet classic in their styling. Gray flannel, in shades from pale to charcoal and sometimes tinged with blue, seemed to be the leading fabric for the seasonal harvest of upscale suits. Subtle stripes added new depth and interest. Deep blue suits were also extremely successful. Substantial shoulders, nipped waists, and comfortably loose

French couturier Jean-Louis Scherrer struck a sophisticated note in his fall 1985 collection: among his designs, a short, slim black sheath worn beneath a swaggering, fire-engine red plaid coat (far left). Meanwhile, the loose look was big during 1985, in the form of oversize shirts and pajama pants; designer Yamamoto added a folkloric flavor to his brightly colored pajama look (left).

trousers comprised the predominant silhouette for virtually all suits.

Casual wear showed more diversity. The ubiquitous uniforms of track suits and sweat clothes began to be challenged by big, slouchy sweaters, flannel shirts, suspenders, cardigans (often with the look of blazers), stadium coats, peacoats, and other weekend trappings of bygone years. Colors such as teal, amethyst, and fuchsia continued to appear in sweaters and sweater vests, often in assertive abstract designs.   E.J.G.

FIJI. See STATISTICS OF THE WORLD.

FINLAND. Finland's economy continued its moderate recovery in 1985 from a slump earlier in the decade. The nation's real gross domestic product was expected to increase by 4.5 percent (compared with 2.5 percent in 1982). Unemployment was projected at 5.5 percent and inflation at 6.25 percent.

The contest between moderate "Eurocommunist" and hard-line Stalinist factions within the Finnish Communist Party deepened. In late 1984 and early 1985 the moderates, in control nationally, created separate party organizations in districts dominated by the Stalinists. The minority Stalinists boycotted a party congress in Helsinki in March, at which Arvo Aalto was unanimously reelected party chairman. In October, eight Stalinist district party organizations were expelled from the party.

Finnish authorities launched a search in early January for a Soviet missile that crashed in northern Finland in late December 1984, during Soviet naval maneuvers in the Barents Sea. The missile had violated both Norwegian and Finnish air space, and Soviet officials expressed regret for the incident. Debris from the object was recovered in Lake Inari and returned to the Soviet Union. Finnish investigators concluded in June that the missile, identified as an SS-N3 Shaddock naval target missile, had strayed because of an electrical defect in its guidance system and then had crashed when its fuel was exhausted.

On June 7 the South Lebanon Army seized 24 Finnish soldiers serving in the United Nations Interim Force in Lebanon. The SLA, largely Christian and supported by Israel, charged that other Finns, earlier the same day, had turned over 11 SLA members, all Shiite Mus-

lims, to the militia of the Shiite Muslim organization Amal. The Finns contended that the 11, whose release was demanded by the SLA, had defected. Three of the captive Finns were released the next day, and on June 15, after an International Red Cross representative convinced the SLA commander that the 11 SLA members had indeed defected, the 21 remaining hostages were released.

See STATISTICS OF THE WORLD.   M.D.H.

FISHERIES. See AGRICULTURE AND FOOD SUPPLIES.

FLORIDA. See STATISTICS OF THE WORLD.

FORMOSA. See TAIWAN.

FRANCE. The auguries in 1985 remained unfavorable for the Socialist government of President François Mitterrand, as public confidence continued to decline in the face of a faltering economy and an uncertain political future. The sinking by French intelligence agents of a ship belonging to the antinuclear group Greenpeace led to the government's worst crisis since it came to power in 1981. Meanwhile, the government confronted a growing independence movement in the French Pacific territory of New Caledonia. Early in the year regional elections saw the Socialists attract less than half of the vote.

Greenpeace Affair. French nuclear testing in the South Pacific continued to be the target of opposition from the antinuclear and environmentalist movement Greenpeace, as well as from nations in the region. In midyear the Greenpeace flagship *Rainbow Warrior* sailed to New Zealand to lead a flotilla into the French test site around Mururoa Atoll, near Tahiti. While berthed in Auckland harbor, the *Rainbow Warrior* was mysteriously sunk on July 10 by limpet mines attached to its hull; a Greenpeace photographer on board was killed. Soon after, New Zealand authorities arrested a man and a woman in connection with the bombing; the pair were identified as French army officers attached to France's intelligence and counterespionage agency, the General Directorate for External Security (DGSE).

An official French investigation concluded in late August—to pronounced skepticism— that the suspects apparently had nothing to do with the sinking and that no government order had been issued to sink the ship. French newspapers called the report a cover-up, and on September 19, Mitterrand, troubled by allegations in the press, "whose accuracy we were unable to appreciate because of the failure of the competent authorities to obtain the necessary information," ordered changes in the personnel and structure of the DGSE. The next day Defense Minister Charles Hernu resigned, and the intelligence agency's head, Admiral Pierre Lacoste, was dismissed.

On September 22, Prime Minister Laurent Fabius finally admitted that the *Rainbow Warrior* had been sunk by DGSE agents. Four DGSE agents and a suspended army officer were indicted a few days later, on charges of disclosing secret information to the press about the operation. In November the two French agents arrested in July pleaded guilty in New Zealand to reduced charges of manslaughter; they were each sentenced to ten years in prison. French Foreign Minister Roland Dumas said negotiations between the two countries had led to the plea, which meant there would be no trial or presentation of evidence possibly

compromising to the French government. New Zealand authorities denied that any deal had been made. In December, France and Greenpeace agreed to negotiate on damages to be paid by France.

New Caledonian Independence Issue. Confrontations heightened between the native Melanesian population, known as Kanakas, and European settlers on the French South Pacific island of New Caledonia. The island has important strategic value for France; it lies in the general area where France conducts its nuclear tests and is an important source of raw materials, particularly nickel. The militantly proindependence Kanaka Socialist National Liberation Front (FLNKS), under the leadership of Jean-Marie Tjibaou, had led a Kanaka boycott of the November 1984 Territorial Assembly elections, which saw anti-independence forces win an overwhelming victory. A period of sporadic violence followed, and on January 7 the French government announced a peace plan, devised by a newly appointed French high commissioner. It proposed that New Caledonia become an independent state linked to France by a special "treaty of association," which would allow the French government to retain control of defense, public order, finances, and broadcasting and would grant special status to the capital city of Nouméa, where most of the European settlers live. In a referendum projected for July the island's residents would choose between independence and remaining part of France.

The main European political group promptly denounced the French plan as a sellout of the settlers' interests, and sporadic armed clashes and several assassinations of Kanakas and whites occurred in mid-January. The territorial government declared a state of emergency; French military and riot police were sent in to reinforce soldiers and police already in place. When two FLNKS leaders were killed by police under suspicious circumstances, Tjibaou also came out flatly against the peace plan. His announcement provoked more violence. On a visit to the island, Mitterrand reiterated his support for the plan.

On April 25, Prime Minister Fabius announced that the referendum would be postponed until the end of 1987. Meanwhile, the

Hand-picked Employees

Some French job-seekers are seeing the handwriting on the wall these days—when their own handwriting is analyzed by a graphologist and they are declared unfit for hiring. Most of France's largest companies now use handwriting analysis to help them decide whom to hire. They find this handy method cheaper and just as reliable as psychological testing: a study at the Laboratoires Upsa showed that 80 percent of the new employees turned out exactly as their handwriting analyses had predicted. One executive claims that every time someone was hired who had done badly on the handwriting test, the individual failed at the job within six months. Graphology is becoming an accepted science in France: graphologists study part-time for four to five years; and there is a journal, *La Graphologie,* and a French Graphological Society with 6,000 members. No single element of handwriting fully reveals an applicant's character; the graphologist must look at all p's and q's before writing off a candidate or handing the lucky person a job.

The French government faced international criticism when it was revealed that its intelligence agents had carried out the July 10 bombing of the Rainbow Warrior (below), flagship of the antinuclear group Greenpeace, while it was docked in Auckland, New Zealand, on its way to a French nuclear test site. Minister of Defense Charles Hernu (far right) resigned as a result of the affair; he was replaced by Paul Quilès (speaking into the microphone).

Territorial Assembly would be abolished, to be replaced by four regional councils together constituting a Congress. Elections for the Congress were conducted on September 29 amid heavy security. French loyalists won a majority of the popular vote and most of the seats, but the Kanakas won control of three of the four regions.

Regional Elections. In March every French department held elections for local officials. Normally such elections do not attract much attention or a large voter turnout. But the sagging popularity of the Mitterrand government and the vigorous attacks on the government from the right-wing opposition parties turned the March elections into a kind of referendum on the regime and a harbinger of what might happen in the 1986 parliamentary elections. The news for the Socialists and their one-time allies, the Communists, was not good. In 1981 the two parties had gained an absolute majority of the French electorate. In the March elections, however, candidates of the left won less than 40 percent of the total vote, while the candidates of the right increased their share by 10–15 percent. Some observers, projecting the results of the elections into 1986, predicted that the Socialists would lose their majority in the National Assembly and the Communists would suffer losses even more catastrophic than those of 1985. The result would be a

The Pont Neuf, Paris's oldest bridge spanning the Seine, was wrapped in 430,000 square feet of luminous sandcolored cloth by the visionary artist, Bulgarian-born Christo, with a crew of hundreds of French assistants. For the wrappers, the experience was exhilarating and fun; for the spectators, the ancient bridge took on a new, transitory beauty.

Socialist president and a right-wing Assembly, raising the likelihood of a deadlock in government.

Electoral Reform. In a move designed to cut the Socialists' possible losses in 1986, the Mitterrand government introduced a new voting system in April. Under the old system, candidates faced each other individually in single-member constituencies in a two-stage vote. The new arrangement established a single vote, with parliamentary seats to be distributed to political parties roughly in proportion to their total vote.

Economic Developments. France continued to suffer from a sluggish economy. Economic growth—which, as measured by the gross national product, had been slower than in most of the other European Economic Community countries—was expected to be only about 1 percent in 1985. The government's deflationary policy, adopted in 1984, reduced inflation to an annual rate of less than 6.5 percent—nearly half of what it had been two years before. But the reduction was purchased at the price of severe unemployment, which stood at more than 10 percent.

Because France had yet to secure a strong position on the world market and because more unemployment loomed in the future, President Mitterrand consistently refused to discuss the elimination of barriers to free trade. At the economic summit of the world's seven

leading industrial democracies in Bonn in early May, he rebuffed U.S. President Ronald Reagan's efforts to set a timetable for a worldwide conference on international trade. However, late in the year trade talks were scheduled for September 1986.

Sanctions Against South Africa. Several days after the government of South Africa declared a state of emergency in late July, in the wake of persistent, often violent demonstrations against apartheid, France recalled its ambassador from Pretoria and suspended all new investment in that country. In May, Prime Minister Fabius had announced that France would impose economic sanctions against South Africa in 18 months unless its human rights record improved markedly. In explaining his government's decision to move up the timetable, Fabius said the South African emergency decrees had only reinforced the repression of blacks by whites. The suspension of new investment in South Africa was no small matter for France; its current investment stood at about $1.6 billion. France was buying 25 percent of its uranium imports from South Africa. That country was also an important source of imported coal and an equally important market for the French electronics industry.

Soviet-bloc Visits. Mikhail Gorbachev went to France in October for his first visit to the West since becoming Soviet leader. During the four-day stay he unveiled new arms control proposals and expressed a willingness to negotiate separate arms accords with Paris and London.

Poland's leader, General Wojciech Jaruzelski, made a controversial visit to Paris in early December, where he met with Mitterrand. Although Mitterrand claimed that the meeting gave him the chance to broach the subjects of religious and worker problems in Poland, it prompted an outcry from a wide spectrum of politicians—including members of the Socialist Party, which has ties with Poland's Solidarity

movement. Joining the fray was Fabius, who declared himself "personally troubled" by the incident.

Department Store Blasts. On December 7, almost 40 people were wounded when incendiary devices exploded in two Parisian department stores. Anonymous callers implicated several groups, but because of the crude nature of the devices, authorities believed they had been planted by a lone individual.

See STATISTICS OF THE WORLD.   S.E.

G

GABON. *See* STATISTICS OF THE WORLD.

GAMBIA, THE. *See* STATISTICS OF THE WORLD.

GEORGIA. *See* STATISTICS OF THE WORLD.

GERMAN DEMOCRATIC REPUBLIC or EAST GERMANY. The Communist Party government continued efforts in 1985 to keep the population of the German Democratic Republic (GDR) politically quiescent. Contacts with the West increased during the year.

Internal Affairs. Party chief Erich Honecker took steps to improve relations with churches and minimize the chance of their becoming an opposition force. In February he met with the chairman of the Federation of Protestant Churches and reaffirmed his 1970 promise that churches could pursue religious activities as long as they did not interfere in politics. Honecker also reached out to East Germany's 1.2 million practicing Catholics when he visited the pope in Rome; a born Catholic and now an atheist, he reportedly told the pope he did not accept Marxist dogma as to the negative social impact of religion.

Soviet leaders attempted to keep East Germans from becoming politically restive by allowing them the highest standard of living of any Eastern bloc state. National income continued to grow, while prices of necessities were kept constant. Quality consumer items such as color television sets, however, remained expensive and scarce.

Contacts with the West. The British foreign minister visited East Berlin in April and the French prime minister went there in June; these

Dresden's legendary Semper Opera reopened on the 40th anniversary of its destruction, with a performance attended by East German leaders and foreign dignitaries. The reconstruction of the opera house, devastated in an Anglo-American bombing during World War II, was a seven-year effort.

were first-time visits for Western officials of such high rank. Conversely, Honecker's trip to Rome, where he met with the Italian prime minister and president as well as with the pope, was his first journey ever into a NATO country.

Death of a U.S. Major. An international incident occurred in March near the East German town of Ludwigslust, when a Soviet sentry shot a U.S. Army major, Arthur Nicholson, who was part of a 14-man military liaison mission in the GDR. (The British and French maintain similar missions there, and the Soviets are allowed about 60 soldiers in West Germany. The real function of all the missions is to gather military information, which is legal as long as no one enters a prohibited area.) When shot, he was photographing Soviet military equipment at a tank depot. Until February the area had been off limits to Americans, but at the time of the incident it was not. The major's driver was not allowed to give him first aid, and in an hour Nicholson bled to death. The Soviets refused an apology or an indemnity for the major's family, but the soldier responsible was apparently court-martialed.

Emigration. In January the last of 168 East Germans who had taken refuge in the West German embassy in Prague, Czechoslovakia, returned to East Germany, following an agreement between the two Germanys that promised them permission to emigrate (which they later received) if they applied through legal channels. However, emigration levels during the year were considerably lower than in 1984, when 40,000 East Germans were allowed to move to the West.

See STATISTICS OF THE WORLD.   R.J.W.

GERMANY, FEDERAL REPUBLIC OF, *or* **WEST GERMANY.** A spy scandal, controversy over the U.S. "Star Wars" program, and continued high unemployment were among the developments that made 1985 a difficult year for West German Chancellor Helmut Kohl, leader of the Christian Democratic Union (CDU), which was the senior partner in the governing coalition. A body identified as that of Nazi death camp doctor Josef Mengele was exhumed in Brazil.

Defection of a Counterspy. Hans-Joachim Tiedge, a senior official in the West German counterintelligence agency, defected to East Germany in August, apparently taking with him a list of 160 West German agents working there. Tiedge was the third government employee to defect in a three-week period, and the incident was a serious embarrassment to the Bonn government. As a result of the Tiedge defection, Chancellor Kohl fired the former chief of Tiedge's agency, Heribert Hellenbroich, from his new position as head of the much larger West German intelligence-gathering agency. Hellenbroich had kept Tiedge on despite knowledge of the latter's public drunkenness, mental depression, and mounting indebtedness.

Star Wars. A major political controversy concerned the degree of support that West Germany should demonstrate for President Ronald Reagan's Strategic Defense Initiative, or "Star Wars" plan, to construct a defensive shield against Soviet nuclear missiles using lasers and other technologies. The conservative wing of the CDU and the party's Bavarian affiliate, the Christian Social Union (CSU), favored a strong West German commitment and participation, both for defense reasons and for the opportunity to share in new technologies. The opposition Social Democratic Party (SPD) and the Greens (an environmental, antinuclear party) were against participation, fearing it would harm nuclear disarmament talks and believing that any funds would be better spent on social or environmental programs.

In April the Bundestag (lower house of Parliament) debated the issue, and the chancellor tried to satisfy all sides in a statement committing his government to a conditional "yes." His government would "explore the possibilities of participation." A top priority would be "a drastic reduction in the nuclear offensive systems on both sides," and Bonn would have to be a full partner in the exchange of technological knowledge. In December the Kohl government announced it would negotiate with the United States on a role for West German industry in the program, but with no participation or funding by the government.

Bitburg Controversy. President Reagan went to West Germany in May to attend a seven-nation economic summit in Bonn and to celebrate the 40th anniversary of the end of World War II in Europe. Normally on such visits U.S.

178

presidents go to former concentration camps and lay wreaths at memorials to victims of Nazism. Kohl wanted a wreath placed at a military cemetery instead, as a gesture of reconciliation between the two nations. The intended visit to the military cemetery at Bitburg aroused a political storm in the United States, however, especially among Jewish and veterans' organizations. In addition to other soldiers buried there, the cemetery contained the graves of 49 members of the Waffen SS, the military arm of the most vicious of Hitler's organizations. In April a majority of both houses of Congress appealed to the president not to go to Bitburg, and a majority in the U.S. House of Representatives asked Chancellor Kohl to release Reagan from his commitment. Kohl did not do so, however. Although a visit to the site of the former Bergen-Belsen concentration camp was added to Reagan's itinerary, the president went through with the ceremony in Bitburg. Kohl's critics charged that the chancellor had indebted himself and the Federal Republic to President Reagan. In a heated Bundestag debate later in May, the SPD opposition leader, Hans-Jochen Vogel, specifically argued that at the economic summit the chancellor had sold out the Federal Republic to the United States on the Star Wars issue.

Elections. West Berlin once had the image of a dying city, as it steadily lost population. In 1985, however, the city was in the midst of a small-scale boom, largely as a result of a changed climate between the two Germanys and the innovative industrial policies of the administration of CDU Mayor Eberhard Diepgen. In March elections, West Berlin voters confirmed the governing CDU/Free Democratic Party (FDP) coalition with 55 percent of the vote. At the same time in the Saarland, however, with unemployment at 14 percent, the CDU/FDP coalition was ousted by the SPD, which won 27 of 51 seats in the state legislature, polling 49 percent of the popular vote.

The CDU also suffered a major defeat in May elections in North Rhine-Westphalia. Under a popular SPD premier, the SPD enlarged its 1980 majority, winning 52 percent of the vote and 125 out of 227 seats. The CDU fell to 36.5 percent, its lowest share ever in the industrial heartland of West Germany. Kohl had campaigned hard for his party there, but the customarily positive "chancellor effect" on the voters did not take place. The Bitburg and Star Wars controversies contributed in part to the CDU defeat. Also, as in the Saarland, a major issue was unemployment. North Rhine-Westphalia's rate of 11 percent was some two points above the national average.

Terrorism. Terrorists of the leftist Red Army Faction, descended from the Baader-Meinhof gang of the 1970's, were active during the year. The RAF took responsibility for the February assassination of Ernst Zimmermann, chief executive of West Germany's largest manufacturer of airplane, tank, and truck engines. In August the group murdered a soldier to get his identification card, which was used to drive a car loaded with explosives into the U.S. Rhein-Main air base. It exploded next to the headquarters building, killing 2 Americans and wounding 20 other people. A bombing at the Frankfurt airport in June killed 3 people and wounded more than 40 others; the RAF did not claim responsibility in this incident.

In March and April, five leading members of the RAF received multiple life sentences, primarily for a series of killings in 1977. In July, 6 core members of the group were arrested in Frankfurt, leaving 9 known members still at large, plus another 250 or so sympathizers, according to police estimates.

In November a car-bomb exploded at an American military shopping complex in northern Frankfurt, wounding 35 people. No group took responsibility for the attack, but West German police announced that they were seeking two Arabs who purchased the car used.

Economic Developments. The West German economy was expanding at a rate of 2.5 percent in the summer, compared with 2.6 percent in all of 1984. About half of the growth was attributed to booming exports aided by a strong U.S. dollar. The trade surplus rose substantially early in the year. Unemployment, though, was not affected, becoming even more severe. In January, because of an exceedingly bad winter, it reached 10.6 percent, its highest level since 1948. In the summer it was still about 9 percent. Consumer prices in July were rising at an annual rate of 2.3 percent, slightly below the 2.4 percent for 1984 as a whole.

179

The search for Josef Mengele ended when Romeu Tuma, of the Brazilian federal police (in dark suit), announced that a skeleton found in a grave near São Paulo had been confirmed by forensic experts as that of the murderous Nazi death camp doctor. Below are pictures of Mengele, from before the war and at stages during the 40-year international manhunt.

Josef Mengele. An international team of forensic experts confirmed on June 21 that a skeleton exhumed earlier in the month from a cemetery near São Paulo in Brazil was that of infamous Nazi Dr. Josef Mengele. As chief physician at the Auschwitz-Birkenau extermination camp in Poland during World War II, Mengele selected the few who would be spared as camp laborers from among the trainloads of victims, mostly Eastern European Jews, sent to the camp to be gassed. He picked out 1,500 sets of twins in order to test some of his bizarre racial theories. Few survived his experiments.

According to German-speaking émigrés from Austria and Hungary residing in São Paulo, Mengele, who left Germany shortly after the war, lived in Argentina and Paraguay before settling in Brazil under an assumed identity in 1961. He died in February 1979 at the age of 67; while swimming at the beach resort of Bertioga he suffered a stroke and drowned. His remains were located about a week after West German police found letters from the émigrés in the home of the retired manager of the Mengele family farm equipment factory in Günzburg, Bavaria.

Hitler Diaries Case. Two men accused of fraud in the 1983 Hitler diaries hoax were convicted and sentenced to prison terms on July 8. Gerd Heidemann, a former reporter for the magazine *Stern* who had obtained the documents for the magazine, received a sentence of four years and eight months. Konrad Kujau, a dealer in Nazi memorabilia who had forged the diaries, received four years and six months. Both were freed pending appeal. An accomplice was sentenced to eight months' probation.

See STATISTICS OF THE WORLD.   R.J.W.

GHANA. *See* STATISTICS OF THE WORLD.

GREAT BRITAIN. The government of Prime Minister Margaret Thatcher (see biography in PEOPLE IN THE NEWS) received the capitulation of the National Union of Mineworkers early in 1985, after a long, bitter, and often violent strike. The economy showed signs of revival, but over 3 million Britons were still without work. Discontent among disadvantaged youth helped fuel riots in depressed urban areas during late summer and early fall. In November, the British and Irish governments signed an accord giving the latter a consultative role in Northern Ireland.

Coal Strike and Its Aftermath. The first week of the year was the 43rd week of a coal miners' strike that was beginning to crumble, as increasing numbers of striking miners, individually and in small groups, straggled back to work. Arthur Scargill, president of the National Union of Mineworkers (NUM), and his left-wing executive committee had failed to bring the productive Nottinghamshire coalfield out on strike. They also declined to hold a national ballot among miners, either before or during the strike. By late February, the National Coal Board, against which the union had pitted itself, was able to claim that most of the miners were at work. Scargill and his executive were still struggling to avoid making the commitment that the board had demanded—acceptance in principle of the need to close down unprofitable mines. But in the end, on March 5, the exhausted NUM executive simply ordered a return to work, and the National Coal Board proceeded with its program of shutting down uneconomical mines. The National Coal Board, the miners' union, and the various associated industries had by then suffered losses totaling more than $4.5 billion. Criminal charges arising out of the strike numbered more than 10,000, and some 1,400 police officers were injured during the walkout.

Urban Riots. A series of violent disturbances broke out in urban areas in September. On September 9–10 in Birmingham, Britain's second-largest city, in a district populated mostly by West Indian and Asian immigrants, at least 137 people were taken into custody during clashes between hundreds of youths and some 1,400 police officers; two people were killed.

On September 28–29 in Brixton, a predominantly black district in south London, black youths, joined by whites, looted and burned shops and set more than 50 vehicles on fire.

According to the authorities, 26 rioters and 10 police officers were injured; between 150 and 200 people were arrested. These clashes were followed on October 1–2 by riots in Liverpool, Britain's third-largest city, where some 300 youths stoned a police station and set cars ablaze, and in Peckham, an area in south London, where about 200 youths threw gasoline bombs and looted shops. On October 6 rioting flared in Tottenham, a district in the northern part of London. Hundreds of black and white youths, armed with shotguns and gasoline bombs, battled with police, setting buildings and cars on fire. During the rioting a constable was stabbed to death and as many as 40 other police officers were wounded, 4 of them seriously.

The next day, in response to the increased mob violence, the police warned that they were prepared to use plastic bullets and tear gas in similar civil disturbances. The government supported the police, contending that the disturbances had been "the result of criminal actions." Critics, however, pointed to what they said were deeper causes. Since 1982 aid to depressed urban areas had been cut by as much as 30 percent, and unemployment among the young had increased significantly; in Brixton it doubled between 1981 and 1985, to about 50 percent.

Party Politics. In May elections for county councils, the Conservatives lost heavily, the Laborites made up some ground, and the middle-of-the-road Liberal-Social Democratic Alliance, composed of the Liberal Party and the Social Democratic Party, scored many gains. The Conservatives lost control of 9 out of a total of 47 counties, while members of the Alliance held the balance of power in 26 other counties. The proportions of votes cast confirmed the suggestion of opinion polls that support for the Conservative Party had been suffering a steep decline.

Some Tories blamed the prime minister for failure to take direct action in alleviating unemployment and providing adequate services. Their misgivings were reinforced by the results of a by-election in Brecon and Radnor, Wales, on July 4, when the Conservatives not only lost the seat but fell into third place, behind the victorious Alliance and Labor.

The world's most famous insurer, Lloyd's of London, is shedding its 18th-century image to achieve a gleaming high-tech look in its new headquarters, designed by avant-garde British architect Richard Rogers. Lloyd's gloved and hatted doorman stands in front of the new building, scheduled to open in 1986.

In September, Thatcher shuffled her cabinet. Norman Tebbit, secretary of state for trade and industry, was appointed chairman of the Conservative Party and given wide latitude to present government policy in a favorable light to the public. Leon Brittan, the home secretary, was demoted to Tebbit's former post. Lord Young of Graffham, a protégé of the prime minister, was given enhanced responsibilities as the new employment minister. The person

he displaced, Tom King, was made secretary of state for Northern Ireland, replacing Douglas Hurd, who was put in charge of the Home Office.

The Economy. At the root of the Thatcher government's difficulties was the high unemployment rate, which was running at more than 13 percent late in the year. Neil Kinnock, leader of the Labor Party, charged that the government's program, as presented to Parliament in November, failed to address the issue of unemployment, concentrating instead on law and order (in the wake of the urban riots), privatization of industries, and reform of Britain's welfare system. Outside of unemployment, however, the economy showed signs of maintaining its recovery. The gross domestic produce was growing at an annual rate of 3.5 percent, inflation was relatively low (about 6 percent), and average earnings were keeping ahead of the inflation rate.

The low value of the British pound in relation to the U.S. dollar was a cause of concern to government and industry alike. The exchange rate moved between slightly over 1.00 dollar to the pound early in the year to above 1.40 late in the year—still a very low level for the pound. During a visit to Washington in February, Thatcher, in addressing the U.S. Congress, had voiced concern about the damage the strong dollar was doing to the world economy. In September, amid strong U.S. protectionist pressures, central bankers and finance ministers from the United States, Britain, and other major industrial nations agreed on steps aimed at lowering the dollar, which helped bolster the pound.

Foreign Policy. The Thatcher government continued to enjoy a close relationship with the Reagan administration. In late October, Defense Secretary Michael Heseltine reached preliminary agreement with his American counterpart, Caspar Weinberger, on Britain's participation in the U.S. space defense research program, popularly known as Star Wars. A pact was signed in December, making Britain the first U.S. ally to join the project.

Relations with the Soviet Union deteriorated in September, after the KGB chief in the Soviet diplomatic mission in London defected to the West. It was said that the defector, Oleg

Gordievsky, had worked as an agent for the British, as well as Danish, secret services for at least ten years. Acting on information provided by Gordievsky, the British government expelled 25 Soviet officials and journalists, accusing them of having spied while in Britain. Moscow retaliated by expelling the same number of Britons from the Soviet Union. Then London expelled six more, and so did Moscow.

On September 25, after two weeks' delay to study the matter, the British government announced it would join the rest of the European Community in imposing certain sanctions on South Africa, including curbs on exports of arms or sensitive materials. The Thatcher government continued to oppose mandatory economic sanctions, contending they would stiffen the Pretoria government's resistance to change. In October, however, at a meeting of Commonwealth of Nations leaders in the Bahamas, Thatcher accepted a compromise resolution calling for limited economic sanctions.

On February 5 the border between Spain and the British colony of Gibraltar was opened for the first time in 16 years. Reciprocal rights were adopted for Spaniards in Gibraltar and for Gibraltar residents in Spain, including the right to own property.

Northern Ireland. On November 15, Thatcher and Irish Prime Minister Garret FitzGerald signed a landmark treaty under which the Irish government was given a formal consultative role and presence in Northern Ireland through an Anglo-Irish Intergovernmental Conference, consisting of cabinet ministers from the two countries. At the same time, the treaty stated that Northern Ireland would remain British as long as a majority of its inhabitants so desired. Predictably, the agreement was strongly denounced by unionists, as well as by nationalists. Ian Gow, Britain's treasury minister of state, resigned in protest, as did the Reverend Ian Paisley, the House of Commons representative who heads the Democratic Unionist Party in Ulster. All 13 of the remaining Protestant representatives from Ulster also eventually resigned, forcing elections for January 1986.

Five days after the treaty was signed, angry Protestants attacked the British secretary of state for Northern Ireland as he entered Belfast City Hall, punching and kicking him and leaving him trapped in the building until police came. Subsequently, an estimated 70,000 to 100,000 unionists attended a protest rally in Belfast. The treaty was nevertheless approved in the British Parliament by a 473-47 vote and went into effect on November 29. The first consultations were held in Belfast on December 11, as Protestant demonstrators protested outside. On December 31, Protestant paramilitary leaders joined a protest march originating in Londonderry.

There was continuing violence in Ulster, including a March 28 mortar attack on a police station, which killed nine police officers, and a December 7 attack that killed two. On December 19, Robert Tohill, an Irish nationalist guerrilla convicted of murdering a British Army reservist, began a hunger strike at Northern

Dismayed Birmingham residents survey the damage done to their neighborhood by mobs of youths who looted and burned businesses and set cars on fire during two days in September.

Ireland's Maze Prison; he was later joined by two other strikers. The strike protested convictions on the basis of uncorroborated evidence from paid informers.

Bermuda. On October 29 the colony of Bermuda held its third parliamentary election in five years. The conservative United Bermuda Party of Prime Minister John Swan captured 31 of the 40 House of Assembly seats, a gain of 5. Swan's new majority was the largest since the introduction of self-government in 1968.

Soccer Tragedies. On May 11 fire broke out at Bradford city stadium in Yorkshire during a soccer match. It swept through a covered grandstand, and within 3½ minutes 56 fans had been fatally burned—many of them unable to escape because of locked safety doors.

On May 29 the European Club Championship match between Liverpool and Juventus of Turin (Italy) was being played at the Heysel Stadium in Brussels. Before the game began, a group of Liverpool supporters broke from their sections to attack Juventus supporters after an exchange of taunts and insults. In the ensuing stampede, a wall collapsed and 38 spectators,

most of them from Italy, were trampled to death; more than 200 others were injured. Subsequently, the official body controlling the European competition banned indefinitely the participation of British soccer clubs in European competitions. Thatcher hurried legislation through Parliament to prohibit the sale and possession of liquor at soccer stadiums (with exceptions).

Royal Family. On August 4 the queen mother celebrated her 85th birthday, receiving the public's good wishes at Sandringham, birthplace of her late husband, King George VI. Prince Charles and Diana, princess of Wales, toured Australia and the United States late in the year; earlier, the couple had visited Italy, where they met with Pope John Paul II.

See STATISTICS OF THE WORLD. *See also* COMMONWEALTH OF NATIONS.   T.J.O.H.

GREECE. A new president and a new Parliament were elected in 1985, as Greece faced increasing domestic unrest and economic woes.

Politics. On March 29, Christos Sartzetakis, widely respected for his role (dramatized in the film Z) in investigating the 1963 murder of a left-wing parliamentary deputy, was narrowly elected by Parliament to serve a five-year term as third president of the republic. He succeeded Constantine Karamanlis, founder of the conservative New Democracy Party, who had resigned shortly before the expiration of his term, on learning that the ruling Panhellenic Socialist Party (Pasok) would not support him for a reelection but instead supported Sartzetakis, a centrist. The speaker of Parliament, Ioannis Alevras, who was appointed interim president, cast the deciding vote in a stalemated Parliament.

In parliamentary elections on June 2, Pasok renewed its majority, giving its leader, Andreas Papandreou, a second four-year term as prime minister. Pasok's victory, after a highly charged three-week campaign, was a decisive one; the Socialists won 46 percent of the popular vote and 161 seats in the 300-member assembly. The next closest party, New Democracy, took 41 percent of the vote to win 126 seats. For the first time since 1974, the Communists won less than 10 percent of the vote.

Demonstrations in November to protest Papandreou's postelection policy of improving

The queen mother travels regally up front during a supersonic birthday jaunt over the coastline of Great Britain aboard a Concorde jet; the flight was arranged to celebrate her 85th birthday on August 4.

Greece's relations with the West turned violent when police shot and killed a 15-year-old demonstrator and clashed with left-wing extremists. Leftists later claimed responsibility for a car-bombing that killed a police officer and wounded 14 others. Three cabinet ministers submitted their resignations, but the prime minister refused to accept them.

Economic Troubles. The 1985 budget reflected the Socialist government's five-year plan for 1983 to 1987, stressing infrastructure projects, tax relief, and increased social benefits. Continued benefits from European Community (EC) credits were counterbalanced by a poor harvest and relatively low EC farm prices. Inflation and unemployment remained serious problems. In October tough austerity measures were introduced—including currency devaluation, wage freezes, import curbs, and new taxes. The measures provoked protest strikes by workers and serious dissension within the ruling party.

Foreign Affairs. Early in the year, Greece concluded economic agreements with Libya. Prime Minister Papandreou received Egyptian President Hosni Mubarak on an official visit and opened a conference in Athens on Greek-Arab economic cooperation. He also visited the Soviet Union, where major economic and technical agreements were signed.

Relations between Greece and the United States were tense early in the year, as the government continued its anti-American rhetoric and remained unwilling to take part in NATO maneuvers on account of its dispute with Turkey. After the June elections, however, the Greek government moderated its rhetoric and relations with the United States appeared to be improving.

The issue of airport security was a continuing irritant in U.S.-Greek relations. After Shiite Muslim gunmen hijacked a TWA jet in June, as it began its flight from Athens, the U.S. State Department warned Americans against flying to Greece because of alleged lax security at the Athens airport. The advisory was rescinded after conditions apparently improved. But new concerns were raised in November by the hijacking of an Egyptian airliner after takeoff from Athens.

See STATISTICS OF THE WORLD.   J.A.P.

GRENADA. See STATISTICS OF THE WORLD.

Dancing in the streets, Athenians celebrate the results of the June national election: a renewal of the Socialists' absolute majority in Parliament and the assurance of a second four-year term for Prime Minister Andreas Papandreou.

GUAM. See STATISTICS OF THE WORLD.

GUATEMALA. In 1985, Guatemala elected its first civilian president since the 1950's; installation of a democratic government under a new constitution was slated for January 1986.

New President. Marco Vinicio Cerezo Arévalo received more than two-thirds of the votes cast in a December 8 runoff, to win election as Guatemala's first civilian president in nearly 30 years. An independent-minded liberal who survived three assassination attempts under military rule, Cerezo was scheduled to be inaugurated on January 14, 1986. Prior to his

185

installation, Cerezo, who distanced himself from U.S. policy in the region and condemned outside intervention in local conflicts, made a tour of foreign capitals, partly to discuss the issue of peace in Central America.

Elections and Constitution. The December 8 runoff was held because no candidate won a majority in November 3 national elections. Cerezo had led with about 40 percent of the votes cast for president, while his Christian Democrats won 51 of 100 seats in the Congress. The first runner-up, Jorge Carpio Nicolle of the National Union of the Center, won about 20 percent of the votes; he took a position more closely aligned with U.S. policy. Candidates of a conservative coalition and of the far-right National Liberation Movement split most of the remaining vote. Neither Marxists nor military officers were allowed to run. The new constitution, delivered in May to chief of state General Oscar Humberto Mejía Víctores and effective in January 1986, legalized all political parties, created the national legislature, established an attorney general's office charged with guarding human rights, set up a constitutional court, and provided for national referenda on important issues.

Internal Security and Human Rights. By early 1985, Guatemala's military regime controlled most of the highland areas where antigovernment guerrillas had been active. Able-bodied adult males had been conscripted into civil defense patrols, and about 50,000 people had been forcibly relocated in "model villages" by the military. Political violence, attributed mostly to the army and police, was continuing, with trade unionists, peasant activists, students, and intellectuals as frequent victims. After a new

organization, the Group for Mutual Support, was formed to seek an accounting of missing persons, two of its six directors were murdered; two more fled the country. Reforms in human rights were expected under the new democratic regime.

The Economy. Nearly one-sixth of the labor force was unemployed in 1985, with another 40 percent estimated to be underemployed. Prices for Guatemala's main exports were depressed, and oil production lagged. The supply of foreign currency was exhausted; $30 million in gold reserves were sold in March to make a payment on the short-term foreign debt. The annual inflation rate hit 60 percent at midyear. Mejía Víctores made efforts to come to grips with the economic situation, but he was pressured by businessmen and landowners who favored slashing social programs and opposed new taxes or stricter enforcement of existing tax laws. Announced increases in food prices and bus fares were rescinded in September, after week-long rioting in which ten persons were killed. Mejía Víctores instead announced price ceilings on 45 consumer items, plus salary increases for government workers.

U.S. Relations. As part of his pre-inauguration tour of foreign capitals, President-elect Cerezo visited the United States in mid-December. He indicated that he was not interested immediately in receiving U.S. military aid but that he did need patience and support from the United States and other democracies as he sought to build up democracy in his own country.

See STATISTICS OF THE WORLD.   L.L.P.

GUINEA. See STATISTICS OF THE WORLD.

GUINEA-BISSAU. See STATISTICS OF THE WORLD.

GUYANA. See STATISTICS OF THE WORLD.

H

HAITI. See STATISTICS OF THE WORLD. See also CARIBBEAN BASIN.

HAWAII. See STATISTICS OF THE WORLD. See also STATE GOVERNMENT REVIEW.

Health and Medicine

In 1985, AIDS cases were reported worldwide, as public concern heightened over the long-range implications of the rapidly spreading epidemic. The importance of early diagnosis and treatment of cancer was spotlighted when President Reagan underwent removal of cancerous growths twice in one month.

MEDICINE

The growing epidemic of acquired immune deficiency syndrome (AIDS) dominated the medical news in 1985. President Ronald Reagan's encounters with cancer captured public attention, and special reports highlighted such public health problems as infant mortality, hunger, and a possible shortage of vaccines.

AIDS Epidemic. The announcement in July that actor Rock Hudson was suffering from AIDS and his death from AIDS in October highlighted concern among scientists and the public about the deadly and fast-spreading disease. First identified in 1981, AIDS is a viral disorder that destroys its victims' immune systems, making them unable to fight off diseases and infections.

The fatality rate was approximately 50 percent among the 16,000 cases diagnosed in the United States by the end of the year, and no one with a full-blown case of AIDS was known to have recovered. AIDS most often affects homosexual men and intravenous drug abusers; a much smaller number of cases have been traced to blood transfusions and other forms of contact.

AIDS is caused by a virus called HTLV-III, or human T-cell lymphotropic virus type III. It was already known that AIDS victims have very few T4 cells, a type of lymphocyte (white blood cell) that activates the body's immune response. Researchers from the U.S. National

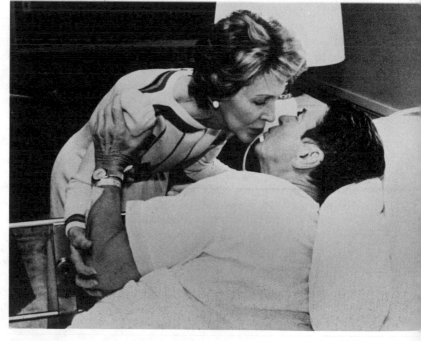

Nancy Reagan comforts President Ronald Reagan after his successful July 13 operation, in which surgeons at the Bethesda Naval Medical Center in Maryland removed a cancerous growth from his colon.

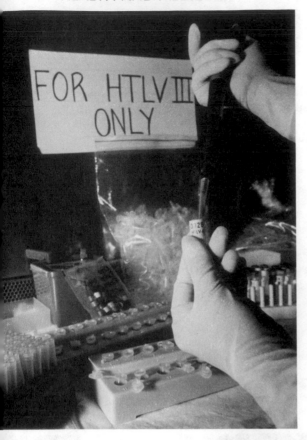

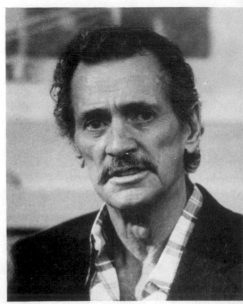

AIDS (acquired immune deficiency syndrome) was the leading medical story of 1985, as the disease spread and scientists still failed to completely understand it or find a cure. Actor Rock Hudson (above) became the first celebrity victim of AIDS; the resulting publicity increased public awareness of the deadly viral disorder. Left, a laboratory worker at a San Francisco blood bank tests blood samples for AIDS-virus antibodies; the availability of this new screening tool helped in safeguarding the U.S. blood supply.

Institutes of Health (NIH) discovered in 1985 that the T4 cells that are present in AIDS victims have an "intrinsic defect" in their ability to recognize and respond to antigens (foreign agents in the body that provoke an immune response). And scientists at Harvard University's Dana-Farber Cancer Institute reported that the AIDS virus—which replicates in the T4 cells—does so at a rate up to 1,000 times faster than any other virus.

Researchers also discovered that the interval between infection with the AIDS virus and development of the disease may be longer than had been previously believed. For example, at the Medical College of Georgia, investigators diagnosed AIDS in a child who had received a blood transfusion 5½ years earlier. When traced, the donor was found to be a homosexual drug abuser who had shown no symptoms of AIDS when he donated blood but who was later found to have antibodies to the virus.

The New England Journal of Medicine reported late in the year that the virus that causes AIDS can also produce meningitis, an infection of the membranes lining the brain and spinal cord. Researchers also found evidence that the virus may grow and reproduce in the brains of AIDS patients.

A new blood test approved in March for use in the United States as a screening tool for the AIDS virus dramatically reduced the chances that the disease would be transmitted through blood transfusions. The test, called ELISA (for enzyme-linked immunosorbent assay), indicates whether donated blood contains antibodies to the AIDS virus, which would mean the donor has been exposed to the virus. Blood that tests positive for antibodies is not used in transfusions, although a positive result does not necessarily mean the donor has AIDS. By July the test was considered so effective that U.S. officials declared the blood supply safe from contamination with the AIDS virus. The test was also showing that many more people had been exposed to the virus than had developed the disease.

The introduction of the test raised fears in some homosexual-rights groups that it would be used to identify homosexuals and would lead to discrimination against them. The Defense Department in August announced it would take the controversial step of screening all military recruits for exposure to the virus. In October the testing was extended to all active-duty military personnel; those who actually had AIDS, as well as those who admitted to drug use or homosexuality during the screening process, would be discharged, and those who tested positive for exposure to the virus would have limitations placed on the duties and areas to which they could be assigned. The U.S. Public Health Service, however, recommended against routine screening of food handlers and healthcare workers for AIDS.

Some evidence was reported suggesting that breast milk might be another body fluid (beside blood and semen) through which the AIDS virus can be transmitted. The virus has also been found in tears and saliva, but there were no reports of actual transmission through either of these, and saliva was found to be seldom infected. The AIDS virus can also be passed from mother to fetus during pregnancy. Whether AIDS might spread significantly through the heterosexual community in the United States remained unknown. The CDC as of late 1985 had recorded only about 150 U.S. cases of heterosexual transmission.

In African nations, AIDS appeared to be spreading almost exclusively through the heterosexual population, with women affected almost as often as men. Researchers suggested that this was the case because homosexual behavior is relatively uncommon in Africa and because of the large number of female prostitutes there who are believed to harbor the AIDS virus. Infected needles and risky blood transfusion practices were also cited as possible causes. Because so many African women have the AIDS virus, a relatively high proportion of African infants and older children are affected (for example, children represent over 20 percent of all reported cases in Rwanda, compared with only about 1 percent in the United States). For various reasons, including an apparent attempt by many African governments to suppress information about AIDS, the disease has been underreported in Africa, but it is clearly a growing public health problem there. (Many scientists now believe that the disease originated in central Africa, but this is uncertain. There is a difference of opinion over whether AIDS originated recently or is an old, previously undetected disease.)

Work toward an AIDS vaccine continued. An encouraging development was the announcement by the New England Regional Primate Center that researchers there had succeeded in infecting monkeys with a virus similar to the one that causes AIDS in humans. Having an animal model to work with was considered a necessary step in developing a human vaccine. However, the prospects for an effective vaccine are lessened by the tendency of the virus to mutate frequently, since a vaccine targeted at one form of the virus will be of no use against a mutated form.

Thus far, effective treatment for the disease has proved elusive, although researchers reported possible indications of progress with drugs that could help AIDS victims either by killing the virus itself or by enhancing or restoring the functioning of the immune system. One drug found to have antiviral effect was HPA-23, which was reportedly administered to Rock Hudson at Paris's Pasteur Institute and was approved for experimental use in the United States in August. Other substances, such as the naturally occurring interleukin 2, have shown some immune-enhancing effect in AIDS patients. There was a flurry of hope in October when French doctors announced, after only a week of testing in a handful of patients, that the drug cyclosporine (generally used to prevent rejection in organ transplants) showed signs of being useful in treating AIDS. By early November three patients being treated with the drug had died; nevertheless, French researchers felt further testing was warranted and planned to expand the experiment.

There was pressure during the year to increase U.S. federal spending for AIDS-related research and treatment, even though spending had grown to nearly $100 million in fiscal

1985. Some members of Congress also complained that the Reagan administration tried to obtain AIDS money by cutting other federal health programs.

Artificial Heart. William J. Schroeder, a retired government employee from Jasper, Ind., in 1985 became the longest surviving recipient of an artificial heart. However, after an initially quick recovery from his November 1984 implant of a Jarvik-7 heart, Schroeder experienced numerous serious complications, including two strokes that impaired his speech and memory. By midyear he had made a trip to his hometown to lead a parade and had moved into an apartment near the Humana Heart Institute in Louisville, Ky., where he was being treated. But his progress toward recovery was interrupted by a third stroke in mid-November. Dr. William C. DeVries, who performed Schroeder's surgery, implanted two more Jarvik-7 hearts during the year. One recipient died only ten days after receiving the implant; the other, Murray P. Haydon, experienced various complications.

In April surgeons at Sweden's Karolinska Thoracic Clinic, using a Jarvik-7, performed the first artificial heart implant outside the United States. The patient did well until late summer, when he suffered a stroke; he died in November. In August, Dr. Jack C. Copeland of Tucson's University of Arizona Medical Center implanted a Jarvik-7 heart as a "bridge" that kept his patient, 25-year-old Michael Drummond, alive, despite a series of small strokes, until a human heart could be implanted a week later.

In October, three men in three different hospitals received artificial hearts of three different designs while they waited for human heart transplants. One of these designs was the so-called Penn State heart, which had been developed at Pennsylvania State University's Hershey Medical Center and approved by the Food and Drug Administration in March for experimental use. Its first recipient, 44-year-old Anthony Mandia, died on November 14, as a result of a severe infection that followed the device's replacement with a human heart. In Minneapolis in December, Mary Lund became the first woman to receive an artificial heart; the device was a modified version of the Jarvik-7 designed for her smaller chest cavity. At year's end she was said to be in a light coma, with prospects for recovery uncertain. Despite problems in patients receiving Jarvik-7 hearts, a federal advisory panel recommended in late December that the procedures be allowed to continue with small numbers of patients, under close supervision by the Food and Drug Administration.

Cancer. The announcement that President Reagan had colon cancer, diagnosed following surgery for removal of a polyp (growth) in his colon, led to a dramatic increase in public concern about the disorder. Reagan underwent the surgery in mid-July and had an uneventful recovery from the operation. A poll taken several days later found many more individuals than before willing to undergo two tests that permit early diagnosis of colon and rectal cancer: a stool blood test and a proctosigmoidoscopy (examination with a device that enables doctors to view the rectum and lower portion of the colon). The survival rate is much higher when the disease is diagnosed early.

The president had problems with another kind of cancer, when malignant skin cells were removed from his nose on two occasions. The events once again heightened public awareness, this time about skin cancer.

A study reported in 1985 supported an increasingly conservative approach to breast cancer surgery. Based on the records of 1,843 women, the study found that for small tumors (up to 1½ inches in diameter) surgical removal of the tumor and a margin of surrounding tissue was just as effective as total breast removal. When combined with radiation therapy, this "segmental mastectomy" was more effective for certain cases than more extensive surgical treatment without radiation. A second, ten-year study found that total mastectomy, or removal of the breast and sometimes the lymph nodes, was as effective in saving lives as radical mastectomy, in which the underlying chest wall muscles are also removed, as well as the lymph nodes in the armpit.

In September an NIH panel recommended that, to prevent recurrence of breast cancer, hormone therapy with tamoxifen should be given after surgery and radiation treatment to patients over age 50 whose lymph nodes showed

First-born septuplet Patricia Ann, one of three surviving infants born in May to Patti and Sam Frustaci in the largest multiple birth ever recorded in the United States, poses with her parents after being released from the hospital. With four infants dead and the survivors facing medical problems, the Frustacis later filed a malpractice suit against the doctor and a California clinic where Mrs. Frustaci was given doses of the fertility drug Perganol.

evidence of cancer. Tamoxifen has not yet been found useful for younger women.

Scientists at the National Cancer Institute reported in December that a procedure called adoptive immunotherapy showed promise in the treatment of cancer. The therapy is a refinement of the concept of directing the body's own natural immune system against malignant cells. White blood cells are removed from the patient and incubated with a synthetic hormone, interleukin-2, that enhances their immune function. The cells are then injected into the body with additional doses of straight IL-2. These "killer cells" attack tumors. Twenty-five patients who had failed to respond to conventional treatment underwent the experimental procedure; tumors were reduced in 11 patients by at least 50 percent; in one patient the tumor appeared to disappear altogether. Dr. Steven Rosenberg, leader of the research team, cautioned that none of the patients had been followed for more than ten months. Side effects of the therapy included weight gains for many patients and serious respiratory difficulties for a few. One patient—not one of the original 25—died after receiving the treatment, apparently in part because of adverse reaction to it. The procedure is also very costly.

Diet and Heart Disease. Several studies found healthful cardiovascular effects from eating fish. Dutch scientists at the University of Leiden monitored 852 middle-aged men for over 20 years. They found that the overall mortality rate from coronary heart disease was more than 50 percent lower among the men who ate an average of at least 30 grams (just over 1 ounce) of fish a day. The 78 men who died of heart disease during the 20-year period ate the least fish. The amount of fish consumed was not related to any other dietary factors. The study had been suggested by earlier findings linking Greenland Eskimos' low death rate from coronary heart disease with their high-fish diet.

At Oregon Health Sciences University, researchers studied the effect of fish oil on high blood levels of the fatty substances called triglycerides, which have been implicated in the development of heart disease. They found that, in 20 people with elevated triglycerides, a fish-oil diet significantly lowered levels of triglycerides—and also cholesterol—in the blood. A low-fat diet also was found to lower triglyceride levels, but to a lesser extent, while a diet with polyunsaturated vegetable oil actually increased triglyceride levels.

At a June meeting of the American Heart Association, scientists from the Johns Hopkins University reported preliminary evidence that people drinking five or more cups of coffee a day had a 2.8 times greater risk of developing heart disease than persons who drink no coffee. The findings were based on a long-term study of 1,000 medical school graduates. However, most previous studies have found little or no link between coffee and heart disease.

Infertility and IUD's. Intrauterine devices, a form of birth control used by 2.2 million U.S. women, increase the risk of infertility, according to two studies reported in 1985. The first study, conducted at the University of Washington, was based on interviews with 159 women who had been diagnosed as having primary tubal infertility (infertility caused by damage to the fallopian tubes). The researchers found that women who had at one time used

In one of the year's incidents of food contamination, listeria bacteria in cheese made by Jalisco Mexican Products sickened hundreds and caused close to 100 deaths. Here a Los Angeles store manager clears the shelves of Jalisco cheese.

IUD's were 2.6 times as likely to develop tubal infertility as those who had not.

A second study, of 4,185 women from seven cities, found that the increased risk of tubal infertility was about twice as great among women who had used IUD's. The level of risk varied considerably depending on the type of IUD. The strongest link was found to be with the Dalkon Shield (no longer sold), the lowest risk among users of various copper-containing IUD's.

Growth Hormone. In October the Food and Drug Administration authorized the marketing of synthetic human growth hormone made by genetic engineering techniques. The synthetic hormone, developed by Genentech, Inc., of South San Francisco, Calif., was given the trade name Protropin. The approval was good news for children with growth problems caused by their bodies' deficient production of growth hormone. Distribution of natural growth hormone to such children had been halted in April after a few cases of a rare fatal brain infection had been found among those using it.

"Designer" Drugs. The desire to produce highly purified drugs that may provide a more intense experience to drug users has led to the problem of so-called designer drugs. Basement chemists, working in many parts of the United States, formulate chemical variants of opium or other illicit drugs that are often far more powerful than the original and that, because they are so new, are not unlawful. Very small amounts of these designer drugs can be lethal. Variations of fenantyl, which is widely used as an anesthetic in prolonged surgery, have been blamed for at least 97 deaths between 1979 and mid-1985. Also, an extremely toxic product can result from the attempt to produce a chemical variant of Demerol. The toxic product, known as MPTP, has produced severe and apparently permanent symptoms of Parkinson's disease among those who ingest it.

Another dangerous designer drug, an amphetamine-like substance called MOMA and nicknamed Ecstasy, was banned by the U.S. Drug Enforcement Administration, effective July 1.

Tobacco Advertising. The American Medical Association called in December for a complete ban on the advertising and promotion of all tobacco products. (Television and radio advertising of tobacco products was already forbidden.) The AMA also called for an end to vending machine sales of cigarettes and for a minimum age limit of 21 for the sale of tobacco products. The tobacco industry argued that such an advertising ban would violate the constitutional right of commercial free speech.

Hunger and Infant Mortality. A report by the Physicians' Task Force on Hunger, released in February, claimed that hunger is "epidemic" in the United States. The task force, based at Harvard University's School of Public Health, uncovered data suggesting that malnutrition is at least as serious a problem as it was in the late 1960's, when a similar report became a major public policy issue. The new report estimated the number of "hungry" Americans—those who could not get enough to eat at least part of the time each month or were chronically unable to afford an adequate diet—at 20 million.

Infant mortality represents another major U.S. public health problem; in 1982, the U.S. infant mortality rate was higher than in 16 other nations, compared with only 6 others in the early 1950's. Most deaths of infants are due to premature delivery; in these cases the infant is of relatively low birth weight and some body systems, especially the lungs, may not be mature enough to cope with the demands of extrauterine life. In February a committee of the Institute of Medicine of the National Academy of Sciences issued a report including a number of recommendations aimed at reducing the incidence of premature delivery and low birth weight. The committee urged increased funding to make early prenatal care and adequate nutrition available to all pregnant women and urged women to avoid smoking and alcohol use during pregnancy.

Contaminated Foods. A milk-borne outbreak of salmonellosis in the Midwest during the spring produced the largest number of culture-confirmed cases ever reported from one epidemic. More than 17,000 persons developed diarrhea, nausea, vomiting, or fever, and 5 died. *Salmonella typhimurium* was found in unopened cartons of 2 percent low-fat milk from Jewel Food Stores' Hillfarm Dairy, located in Melrose Park, Ill. A joint federal-state task force concluded that a plumbing cross-connection had probably allowed raw milk to mix with pasteurized milk before packaging, causing contamination.

Almost as mysterious was an outbreak of a serious disease caused by the bacterium *Listeria monocytogenes* in Mexican-style cheese made in California. This outbreak caused hundreds of cases of disease and close to 100 deaths from March through July. The organism infected two brands of cheese, Cotija and Queso Fresco, produced by Jalisco Mexican Products, Inc. Most of those affected were pregnant women and their fetuses and newborn infants, who are at especially high risk. Los Angeles officials suspected that untreated milk had been processed with pasteurized milk in the manufacture of the contaminated cheese.

Immunization Concern. The United States has had an adequate supply of vaccines for so long that many Americans were startled to learn of a shortage of DPT, a vaccine for diphtheria, pertussis (whooping cough), and tetanus, used in basic immunizations of infants. The shortage developed after two of the three manufacturers making the vaccine restricted production. Over the last two decades, a number of companies have decided that the limited profits from vaccine manufacture do not justify the risks of lawsuits over occasional adverse reactions.

A committee of health experts warned in July that the U.S. supply of vaccines is "precarious," because often a vaccine is made or distributed primarily by only one or two companies, which may decide to stop making and distributing the vaccine. Drug companies argue they should not be held liable if problems arise, because their vaccines are tested and approved by the federal government.

A major goal of the U.S. immunization program was to eliminate measles from the continental United States by 1982. Yet more than 1,800 measles cases were reported in the United States during the first seven months of 1985. Of these, 334 cases had been registered on 25 college campuses, and there were 3 reported deaths.

These institutions and others with isolated outbreaks responded by requiring students to provide proof of measles immunization and by sponsoring mass measles immunization programs on the campus. Part of the problem is that the current generation of college students was born shortly after measles vaccination had been introduced. During this period most children, unlike their elders, were not exposed to the disease and did not acquire natural immunity. At the same time, some were never vaccinated and others were vaccinated at what proved to be too early an age.

Legionellosis. Legionellosis (popularly called Legionnaires' disease because the outbreak that led to its discovery occurred at an American Legion convention in Philadelphia) is a form of pneumonia caused by the bacterium *Legionella pneumophila.* Two noteworthy outbreaks occurred in 1985. One was at Stafford General Hospital, England, where 163 persons were affected and 37 died during April and May. The source was water in the cooling tower of the air-conditioning system, which spread contaminated droplets to people in the waiting room of the outpatient department. In April there was an outbreak of 46 confirmed or suspected cases, including 3 deaths, among persons attending a church banquet at a Detroit-area hotel. Washings from the cooling coils of the air-conditioning system cultured out the legionella organism.

MENTAL HEALTH

Renewed attention was focused in 1985 on an age-old question—the effect of mental health on disease.

Emotions and Disease. A long-standing debate on the relationship between mental state and disease was renewed with the June publication of an editorial in the *New England Journal of Medicine* claiming there is no scientific proof for believing that a patient's psychological state may cause or cure disease. It said that the patient who does not get well may experience guilt and a sense of personal failure for an outcome that is in fact biologically controlled. Moreover, in depending on "positive thinking," patients may neglect to seek medical attention. The editorial was prompted by the journal's publication of a study of 359 cancer patients that showed no correlation between psychosocial factors and the course of the disease.

In sometimes angry response from readers, psychologists and others cited studies appar-

ently showing that psychological help can influence disease outcome, possibly by affecting the workings of the immune system in some way not yet understood. For example, a recent German study of 100 women with breast cancer found longer average survival rates in patients who received a combination of chemotherapy and psychotherapy than in those who received chemotherapy alone.

Anxiety Peptide. Investigators at the National Institute of Mental Health reported in February that they had found in rat and human brains a peptide—a string of amino acids—that increases anxiety. The peptide, which resembles no other known mammalian peptide, binds to the same receptor in the brain as do the tranquilizers diazepam (commonly sold as Valium) and Librium, even though its effect is the opposite of those drugs.   S.W. & J.F.J.

HONDURAS. On December 23, 1985, Honduras's National Elections Tribunal declared Liberal Party member José Azcona del Hoyo as winner of the November presidential election; he was scheduled to be inaugurated on January 27, 1986. Nine candidates from four parties had run for the presidency on November 24, under an electoral law enacted in the fall that would give the victory to the leading vote-getter of the party whose candidates in combination received the most votes. According to the elections panel, the Liberals won 786,594 votes for their four candidates combined, or 49 percent of the total, while the National Party came in second, with 701,406, or 44 percent. Two other parties, with one candidate each, trailed.

The panel did not disclose individual votes for each candidate, but unofficial results indicated that the leading National Party candidate, Rafael Leonardo Callejas, had outpolled Azcona by a wide margin. Oscar Mejía Arellano, a Liberal candidate favored by incumbent President Roberto Suazo Córdova, trailed behind Azcona. The election was marked by intrigue, and there were frequent rumors that a coup would preempt the results. On one occasion, President Suazo reportedly used a U.S. helicopter to drop campaign material accusing Callejas of being a "sodomist" suffering from acquired immune deficiency syndrome. Supporters of Callejas denounced th

U.S. tanks and helicopters on military maneuvers with Honduran troops show their might near the Nicaraguan border, as Honduran civilians look on.

electoral law as contravening the constitution, which provides for direct election of the president by a majority vote.

The electoral system had arisen as a compromise, after President Suazo had called an "extraordinary assembly" of the Liberal Party at which his choice for a successor, Mejía Arellano, was nominated. Other aspirants denounced the assembly and called for direct party primaries. In the ensuing constitutional crisis, the Congress impeached five Suazo-appointed judges, and Suazo responded by arresting the new chief justice. After the armed forces commander refused to approve a declared state of emergency, a compromise was reached, providing that all candidates from each party could run in the November elections, and legislation was subsequently enacted to that effect.

Meanwhile, economic conditions remained extremely harsh, with unemployment estimated at about 20 percent and perhaps another 60 percent underemployed. On May Day, some 80,000 people demonstrated in the streets of the capital, Tegucigalpa, protesting economic conditions, as well as alleged human rights violations. In the weeks that followed, the unions flexed their muscles; at La Ceiba, a general strike paralyzed Atlantic Coast and Standard Fruit operations.

U.S. military exercises continued, and Nicaraguan antigovernment guerrillas (contras) continued to use Honduran bases, but Salvadoran training camps were closed in midsummer, the Honduran military being unwilling to strengthen the forces of a traditional enemy. Relations with Nicaragua grew increasingly tense over a series of border incidents. After the U.S. Congress approved aid to the contras in June, they attacked inside Nicaragua, reducing their presence in Honduras.

See STATISTICS OF THE WORLD.   D.E.S.

HOUSING AND CONSTRUCTION

HOUSING AND CONSTRUCTION. Mortgage rates declined and home values remained relatively stable in the United States during 1985. Lower rates meant that an estimated 4 million more U.S. households than before could afford a home, so that the stage was apparently set for an all-out real estate boom. However, an all-out boom did not materialize. Part of the reason was that much of the pent-up demand for home ownership had been satisfied in 1983 and 1984. The baby boom generation had largely filled its needs, and households now coming into the prime home-buying age were fewer in number. Slow growth in personal income and a decline in the rate of personal savings were also blamed.

Housing starts rose and fell sharply from month to month. A steep decline in November dampened earlier, more optimistic projections. For the first 11 months of the year, new housing came to a total of 1.62 million units, a decline of 2.2 percent from the same period in 1984.

Construction Spending. Overall construction spending was, however, high; it was reported in October at an annualized rate of $348 billion—a record. Total construction spending had increased sharply in January from December 1984 and then increased moderately virtually every month thereafter. In October, construction of nonresidential buildings was valued at an annual rate of nearly $90 billion, spending on residential building was just over $150 billion, and other construction spending was more than $60 billion.

Home Costs. Housing affordability reached a level not seen since 1979. A household with the U.S. median income of $27,563 had 98 percent of the income needed to qualify for an 80 percent mortgage on a median-priced existing home. In September the median price of an existing home was $75,300, up about $3,400 from September 1984. The median price of a newly built house was $86,200 as of October.

The Buffalo/Niagara Falls, N.Y., metropolitan area had the most affordable existing homes in the United States—with a median price of around $46,000. The Louisville, Ky., Detroit, and Indianapolis metropolitan areas also had some of the nation's best housing buys. The San Francisco Bay area had the highest median prices—well over $140,000. Other high-priced metropolitan markets included Santa Clara County, Calif.; Boston; New York City; and Orange County, Calif.

Construction Activity. The Northeast fared well, the South less well in the number of building permits issued for new housing during the year. The biggest increases were in New Jersey, New York, California, Massachusetts, and North Carolina. States where permits decreased the most from 1984 to 1985 were Texas (down almost 50,000), Colorado, Oklahoma, Arizona, and Louisiana.

The ten metropolitan areas with the most housing starts, according to projected figures, were Los Angeles/Anaheim/Riverside, Calif.; Dallas/Ft. Worth; Phoenix; Atlanta; San Francisco/Oakland/San Jose, Calif.; San Diego; Tampa/St. Petersburg/Clearwater, Fla.; Washington, D.C.; Denver/Boulder, Colo.; and Seattle/Tacoma, Wash.

Home ownership rates in the United States remained virtually unchanged from 1984; as of the second quarter of 1985, 64 percent of U.S. households owned their own home. Americans spent an estimated $83 billion to repair, maintain, and remodel their homes; about one fourth of this amount was spent by home owners on do-it-yourself projects.

An increasing trend was the use of federal tax credits in attracting capital to build low-income housing in urban areas. Such credits, widely available for older buildings in cities, fill a gap left by budget cuts in federal housing rehabilitation programs and were being used extensively, particularly in Northeastern and Midwestern urban areas. The Reagan administration tax reform plan called for eliminating such credits; tax reform legislation approved late in the year by the U.S. House merely reduced the amount of the credit slightly, but the ultimate fate of the credits was in suspense.

The Reagan administration dropped the Minimum Property Standards of the Federal Housing Administration in favor of adherence to local building codes and marketplace acceptance. In addition, tax credits for winterizing homes and for using solar-energy equipment were mostly phased out.

High Unemployment. Construction employment increased by 33,000 jobs in September and by 22,000 jobs in October; in November the workforce amounted to about 4,750,000 persons. Average hourly wages for construction workers were $12.21. Despite the new construction jobs, the unemployment rate for construction workers was up to nearly 14 percent in November, from about 13 percent in August.

Mortgage Practices. Mortgage loan interest rates decreased steadily from a high of 13.81 percent in April to 12.65 percent by September. The Veterans Administration in November lowered its rate to 11 percent, the lowest rate since September 1979. Fixed-rate mortgage loans were becoming more popular and the adjustable-rate loan, in which monthly payments vary, was rapidly losing favor. Mortgage delinquencies were up in the first quarter of 1985, to 6.19 percent. To reduce loan defaults, the Federal National Mortgage Association, or Fannie Mae, required tighter lending practices from mortgage lenders. Fannie Mae, which buys loans from lenders and then resells them on the secondary market, is the nation's largest single supplier of home mortgage funds.

Mobile Homes Scandal. The Veterans Administration investigated the mobile home industry and accused several manufacturers of overcharging buyers of mobile homes. The VA said kickbacks and invoice padding may have cost it more than $3.5 billion as manufacturers inflated a home's value, then rebated the difference between the invoice price and the true price to retailers of mobile homes. The VA insures mobile-home loans and thus is at risk if an owner cannot meet monthly payments.

New Systems. A major innovation in home building got underway in 1985. The Smart House, a project undertaken by the National Association of Home Builders and 30 U.S. companies, was designed to develop a wiring system that would allow appliances to interact with one another, reducing fire and shock hazards while expanding capabilities for communications and home automation. In a separate development, the plumbing code, based on 40-year-old standards, was revised to allow more flexibility in kitchen and bathroom design. J.C.

HUNGARY. The regime of Communist Party leader János Kádár continued to employ tough measures to curb dissent in Hungary during 1985. Dissidents were sporadically harassed by house searches, detention for questioning, stiff fines, confiscation of unauthorized materials, denial of passports, and loss of jobs. New sources of opposition managed to be heard, however—for example, a hitherto unknown Jewish organization and a spontaneous ecological movement.

At the 13th Congress of the Hungarian Socialist Workers' (Communist) Party in Budapest in March, Kádár was reelected as head of the party, but his title was changed from first secretary to general secretary. Karoly Nemeth, Kádár's deputy in the secretariat of the Central Committee since 1978, was officially appointed as deputy general secretary.

In January the government announced a round of extensive price increases. Food, restaurant and factory meals, gas and electricity, postal services, public transportation, automobiles, books, and many other items were affected.

At the same time, Hungary became the first Soviet-bloc country to introduce a system (already followed in Yugoslavia and China) in which workers' representatives could have a say in how the enterprise was run and in some cases in the appointment of a manager.

The increasing prevalence of a so-called third economy continued to trouble the government. Based on economic manipulation, the clandestine—or at least undocumentable—system was estimated to yield about $2 billion a year, or approximately 20 percent of the total income of the population. Sources of such unauthorized income included illegal moonlighting, renting property, violating customs regulations, evading taxes, fraud, misappropriation of labor, and "income correctives" achieved through acceptance of illegal tips and gratuities, overcharging, and giving short weights.

Under growing public pressure, the Kádár regime began to pay more attention to the issue of Hungarian minorities living in Romania and Czechoslovakia. Hungary asked that equal rights be accorded to these communities. U.S. Secretary of State George Shultz visited Budapest in December and had cordial discussions with Kádár.

See STATISTICS OF THE WORLD. R.A.P.

I

ICELAND. The prime ministers of all five Nordic nations attended the 33rd session of the Nordic Council in Reykjavík in March 1985. A long-awaited common policy on economic development and full employment was formulated, and a "Northwest Fund" with initial capital of $13.5 million was established. The fund was to make loans to Greenland, Iceland, and the Faeroe Islands to help in their economic diversification.

U.S. Secretary of State George Shultz stopped in Iceland in March, on a return trip from the

Moderate Sikh leader Harchand Singh Longowal, shown here in New Delhi after his release from jail in March, was assassinated by extremist Sikhs on August 20. As president of the major Sikh party, he had signed an accord with Prime Minister Rajiv Gandhi in an attempt to end the three-year separatist crisis in Punjab that had already claimed thousands of lives.

funeral of Soviet leader Konstantin Chernenko. Shultz met with Foreign Minister Geir Hallgrímsson and discussed a 1975 Pentagon contingency plan that had been drawn up with Iceland's knowledge and released without authorization in late 1984. The document spoke of deploying, in an unspecified emergency, antisubmarine nuclear depth charges in Iceland and at several other sites. Hallgrímsson said he told Shultz that Iceland must be informed about any military plans affecting it.

The government made plans to control the nation's increasing foreign debt as well as the foreign trade deficit. A reduction in government borrowing, sales of government bonds, reduced tax rates, and stringent actions against tax evaders were among the steps decided upon.

A three-week seamen's strike won them increases in pensions and food allowances on board as well as a 50 percent raise in wages. Teachers ended a prolonged strike when Prime Minister Steingrímur Hermannsson guaranteed in writing to improve their salaries and working conditions to resemble those of similarly qualified private-sector employees.

Parliament ended the 55-year monopoly held by the State Broadcasting Service by legislating that, after January 1, 1986, private radio and television stations could be established.

See also STATISTICS OF THE WORLD.   E.J.F.

IDAHO. *See* STATISTICS OF THE WORLD.

ILLINOIS. *See* STATISTICS OF THE WORLD.

INDIA. Prime Minister Rajiv Gandhi made progress in 1985 toward restoring stability to his strife-torn country and improving relations with other nations.

Rajiv Gandhi in Power. Rajiv Gandhi had become prime minister after the assassination of his mother, Prime Minister Indira Gandhi, on October 31, 1984. Assured of a popular mandate following his Congress-I Party's landslide victory in December 1984 general elections, he began the new year with a streamlined cabinet and staff, having dismissed several of his mother's top aides and advisers. By the first anniversary of her death he had made little progress as yet toward his stated goal of reforming the often corrupt government bureaucracy, but he had reached important settlements with dissident groups in Punjab and Assam and adopted an approach of conciliation, rather than confrontation, with opponents both at home and abroad.

Gandhi's popularity was evidenced by the results of state elections in March. His Congress-I party won majorities in 8 of the 11 states involved. The only losses were in Karnataka and Andhra Pradesh in the south and Sikkim and Assam in the Himalayan north.

Punjab and the Sikhs. Indira Gandhi's assassination at the hands of Sikh bodyguards led to riots that by the end of 1984 had killed nearly 3,000 people, mostly Sikhs. Hindu-Sikh mistrust and sporadic violence continued, with extremist Sikhs turning to random terrorism in response to what many of them considered a national Hindu conspiracy against Sikhs. Rajiv Gandhi tried to appease the leadership of the major Sikh political party, Akali Dal, by releasing Sant Harchand Singh Longowal from prison in March, together with other moderate Sikh leaders. The prime minister visited Punjab in April and offered concessions to win over Sikh opponents to his government. However, terrorism continued to claim the lives of Gandhi's supporters in the Punjab. Sikh terrorists were also suspected of possible sabotage of an Air-India jet that crashed off the Irish coast on July 23, killing 329 people.

On July 24, Gandhi signed a seven-point accord with Longowal and other Akali leaders that was hailed as marking a possible end to the tragic unrest in Punjab. Among other things, it provided for Chandigarh to become the sole capital of the state of Punjab, which would be expanded to include Sikh-populated regions in the Hindu-majority state of Haryana, carved out of Punjab in 1966. The agreement did not satisfy Sikh militants, however, and Longowal was gunned down on August 20. The Akali Dal chose another moderate, Surjeet Singh Barnala, as its new leader.

Despite renewed requests to postpone elections in the volatile Punjab until 1986, Gandhi decided they would be held on September 25, just three days later than originally scheduled. The militant wing of the Akali Dal announced

it would boycott the elections, and terrorist acts continued, but election day was surprisingly peaceful. The Akali Dal scored a lopsided victory, winning 73 of the 115 legislative seats at stake. Direct rule of Punjab by the central government, in effect since 1983, was formally ended.

Assam Agreement. On August 15, Gandhi signed an accord with militant leaders in Assam, aimed at ending agitation there against Muslim immigrants from Bangladesh, of whom more than 3,000 had been slain during 1983 state elections. The agreement called for deportation of some 2.6 million immigrants who had arrived after Bangladesh became a nation in 1971; it also called for disenfranchising for ten years all Muslim immigrants who had arrived between 1966 and 1971. In elections held on December 16 using the new voting roles, Gandhi's Congress Party was defeated, as the Assam People's Party, a new, regionally oriented group, won 64 of the 126 legislative seats. The latter party's leader, Prafulla Kumar Mahanta, was installed as chief minister.

Gujarat Riots. Riots also rocked Ahmadabad, capital of the state of Gujarat, and several of the state's major ports, as angry Hindus attacked slums inhabited by former untouchables and Muslims. Close to 200 people were killed in the upheaval, which reportedly stemmed from resentment over government programs to aid disadvantaged groups.

Economy. Prime Minister Gandhi indicated a strong commitment to modernizing industry and increasing productivity, so as to strengthen India's slowly expanding economy and raise the often low standard of living for its masses of people. He acted to remove restrictions from many imports, especially high-technology products. He also proposed sweeping tax reform measures and was preparing to introduce anticorruption measures designed to clean up the economy and help inspire foreign investment. India's economic problems remained formidable, however, and a projected budget deficit of $3 billion, in a total budget of under $40 billion, raised questions from government critics.

Spy Scandals. Members of the prime minister's secretariat were implicated in what appeared to have been a long-standing spy ring selling top secret defense and finance information to foreign businessmen and diplomats. Several assistants of P. C. Alexander, Indira Gandhi's private secretary before he became her son's, were among those charged. (Alexander resigned his post.) France appeared to be deeply involved in buying up secrets to help it compete more effectively in contract-bidding. As a result of the scandal, a billion-dollar deal for French heavy artillery weapons was derailed. In mid-April, 19 Indians were formally charged with espionage and 6 foreign diplomats were named as "buyers" of state secrets.

Bhopal. In late 1985, 627 former workers at the Bhopal plant of the U.S.-based Union Carbide Corporation, who lost their jobs when the plant closed in July following a 1984 poison gas leak that killed more than 2,000 people, agreed to a $1.8 million settlement on compensation issues. Disaster lawsuits claiming more than $200 billion in damages were still pending. Meanwhile, thousands participated in a demonstration outside the Bhopal plant on December 2, 1985, the anniversary of the disaster.

Foreign Affairs. Visiting Moscow in May, Gandhi assured his hosts of India's continuing faith in Soviet friendship and cooperation, in keeping with a 20-year treaty signed in 1971. Agreement was reached on a $1.15 billion credit to India for trade and investment. Visiting Washington, D.C., the next month, Gandhi addressed both houses of Congress and affirmed his faith both in democracy and in nonalignment. He appeared more pro-Western than his mother had been and was committed to closer contacts and increased trade with the United States.

The violent struggle in Sri Lanka between separatist Hindu Tamil "Tigers" and the Buddhist Sinhalese majority escalated. Sri Lanka's President J. R. Jayewardene met Gandhi in New Delhi and agreed to a formula that would give Sri Lanka's Tamils greater autonomy over their domain in the island's north. A truce was called in late June, and talks among the parties were begun in Bhutan the next month. Putting pressure on the guerrillas to negotiate a settlement, the Indian government in August expelled three insurgent leaders who had been using southern India as their base; a civil disobedience campaign erupted in India as a result, leading to about 1,000 arrests. After weeks of cease-fire violations, a new truce was announced between the Sri Lankan government and a key rebel group, but it appeared ineffective, and talks were resumed in New Delhi.

India remained deeply concerned that neighboring Pakistan might turn its modern arsenal eastward. Gandhi expressed fears about Pakistan's alleged "nuclear threat," and many advisers urged him to restart nuclear weapons testing and development in India. While visiting the United Nations in October, the Indian prime minister met with Pakistani President Muhammad Zia ul-Haq; the two agreed that their countries would begin talks on improving border security and expanding trade and would also address the issue of nuclear armaments. Gandhi and Zia met again in December in New Delhi and pledged that India and Pakistan would not attack each other's nuclear facilities.

See STATISTICS OF THE WORLD.   S.A.W.

INDIANA. See STATISTICS OF THE WORLD.

INDIANS, AMERICAN. The Reagan administration was criticized in 1985 for allowing the Interior Department's Bureau of Indian Affairs (BIA) and the Department of Health and Human Services' Indian Health Service (IHS) to remain leaderless for a long period of time.

Ross Swimmer, chief of the Cherokee Nation of Oklahoma, and also a lawyer and a banker, was nominated as the Interior Department's assistant secretary for Indian affairs, and thus head of the BIA, in late September, nine months after Kenneth L. Smith had resigned from the post. Swimmer was controversial in the Indian community because of his views that Indians should not be economically dependent on the federal government and because he chaired a presidential commission that, in late 1984, recommended the dismantling of the BIA. For most of 1985, the agency was run by a deputy assistant secretary and was without directors for two of its three program offices. Interior Secretary Donald Hodel promised that the BIA, under Swimmer, would become a "well-managed organization" and would begin implementing "appropriate" recommendations of the 1984 commission report. On December 14, one day after Swimmer was sworn in, Wilma P. Mankiller replaced him as chief of the Cherokee Nation of Oklahoma; she was the first woman to be chief of a major American Indian tribe.

At the IHS, Dr. Everett Rhoades, the first Indian to hold the post of director, was suspended from office in June, pending investigation of charges that he had shown favoritism in the awarding of $33,000 in scholarship grants to his daughter. A report by the inspector general's office found he had acted improperly, but he was reinstated with a reprimand after 5½ months.

Reservation Economies. Indian tribes throughout the United States complained about federal budget cuts and increased unemployment caused by the reductions in programs. Many tribes claimed that high-stakes bingo and other gambling were needed to make up for the loss of federal funds. There also was a surge of other entrepreneurial activities affecting reservation economies. Among the most notable were the innovative economic policies of the Passamaquoddy and Penobscot tribes of Maine. The tribes invested two-thirds of the $81.5 million award they received in a 1980 land

claim settlement in timberlands and liquid government securities. The Passamaquoddies then bought two profitable radio stations, a blueberry farm, and a large cement company, while the Penobscots built a $1.5 million ice hockey rink and a $2.5 million electronics plant, besides starting a venture investment firm to gain equity in various small, growing companies in the state.

In other developments, the Papago tribe of Arizona and the Lummi tribe of Washington opened foreign trade zones on their reservations. The Sac and Fox tribe of Oklahoma used its exemption from federal excise taxes and certain other taxes to become a U.S. purchasing agent for a Saudi trading and construction company. The Lac du Flambeau Band of Chippewas in Wisconsin issued tribal government tax-exempt bonds to help finance purchase of the Simpson Electric Company for $23 million.

Navajo Relocation. President Ronald Reagan in February appointed a close associate, former Interior Secretary William Clark, as his special envoy to effect "a speedy and final resolution" to a dispute between the Navajo and Hopi

A Navajo family, among thousands resisting relocation by the federal government, remains on land allocated in 1974 to the Hopis.

tribes in Arizona. In 1974, Congress had partitioned 1.8 million acres of land jointly used by the two tribes, leaving about 10,000 Navajos on land allocated to the Hopis. Approximately $50 million was spent on a voluntary relocation plan, but most of the Navajo families remained on the lands their ancestors had occupied for generations. After Senate hearings and an unsuccessful negotiating session at the White House, Clark conceded that an agreement was not imminent. Under the current mandate, the relocation had to be completed by June 30, 1986.

Chippewa Land Dispute. In December the Senate voted in favor of Minnesota in a land dispute between the state and the White Earth band of Chippewa Indians. The settlement, which awaited a House vote, would give $17 million to the Chippewas. It would also result in a reservation of under 70,000 acres; in 1865 the Chippewas signed a treaty with the United States delineating a reservation totaling 762,000 acres.

Reservation Gambling. High-stakes bingo games continued to be a primary producer of jobs and revenues on reservations. In Alabama, bingo's opening night on the new reservation for Poarch Creek Indians attracted nearly 1,500 players from at least four states. The Fond du Lac Band of Chippewa Indians in Minnesota created an urban "bingo reservation" by expanding their successful operation to the economically depressed city of Duluth.

Indian bingo games have been free of state regulation because federal reservations are not generally considered subject to state jurisdiction. However, there has been dispute over this position as it applies to gambling. The Oklahoma Supreme Court ruled in July that Indian bingo games were subject to state regulation and taxes, but in this case a federal district court later issued an injunction against any state action. In Michigan, on the other hand, a federal district court supported the state's contention that casino gambling on the L'Anse reservation violated federal legislation dealing with organized crime. In New Mexico and Arizona, state attorney generals argued that reservation-based parimutuel betting on dog racing and jai alai was illegal and should be opposed by the secretary of the interior.

Interior Secretary Hodel replied that he supported the bingo games but intended to take steps against "hard-core gambling" such as casinos and parimutuel betting. Meanwhile, legislation designed to bring federal regulation to reservation gambling had been introduced in Congress.

Indians Honored. Mark Trahant, editor of Navajo Times Today, was cited by the National Press Foundation in February for having remade the former tribal weekly into an aggressive daily paper, keyed to Indian concerns. Tim Giago, editor of The Lakota Times in South Dakota, received the H. L. Mencken Writing Award, sponsored by the Baltimore Sun. Also, Ovetta Wilson, a 56-year-old Navajo Indian, was honored by the White House for helping to rescue Indian children from rising floodwaters in 1984. Another Navajo, Mae Chee Castillo, 72, caused a stir in April when she used a White House ceremony honoring her and other senior citizens to tell President Reagan, through a translator, that he should not cut funding for social programs needed on the reservations.

Wind River Suicides. Over a period of less than two months, starting in early August, nine young men on the Wind River Reservation in Wyoming hanged themselves. The rash of suicides focused attention on widespread reservation problems; unemployment at Wind River was about 70 percent. Alcohol problems also were said to be widespread on the reservation, though most of the suicides were not thought attributable to alcohol or drugs. V.L.

INDONESIA. A series of disruptive events drew governmental and public attention in 1985. Not all were deliberate, politically or religiously motivated acts, but some appeared to be so. Violence in Jakarta's harbor area in September 1984 was followed in 1985 by bombings in the city's business district, in its outlying industrial area, and at ammunition storehouses in Jakarta and Bandung. There were also fires at the famous Sarinah department store, at the Liberty shopping center in Yogyakarta, at the traditional palace at Surakarta, and at another Jakarta department store, as well as at the headquarters of the government broadcasting system. The most shocking event, however, was the January bombing of the Central Java-

President Ronald Reagan talks with Prime Minister Yasuhiro Nakasone of Japan at a seven-nation economic conference in Bonn; others at the table were, from left, Prime Minister Bettino Craxi of Italy (mostly hidden behind Reagan), Prime Minister Brian Mulroney of Canada, President François Mitterrand of France, Chancellor Helmut Kohl of West Germany, Prime Minister Margaret Thatcher of Great Britain, and Jacques Delors, president of the European Community.

nese ninth-century Borobudur temple, a Buddhist monument regarded as one of the archaeological wonders of the world. Nine bombs exploded on the upper level, doing extensive damage to the edifice, which had been reopened in 1903 after an eight-year, multimillion-dollar restoration.

In June the last of five laws regulating Indonesian political life—the so-called "social organization laws"—was passed. These measures require, among other things, that all organizations, including Islamic ones, accept the secular state philosophy of Pancasila as their basic creed—a requirement bitterly opposed by orthodox Muslims. (The new system, for example, would force Islamic political groups to open membership to non-Muslims.)

Top leaders of a separatist movement in the province of West Irian surrendered in December to authorities across the border in Papua New Guinea. The government there said it would not return the individuals to Indonesia.

During the 1985 fiscal year, the Indonesian economy performed somewhat better than expected, growing slightly more than 1984's 4.2

percent but far below the 7.3 percent average annual growth for the previous 15 years. A bright spot was the record rice harvest. Direct trade with China was resumed after an agreement in July.

In April, Indonesia hosted celebration of the 30th anniversary of the Bandung Conference of Asian and African nations. The original conference, hosted by then-President Sukarno, had brought world recognition to his country as a leader in what became known as the nonaligned movement. The anniversary meeting, attended by representatives of more than 80 countries, seemed designed in part to counter critics of Suharto, who repeatedly complained that Indonesia had lost its prominence in world affairs. The meeting did not attract the attention hoped for, however, and Indonesian efforts to exert leadership on major issues met with little success.

See STATISTICS OF THE WORLD. W.F.

INTERNATIONAL CONFERENCES. A variety of international conferences were held in 1985. For some not covered below, see AFRICA; COMMONWEALTH OF NATIONS; ECONOMY AND

INTERNATIONAL CONFERENCES

BUSINESS; NORTH ATLANTIC TREATY ORGANIZATION; ORGANIZATION OF AMERICAN STATES; ORGANIZATION OF PETROLEUM EXPORTING COUNTRIES; UNION OF SOVIET SOCIALIST REPUBLICS; UNITED NATIONS; UNITED STATES; WOMEN.

Helsinki Accords. Representatives of 35 nations met in Helsinki from July 30 to August 1, to mark the tenth anniversary of the signing of the Final Act of the Conference on Security and Cooperation in Europe. The Helsinki accords, signed in that city on August 1, 1975, by delegates from Eastern and Western European nations, plus the United States and Canada, recognized existing post-World War II boundaries in Europe, while committing countries to respect human rights and to facilitate scientific and cultural exchanges. Not officially a treaty, the accords contained no enforcement mechanism, only a provision for periodic review conferences. At the formal Helsinki meeting, U.S. Secretary of State George Shultz criticized Soviet human rights policies, while Soviet Foreign Minister Eduard Shevardnadze accused the United States of engaging in an arms buildup; in private meetings, the two mapped out the groundwork for a November U.S.-Soviet summit conference in Geneva.

The eighth session of the European Security Conference concluded in December in Stockholm; representatives reported some progress as talks focused specifically on the issue of preventing accidental wars from breaking out. Among other meetings relating to the Helsinki accords was a meeting convened in Ottawa in June to discuss human rights; conferees reportedly made little headway.

Bonn Summit. The 11th annual summit conference of the seven major non-Communist industrialized nations was held May 2–4 in Bonn, West Germany. The heads of state or government of Canada, France, Great Britain, Italy, Japan, the United States, and West Germany, as well as the president of the European Community, issued general statements promising to follow "prudent" economic policies and to seek sustained economic growth, higher employment, reduction of trade barriers, and stabilization of the world monetary system.

New Association. The government leaders of Bangladesh, Bhutan, India, the Maldives, Nepal, Pakistan, and Sri Lanka met in Bangladesh on December 7–8 and created the South Asian Association for Regional Cooperation. The conferees pledged not to interfere in other members' internal affairs. Members hoped to reduce regional tensions and promote cooperation.

Asean Meetings. At a February 11 meeting of the Association of Southeast Asian Nations (Asean), members called for military aid for the Cambodian rebels, both Communist and non-Communist, fighting Vietnamese occupation troops. On July 8–9, the Asean foreign ministers, meeting in Kuala Lumpur, proposed "proximity talks" between Cambodian resistance groups and a Vietnamese delegation including members of the Heng Samrin government. Vietnam rejected the proposal.

Bandung Anniversary. On April 24–25, Indonesia hosted a meeting of delegates from more than 80 Third World countries and liberation movements in Bandung, 30 years after the first Bandung Conference brought together 29 African and Asian countries in the fledgling movement of so-called nonaligned nations. The 1985 conferees expressed concern about the arms race and its possible extension to outer space, attacked economic protectionism, and called for the relief of Third World nations' debt problems.   K.C.

IOWA. See STATISTICS OF THE WORLD.

IRAN. The costly war with Iraq remained at the center of events in 1985. Domestically, President Sayed Ali Khamenei was reelected, and a future successor to Ayatollah Ruhollah Khomeini was named.

War With Iraq. Although larger in numbers, Iran's army did not make significant headway against Iraq's better-equipped forces. On March 12, Iran launched a major offensive north of the Iraqi city of Basra, which failed, despite some initial gains, when Iraq counterattacked a day later. Iranian casualties were estimated at 15,000–20,000. U.S. intelligence analysts supported Iran's claims that Iraq had used chemical weapons in the battle. At about the same time, each country was engaged in bombardments of the other's towns and cities, despite a 1984 UN-mediated agreement to refrain from such attacks. Iran conducted heavy artillery attacks on Basra and used long-range surface-to-surface missiles against Baghdad.

The continuing "tanker war" at sea escalated on August 15 when Iraq launched the first in a series of major attacks against Iran's main oil facilities on Kharg Island. On September 19, in Iraq's tenth raid in five weeks, much of Kharg's Sea Island loading area was destroyed, reportedly cutting Iran's oil export capacity in half. Iran moved some operations to a safer, makeshift terminal at Sirri Island.

Iraqi attacks continued late in the year. On November 5 the Iraqis hit a Greek supertanker off the Iranian coast; two days later, Baghdad reported that it had bombed Iranian troop concentrations in the Hawizah Marshes on their common border. On December 29, Iraq announced it had mounted its 60th air raid on Kharg since mid-August. Iran was said to be planning to abandon the heavily damaged Kharg Island facility as its main oil terminal in favor of other export sites completed or under construction by year's end.

Despite international efforts at mediation, Iran showed little willingness to negotiate an end to the war, merely reiterating demands unacceptable to Iraq.

Foreign Relations. Most Arab states in the region, including Saudi Arabia, were supporting Iraq, but there was an improvement in Iran's relations with Saudi Arabia, aided by the visit of the Saudi foreign minister to Iran in May.

Prime Minister Mir Hussein Moussavi visited Nicaraguan, Cuban, and Venezuelan leaders in January, and Majlis (Parliament) Speaker Hojatolislam Hashemi Rafsanjani traveled to Japan and China in July. Soviet-Iranian relations

Civilian bombings escalated in the Iran-Iraq war, despite a 1984 UN-negotiated agreement by both sides to refrain from such attacks. Here, a street scene in the Iranian city of Khorramabad, hard hit during an Iraqi strike in March.

improved for a time, after an April meeting, but then deteriorated, as strains over Afghanistan and over Iran's suppression of the Tudeh (Communist) Party resurfaced and the Soviet Union withdrew its technicians from Iranian development projects. Iranian-U.S. relations remained implacably hostile; meanwhile, smuggling of U.S. military equipment to Iran seemed to be on the increase.

Economic Developments. Iraqi air attacks against shipping and against oil facilities continued to pose a serious threat to Iran's economy, which was also beset by weak international demand for crude oil and falling world oil prices. A shuttle service from vulnerable Kharg Island to tankers waiting at Sirri Island and a system of discounts for oil loaded at Sirri and Kharg were instituted by the government, with some success.

Presidential Elections. Incumbent President Khamenei, who was believed to enjoy the support of Ayatollah Khomeini, the supreme authority in Iran, easily won reelection over two other candidates (both supporters of the regime) with 12.2 million votes out of 14.2 million cast. Former Prime Minister Mehdi Bazargan of the Freedom Movement (Iran's only remaining legal opposition party) was rejected as a candidate by the country's 12-member Council of Constitutional Guardians. Opposition groups had urged an election boycott, and 355,000 blank ballots were cast as a sign of protest. After winning, Khamenei called for a foreign policy designed to win allies for Iran and expressed support for a mixed economy. On meeting the new 22-member cabinet on October 31, Ayatollah Khomeini supported the latter goal, advising the cabinet not to "nationalize everything."

Khomeini Successor Named. In November, Ayatollah Hussein Ali Montazeri was designated by a special 83-man Council of Experts as the eventual successor to Khomeini. Montazeri, long an ally of Khomeini's, was considered to be Khomeini's personal choice for the job.

Political Turmoil. On March 15 a suicide bomber believed to be associated with the Paris-based Mujahedeen guerrillas attempted to assassinate President Khamenei. He survived, but 14 people were killed and 88 wounded. Other terrorist incidents were reported during the year. Despite moves by Khomeini to ease harsh prison conditions, the government was believed to be holding 10,000–20,000 political prisoners in 1985.

See STATISTICS OF THE WORLD.　　J.S.I.

IRAQ. Iraqi policy in 1985 was directed toward strengthening the country in its war against Iran and applying pressure on Iran to negotiate an end to the conflict.

War With Iran. A substantial edge in nearly all categories of military equipment enabled Iraq to offset Iran's superiority in raw manpower and carry the war to Iranian economic targets. In late January, Iraq launched its first major ground attack against Iran in nearly three years, in an unsuccessful attempt to recapture the Majnoon oil fields north of the Iraqi city of Basra. In March, an Iranian offensive in the same area, which threatened to cut off the vital Baghdad-Basra highway, was promptly repelled by counterattacking Iraqi forces (reportedly using chemical weapons), with heavy casualties to both sides. Strategic bombardment of civilian population centers by both sides escalated within the same period, despite a 1984 moratorium arranged by the United Nations. Iraq also bombed a nuclear reactor being built at Bushire and economic targets in Ahwaz. Its March 17 threat to destroy any plane flying through Iranian airspace forced suspension of most commercial air flights to Iran.

The so-called tanker war also escalated, as Iraq attempted to cut off Iranian imports and vital oil exports through the Persian Gulf, with Iran periodically retaliating against neutral shipping. In late December, Iraq reportedly launched the 60th in a series of air raids since August against Iran's principal oil export facilities at Kharg Island; the attacks reportedly inflicted severe damage.

Foreign Relations. Regionally, Iraq enjoyed the support of most Arab countries except Algeria and South Yemen (which remained neutral) and Syria and Libya (which supported Iran). In March the Arab League Council declared its "total solidarity" with Iraq, while Jordan, Egypt, and the Persian Gulf states—all opponents of Iraq before the war—continued giving generous financial aid. Iraq improved its relations with the United States, which agreed to $633 million

Clearing the battlefield, Iraqi soldiers stockpile arms recovered after their forces pushed back an Iranian offensive aimed at cutting the important Basra-Baghdad highway link. The Iraqi troops inflicted heavy casualties on the Iranians.

in agricultural credits during the year and seemed to be tilting toward Iraq despite its declared neutrality in the war. The Soviet Union remained one of Iraq's major weapons suppliers. Iraq reached an agreement in principle in September to buy 24 combat planes from France, its other major arms source.

Economic Scene. The crux of Baghdad's economic problems was its costs of $1 billion a month for the war and its continued low oil export earnings, worsened by the falling world price of oil. Foreign currency reserves were nearly exhausted, requiring large-scale foreign borrowing. By mid-1985, the nation's external indebtedness was about $40 billion, a sixfold increase from 1982. Left with only a single export pipeline (through Turkey) because of the war, the government made real progress toward coping with these problems. A pipeline nearly 400 miles long linking southern Iraqi oil fields to Saudi Arabia's oil distribution network was completed in the fall, and plans became final for a second Iraqi-Saudi pipeline. Other pipeline construction and improvements

were planned, and Iraq predicted that these projects together would soon start raising its oil export capacity back toward prewar levels.

Domestic Opposition. Evidence that the regime of President Saddam Hussein and the Arab Baath Socialist Party remained securely in power came early in the year, as the Revolutionary Command Council on February 13 announced an amnesty for most political opponents of the government as well as for army deserters. The move also served to improve Iraq's image abroad. The various Kurdish separatist organizations were able to escalate their struggle against the regime beyond sporadic terrorism, but with the country's armed forces at peak strength, Iraq seemed unthreatened by the upsurge in Kurdish separatism.

See STATISTICS OF THE WORLD. T.I.

IRELAND, NORTHERN. *See* GREAT BRITAIN.

IRELAND, REPUBLIC OF. On November 15, 1985, Prime Minister Garret FitzGerald of Ireland and Prime Minister Margaret Thatcher of Great Britain signed an important agreement granting the Irish Republic an official consul-

207

tative role and presence in Northern Ireland, through an ongoing conference involving ministers from the two countries. The treaty, which was greeted with strong protest by unionists and nationalists alike, also specified that Northern Ireland would remain British as long as a majority of its (mostly Protestant) inhabitants chose. Partly because it thus recognized Northern Ireland as a part of the United Kingdom, the accord was strongly criticized by Irish opposition leader Charles Haughey, of Fianna Fáil. But it won the support of the two parties in Ireland's ruling coalition and was approved by the parliaments in both countries. It took effect on November 29, and consultations under its aegis were held in Belfast on December 11.

With little improvement in living standards and unemployment around 17 percent, the popularity of the Irish government sank during the year. This was recorded in the nationwide local government elections in mid-June, when Fianna Fáil made large gains, showing a clear lead in the popular vote over the two coalition parties together.

In February the government introduced a bill to liberalize restrictions on the sale of contraceptives to persons over the age of 18. The measure was denounced by the new and conservative archbishop of Dublin, Kevin McNamara, as calculated to encourage premarital sexual activity; the Irish Parliament, or Dáil, nevertheless passed the bill, by 83 votes to 80.

There were many expressions of public alarm at the prevalence of drug abuse and violent crime, some of it (such as robberies, kidnappings, and protection rackets) associated with the troubles in the North. Stiffer measures were introduced by the minister of justice. Official crime statistics did not altogether bear out the public's perception of rapidly growing lawlessness.

The Irish took pride in the initiative of Bob Geldof, a rock musician of their own, whose "Live Aid," an international rock concert to benefit African famine victims, raised more than $65 million in charitable donations. The Irish people themselves gave generously to the cause.

See STATISTICS OF THE WORLD.   T.J.O.H.

Prime Minister Margaret Thatcher of the United Kingdom and Prime Minister Garret FitzGerald of Ireland at ceremonies following the signing of a treaty giving the Irish Republic a consultative role in Northern Ireland affairs for the first time.

Young Ethiopian Jews who were evacuated from Sudanese refugee camps during a secret Israeli airlift learn Hebrew at a youth center north of Haifa.

ISRAEL. Developments dominating the news in Israel in 1985 included the rescue of more than 10,000 Ethiopian Jews, the withdrawal of Israeli troops from Lebanon, the continuing economic crisis, the increasingly sharp debate over the peace process, and speculation over whether the shaky national unity government would survive.

Ethiopian Airlift. In January it was revealed that about half of the 25,000 Jews in Ethiopia, who are known as Falashas and who had suffered from centuries of persecution and more recently from famine and civil war, had been airlifted to Israel by way of Sudan. The premature revelation of the airlift by a Jewish Agency official had led Sudan (still theoretically in a state of war with Israel) to cut off the flow of immigrants. However, two months later the United States was able to evacuate the Ethiopian Jews in Sudanese refugee camps to Israel.

Withdrawal From Lebanon. After talks with Lebanese military leaders under United Nations auspices broke down in January, Israel decided to undertake a unilateral withdrawal from Lebanon, which it had invaded in 1982. By the beginning of June, all Israeli combat units had been withdrawn from Lebanon, but only after a spate of violence that included car bombings and other attacks by Shiite Muslim guerrillas against Israeli forces and Israeli retaliation against Shiite villages. Israel subsequently established a 6-mile-wide, 50-mile-long "security zone" along its entire northern border, policed by the predominantly Christian South Lebanon Army. Approximately 1,000 Israeli troops remained in Lebanon at year's end working with the South Lebanon Army.

In a controversial move, Israel transferred to an Israeli prison approximately 1,100 Lebanese, predominantly Shiites, who had been detained in Lebanon on suspicion of guerrilla activity. While the troop withdrawal was going on, Israel began releasing the detainees in groups as a hedge against Shiite attacks. The process was temporarily slowed following the June hijacking of an American TWA jetliner by Shiite terrorists who demanded the immediate release of all of the remaining detainees. Following the release of the American hostages, Israel resumed freeing detainees; the final prisoners were released in September.

209

Israeli troops start their pullout from the port city of Tyre in southern Lebanon. All combat units were out of Lebanon by the beginning of June.

U.S.-Israeli Relations. Relations between Israel and the United States remained strong despite some tension. The primary source of friction was President Ronald Reagan's decision to lay a wreath at a military cemetery in Bitburg, West Germany, where Nazi SS troops were buried, as part of ceremonies marking the 40th anniversary of the end of World War II. Prime Minister Shimon Peres severely criticized the Bitburg visit. The other major note of discord came late in the year when a U.S. Navy intelligence analyst was charged with selling secret documents to Israel. Israel apologized for the espionage and said an investigation would be conducted. Questions remained as to who in the Israeli government ordered and knew of the operation.

The Peace Process. The divisions between the two main components of the national unity government, the Likud coalition and the Labor Party, were at their most apparent following the February 11 "agreement" between King Hussein of Jordan and Yasir Arafat, leader of the Palestine Liberation Organization, that called for a joint Palestinian-Jordanian team to negotiate with Israel at an international peace conference. Likud, objecting to the vagueness of Arafat's commitments, dismissed the initiative out of hand; Labor said it had some possibilities. Prime Minister Peres also gave a cautious endorsement to a similar proposal later in February by Egyptian President Hosni Mubarak. Peres was concerned that the PLO was angling for U.S. recognition without explicitly recognizing Israel's right to exist or renouncing terrorism.

In October, Peres declared, in a speech before the UN General Assembly, that he was not opposed to an international peace conference provided the Soviet Union restored diplomatic relations with Israel. King Hussein welcomed Peres's remarks, but agreement on the form of Palestinian participation was still a major sticking point. Peres's speech provoked sharp debate within the Israeli government, but he won a parliamentary vote of confidence on the issue. In November it was reported that Peres and Hussein had reached an informal agreement to work toward peace negotiations.

Domestic Politics. Bitter exchanges between Labor and Likud became increasingly common. In August several Likud cabinet ministers, including Ariel Sharon (the minister of industry and trade), defied Peres by visiting an illegally acquired apartment in Hebron to demonstrate solidarity with seven right-wing members of the Knesset who had established themselves there to symbolize the right of Israeli Jews to settle anywhere on the West Bank. Defense Minister Yitzhak Rabin, of the Labor Party, had the ministers evicted.

The rising popularity of Rabbi Meir Kahane troubled many Israelis. Kahane openly preached a simplistic solution to increased Arab terrorism and the seemingly interminable conflict: the expulsion of all Arabs from Israel, the West Bank, and the Gaza Strip.

Terrorism. One of the most politically divisive developments of the year was the government's decision at midyear to free 1,150 Arab and other terrorists in exchange for 3 Israeli soldiers captured during the Lebanese war who were being held in Syria. The release led to demands for the pardoning of 27 Jewish terrorists who were arrested in 1984 for killing and/or maiming Arabs on the West Bank. The Jewish terrorists were not released: 3 received life sentences, and by late in the year 22 had been given prison terms of up to ten years.

Amid a general increase in terrorist attacks—including the killing of three Israelis in a Larnaca, Cyprus, marina on September 25—Israeli planes bombed the PLO headquarters in Tunisia on October 1, killing about 70 Palestinians and Tunisians. The raid was condemned by the Arab world and other countries. The United States, which at first supported the attack as a "legitimate response" to terrorism, later said the raid could not be condoned. Terrorist attacks by Palestinians later in the year were said to be responses in part to the Israeli raid in Tunisia. (*See also* MIDDLE EAST.)

Economic Crisis. The Israeli economy was in an almost continual state of crisis in 1985. Only in July was an austerity program introduced that seemed to hold out the possibility of controlling Israel's runaway inflation. The measures, designed to reduce the purchasing power of Israelis by 30 percent, included an 18.8 percent devaluation of the shekel against the U.S. dollar, sharp price increases on subsidized products, and a three-month freeze on wages and prices. In September a new shekel, worth 1,000 times the existing shekel, was introduced.

See STATISTICS OF THE WORLD.   R.O.F.

ITALY. The government of Socialist Prime Minister Bettino Craxi fell temporarily over its handling of a hijacking crisis—one of several terrorist incidents that affected Italy during 1985. However, the five-party coalition was reconstituted and in November became Italy's longest-lived government since the end of World War II.

Hijacking and Government Crisis. On October 7 the Italian cruise ship *Achille Lauro* was seized, shortly after it left the Egyptian port of Alexandria, by four gunmen, who demanded the release of 50 Palestinian prisoners in Israel. Negotiations were conducted by Italy, Egypt, and Palestine Liberation Organization officials

including Muhammad Abbas, leader of the PLO faction to which the hijackers belonged and alleged mastermind of the plot. On October 9 the gunmen surrendered in exchange for a promise of safe passage out of Egypt. The following day, an Egyptian airliner carrying the four Palestinians, Abbas, and other officials to Tunisia was intercepted by U.S. Navy jet fighters and forced to land at a joint U.S.-NATO base in Sicily. The gunmen were taken into custody by Italian authorities and charged with the kidnapping and murder of an elderly, wheelchair-bound American passenger, Leon Klinghoffer. Amid intense objections from the United States, Abbas was later allowed to leave Italy, a move that precipitated a government crisis in Rome.

Defense Minister Giovanni Spadolini, leader of the Republican Party and a rival of Craxi's throughout the 1980's, withdrew his party from the government coalition, saying that he had been left out of the decision-making process concerning Abbas's release, which he opposed, and objecting to what he called Italy's "close relations" with the PLO. On October 17, Craxi himself submitted his resignation. (Late in the month, Sicilian prosecuters issued an arrest warrant for Abbas and his bodyguard. In November warrants were issued in Genoa for 16 Palestinians accused of involvement in the hijacking.)

On October 21, President Francesco Cossiga asked Craxi to form a new government, but this proved unnecessary after members of the coalition agreed on a policy document promising consultations on major issues. Cossiga rescinded his provisional acceptance of Craxi's resignation, and Craxi retained office by winning votes of confidence in November in the Senate and Chamber of Deputies—although he provoked a new storm by defending the PLO's right to resort to arms.

Meanwhile, the four hijackers and a fifth man arrested in Genoa before the ship sailed were convicted and sentenced to prison on weapons charges. (One of the men, a 17-year-old, had to be retried subsequently because he was a juvenile.) Trial on the major charges was pending.

Elections. Popular support for the Communist Party continued to slip. In regional elections on May 12–13, the Communists garnered 30.1 percent of the vote, compared with 31.5 percent in the previous regional elections in 1980. And a Communist-backed referendum proposal to reverse wage cuts mandated in 1984 was defeated.

On June 24, Parliament elected Cossiga, a Christian Democrat, to succeed Socialist President Alessandro Pertini, whose seven-year term expired in July. Pertini, 88, a popular president, had declined to seek a second term.

Terrorism and Crime. The cruise ship hijacking was not the only terrorist incident to affect Italy. On December 27, four Arab terrorists launched an attack with machine guns and hand grenades near the check-in counter of El-Al Israel Airlines at the Leonardo Da Vinci Airport in Rome, killing 13 people and wounding about 70 others. Three of the terrorists were killed in a gun battle with police and security personnel, and one was captured. (A similar attack at Schwechat Airport in Vienna occurred just minutes after the Rome massacre, leaving four fatally wounded or dead, including one of the terrorists.) Most analysts considered the attacks to have been carried out by followers of Abu Nidal (real name, Mazen Sabry al-Banna), leader of a dissident Palestinian extremist group allegedly having ties to Libya.

Earlier, on January 13, the press attaché at the Libyan embassy in Rome was shot dead; a terrorist organization opposed to Libyan strongman Muammar al-Qaddafi took responsibility. On September 16, two grenades were thrown at an outdoor café on Rome's Via Veneto; one grenade exploded, wounding 38 people, many of them tourists. And on September 25, a bomb exploded at a British Airways terminal in Rome, wounding at least 14 people. Palestinians were arrested in both cases.

The struggle continued against the Mafia, in Sicily as well as on the mainland, and against its Neapolitan manifestation, the Camorra. On November 9, Sicilian magistrates indicted 475 Mafia suspects, in the largest crackdown ever on Italy's underground.

Economic Affairs. The large public sector borrowing requirement continued to increase; by July it had reached over 13 percent of the gross domestic product. On Friday, July 19—"Black Friday"—when the foreign exchange markets closed, the lira fell by about 20 percent against the U.S. dollar, after the state-owned energy company ENI, against official advice, tried to buy $125 million to settle a debt. The next day, the finance ministers of the European Community agreed to a devaluation of the lira within the European Monetary System.

Bodies tagged for identification lie strewn over Leonardo da Vinci Airport, following a massacre by Arab terrorists on December 27.

A massive wave of mud and water, released by the collapse of a dam, swept through Stava, Italy, destroying much of the Dolomite resort village and leaving more than 200 people dead.

The government also introduced a package of fiscal measures designed to reduce its huge deficit. Its program secured a vote of confidence in the Senate on August 1.

Foreign Affairs. On February 25–28, Italy played host to Soviet Foreign Minister Andrei Gromyko; Gromyko was received by President Pertini and by Pope John Paul II, and he had talks with Craxi and Foreign Minister Giulio Andreotti on U.S.-Soviet arms negotiations. Three months later, Craxi and Andreotti visited Moscow, where they met the new Soviet leader, Mikhail Gorbachev. In early March, Craxi had visited the United States, where he met with President Ronald Reagan and addressed a joint session of Congress, reiterating Italy's support for U.S. policy in Europe. Italy also continued to seek close ties with China. In April, Defense Minister Spadolini, on a visit to the People's Republic, negotiated an agreement for the sale of arms to Peking.

Papal Plot Trial. On May 27 the trial of five Turks, including Mehmet Ali Agca, and three Bulgarian government officials opened in Rome. The defendants were accused of having plotted to assassinate Pope John Paul II in Rome in May 1981. Much of the evidence had been provided by Agca himself in a series of statements to Italian authorities after his conviction in the shooting of the pope. The plot, Agca had claimed, involved Bulgaria, the Soviet Union, and a right-wing Turkish organization. He testified during the trial, often making bizarre statements and claims.

In October, after a summer recess, Sergei I. Antonov, a Bulgarian airline official charged with being an accomplice of Agca's, testified that he had nothing to do with the assassination attempt. In mid-month one of the accused Turks, who was being tried in absentia, died of a heart attack in Turkey. In November, Turkish businessman Omer Mersan testified that in 1980, on behalf of a Turkish underworld figure and for a purpose unknown to him, he had given Agca money. The court also heard evidence in Bulgaria from two defendants there who denied any involvement.

Disasters. On May 29, a riot at Heysel Stadium in Brussels before the European Cup soccer championship match between Liverpool and

213

the Italian team Juventus of Turin resulted in the death of 38 people, most of them Italian spectators; more than 200 others were injured. The majority of the casualties came when a brick wall collapsed as Italian fans pressed against it while seeking to flee British rioters.

On July 19 an earthen dam collapsed above the hamlet of Stava, north of Tesero, in the Dolomites near the Austrian border, bringing down a 130-foot-high wall of mud and water that crashed through hotels, homes, and a holiday camp. Over 230 people were killed. On December 25, Mount Etna erupted, causing lava flows and a series of earthquakes in the vicinity; one person was killed and a dozen were injured.

See STATISTICS OF THE WORLD.   M.G.

IVORY COAST. See STATISTICS OF THE WORLD.

J

JAMAICA. See STATISTICS OF THE WORLD. See also CARIBBEAN BASIN.

JAPAN. Factional maneuvering was intense within Japan's political parties in 1985. The nation's outstanding success as an exporter continued to complicate its relationship with the United States.

Political Maneuvering. On February 27, Kakuei Tanaka, who had long played a dominant role within the ruling Liberal Democratic Party (LDP), suffered a stroke, which required a long period of hospital recovery. His absence set off an open struggle within his faction—the LDP's largest—between Susumu Nikaido (Tanaka's longtime right-hand man) and Noboru Takeshita. Meanwhile, Kiichi Miyazawa and Shintaro Abe, younger leaders in two other LDP factions, began maneuvering in an attempt to succeed current Prime Minister Yasuhiro Nakasone in the 1986 party election, focusing their opposition on Nakasone's tight budget policies.

Within the Japan Socialist Party, chairman Masashi Ishibashi successfully promoted a draft platform that abandoned Marxist-Leninist principles for a more pragmatic approach. The party's new mood was seen in its attempts to step up cooperation with Komeito, a centrist, Buddhist-oriented party.

On July 17 the Japanese Supreme Court ruled the 1983 election for the Diet's House of Representatives unconstitutional (but not invalid) because of a disproportionate distribution of seats between rural districts—the basis of the LDP's strength—and urban districts, many of which were under-represented. An LDP reapportionment plan was put before the Diet but failed to gain passage.

On December 28 a new cabinet was installed; most members of the old cabinet were replaced, but the ministers of foreign affairs,

What's Your Blood Type?

This new question is rapidly replacing "What's your sign?" as the conversational icebreaker on the Japanese social scene. Toshitaka Nomi revived a 50-year-old theory with his bestseller, *Advice on How to Form a Good Combination of Blood Types,* and a host of subsidiary books, articles, and TV appearances; the theory, originally posited by a Japanese psychologist, holds that blood groups correspond directly with personality characteristics. A person with type A blood is said to be a hard-driving perfectionist, type O an aggressive go-getter, type B a free spirit who requires a structureless environment, and type AB a bloodless conformist. Since types A and O account for at least 70 percent of Japan's population, Nomi's book supposedly divulges the secret behind the country's technological supremacy. The scientific community, however, is not persuaded, pointing to the worldwide predominance of types O and A, to the real number of blood groups—more than 240—and to the lack of any proven connection between blood type and personality.

defense, and finance were retained. Also retained was the usual balance of power among the five main LDP factions.

Economy. Japan's gross national product rose 5.7 percent in the fiscal year ending March 31, 1985, the largest gain in 12 years. The trade surplus reached a record $46 billion, but much of it was offset by a massive flow of capital out of Japan to foreign markets, especially the United States.

On September 22, Japan, Great Britain, France, West Germany, and the United States agreed to work together to lower the value of the U.S. dollar, with a key role to be played by Japanese efforts to strengthen the yen. The Bank of Japan intervened aggressively in the currency market, buying up yen. On October 15 the Japanese government also adopted measures to stimulate economic growth and thereby curb the trade surplus.

The Nakasone administration, struggling to reduce a huge budget deficit, presented a fiscal 1985 budget (adopted by the Diet in April) that was up only 3.7 percent from the initial fiscal 1984 budget. One of the few budget items to show substantial growth was defense, with a 6.9 percent increase over fiscal 1984. This increase was controversial both within Japan, where there is pressure to keep defense spending extremely low as a proportion of GNP, and in the United States, which believed that Japanese defense spending should be substantially higher.

U.S.-Japanese Trade. Against a backdrop of growing Japanese exports of manufactured goods and a record U.S. bilateral trade deficit with Japan, Prime Minister Nakasone, meeting with President Ronald Reagan on January 2 in California, promised further efforts to open the Japanese market and increase imports. Early in the year, high-level bilateral trade negotiations were held in the areas of telecommunications, electronics, medical equipment and pharmaceuticals, and forestry products, producing orders for U.S. satellites and supercomputers as well as concessions involving telecommunications.

There was growing U.S. domestic political pressure for restraints on Japanese exports, and in March the Japanese agreed to voluntarily restrict their U.S. steel exports to 5.8 percent

Fashionable Japanese shoppers appear to be following Prime Minister Nakasone's urgings to buy imported goods, at least when it comes to putting together a stylish wardrobe, which might include a few items from the Ivy League clothing mainstay, Brooks Brothers (of Tokyo).

of the U.S. market for five years. Despite a Reagan administration decision not to request extension of a four-year-old voluntary limit on Japanese automobile exports to the United States, Japan announced on March 28 that it would continue the restraints, raising the quota from 1.85 million to 2.3 million cars. This move embarrassed the Reagan administration and members of Congress who were resisting import limitations; it also failed to appease other members of Congress who wanted stronger action. By fall more than 300 pieces of legislation relating to the trade deficit had been introduced in Congress; one bill passed but was vetoed by Reagan.

U.S. officials met with Nakasone in Tokyo on March 31, and on April 9, Japan announced a package of measures to promote imports.

In memory of atomic bomb victims, thousands of paper lanterns were sent by friends and relatives to float down Hiroshima's Motoyasu River, past the A-Bomb Dome. A series of rites were held in Hiroshima on August 6 to mark the 40th anniversary of the bombing.

Nakasone, in a nationwide speech on Japanese television, expressed his concern over the problem and urged Japanese consumers to buy imported goods. He followed up with a much-publicized shopping trip to a Japanese department store to personally purchase foreign-made items. Details of the measures were released in July; they included tariff cuts of about 20 percent on more than 1,800 items; simplification of standards, certification systems, and import procedures; an increase from 45 to 61 in the number of government agencies that can purchase imports; market access for foreign services, including lawyers; and removal of the interest ceiling on big-denomination deposits in banks.

Foreign Affairs. After visiting President Reagan in California in January, Nakasone made a round of good-will trips to Fiji, Papua New Guinea, Australia, and New Zealand. In May he attended a meeting of leaders of six other major industrial democracies in Bonn, West Germany, and in July he visited member countries of the European Economic Community;

much of the talk at these meetings focused on the need to open Japanese markets. In July, agreements on low-interest loans and nuclear power cooperation were concluded with China, which since 1984 has been Japan's second-largest export market.

Other Events. March saw digging completed on the 34-mile Seikan Tunnel (begun in 1964) between the main island of Honshu and the northern island of Hokkaido. Rail service in this longest of the world's underwater transportation tunnels was expected to begin in 1987. On August 6, Hiroshima marked the 40th anniversary of its destruction by a U.S. atomic bomb, with a gathering of some 50,000 people at the city's Peace Memorial. On August 12, a Japan Air Lines Boeing 747 jet crashed an hour after takeoff from Tokyo's Haneda airport, killing 520 people in the worst single-plane disaster in aviation history.

See STATISTICS OF THE WORLD.   M. S. B.

JORDAN. A peace initiative launched by King Hussein and Palestine Liberation Organization chairman Yasir Arafat dominated Jordanian events during 1985. The initiative, announced on February 11 in Amman, had as its centerpiece the formation of a joint Jordanian-Palestinian delegation to negotiate with Israel on a possible peace accord, providing for a Palestinian state on the West Bank and Gaza Strip in confederation with Jordan. A five-stage process was envisioned, which included a U.S. meeting with a Jordanian-Palestinian delegation having no PLO members, a formal declaration by the PLO declaring its readiness to recognize and negotiate with Israel on the basis of the appropriate UN resolutions, a U.S. declaration of support for Palestinian self-determination in confederation with Jordan, an American meeting with a new Jordanian-Palestinian delegation including PLO members, and an international conference with direct Arab-Israeli negotiations.

Within the Arab bloc, only Egypt and Iraq supported the initiative, while Saudi Arabia and other Arab moderates remained officially silent. Syria and radical elements within the PLO rejected it totally; radicals in the PLO were implicated in the assassination of a Jordanian diplomat in Ankara, Turkey, in July and in terrorist attacks on other Jordanian targets. Israeli reaction was mixed, with the right-wing Likud bloc rejecting discussions with any Palestinians while the Labor Party left the door open for talks with non-PLO Palestinians.

The Reagan administration welcomed the initiative but refused to give it unqualified support. Hussein assured the United States during his May visit to Washington that the PLO would approve UN Resolution 242, a condition the United States has set for talks with the organization. But amid conflicting signals from the PLO itself, the organization's participation in the talks remained a stumbling block. A second problem was the proposed participation of the Soviet Union, which the United States and Israel opposed.

New efforts to break the diplomatic deadlock began in September when Hussein and Israeli Prime Minister Shimon Peres made speeches before the UN General Assembly in which each expressed his willingness to enter negotiations. Peres said that such talks could occur in the framework of an international conference provided the Soviet Union restored diplomatic relations with Israel. Israel continued to oppose PLO participation in the proposed talks. Hussein met with Arafat in late October in an apparent effort to induce the PLO leader to make the compromises necessary to advance the peace process, but their talks appeared to make little headway. In November an informal understanding between Hussein and Peres on terms for negotiations was reported; it envisioned acceptance by Israel of an international framework and a pledge by Jordan to include in the talks only those Palestinians acceptable to the Israelis.

Aside from complications which arose because of the peace initiative, Jordan's relations with its Arab neighbors were generally good. Saudi Arabia did not cut off economic aid, and relations with Iraq remained strong, as Jordan continued to support its Arab neighbor in the war with Iran. There were even signs of a rapprochement with Syria. As part of a general crackdown against Muslim fundamentalists, Hussein said in November that Jordanian territory would never again be used as a base for fundamentalist terrorist operations against Syria. The following month, Hussein had a two-day meeting with Syrian President Hafez al-Assad in Damascus.

On October 23, President Ronald Reagan, who had announced his intention (subject to congressional veto) to sell Jordan $1.5–$1.9 billion in arms, bowed to congressional opposition and instead endorsed a congressional resolution that would bar any such deal at least until March 1986, unless Jordan entered "direct and meaningful peace negotiations" with Israel before then. Hussein called the resolution "demeaning." Earlier in the year, the king made good on a 1984 threat to diversify his arms purchases by arranging to obtain weapons from the Soviet Union, Spain, Great Britain, and France.

See STATISTICS OF THE WORLD.   C.H.A.

JOURNALISM. Two widely publicized libel cases ended in 1985 in technical victories for the news media, although the credibility of the media suffered in the process. Relations between the media and the Reagan administration were sensitive at times.

Sharon Case. Former Israeli Defense Minister Ariel Sharon's $50 million libel suit against

Two major news organizations defended themselves against libel suits brought by public figures. A jury ruled that Time magazine had defamed but not libeled former Israeli Defense Minister Ariel Sharon (above); U.S. General William Westmoreland (right) dropped his suit against CBS before it came to trial.

Time Inc. ended in January. The case had grown out of the assassination in 1982 of Lebanon's President-elect Bashir Gemayel and the murder two days later of hundreds of Palestinians, when refugee camps in an Israeli-controlled area were overrun by vengeful Christian Phalangist supporters of Gemayel. An Israeli commission found Sharon indirectly responsible, for having allowed the Phalangists into the camps; a Time magazine article further concluded that, on a visit to the grieving Gemayel family prior to the massacre, Sharon had "reportedly discussed the need for the Phalangists to take revenge." This information, Time said, was in a secret "Appendix B" to the commission's report.

Sharon sued, charging that Time had falsely and maliciously accused him of inspiring the massacre. In the trial, which began in November 1984, Time correspondent David Halevy conceded that his report to Time editors never said Sharon "discussed" vengeance with the Gemayels, only that he "gave them the feeling . . . that he understood their need to take revenge." Halevy also said he had not seen Appendix B but had relied on information from confidential sources.

The jury decided that the Time article con-

tained false information and had defamed Sharon. But, while criticizing "certain Time employees" for negligence and carelessness, the jury concluded that Time had not knowingly or maliciously defamed the general and therefore was not guilty of libel. However, many journalists feared that the case had increased public doubts about the reliability of the press.

Westmoreland Case. Another major libel case grew out of a 1982 CBS documentary, "The Uncounted Enemy: A Vietnam Deception," which depicted General William Westmoreland as having conspired to mislead the president and the public during the Vietnam war by systematically understating enemy troop strength levels. When a subsequent TV Guide article charged that CBS had coached interviewees and left out material favorable to the retired general, CBS ordered an internal investigation. The investigation criticized the program for nonstandard procedures, but the network said it still "stood by" the broadcast; Westmoreland, accepting an offer of financial help from the Washington Legal Foundation, sued for $120 million.

The expensive, highly publicized trial never went to the jury, however. In February 1985, after 16 weeks of testimony, Westmoreland abruptly agreed to drop his suit in return for a statement from CBS in which it said it "never intended to assert" that he "was unpatriotic or disloyal." Westmoreland called the outcome a victory and the statement "in essence an apology," but CBS said it still believed that the program had been "fair and accurate."

Viceroy Suit. The media lost a less publicized libel suit late in the year, when the Brown & Williamson Tobacco Corporation, manufacturer of Viceroy cigarettes, was awarded $5.05 million in damages, in an action brought against CBS Inc. and Chicago television commentator Walter Jacobson. In an on-the-air commentary, Jacobson had accused Brown & Williamson of trying to lure children to smoking by using ads associating it with such "adult" habits as alcohol, drugs, and sex. He did not note that the ads in question were a proposal by an ad agency and that the company never used them.

Press and Government. The U.S. Defense Department, faced by protests from newspapers and press groups, backed off in late 1984 from a decision to exclude newspaper reporters from the pool of 11 journalists who would be alerted on short notice to cover military actions; it expanded the pool to include representatives of 24 newspaper organizations. In April the Defense Department tested the plan by alerting eight news organizations, on ten hours notice, to send reporters to Andrews Air Force Base, prepared to spend a week in hot, rainy weather. Although the journalists were not told they would be watching U.S. military training exercises in Honduras, the mission's cover was blown in a very short time. The Pentagon said it would stage more trials to iron out problems. A second test, in September, in which reporters were secretly flown to a training exercise in Kentucky, was more successful, with no leaks reported.

Coverage of the June hostage crisis in Beirut led to criticism of the U.S. news media, particularly of broadcasters. Most journalists seemed to agree that American news organizations had handled the story responsibly, except for minor lapses. But many members of the public, and some government officials, believed media coverage had been too sensational and had played into the hands of the terrorists by giving them the publicity they sought.　　　　J.L.

K

KAMPUCHEA. See CAMBODIA.
KANSAS. See STATISTICS OF THE WORLD.
KENTUCKY. See STATISTICS OF THE WORLD.
KENYA. In January 1985, Kenya's President Daniel arap Moi initiated a membership recruitment drive for the Kenya African National Union (Kanu), the ruling and only legal party. By April, the party had more than 4 million members, and President Moi called an election for party officers in June. Of the nine national officeholders, only President Moi, Vice-President Mwai Kibaki, and the party's national treasurer were reelected. The president's Kalenjin people and the Luhya were now clearly at the forefront in party leadership, at the expense of the once-dominant Kikuyu.

In July, Nairobi hosted a United Nations conference attended by 2,000 delegates from 157 countries, marking the end of the UN Decade for Women, as well as Forum '85, a conference for nongovernmental participants, attended by around 13,000 women. The Kenyan delegation to the UN conference, led by Margaret Kenyatta (daughter of the late President Jomo Kenyatta), reportedly played a major role in achieving the final consensus document. In August, Kenya hosted the 43rd Eucharistic Congress of the Roman Catholic Church, under the theme "The Eucharist and the Family." With 4 million Catholics and the world's highest birthrate, Kenya was at the center of struggle between the church, with its strictures against birth control, and family-planning-minded Third World governments. At the conference, Pope John Paul spoke out strongly against contraception.

Although high prices for coffee and tea helped somewhat to mitigate the effects of generally poor agricultural performance, drought in 1984 had caused heavy food imports and a reduction by almost half in the balance-of-payments surplus. The March-to-May rains in 1985 were satisfactory, however, and agricultural outputs were expected to show improvement. Overall economic growth was also expected to rise, after a meager 0.9 percent rate for 1984.

See STATISTICS OF THE WORLD.   P.S.

KHMER REPUBLIC. See CAMBODIA.

KIRIBATI. See STATISTICS OF THE WORLD.

KOREA, DEMOCRATIC PEOPLE'S REPUBLIC OF, or **NORTH KOREA.** Relations with the Soviet Union grew closer in 1985. Foreign Minister Kim Yong Nam visited the Soviet Union in April, meeting with Soviet leader Mikhail Gorbachev and then-Foreign Minister Andrei Gromyko. The Soviets reciprocated on North Korean Liberation Day in August, with

Reunited for a day, a North Korean brother and South Korean sister embrace; they were among a small number of the many families separated by war and politics who were allowed in September to briefly cross the border between the two hostile Koreas.

a visit by Vice-Premier Geidar Aliyev. Relations with China were highlighted by the visit of Chinese Communist Party chief Hu Yaobang to the North Korean border city of Sinuiju in May.

North and South Korean delegations met in Panmunjom for economic talks, and Red Cross talks resumed in Seoul and Pyongyang for the first time since 1973. In September members of divided families from each side were allowed brief reunions, for the first time in over 30 years.

In October, North Korea freed several crewmen from a captured South Korean fishing boat. At about the same time, South Korea reported it had sunk an alleged North Korean spy ship; the sinking was the first incident of its kind in nearly two years.

The slow process of establishing Kim Chong Il as successor to his father, President Kim Il Sung, continued. He frequently made "on-the-spot guidance" appearances in the manner of his father, his name appeared second to Kim Il Sung's in official lists, and his writings were quoted as authority for party and state policies.

The 1985 budget was increased 4 percent. The chairman of the Agricultural Committee announced in January that the 1984 grain crop had exceeded 10 million tons, leading to a surplus.

While continuing to urge three-way North Korea-South Korea-U.S. talks for relaxation of tensions, North Korea kept up its anti-American propaganda. The tone, however, was less vituperative than in previous years.

See STATISTICS OF THE WORLD.   D.S.M.

KOREA, REPUBLIC OF, or **SOUTH KOREA.** In 1985 a strong opposition party emerged, and student protests accelerated. Economic growth slowed slightly.

Politics and Government. A new opposition party, the New Korea Democratic Party, surprised observers by capturing 67 of the National Assembly's 276 seats and 29 percent of the popular vote in February 12 elections. The progovernment Democratic Justice Party, with a plurality of 35 percent of the total vote, kept its legislative majority, with over 140 seats. After the election, President Chun Doo Hwan named Roh Tae-woo, an ex-military associate, as chairman of the government party. Chun also named Lho Shin Yong as prime minister and replaced 12 other cabinet members.

Following the election, the ban on political activity was lifted on the last 14 of more than 800 leaders on whom it had been imposed in 1980. However, Kim Dae Jung, an unsuccessful 1971 presidential candidate, was still forbidden to engage in political activity because of a suspended 20-year sentence for sedition. Kim had returned from two years in the United States just before the election, accompanied by a group of Americans who vowed to protect him. Security forces hustled him away from the Americans and the welcoming crowd of thousands; two U.S. congressmen and two other Americans later said they and Kim had been beaten during the incident. Kim himself was placed under house arrest until after the election; he was also placed under occasional house arrest later on. Despite governmental restrictions, he continued to exert political influence.

In April a National Federation of Students was organized by 1,200 students from 62 colleges. The more radical members were involved in a nebulous group known as Sammint'u, whose ideology had antiforeign and anticapitalist overtones. In May, 73 students broke into the U.S. Information Service building in Seoul and occupied it for four days; they were induced to leave peacefully. Warnings or short jail terms were given to 53 of the students. The other 20 received prison sentences in October, ranging from a two-year suspended sentence to as long as seven years in jail. Later, more than two dozen other students or former students were arrested and accused of organizing the occupation.

The upsurge in student protests, along with increasing labor unrest, led the government to modify its political liberalization policies. For the first time in over a year, police were allowed onto college campuses in the fall to disperse protests. A crackdown on subversive literature spread from Seoul to other parts of the country, and the national police force was expanded. Human rights groups and opposition leaders charged that in some instances political prisoners were being tortured to obtain confessions.

Economic Developments. Early economic projections of 7.5 percent growth in gross national product for 1985 were revised downward at midyear to 6–7 percent. Exports through September were down slightly from the same period in 1984. Measures to boost exports included an "early warning system" to alert Korean exporters to possible retaliatory action by the United States. Motor vehicle exports continued to rise. Foreign investment rose by over 50 percent in 1984, and ambitious goals were set for 1985.

Foreign Affairs. On a visit to the United States in April, President Chun met with President Ronald Reagan, and a joint statement by the two leaders reaffirmed the American security commitment to South Korea. Growing South Korean penetration of U.S. markets led to continuing complaints by U.S. clothing, footwear, electronics, and steel producers. South Korea agreed to limit its steel exports to the United States for five years to 1.9 percent of the U.S. market.

See STATISTICS OF THE WORLD. See also KOREA, DEMOCRATIC PEOPLE'S REPUBLIC OF.　　D.S.M.

KUWAIT. Terrorism continued to plague Sunni Muslim-led Kuwait in 1985, largely because of its support of Iraq against Shiite Iran in the protracted Iran-Iraq war. Radical Shiite Muslims also were seeking the release of 17 Shiites imprisoned in Kuwait, convicted for December 1983 bombings. In September, when an American hostage, the Reverend Benjamin Weir, was released by terrorists in Lebanon, he reported that his captors, holding six other Americans there, were demanding the release of the 17 prisoners in Kuwait. Kuwaiti officials declared they had no intention of complying.

An Iraqi diplomat and his son were murdered in February. In May, Sheikh Jabir al-Ahmad al-Jabir al-Sabah, Kuwait's emir, escaped with minor scratches from a suicide car-bomb attack on his motorcade, but four people were killed. In July, 11 people were killed when two seaside cafés were bombed. Five Iranians were tried early in the year for subversive actions; most observers believe that they were convicted but that Kuwait made no formal announcement for fear of Shiite retaliation. To bolster its internal security, Kuwait in May began deporting hundreds of Lebanese, Iranians, and Iraqis and also barred Lebanese citizens from traveling on its national airline.

Kuwait, the only Persian Gulf country with an elected Parliament, held elections in February. Only males over 21 years old who can trace their Kuwaiti roots back to before 1920 may vote. More than half of the 40 incumbents were defeated, and voters ousted two prominent Islamic fundamentalists. Later, cabinet changes were made in key economic posts.

Government spending was cautious, partly because of depressed world oil markets. In addition, collapse of the unofficial stock market in 1982 was still taking its toll.

In June a Kuwaiti freighter was seized by Iran in international waters. Kuwait protested, but Iran did not release the ship.

See also STATISTICS OF THE WORLD.   L.A.K.

L

LABOR UNIONS. Economic hard times and increasing trade competition in 1985 brought a dramatic shift away from the pattern wage bargaining that was prevalent in U.S. labor negotiations during the 1970's. Employers instead were pursuing tougher wage and non-wage bargaining stances.

Continued Air Turbulence. One of the most disruptive strikes of the year began on May 17, when 5,200 United Airlines pilots stopped work to protest management's proposal for a two-tier wage system. The proposal called for a substantial gap between current pilots' salaries, which averaged $86,450, and salaries for newly hired pilots; United, the nation's largest air carrier, claimed it needed a reduction in its labor costs to remain competitive with other airlines. The strike was the first by United pilots since 1951 and resulted in a drastic reduction in the airline's operations—only 14 percent of United's 1,500 daily flights, carrying 120,000 passengers, were able to continue. Nonetheless, United vowed to keep flying and recruited new pilots to help it do so. An agreement was reached on June 12; it provided for a two-tiered pay scale for five years, after which the issue would be submitted to binding arbitration. All outstanding issues in the back-to-work settlement were submitted to a federal judge for resolution.

In another major settlement, the International Association of Machinists and the independent Union of Flight Attendants decided in April to call off a strike against Continental Air Lines that began in 1983. The offer to return to work

ended the longest strike ever held against a major airline. A third union on strike at Continental, the Air Line Pilots Association, said it would not return to work until it achieved an "equitable agreement." The carrier continued operations during the strike, employing new hires and union members who crossed picket lines. In October a federal bankruptcy judge ordered the pilots to end their strike and accept a settlement.

New Directions for Autos. The automobile industry provided some of the most important developments of the year in collective bargaining. The first was the arrangement between the United Automobile Workers (UAW) and New United Motor Manufacturing, Inc., or NUMMI, the General Motors-Toyota joint venture in Fremont, Calif. NUMMI is designed to enable GM to learn from the Japanese the manufacturing and management techniques that have made them so successful as automakers. The deal permits Toyota to test the water for producing cars in the United States with a modest investment. Pay and benefits under the agreement are "comparable" to base levels at General Motors and Ford, and a job security provision was described by the unions as "a virtual guarantee of no layoffs." For the first time in the domestic auto industry, the union won the right to join management in reviewing any unusual or mitigating circumstances in cases where the discharge or suspension of an employee is being considered.

Path-breaking negotiations also took place between the UAW and the Saturn Corporation, a new, wholly owned GM subsidiary formed to produce a small car competitive with Japanese imports, using new manufacturing and management techniques (see AUTOMOBILE INDUSTRY).

U.S. and Canadian Chrysler workers walked off their jobs on October 16 after contract negotiations bogged down. Canadian workers settled first, ratifying an October 20 tentative agreement bringing wages and benefits up to the levels enjoyed by GM and Ford workers in Canada. An agreement reached in the United States on October 23 was approved by 87 percent of the union membership. In addition to providing wage and benefit parity with GM and Ford workers, the new contract gave each active worker an immediate bonus of $2,120 and each retired worker a payment of $1,000, in compensation for past concessions.

Rubber Bandwagon. Unlike most other industries, bargaining in the rubber industry followed a familiar pattern, with one firm (B. F. Goodrich Company) setting the standard and the other three major producers (Goodyear Tire & Rubber, Firestone Tire & Rubber, and Uniroyal Tire) following along with similar settlements. All four major rubber producers settled with the United Rubber Workers with nearly identical contracts covering their 36,000 workers. The contracts, reflecting the generally profitable conditions in the industry, provided for specified wage increases, unlike the 1982 contracts negotiated during a period of operating losses.

No Electrical Sparks. The Coordinated Bargaining Committee of General Electric and Westinghouse unions—founded in 1965 to thwart the divide-and-conquer tactics that had been used against the 13 individual unions—reached agreement with the two companies during nearly three months of negotiations. The settlement with GE, reached in late June, embodied several breakthroughs, including an agency shop agreement which the union had been seeking for years. It specified that workers who refuse to join the union representing them at the bargaining table must pay a fee for those services in lieu of union dues. Another major gain was improved job security, particularly the provisions giving preferential hiring rights at other plants to workers hurt by a plant closing. Salaried workers at Westinghouse

Striking United Airlines pilots and their supporters are joined by Lane Kirkland, president of the AFL-CIO (right), on the picket line at National Airport in Washington, D.C. United's service was cut drastically as over 5,000 pilots stayed on the ground for nearly a month to protest a new wage system.

reached agreement in late July on a new contract; soon afterward, the blue-collar workers settled on terms mostly following the GE pattern, including an agency shop provision, but with no provision on job security.

Trucking Agreement. The Teamsters union opened negotiations in mid-January on behalf of more than 20,000 employees covered by the National Master Freight Agreement, and a settlement with the two largest trucking employer federations was reached on April 3. The new national agreement calls for wage hikes of $1.50 per hour over three years and provides employers with a limited two-tier system by establishing lower pay for new hires during the first three years of employment.

Steel Woes. Unified collective bargaining in the steel industry ended when the five remaining members of the coordinating committee of steel companies voted to disband and bargain individually with the United Steelworkers upon the expiration of their contracts in July 1986.

In April the Wheeling-Pittsburgh Steel Corporation, the industry's seventh largest producer, filed for protection under Chapter 11 of the federal bankruptcy code. The move came after the United Steelworkers Union had refused to accept a debt restructuring plan. The company then went to a federal bankruptcy judge for relief, and in July he granted it authority to void its collective bargaining agreement with the steelworkers. Judge Warren W. Bentz's ruling endorsed a management proposal to reduce the wage rate to $15.50 per hour for a five-year period, from $21.40 in the existing contract. A strike called by the steelworkers to protest the company's plans and the judge's decision began on July 21. The walkout ended in late October after union members overwhelmingly ratified a contract cutting pay by 16 percent.

Coal Strike Ends. In December the United Mine Workers of America ended the union's bitter 15-month strike against the A. T. Massey Company. The dispute centered on whether Massey was required to sign a single, companywide contract with the union or whether Massey's affiliates in West Virginia, Kentucky, and Pennsylvania constituted separate and distinct operations. After hearings before the National Labor Relations Board, Massey agreed that its affiliates constituted one company. The UMW, claiming victory, ordered members to return to work "unconditionally."

Other Industries. Hard hit by low world copper prices and a flood of foreign imports, U.S. copper producers requested midcontract revisions from the unions representing their workers. After a week of negotiations in mid-January, the unions' national nonferrous industry conference—representing 20 unions—voted to reject a tentative agreement that would have cut pay immediately by $2.50 per hour, suspended cost-of-living adjustments, and extended the current contracts by one year.

Postal Service clerks, mail carriers, mail handlers, and rural letter carriers received an arbitration award that provided for a 2.7 percent annual pay increase but markedly lower salaries for new employees. The award affected about 650,000 workers—more than any other arbitration agreement in U.S. history.

Leadership Changes. A more positive tone in relations between the Reagan administration and organized labor was established with the resignation of beleaguered Secretary of Labor Raymond J. Donovan and his replacement by William E. Brock, III, U.S. trade representative and former chairman of the Republican Party. Donovan resigned on March 15 after a New York State judge denied a motion to dismiss an indictment accusing the labor secretary, with nine other defendants and two companies, of defrauding the New York Transit Authority of approximately $7.4 million.

Teamster Trouble. In December former Teamsters union president Roy Williams, convicted in 1982 of conspiracy to bribe then Senator Howard W. Cannon (D) of Nebraska, was ordered to begin serving a 10-year prison term. Williams had been free pending legal actions. Of the four others convicted of taking part in a scheme to block legislation opposed by the union, three were already in prison, and one had been slain.   G.H.

LAOS. In 1985 the Lao People's Democratic Republic (LPDR) remained in its subordinate "special relationship" to Vietnam. The Soviet Union and its Eastern European allies supplied Laos with most of its foreign aid, and Laos followed the Vietnamese lead in important foreign policy issues, particularly those involving Vietnam's occupation of Cambodia and its tense relations with China. Laos, Cambodia, and Vietnam did, however, express a willingness to discuss proposals made by the Association of Southeast Asian Nations (Asean) for negotiations among the parties concerned in Cambodia, withdrawal of Vietnamese troops, and elections supervised by foreign observers.

Vietnamese advisers in Laos were estimated to number from 5,000 to 8,000, and Vietnamese troops were estimated at 40,000. Some 1,600 advisers from the Soviet Union reportedly worked on economic development projects and military affairs. Meanwhile, economic exchanges with Thailand increased. Thailand continued to purchase electricity generated at Laos's Nam Ngum dam, thus providing Laos with its major source of foreign exchange.

Early in the year a U.S. technical team was admitted to southern Laos to search for the remains of 13 American airmen who had crashed there in 1972. The remains were located and identified. In November the United States reached an agreement with Laos on future "multiple site excavations."

The government reported that, according to a census taken in March, the republic's total population was 3,584,803, consisting of 1,757,115 men and 1,827,688 women. A flow of refugees continued from Laos to Thailand, though their numbers were greatly reduced from the peak years of 1978 through 1980. Approximately 7,000 Lao refugees were reported to have reached Thailand in the first six months of 1985. Some 50,000 tribal highlanders from Laos remained in refugee camps administered by the UN High Commissioner for Refugees in Thailand, reluctant to undertake resettlement in other countries. Several passes were opened on the border in a program to promote repatriation.

See STATISTICS OF THE WORLD. J.J.Z.

LEBANON. As Lebanon endured its tenth year of civil war, the violence and internal divisions seemed only to get worse. A truce mediated between warring factions late in December raised some hopes for peace, but these were soon to be frustrated.

Israel's Withdrawal. After fruitless negotiations with a Lebanese delegation, Israel decided in January to withdraw unilaterally from Lebanon, which it had invaded in 1982. By June 10, Israel had removed all of its combat forces from the country but had set up a narrow "security zone" in southern Lebanon, just above the frontier, which was policed by the Israeli-supported, predominantly Christian South Lebanon Army (SLA). The withdrawal was plagued by violence: frequent guerrilla attacks against Israeli and SLA forces, Israeli retaliation against the civilian village population, and factional fighting among groups looking to fill the power vacuum.

Internal Conflicts. Lebanon's internal chaos defied attempts at resolution. The "national unity" cabinet, formed with high hopes in April 1984, collapsed in April 1985, after being boycotted by key leaders. The year also witnessed bloody breakdowns within the opposing Muslim and Christian coalitions.

Christian Revolt. In March, Samir Geagea, a hard-line militant within the (Christian) Phal-

Speaking Up for the Shiites
Nabih Berri became a household name to millions of Americans in June during the hostage crisis in Lebanon, after Shiite Muslims hijacked a TWA jetliner. Berri, 47, head of Lebanon's Shiite Amal movement since 1980 and a member of President Amin Gemayel's cabinet, stepped in as negotiator for the release of the 40 American captives; at the same time, he pressed the demands of the hijackers. When the crisis was resolved successfully, his prestige soared. In seeking greater political power for Lebanon's Shiite community, now the country's largest religious grouping, Berri has been a reformer, not a revolutionary; and as such he is politically vulnerable to extremists in the Shiite movement. Nevertheless, the soft-spoken one-time resident of Dearborn, Mich., achieved what many consider an impressive diplomatic victory and has become an important spokesman for Shiite grievances.

Nabih Berri

Life returns to a devastated street in the Shatila Palestinian refugee camp in Beirut, after intense fighting in May and June between the Shiite Amal militia and Palestinians. The Amal, believed to have been backed by Syria, had attacked Palestinian camps to prevent PLO members loyal to Yasir Arafat from reestablishing a presence in Lebanon.

angist Party's military wing, led a revolt within Phalangist ranks in which several prominent Christians vowed to fight the increasing Syrian and Muslim dominance of Lebanese affairs. Geagea ordered his forces to open fire on the Muslim Sunnis, Shiites, and Palestinians in and around Sidon. The Muslim groups retaliated fiercely, driving thousands of Christians southward; their abandoned villages were subsequently ransacked and looted. As the revolt crumbled, Syria was seen to have gained even greater dominance over Lebanon's Christians.

The Amal Movement. The Shiite Amal movement, under the leadership of Nabih Berri (also the country's minister of justice, water and electricity, and south Lebanon affairs), increased its power vis à vis the Christians early in the year. But Amal suffered political losses after it attacked Palestinian refugee camps in West Beirut during May and June, in an attempt to prevent Palestine Liberation Organization cadres loyal to Yasir Arafat from reestablishing a political and military presence in Lebanon. Syria was widely believed to have encouraged Berri to attack the camps as part of its campaign to unseat Arafat and establish control over the Palestinian movement. However, Amal failed to capture the camps and lost around 500 of its fighters; hundreds of Palestinian fighters and civilians were also killed.

Peace Efforts. In July, a Syrian-backed peace plan was put into effect, but the truce soon broke down in a murderous series of car-bombings. In a single week in August, five car-bombs exploded in East and West Beirut and in Tripoli, killing over 100 people. Massive shelling between the Christian and Muslim sectors of Beirut broke out as well. By the time another Syrian-sponsored cease-fire could go into effect on August 23, 282 people had been killed and 862 wounded.

Fighting between rival militias in Tripoli

intensified in September, with Muslim fundamentalists pitted against several pro-Syrian militias. Hundreds of dead and wounded were reported as the Syrian-backed forces attempted to take control of the city. After 19 days of fighting, a Syrian-brokered truce was agreed upon. Another Syrian attempt at ending Lebanon's internal strife was reported in October, when leaders of the Shiite, Christian, and Druze communities were said to have reached an agreement after talks in Damascus. This peace effort also appeared to falter, because of opposition by Christians to any lessening of their governmental power. In November new fighting broke out in West Beirut between Amal and Druze militiamen.

On December 28, a truce was signed in Damascus by Druze leader Walid Jumblat, Amal leader Nabih Berri, and Christian militia leader Elie Hobeika. It provided for dissolution of all private militias over a 12-month period and for parity between Muslims and Christians in power-sharing within the Lebanese government. The terms of the pact were controversial, and its chances of bringing peace were regarded with some skepticism. On December 31, Hobeika's chief aide, who played a key role in negotiating the accord, narrowly escaped being killed in an ambush by unknown forces, in a Christian area.

Hostage Crisis. On June 14, two Lebanese Shiite gunmen hijacked TWA flight 847, carrying 153 passengers and crew, which was en route from Athens to Rome. After shuttling back and forth between Beirut and Algiers, during which time a U.S. Navy diver was killed and most of the passengers were released, the plane landed in Beirut, where the remaining passengers were removed and held captive at different locations in the city. The hijackers demanded the release of over 700 prisoners (mostly Shiites) captured by Israel during its occupation of Lebanon and then being held in an Israeli prison. Nabih Berri, leader of the more moderate Amal, stepped in at this point, said that he backed the hijackers' demands, and became a mediator.

On June 20, at a press conference organized by their captors, five of the hostages appeared and urged that the United States refrain from any military rescue operation. On June 24,

Israel released 31 of its Shiite detainees, but both Israel and the United States said there was no link between the hostages' freedom and that of the prisoners in Israel. Israel, it was noted, had already released some of the detainees and had been proceeding with their gradual release when the process was interrupted by the hijacking. On June 26, one of the 40 hostages was released because of medical problems.

Intercession by Syrian President Hafez al-Assad finally succeeded in obtaining the hostages' release on June 30, 17 days after their flight had been interrupted. They were driven to Damascus and then flown to West Germany en route to the United States. Israel released the remaining prisoners in large groups, starting with 300 on July 3 and ending in early September.

Other Captives. Two of eight other Americans who had been kidnapped In Lebanon by Islamic extremists gained their freedom in 1985. In February an American television reporter escaped, or was permitted to escape, from Islamic captors in a Syrian-controlled region of Lebanon. In September the Reverend Benjamin Weir, an American missionary, was set free; he said upon release that his captors would kill the other hostages if their demand—release of 17 Shiites imprisoned in Kuwait for 1983 car-bomb attacks—was not met. In October the Islamic Holy War organization claimed it had killed one hostage, former U.S. Embassy political officer William Buckley. Four other hostages signed a letter to the archbishop of Canterbury, which instigated a mediation effort by the archbishop's special envoy, Terry Waite; but at year's end, after three trips to meet with the group holding the Americans, he was unable to win an agreement or meet personally with the hostages.

In late September, four Soviet diplomats were abducted in West Beirut. The kidnappings were believed to be related to the fighting then going on in Tripoli; Syria, the Soviet Union's main client in the Middle East, was said to be behind the antifundamentalist battles raging there. On October 2 one of the kidnapped diplomats was found shot to death. On October 30, after the truce in Tripoli had calmed hostilities, the three remaining hostages were released unharmed.

Economic Conditions. The Lebanese economy continued its slow collapse. The Chamber of Commerce estimated that the gross domestic product had declined by almost half between 1974 and 1983. Perhaps the most dramatic indicator of Lebanon's economic decline was the precipitous fall in customs receipts, a chief source of government revenue. This fact helped account for a real deficit between government revenues and expenditures in 1984 of $1.12 billion.

See STATISTICS OF THE WORLD.   M.C.H.

LESOTHO. See STATISTICS OF THE WORLD.

LIBERIA. See STATISTICS OF THE WORLD.

LIBRARIES. The trend toward increasing computerization of libraries continued in 1985. With federal aid to libraries running at low levels, state and local fund-raising were increasingly important.

Technological Advances. While microcomputers remained at the forefront of library computerization, computerized catalogs were making their way into many libraries, replacing the familiar card catalogs. The New York State Library, in a research project, found that the on-line catalog led to dramatically increased catalog use. At the New York Public Library in New York City, 1985 saw the elimination of 10 million catalog cards, as a central memory bank was readied, with 50 terminals. Full operation of the new system was expected by mid-1986.

Computers were not the only technical in-

A stylized image of a reader with a book, white on a green background, has been adopted by the U.S. Federal Highway Administration as a standard road sign indicating the presence of a library nearby. The symbol is based on the existing national library symbol.

novation found in libraries. Storage of data on laser disks (also called optical disks) offers a way to contain telecommunications costs. One system using laser disks, devised by International Standard Information Systems of Framingham, Mass., charges users a fixed monthly fee (rather than per-use costs) to tap into on-line databases. Optical-disk technology has also made its mark at the Ramapo Catskill Library System (Middletown, N.Y.), where library holdings for eight counties were placed on laser disks in the spring. The National Archives was planning to launch a pilot project in converting archival records to optical-disk storage, and OCLC, Inc., a nationwide data network, was actively pursuing applications of optical-disk technology.

Library data networks continued to grow, with numerous states centralizing on-line access to their libraries' holdings. The use of facsimiles for interlibrary loan spread as well, with some libraries even trying satellite dishes for this purpose. In March fiber optics made its debut at the Dallas Public Library, which converted to fiber optics lines to link its computer and the 88 terminals in the main library.

Funding. The University of Illinois reported that, while U.S. public library circulation increased by 1.9 percent in 1984 over the previous year, spending rose 11.5 percent, the biggest jump in a decade. State aid gained in importance in 1985, and fund-raising was more prominent and innovative. Of the $2 billion spent on U.S. libraries, only 5 percent was from federal funds, compared with 13 percent from state money and 82 percent from local funding. Federal funds appropriated for libraries for fiscal 1986 were cut back slightly from the level of the previous year.

An unusual student initiative at the University of Utah was responsible for an allocation from the Utah legislature. Students agreed to shoulder a $1 million, one-time-only tuition surcharge if the legislature matched the surcharge with $2 million in funding.

Access to Information. In March the U.S. Office of Management and Budget proposed that it receive authority over all information-gathering efforts by federal agencies. According to the proposal, federal agencies would have to show that the data were essential to

Better Late Than Never?

The longest overdue library book in Britain, appropriately entitled the *Book of Fines,* has finally found its way home to the Somerset County records office. The London *Times* reported in March that this venerable record of property transactions in the town of Taunton from 1641 to 1648 was originally borrowed by the bishop of Winchester over 300 years ago, for his reading pleasure. After two centuries in the bishop's office, the book went to the Church Commissioners, who held onto it for another hundred years. An archivist discovered it in the Hampshire County records office, and it was returned to its rightful county. On the basis of days overdue, officials estimated that the fine on *Fines* would come to more than £3,000.

their mission, were not likely to be gathered by the private sector, and would offer benefits outweighing the collection costs. Eileen D. Cooke, of the American Library Association, called the proposal in keeping with a "trend of this administration to limit public access to information." A revised version of the proposal was in preparation by OMB, based on comments it had received from interested parties.

Paperbacks and Videos. The proper role of libraries was debated by librarians. One issue involved whether or not to go into the "entertainment" business. Bookstore-type shelving and record-store bins rapidly emerged in libraries across the United States, along with renovations to accommodate the equipment, and paperbacks were in wide use. The acquisition of paperbacks came in for much discussion—most notably over whether to choose mostly quality books or give patrons popular books of little or no literary merit. Videocassette and computer software collections continued to grow, and these items were being widely circulated. Feature films were the most popular items within videocassette collections, and word-processing programs within computer software collections. S.A.

LIBYA. In 1985 there were at least two reports of attempts to assassinate Libyan leader Muammar al-Qaddafi. The first attempt was believed to have occurred in early March at a presidential villa near Tripoli; some 15 officers were said to have been executed after the attempt. In April another attack apparently took place, this time on a convoy in which Qaddafi was mistakenly thought to be traveling; at least 60 officers were reportedly executed in retaliation. In May the regime crushed an apparent coup attempt and arrested at least 2,000 people in its wake. In November, reports of a CIA plan to destabilize the Qaddafi regime were leaked to the U.S. press. The Reagan administration was convinced that the Qaddafi regime played a major role in supporting terrorism against Western targets around the world.

There was some evidence linking Libya specifically to the terrorist attacks by Palestinians at the Rome and Vienna airports in late December, in which 20 people (including four of the terrorists) were killed. The Libyan press agency subsequently described the raids as "heroic," a characterization that caused an uproar in Italy and Austria. Libya denied any involvement, however.

Qaddafi did take credit for the ouster of Sudan's President Jaafar al-Nimeiry in a military coup on April 6; later in the month it was announced that diplomatic relations between Libya and the new regime had been established. Anti-Qaddafi exiles were expelled from Sudan, and Libya agreed to supply equipment and training for Sudanese armed forces.

Libya's relations with Egypt remained poor. On May 23, Egypt claimed to have foiled a plot, involving a Libyan-recruited terrorist, to bomb an embassy in Cairo. In November, Egypt announced the arrest of four Libyans accused of a plot (the second in a year) to assassinate a prominent Qaddafi opponent living in Cairo. Adding to the tension between Egypt and Libya was Libya's expulsion of some 10,000 Egyptian workers. Libya's expulsion of about 29,000 Tunisian workers in August also increased tension with Tunisia. The Tunisian government responded by expelling nearly 300 Libyans (including 30 diplomats who were accused of spying), recalling all its workers, and severing trade relations; finally, amid border tensions and other irritants, Tunisia broke diplomatic relations on September 26. Iraq had already broken relations with Libya, on June 26, after Libya openly expressed support for Iran in the

Iran-Iraq war. Libya's ties with its ally Syria were also strained, partly because of Libya's expulsions of Syrian workers.

Libyan troops remained in Chad, as Qaddafi continued to support rebels seeking to overthrow the Chadian government, which is backed by France and the United States. Libya had failed to live up to its part of a September 1984 agreement with France specifying that both countries would withdraw their forces simultaneously from Chad.

In late December the U.S. State Department asserted that Libya had received sophisticated SA-5 long-range ground-to-air missiles from the Soviet Union. The United States said it had sought unsuccessfully to deter the Soviets from providing Libya with the missiles; it stated that the missiles could pose a serious threat to aircraft in disputed areas of the Mediterranean, where there had been sporadic clashes between Libya and the United States.

See STATISTICS OF THE WORLD.   A.D.

LIECHTENSTEIN. See STATISTICS OF THE WORLD.

LIFE SCIENCES. Biochemical research, including genetic engineering, made important strides forward in 1985. Other findings involved mummies, dinosaurs, plants and pollinators, deer, chimpanzees, and humpback whales.

BIOLOGY

A court action and new federal guidelines appeared to open the way toward new experiments in genetic engineering, which involves isolating a gene from one organism and inserting it into another, thereby transferring to the other organism the specific trait coded for by the gene.

Biotechnology. On February 27 a U.S. court of appeals modified a 1984 federal court ruling halting a proposed experiment by researcher Steven Lindow that would have represented the first release of a genetically engineered organism into the environment. The experiment involved spreading a modified strain of bacteria on a field of potatoes to test its frost-inhibiting ability. In effect, the appeals court narrowed the scope of the environmental impact assessment needed before Lindow's experiment could be approved. Meanwhile, the EPA approved an experiment by Advanced Genetics Sciences, Inc., of Oakland, Calif., testing the same bacteria on strawberries and other plants.

On September 23 a U.S. government advisory panel approved guidelines for transplanting genes to correct a range of fatal hereditary diseases in humans. Under the guidelines, proposed experiments in gene therapy would still have to be cleared by local review committees and the federal government, but researchers were now in a position to begin submitting proposals. The first diseases on which gene therapy is likely to be used are rare hereditary conditions that leave the patient without normal immune defenses against infection and disease.

New Products. Many new products produced by genetic engineering techniques in 1984 were being tested in humans in 1985. The products include factor VIII, a component of the blood-clotting mechanism that is absent in most hemophiliacs; epidermal growth factor, which stimulates the healing of wounds and may be useful in the treatment of burns and peptic ulcers; and human superoxide dismutase, which reduces damage to tissues deprived of blood flow by blockage of an artery or by interruptions of blood flow during transplants.

Biotechnologists also produced human renin—not to be confused with rennin, an enzyme used in making cheese—the most potent peptide known for raising blood pressure. Having significant amounts of renin available for research may make it possible to develop an inhibitor of its activity, which would be useful in the treatment of high blood pressure.

Vaccines. Investigators were using the techniques of genetic engineering to produce proteins normally found on the surfaces of disease-causing viruses and bacteria. These proteins could then be used in vaccines to stimulate immunity to those pathogenic microorganisms. This approach should be useful for diseases caused by microorganisms that are difficult to grow in the laboratory.

In March investigators at Genentech, Inc., of South San Francisco, Calif., reported that they had used this technique to protect guinea pigs against herpes infections. In June, Gary Schoolnik of the Stanford University Medical Center reported that he had used surface proteins to make vaccines that protected mice from pyelonephritis, a severe infection of the

Paleontologist Robert Long displays 225-million-year-old bones from a skeleton found in Arizona, believed to belong to the earliest known dinosaur. About the size of a German shepherd, this creature existed at the dawn of the dinosaur age, long before mammals, birds, or flowering plants.

kidneys caused by a virulent strain of the common bacterium *Escherichia coli*. Schoolnik also successfully tested in rabbits a similar vaccine against gonorrhea.

In May a team of investigators from five institutions reported that they had used genetic engineering techniques to produce surface proteins from one life stage of the human malaria parasite *Plasmodium falciparum*. This species causes the most severe form of malaria. Mice injected with the proteins produced antibodies to the *Plasmodium* species. Protection against malaria has been very difficult to achieve because of difficulties in growing *Plasmodium*, and this achievement represents a major breakthrough. Tests in humans were the next step.

Alternatives to Bacteria. Most attempts to produce biological products by genetic engineering have used bacteria or yeast as miniature "chemical factories." Other organisms might be more useful, however, because they would introduce less contamination. Investigators in Japan reported in June that they had produced alpha interferon, a potent antiviral agent, in silkworm larvae that they infected with engineered viruses. The product was harvested four days after the infection by pricking the worms with a pin and collecting the interferon-rich material that seeped out.

Monoclonal Antibodies. Scientists have great hopes for the treatment of cancer with monoclonal antibodies, which are laboratory-produced clones of antibodies against specific cells, bacteria, or viruses. The investigators are trying to produce monoclonal antibodies that can bind specifically to cancer cells in a tumor; the cells would then be killed by the antibodies themselves or by drugs or radioactive isotopes attached to the antibodies. Ronald Levy and his colleagues at Stanford University reported in July that they had obtained complete remission of lymphoma, a cancer of the lymph glands, in 1 of 11 patients treated with monoclonal antibodies and improvement in 4 others. None of the patients had responded to conventional therapy.

In August radiologists at Johns Hopkins University reported what they termed "the first effective treatment" for liver cancer, or hepatoma. They treated 104 hepatoma patients with monoclonal antibodies linked to radioactive elements; the therapy shrank tumors by 30 percent or more in 50 patients and produced total remission in 7. Conventional treatment has been almost completely ineffective against hepatomas.

Cloning DNA From Long-Dead Sources. Scientists have successfully cloned the genetic material DNA (deoxyribonucleic acid) from an Egyptian mummy and an extinct mammal. The mummy experiment was reported in April. Svante Pääbo, of the University of Uppsala in Sweden, took some well-preserved DNA from the left leg of a 2,400-year-old mummified Egyptian child, purified it, and copied it in quantity by inserting a section into a bacterial host. Subsequent examination determined that the fragment of ancient genetic material was almost identical to a contemporary human gene sequence called *Alu*. The discovery may help scientists to investigate the racial descent of people now living in the Nile Valley and even assess how closely members of the notoriously incestuous ancient Egyptian royal dynasties were related. Similar methods were used to clone fragments of DNA from dried muscle attached to a quagga hide, according to research reported in late 1984. The quagga, a close relative of the zebra, became extinct in the 1880's.

Virus Structures. Scientists from four U.S. institutions reported in September that they had finally determined the three-dimensional structure of two viruses—a cold virus and a poliovirus—that infect humans. The preceding several years had seen successes in producing atomic-scale models of some plant viruses, but never before had human (or animal) viruses been mapped out in such detail. The method used was X-ray crystallography: a crystalline form of the virus was subjected to intense X

rays, and hundreds of photographs were produced showing how the X rays were deflected by the virus structure; the massive amounts of information contained in the photographs were then analyzed by computer to produce an image of the virus. Both viruses were found to be 20-sided and to have 60 copies each of 4 proteins; their structure was similar to that of 20-sided plant viruses, suggesting a common evolution.

Cystic Fibrosis Gain. The search for the faulty gene responsible for cystic fibrosis, the most common hereditary disease among Caucasians, was advanced when researchers announced late in the year that they had discovered genetic markers closely linked to the faulty gene. The finding enhances the prospects that researchers will be able to locate the gene itself, which in turn could help in understanding and treating this usually fatal affliction.

Dinosaurs. The largest dinosaurs of prehistoric times were far larger and heavier than any of today's land animals. As animals get bigger, however, the strength of their bones and muscles decreases relative to their rapidly increasing weight; this may have placed restrictions on the largest species' posture or on how they walked. But how can scientists investigate the biomechanics of long-dead animals? R. McNeil Alexander of the University of Leeds in England reported in January on a surprisingly simple approach: he used plastic souvenir models of dinosaurs from the British Museum (Natural History). Although mainly appreciated by children, these models are based on recent anatomical studies and are accurate.

Alexander suspended the models on cords, estimated the real animal's center of gravity, and measured the distribution of weight along the body by weighing the models while sections of them were immersed in water. Scaling up from his models' weights, he estimated that a *Diplodocus* about 12½ feet high would have weighed as much as 20½ tons. Both the *Diplodocus* and the *Stegosaurus* supported most of their weight on their hind legs; the huge creatures could probably rear up on their hind legs to feed or defend themselves. The *Diplodocus* would have needed nearly a quarter of a ton of muscle just to lift its long neck and head. Alexander was even able to calculate the pressure that each animal's foot exerted on the ground. Despite their great size, bipedal dinosaurs such as the *Iquanodon* may have been no more likely to get bogged down in soft ground than modern cattle.

In June, a very important hunk of sedimentary rock was airlifted by helicopter from the site of its discovery in Arizona's Petrified Forest National Park and taken to the University of California at Berkeley. The rock, which contained fossil remains of specimens of the world's oldest known dinosaur, was part of a dinosaur bone find made in 1984 by Brian Small, a student working under Robert Long of Berkeley. Some bones lying on or near the surface were taken to Berkeley for analysis soon after Small spotted them. From a study of pollen grains preserved in the sediment, Sidney Ash of Weber State College in Utah estimated that the deposit was 225 million years old. The fossils, of a small dinosaur probably weighing about 100 pounds, are a few million years older than any others found so far.

BOTANY

Recent studies have cast new light on the complex relationship between plants and the insects and birds that pollinate them. Botanists pursued a comprehensive effort to save endangered American plant species.

Plants and Pollinators. While many insects damage the plants on which they feed, others, such as bees, moths, and butterflies, play a vital role in pollination. Successful pollination requires the transfer of male pollen from one flower to fertilize the female parts of another of the same species. Plants that rely on insects to perform the transfer usually reward the helpmate with sugary nectar. However, insects can be very selective, and have many different flowers to choose from. Plants therefore have evolved just the right combinations of shape, size, scent, and color to be maximally attractive to their chosen pollinators. But there is an inherent snag in this approach. What if a plant has a prolonged flowering time but is adapted to a pollinator that only flies during a short part of that period? Presumably, flowers opening before or after the time when the pollinator is flying will fail to be fertilized and represent a waste of reproductive effort.

Recent studies on the scarlet gilia flower on Fern Mountain, in Arizona, have revealed that this plant at least is capable of altering its appearance to attract different pollinators. In research findings published early in 1985, Ken Paige and Thomas Whitham of Northern Arizona University observed that the scarlet gilia at high altitudes can produce flowers colored from red through pink to white and that each plant produces a succession of flowers during a long flowering season from mid-July to September. Flowers set early in the season are significantly darker red in color than flowers set later—even within individual flower heads. The plants are pollinated by two species of hummingbird which fly by day and by a single night-flying hawk moth species. During the day, brightly colored red flowers were the most attractive to the hummingbirds, while at night the pale pink and white varieties had the advantage for attracting moths. The seasonal shift from predominantly red to paler flower color coincided with the annual emigration of the hummingbirds away from the high altitude sites. Paige and Whitham observed that the seasonal color changes in high-altitude plants ideally suit them to track changing populations of pollinators, ensuring maximum efficiency throughout the prolonged flowering period. At lower altitudes, where hummingbird populations are stable, this mechanism is not needed.

Endangered Plants. Botanists say that plant species are disappearing year by year, with perhaps 3,000 of the more than 20,000 native U.S. species now in danger of extinction. (Tens of thousands of other plant species around the world are in similar danger.) Many of these species are, or may be found to be, useful in medicine, agriculture, or other fields; even those that have no practical value may be worth preserving for their own sake. In an effort to save threatened species, the Center for Plant Conservation, based at Harvard University's Arnold Arboretum, has begun a comprehensive program to grow specimens of each species, besides stockpiling seeds for added insurance. The center and affiliated institutions, aided by $500,000 in start-up funds, collected more than 90 species during the summer and hoped to build up a fund totaling $15 million to save virtually all threatened plant species within the next ten years.

Psychologist Francine Patterson gives a new Manx kitten to her full-time student Koko, a gorilla who has learned 600 words in American Sign Language; the pet replaced a favorite kitten run over some months earlier.

ZOOLOGY

Recent findings include studies on the survival of male red deer and the learning capacity of chimpanzees. Fires on the Galápagos Islands threatened their unique fauna. A humpback whale that swam up the Sacramento River helped give scientists new knowledge about that species, besides providing a diversion for onlookers.

Male and Female Survival. Tim Clutton-Brock of Cambridge University's Zoology Department has studied red deer on the Scottish island of Rhum for many years. In 1985, Clutton-Brock and colleagues provided a simple new hypothesis to explain the difference in survival rates between the males and the females. The greater the eventual body weight differences between males and females, the more food the growing males need to eat compared with the females. Although young males grow faster than young females, they add much less body fat. Since they have smaller fat reserves and a greater physiological requirement, they must be more vulnerable to temporary food shortages. When faced with inadequate diets (as would be the case for the offspring of low-status mothers), fast-growing young males must be at a considerable disadvantage compared with their sisters, and this would account for their higher mortality. This new theory is sup-

ported by the observation that a difference in mortality is most marked in species with large male-female size differences and in areas where the species population density is high or food availability low.

Math Ability in Chimps. Although chimpanzees cannot speak, they can communicate complex ideas by using forms of sign language. Despite growing interest in chimp linguistic ability, no one seriously investigated their numerical skills until this year. Tetsuro Matsuzawa of the Psychology Department of Kyoto University in Japan trained a five-year-old chimp named Ai to recognize symbols for 14 objects and 11 colors; Ai was taught to press appropriate buttons to describe objects presented. Matsuzawa then introduced Ai to Arabic numerals. After 104 training sessions, she had learned to count to six and could identify a test subject, such as six red pencils, by name, color, and number with 98.5 percent accuracy. Ai seemed to find numbers more tricky to master than names or colors, but of course so do the majority of five-year-old humans!

Galápagos Fires. Many species on the island of Isabela in Ecuador's Galápagos Islands were threatened by a fire that started in February and burned for several months. Other fires also broke out during the year. Concern focused on the islands' famous giant tortoises, which weigh up to 500 pounds; some of them were transported to safe areas, and only a few perished. Other species, including penguins and flamingos, fled the flames, abandoning their young and eggs. Many species and subspecies are unique to the remote islands, where Charles Darwin conducted research that led to his theory of evolution.

Whale of a Mistake. On October 11 a 40-foot, 45-ton humpback whale headed inland into San Francisco Bay, rather than out to sea, during the herd's yearly migration south, eventually swimming almost 70 miles up the Sacramento River. Scientists knew that Humphrey, as the whale was soon nicknamed, could not survive long in a freshwater environment, and officials from a hastily set-up Whale Rescue Coordination Center began full-scale efforts to lure him back to sea, spending about $60,000 on the project. Attempts to scare him downriver by playing tapes of menacing killer whale sounds failed, but friendly humpback sounds seemed to work better; Humphrey never strayed far from the boat broadcasting the recordings, as it coasted toward the sea. On November 4, to the cheers of hundreds of observers, he slid under the Golden Gate Bridge and out into the salty Pacific—hopefully headed south toward the humpbacks' tropical breeding grounds.

The effort gave scientists a chance to study the elusive species at close range. Humphrey was believed to have been attracted by the humpback whales' sounds because he was lonely, an indication that humpback whales are sociable creatures. They also apparently prefer to swim against tides and currents instead of drifting with them; this gives them greater control.   S.M.H. & T.H.M.

LITERATURE. Among the major literary developments of 1985 were:

AMERICAN

A new generation of exciting, often very young writers began to publish, and established masters brought out new, often distinguished, work.

Fiction. William Gaddis's style, ambitious and demanding, marked by a flawless ear for American speech, has never won him a popular audience, but fellow writers regard him as a master. In *Carpenter's Gothic,* about three people, a strange house, and a fundamentalist cult, he returns to his obsessions: authenticity and phoniness, the American business ethic, and the way we talk now. Equally revered, if much more accessible, is Peter Taylor, a veteran short-story writer. In *The Old Forest and*

In October a 45-ton humpback whale strayed into San Francisco Bay and up the Sacramento River during his herd's yearly migration south. While tourists flocked to watch the whale frolic (below), scientists managed to lure him back to the Pacific Ocean; their success was attributed to tape recordings of friendly humpback sounds.

Other Stories, Taylor gathered his favorite work of the past 40 years, seemingly easygoing but consummately structured stories detailing the life of genteel Southerners.

W. M. Spackman's *A Little Decorum, For Once* treated the love affairs of an old couple and of their grandchildren in the elliptical, brittle manner that has become his trademark; the style is a bit fey, but to many it makes exquisite reading. Like Gaddis, Stanley Elkin is known for his impeccable ear for speech, his black humor, and his audacity, all of them evident in *Stanley Elkin's The Magic Kingdom.* Here Elkin imagines a visit by a handful of dying children to Disney World; the kids banter wryly about their various diseases, their adult guardians carry on affairs, and the Angel of Death disguised as a Disney cartoon character hovers in the distance.

The novels of Don DeLillo and Gilbert Sorrentino made a similar impact. DeLillo's *White Noise* describes the family of a professor of Hitler studies at a small university town. What happens when the town is exposed to a cloud of toxic gas makes for a comic, bitter, and admonitory tale. In *Odd Number,* Sorrentino rounds up his usual cast of characters—phony intellectuals, burned-out artists, promiscuous hangers-on—and plunks an unsolved murder in their midst. The result is a comic exercise with echoes of Beckett and the French New Novel. Kurt Vonnegut also came out with a zestful new novel, *Galapagos,* which somersaults from 1986 to a far-off future. In *World's Fair,* E. L. Doctorow returned with another mixture of fact and fiction—the tale of a Jewish boy growing up in the Bronx in the 1930's.

The nature of the artist provides the theme for Philip Roth's *Zuckerman Bound,* a trilogy of previously published novels supplemented with a new novella, "The Prague Orgy." In these episodes Roth examines the intertwinings of art and reality, especially the writer's relationship to his family and Jewish heritage. Artists also figure largely in Mary Gordon's third, highly praised novel, *Men and Angels,* which revolves around a devoted mother and art historian, the Impressionist artist she researches, and the ultimately dangerous young woman she hires as a baby-sitter. The issue of abortion and all the controversies surrounding it are at the heart of John Irving's *The Cider House Rules,* the tale of a Maine doctor.

Other established novelists produced works of particular merit. Many reviewers acclaimed Larry McMurtry's *Lonesome Dove,* an epic tale

Radio host Garrison Keillor (left) hit the best-seller lists with Lake Wobegon Days, *a collection of tales about a mythical small town in the Midwest. Keillor had invented the town for his offbeat monologues on* A Prairie Home Companion, *a popular weekly program broadcast over Minnesota Public Radio.*

of a Texas cattle drive, as one of the best novels ever written about the American West. Anne Tyler, in *The Accidental Tourist,* built on the achievement of the much-admired *Dinner at the Homesick Restaurant;* the new novel tells the story of Macon Leary, devastated by the death of his son and the desertion of his wife, who finds love with a very unlikely woman.

Two short-story writers who focus on the Jewish experience put out fine collections. Nobel laureate Isaac Bashevis Singer once more visited with dybbuks, demons, and retired New Yorkers in *The Image and Other Stories,* while Grace Paley issued her third collection of short fiction about intellectuals, pacifists, and Greenwich Villagers, *Later the Same Day.* The year also brought *The Collected Stories of John O'Hara,* which, edited by Frank Mac-Shane, highlights the achievements of one of America's finest storytellers.

Half a dozen newer writers of already daunting achievement had books out in 1985. In his second novel, *Ransom,* Jay McInerney showed remarkable range, this time relating the experiences of a young American in Japan studying the martial arts. Poet Brad Leithauser also set his evocative first novel, *Equal Distance,* in Japan. It traces a young man on the loose, slyly looking for love and a meaning to life. Carolyn Chute's debut, *The Beans of Egypt, Maine,* was a surprise best-seller in 1985; it chronicles the fascination of a nice Maine girl for a family of white trash. Madison Smartt Bell's second novel, *Waiting for the End of the World,* confirmed his talent; he spins a tale of lowlifes who plan to set off an atomic bomb under Times Square. Gloria Naylor's second novel, *Linden Hills,* didn't fare so well; this journey through a bourgeois black neighborhood struck many as too obviously allegorical. Bobbie Ann Mason's first novel, *In Country,* dealt with the Vietnam war and its impact on a Kentucky woman.

Mary Morris's *The Bus of Dreams,* focusing on yuppies, was one of the most memorable short-story debuts. Among more established story writers, T. Coraghessan Boyle's *Greasy Lake & Other Stories* was notable for its zany humor and rococo wordplay. But the most exciting story collection was Garrison Keillor's *Lake Wobegon Days,* a lighthearted, nostalgic

Who Is That Writer in the Window?

Writing is usually considered a solitary art, but author Georgelle Hirliman clearly disagrees. A new career as sit-down comic and wordsmith-on-view opened up for her after she went public and began writing stories in store windows. Window work in her native Santa Fe, N.M., was originally a means of breaking through writer's block and finding fresh ideas; she encouraged audience participation, in the form of questions and comments, and taped witty responses to the window for the edification of onlookers. She now travels around the United States displaying her talents and claims that the stories composed behind glass are her best work.

history of the imaginary Minnesota town made famous on Keillor's radio program, *A Prairie Home Companion.*

Poetry. Books of poetry issued from the pens of America's two most versatile men of letters: Robert Penn Warren and John Updike. Warren's *New and Selected Poems: 1923–1985* gathered the best work by the novelist, critic, teacher, and poet. Updike is best known as a novelist and reviewer, but *Facing Nature* is in fact his fifth collection of verse, much of it light and comic, but with every page revealing steely artistry.

James Merrill and Kenneth Koch, leading lights of the New York School, also reminded readers of their brilliance. Merrill's *Late Settings* offers dazzling verbal filigree that can be utterly magical. Koch's *Selected Poems: 1950–1982* showed this often hilarious poet at his best, especially in such brilliant tours de force as "The Art of Poetry."

Among works by women poets, Mary Jo Salter's *Henry Purcell in Japan* and Amy Clampitt's *What the Light Was Like* stand out. Clampitt's volume extends the achievement of her startling debut, *The Kingfisher,* and continues to show her dexterity with thickly textured lines. Also, Adrienne Rich assembled her work in a volume of strong, opinionated, and often poignant verse called *The Fact of a Doorframe: Poems Selected and New 1950–1984.*

One of the year's surprise best-sellers was a first novel by Carolyn Chute (shown here with her husband); The Beans of Egypt, Maine portrayed a poor and raffish family in backwoods Maine.

Biography. Literary biographies of note included *Louise Bogan: A Portrait,* in which Elizabeth Frank evoked the tortured, neurotic life of a fine poet and critic, as well as a remarkable woman. Donald Spoto's *The Kindness of Strangers* looked at the equally tortured life of playwright Tennessee Williams. Peter Manso edited a collection of oral tributes and verbal punches in *Mailer,* a sort of collage biography of the writer sometimes referred to as today's Hemingway. The real Hemingway was the subject of a new full-scale biography by Jeffrey Meyers. Also published was a comprehensive biography of the enigmatic Wallace Stevens, by Milton J. Bates, and a shortened version of the celebrated five-volume biography of Henry James, by Leon Edel.

Science Fiction, Thrillers, Crime. Science fiction fans mourned the death of Theodore Sturgeon, a master of the short story, in May. Frank Herbert added yet another volume to his popular series, with *Chapterhouse: Dune,* while masters Isaac Asimov and Robert A. Heinlein added to their science fiction oeuvre. Meanwhile, posthumous books by the great Philip K. Dick continued to arrive, among them *Puttering Around in a Small Land* and *The Man Whose Teeth Were All Alike.* In *Always Coming Home,* Ursula LeGuin unveils the world of the Kesh, a postnuclear holocaust society encamped in northern California.

Stephen King's new book, *Skeleton Crew,* was a collection of 20 short thrillers, including some of his finest work: the frightening creature novella "The Mist" and the downeast folktale "Mrs. Todd's Shortcut." One of the biggest and least expected best-sellers of the year was Tom Clancy's *The Hunt for Red October,* a novel about the commander of a Soviet super sub who decides to defect.

In crime fiction, Tony Hillerman's *The Ghostway* was an expert mystery that also evoked contemporary Navajo life. Andrew Vachss's naturalistic thriller *Flood* announced a new talent so gritty that Mickey Spillane almost looked soft by comparison. And Elmore Leonard's blockbuster *Glitz* transported his many readers to the bright lights and dark corners of Atlantic City.   M.D.

AUSTRALIAN
The reputation of Australian women writers was enhanced in 1985 by the publication of several notable novels and collections of short stories.

Lilian's Story represents Kate Grenville's impressive debut as a novelist. She writes with insight, wit, and style about an eccentric Sydney woman. Olga Masters's *A Long Time Dying* depicts a country town in mid-Depression, through 17 interrelated stories unified by the theme of shame. Elizabeth Jolley confirmed her status as a major novelist with *Foxybaby,* a highly original story about a summer school. *Beachmasters,* by Thea Astley, another mature novelist, deals with universal themes in the setting of a Pacific island undergoing political change. Three other women displayed their considerable talents in collections of short stories: Helen Garner with *Postcards From Surfers,* Beverley Farmer with *Home Time,* and Renate Yates with *Fine Bones.*

The success of these women writers nearly overshadowed distinguished achievements by a number of Australia's male novelists. The prolific Thomas Keneally's latest novel, *A Family Madness,* was acclaimed by critics as one of his best. Its theme was the juxtaposition of native Australian and Eastern European immigrant life experiences. Christopher Koch's *Double-Man,* a novel about the essentially dual nature of human beings, was also warmly received. Peter Carey's entertaining picaresque novel *Illywhacker* dealt with a professional confidence man. Two contrasting collections of short stories were *This Freedom,* by John Morrison, representing a traditional approach, and *Memories of the Assassination Attempt,* a witty, more contemporary entry by Gerard Windsor.

One of the growing number of successful Australian women writers, Elizabeth Jolley this year published Foxybaby, *a novel about a group of middle-aged matrons taking a summer course at a run-down college campus.*

Readers interested in sampling the Australian literary output were well served by the publication of the two-volume *My Country: Australian Poetry and Short Stories—Two Hundred Years.* The texts were chosen by Professor Leonie Kramer, who enhanced the work with illustrations of selected Australian paintings to demonstrate affinities between literature and painting. Geoffrey Dutton put together *The Australian Collection: Australia's Greatest Books,* a one-volume anthology with brief selections from 97 classics, together with an essay on each work and a brief biographical account of the writer. It is a good introductory guide for anyone interested in Australia's favorite books.

A 24-year-old, Tim Winton, won the prestigious Miles Franklin Award for his second novel, *Shallows,* described as "a finely wrought work, extraordinarily vivid in its writing." A Canadian panel named Les Murray, widely known for his collections of poems and his verse novel *The Boys Who Stole the Funeral,* as the winner of the Canada-Australia Literary Prize. Elizabeth Jolley won the fiction prize in the New South Wales Premier's Awards for her novel *Milk and Honey.* In the Victorian Premier's Literary Awards, poetry honors were shared by Kevin Hart's *Your Shadow* and Rosemary Dobson's collection *The Three Fates and Other Poems.* Earlier in the year, Dobson had won the 1984 Patrick White Literary Award. The Vance Palmer award for fiction went to David Malouf for a collection of stories, *Antipodes.* Bernard Smith's unconventional autobiography, *The Boy Adeodatus,* won the Nettie Palmer prize for nonfiction. It already had been named the National Book Council's 1984 Book of the Year.   I.K.

CANADIAN

The major Canadian publishing event of 1985— a new general encyclopedia—was important far beyond the field of literature. There were some distinguished literary works, especially in fiction.

Encyclopedia. *The Canadian Encyclopedia* was the most ambitious undertaking of its kind in Canadian publishing history. The result of over five years of labor by publisher Mel Hurtig and his team of 250 consultants and more than 2,500 expert contributors, the encyclopedia is a relatively low-cost three-volume work that

contains more than 8,000 entries and 2,000 maps, illustrations, and photographs. A French edition was planned for 1987.

Fiction. Perhaps the most interesting and important novel of 1985 was Margaret Atwood's *The Handmaid's Tale,* her sixth and most daring work, set in a future United States where the fundamentalism of the ultraconservative "moral majority" has led society into a terrifying state. In *What's Bred in the Bone,* Robertson Davies returned to the small-town world that proved so effective in his *Fifth Business* (1970); the new novel was said by some critics to lack the charm and tight structure notable in the earlier classic. Brian Moore's *Black Robe,* an account of the Jesuit missionaries in 17th-century Canada, was disappointing as a historical novel, but illustrated the author's growing interest in creating scenarios suitable for films. Anthony Hyde's *The Red Fox,* an ingenious spy thriller, won immense attention not only for its superb plot and structure, but also for the approximately $1 million in advance royalties received by the author—the highest amount ever for a Canadian novel.

Morley Callaghan, who began publishing in the 1920's, gathered together 20 previously uncollected short stories under the title *The Lost and Found Stories of Morley Callaghan.* Other fine short-story collections were Austin Clarke's *When Women Rule,* Marian Engel's *The Tattooed Woman* (published after her death in February), Mavis Gallant's *Overhead in a Balloon,* Katherine Govier's *Fables of Brunswick Avenue,* Bharati Mukherjee's *Darkness,* Jane Rule's *Inland Passage,* and Carol Shield's *Various Miracles.* Especially impressive was *Digging Up the Mountains,* a first volume by Neil Bissoondath, a nephew of V. S. Naipaul.

Among noteworthy novels published in French were Gérard Bessette's poignant evocation of an inner life, *Les Dites d'Omer Marin* (The Sayings of Omer Marin), and Victor-Lévy Beaulieu's *Steven le hérault* (Steven the herald). A large number of English-Canadian novels were published in French translations, including works by Margaret Atwood, Robert Kroetsch, Stephen Leacock, Heather Robertson, and Rudy Wiebe.

Poetry. The relatively few volumes of verse published in 1985 were generally of poor quality. Exceptions included new volumes by P. K. Page, Alden Nowlan, Erin Mouré, and Robert Kroetsch.

Nonfiction. Autobiography and biography dominated the ranks of nonfiction. Autobiographical volumes by Jean Chrétien, George Ignatieff, and Paul Martin were released. Also published were journals penned by Elizabeth Smart and Lucy Maud Montgomery, as well as letters by Susanna Moodie and Jacques Ferron (who died in April).

Awards. The Governor General's Awards for 1984 went to Josef Skvorecky for *The Engineer of Human Souls* and Jacques Brault for *Agonie* (Agony) in the fiction category; to Paulette Jiles for *Celestial Navigation* and Nicole Brossard for *Double Impression: poèmes et textes 1967–1984* (poetry); to Judith Thompson for *White Biting Dog* and René-Daniel Dubois for *Ne blâmez jamais les Bédouins* (Don't ever blame the Bedouins) in the drama classification; and to Sandra Gwyn for *The Private Capital: Ambition and Love in the Age of Macdonald and Laurier* and Jean Hamelin and Nicole Gagnon for *Le XXe Siècle: Histoire du catholicisme québécois* (The 20th century: history of Quebec Catholicism), Volumes 1 and 2 (nonfiction).

D.S.

ENGLISH

Historical settings were prominent in many of the year's outstanding novels. Biographies provided fascinating and sometimes surprising new insights into the lives of leading literary figures.

Fiction. *The Kingdom of the Wicked,* by Anthony Burgess, was an ebullient historical chronicle of ancient Rome. The vigorous narrative, peopled with familiar biblical figures, reinterpreted the beginnings of Christianity and its conflicts with society. Brian Moore in *Black Robe,* set in 17th-century Canada, also depicted conflict between sharply opposed beliefs and customs. His central characters were Jesuit priests on a perilous mission into the territory of Indian tribal chiefs. *A Maggot,* by John Fowles, was a difficult tale of mystery, superstition, and faith, set in 18th century England.

Graham Greene's *The Tenth Man* was originally written as a film script in 1944 and then forgotten until its recent publication. This taut, compelling tale, about French prisoners drawing lots to decide which should face a German firing squad, explored the later attempted expiation of the guilt-stricken lawyer who had bought himself off.

Quinx, by Lawrence Durrell, was the fifth and final volume of his "Avignon Quintet." A. S. Byatt's *Still Life* was likewise part of a larger contemporary canvas with an author-figure as protagonist.

Janice Elliott's deftly organized *The Italian Lesson* contained pervasive echoes of E. M. Forster, updated to include such topicalities as terrorist bombs. Another look at "revolutionaries," this time in London, was provided in Doris Lessing's *The Good Terrorist.* Difficulties in achieving goodness were likewise examined in Iris Murdoch's new novel *The Good Apprentice.*

In *The Swimming Pool Season,* by Rose Tremain, a mood of elegiac melancholy was rendered as its middle-aged heroine found late fulfillment as a painter. *Valley of Decision,* by Stanley Middleton, was a quiet laconic story of crisis in the marriage of two talented amateur musicians.

Biography. *The Life of Jane Austen,* by John Halperin, concentrated on the sharper aspects of Austen's personality: the tartness in her wit, a detected dislike of her hypochondriac mother, and the politics of money and marriage as a dominant theme in her life as well as her novels. In *Immortal Boy: A Portrait of Leigh Hunt,* Ann Blainey provided the first biography of its subject in more than 50 years; the emphasis was on domestic detail, including the poet's touching love for an ailing wife and a horde of unruly children.

Robert Bernard Martin, in his study of Edward Fitzgerald, *With Friends Possessed,* drew a satisfying portrait of this paradoxical figure from the Victorian Age. In *John Ruskin: The Early Years, 1819–1859,* Tim Hilton offers a vigorous portrayal of another eminent Victorian, focusing on Ruskin's religious beliefs and early

In her newest novel, The Good Terrorist, *Doris Lessing examines the relations between a middle-class woman and a group of revolutionaries who take over an abandoned house in London.*

politics, the fiasco of his marriage, and his dealings with painter J. M. W. Turner.

Among notable biographies of theater people, Stanley Ayling's *A Portrait of Sheridan* charted the meteoric rise and fall of the picturesque 18th-century playwright Richard Sheridan from early success to a squalid old age. In *Lady Gregory: The Woman Behind the Irish Renaissance,* Mary Lou Kohfeldt paid a lively tribute to the cofounder of the Abbey Theatre, Dublin.

Drama. *Pravda,* by Howard Brenton and David Hare, anatomized the exercise and abuse of editorial power in the press, as exemplified by a predatory tycoon who swallows up tabloid and "quality" newspapers alike. *Deadlines,* by Stephen Wakelam, took another disenchanted look at the media, depicting an unemployed teenager's suicide in a strikebound mining town and its progressive glib distortion in radio and television reports.

Unemployment was also featured in Stanley Price's *Why Me?,* which observed the effects of economic recession on a middle-class marriage. Another topical theme was investigated by Louis Page in *Golden Girls,* which portrayed the experiences of a group of women relay runners gathered in Greece for a race being sponsored by a big shampoo company. *My Brother's Keeper,* by Nigel Williams, focused on a family reunion at the deathbed of a retired actor.

Long Lost Shakespeare Lyric? In November, Gary Taylor, an American scholar studying at Oxford University, announced that he had discovered in the library's extensive manuscript collection an untitled, little-noticed poem which he claimed was written by Shakespeare. The poem, which would be the first addition to Shakespeare's known works since the 17th century, attracted considerable attention and debate, with some critics arguing on the basis of internal evidence that it was not Shakespeare's. Oxford University Press was planning to include the poem in an edition edited by Taylor and by Stanley Wells, a leading Shakespeare scholar. M.W.

WORLD

The continuing vitality of Latin American writers in 1985 was especially well exemplified by the debut in English translation of an extremely talented novelist, Isabel Allende. The flow of English translations also brought new recognition to many familiar names.

Latin American, Spanish. Omar Cabezas, who had fought in the Sandinista revolution in Nicaragua and later became a member of the Sandinista government, gained wide readership with the English translation of his graphic memoirs of guerrilla life, *Fire From the Mountain (La montaña,* 1984). A stimulating collection of essays by Mexican poet Octavio Paz, entitled *One Earth, Four or Five Worlds (Tiempo nublado,* 1983), appeared in 1985. Also published was a newly translated novel by Mexican writer Carlos Fuentes, *The Old Gringo,* recounting an imaginary conclusion to the life of American writer Ambrose Bierce, who disappeared in Mexico in 1914; it was the first novel by a Mexican to become a best-seller in the United States. Perhaps of even greater interest was the publication in English of Isabel Allende's much admired first novel, *The House of the Spirits (La casa de los espíritus,* 1982), stunningly unfolding a four-generation family chronicle in tragicomic dimensions.

Late in the year, a new novel by Nobel Prize laureate Gabriel García Márquez was published in Colombia, amid great excitement. Entitled *El amor en los tiempos del cólera (Love in the times of cholera),* it tells the story of a man and woman who are prevented by various obstacles from marrying in their youth and finally become too old to marry, though they love each other greatly. The book was expected to be translated and published in English in early 1987.

French. The poetry and prose of Jules Laforgue influenced a generation of American and British poets; now his *Moral Tales (Moralités légendaires,* 1887) are available in English in a fine new translation. René Crevel (1900–1935), who won renown for the surrealistic novel *Babylone,* was revived in a superlative translation, *Babylon,* by Kay Boyle. Marguerite Yourcenar's *Oriental Tales (Nouvelles orientales,* 1937) delicately re-creates stories from a range of Eastern sources. Marguerite Duras's acclaimed *L'Amant (The Lover),* which won the Prix Goncourt for 1984, also appeared in translation during the year. In the novel, an aged narrator relives her troubled adolescence

New Latin American Novelist

The bloody 1973 military coup that toppled Marxist President Salvador Allende Gossens of Chile created cultural aftershocks in journalism and literature; one of them was *La Casa de los Espiritus* (*The House of the Spirits*), a powerful first novel by Isabel Allende, the late president's niece and godchild. A narrative of four generations of an exuberant Latin American family, the novel has strong political and feminist overtones; at the same time it is shot through with the fantasy and humor that dominates much of modern Latin American literature. The book was received so enthusiastically around the world, in the original Spanish and in translation, that the Chilean dictatorship relaxed its normally harsh censorship to allow sales in Chile. Isabel Allende was born in 1942 in Lima, Peru, and now lives with her family in Venezuela. Her second novel *De Amores e Ombres* (*Love and Shadows*), about a pair of young lovers living under a dictatorship, was published in Spain in 1984 and slated for eventual English translation; she was working on a third novel in 1985.

Isabel Allende

in French Indochina. Of the newer novelists, Michel Rio scored impressively with *Parrot's Perch* (*Le Perchoir du perroquet,* 1983), about a victim of political persecution who becomes a monk but cannot reconcile his religious beliefs with the existence of evil. The 1985 Prix Goncourt went to Yaan Queffelec for his second novel, *Les Noces barbares* (*Barbarous Wedding*), about the torment of an illegitimate boy.

Austrian, German, Swiss. The Austrian Peter Handke, in the now translated novel *Slow Homecoming* (*Die langsame Heimkehr,* 1979), used various techniques to illustrate the attempts of a world traveler to identify himself with what he sees. German readers had a chance to enjoy the heretofore unpublished first novel by Uwe Johnson, *Ingrid Babendererde; Reifeprüfung 1953* (untranslated), which offers a pretaste of his many later novels about the divided Germanies. Heinrich Böll's *A Soldier's Legacy* (*Das Vermächtnis,* 1947), translated in 1985, realistically portrays war action on the Russian front. Johnson died in 1984 and Böll in 1985.

A novelistic account of what life was like in Germany and Austria between 1935 and 1955 is Gregor von Rezzori's *The Death of My Brother Abel* (*Der Tod meines Bruders Abel,* 1976), made available in English in 1985. Meanwhile, the reputation of novelist Martin Walser was enhanced with publication of the untranslated *Messners Gedanken* (Messner's thoughts), whose narrator gives us the raw materials of his life as he tried to shape them into an autobiography. Walser was also represented by two translated novels: *Letter to Lord Liszt* (*Brief an Lord Liszt,* 1982), in which two business competitors exchange self-revealing letters; and *The Inner Man* (*Seelenarbeit,* 1979), a portrait of a modern German family spoiled by affluence. The Swiss essayist and fiction writer Adolf Muschg finally received attention among English-speaking readers with selections from his short stories in *The Blue Man,* featuring brisk social satire. The common-sense polemics of German writer Günter Grass are anthologized in his essays *On Writing and Politics, 1967–1983.*

Italian. As a critic and writer Natalia Ginzburg is a powerhouse, although she is barely known through translations into English. Her current

243

Italo Calvino, Italy's leading contemporary novelist and a master of allegorical fantasy, died in September from the effects of a stroke.

(untranslated) novel *La Città e la Casa* (The city and the house) contrasts urban and peasant cultures. An earlier novel, *All Our Yesterdays* (*Tutti i nostri' ieri,* 1952), which now has been translated, unforgettably etches scenes from the days of Italian and German fascism. Italo Calvino, who died during the year, entertained with his newly translated novel *Mr. Palomar* (*Palomar,* 1983), in which the narrator comments with understated comedy on life's commonplaces. Primo Levi has a dual reputation as both scientist and novelist. His recently translated memoir, *The Periodic Table* (*Il sistema periodico,* 1975) gained a wide audience in the United States; not far behind was his novel *If Not now, When?* (*Se non ora, quando?,* 1982), which portrays Russian-Jewish partisans on World War II battlefields.

Czech. Smuggled out of Czechoslovakia and translated, Ivan Klima's *My Merry Mornings,* with a story for each day of the week, gives the feel of state-monitored everyday life in Prague. Poems of protest and autobiographical impressions from the 1970's by Jaroslav Seifert, who won the Nobel Prize for literature in 1984, are included in the English anthology *An Umbrella From Piccadilly.* Rudolf Tesnohlidek's *The Cunning Little Vixen,* written as a news-

paper serial in 1920, was published in English for the first time, with illustrations by Maurice Sendak. This earthy, satirical novel (more suitable for adult readers than for children) observes its human characters in detail through the often perceptive eyes of its shrewd animal characters.

Russian. *Soviet Dissent: Contemporary Movements for National, Religious, and Human Rights* is a comprehensive history of modern "movements for self-determination" by national and religious groups, workers, and human rights advocates seeking to overcome repression in the Soviet Union; the author, former Soviet dissident Ludmilla Alexeyeva, left for the West in 1977 to have the work translated and published.

Chinese. Assessments of the Cultural Revolution were given factual and fictional form by Yang Jiang's *Six Chapters From My Life "Downunder"* and Feng Jicai's *Chrysanthemums.* Yang's memoirs show why sending intellectuals to farming communities was a failure. Feng's stories, which appeared in Chinese periodicals over the last six years, seek to reclaim literature from political ends. S.M.

BOOKS FOR CHILDREN

The continuing rise in U.S. sales of children's books in 1985 was reflected at the annual American Booksellers Association convention, where publishers allotted more space than ever to the display of their juvenile titles. The growing interest led to formation of the Association of Booksellers for Children, which was designed to promote excellence in juvenile publishing and to create a network of communication among children's booksellers.

Trends. Sales of paperback children's books slowed somewhat after the phenomenal growth of 1984. Estimated consumer sales for the year, reported in August by the Book Industry Study Group, showed a (still substantial) increase of about 19 percent over 1984, as compared with an increase of over 60 percent between 1983 and 1984. Hardcover juvenile book sales showed an estimated increase of 10 percent, after a decrease in 1984.

Paperback publishing was clearly a booming industry, with companies producing softcovers for all age levels and in a variety of formats, from picture books to young adult novels.

Paperback publishing history was made when *Perfect Summer* became the first teen title in the history of The New York Times *Book Review* to appear on the best-seller list. On August 25 it reached the number 14 spot on the paperback fiction list.

"Baby lit"—books for children aged two months and up—was still growing. More and more companies turned to the production of board books, wordless books, pop-up books, and floating books. Leo Lionni, creator of such popular picture books as *Swimmy* and *Inch by Inch,* introduced a series of four board books in which mice show toddlers basic concepts such as numbers and colors. First Experience Books by Fred Rogers, star of the long-running public television show *Mr. Rogers' Neighborhood,* were illustrated with color photographs by Jim Judkis. The books, for children aged two to seven, describe family experiences like the arrival of a new baby and going to day care. *The Baby's Story Book,* collected and illustrated by Kay Chorao, was published as a companion volume to *The Baby's Lap Book* and *The Baby's Bedtime Book.* It contains 15 simply told tales for children from one to six.

Business News. Trumpet Club, a paperbook book club for grades four to six, was launched

A terrifying flight in the claws of a fiery dragon is one of the perils depicted by Trina Schart Hyman in Saint George and the Dragon, *winner of the 1985 Caldecott Medal for the best illustrated children's book.*

in September, offering up to 35 titles each month. Scholastic, for decades a publisher of school magazines and juvenile paperbacks, started the company's first cloth children's line, called Scholastic Hardcover; its list was intended as an extension of the paperback program, providing a means for Scholastic to publish in hardcover its current softcover authors who were felt to deserve such distinction.

The rise in licensing, including tie-ins and spin-offs from television shows, movies, and comics, continued, with new characters featured. The Smurfs, Care Bears, and Muppets of 1984 shared shelf space with The Transformers, Gummy Bears, and Muppet Babies of 1985. Books based on these creatures continued to be a lucrative source of income for publishers.

New and Old Favorites. Several old favorites resurfaced, most notably Beatrix Potter's beloved Jemima Puddle-Duck in the *Jemima Puddle-Duck Pop-Up Book.* Potter's illustrations now leap off the page and are animated by ingenious devices of paper engineering. Also making a recent reappearance was Corduroy, the little bear who made his debut almost 20 years ago in Don Freeman's picture book classics *Corduroy* and *A Pocket for Corduroy.* Corduroy returned in three new stories—two board books and a "pudgy" book.

The late Margaret Wise Brown, prolific author of picture books, captured audiences once again with *Margaret Wise Brown's Wonderful Storybook,* illustrated by J. P Miller. Eric Carle, author and illustrator of the enduring best-seller *The Very Hungry Caterpillar,* presented his latest innovation, *The Very Busy Spider.* The brilliantly colored pages portray a farmyard in which the animals invite children to explore their sense of touch through textured additions to each page.

Madeline, the favorite little girl of many young readers, first appeared in 1939 in the award-winning *Madeline,* by the late Ludwig Bemelmans. Published in 1985 was a new Madeline book called *Madeline's Christmas;* it was taken from a Bemelmans story that originally appeared in the December 1956 issue of *McCall's* magazine.

In 1974, Robert Cormier wrote a controversial novel for teenagers, *The Chocolate War,* which has remained a best-seller. The story centers on Jerry, a boy who struggles against the peer pressures of his private high school. In 1985, 11 years later, Cormier published a sequel, *Beyond the Chocolate War,* in which Jerry returns to Trinity School.

Prizes. The winner of the Delacorte Press Prize for an Outstanding First Young Adult Novel was 18-year-old Cin Forshay-Lunsford's *Walk Through Cold Fire,* about a motherless teen, living with relatives, who becomes involved with a street gang. The winner of the Avon/Flare Young Adult Novel Competition was 18-year-old Tamela Larimer, whose novel *Buck,* about a teen runaway, was to be published in 1986. The American Library Association's Newbery Medal was awarded to Robin McKinley for *The Hero and the Crown.* McKinley's *The Blue Sword* had been selected as a Newbery Honor Book in 1983. The Caldecott Medal for the best American picture book was presented to Trina Schart Hyman, illustrator of *Saint George and the Dragon,* as retold by Margaret Hodges. A.M.

LOUISIANA. See STATISTICS OF THE WORLD. See also STATE GOVERNMENT REVIEW.

LUXEMBOURG. In 1985 the Christian Social-Socialist coalition government of Premier Jacques Santer continued a program broadly similar to that of the previous Christian Social-Liberal coalition. The major change was a decision to reintroduce the practice by which wage increases are tied to increases in the cost of living, beginning in January. However, in order to keep exports competitive in price, it was agreed that indexing wages to prices would not be applied if wage rates increased out of proportion to those of Luxembourg's trading partners.

The 1985 budget included a projected surplus intended to build up reserves and to continue aid to the steel industry. While the steel industry has declined in relative importance to the overall economy, it continues to be a major employer and the source of about 40 percent of total exports. In order to cushion the effects of declining employment and reduce economic dependence on steel, the government continued to promote greater diversification of the economy.

See STATISTICS OF THE WORLD. W.C.C.

M

MADAGASCAR. *See* STATISTICS OF THE WORLD.
MAINE. *See* STATISTICS OF THE WORLD.
MALAWI. *See* STATISTICS OF THE WORLD.
MALAYSIA. During 1985, turbulence within Malaysia's ruling National Front threatened to erode the coalition's dominance. Human rights issues loomed large, and there was serious rioting involving Muslims.

In the East Malaysian state of Sabah, the Berjaya Party, which had governed the state since 1976, was routed in April elections by the newly formed Parti Bersatu Sabah and a resurgent United Sabah National Organization. The PBS captured 25 seats, the USNO won 16, and the Berjaya Party only 6. The PBS has been formed by dissident Berjaya members who felt that the Berjaya Party's professed multiracial orientation actually was tilted against Kadazans and Catholics. In a surprise move, defeated chief minister and Berjaya leader Harris Salleh threw his party's support behind his former arch foe, USNO leader Tun Mustapha Harun, in an attempt to name Mustapha chief minister instead of PBS leader Joseph Pairin Kitingan. Kitingan gained the office and a vote of confidence from the state assembly, but sporadic bomb blasts accompanied the government transition. Meanwhile, court cases challenging the outcome continued late in the year.

In West Malaysia, the power struggle within the Malaysian Chinese Association (MCA) continued between the party president, Neo Yee Pan, and the MCA's former vice-president, Tan Koon Swan. Prime Minister Mahathir Mohamed, who had repeatedly called for settlement of the dispute, ousted Neo from the cabinet. Finally, in November, Tan was reportedly elected as MCA president.

Rioting broke out in northern Kedah state on November 19, when police tried to arrest the leader of the Pan Malaysian Islamic Party on charges of extremist activities. The leader, 13 followers, and 4 policemen were killed. In response, the government banned public gatherings in five predominantly Muslim states.

Human rights remained an issue as Fan Yew Teng, member of the opposition Social Democratic Party, was arrested under a government security act for publishing a book banned in Malaysia. In August the vice-president of the Malaysian Bar Council was charged with sedition after he presented an appeal to the pardons board claiming that different standards of justice were being applied to the poor than to the rich. Later in the year, James Clad, a foreign correspondent, was fined $4,150 for reporting on an unpublished cabinet document relating to Malaysian policy toward China. On the religious front, female teachers and civil servants were ordered not to wear the type of dress adopted by some Muslim fundamentalist groups that conceals the entire body except for the eyes.

On September 1, Malaysia's "national car," named the Proton Saga, was launched as the joint venture of a state-owned company and the Mitsubishi Corporation. Otherwise, economic recovery was slow because of lagging international commodity markets for key Malaysian exports, especially tin and rubber. On October 24 trading in tin was suspended on commodity markets in London and Kuala Lumpur, following disclosure that the International Tin Council, which buys and sells the metal, had run out of cash. It was uncertain whether a further serious collapse in tin prices could be prevented.

See STATISTICS OF THE WORLD.   K.M.

MALDIVES. *See* STATISTICS OF THE WORLD.
MALI. *See* STATISTICS OF THE WORLD.
MALTA. Malta's new prime minister, Carmelo Mifsud Bonnici, undertook several foreign policy initiatives during 1985 that were intended to normalize ties with countries that his predecessor, Dom Mintoff, had either neglected or alienated. For example, he attended the party leaders' conference of the Socialist International in Brussels, Belgium, in April. While there, he met with Claude Cheysson, a commissioner of the European Community, to renew talks on a financial protocol. He also held talks with British and Italian officials, and he finalized an agreement with the Vatican over

Malta's requirement that the island's Catholic schools be tuition free. His overtures in Western Europe were balanced by Malta's continuing cooperative relations with other nations inside and outside the Communist bloc.

Bonnici, who had taken office in December 1984, after the resignation of Mintoff, said that as prime minister he would continue Mintoff's efforts to create a welfare state and to pursue a nonaligned foreign policy. His cabinet was almost a replica of Mintoff's.

In November an Egyptian airliner was hijacked and forced to land in Malta; the hijackers shot eight people, killing two, before an Egyptian commando team stormed the plane. An additional 58 people were killed in the rescue attempt. The hijackers, one of whom survived, were said by Egypt to be pro-Libyan Palestinians opposed to Palestine Liberation Organization leader Yasir Arafat. In December the surviving suspect was charged with 16 counts of hijacking, murder, and assault. (*See also* EGYPT; MIDDLE EAST.)

See STATISTICS OF THE WORLD.   P.J.M.

MANITOBA. *See* STATISTICS OF THE WORLD. *See also* CANADA.

MANUFACTURING INDUSTRIES. As 1985 neared its conclusion, leading U.S. manufacturing executives and professional "business watchers" were cautiously optimistic about the future. A survey of business leaders revealed that most of them foresaw increased sales and rising profits, while fewer than one third expected to see an accompanying rise in prices. However, for a representative sampling of U.S manufacturing industries—steel, textiles, paper, and machine tools—participants and analysts detected notable pitfalls ahead, especially in the controversial and interconnected areas of tax reform and tariff imposition. Many experts stressed taxation as a major factor in production costs, noting that the U.S. tax system helps to boost labor and capital costs over those of competitors abroad. To these experts, tariff protection for industries damaged by heavy foreign import competition makes little sense when gains are canceled out by tax law changes that raise the cost of capital.

Foreign imports clearly were a major problem. The U.S. trade deficit for 1985 was projected to approach a record $150 billion,

with the manufacturing sector especially hard hit. The United States was experiencing significant net trade deficits in such areas as automobiles, consumer electronics, iron and steel, footwear, clothing, and petroleum products. There was strong sentiment in the U.S. Congress for protectionist measures, which the Reagan administration opposed as being ineffective means to deal with trade deficit problems. A symbolic showdown occurred when the U.S. International Trade Commission, a quasijudicial advisory agency, recommended that protective quotas be placed on U.S. shoe imports because of hardships suffered by American footwear manufacturers. (The imports' share of the shoe market had increased from 22 percent in 1968 to 76 percent by 1984.) In late August, President Ronald Reagan rejected the commission's recommendation.

The administration did, however, step up efforts to discourage unfair and restrictive practices by foreign trading partners and thus, at the same time, seek to reduce domestic pressures for protectionist legislation. In early September the United States announced proceedings against Japan, Brazil, South Korea, and the European Economic Community (EEC) for restrictions and subsidies in various industries. Later in the month, the administration also called a meeting with finance ministers and central bank presidents of four other major industrial nations. The countries pledged to work together toward lowering the value of the U.S. dollar, a key factor in the current mounting trade deficit. Declines in the dollar were expected to alleviate the trade deficit, though not in the short term. Reagan also announced new U.S. measures designed to blunt congressional pressures for protectionism; these included a $300 million fund to provide low-cost loans to support certain exports. One major protectionist measure did clear Congress, in early December. The bill, providing for reductions of up to 30 percent on imports of textiles, apparel, shoes, and copper, was vetoed by Reagan.

Meanwhile, U.S. industrial production continued to edge upward slowly. In December it was at 126 percent of its 1977 base, but only 2.1 percent above where it had been a year earlier. Spending on plants and equipment,

Faced with increased foreign competition, the U.S. textile industry has had to make major cutbacks. Mayor Tony Paulos of Great Falls, S.C. (below), stands at the locked gate of one of the three J. P. Stevens textile factories that have been shut down in that city since 1981, with a loss of 1,500 jobs.

through the first nine months of 1985, increased $37.86 billion, compared with the same period in 1984. The Labor Department reported in December that 10 million new jobs had been created in the United States since the business expansion began in December 1982. But growth in manufacturing jobs had been weak. In a long-term trend from 1950, factory jobs as a proportion of all nonfarm jobs had declined from 50 percent to 20 percent.

Steel. In late 1985 the U.S. steel industry employed 210,748 workers who received a $16.45 average hourly wage over a 38.7-hour work week. During the late 1970's, twice as many people had worked in the industry. In the first nine months of 1985, according to the American Iron and Steel Institute, domestic mill shipments totaled 54,665,613 tons, imports 19,129,024 tons, and exports only 700,790 tons.

With America's largest producer, U.S. Steel, receiving only 35 percent of its revenue from steel, and its steel division lopping off 100,000 jobs and shutting down about 150 plants, the industry's belt-tightening process had clearly begun. Although LTV Corporation moved into the number-two spot, it suspended payment on its four classes of preferred stock for an indefinite period. The company also put its specialty steel division up for sale and, with other big producers, planned to follow U.S. Steel in raising sheet steel prices, effective January 1, 1986. Unlike U.S. Steel and LTV, number-three Bethlehem Steel Corporation remained mainly a steel company. Chairman Donald Trautlein saw little or no profits for 1985, but the firm invested heavily in new equipment, betting on an industry turnaround.

The most volatile upheavals among steelmakers took place at Wheeling-Pittsburgh Steel Corporation, whose application for bankruptcy in April was complicated by a strike in July by the firm's 8,200 workers. Major stockholders forced out Dennis Carney as chief executive officer and replaced him with former Ford Motor Company executive George Ferris. The strike was settled in October, with employees accepting a wage cut, and the company then focused on its reorganization plan for bankruptcy court. Meanwhile, the company reported a third-quarter loss of $133 million.

The once sedate steel industry was a battleground for market share and a competitive edge. U.S. Steel held the lead, having boosted its market share to 17.6 percent by the second quarter. Price cutting was in evidence everywhere, with some steel products falling by as much as $70 a ton. Meanwhile, pressure from

U.S. automakers—representing about 30 percent of the steel industry's annual shipments—led steel producers to improve quality. Electrogalvanized steel, for example, was much in demand. General Motors signed a purchasing agreement with a Bethlehem/Pre Finish Metals joint venture for sheet steel electrogalvanized on two sides; car manufacturers wanted sheet steel with zinc or zinc alloy coatings in order to offer automobiles with a ten-year warranty against rust and corrosion. Most domestic steel companies were installing electrogalvanizing facilities and expected to be producing coated steel early in 1986.

With imported steel gobbling up about one-fourth of the U.S. market in 1984, President Reagan had directed his trade representative, William Brock, to negotiate "voluntary" import restrictions that would hold the import line to 18.5 percent of the market. U.S. negotiator Charles Blum reported in September 1985 that he had worked out 14 voluntary agreements with foreign steelmakers. However, import levels late in the year had still not declined to the extent envisioned by the administration, and the efficacy of the administration program remained in doubt. On December 30 the United States imposed unilateral quotas on exports of semifinished steel products by the European Community, which vowed retaliation.

Textiles. The $50 billion American textile industry was in deep trouble during the year. The industry's single largest market, the apparel trade, was breaking down at an alarming rate, with garment imports (by value) having doubled since 1980. Major U.S. mills were responding with automation and tighter cost control. An $11 million publicity program entitled "Crafted With Pride in USA" was introduced to promote purchases of American goods.

Aggregate demand for all textile products, imports and U.S.-made combined, was expected to decline 5 percent in 1985, and the American Textile Manufacturers Institute reported a 9 percent drop in mill production. Textile profits in the first six months of the year were half those of the same period in 1984. Capital expenditures by textile manufacturers, though at a record high, threatened to curb cash flow and cut deeply into 1986 outlays.

Production capacity dropped about 5 percent from mid-1984 to mid-1985—which translates into about 600 million pounds of textile products. The capacity utilization rate, although exceeding 80 percent, left 2 billion pounds of unused capacity, and textile mill employment by midyear had dropped to 699,000, the lowest level recorded by the Bureau of Labor Statistics since it began keeping such records in 1939.

The darkest cloud in the industry's sky was the exploding rate of imports and the seriousness of their impact on American mills. In August the administration warned 18 nations of its intention to limit imports in 80 product categories, still only about 5 percent of first half 1985 trade volume. In October the U.S. House approved a bill intended to roll back textile and apparel imports from major suppliers by up to 30–40 percent; the measure was stronger than the one ultimately cleared by Congress in early December, but it did not extend to footwear or copper.

Paper. Business activity in the paper industry established record highs in 1984 in both paper and paperboard production, but it appeared that production would fall by about 2.5 percent in 1985. Production was affected by shutdowns of kraft paperboard mills because of the need to reduce inventories. Imports of paper and paperboard exceeded 1984 nine-month totals by 4 percent, while exports declined by 10 percent.

Awaiting the final shape of tax reform legislation in Congress, the industry faced the possibility of major changes in the tax structure that could discourage investment in new plants or equipment. This capital-intensive industry has widely employed the available tax incentives, such as accelerated capital recovery and investment tax credit, in financing new capacity. Removing or reducing these would sharply curb investment.

Despite some problems, American paper and paperboard producers were boosting their capacity. U.S. Department of Commerce data indicate that firms would invest more than $8 billion in new plants and equipment during all of 1985, a tangible expression of industry self-confidence. More expansion was seen for 1986 and 1987, with most of the gains taking place

A huge earthquake and its aftershocks destroyed much of downtown Mexico City in September; buildings crashed into the streets, killing thousands of people and leaving rescue workers with the grim and exhausting task of searching for survivors and bodies in the rubble.

in strong demand areas such as coated paper and uncoated sheet papers.

Machine Tools. The National Machine Tool Builders' Association reported that machine tool orders for the first nine months of 1985 totaled $1.93 billion, off 11 percent from the same period in 1984. The full-year total for 1984 had been $2.92 billion, a sharp increase over 1983 because of the surging economy. Employment in the industry stood at about 73,500 in 1985. Sharp increases in imports—in metal cutting machines and other tools—were a major problem. L.R.H.

MARYLAND. See STATISTICS OF THE WORLD.

MASSACHUSETTS. See STATISTICS OF THE WORLD.

MAURITANIA. See STATISTICS OF THE WORLD.

MAURITIUS. See STATISTICS OF THE WORLD.

MEXICO. During 1985, Mexico was hit by a severe earthquake and besieged by serious economic problems. July elections led to no

erosion in the pervasive political power of the government party.

Earthquake. A devastating earthquake struck populous Mexico City and several Mexican states to the west on the morning of September 19, 1985. Compounded by a heavy aftershock the next day, it left more than 7,000 dead according to official estimates (other estimates ran as high as 10,000). In the capital alone, hundreds of buildings collapsed, among them 7 hotels, 3 large hospitals, more than 100 government buildings, and 2 large apartment complexes. Collapse of the Communications Tower and of Televicentro, headquarters of the major television networks, led to early reports that Mexico City had virtually been destroyed. International rescue workers labored for days to rescue survivors trapped in the fallen debris, and many were found to have almost miraculously clung to life. City authorities decreed that no new buildings would replace those destroyed, ordering the sites to be converted into parks. As aid poured in to Mexico from other countries and from international agencies, the United Nations Commission on Latin America assessed earthquake damages at $4 billion.

Elections. Earlier in the year, on July 7, city, state, and legislative elections were held. The main question was whether the ruling Institutional Revolutionary Party (PRI) would suffer any significant defeats. It has held a virtual monopoly on political power in Mexico since its formation in 1929, never having lost a statewide, much less a nationwide, election, but charges of corruption and electoral fraud have frequently been made against it. The right-of-center National Action Party (PAN) was hoping to win the governorship of both Sonora and Nuevo León states. It won in neither place, according to official vote tallies. There were, however, widespread reports of "irregularities" in many areas of the country—including ballot boxes that had been stuffed or stolen outright.

Despite making some inroads into PRI strength in the popular vote, the PAN ended up with fewer deputies in the lower house of Congress than before. It protested vigorously, noting that the Electoral College, which assigns 100 of the seats to different opposition parties under a proportional representation scheme, was controlled by the PRI. The PAN charged that the ruling party gave tiny parties individual representation that they did not merit, in order to keep the opposition splintered.

Economic Developments. In the weeks following the elections, Mexicans learned that the country's desperate economic situation was growing worse. With a foreign debt of nearly $100 billion, much of the federal budget was used up simply to cover interest payments. Petroleum prices continued to fall, and tourism—Mexico's second largest earner of foreign currency—had declined.

On July 24, the peso's controlled rate, used for 80 percent of transactions, was devalued by 16.7 percent in relation to the U.S. dollar. The president announced that some 30,000 top-level and middle-level government employees would be laid off. Of the nearly 400 government companies, all running in the red,

more than 80 were offered for sale, with the possibility that they would be closed if no buyers were found. It was estimated that up to half of the work force was unemployed or underemployed in 1985.

During the late 1970's, Mexico had borrowed heavily, counting on petroleum exports to pay the debt. By mid-1985, however, it became apparent that continually dropping petroleum prices might cost Mexico as much as $2 billion in anticipated earnings for the year. Mexico's difficulties were eased somewhat on August 29, when Mexico and representatives of more than 600 commercial banks signed the final part of an agreement to stretch out repayment of outstanding loans totaling $48.7 billion. On October 1, following the disastrous earthquake, a group of major international banks agreed to reschedule nearly $1 billion in loan repayments due shortly.

Foreign Affairs. Mexico's relations with the United States fell for a time to their lowest ebb in many years, in response to relatively small-scale incidents. Trouble began with the kidnapping and murder in Guadalajara of Enrique Camarena, an officer of the U.S. Drug Enforcement Administration whose body was found in March. (Later in the year, in November, 21 police officers were killed by drug smugglers who had been discovered with a large quantity of marijuana believed destined for the United States.) Washington charged that Mexican authorities were not working hard to find Camarena's killers; in apparent retaliation, nine border crossings were temporarily closed by U.S. authorities. The U.S. State Department announced it might issue a travel advisory warning of dangers to Americans in Mexico. Privately, many Mexican officials maintained that the United States was raising difficulties in an effort to change Mexico's policies toward the government in El Salvador, to which it has been cool, and toward the Sandinista regime in Nicaragua, which Mexico has supported. Toward the latter part of the year, Mexico appeared to be coming closer to Washington's position. In one significant step, Mexico restored full relations with El Salvador.

See STATISTICS OF THE WORLD.   J.H.B

MICHIGAN. *See* STATISTICS OF THE WORLD.

MICRONESIA. *See* PACIFIC ISLANDS.

Middle East

Peace initiatives in 1985 gave some hope for progress in resolving the Arab-Israeli conflict. But hopes were frustrated by a series of terrorist incidents and internal quarrels in the Israeli and Arab camps.

The peace initiatives polarized Arab states into moderates such as Egypt and Jordan, who were pursuing an active peace diplomacy, and those of the so-called "rejectionist front," such as Syria and Libya, which were adamantly opposed to negotiations with Israel. The Palestine Liberation Organization (PLO) was divided along similar lines. In Israel, differences between the Labor and Likud parties over the peace process and other issues threatened the existence of their national unity government. In Lebanon, the withdrawal of Israeli troops after three years of occupation left Syria as the only foreign

power with significant influence over the country's warring sectarian factions. The latest in a series of Syrian-mediated truces was signed in December, but its prospects of bringing peace to Lebanon were uncertain.

Hussein-Arafat Agreement. An agreement signed between Jordan's King Hussein and PLO Chairman Yasir Arafat in Amman during February marked an important step in Hussein's effort to bring the PLO into the Mideast peace process. The agreement delineated five principles as forming the basis for peace: total withdrawal by Israel from the Arab territories it occupied

The gutted headquarters of the Palestine Liberation Organization in Tunisia; the compound was the target of a long-range Israeli air strike on October 1, in which approximately 70 Palestinians and Tunisians were killed.

Egyptian soldiers guard the Italian cruise ship Achille Lauro *(above), which was hijacked by four Palestinians. The gunmen murdered an American tourist, Leon Klinghoffer; below, his widow is helped from the ship.*

in the 1967 war; the right of self-determination for the Palestinian people within a Jordanian-Palestinian federation; solution of the Palestinian refugee question in accordance with the appropriate United Nations resolutions; solution of the "Palestinian question in all its aspects"; and "peace negotiations . . . under the auspices of an international conference [with] the five permanent members of the [UN] Security Council and all the parties to the conflict . . . including the PLO." A joint Jordanian-Palestinian delegation was to be formed to negotiate with Israel. The agreement was considered a significant step toward peace because it implied that for the first time the PLO was publicly recognizing Israel's right to exist. However, though King Hussein asserted that both Jordan and the PLO were signifying such recognition, Arafat and other prominent PLO figures refused to say as much.

Egypt acclaimed the agreement, but it raised a storm of protest among the hard-line Arab states and their supporters. In Damascus, six PLO factions, including a dissident faction of Arafat's own Fatah organization, announced in March the formation of a Palestinian National Salvation Front to oppose Arafat's peace policies and to continue the struggle against Israel; the six factions were clients of Syria and sympathized with that country's hostility to Arafat's leadership. Initial Israeli reaction was also highly critical. The Likud coalition dismissed the initiative immediately, while Defense Minister Yitzhak Rabin of the Labor Party called it nothing more than a "propaganda maneuver." Prime Minister Shimon Peres adopted a wait-and-see attitude.

In July, Jordan passed on to the United States a list of seven Palestinians who would be acceptable to the PLO as part of a negotiating team. But because several of the proposed figures had overt PLO ties—Israel will not deal with the PLO, nor will the United States until the organization recognizes Israel—the initiative appeared to be stalled.

Peres Initiative. In a speech to the UN General Assembly in October, Peres laid the framework for a new Israeli initiative that called for direct negotiations without any preconditions between Israel and Jordan, based on UN Resolutions 242 and 338. The negotiations, Peres said, could begin in Israel, Jordan, or any other mutually agreed-upon location before the end of 1985; Jordanian representation could consist of either a Jordanian or a Jordanian-Palestinian delegation "comprising delegates that represent peace, not terror"; the negotiations, if necessary, could "be initiated with the support of an international forum"; and the permanent members of the UN Security Council could be invited to "support the initiation of these negotiations."

Aside from his failure to attack the PLO, the most significant component of the Peres proposals was his willingness to allow for a Soviet role in peace talks; previously both the United States and Israel had sought to exclude the Soviets from any possible peace parley. Peres's apparent concession had a proviso, however: that Moscow renew diplomatic ties with Israel, broken since the 1967 war. Both King Hussein and Egyptian President Hosni Mubarak responded favorably to the initiative, but it caused dissension within the Israeli government.

Egyptian-Israeli Relations. Both Israel and Egypt took steps to improve what had been characterized as a "cold peace" between them. In January the two countries resumed talks on Taba, the tiny enclave on the Gulf of Aqaba that is controlled by Israel but claimed by Egypt. Resolution of the dispute was seen as an important barometer of relations; Mubarak declared that he would be prepared to meet with Peres if the sides achieved a Taba settlement, if Israel withdrew its forces from Lebanon, and if progress was made in the overall peace process. However, several incidents cast a shadow over steps to improve relations. In August an Israeli diplomat was assassinated in Cairo, and in October seven Israeli tourists were killed in Sinai by an Egyptian soldier or policeman who the government claimed was mentally disturbed. The violence provided ammunition for Israeli opponents of Peres's efforts to compromise differences with Egypt, especially over the Taba issue. There was also growing criticism in Egypt of the 1979 peace treaty with Israel.

The Palestine Liberation Organization. Peace efforts were also set back by Israel's bombing of the PLO headquarters in Tunis, the capital of Tunisia, on October 1 and by the seizure of

an Italian cruise ship off the Egyptian coast about a week later by members of a PLO faction known as the Palestine Liberation Front (PLF). Israel asserted that its air attack, in which some 70 Palestinians and Tunisians were killed, was a response to growing PLO terrorism, including the recent murder of three Israelis in Cyprus. The attack was condemned by the Arab world, including Egypt and Jordan, and by the UN Security Council (the United States abstained from the 14-0 vote). President Ronald Reagan's initial approval of the raid as "a legitimate response" to "terrorist attacks" strained relations with Tunisia, a moderate pro-American Arab state. In Cairo thousands of demonstrators demanded that Egypt sever relations with the United States and Israel; in response, Mubarak suspended the Taba talks (they resumed in December).

Seizure of the Italian ship *Achille Lauro* by PLF members greatly embarrassed Arafat when it was reported that the alleged mastermind behind the hijacking was Muhammad Abbas, a PLF leader considered an Arafat protégé. After surrendering to Egyptian authorities in exchange for a promise of safe passage out of Egypt (Abbas was involved in the negotiations), Abbas and the four gunmen were flown out of Egypt aboard an Egyptian airliner. However, the airliner was intercepted by U.S. Navy jet fighters and forced to land at a joint U.S.-NATO base in Sicily, where the hijackers were arrested by Italian authorities. Italy later permitted Abbas to leave the country; the hijackers were convicted on weapons charges and awaited trial for the hijacking and for the murder of an American Jewish passenger who had been shot and thrown overboard.

Interception of the Egyptian airliner by American planes sparked a new wave of protest in Cairo and other Arab capitals. Mubarak's demand for an apology was rejected by President Reagan; instead a special U.S. envoy was sent to Egypt to ease the tension.

PLO involvement in the *Achille Lauro* incident and the organization's inability to agree on its stance toward Israel prior to a scheduled Jordanian-Palestinian meeting with the British foreign secretary led to renewed tensions between Arafat and Hussein. The meeting with British officials was canceled by the Foreign

President Hafez al-Assad of Syria (right) welcomes Lebanese President Amin Gemayel to Damascus in March for a discussion of the Phalangist revolt against Syrian influence in Lebanon.

objected to Mubarak's and Arafat's moves toward peace negotiations with Israel. The group was believed to be linked to Libya.

Airport Attacks. On December 27 Arab terrorists attacked the check-in counters of El-Al Israel Airlines at airports in Rome and Vienna, killing 16 innocent persons and wounding more than 100 others, in volleys of machine gun fire and grenades. Four of the terrorists were killed in gun battles with police and security personnel, and three attackers were captured. The attacks occurred within minutes of each other. Most analysts attributed them to followers of Abu Nidal. A note carried by one of the surviving terrorists in the Rome attack said it had been done in response to Israel's bombing of the PLO headquarters in Tunisia; some reports interpreted the attacks as designed to block the Arafat-Hussein peace effort. Israel blamed the PLO and said it would retaliate; the PLO denied involvement in the attacks. Libyan links were, again, suspected.

Lebanon. During June a TWA airliner en route from Athens to Rome was hijacked by Lebanese Shiites. After several trips back and forth across the Mediterranean between Beirut and Algiers, during which time U.S. Navy diver Robert D. Stethem was killed and most of the other passengers were released, the plane came to a halt in Beirut, where the remaining passengers were removed and held captive at different locations in the city. The hijackers, who claimed to represent a Muslim fundamentalist faction, demanded the release of more than 700 prisoners, mostly Shiites, who had been captured by Israel during its occupation of South Lebanon and transferred to an Israeli prison. Nabih Berri, leader of Amal, a moderate Shiite group, stepped in to take control of most of the hostages and became the intermediary between the hijackers and U.S. and Lebanese authorities. With backing from Syria, Berri eventually persuaded the hijackers to release the last hostages after 17 days in captivity. They were driven to Damascus and then flown to West Germany en route to the United States. Israel released its prisoners, in several large groups, in operations lasting several weeks. Analysts pointed out that Israel had begun releasing the prisoners even before the hijacking incident and that the process was actually slowed by

Office when Palestinian members of the delegation refused to sign a statement recognizing Israel. In October, Hussein summoned Arafat to Amman and was reported to have warned him that he would be dropped from Jordan's peace initiative unless the PLO took steps to make itself a reliable bargaining partner. Arafat was said to have responded that there would not be "peace and stability in the region" if the PLO was left out. Although Arafat later issued a statement condemning terrorist acts outside Israel and the occupied territories, the tension with Hussein persisted.

Hijacking to Malta. In November an Egyptian airliner was hijacked after takeoff from Athens by Arab gunmen who forced the plane to land in Malta and shot eight passengers, killing two (an American and an Israeli). Hours later an Egyptian commando team stormed the plane in a rescue attempt, during which 58 people were killed or fatally wounded. Mubarak was criticized for his handling of the affair. The hijackers, one of whom survived, were believed to be radical anti-Arafat Palestinians belonging to a faction led by Abu Nidal, who the affair; thus, Israel and the United States were able to claim that no deal had been made with the terrorists.

At the end of the year, Muslim extremists were still holding at least four other American hostages in Lebanon, seeking the release of 17 Shiites being held in a Kuwaiti prison for their role in 1983 car-bomb attacks there; the fate of two other Americans who had been abducted was uncertain. A seventh hostage, the Reverend Benjamin Weir, was released in September. Four Soviet diplomats were abducted in Beirut in late September to protest Syria's involvement in antifundamentalist battles raging in Tripoli. (Syria is the Soviet Union's chief ally in the Middle East.) One of the men was found shot to death a few days later; the three others were released unharmed shortly after a truce had gone into effect in Tripoli.

Israel completed the withdrawal of its forces from Lebanon in June, although it left behind about 1,000 security personnel in a border security zone controlled by the Israeli-backed South Lebanese Army, a largely Maronite Christian force. Sporadic fighting between rival factions continued in Beirut, as Syria continued efforts to bring about a settlement. On December 28, leaders of Lebanon's rival militias signed a Syrian-mediated peace pact in Damascus. Announcement of the pact was greeted with cheers, but there was also widespread skepticism as to its likely effectiveness.

See also articles on individual countries mentioned and other Middle Eastern countries.   D.P.

MILITARY AND NAVAL AFFAIRS. Military affairs in 1985 were overshadowed by the Geneva summit meeting in November between American and Soviet leaders, although little actual headway was made at that time in the area of arms control. The United States responded forcefully against terrorist activity in intercepting an airliner carrying hijackers of a Mediterranean cruise ship. A series of espionage cases jolted the U.S. intelligence community (see CRIME AND LAW ENFORCEMENT), and controversies over waste, fraud, and mismanagement in the Pentagon continued. Factional fighting continued in Lebanon (see MIDDLE EAST). War dragged on between Iran and Iraq, and the Sudanese government was overthrown in a coup.

A nuclear-powered X-ray laser aims at approaching Soviet missiles in an artist's conception of the "Star Wars" defense system.

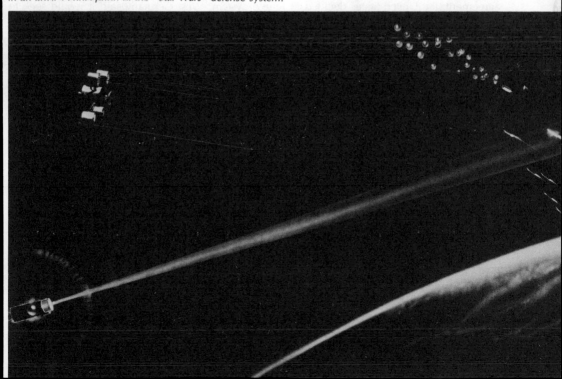

Superpower Relations. President Ronald Reagan and Soviet leader Mikhail Gorbachev met in Geneva in November. However, progress in arms control foundered because of differences over the U.S. Strategic Defense Initiative—popularly known as Star Wars—which Reagan intended to pursue despite Soviet opposition. Regional conflicts also were a major topic of discussion.

Negotiations to curb the nuclear weapons stockpiles of the two superpowers were resumed earlier in the year, in March, 15 months after the Soviet Union had walked out of the talks to protest the stationing of new U.S. missiles in Europe. In September, Gorbachev proposed a 50 percent reduction in strategic missiles but excluded Soviet medium-range missiles and bombers in Europe from the limit. An American counteroffer in November proposed limiting land-based nuclear missile warheads to 3,000, freezing the deployment of U.S. Pershing II and cruise missiles in Europe at 140 in exchange for major reductions of Soviet SS-20 missiles in Europe and Asia, and reducing the ceiling on air-launched cruise missiles from approximately 4,000 to 1,500. Each proposal envisioned an overall limit of 6,000 nuclear warheads.

Despite the inability to achieve an arms agreement, the United States decided in June to dismantle an obsolescent Poseidon nuclear missile submarine to comply with the limits of the 1979 Strategic Arms Limitation Treaty (SALT II) with the Soviets, even though the treaty was never ratified by the U.S. Senate. Nevertheless, an aggressive buildup of strategic systems by both sides proceeded. The first B-1B strategic bomber became operational in June. Development continued on a single-warhead ICBM, nicknamed Midgetman, and a "stealth" bomber that could escape detection by enemy air defenses. But Reagan's controversial MX land-based ICBM system again experienced legislative difficulties; his plan to deploy 100 MX missiles in underground silos was cut in half by Congress. The Soviets continued developing a new generation of ICBM's, began deploying the SS-25 mobile missile, and prepared to deploy their own antisatellite weapon system.

It was Star Wars, however, that provoked the most acrimony between the superpowers. Reagan had ordered research on his Strategic Defense Initiative in 1983, but only in 1985 did work on SDI get fully under way. SDI research is ultimately aimed at devising a system that would neutralize attacking ballistic missiles and render offensive nuclear weapons largely useless. Various technological options are available, none of them known to be able to work effectively. In very preliminary testing, a laser beam aimed from a mountaintop in Hawaii in June hit an 8-inch mirror on the side of a U.S. space shuttle as it passed 220 miles overhead. In September it was announced that a missile section had been destroyed on the ground by a test laser. In December an underground nuclear test reportedly involving an X-ray laser was carried out in Nevada and said to be successful.

Some critics of SDI contend it violates the 1972 antiballistic missile treaty, which generally bars the testing or deployment of antimissile systems. Opponents also charge that SDI won't achieve its objective but will trigger a new round in the arms race. Gorbachev told Reagan at Geneva that the Soviet Union would build its own defensive system if the United States pursued SDI. In December, Great Britain agreed to participate in research on the missile-defense system; West Germany said it would seek to negotiate an agreement for participation by West German industry, as part of an overall accord on exchange of scientific and technological research. (*See also* TECHNOLOGY.)

In early August the Soviet Union instituted a temporary moratorium on nuclear testing, scheduled to last until the end of the year. The United States refused to join, citing, for one thing, the absence of provisions for on-site inspection. In December the Soviet Union said it would allow limited on-site inspection if the United States agreed to participate in a moratorium on testing; the United States declined, citing a need for U.S. tests and expressing doubts as to the verification procedure proposed. Reagan wrote a letter to Gorbachev proposing that experts meet to discuss ways of improving verification of agreements on underground testing.

Terrorism. In a daring display of aerial warfare, F-14 jet fighters from the U.S. aircraft carrier

In the aftermath of the June hijacking of TWA flight 847 by Lebanese Shiite Muslim gunmen, an honor guard salutes Robert Stethem, a U.S. seaman killed by hijackers, as his body is returned from Beirut.

Saratoga intercepted a chartered Egyptian airliner over the Mediterranean Sea on October 10 and forced the plane to land at a joint Italian-NATO air base at Sigonella, Sicily. The plane was carrying four Palestinian terrorists implicated in the murder of an American passenger, Leon Klinghoffer, during the hijacking of the Italian cruise ship *Achille Lauro* three days earlier. The United States had insisted the terrorists be brought to justice for the murder and acted after Palestine Liberation Organization negotiators sent aboard the ship by Egyptian authorities turned the hijackers over to Egypt, which had guaranteed them safe-passage. U.S. officials later confirmed that an elite military counterterrorist unit had been preparing to assault the ship when the hostages were released.

The dramatic military intervention was the first successful antiterrorist action by the Reagan administration in the wake of several acts of violence against U.S. citizens. In June, U.S. Navy diver Robert Stethem was tortured and murdered by Palestinian terrorists during the hijacking of a Trans World Airlines jet in the Middle East. U.S. antiterrorist commandos had been dispatched to Algiers to storm the jet, but the plane was flown to Beirut, where 39 Americans were held hostage for two weeks (a 40th was released early for health reasons).

During the same month, four Marine guards at the U.S. embassy in El Salvador and nine others were gunned down at a strip of sidewalk restaurants in San Salvador.

Later in the year, in November, terrorists seized an Egyptian airliner and, after forcing it to land at an airport in Malta, began shooting passengers, killing two. A total of 58 others, including most of the gunmen, were killed when Egyptian commandos stormed the plane. Most of the deaths were attributed to smoke inhalation, from fire possibly caused by explosions set by the Egyptians to gain access to the plane. The Egyptian commandos also reportedly used heavy gunfire in the assault, and the terrorists fired grenades. Three U.S. military officers were at the airport, but there were conflicting accounts of what assistance they gave or were allowed to give. Antiterrorist experts from the U.S. Delta Force were initially refused permission to come to Malta; they later received permission, but it was too late. On December 27, terrorists launched attacks at the Rome and Vienna airports that led to the deaths of 16 innocent persons. The attacks highlighted the difficult question of what could be done to punish or deter such terrorism.

Arms Sales. A U.S. congressional study disclosed in May that worldwide arms sales to developing countries had decreased during

1984, to a (still sizable) $32.3 billion. The Soviet Union remained the world's leading arms merchant, selling $10.4 billion in military equipment to other nations. France sold $9.1 billion in arms, quadruple the previous year's sales, while the United States sold $7.3 billion, $3 billion less than in 1983.

The United States announced plans in March to sell F-16 jets to Thailand and Sidewinder air-to-air missiles to Pakistan. But the bulk of U.S. arms sales were to Middle Eastern countries. Despite a moratorium on arms sales to the region for several months, nearly $2 billion in military grants was approved for Israel in 1984, and in May 1985 the Pentagon said it would sell more M-60 tanks to Egypt. In September the Reagan administration disclosed plans to sell $1.5–$1.9 billion in arms to Jordan, including either F-16 or F-20 jet fighters and improved Hawk surface-to-air missiles. But the proposal prompted overwhelming opposition in Congress, and in October, Reagan reluctantly agreed to delay the sale until March 1, 1986, unless peace negotiations between Israel and Jordan began in the interim.

After similar congressional criticism delayed a proposed sale of U.S. F-15 jets to Saudi Arabia, the Saudis decided instead in September to purchase $3 billion to $4 billion in military aircraft from a British, West German, and Italian consortium. Those three governments agreed in August to build jointly a new European jet fighter. The project reportedly involved the production of as many as 700 aircraft at an estimated cost of $14 billion to $25 billion.

Central America. The United States continued to maintain a sizable military presence in Central America. Several thousand U.S. troops participated in major military training exercises in Honduras and El Salvador, and the show of force in the region appeared to stabilize the pro-American government of El Salvador in its civil war against guerrillas supported by the Marxist government of Nicaragua. The Reagan administration also maintained its controversial policy of support for rebels seeking to overthrow the Sandinista regime in Nicaragua. The U.S. House had banned all aid in April, but after intensive White House lobbying, Congress approved nonmilitary assistance.

Despite a congressional ban on military aid to the contras, the White House acknowledged in August that staff members of the National Security Council had helped contra officials raise money from nongovernmental sources in the United States and had also given advice on military operations to contra leaders. The Reagan administration continued to maintain that it had no intention of sending U.S. combat forces to Central America. Even so, published reports claimed U.S. military planners had concluded that a hypothetical invasion of Nicaragua could quickly rout the Sandinista government instead of miring American forces in a Vietnam-style guerrilla war.

Iran-Iraq War. The war between Iran and Iraq slogged into its sixth year of stalemate with little prospect for either a military or diplomatic solution. As casualties skyrocketed, it appeared the military balance had shifted in favor of Iraq; in what some Western analysts described as the heaviest fighting of the conflict, the Iraqis repelled a massive Iranian offensive near the oil port of Basra in March. But the stalemate on the ground prompted the Iraqis to shift to a strategy of economic warfare. By late summer the Iraqis had begun a fierce air war against Iranian oil facilities, repeatedly bombing the huge oil terminal at Kharg Island. The attacks severely damaged Iran's crude oil production facilities and gave Iraq a clear financial and economic advantage. Some intelligence estimates placed the number of combined war dead at close to 1 million, the largest casualty toll in any one conflict since World War II.

Cambodia and Vietnam. In an unusually strong four-month offensive ending in March, Vietnamese troops overran base camps inside Cambodia of three forces (one Communist and two non-Communist) that were resisting Vietnamese domination of Cambodia. Resistance forces were dispersed and had to resort to guerrilla tactics. The Vietnamese also invaded Thai territory, asserting that Thailand was harboring Cambodian rebels. Vietnam's dry-season offensive had become an annual event, but despite the stepped-up action in 1984–1985, the crushing of Cambodian resistance did not yet seem to be at hand.

Military Coups and Coup Attempts. Jaafar al-Nimeiry, the pro-American president of Sudan,

American and Soviet World War II veterans gathered in Torgau, East Germany, in April to mark the 40th anniversary of the "Meeting at the Elbe," the famous linkup of U.S. and U.S.S.R. forces that took place there in 1945.

was ousted in April in a bloodless coup led by senior Army generals. Nimeiry, who held power for 16 years, had been under fire for his inability to curb domestic unrest. He was replaced by General Abdul Rahman Swar al-Dahab, who had been named defense minister and commander of the armed forces by Nimeiry three weeks before the coup. In Uganda the five-year-old regime of President Milton Obote was toppled in July; the military junta suspended the constitution but pledged to hold elections in a year. In Nigeria, Major General Mohammed Buhari was forced from power in August in a bloodless coup led by the army chief of staff; Buhari had come to power 20 months earlier in another coup.

In Liberia, a former military commander, Thomas Quiwonkpa, led an unsuccessful coup in November against the regime of General Samuel Doe. An unknown number of people were killed or wounded in the revolt, said to be the seventh attempt to oust Doe since he seized power in 1980. Another coup attempt, in Thailand during September, failed to bring

down the government there; several senior military officers were implicated.

Other nations were fighting military insurgencies. U.S. intelligence sources concluded that the threat to the pro-Western government of Philippines President Ferdinand Marcos from a Communist-backed military insurgency had increased significantly. In Afghanistan, Western-backed guerrillas continued to impose heavy casualties on Soviet occupation forces backing the government. South Africa was discovered to have infiltrated troops into Angola and was also reportedly continuing to supply antigovernment guerrillas in Mozambique, despite a 1984 nonaggression pact between the two countries.

U.S. Developments. The Pentagon submitted a $322 billion defense budget request to Congress in February for the 1986 fiscal year beginning October 1, 1985. The proposal was $29.1 billion higher than fiscal 1985 outlays and reflected a 5.9 percent increase above inflation. The Pentagon sought substantial funding increases to finance major weapons programs,

261

including $6.2 billion for the B-1 bomber, $4.7 billion for Trident submarines and missiles, $4 billion for the MX missile, $3.7 billion for the Star Wars space defense program, $2.8 billion for Aegis-class cruisers, and $2.2 billion for M-1 tanks. The budget proposal was seen as excessive on Capitol Hill, although Congress did approve funds for all major weapons systems. Before adjourning in December, Congress approved a military appropriation of $297.4 billion for fiscal 1986, well below Reagan's request; it did carry forward $6.3 billion in unused appropriations that could also be drawn upon.

Conventional Arms and Equipment. In conventional weapons developments, the Pentagon cited poor testing performance in canceling the Army's $4.8 billion Sergeant York air defense gun in August. The Pentagon had already spent $1.8 billion on the weapon but said it was not worth another $3 billion in projected costs. After a 16-year moratorium, Congress approved the production of chemical weapons in July, and the Army began replacing its venerable .45 caliber pistol with an Italian-made Beretta 9-mm automatic sidearm.

Waste and Abuse. Instances of waste, fraud, and abuse within the military created a growing backlash against defense spending practices and fueled the debate over whether the $1

trillion spent by the Pentagon during Reagan's first four years in office had produced a more efficient military. A host of prominent defense contractors, including General Dynamics and General Electric, were accused of overcharging the government; several contractors, including both of these companies, were temporarily barred from receiving new contracts from the Pentagon. GE pleaded guilty in May to defrauding the Air Force of $800,000 in 1980 on Minuteman missile components; a federal judge fined the company $1.04 million and ordered it to repay the $800,000. After pleading guilty to similar charges in October, Rockwell International Corporation agreed to pay $1.5 million in fines and repayments. GE and the Pratt & Whitney division of United Technologies had already been ordered to return $208 million in excess profits on spare parts for Air Force and Navy jet engines.

In May, Navy Secretary John Lehman announced that he was fining General Dynamics $676,283 for giving gratuities to Admiral Hyman Rickover, former director of the Navy's nuclear submarine program. Lehman sent a letter of censure to the 85-year-old retired admiral. Amid revelations and allegations of many major abuses, the issue was dramatized for the general public by reports on small items; in May, for example, it was learned that a

General Dynamics Corporation, a leading U.S. defense contractor, came under fire for a variety of alleged financial and management violations. In December the company was named in a federal fraud indictment and barred from receiving government contracts of any kind.

California naval air station had purchased $659 ashtrays for several of its warplanes.

On December 2, James M. Beggs, administrator of the National Aeronautics and Space Administration, was indicted on charges of having defrauded the Army on a weapons contract while he was an executive with General Dynamics. The company itself and three of its other officers were also indicted. The charges related to the alleged overbilling to the government (reportedly of about $7.5 million) on a prototype of the Sergeant York gun. On December 3, General Dynamics was barred from receiving new government contracts of any kind; it had previously been barred for a time from receiving new defense contracts.

Staff Report. In October the Senate Armed Services Committee released a sharply critical staff report on the state of the armed forces. The bipartisan study claimed a drastic reorganization of the military was necessary to eliminate interservice rivalries and mismanagement that had endangered the Pentagon's ability to wage war.

Personnel. In an effort to improve combat readiness of conventional forces, the Army expanded the number of light infantry divisions, beefed up its special forces operations, and expanded its reserve force to more than 1 million for the first time in a decade. The Army also announced it was toughening its physical fitness standards for personnel, effective in October 1986, because too many soldiers were passing the tests without having to exercise regularly. All the services met recruiting and reenlistment objectives for 1985, but an improving economic climate and a decline in the number of available young people led the Pentagon to increase its retention incentives and prompted speculation about a possible resumption of the military draft.

Pentagon officials announced in October that all members of the armed forces would be required to undergo testing for exposure to the deadly virus that causes acquired immune deficiency syndrome. Screening for AIDS had originally been ordered only for all new recruits. Personnel who actually had the disease were to be issued medical discharges; troops merely exposed to the virus could remain on duty but would not be deployed overseas.

Admiral William J. Crowe, Jr., became chairman of the Joint Chiefs of Staff on October 1. Crowe, previously commander of U.S. forces in the Pacific, succeeded Army General John W. Vessey, Jr.

Gander Crash. On December 12 a chartered jetliner crashed on takeoff from the international airport at Gander, Newfoundland, killing all 256 persons aboard. Those aboard, except for a crew of 8, were all soldiers of the 502nd Infantry of the 101st Airborne Division, en route to Fort Campbell, Ky., from peacekeeping duties in the Sinai. Investigations into the tragedy began immediately. The multinational peacekeeping force had selected the carrier, Arrow Air, from a list of carriers approved by the Air Force; the Pentagon said it would review its policy of chartering aircraft to transport military personnel.   T.D.

MINERAL AND METAL INDUSTRY. *See* ENERGY; LABOR; MANUFACTURING INDUSTRIES; MALAYSIA.

MINNESOTA. *See* STATISTICS OF THE WORLD.

MISSISSIPPI. *See* STATISTICS OF THE WORLD.

MISSOURI. *See* STATISTICS OF THE WORLD.

MONACO. *See* STATISTICS OF THE WORLD.

MONGOLIAN PEOPLE'S REPUBLIC. *See* STATISTICS OF THE WORLD.

MONTANA. *See* STATISTICS OF THE WORLD.

MOROCCO. In the tenth year of its struggle with Polisario Front guerrillas over the Western Sahara, a former Spanish colony annexed by Morocco, the Moroccan Army consolidated its control over more of the disputed territory. In August engineer units completed construction of the fifth and probably final section of a 9-foot-high sand-and-dirt wall that now stretched more than 1,500 miles across the Sahara, enclosing about two-thirds of the disputed territory. Polisario forces temporarily breached the wall at various points but were beaten back by superior Moroccan firepower.

On March 8, Morocco's King Hassan II declared that the only acceptable solution of the Western Sahara conflict was a referendum in which residents of the territory would choose between integration into Morocco and independence. In October, Morocco declared a unilateral cease-fire in the Western Sahara and asked the United Nations to supervise a referendum there in 1986. Morocco warned that the proposal would be withdrawn if "aggression against the territories under its responsibility" continued. The Polisario Front said its attacks would continue and demanded direct negotiations with Morocco and withdrawal of all Moroccan troops from the area as conditions for peace.

To the surprise of many outside observers, Morocco's federation with Libya, initiated in August 1984, survived its first year. In July the joint Moroccan-Libyan legislature held its first three sessions. However, there were stresses and strains in the relationship.

On April 11, nearly seven months after the September 1984 parliamentary elections, King Hassan named a new government. Like its predecessor, it was headed by Prime Minister Muhammad Karim Lamrani, and 21 of its 30 cabinet members were holdovers from the previous government, which had collapsed because of opposition to its austerity program. The new government unveiled an economic program calling for selective liberalization of economic constraints and a widening of the private sector.

The gross domestic product grew by slightly over 2 percent in real terms during 1984, and growth was expected to continue through 1985,

partly because of a good harvest. Still, Morocco needed to import about 2 million tons of wheat. Double-digit inflation and high unemployment were expected to continue through 1985, along with a substantial trade deficit.

See STATISTICS OF THE WORLD.   J.D.

MOTION PICTURES. During 1985, movie fans were spending more and more money on buying or renting videocassettes, and there was a lag in movie box office revenues. Many of the films that did well at the box office were undistinguished efforts designed to appeal to the lucrative youth market, but the year also had its share of interesting quality films.

Videocassettes. Revenue from the sale and rental of videocassettes reached a point almost equal to movie business at theater box offices. Projected gross revenues from the cassette market came to $3.3 billion, while the projected box office tally dipped to $3.6 billion, from more than $4 billion in 1984. In addition to affecting the economics of the industry, the popularity of videocassettes began to change the life expectancy of certain films. Films like *The Cotton Club, Red Dawn, Dune, The Pope of Greenwich Village,* and *Crimes of Passion* showed up well on the cassette charts after having disappointing theatrical runs.

No More Kid Next Door
Ron Howard tried for years to live down his reputation as the red-headed, freckled-faced kid next door, earned in the 1960's when he played Opie on television's *The Andy Griffith Show* and reinforced in the 1970's when he starred as Richie Cunningham on the TV series *Happy Days.* Now, after directing two hit movies—*Cocoon* (1985), a light fantasy about three aging men rejuvenated by a visit from extraterrestrials, and *Splash* (1984), a romantic comedy in which a young businessman falls in love with a mermaid—he may have achieved his goal. Howard was born in 1954 in Oklahoma and made his acting debut at the age of 18 months. A few years after graduating from *The Andy Griffith Show,* he played a high-school class president in the 1973 movie *American Graffiti;* that role led to his stint on *Happy Days.* Howard married his own high school sweetheart in 1975.

Ron Howard

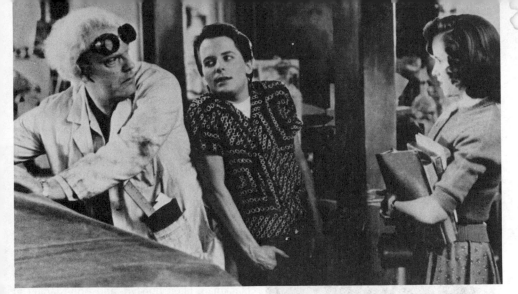

One of the year's best summer youth films was Back to the Future, *produced by Steven Spielberg and directed by Robert Zemeckis. Michael J. Fox starred as a high school student who goes back 30 years in a time machine, meets his parents as teenagers, and has to make them fall in love. Above, Christopher Lloyd as a mad scientist, Michael J. Fox, and Lea Thompson as his mother.*

The Youth Market. There were indications that Hollywood's slavish attention to the teenage market might have reached the point of diminishing returns. The summer saw a depressing glut of teen pictures. One of the few hits was Robert Zemeckis's *Back to the Future,* an attractive vehicle starring Michael J. Fox as a youth who travels back in time 30 years, meets his parents-to-be, and changes their lives. The film grossed close to $200 million by the end of the year.

In many cases, it was hard to distinguish one teenage movie from another, because of similar titles such as *Real Genius, Weird Science, My Science Project,* and *Explorers. Real Genius,* starring Val Kilmer and directed by Martha Coolidge, was superior to these other three. The humor was brighter, and the film had something to say about the misuse of idealistic science students by a professor exploiting them on a secret military project.

Among films suited to young children, *The Goonies* was the slickest entry. Produced under the aegis of Steven Spielberg and directed by Richard Donner, the well-made fantasy featured youngsters propelled on an unexpected adventure. On the other hand, the Disney studio's *Return to Oz* was a frightening downer

in comparison with the original classic *Wizard of Oz. The Black Cauldron,* also from Disney, was a disappointing animated reprise of the familiar action fantasy involving a boy on a mission to save the world from evil.

Some Adult Fare. Among the year's most fascinating and successful grown-up films was Peter Weir's *Witness,* which demonstrated that Harrison Ford, best known for his action work in *Star Wars* and *Raiders of the Lost Ark,* could handle a more complex leading role, as a detective thrown among the pacifist Amish, with their spartan life-style. Woody Allen's *The Purple Rose of Cairo* was a sophisticated comic and romantic exploration of the relationship between movies and audiences. French director Louis Malle looked at conflict between Vietnamese refugees and Texas fishermen in *Alamo Bay.*

Rebecca West's novel *The Return of the Soldier* was made into a movie, teaming Glenda Jackson, Julie Christie, Ann-Margret, and Alan Bates. This drama of a shell-shocked World War I soldier (produced in 1982 but released in the United States in 1985) was directed by Alan Bridges. He also made *The Shooting Party,* exploring Edwardian England on the eve of World War I and presenting James Mason in

Rambo: First Blood Part II *was a phenomenal success with audiences if not critics. Sylvester Stallone, who co-wrote the film, starred as a veteran who returned to Vietnam to singlehandedly free some American prisoners of war; heavy promotion made Rambo/ Stallone into a new macho symbol.*

his last movie role. Destruction of the environment was the subject of John Boorman's *The Emerald Forest,* with Powers Boothe as an engineer searching for a son who was kidnapped and raised by an Amazon tribe.

Summer and Fall. The summer yielded at least two welcome surprises. The fantasy comedy *Cocoon,* directed by Ron Howard, featured oldsters at a Florida retirement community, played by such veterans as Don Ameche and Hume Cronyn, who suddenly become rejuvenated after swimming in a pool given restorative properties by extraterrestrials. A dark, gallows-humor comedy, *Prizzi's Honor,* offered colorful, satirical performances by Jack Nicholson and Kathleen Turner as professional killers; it also showed veteran director John Huston to be in firm control of his extraordinary talent.

The fall brought an onrush of heavyweight pictures with performances by some of Hollywood's biggest stars. Meryl Streep proved her acting prowess again in *Plenty,* a film version of David Hare's play about a British woman who distinguishes herself in the French resistance, only to be disillusioned by unfulfilled postwar expectations that parallel the frustrations of her countrymen. Kate Nelligan returned in *Eleni,* based on reporter Nicholas Gage's book about his search for the facts about his mother's execution during the Greek civil war.

Jane Fonda, Meg Tilly, and Anne Bancroft made a formidable ensemble in *Agnes of God,* Norman Jewison's film based on John Pielmeier's play about a young nun (Tilly) who can't remember conceiving a child, giving birth, or killing the newborn infant. Another strong acting combination consisted of Gene Hackman, Ellen Burstyn, and Ann-Margret in Bud Yorkin's *Twice in a Lifetime,* dramatizing the family conflict that erupts when a steelworker decides to leave his wife and start over with another woman.

Rising star Glenn Close played a woman lawyer involved with a client accused of murder in the taut mystery thriller *Jagged Edge.* Jessica Lange gave a stunning performance as the ill-fated country singing star Patsy Cline in *Sweet Dreams,* directed by Karel Reisz. In *Marie,* Sissy Spacek starred in the true story of a woman who bravely exposed political corruption. And Geraldine Page won wide praise for her performance in *The Trip to Bountiful,* Peter Horton's film adaptation of his own play, about an eccentric elderly woman seeking to return to her rural Texas hometown.

Mordecai Richler's novel *Joshua Then and Now* was scripted for the screen by the author and directed by Ted Kotcheff. It featured outstanding performances by James Woods as a Jewish writer struggling in a gentile environment and Alan Arkin as his larger-than-life father who has a prison record. Robert Altman adapted Sam Shepard's play *Fool for Love,* depicting a turbulent relationship, and cast Shepard in the leading male role opposite Kim Basinger. Michael Douglas and Kathleen Turner teamed up again in *The Jewel of the Nile,* which some critics said was not as good as its rollicking predecessor, *Romancing the Stone. Young Sherlock Holmes,* a Steven Spielberg "presentation," was an exuberant look at the early life of the famous fictional detective.

Directors' Entries. Among major directors entering the lists, Martin Scorsese unveiled his gallows-humor comedy *After Hours,* a funny but jarring odyssey of a computer programmer enduring a series of weird misadventures in New York during one long night. Arthur Penn was back with *Target,* starring Gene Hackman as an ex-CIA agent whose past is revealed to his son, played by Matt Dillon, when Hackman's wife is kidnapped. Paul Schrader went to Japan to base a film, *Mishima,* on the life and suicide of novelist Yukio Mishima. Taylor Hackford filmed *White Nights,* starring Mikhail Baryshnikov as a Soviet defector. Richard Attenborough turned the Broadway hit *A Chorus Line* into a movie. Hugh Hudson released *Revolution,* a film about the American Revolution, starring Al Pacino. William Friedkin starred William Petersen in *To Live and Die in L.A.,* about a secret service agent. Michael Cimino's *Year of the Dragon,* a melodrama about corruption in New York's Chinatown, was coolly received and drew protests of racism from Chinese-American organizations.

Spielberg's eagerly awaited film of Alice Walker's Pulitzer Prize novel *The Color Purple* opened to acclaim from some critics; the story of a black woman's experiences in the rural South in the early part of this century, which starred Whoopi Goldberg, marked the director's first foray in many years into moviemaking not geared to the youth or sci-fi market. Sidney Pollock's lush film *Out of Africa,* based on the life of writer Isak Dinesen, was also a showcase for its two stars, Robert Redford and (once again) Meryl Streep.

Foreign Films. Some of the year's most impressive movies came from outside the United States. Brazil's *Kiss of the Spider Woman,* directed by Héctor Babenco, starred William Hurt as a homosexual and Raul Julia as his political prisoner cellmate under repressive conditions in a Latin American country. Japanese master Akira Kurosawa made *Ran,* chosen to open the New York Film Festival; the film was an ambitious epic based in part on Shakespeare's *King Lear.* Luis Puenzo's *The Official Story* skillfully recalled horrors under

A black comedy summer release, John Huston's Prizzi's Honor *starred Jack Nicholson as a mob hit man and Kathleen Turner as the mystery woman he marries who turns out to be in the same business. Here they join forces for a bit of connubial killing.*

Closing in on stardom is Glenn Close, who played an attorney in Jagged Edge, *released in October; her client, a newspaper publisher accused of killing his wife, was portrayed by Jeff Bridges.*

repression in Argentina. Jean-Luc Godard inspired even more controversy than usual with *Hail Mary,* his freewheeling modern interpretation of the birth of Christ. *Shoah,* a monumental, in-depth nine-hour documentary searching for explanations of the Holocaust, was made by Frenchman Claude Lanzmann.

Macho Heroes. Just when Sylvester Stallone appeared to have peaked, he came bursting back with *Rambo: First Blood Part II.* Garnering over $150 million at the box office, it exploited deeprooted resentful feelings related to the loss of the Vietnam war. Rambo, a Vietnam veteran, returns there on a secret mission to free U.S. soldiers still held prisoner. Singlehandedly, he demolishes their Vietnamese and Soviet captors. He also defies the military brass who want to sabotage the mission. "Do we get to win this time?" Rambo asks. The implication was that the United States could have won in Vietnam if men like Rambo had been running things. In November, Stallone appeared again, this time fighting the Soviets in the boxing ring, in *Rocky IV,* which opened at an unprecedented 2,000 theaters, accompanied by a flood of "Rocky" merchandise.

Resentments about the Vietnam war were also mined by Chuck Norris in *Missing in Action 2—The Beginning,* dealing with a sim-

ilar mission. But Norris was also breaking out to become a new macho hero on other terms. His *Code of Silence* depicted him as a Chicago detective having to go it alone against mobsters because he would not join a coverup for a fellow cop. In *Invasion U.S.A.* He took on the task of wiping out terrorists on U.S. soil. Norris, who first achieved recognition as a karate champion, moved into a position as a top box-office attraction.

Awards. In the Oscar race for 1984 films, Milos Forman's *Amadeus* was the big winner, receiving eight awards, among them best picture, best director, and best actor (F. Murray Abraham). Among other Oscar winners, Sally Field was named best actress for *Places in the Heart;* Haing S. Ngor, best supporting actor for *The Killing Fields;* Dame Peggy Ashcroft, best supporting actress for *A Passage to India;* and Robert Benton, best original screenplay for *Places in the Heart.*

At the Cannes Film Festival the top prize was a surprise choice, the Yugoslav film *When Father Was Away on Business,* directed by Emir Kusturica. A special jury grand prize was awarded to *Birdy,* Alan Parker's movie about a catatonic Vietnam veteran and the friend who tries to snap him out of his withdrawal. The best actor prize went to William Hurt for

Kiss of the Spider Woman. Cher, who played the mother of a disfigured teenager in *Mask,* shared top actress honors with Norma Aleandro, who won for *The Official Story.*

Behind the Scenes. One of the major developments in the configuration of the Hollywood studios was the broadened activity under the Disney banner. The company's new chairman, Michael Eisner, launched into a revitalization of the firm, with plans to produce a greater number of films and to concentrate anew on the kind of animation projects for which the studio earned its reputation. A key step was taken with respect to the cassette market. Disney films have long been viewed as a major asset, judiciously rereleased at intervals. But a decision to put *Pinocchio* on sale as a videocassette recognized new marketing techniques and potential.

Other significant business developments included the purchase by broadcasting and publishing tycoon Rupert Murdoch of 20th Century-Fox and the attempted move into MGM/UA by broadcasting mogul Ted Turner. Both opened the prospect of new links between motion picture companies and television stations. W.W.

MOZAMBIQUE. In 1985 the South-African sponsored Mozambique National Resistance continued its attacks aimed especially at disrupting transport and development projects in Mozambique. Attacks on buses in Maputo Province alone resulted in at least 88 deaths by July. In September the MNR claimed responsibility for explosions at an army ammunition depot in a Maputo suburb after the seizure of its principal base in August by Mozambican and Zimbabwean troops. In December the MNR claimed to have seized control of two district capitals, killing at least 124 soldiers.

Under the 1984 Nkomati Accord, South Africa had pledged to stop its acknowledged support of the MNR guerrillas. In mid-September, however, South African Foreign Minister Roelof F. Botha admitted that South Africa had committed "technical violations" of the accord, including radio communication with insurgents, air drops of supplies, and preparation of a landing strip for rebel use.

Mozambique sought outside aid in its effort to control the insurgents. After a midyear summit between Mozambican President Samora Machel and Zimbabwean and Tanzanian leaders, it was reported that additional Zimbabwean and Tanzanian troops would be sent to help guard the railway and oil pipeline from the Mozambican port of Beira to Zimbabwe.

In June, Mozambicans celebrated the tenth anniversary of their independence in a somber mood owing to the internal strife. Prior to the anniversary, the body of nationalist resistance hero Gungunyane, who was exiled to Portugal in 1896, was returned to Mozambique and buried in his home province of Gaza.

See STATISTICS OF THE WORLD. W.M.

MUSIC. Highlights of the year in music included the Live Aid rock benefit for African famine relief and commemoration of the births of Johann Sebastian Bach and George Frideric Handel 300 years ago.

POPULAR MUSIC

Had it not been for widespread starvation in Africa and the plight of the small farmer in America, the popular music story in 1985 would have been generally boring. Few new performers of note appeared, and few new trends showed themselves.

Rock. Early in the year, Ken Kragen, manager of Kenny Rogers and Lionel Richie and a longtime antihunger crusader himself, teamed up with Harry Belafonte and producer Quincy Jones to form United Support of Artists for Africa (USA for Africa). Emulating a group of British rock stars who in late 1984 recorded a single for the benefit of famine relief in Ethiopia, USA for Africa released the single "We Are the World," penned by Richie and Michael Jackson, plus a video, an album, and a home videotape on the making of the single. "We Are the World" also featured a wide variety of performers, including Dan Aykroyd, Ray Charles, Bob Dylan, Bob Geldof (the Boomtown Rats leader who had organized the British effort), Hall & Oates, Billy Joel, Cyndi Lauper, Bette Midler, Willie Nelson, the Pointer Sisters, Kenny Rogers, Diana Ross, Paul Simon, Bruce Springsteen, Tina Turner, Dionne Warwick, and Stevie Wonder. Millions of dollars were raised for famine relief. Within weeks, similar efforts by African, reggae, Canadian, and Latin musicians were also released.

Early in the summer, Geldof met with Belafonte and Kragen about an even more ambitious project: a gala, mammoth benefit show consisting of two concerts, one to be held at Wembley Stadium outside London and the other at Philadelphia's John F. Kennedy Stadium, with the two telecast worldwide by linked intercontinental television satellites. Hundreds of rock's most prominent artists were asked to perform, and two of the biggest bands of the past two decades, the Who and Led Zeppelin, agreed to stage reunions of their surviving members. On July 13, the largest rock benefit of all time took to the stage and the airwaves: Live Aid, as it was called, was a financial triumph—more than $65 million was raised—though few objective observers called it a musical one. There were some highlights—Elvis Costello opening the Wembley show singing the Beatles' "All You Need Is Love," Mick Jagger and Tina Turner trading leers and looks while singing the Jacksons' "State of Shock," David Bowie's performance, and an acoustic set by Bob Dylan, who was accompanied by Rolling Stones Ron Wood and Keith Richards. The World Hunger Media Awards, sponsored by Kenny Rogers and his wife, later named Geldof to receive a special achievement award of $20,000 for his efforts.

The activism didn't stop at famine relief. Notable endeavors included the angry, partisan "Sun City" (along with an album by that name)—recorded by Artists United Against Apartheid, a collection of such performers as Bruce Springsteen, Miles Davis, Rubén Blades, George Clinton, and Bob Dylan—and "That's What Friends Are For," a song whose royalties and profits were to benefit AIDS research, by performers Dionne Warwick, Stevie Wonder, Elton John, and Gladys Knight.

Bob Dylan was also active in other areas. In June he released his 29th album, *Empire Burlesque,* and later in the year he released a five-album retrospective of his still-flourishing career, entitled *Biography.*

On the down side, pop singer Ricky Nelson was killed on December 31, with his fiancée and five members of his band, when his private plane crashed en route to a New Year's Eve concert. Also, two of the biggest bands of the decade apparently broke up. It seemed as if the Police, who had emerged from Britain's punk era with a melodic pop-reggae sound that they refined until they had become one of the world's top-selling bands, would no longer record or perform together—at least for the

"The Boss"
Bruce Springsteen, the singer/songwriter once called "rock and roll future," is indisputably rock and roll present. His hit album *Born in the U.S.A.,* released in mid-1984, was still among the best-selling records of 1985; the single "Dancing in the Dark" garnered him a 1985 Grammy Award—his first—for best male rock vocalist; and his worldwide concert tour was a sellout. Springsteen's phenomenal popularity derives from his role as the gritty, passionate voice of the common people, such as those he grew up with in Freehold, N.J., where he was born in 1949. Though his early albums (*Greetings From Asbury Park, N.J.* and *The Wild, the Innocent, and the E Street Shuffle*) sold few copies when first released, subsequent albums—beginning with the powerful *Born to Run* (1975)—turned him into a superstar. Springsteen married model and actress Julianne Phillips in May 1985; they live in Rumson, N.J.

Bruce Springsteen

foreseeable future—largely because bassist/lead singer Sting was concentrating on a solo singing and acting career. Then Van Halen, the heavy metal band that showcased the guitar work of Eddie Van Halen, one of rock's most inventive guitarists, split up after the departure of flamboyant lead singer David Lee Roth, who was also pursuing a successful solo career.

The media, casting about for someone to focus on—as it had on Michael Jackson in 1983 and Prince in 1984—found Bruce Springsteen, whose rock populism had made his popularity rise to the point where he was finally playing the largest venues—mostly stadiums—available. Oddly, his audience seemed unaware of the left-leaning messages in his songs and seemed to treat hits like "Born in the U.S.A.," a tale of a disillusioned Vietnam veteran, as superpatriotic anthems.

Nor was that the only way that politics and rock 'n' roll interacted. A group of congressional wives headed by Tipper Gore, wife of Senator Albert Gore, Jr. (D, Tenn.), calling themselves the Parents' Music Resource Center, petitioned the Recording Industry Association of America (RIAA) to institute a record-rating system similar to that used in the motion picture industry. Enforced by congressional

In Live Aid—a trans-Atlantic, 16-hour, satellite-telecast charity concert—the rock world banded together to raise money for drought-stricken African countries. Above, the scene at JFK stadium in Philadelphia. Below, Tina Turner and Mick Jagger perform in an electric duet.

271

Country and western singer Willie Nelson organized the "Farm Aid" concert, held in Illinois in September, to raise funds and draw attention to the financial plight of America's farmers. More than 50 popular acts participated in the event.

legislation if necessary, the ratings would be intended to protect young children from what the PMRC saw as sexually explicit lyrics; songs glorifying drug use, satanism, and disobedience to authority; music videos containing violence; record covers with obscene images; and the like. At congressional hearings such unlikely allies as John Denver and Dee Synder, of the heavy-metal group Twisted Sister, decried the PMRC's objectives. As a compromise, the RIAA recommended use of a warning sticker ("Parental Guidance: Explicit Lyrics") or the printing of lyrics on appropriate albums, but some record companies refused to go along.

Country. Many of today's country stars grew up on farms or doing farm labor, so when word got out that Bob Dylan had said during the Live Aid proceedings that there was an agricultural crisis in the United States, a group of country stars decided to do something for America's farmers. The result was a Live Aid-like show held on September 22 in Champaign, Ill., called Farm Aid. Willie Nelson volunteered to take charge of the organization administering the funds raised and, with partner Tim O'Connor, helped to plan the show. Not strictly a country event, the 14-hour show included more than 50 acts, including the Beach Boys, John Cougar Mellencamp, Neil Young, For-eigner, Bob Dylan, Randy Newman, Roy Orbison, Alabama, Loretta Lynn, Billy Joel, George Jones, X, Ry Cooder, Glen Campbell, and Lou Reed.

Soul. If there was a trend in soul music, it was the presence of rock. Tina Turner's album *Private Dancer* was one of 1985's best-sellers. Nearing 50 years old, Turner recorded *Private Dancer* with a number of British rock musicians and found her career revived in a way nobody could have predicted. Though she alienated members of her black audience by disparaging black musicians in some of the interviews she gave, other black fans saw in her a symbol of strength and triumph over adversity.

Meanwhile, whites made very strong inroads into soul music. Madonna (see biography in PEOPLE IN THE NEWS) dominated the charts with her canny exploitation of a brassy, sex-symbol image and songs such as "Material Girl" and the title track from her *Like A Virgin* album. Hall & Oates, in the blue-eyed Philadelphia soul tradition of the Righteous Brothers, had hit after hit on the black charts, and late in the year they released an album recorded live at Harlem's legendary Apollo Theatre with members of the Temptations, the great Motown act. The Apollo itself was revived during the year under new management and was the subject of a long television special called *Motown at the Apollo* that featured many white rock acts.

One black performer who didn't venture too near rock was Aretha Franklin, who staged a comeback with a best-selling album,*Who's Zoomin' Who?*, and a single, "Freeway of Love." The video of the single conquered MTV.

As sometimes happens when a clear trend isn't in the air, an odd novelty record wound up making a lot of noise. Until 1985, Sidney Semien, known as Rockin' Sidney, was an obscure purveyor of the accordion-based Louisiana black Cajun music called zydeco. Sidney, who is not even zydeco's best-known performer, toured the circuit, occasionally releasing albums on his Maison de Soul label. Then he released a song called "My Toot-Toot," a catchier-than-usual zydeco tune with silly lyrics which, for some reason, took off. Sidney found himself in demand as never before, and versions of the song abounded: New Orleans-based soul singer Jean Knight, Mississippi-based Denise LaSalle, fiddler Doug Kershaw and rock legend Fats Domino, and John Fogerty, prime mover behind the 1960's powerhouse rockers Creedence Clearwater Re-vival, all enthusiastically boarded the "Toot-Toot" bandwagon.

Hip-hop and rap music continued to do well with younger record buyers, and one rap tune, "Roxanne" by U.T.F.O., managed to spawn over 25 "answer" records. Some of this music crossed over into the mainstream pop market, most notably that by rappers Run-D.M.C. Traditional soul balladeers placed a higher-than-usual number of songs on the charts, while superstars like Michael Jackson and Prince kept a low profile, with the latter releasing a new album, *Around the World in a Day,* and announcing retirement from touring.   E.W.

CLASSICAL MUSIC

The classical music world in 1985 celebrated the 300th anniversary of the births of Johann Sebastian Bach and George Frideric Handel. Concert halls, opera houses, and auditoriums rang out with the composers' music.

The Pepsico Summerfare's Handel Opera Festival at the State University of New York at Purchase featured three radically differing approaches to three largely forgotten works—*Giulio Cesare, Tamerlano,* and *Teseo.* In the first, staged by the iconoclastic young director

Minimalist Musician
Philip Glass's avant-garde music captivated a growing international audience in 1985. His opera *Akhnaten* received its British premiere in June. A collaborative opera by Glass and composer Robert Moran, *The Juniper Tree,* had its world premiere in Massachusetts in December. Australia's Adelaide Festival commissioned a new dance-theater work. The year also saw the release of the film *Mishima,* with a score by Glass, and a minifestival of Glass works. Though his recent scores are more elaborate, Glass is best known for what critics call his minimalist style of music, characterized by repetitive melodies, steady rhythms, and lengthy unchanged harmonies. The style is exemplified by his famous opera *Einstein on the Beach,* in which he collaborated with playwright-director Robert Wilson. He also collaborated with Wilson and others on a mammoth 12-hour stage work called *the CIVIL warS: a tree is best measured when it is down.* Glass was born in 1937 in Baltimore; he lives in New York City's East Village.

Philip Glass

Peter Sellars, Caesar was depicted as a modern political strongman and Cleopatra as a giddy playgirl. On the other hand, *Teseo*, directed by Nicholas McCegan, hewed closely to the static staging style of Handel's day. (This acclaimed production was first seen at the Boston Early Music Festival.) Finally, *Tamerlano*, directed by *New Yorker* music critic Andrew Porter, was neither fastidiously baroque nor drastically modernized. (It had first been given at Indiana University in Bloomington.) At the Kennedy Center in Washington, D.C., conductor Stephen Simon led the ninth installment of his annual Handel opera series, presenting *Giulio Cesare* and the U.S. premier of *Alessandro*. The latter was also given at Carnegie Hall in New York City as part of a four-opera Handel celebration.

Some 120 artists and ensembles took part in a wide-ranging grassroots Bach celebration in Birmingham, Ala. The Metropolitan Museum of Art presented 16 Bach evenings, including two sets of the complete Cello Suites. The New York City chapter of the American Guild of Organists sponsored Bach's complete organ works in 16 programs, while the Bach-Gesellschaft of New York sponsored 26 harpsichord recitals by Judith Norell. And at Yale University, 33 newly discovered chorale preludes by Bach were played by organists John Ferris and Charles Krigbaum.

Opera. The Metropolitan Opera in New York staged Gershwin's *Porgy and Bess* for the first time in the house, stirring discussion about the blurring of lines between "serious" opera and popular musical theater. Critics gave the production an A for effort. There also was a splendid production of Wagner's *Parsifal*, with Jon Vickers, Leonie Rysanek, and Kurt Moll. Later, Mussorgsky's *Khovanshchina*, a powerful work set in the time of Peter the Great, was revived by the Met after 35 years.

The New York City Opera's productions of Bizet's *Carmen* and Rossini's *La Cenerentola* featured the rising young coloratura mezzo-soprano Judith Forst. Its *Atilla* by Verdi showed off the fine talents of basso Samuel Ramey and soprano Linda Roark-Strummer. The San Francisco Opera, completing its third Wagner *Ring* cycle in 50 years, brought back horned helmets, silvery shields, and other remnants of a kind of realism that disappeared in the 1950's; the excellent cast included Eva Marton and James A. Morris. Meanwhile, the Seattle Opera inaugurated its own new *Ring* cycle with *Die Walküre*, conducted by Armin Jordan.

Harriet, the Woman Called Moses, by Thea Musgrave, was unveiled by the Virginia Opera in Norfolk. Based on the story of a heroic slave, *Harriet* made attractive use of Negro spirituals; Cynthia Haymon won great praise in the title role. Another new work, *Casanova's Homecoming* by Dominick Argento, presented by the Minnesota Opera in St. Paul, succeeded with its generally frothy, brilliant, and delicate score. (The production was to move on later to the New York City Opera.) The Minnesota Opera also staged the U.S. premiere of *Where the Wild Things Are*, with costumes and set designs by children's author and illustrator Maurice Sendak. Santa Fe saw the U.S. premiere of Hans Werner Henze's bubbling *The English Cat* and the world premiere of John Eaton's *The Tempest*.

Porgy and Bess, George Gershwin's popular opera/musical drama, received its first Metropolitan Opera staging ever in 1985. The lavish Met production starred Simon Estes and Grace Bumbry as the chief denizens of Catfish Row.

The 300th birthday anniversaries of Baroque composers Bach and Handel were celebrated by music lovers throughout the world in 1985. Johann Sebastian Bach (left), unappreciated in his own day, is now recognized as one of the most innovative composers of all time. Fellow German George Frideric Handel (right) is renowned for his Italianate operas and oratorios.

Instrumental Music. During the first-ever American Music Week, held November 4–10, more than 300 events were scheduled throughout the United States, with artists and ensembles performing works by such elder statesmen as Virgil Thomson, Aaron Copland, William Schuman, and John Cage, in addition to works by younger composers.

Premieres by prominent American composers abounded. In addition to Charles Wuorinen's Concertino (performed by the Winds of Parnassus ensemble in New York), Rhapsody for Violin and Orchestra (San Francisco Symphony), and *Crossfire* (Baltimore Symphony), they included David del Tredici's *March to Tonality* (Chicago Symphony), Henry Brant's *Desert Forests* (Atlanta Symphony), Elie Siegmeister's Violin Concerto (Oakland Symphony), Ned Rorem's *An American Oratorio* (Pittsburgh's Mendelssohn Choir and Pittsburgh Symphony), and Ellen Zwilich's *Celebration*

(Los Angeles Symphony) and Symphony No. 2 (San Francisco Symphony). Lou Harrison wrote a concerto for pianist Keith Jarrett for the opening concert of the American Composers Orchestra's tenth anniversary season.

Personalities. Leontyne Price sang her farewell to opera on January 3 in *Aïda* at the Metropolitan Opera. Composer Stephen Albert won the 1985 Pulitzer Prize for music for *Symphony, RiverRun,* while William Schuman received a special Pulitzer citation for his contribution to American music as composer and educator. Elliott Carter was awarded the new National Medal of Arts created by Congress in 1985. American pianist Murray Perahia won France's highest recording award for his performance of the complete Mozart piano concertos. Polish composer Witold Lutosławski received the first Grawemeyer Award, a $150,000 prize, from the University of Louisville for his Symphony No. 3.

MUSIC

Europe. In East Germany, the beautifully reconstructed Dresden Semper Opera opened in February, 40 years after it was destroyed in World War II. A world premiere, *The Song of the Life and Death of Standard-Bearer Christoph Rilke* by Siegfried Matthus, East Germany's leading composer, was a highlight of the first season.

At La Scala, in Milan, Polish composer Krzysztof Penderecki led the premier of his *Polish Requiem*, described as "a magnificent and profoundly moving work." In Italy, as elsewhere, Bach/Handel commemorations flourished. The works of Domenico Scarlatti, the tercentenary of whose birth was also celebrated in 1985, were featured as well in many concerts.

In Toulouse, France, the new *Montségur* by Marcel Landowski called for an orchestra of 100, plus synthesizer, electric guitar, and ondes martenot (an electronic instrument that produces musical tones by oscillating electric circuits). The opera proved astonishingly varied in instrumental sound and was at the same time sympathetic to the voices.

In London, the English National Opera produced the opera *Akhnaten* by Philip Glass, a leading U.S. minimalist composer whose work has been evoking growing enthusiasm. A new ENO production of Sir Michael Tippett's *The Midsummer Marriage* confirmed its status as one of the most exuberant modern operas. A Covent Garden production of Tippett's *King Priam* featured singers in American football gear to emphasize the modern relevance of the work. S.F.

RECORDINGS

Most of the top classical recording labels had contributions honoring the tercentenaries of Bach and Handel.

Bach Cornucopia. A torrent of elaborate, multivolume Bach editions flooded stores across the United States. The East German label Capriccio offered a total of 22 long-playing records, or LP's—and an equal number of prerecorded cassettes or compact disks. The West German company Deutsche Grammophon weighed in with a new Bach edition on its subsidiary Archiv label, comprising 130 LP's. This set enlarged upon the company's original Bach edition of 1974. Included were some of the last recordings conducted by Karl Richter in the late 1970's. Archiv also released an edited-down Bach edition on compact disks. From another West German label, Teldec, came a Bach edition (in ten two-record or two-cassette packages) consisting of recordings by the conductors Nikolaus Harnoncourt and Gustav Leonhardt.

Among individual works that came in for considerable attention were the *St. Matthew Passion* (three new recordings, one conducted by Peter Schreier for Philips, a second by Philippe Herreweghe for the Harmonia Mundi label, and the third by Helmuth Rilling for CBS), the suites for solo cello (by Janos Starker for Sefel and Lynn Harrell for London, with recent ones by Yo-Yo Ma and Paul Tortelier appearing for the first time on compact disks), and the keyboard partitas (by Kenneth Gilbert for Harmonia Mundi and by pianists András Schiff for London and Jean-Louis Steuerman, in a recording debut on Philips).

Added to these were recordings of the *Magnificat* (conducted by John Eliot Gardiner on Philips), the French Suites (by pianist Andrei Gavrilov on Angel), the Two- and Three-Part Inventions (by Schiff for London and Gilbert for Archiv), and Book I of the *Well-Tempered Clavier* (by Schiff, again, for London and Daniel Chorzempa for Philips). Angel's release of the B-Minor Mass, conducted by Andrew Parrott, was followed by a CBS recording by Rilling. Teldec's series of the complete Bach cantatas reached Volume 36.

In a gesture to history, the French EMI company, Pathé Marconi, released a set of Bach recordings made by the harpsichordist Wanda Landowska at her music school near Paris in 1935. Released almost simultaneously were two recordings historic in a different sense: the 33 Bach organ chorales discovered in 1984 at the Yale University Library (by a Harvard man)—one by Joseph Payne on Harmonia Mundi and the other by Werner Jacob on Angel.

Handel Selections. Two new modern-dress recordings of Handel's *Messiah* appeared. One, on the London label, was conducted by Sir Georg Solti, with the Chicago Symphony Chorus and Orchestra. The other, on Philips, featured Sir Colin Davis conducting the Bavarian Radio Chorus and Orchestra. An "early music" *Messiah*—using historically authentic practices and early instruments—was released by Erato. For this set, Ton Koopman conducted a Dutch-based chorus, the Sixteen, along with the Amsterdam Baroque Orchestra.

At least five new recordings of the *Water Music* were released. Early-music treatments by Hans-Martin Linde and the Linde Consort on Angel Reflexe and Jean-Claude Malgoire's La Grande Écurie et la Chambre du Roy on CBS joined latter-day versions of the *Water Music* by the Chamber Orchestra of Europe under James Galway on RCA, the Scottish Chamber Orchestra under Alexander Gibson on Chandos, and the Berlin Philharmonic under Riccardo Muti on Angel.

Deutsche Grammophon reissued *Israel in Egypt, Saul,* and *Judas Maccabaeus,* conducted by Sir Charles Mackerras, and *Giulio Cesare, Samson,* and the *Messiah,* conducted by Richter. London's affiliate Argo label reached back to the 1960's to reissue a recording of *Acis and Galatea* with Dame Joan Sutherland and Peter Pears, conducted by Sir Adrian Boult. Among the few new recordings of Handel's works for the stage were his operas *Tamerlano,* performed by Malgoire's ensemble for CBS, and *Julius Caesar,* an EMI/English National Opera production conducted by Mackerras, marking Dame Janet Baker's farewell to the opera stage.

Scarlatti and Schütz. The year 1985 also marked the 300th anniversary of (Giuseppe) Domenico Scarlatti. He was honored more by the promise of recordings to come than by actual releases. In France, the young American harpsichordist Scott Ross was making his way through all 555 of Scarlatti's keyboard sonatas, for release by Erato in 1986.

Heinrich Schütz, founder of the German baroque style, was born a hundred years earlier than the tercentenary trio. Schütz's *St. Matthew Passion* was newly recorded by Paul Hillier and his Hilliard Ensemble and released by Angel. A set of the composer's delightful "Italian" madrigals, performed by Concerto Vocale, was imported from France by Harmonia Mundi.

Berg. A relative parvenu in the anniversary group was Alban Berg, born in 1885. His birthday was virtually ignored, except by Deutsche Grammophon, which came up with a handsome ten-record boxed set issued on LP's only. *Alban Berg: The Published Works* included the operas *Wozzeck* and *Lulu.* Both of these recordings, dating from the 1960's, were conducted by the late Karl Böhm and featured baritone Dietrich Fischer-Dieskau in leading roles.

Other Releases. Notable new recordings of 20th-century opera ranged from Arnold Schoenberg's *Moses und Aron* (with baritone Frank Mazura and tenor Philip Langridge in the title roles under Solti's direction) and Igor Stravinsky's *The Rake's Progress* (with Langridge as Tom Rakewell under Riccardo Chailly), both on London Records, to a first recording on CBS of Philip Glass's *Satyagraha,* with Douglas Perry as the Indian leader Mohandas Gandhi, in a New York City Opera production conducted by Christopher Keene.

Outstanding among mainstream opera recordings were Verdi's *Il Trovatore,* with Placido Domingo and Rosalind Plowright, Carlo Maria Giulini conducting, on Deutsche Grammophon; Wagner's *The Flying Dutchman,* with José van Dam in the title role, Herbert von Karajan conducting, on Angel; and Mussorgsky's *Boris Godunov,* with Alexander Vedernikov as the doomed tsar, Vladimir Fedoseyev conducting, on Philips.

Other major releases included the complete horn music of Mozart, played by Barry Tuckwell on three imported Decca LP's; the complete songs of Sibelius, another import, from Argo, sung by soprano Elizabeth Söderstrom and baritone Tom Krause; the complete works for string quartet by Dvořàk, a Deutsche Grammophon import, performed by the Prague Quartet; and a rerecording by Daniel Barenboim, for Deutsche Grammophon, of the 32 Beethoven piano sonatas. A curious hybrid amid all this, and a furious best-seller, was a setting of the *Requiem* by Andrew Lloyd Webber, probably best known as the composer of the Broadway musical *Cats.* For this Angel recording the composer used his wife, Sarah Brightman, and Placido Domingo as the vocal soloists, and the Winchester Cathedral Choir and the English Chamber Orchestra under Lorin Maazel. C.B.

N

NAMIBIA. *See* SOUTH WEST AFRICA.
NAURU. *See* STATISTICS OF THE WORLD.
NEBRASKA. *See* STATISTICS OF THE WORLD.
NEGROES IN THE UNITED STATES. *See* BLACKS IN THE UNITED STATES.
NEPAL. *See* STATISTICS OF THE WORLD.
NETHERLANDS, THE. In 1985 the center-right coalition government of Christian Democratic Prime Minister Ruud Lubbers continued its austerity program, aimed at reducing the public sector deficit by restraining growth in government spending and by enhancing revenues through stimulation of the private sector. Government spending cuts focused on the social welfare program, one of the most ample in Europe, and on wages for public employees.

Unemployment benefits, previously noted for their lengthy duration and generous eligibility criteria, were trimmed back, and reductions were made in disability and sickness benefits as well. Compensation for civil servants was also lowered, in exchange for a shorter work week.

On November 1, Lubbers said his government would join those of four other NATO members in accepting new U.S. medium-range missiles. The Parliament had voted in June 1984 to accept deployment of 48 cruise missiles on Dutch soil no later than 1988, unless a U.S.-Soviet arms limitation agreement was reached by November 1, 1985, or unless the Soviet Union by that time agreed to freeze

Anti-pope slogans are paraded by youths in Utrecht; the demonstration, which later turned into a riot, was one of the incidents that marred John Paul's difficult May trip to the Netherlands.

deployment of SS-20 missiles at June 1984 levels. According to the United States, the Soviets by April had increased the number of SS-20 missiles well beyond June 1984 levels and enjoyed a ten-to-one advantage in intermediate-range nuclear missiles. The announcement, which triggered protests from the nation's strong antinuclear movement, was tempered by a government decision to remove the nuclear capability from Dutch F-16 fighter planes and Orion sea patrol planes.

The economy continued its recovery in 1985, although at a slower pace than the previous year. Real gross domestic product was expected to increase by about 1.75 percent, compared with 2.25 percent in 1984. Other positive signs in the economy included a modest growth in private consumption and an expected rise in consumer prices of only 2 percent, one of the lowest in Western Europe. This general economic recovery did little to ease the problem of unemployment, expected to remain at about 15 percent, one of the highest levels in Western Europe. While business activity did result in new jobs, the gain was largely offset by a continuing influx of youth, women, and a sizable immigrant population into the labor market.

Pope John Paul II visited the Netherlands in May as part of an 11-day trip to the low countries. It was the pope's 26th foreign journey and, by many accounts, one of his most difficult. Dutch Catholics, considered to be among the most liberal Catholics in the world, were deeply divided on numerous social and religious issues. During meetings with church representatives, John Paul often encountered strong resistance to official Vatican policies opposing abortion, premarital sex, artificial birth control, homosexual activity, the marriage of priests, and the ordination of women. For their part, many Dutch Catholics strongly objected to the Vatican practice of appointing conservative bishops in the Netherlands in order to uphold church doctrine there.

The pope's visit attracted several demonstrations. On one occasion, protesters threw rocks and bottles at the pope's car. On another, violence erupted after police tried to prevent throngs of young marchers, many in punk attire, from approaching the area where the pontiff was speaking. At least eight people were reported injured, including three police officers.

See STATISTICS OF THE WORLD.   W.C.C.

NEVADA. See STATISTICS OF THE WORLD.

NEW BRUNSWICK. See STATISTICS OF THE WORLD. See also CANADA.

NEW CALEDONIA. See PACIFIC ISLANDS.

NEWFOUNDLAND. See STATISTICS OF THE WORLD. See also CANADA.

NEW HAMPSHIRE. See STATISTICS OF THE WORLD.

NEW JERSEY. See STATISTICS OF THE WORLD.

NEW MEXICO. See STATISTICS OF THE WORLD.

NEW YORK. See STATISTICS OF THE WORLD.

NEW ZEALAND. During 1985, in his first full year as prime minister of New Zealand, David Lange (see biography in PEOPLE IN THE NEWS) sought to project an image of nondoctrinaire, consensus-style leadership. At home, his government achieved a reduced budget deficit, partly through curbs on government spending. However, inflation and interest rates were up, and the government party, in a May by-election, lost a seat it had held for 57 years.

Nuclear issues were conspicuous in the year's developments. New Zealand's friendship with the United States and its commitment to the Anzus military defense pact with Australia and the United States appeared jeopardized by the government's policy decision to ban nuclear-powered or nuclear-armed ships from New Zealand waters. In February the U.S. State Department announced that a request for a visit to New Zealand by the destroyer *Buchanan* had been turned down since the United States was unwilling to state that the ship was not nuclear-armed. Scheduled Anzus maneuvers were subsequently canceled by the United States. Lange enjoyed wide domestic support for his position. In an apparent bid to improve U.S. ties, New Zealand proposed a plan that removed the need for U.S. notification if a visiting ship carried nuclear weapons; New Zealand would decide on its own. But the plan was unacceptable to the United States since it still meant that New Zealand would bar any nuclear presence.

On July 10 the antinuclear protest vessel *Rainbow Warrior*, owned by the Greenpeace environmental group, was bombed in Auckland harbor, and a Dutch photographer for the environmentalist group was killed; the ship had been about to sail for Mururoa Atoll to protest French nuclear testing in the Pacific. New Zealand police arrested two French intelligence agents on murder charges. A report by the French government sought to refute suggestions that French agents had been involved, but Lange rejected this conclusion, and in September the French acknowledged involvement. The two captured agents—who reportedly were not the ones directly involved in the bombing—were later allowed to plead guilty to reduced charges of manslaughter and arson; Lange denied that the reduced pleas were the result of a deal with France. The two were sentenced on November 22 to ten years in prison.

Meanwhile, the government in early December introduced a measure that would ban nuclear-armed ships and aircraft from New Zealand by law, and also outlaw the dumping of radioactive wastes. The bill did not ban nuclear-capable ships as such, but there was no indication as to how New Zealand would determine whether a ship actually was carrying nuclear arms or not. The measure passed on preliminary vote, 48-30, with a final vote expected in 1986.

See also STATISTICS OF THE WORLD.   F.D.S.

NICARAGUA. Fighting between the Nicaraguan Army and U.S.-supported rebels intensified in 1985, with the outcome uncertain. The Reagan administration, apparently seeking the overthrow of the leftist Sandinista regime, stepped up its rhetoric in behalf of the rebels.

Internal Politics. Elected president of Nicaragua in late 1984, Daniel Ortega Saavedra took office in January 1985. He declared an interest in improving relations with the United States and offered amnesty to rebels who would lay down their arms. Ortega faced many problems. Foreign exchange losses (caused largely by rebel attacks on export crops and the drying up of financing from the United States and its allies) had slowed production, reduced fuel purchases, and limited Nicaragua's ability to pay its $4 billion foreign debt. Rising unemployment, declining real wages, shortages, and the institution of the draft undermined the regime's popularity. In October the government suspended civil liberties, blaming "brutal

aggression" by the United States and its "internal allies."

Relations with the Roman Catholic Church were tense. The Vatican suspended two priests serving as government ministers, and in April, Pope John Paul II named the anti-Sandinista archbishop of Managua, Miguel Obando y Bravo, to the College of Cardinals. On another front, negotiations with the Miskito Indians, who had been fighting the regime since 1981, led to agreement with a major Miskito group, with pledges by both sides not to initiate armed actions. The government freed jailed Indians and promised to allow the repopulation of evacuated Indian villages; however, Miskitos returning to their villages had to rebuild their homes and replant crops, with little help from the government. A group of Miskitos was organized to receive American aid; one Indian leader excluded from the group charged that the Reagan administration, trying to get a group it could control, was blocking Miskito unity.

Economic Problems. In the face of accelerating inflation and other economic ills, the government in February devalued the currency, increased interest rates, eliminated subsidies on basic goods and services, and entered the black market trade in U.S. dollars. Prices were raised for gas and electricity, meat, sugar, and rice. Responding to the predictable grumbling, the government in May gave big pay boosts to nonrural workers and unskilled agricultural day workers. It sought to help agriculture through easier credit access and higher producer prices.

Civil War and U.S. Relations. In January the Reagan administration suspended negotiations with Nicaragua and began military maneuvers in Honduras and Panama. Ortega announced in February that 100 Cuban military advisers would be sent home, that weapons acquisitions would be suspended, and that a U.S. congressional committee could inspect Nicaraguan military bases; but these moves had no effect on U.S. relations. In April the Reagan administration made a new peace proposal—under this plan the antigovernment guerrillas (contras) would lay down their arms until June while negotiating with the government; if no progress was made, the war would resume. The plan did not win acceptance. Reagan also asked Congress to approve $14 million in aid to the

Nicaraguan contra recruits train in Honduras for anti-Sandinista raids across the border. Backed by the United States, the rebel forces are a persistent threat to the Nicaraguan government.

contras for food, clothing, and medicine. At first, Congress rejected even humanitarian aid, and in May the United States announced a trade embargo against Nicaragua. Ortega then traveled to Communist-bloc capitals in search of aid, angering many members of Congress who had opposed aid to the contras. Administration critics felt betrayed, and Congress then approved $27 million in "nonlethal" aid for the contras.

This action lifted the contras' morale at a time when they were being pushed back by the army. In June the creation of the Unified Nicaraguan Opposition united moderate rebel leaders with former members of the National Guard, notorious for its human rights abuses under ousted Nicaraguan dictator Anastasio Somoza Debayle. The contras regrouped and struck deep into Nicaragua. Although they were repulsed by superior manpower and firepower, the contras now appeared to be more of a threat than in the past. A Nicaraguan official said in October that the Soviet bloc was increasing its aid to Nicaragua, and government forces began using Soviet-made as-

sault helicopters. The United States claimed that Cuban military advisers were assuming an increased combat role. Nicaragua's relations with Honduras and Costa Rica deteriorated as fighting flared along its borders.

It was revealed in August that National Security Council aides were advising the contras and helping them find financing; the Reagan administration indicated that U.S. differences with Nicaragua could not be resolved so long as the Sandinistas held power. In an October speech to the UN General Assembly, Ortega, for his part, strongly attacked U.S. policy in Central America. In December, Nicaragua took a conciliatory step by holding talks with opposition leaders, as part of a new peace initiative sponsored by Spain.

Nicaragua's case against the United States in the World Court, arising out of a 1984 CIA operation to mine Nicaraguan harbors, moved forward, with presentation of evidence beginning in September. The United States had already withdrawn from involvement in the court proceedings.

See STATISTICS OF THE WORLD.   D.E.S.

NIGER. *See* STATISTICS OF THE WORLD.

NIGERIA. The 20-month-old government of Major General Mohammed Buhari was overthrown on August 27, 1985, in a bloodless military coup led by Army Chief of Staff Ibrahim Babangida and other top-ranking officers. The coup was Nigeria's sixth in 25 years of independence. General Babangida was named president. Thirteen of 19 state governors were replaced, but most members of the former Supreme Military Council were reappointed to a new, enlarged Army Forces Ruling Council.

The primary targets of the coup were Buhari and his chief of staff, who were said to have made dictatorial use of their power. Particularly unpopular was the Buhari government's Decree 4, which forbade publication of anything that might ridicule or denigrate government officials. The decree had shackled Nigeria's vigorously independent, increasingly sophisticated press and led to the arrest of prominent journalists. Also bitterly resented was a decree providing for the detention of any citizen deemed a security risk. Under this provision, the Nigerian Security Organization (NSO) had been given a virtual blank check to arrest critics and dissidents. Perhaps the most shocking act of the Buhari government was the execution in April of three persons convicted of cocaine use under yet another decree. In one of his first acts as president, Babangida announced the repeal of Decree 4 and the release of all journalists in detention. A number of prominent former politicians were also freed, and the top leadership of the NSO disbanded.

The new government made revival of the economy a high priority. Criticizing the increasing reliance of the Buhari government on trade agreements in which Nigerian oil was bartered for foreign goods, Babangida pledged to restructure Nigeria's foreign debts and obtain urgently needed new foreign exchange. Industrial production was lagging in 1985, following a decline of 12 percent in 1984. Agriculture appeared to be continuing its growth, buoyed by a government decision to raise producer prices for most crops. However, with oil production slumping, it was not clear that the economy would meet even the modest goal of 1 percent growth envisioned in the 1985 budget, and in October the government announced a 15-month economic state of emergency, stating that Nigerians faced "bad times" and "sacrifice."

On April 15, for the second time in three years, the Buhari government had ordered the expulsion of all illegal aliens. The sudden order, which gave undocumented alien residents 25 days to regularize their status or leave, was reminiscent of the traumatic 1983 expulsion of illegal immigrants and occasioned some of the same panic and hardship, with many injuries and a few deaths reported. Although the government claimed that an estimated 700,000 aliens were illegally residing in Nigeria, a far smaller number actually left.

In December the Babangida regime announced it had foiled a coup attempt. Fourteen military officers were arrested in connection with the plot, including General Mamman Vatsa, a member of the Armed Forces Ruling Council.

See STATISTICS OF THE WORLD.   L.D.

NORTH ATLANTIC TREATY ORGANIZATION. Among the areas of concern to the members of NATO in 1985 were the Geneva arms talks between the United States and the Soviet Union, the relative preparedness of NATO and the Warsaw Pact in conventional weapons, and, within the alliance, the disruptive behavior of Greece.

U.S.-Soviet Arms Proposals. As the late November summit meeting between U.S. President Ronald Reagan and Soviet leader Mikhail Gorbachev drew near, the arms reduction proposals of the two superpowers began to show greater flexibility. Both Gorbachev and Reagan offered to cut different strategic weapons by 50 percent; Reagan also proposed to scrap the U.S. Midgetman program in return for a promise by the Soviets to eliminate their SS-24 and SS-25 mobile missiles. But Reagan declared that he would not negotiate away his Strategic Defense Initiative, the missile defense system popularly known as Star Wars.

The new Reagan offers had some favorable effect on the NATO allies. At a NATO meeting in Brussels, Reagan was promised "full support and solidarity" for his proposals. However, only the British government agreed to take part in Star Wars research. (The West German government said it would seek to negotiate a role for private West German companies.) Meanwhile, the Dutch parliament finally consented to the deployment in the Netherlands of 48 U.S. cruise missiles; the Dutch action marked the final failure of Soviet propaganda efforts to block the installation of intermediate-range missiles in Europe.

Ministerial Meetings. At a meeting of NATO defense ministers in Luxembourg in March, there was general approval for SDI. U.S. Defense Secretary Caspar Weinberger exhorted all NATO nations—as well as such other U.S. allies as Australia, Japan, and Israel—to join in an effort now budgeted at about $26 billion. It quickly became apparent, however, that there was an important distinction between approval and support. Australia, Norway, and Denmark refused to take part in SDI; Canada said it needed to study the administration's plans further (it later declared it would not join SDI); and the French acted interested but cautious. Moreover, the approval given to Star Wars by the defense ministers was not echoed at a foreign ministers' meeting in Portugal in May; France, Greece, Norway, and Denmark all refused to allow any mention of SDI in the communiqué issued at the conclusion of the meeting.

The defense ministers met again in May, this time to discuss the alliance's conventional weapons readiness. With the Soviets and their Warsaw Pact allies in an allegedly superior position to fight a conventional war in Europe, the European NATO members feared that the United States would resort to nuclear retaliation if it appeared that the Warsaw pact had gained an early upper hand in an armed conflict. The ministers agreed, therefore, to develop a program to reduce or eliminate shortfalls in NATO's conventional weaponry. The need for drastic improvements in conventional forces and weapons was restated at a one-day defense ministers' gathering in Brussels in early December. Later in the month, the foreign ministers approved a plan for cooperation in the development of new conventional weapons systems, in order to reduce costs.

At the May meeting, calls also came for an improvement in antisubmarine defenses and in the availability of ammunition. Weinberger urged his NATO counterparts to develop a chemical warfare deterrent as well, pointing out that the United States had information showing the Soviets ahead in this area. But the other ministers declined to accede to the U.S. request. Lord Carrington, NATO's secretary-general, asserted forcefully that chemical warfare had no place in the NATO arsenal and expressed hope that pressure from the alliance would lead to a bilateral ban on such weapons. (At the Geneva summit, Reagan and Gorbachev reaffirmed their support for a "complete prohibition" of chemical weapons.)

"Eurofighter." Britain, Italy, and West Germany agreed in August to produce jointly a new fighter plane, dubbed the Eurofighter. The plane will be designed to replace the U.S. F-4 and F-104, which the Europeans feel are aging. It was clear also, however, that the participating nations wished to lessen their dependence on the U.S. arms industry, which at present builds 85 percent of NATO's weapons. France refrained from joining the partnership when its bid for leadership of the project failed. The French had pushed for a light plane designed for ground attacks, while the others preferred a heavier plane designed for air-to-air combat. The target date for completion of the Eurofighter is 1995.

Greece. The maverick policy of Greece continued to cause concern in NATO circles. Early in the year, Prime Minister Andreas Papandreou announced that his country would not participate in NATO's Defense College in Rome; he also indicated he would not allow the United States to modernize its nuclear weapons installations in Greece. In February, Papandreou visited the Soviet Union, where he denounced Turkey, a NATO ally, and suggested that he would continue to pursue an independent course within the Atlantic alliance. In May the Greek government refused to allow a British naval vessel to refuel on Crete; NATO officials, furious, called the incident an "unprecedented snub" of one NATO member by another.

NATO officials were somewhat relieved when Papandreou and his Socialists won a convincing electoral victory in June. Observers speculated that Papandreou's easy reelection might persuade the Greek leader to adopt a more cooperative attitude within NATO, as he would no longer find it so necessary to curry favor with leftists in his own party who are hostile to the United States and to the Atlantic alliance.

Terrorist Attacks. NATO installations were plagued by terrorist attacks in 1985. In January, a bomb destroyed a U.S. military recreation center in Brussels. An organization calling itself the Communist Combatant Cells, the same group thought to be responsible for several anti-NATO bombings late in 1984, claimed responsibility. Later that same month, three grenades were thrown at NATO warships anchored in Lisbon harbor. The leftist Portuguese guerrilla group Popular Forces of April 25th took responsibility. In the face of the escalating violence, West Germany and France announced that they were coordinating their antiterrorist efforts.

See also COMMUNIST WORLD; MILITARY AND NAVAL AFFAIRS; and articles on NATO member nations. J.O.S.

NORTH CAROLINA. See STATISTICS OF THE WORLD.

NORTH DAKOTA. See STATISTICS OF THE WORLD.

NORTHWEST TERRITORIES. See STATISTICS OF THE WORLD. See also CANADA.

NORWAY. Norwegian Prime Minister Kaare Willoch and his Conservative-led three-party coalition government secured a narrow victory in national parliamentary elections on September 8–9, 1985. The Conservatives, the Christian People's party, and the agrarian-based Center Party jointly won 78 seats, compared with a combined total of 77 seats for the opposition Norwegian Labor Party (71 seats) and the Socialist Left Party (6 seats). The ultraconservative Progressive Party chose to add its 3 seats to the incumbent coalition rather than ally with the minority Labor government, slightly bolstering Willoch's hairline majority.

On the eve of the campaign, Norway's recent economic performance had seemed to give the nonsocialist coalition a pronounced edge. According to data compiled by the Organization for Economic Cooperation and Development, the economic recovery that began under Conservative auspices in 1982 had continued into 1985. Inflation was projected at 5 percent for the year. However, there was a surge in public support for the Labor Party during the closing weeks of the campaign, due above all to its emphasis on the need for greater government activism to reduce unemployment. (The unemployment rate was up from 1.7 percent in 1981, when the Labor Party lost control of the government, to 4 percent by mid-1985, an unusually high figure by Norwegian standards.) Labor also called for increased welfare expenditures.

Willoch and his coalition partners said such measures would be inflationary and instead advocated tax cuts and other measures to stimulate economic growth. The election, which resulted in a gain of five seats for Labor and a loss of three for the Conservatives, proved a moral victory for Labor Party leader and former Prime Minister Gro Harlem Bruntland, even though she did not regain office.

A decline in world prices for oil prompted the state-owned Statoil company to abandon a system of fixed prices for Norwegian petroleum exports in mid-January in favor of a system based on prevailing spot-market prices. The Organization of Petroleum Exporting Countries responded angrily to consequent price reductions of Norwegian oil with a price cut of its own in late January. Great Britain disappointed public and private officials by retracting in February an earlier agreement to purchase $30 billion worth of natural gas from the Sleipner field, off Norway's western coast. Prompting the decision was the discovery of some 6.2 trillion cubic feet of natural gas in Britain's own territorial waters.

Government officials declared in April that Norway, rejecting an invitation by the United States, would not participate in the U.S.-sponsored Strategic Defense Initiative, a controversial project, popularly known as Star Wars, to construct a laser-based defensive system in outer space. However, Willoch later said Norwegian scientists could be involved in basic research that was not "of military nature."

Arne Treholt, once a promising young member of Norway's diplomatic service, was convicted in Oslo on June 20 of having engaged in espionage activities for the Soviet KGB from sometime before 1970 until his arrest in 1984. Treholt was sentenced to 20 years in prison.

See STATISTICS OF THE WORLD. M.D.H.

NOVA SCOTIA. See STATISTICS OF THE WORLD.

NUCLEAR POWER. See ENERGY.

O

OBITUARIES. Each entry below contains the name of a notable person who died in 1985. It also contains a brief description of the accomplishments and events that contributed to making each person notable.

Abbas, Ferhat, 86, Algerian political figure who led Algeria to independence from France, serving as the first president of its provisional government in 1958–1961; he retired from public life in 1964 following house arrest by the National Liberation Front government. December 24 in Algiers.

Abruzzo, Ben, 54, American ballooning adventurer who took part in the first Atlantic and Pacific balloon crossings. Killed February 11, in a plane crash at Albuquerque, N.M.

Adams, Tom (John Michael Geoffrey Manningham Adams), 53, prime minister of Barbados since 1976; he was one of the Caribbean's strongest supporters of the 1983 U.S.-led invasion of Grenada. March 11 In Bridgetown, Barbados.

Arends, Leslie (Cornelius), 89, Republican U.S. representative from Illinois for more than 40 years before his retirement in 1975; from 1943 he served as Republican House whip. July 16 in Naples, Fla.

Ashley, Laura, 60, British fabric and clothing designer and founder of the clothing and furnishings empire that bore her name. September 17, in Coventry, England, from injuries sustained in a fall.

Baxter, Anne, 62, American actress best known for her title role in *All About Eve* (1950), for which she received an Academy Award nomination as best actress; she won an Oscar as best supporting actress for *The Razor's Edge* (1946). December 12 in New York City.

Beard, James (Andrews), 81, epicurean American cookbook writer and chef whose more than 20 books, countless articles and TV appearances and cooking school helped develop an appreciation of fine food among Americans. January 23 in New York City.

Blood, Johnny (John Victor McNally), 82, colorful U.S. National Football League halfback who was one of the original 17 players inducted into the Pro Football Hall of Fame. November 28 in Palm Springs, Calif.

Böll, Heinrich (Theodor), 67, West German novelist, short-story writer, essayist, and translator who won the 1972 Nobel Prize for literature; a pacifist and foe of oppressive institutionalized power of any kind, he wrote of German life under the Nazis and after the war in a generally plain and accessible style, gaining a wide readership and a reputation as "the conscience of the nation." Among his best-known novels were *Billiards at Half-Past Nine*

James Beard, one of the country's foremost experts on cooking and dining, was an enthusiastic spokesman for American cuisine.

Actor Yul Brynner gave one of the longest star turns in theater history—more than 4,600 performances as the King of Siam in the musical The King and I.

(1959), *The Clown* (1963), and *Group Portrait With Lady* (1971). July 16 in Hürtgenwald, West Germany.

Boulting John (Edward), 71, British filmmaker who as producer, director, or writer collaborated with his twin brother, Roy, on over 30 movies, most of them light, satirical comedies, including *Private's Progress* (1956), *I'm All Right Jack* (1959), and *The Family Way* (1966). June 17 in Sunningdale, England.

Boyle, William Anthony (Tony), 83, ironfisted president of the United Mine Workers of America from 1963 to 1972; subsequently convicted of arranging the 1969 murder of a union rival and his family, Boyle died in prison, May 31 in Wilkes-Barre, Pa.

Brooks, Louise, 78, raven-haired American star of silent films, most notably *Pandora's Box* and *Diary of a Lost Girl* by German director G. W. Pabst (1929); years later, she published her memoirs, *Lulu in Hollywood* (1982), to wide acclaim. August 8 in Rochester, N.Y.

Brynner, Yul, 65(?), actor of Mongolian-gypsy origin whose award-winning stage and screen portrayal of the king of Siam in the musical *The King and I* made him for Americans the incarnation of the oriental potentate; he was also a talented TV director and photographer. October 10 in New York City.

Burnet, Sir (Frank) MacFarlane, 85, Australian immunologist who shared the 1960 Nobel Prize in medicine for work on acquired immunological tolerance. August 31 in Melbourne.

Burnham, (Linden) Forbes Sampson, 62, flamboyant leftist president of Guyana; a charismatic orator who came to power as prime minister in 1964, he espoused a policy of nonalignment and economic self-sufficiency. August 6 in Georgetown, Guyana.

Burrows, Abe, 74, American author, director, songwriter, and comic who wrote or co-wrote (and in many cases directed) such hit Broadway musicals as *Guys and Dolls* (1950), *Can-Can* (1953), *Say Darling* (1958), *How to Succeed in Business Without Really Trying* (1961), and *What Makes Sammy Run* (1964). May 17 in New York City.

Caldwell, Taylor, 84, best-selling English-born author of over 40 historical romances and family sagas including *Dynasty of Death* (1938), *Dear and Glorious Physician* (1959), and *Answer as a Man* (1981). August 30 in Greenwich, Conn.

Calvino, Italo, 61, leading Italian novelist and short-story writer whose often folk-inspired allegorical fantasies earned an international following; his books included *Mr. Palomar* (1985), *If on a Winter's Night a Traveler* (1979), *Cosmicomics* (1966), and *Italian Folktales* (1956). September 19 in Siena, Italy.

Canaday, John, 78, influential American art critic who wrote gracefully yet combatively about art for the New York *Times* from 1959 to 1977; he also wrote mystery novels under the pseudonym Matthew Head. July 19 in New York City.

Chagall, Marc, 97, Russian-born giant of modern art, noted for his celebration of love and life in a highly personal style featuring lush colors and fanciful, dreamlike imagery. The Jewish life and folklore of his birthplace, Vitebsk, provided much of his subject matter. His long career saw him work in all media, forging a permanent legacy; he created a magical, gravity-defying world of blue angels, levitating fiddlers, melancholy clowns, and fantastic animals. March 28 in St. Paul de Vence, France.

Charlotte, Grand Duchess, 89, beloved constitutional ruler of Luxembourg from 1919 to 1964, when she stepped down in favor of her son Jean. During World War II her radio broadcasts from exile in Montreal helped keep up morale; after the war she helped guide Luxembourg to prosperity. July 9 in Fischbach Castle, Luxembourg.

Taylor Caldwell, one of the world's best selling authors, wrote more than 40 romantic novels and historical sagas.

Chase, Stuart, 97, American economist and key adviser to President Franklin D. Roosevelt; he coined the phrase "New Deal" and was an ardent proponent of government intervention in the economy. November 16 in Redding, Conn.

Chernenko, Konstantin Ustinovich, 73, Soviet leader—general secretary of the Central Committee of the Communist Party—since February 1984; already in poor health when named general secretary, he was widely regarded as an interim choice and did not seem able to put his personal stamp on policy decisions, made collectively by the ruling Politburo. During his tenure, a decision was made to resume arms talks with the United States. Shortly after becoming general secretary, he was also named chairman of the Defense Council and chief of state. Chernenko owed his rise to the top ranks of the party to his long association with the late General Secretary Leonid Brezhnev. March 10 in Moscow.

Claire, Ina (Ina Fagan), 92, American comic actress celebrated for her droll and sophisticated style; after beginning her career in vaudeville and musical comedy, she scored triumphs in straight comedy roles in such plays as *The Last of Mrs. Cheyney* (1925), *Biography* (1932), and *The Confidential Clerk* (1954) and appeared in several films, including *Ninotchka* (1939). February 21 in San Francisco.

Colasanto, Nick, 61, American stage, screen, and TV actor best known for his role as the lovable bartender Coach on the NBC comedy series *Cheers.* February 12 in Los Angeles.

Collingwood, Charles, 68, award-winning American news correspondent and commentator whose 41-year career with the CBS network took him throughout the world. October 3 in New York City.

Coots, John Frederick ("J. Fred"), 87, Tin Pan Alley-era American composer who wrote the tunes for hundreds of songs, including "Santa Claus is Coming to Town," and "Love Letters in the Sand." April 8 in New York City.

Cowsill, Barbara C., 56, American singer who with six of her children formed the 1960's soft-rock group known as the Cowsills that recorded such hits as "We Can Fly" and the title song of the musical *Hair.* January 31 in Tempe, Ariz.

OBITUARIES

Cushman, Robert Everton, Jr., 70, retired U.S. Marine Corps general; during the Vietnam war he commanded the largest combat unit ever led by a marine, and later served as deputy director of the CIA (1969–1971) and as commandant of the Marine Corps (1972–1975). January 2 in Fort Washington, Md.

Deckers, Jeanine, 52, Belgium's guitar-playing "singing nun" whose 1963 song "Dominique" was an international hit; she left her Dominican order in 1966. Found dead, from a drug overdose, April 1 in Wavre, Belgium.

De Quay, Jan Eduard, 83, conservative Dutch prime minister from 1959 to 1963; during World War II he helped found the Netherlands Union, an unsuccessful attempt to preserve Dutch law through accommodation with the German occupiers. July 4 in Beers, the Netherlands.

De Rivera, José, 80, American sculptor highly praised by critics for his bold yet delicate curvilinear works in stainless steel and bronze; his best-known effort is the revolving sculpture (1967) at the Smithsonian Institution in Washington, D.C. March 19 in New York City.

Desmond, Johnny, 65, American singer and actor who rose to fame with Glenn Miller's Army Air Force Band during World War II; his later hit songs included "C'est Si Bon" and "Play Me Hearts and Flowers." September 6 in Los Angeles.

Diamond, Selma, 64, Canadian-born comedy writer and character actress who played the wisecracking bailiff Selma Hacker on the TV series *Night Court;* she wrote for such comedians as Groucho Marx, Milton Berle, and Sid Caesar. May 13 in Los Angeles.

Donghia, Angelo, 50, influential American interior designer whose eclectic approach, featuring bold, clean lines and distinctive patterns, won him many celebrity and corporate clients; mass-produced furniture, fabrics, sheets, and glassware also carried his name. April 10 in New York City.

Dubuffet, Jean, 83, French painter, sculptor, and printmaker widely regarded as the most important artist to emerge from France since World War II; stressing the importance of energy and spontaneity, he favored a caricatural, graffitilike form and had a marked influence on neoexpressionism. May 12 in Paris.

Sam Ervin, who usually described himself as "just an ol' country lawyer," was best known to the American public for having directed the Senate Watergate investigation.

Eisenhower, Milton S(tover), 85, American educator, diplomat, and adviser to several U.S. presidents, most notably his brother Dwight; he served as president of Kansas State College, Pennsylvania State University, and the Johns Hopkins University and chaired the inquiry into the causes of violence following the 1968 assassinations of Robert Kennedy and Martin Luther King, Jr. May 2 in Baltimore.

Enders, John Franklin, 88, American virologist who shared the 1954 Nobel Prize in medicine for helping to develop a way to culture polioviruses in large quantities, paving the way for vaccine development. September 9 in Waterford, Conn.

Engel, Marian, 51, Canadian novelist much admired for her lyrical, harmonious prose and ability to recreate women's perceptions. Her novel *Bear* won the 1976 Governor General's Award. February 16 in Toronto.

Erlander, Tage F(ritiof), 84, Swedish Social Democratic statesman who as prime minister (1946–1969) maintained Sweden's foreign policy of armed neutrality while leading the country into economic prosperity and overseeing development of a cradle-to-grave welfare system. June 21 in Huddinge, Sweden.

Ervin, Samuel J(ames), Jr., 88, courtly former Democratic U.S. senator from North Carolina who headed the Senate Watergate investigation that contributed to the resignation of President Richard Nixon; named to the North Carolina Supreme Court in 1948, he entered the Senate in 1954, where he served for two decades, becoming its leading expert on constitutional law. April 23 in Winston-Salem, N.C.

Fetchit, Stepin (Lincoln Theodore Perry), 83, the first black American performer to be given featured billing in Hollywood films; his typical role as a shuffling, dimwitted servant in films of the 1920's and 1930's was later criticized as a racist stereotype, but he helped blaze a trail for other black film stars. November 19 in Los Angeles.

Flory, Paul J(ohn), 75, American polymer chemist who won the Nobel Prize in 1974, subsequently becoming a noted fighter for human rights. September 9 in Big Sur, Calif.

Foster, Phil (Fivel Feldman), 72, American stand-up comic and stage and TV actor best known as Laverne DeFazio's Brooklyn-tongued father in the series *Laverne and Shirley* (1976–1983). July 8 in Rancho Mirage, Calif.

Gernreich, Rudi (Rudolf Gernreich), 62, Austrian-born avant-garde women's fashion designer who introduced the topless bathing suit in 1964 and helped popularize the miniskirt. April 21 in Los Angeles.

Gilels, Emil Grigoryevich, 68, world-renowned Soviet pianist whose playing was noted for its power, dexterity, and lyricism. October 14 in Moscow.

Gordon, Ruth (Ruth Gordon Jones), 88, distinguished American actress who made her Broadway debut in 1915 and was best known for her starring role in the 1971 film *Harold and Maude* and for her Oscar-winning performance as a witch in *Rosemary's Baby* (1968). She also wrote the 1940's hit plays *Over 21* and *Years Ago* and coauthored such screenplays as *Adam's Rib* (1949), and *Pat and Mike* (1952). August 28 in Edgartown, Mass.

Gould, Chester, 84, American cartoonist, creator of Dick Tracy, the comic-strip detective who fought such unsavory criminals as Flattop, Pruneface, and B. B. Eyes; he wrote and drew "Dick Tracy" from 1931, when its graphic violence and serious hero made it the first uncomic comic strip, until 1977. May 11 in Woodstock, Ill.

Graves, Robert (von Ranke), 90, brilliant, versatile English poet, novelist, classical scholar, biographer, and translator best known as the author of *I, Claudius* (1934), which, with its sequel, was made into an esteemed television series. December 7 in Majorca.

Grimes, Burleigh, 92, American baseball player; the last legal spitball pitcher, he compiled 270 victories in 19 years in the major leagues and was elected to the Hall of Fame in 1964. December 6 in Wisconsin.

Groppi, James, 54, American civil rights activist who, as a Roman Catholic priest (until 1976), led some 200 open-housing marches in Milwaukee in the 1960's and was later involved in Vietnam war protests. November 4 in Milwaukee.

Guarnieri, Johnny, 67, American jazz pianist of the swing era who played with such jazzmen as Benny Goodman, Artie Shaw, and Jimmy Dorsey. January 7 in Livingstone, N.J.

Ruth Gordon's acting career spanned 70 years of theater, film, and television work; one of her most popular roles was in the film Harold and Maude.

Film character actress Margaret Hamilton was best known for her spine-chilling portrayal of the Wicked Witch of the West in The Wizard of Oz.

Hamilton, Margaret, 82, American character actress, and onetime kindergarten teacher, best known for her performance as the cackling, green-skinned Wicked Witch of the West in the movie *The Wizard of Oz* (1939). May 16 in Salisbury, Conn.

Hanley, James, 84, acclaimed but neglected English novelist whose works, beginning with *Drift* (1930), often dealt with simple, inarticulate characters. November 11 in London.

Harris, Patricia R(oberts), 60, American lawyer, educator, and civil rights activist; the first black woman to be a U.S. ambassador and hold a cabinet post, she was ambassador to Luxembourg and, under President Jimmy Carter, successively secretary of housing and urban development, secretary of health, education, and welfare, and secretary of health and human services. March 23 in Washington, D.C.

Hayward, Louis (Seafield Grant), 75, South African-born actor best known for his leading roles in such Hollywood adventure films as *The Man in the Iron Mask* (1939) and *The Return of Monte Cristo* (1946). February 21 in Palm Springs, Calif.

Hecht, Harold, 77, American film producer who helped break up the traditional Hollywood studio system, joining with actor Burt Lancaster in the late 1940's to form an independent production company that proved enormously successful; among his films was *Marty* (1955), which won four Academy Awards. May 25 in Beverly Hills, Calif.

Hewitt, Foster W(illiam), 82, dean of Canadian sportscasters whose signature phrase "He shoots, he scores!" became part of hockey legend; broadcaster of Toronto Maple Leafs' games between 1923 and 1978, he was elected to the Hockey Hall of Fame in 1965. April 21 in Toronto.

Holt, John (Caldwell), 62, maverick American educator and author whose 1964 book *How Children Fail* touched off a national debate on the quality of American education. September 14 in Boston.

Horrocks, Sir Brian, 89, British World War II general who helped turn back the Germans in North Africa and took part in the D-day landings in Normandy; after the war he hosted the BBC series *Men in Battle*. January 6 in Fishbourne, England.

Hoxha, Enver, 76, longtime Albanian leader as chief of the Albanian Workers' (Communist) Party; having risen to power by leading resistance forces against the Italian and German occupation during World War II, he imposed a rigidly Stalinist and isolationist regime. April 11 in Tiranë, Albania.

Hudson, Rock (Roy Scherer, Jr.), 59, tall, handsome, low-key American actor who made over 60 films, among them *The Magnificent Obsession* (1954), *Giant* (1956), and *Pillow Talk* (1959)—the first of a series of romantic comedies with Doris Day; his television work included starring roles in the series *McMillan and Wife* and *The Devlin Connection*. The disclosure in July 1985 that he was suffering from AIDS focused wide attention on the threat presented by that deadly disease. October 2 in Los Angeles.

Jenner, William E(zra), 76, former Republican U.S. senator from Indiana (1944–1945,

1947–1959); a conservative and isolationist, he investigated supposed Communist infiltration of the teaching profession. March 9 in Bedford, Ind.

Jones, Jo, 73, American jazz drummer and swing-era pioneer whose light, precise four-beat pervaded the music of the original Count Basie Band. September 3 in New York City.

Jones, Philly Joe, 62, American jazz drummer and leader of the repertory group Dameonia; during the 1950's and 1960's he played with such jazz greats as John Coltrane, Miles Davis, and Charlie Parker. August 30 in Philadelphia.

Joy, Leatrice (Leatrice Joy Zeidler), 91, legendary American actress of the silent-film era who starred in comedies and in Cecil B. DeMille films, including *The Ten Commandments* (1923); she often played elegant career women and socialites, and she was responsible for the popularity of bobbed hair in the 1920's. May 13 in New York City.

Kelly, John B. (Jack), Jr., 57, newly elected president of the U.S. Olympic Committee; a brother of the late Princess Grace of Monaco, he won a bronze medal in sculling in the 1956 Olympics. March 2 in Philadelphia, of a heart attack while jogging.

Kertész, André, 91, Hungarian-born master of the hand-held camera whose spontaneous, lyrically composed pictures, taken over a career spanning 70 years, exerted a great influence on 20th-century photojournalism and helped establish photography as a legitimate art form. September 27 in New York City.

Kimball, Spencer W(oolley), 90, American religious leader who, as president and prophet of the Mormon church since 1973, steered it through a period of rapid growth and changing times. November 5 in Salt Lake City.

Koo, Vi Kyuin Wellington, 97, Chinese Nationalist politician and diplomat who served the republic of China for more than 50 years, including a brief period as acting prime minister. November 14 in New York City.

Koopmans, Tjalling Charles, 74, Dutch-born economist, long a professor at Yale University, who was cowinner of the 1975 Nobel Prize in economics for his contribution to the theory of optimum allocation of resources. February 26 in New Haven, Conn.

Kuznets, Simon, 84, Ukrainian-born professor emeritus of economics at Harvard who was awarded a Nobel Prize in 1971 for this development in the 1930's of an effective system for measuring national income and growth. July 8 in Cambridge, Mass.

Kyser, James King Kern ("Kay"), 79, popular American radio program host who as the "Old Perfesser" led the swing-era band called the Kollege of Musical Knowledge. July 23 in Chapel Hill, N.C.

Lander, Toni, 53, statuesque and versatile Danish ballerina who gained renown as a principal with the London Festival Ballet, the American Ballet Theatre, and the Royal Danish Ballet; she later became principal teacher with Salt Lake City's Ballet West. May 19 in Salt Lake City.

Lang, Harold, 64, American classical ballet dancer and musical-comedy star best known for his performance in the title role in a 1952 revival of *Pal Joey;* he was a three-time winner of the Donaldson Award for best dancer on Broadway. July 26 in Chico, Calif.

Langer, Suzanne K(atherina), 89, American philosopher whose writings on the connections between emotion and art helped mold 20th-century aesthetic theory; her seminal book *Philosophy in a New Key* (1942) sold more than 500,000 copies. July 17 in Old Lyme, Conn.

Larkin, Philip Arthur, 63, esteemed English poet and librarian whose verse, published in four volumes between 1945 and 1974, often explored themes of deprivation and disappointment. December 2 in Hull, England.

Lindbergh, Pelle, 26, Swedish goalie for the Philadelphia Flyers, voted the National Hockey League's top goaltender for 1984–1985. November 12 in Stratford, N.J., after an automobile accident.

Lodge, Henry Cabot, 82, Republican politician and diplomat who won election to three terms in the U.S. Senate from Massachusetts, served as U.S. ambassador to the UN from 1953 to 1960, and was his party's candidate for vice-president in 1960; during the Vietnam war he served twice as ambassador to South Vietnam and headed the U.S. delegation at unsuccessful Paris peace talks in 1969. February 27 in Beverly, Mass.

Lon Nol, 72, Cambodian general who ousted Prince Sihanouk and ruled his country for five years, until the Khmer Rouge took control in 1975. In the early 1950's he fought the Vietminh; he later became defense minister and held other cabinet posts in Sihanouk's government. November 17 in Fullerton, Calif.

London, George (George Burnstein), 64, famed Canadian-born bass-baritone whose rich, dark-hued voice produced authoritative interpretations of such roles as Wotan in Wagner's *Ring* and the title character of Mussorgsky's *Boris Godunov.* March 24 in Armonk, N.Y.

Long, Gillis W(illiam), 61, liberal U.S. congressman from Louisiana, elected to Congress in 1962 and in each election from 1972 on; he chaired the House Democratic Caucus from 1981 to 1984. January 20 in Washington, D.C.

Longowal, Harchand Singh, 57, Indian Sikh separatist leader and proponent of nonviolent protest who in late July signed an accord aimed at ending the separatist crisis in Punjab that had seen thousands die. Assassinated at a Sikh temple in Sherpur, Punjab, on August 20.

Lule, Yusufu K., 72, Ugandan educator and public figure who served as his country's president for 68 days after the overthrow of Idi Amin in 1979. January 21 in London.

MacInnes, Helen, 77, Scottish-born novelist recognized as the queen of espionage fiction; her 21 best-sellers included *Above Suspicion* (1941), *Assignment in Brittany* (1942), and *The Venetian Affair* (1963). September 30 in New York City.

Mahler, Margaret S., 86, Hungarian-born psychiatrist who pioneered the theory that a person's character is basically shaped in the first three years of life. October 2 in New York City.

Maltz, Albert, 76, American screenwriter, playwright, and novelist whose pictures included *This Gun for Hire* (1942) and *The Naked City* (1948); as one of the "Hollywood Ten" who refused to answer questions by the House Committee on Un-American Activities, he was jailed in 1950 and also blacklisted by the film industry. April 26 in Los Angeles.

Maris, Roger Eugene, 51, American baseball player; a star batter and excellent fielder, he played in the major leagues from 1957 to 1968 and, as a New York Yankee in 1961, hit 61

New York Yankee outfielder Roger Maris hit 61 home runs in 1961 to break the record set by the immortal Babe Ruth.

home runs to break the famous record of 60 set in 1927 by Yankee Babe Ruth. December 14 in Houston.

Marks, Johnny, 75, American songwriter who composed "Rudolph the Red-Nosed Reindeer," one of the most popular songs of all time, with 150 million records sold. September 3 in New York City.

Marriott, John Willard, 84, American businessman; chairman of the board of the Marriott Corporation, a multibillion-dollar food and lodgings empire that he built from an initial 1927 investment of $500 in a root beer stand. August 13 in Wolfeboro, N.H.

Miller, Arnold R(ay), 62, American labor leader; he ousted Tony Boyle as head of the United Mine Workers in 1972 and served seven years as union president. July 12 in Charleston, W. Va.

Morante, Elsa, 67, leading Italian novelist and short-story writer whose translated works included the prizewinning *House of Liars* (1951) and *Arturo's Island* (1956), as well as the popular *History: A Novel* (1977). November 25 in Rome.

Nash, Clarence ("Ducky"), 80, American entertainer who for five decades did the voice of Donald Duck, his nephews, and his girlfriend, Daisy, in English and in six foreign languages. February 20 in Burbank, Calif.

Nathan, Robert, 91, prolific American novelist, poet, and playwright best known for his whimsical novels *One More Spring* (1933) and *Portrait of Jennie* (1940). May 25 in Los Angeles.

Nelson, Ricky (Eric Hilliard Nelson), 45, American pop singer and former teen idol who played himself from age 11 to early adulthood on *The Adventures of Ozzie and Harriet,* the popular television series of the 1950's and 1960's in which he joined his parents and brother as stars; among his hit records were "Mary Lou" and "Travelin' Man." Killed December 31 in De Kalb, Texas, with six others in a crash of his private plane.

Neves, Tancredo (Tancredo de Almeida Neves), 75, popular Brazilian political figure whose election as president in January signaled an end to two decades of military rule. A moderate pragmatist, he served as a congressman, senator, governor, and prime minister; prevented by an abdominal illness from taking office as president, he underwent seven operations in the 38 days before his death on April 21 in São Paulo.

Nolan, Lloyd (Benedict), 83, American character actor best known for his mid-1950's Broadway and TV performance as Captain Queeg in *The Caine Mutiny Court Martial* and later as costar of the TV series *Julia.* September 27 in Los Angeles.

North, John Ringling, 81, flamboyant American showman who headed the Ringling Brothers and Barnum & Bailey Circus, started by his uncles, for many years; under his management the circus moved indoors in 1956. June 4 in Brussels.

O'Brien, Edmond, 69, versatile American stage, screen, and TV actor who won an Academy Award as best supporting actor for his performance in *The Barefoot Contessa* (1954); among his many other films were such classics as *The Hunchback of Notre Dame* (1939), *The Killers* (1946), *White Heat* (1949), *Julius Caesar* (1953), and *The Wild Bunch* (1969). May 9 in Inglewood, Calif.

Ormandy, Eugene (Jeno Blau), 85, Hungarian-born conductor, trained as a violinist, who was music director of the Philadelphia Or-

Eugene Ormandy spent more than four decades as director of the Philadelphia Orchestra; he achieved worldwide fame for his classic renderings of music from the romantic period.

Karen Ann Quinlan, comatose for ten years, was the focus of a national debate over the "right to die."

to-die controversy when her adoptive parents filed suit asking that doctors disconnect her respirator; the request was granted in a 1976 state Supreme Court decision, but she remained alive after the respirator was turned off. June 11 in Morris Plains, N.J., of pneumonia.

Ramgoolam, Seewoosagur, 85, Mauritian political figure who led the country to independence from Britain in 1968 and was prime minister until electoral defeat in 1982; he subsequently held the ceremonial post of governor general. December 15 in Port Louis, Mauritius.

Redgrave, Sir Michael, 77, distinguished British actor who gained acclaim in the mid-1930's playing Shakespearean roles on the stage, became an instant film star in the 1938 Hitchcock classic *The Lady Vanishes,* and appeared in 35 films in all. His stage triumphs include Chekhov's *Uncle Vanya* and Ibsen's *The Master Builder.* Redgrave came from a family of eminent actors, whose tradition has been carried on by his daughters, Vanessa and Lynn. March 21 in Denham, England.

Richter, Charles F(rancis), 85, American seismologist who helped devise the Richter

chestra for 44 years, until his retirement in 1980; he was particularly famed for his masterly interpretations of music from the romantic era. March 12 in Philadelphia.

Pereira, William, 76, American architect and planner who designed San Francisco's Transamerica building and the planned community of Irvine in California. November 13 in Los Angeles.

Porter, Rodney Robert, 67, British biochemist who shared the 1972 Nobel Prize for medicine for his research on antibodies. Killed in a car crash September 6 at Beacon Hill, England.

Pritikin, Nathan, 69, controversial self-taught American nutritionist who in such best-selling books as *The Pritikin Program for Diet and Exercise* (1979) advocated a strict low-cholesterol, low-fat, and salt-free diet and regular exercise to combat heart disease and other ailments. February 21, of self-inflicted razor wounds, while suffering from terminal leukemia, in Albany, N.Y.

Quinlan, Karen Ann, 31, New Jersey coma victim who became the center of a U.S. right-

At the head of the Redgrave acting clan was Sir Michael, one of Britain's most accomplished stage and film thespians.

294

magnitude scale that measures an earthquake's intensity. September 30 in Pasadena, Calif.

Riddle, Nelson (Smock), 64, famed American composer-arranger who worked with such stars as Tommy Dorsey, Frank Sinatra, and Linda Ronstadt and composed "Lisbon Antiqua" and "Port au Prince" (1956); his score for the 1974 film *The Great Gatsby* earned him an Oscar. October 6 in Los Angeles.

Romulo, Carlos Pena, 86, Filipino diplomat and writer; a cofounder of the UN in 1945, he served as the Philippines' chief delegate to the UN from 1945 to 1954 and as foreign minister from 1968 to 1984. An eloquent advocate of anticolonialism, he was a leading spokesman for Third World countries and an ally, if sometimes a critic, of the United States. December 15 in Manila.

Roy, Maurice Cardinal, 80, former longtime archbishop of Québec and Roman Catholic primate of Canada. October 24 in Montréal.

Ryskind, Morrie, 89, American comedy writer who collaborated on several Marx brothers screen and stage hits, including *The Coconuts* (1929) and *A Night at the Opera* (1935), and on the Pulitzer Prize-winning musical *Of Thee I Sing* (1932). August 24 in Washington, D.C.

Sarkis, Elias, 60, president of Lebanon from 1976 to 1982 whose quiet, bureaucratic style was unable to end the civil strife ravaging the nation; a Maronite Christian and lawyer, he held the powerful post of governor of the central bank for several years. June 27 in Paris.

Scott, Francis Reginald (Frank), 85, Canadian poet, politician, and authority on constitutional law who helped found the forerunner of the New Democratic Party in the 1930's and later was dean of McGill University's law school; he received a Governor General's Literary Award in 1978 for *Essays on the Constitution* and in 1982 for *Collected Poems.* January 31 in Montréal.

Scourby, Alexander, 71, American actor who used his rich bass voice to narrate films and television programs, including *Victory at Sea,* and to record hundreds of books for the American Foundation for the Blind. February 23 in Boston.

Sessions, Roger (Huntington), 88, eminent American composer and educator; although his difficult, intellectually complex music failed to attract a wide audience, he was awarded a special Pulitzer Prize citation in 1974 and received in 1982 a Pulitzer Prize for his Concerto for Orchestra. March 16 in Princeton, N.J.

Shivers, (Robert) Allan, 77, U.S. politician who was governor of Texas from 1949 to 1957; a Democrat, he from 1952 consistently supported Republican presidential candidates. January 14 in Austin, Texas.

Shklovsky, Josif Samuilovich, 68, distinguished Soviet astrophysicist widely known for his 1962 book suggesting that intelligent life may exist on other worlds; an English translation expanded by Carl Sagan came out in 1966 under the title *Intelligent Life in the Universe.* March 3 in Moscow.

Shore, Edward W. (Eddie), 82, Canadian National Hockey League star who played for the Boston Bruins in the 1920's and 1930's; the only defenseman to win the Hart Trophy four times, he was elected to hockey's Hall of Fame. March 16 in Springfield, Mass.

Signoret, Simone (Simone Kaminker), 64, internationally acclaimed French actress whose

Simone Signoret, celebrated French actress, won the Oscar for best actress in 1959, for her role in Room at the Top.

movies included *Room at the Top* (1958), for which she won an Oscar, *Diabolique* (1954), *Ship of Fools* (1965), and *Madame Rosa* (1978). September 30 at Autheuil-Authouillet, France.

Silvers, Phil, 73, American actor and comedian best known for his starring role as Master Sergeant Ernie Bilko on the 1950's TV series *The Phil Silvers Show;* he also performed as a stand-up comic, in Broadway plays, in films, and on television. November 1 in Los Angeles.

Sims, John Haley (Zoot), 59, American jazz saxophonist who played with the big bands of Benny Goodman, Woody Herman, and Stan Kenton and made over 40 recordings under his own name in his "cool" tenor sax style. March 23 in New York City.

Smith, Samantha, 13, American schoolgirl whose plea for peace addressed to Soviet leader

As the fast-talking, always-gambling Master Sergeant Ernie Bilko, comedian Phil Silvers made his series a fixture on 1950's television.

Yuri Andropov earned her a trip to the Soviet Union in 1983 and celebrity status in the United States. Killed August 25 in a plane crash near Auburn, Me.

Sondergaard, Gale, 86, American film actress best known for her villain roles in the 1930's and 1940's; her debut in *Anthony Adverse* (1936) won her an Oscar as best supporting actress. August 14 in Woodland Hills, Calif.

Sparkman, John, 85, Alabama Democrat who served 10 years in the U.S. House and 32 years in the Senate, retiring in 1978. He was Adlai Stevenson's vice-presidential running mate in 1952 and became chairman of the Senate Foreign Relations Committee in 1975. November 16 in Huntsville, Ala.

Spiegel, Sam, 84, Austrian-born American film producer considered the quintessential Hollywood wheeler-dealer; among his classic productions were *The African Queen, On the Waterfront, Lawrence of Arabia,* and *The Bridge on the River Kwai.* December 31 in St. Martin, Netherlands Antilles.

Stewart, Potter, 70, American jurist who served as a U.S. Supreme Court associate justice for 23 years, until retiring in 1981. Appointed by President Dwight Eisenhower in 1958, Justice Stewart was a conservative on the Warren Court and generally a centrist on the more conservative Burger Court. December 7 in Hanover, N.H.

Sturgeon, Theodore (Edward Hamilton Waldo), 67, prolific American science fiction writer noted for his realistic depiction of unlikely events and unexpected points of view; he received the International Fantasy Award in 1954 for his novel *More than Human* and the Nebula (1970) and Hugo (1971) awards for the short story "Slow Sculpture." May 8 in Eugene, Ore.

Tanny, Vic (Victor Iannidinardo), 73, American body builder and fitness pioneer who founded a chain of innovative "health spas" in the United States and Canada that offered bright colors, carpeting, music, and catchy slogans instead of the traditional dingy gym. June 11 in Tampa, Fla.

Thuy, Xuan, 73, longtime Vietnamese diplomat best known as North Vietnam's chief representative at the Paris peace talks that led

Samantha Smith's 1983 letter to Soviet premier Yuri Andropov concerning the threat of nuclear war won the girl, then 11 years old, a highly publicized trip to the Soviet Union.

to the withdrawal of U.S. troops from South Vietnam in 1973. June 18 in Hanoi.

Tillstrom, Burr, 68, American puppeteer; creator of television's *Kukla, Fran and Ollie;* he won 5 Emmys during his long career on commercial and public television. December 6 in Palm Springs, Calif.

Turner, Joseph (Big Joe), 74, American blues singer who teamed with boogie-woogie pianist Pete Johnson in the 1930's and later sang with Duke Ellington, Count Basie, and others. His 1954 hit "Shake, Rattle and Roll" became an early rock classic in an expurgated version recorded by Bill Haley and the Comets. November 24 in Englewood, Calif.

Welch, Robert H. W., Jr., 85, American candy company executive and political activist who founded the ultraconservative, fiercely anti-Communist John Birch Society in 1958 and served as its president for 25 years. January 6 in Winchester, Mass.

Welles, (George) Orson, 70, brilliant American actor, director, producer, and writer particularly remembered for his 1938 radio version of H. G. Wells's *The War of the Worlds,* which caused many listeners to believe Martians had actually landed, and for his film *Citizen Kane* (1941), called by some critics the greatest ever made. His other films included *The Magnificent*

Ambersons (1942) and *Touch of Evil* (1958). October 10 in Los Angeles.

Wells, Dicky, 78(?), acclaimed and imaginative American jazz trombonist who starred with Count Basie's orchestra starting in 1938. November 12 in New York City.

White, Dan, 39, former San Francisco city supervisor who in 1978 shot to death gay rights activist Supervisor Harvey Milk and Mayor George Moscone; convicted only of voluntary manslaughter, he served five years in prison for the killings. Committed suicide October 21 in San Francisco.

White, E(lwyn) B(rooks), 86, distinguished American essayist and longtime *New Yorker* contributor; his books included the children's classic *Charlotte's Web* (1952) and a best-selling revision of the writing guide known as *The Elements of Style.* October 1 in North Brooklin, Me.

Wirkkala, Tapio, 69, celebrated Finnish sculptor and designer known for his simple yet elegant works in glass, ceramics, wood, and metal; he was regarded by many experts as the leading modern designer of such objects as cutlery, vases, and glassware. May 19 in Espoo, Finland.

Wolfenden, Lord (John Frederick Wolfenden), 78, British educator and social reformer;

Said by many to have made the greatest film ever (Citizen Kane), yet often said to have fallen short of his potential, Orson Welles was a towering figure in modern cinema.

E. B. White was an esteemed essayist and stylist and the author of the classic children's books Charlotte's Web and Stuart Little.

he headed a government committee that in 1957 made recommendations, subsequently adopted, that homosexual acts between consenting male adults be decriminalized and that prostitution, except for street solicitation, remain legal. January 18 in London.

Wood, Smoky Joe, 95, American baseball player; as Boston Red Sox pitcher in 1912 he won an American League record 16 straight games, threw 10 shutouts, and had a 1.92 earned run average. July 27 in West Haven, Conn.

Woodruff, Robert W(inship), 95, American businessman who took over the Coca-Cola Company at the age of 33 and transformed it from a debt-ridden soda fountain business into an international financial empire. March 7 in Atlanta.

Zimbalist, Efrem, 94 or 95, Russian-born violinist who in over 40 years on the concert stage earned wide acclaim for his technique and musicianship; he was also a composer—his works included songs, chamber music, tone poems, and the opera *Landara*—and a music educator, serving as director of Philadelphia's Curtis Institute from 1941 to 1968. February 22 in Reno, Nev.   R.F.

OHIO. See STATISTICS OF THE WORLD.

OKLAHOMA. See STATISTICS OF THE WORLD.

OMAN. See STATISTICS OF THE WORLD. See also PERSIAN GULF STATES.

ONTARIO. See STATISTICS OF THE WORLD. See also CANADA.

OREGON. See STATISTICS OF THE WORLD.

ORGANIZATION OF AMERICAN STATES. The 15th General Assembly of the Organization of American States (OAS) held a special session during early 1985, in Cartagena, Colombia, to amend the OAS charter. The proposed amendments will take effect if and when they are ratified by two-thirds of the 32 member nations. They provide an expanded role for the organization's Permanent Council, allow the secretary-general to participate in General Assembly deliberations, and allow the admission of new members having certain unresolved territorial disputes.

During early December, Argentina, Brazil, Peru, and Uruguay also joined with the Contadora nations (Colombia, Mexico, Panama, and Venezuela), which seek to negotiate a peace treaty for Central America, in submitting a draft resolution to the UN General Assembly. The resolution urged the U.S. government to resume direct talks with Nicaragua's Sandinista government and called for an end to military maneuvers in Central America by foreign powers—a reference to the United States. U.S. officials declined participating in bilateral talks with Nicaragua, citing its failure to seek "internal reconciliation." In November, Nicaragua had rejected the latest draft treaty prepared by the Contadora group because it did not ban U.S. military maneuvers and because it provided for freezes in regular armies but not in guerrilla forces such as the anti-Sandinista "contras" backed by the United States. A new peace initiative sponsored by Spain was underway in late December, but prospects for peace remained dim.

On May 30 the OAS censured the construction by Great Britain of a strategic air base in the Falkland Islands, by a vote of 20-0, with abstentions by 9 English-speaking nations of the Caribbean and by the United States. Earlier in May, after the United States declared a trade embargo against Nicaragua, the Permanent Council approved by consensus a resolution opposing the use of political intervention and economic sanctions.

In November the Inter-American Court of Human Rights, a judicial body of the OAS, ruled, 7-0, in an influential but nonbinding decision, that laws requiring licensing of journalists violate the right to free expression. Eleven OAS nations had such laws at the time.

In December the 11 regional debtor nations, the so-called Cartagena Group, met in Uruguay and agreed that the five largest debtors—Argentina, Brazil, Colombia, Mexico, and Venezuela—would act together in lobbying banks and governments on proposals to deal with the debt crisis.   L.L.P.

ORGANIZATION OF PETROLEUM EXPORTING COUNTRIES. In 1985, world economic conditions and disagreements among the 13 members of the Organization of Petroleum Exporting Countries led to a progressive deterioration in OPEC's control over petroleum production and prices. At the cartel's final meeting of the year, in December in Geneva, OPEC decided to abandon its stated policy of defending oil prices through cuts in production (already flouted by its members) and instead seek to preserve a "fair share" of the world oil market by cutting prices as needed to compete with major non-OPEC oil producers such as Great Britain, Mexico, Egypt, and Norway. A committee was appointed to work out details of the new approach, which appeared to set the stage for a price war. OPEC nations hoped that other countries would cut their production to help sustain higher prices for everyone. After the OPEC decision, oil prices plunged quickly, then rallied. The long-range trend remained to be seen.

Earlier in the year, at a meeting during January in Geneva, nine members had agreed on a modest price cut in an effort to bring the cost of OPEC oil more in line with free market prices—only the second time in the organization's history that it actually agreed to lower prices. The agreement brought the official price of light crude from about $29 to $28. Algeria, Libya, and Iran dissented, but by February, Iran also had dropped its price for light crude. OPEC members were trying to keep within their collective production quota of 16 million barrels a day (b/d), but competition from non-

A worldwide oil glut undermined the power of OPEC to determine the price of oil, forcing cartel members to cut production and prices.

OPEC producers helped create a temporary surplus of oil in world markets and contributed to pressure for lowering prices. The surplus was exacerbated by OPEC members themselves; by midyear Saudi Arabia and Iran were the only members adhering to their quotas.

In April the OPEC monitoring committee (the United Arab Emirates, Iraq, Iran, Libya, Algeria, and Ecuador) reaffirmed the overall production quota of 16 million b/d. It warned, however, that members "must stop giving more or less overt discounts to their clients." It also approved a small price cut. The committee observed that the anticipated reserves of members were considerably larger than previously estimated; reserves were now expected to last 240 years in Kuwait, 140 in Iraq, 120 in Saudi Arabia, and 85 in the UAE.

At a July meeting in Geneva, OPEC oil ministers, by a 10-3 vote, agreed to Saudi Arabia's demand for small additional price reductions in medium and heavy crude. The cuts amounted to 50 cents a barrel for heavy crude, bringing it down to $26 a barrel, and 20 cents a barrel for medium crude, lowering it to $27.20. A major goal of the new cuts (not accepted by Algeria, Libya, and Iran) was to help Saudi Arabia expand oil production by making its heavier crude more attractive to buyers. Saudi Arabia was caught in a financial squeeze, caused by its efforts to shore up OPEC prices by setting limits on its own oil output, which was reaching a 20-year low. Meanwhile, to help reverse the sharp decline in Saudi oil sales, King Fahd announced in September that Saudi Arabia asserted freedom to cut prices on its own.

At an OPEC meeting in Vienna during October, the ministers could not resolve demands for higher production quotas by six members and postponed additional discussion until their December meeting. In the fall, prices at first held relatively steady because of such factors as prewinter buildups of stocks by oil companies and reduced Iranian production (owing to bomb-damaged oil facilities). Then, however, the organization seemed to be losing control of prices, and in November the UAE oil minister unofficially announced that OPEC members were free to set oil prices as they wished. The statement foreshadowed the action taken at the December meeting.   D.P.

P

PACIFIC ISLANDS. Visits to the Pacific Islands in 1985 by the Japanese prime minister and the Chinese Communist Party general secretary indicated increased interest in the region on the part of the outside world. In other developments, the U.S. Congress approved legislation ending its stewardship of the Micronesian Islands.

The Pacific region attracted attention partly because of nuclear issues. In August all the independent island states except Vanuatu joined Australia and New Zealand in giving preliminary approval to a treaty establishing a nuclear-free zone in the South Pacific. The treaty did not prohibit the passage or docking of nuclear-capable ships in the region (a matter which continued to be a source of tension between the United States and New Zealand). But it did ban the testing, acquisition, or stationing of nuclear devices on the territory of the signatories, in opposition to the French nuclear testing program at Mururoa Atoll, near Tahiti. The July 10 bombing of the antinuclear protest vessel *Rainbow Warrior* in New Zealand, by French agents, had brought the issue of nuclear testing into particular prominence, and the environmental group that had sponsored the *Rainbow Warrior* subsequently sent other vessels to the Mururoa vicinity.

The issue of independence from France continued to arouse violent controversy in New Caledonia, where clashes between those favoring independence and those opposing it had caused 20 deaths by early 1985. In April the French announced changes in the political structure and moved an independence referendum from mid-1985 to 1987. In September elections, antiindependence groups won a majority in a newly created Congress, while proindependence majorities were elected in three of four new regional assemblies.

In December, the U.S. Congress approved

Hoping to defuse the tense political situation in New Caledonia, France's President François Mitterrand (fourth from left, in dark suit) visited Nouméa in January. Demonstrations and riots continued to disrupt the French South Pacific island.

legislation for a compact of free association that would grant the Marshall Islands and the Federated States of Micronesia self-governing status, while allowing the United States to maintain a military presence in the region. Islanders and Congress had disagreed over terms of the pact for many years. On Palau, another entity of the U.S. Trust Territory (where a similar self-governing status was expected), President Haruo Remeliik was assassinated on June 30.

In Papua New Guinea, the government of Michael Somare was defeated in late November on a vote of no-confidence. Deputy Prime Minister Paias Wingti, who had crossed over to the opposition earlier in the year, became prime minister. In Western Samoa, Prime Minister Tofilau Eti Alesana resigned over a budget impasse; he was succeeded by opposition leader Va'ai Kolone.

See STATISTICS OF THE WORLD.   G.F. & R.M.

PAKISTAN. On December 30, 1985, Pakistan's president, General Muhammad Zia ul-Haq, declared an end to martial law as promised, after 8½ years. He also announced a restoration of basic human rights. Zia remained president of the country, presiding over a civilian government which, since August, had been led by a prime minister. He also retained his title as army chief of staff, and his regime continued to have broad powers, partly in virtue of aspects of martial law that had previously been carried over into the civil code at the government's behest. Nevertheless, the cessation of military rule was regarded as an important step in a possible movement toward democracy in Pakistan.

Earlier in the year, on February 25, voters went to the polls to elect a new National Assembly, as well as four provincial assemblies. Zia, however, had disqualified some politicians from participating and denied political parties the right to campaign. The government also arrested several hundred persons allegedly planning to disrupt the election, which the opposition had denounced as a sham. The electorate failed to give Zia's slate of candidates a strong endorsement. Only two of the nine cabinet-level officials contesting the elections gained seats in the National Assembly, and voters turned out more than 30 members re-

puted to be intimates of the president. Zia himself remained firmly ensconced in office by a December 1984 referendum that he interpreted as renewing his presidential term for five years. Only days after the February elections, the 1973 constitution also was amended to bolster Zia's powers.

Shahnawaz Bhutto, a son of the late Prime Minister Zulfikar Ali Bhutto, was found dead July 18 under mysterious circumstances in his apartment in Cannes, France. His death gave impetus to the opposition's Movement for the Restoration of Democracy, of which Bhutto's former party, the Pakistan People's Party (PPP) was the dominant member. Shahnawaz had reputedly been a leader of the Al-Zulfikar terrorist organization, dedicated to Zia's overthrow; the organization was perceived as a militant extension of the PPP, which was led by Shahnawaz's sister Benazir Bhutto. She returned from exile in London with her brother's body August 20 and led a massive funeral procession. On August 29 she was placed under house arrest, but she was later allowed to leave the country.

Muhammad Khan Junejo, appointed to the newly revived post of prime minister, had announced in August that martial law would be lifted by the end of the year. The president reiterated the same promise the following month; he added that political parties would eventually be allowed to resume activity.

Relations between Pakistan and India were marred by disputes over nuclear arms and by border clashes; after Zia met with Prime Minister Rajiv Gandhi at the United Nations in October, however, it was announced that the two countries would hold talks on these issues and on economic cooperation.

The war in Afghanistan continued to cause an influx of refugees into Pakistan, and Pakistani villages along the Afghanistan border continued to be bombed and strafed. Separate Afghan and Pakistani peace talks with a UN mediator recessed in December.

See STATISTICS OF THE WORLD.   L.Z.

PALESTINE LIBERATION ORGANIZATION
See MIDDLE EAST.

PANAMA. Saying he lacked the military and political support to lead debt-burdened Panama out of its economic crisis, President Nicol-

Ardito Barletta Vallarina resigned on September 28, 1985. Vice-President Eric Arturo Delvalle, a prominent figure in the rightist Republican Party, replaced him.

Barletta's government had faced increasing opposition, both from supporters of the late General Omar Torrijos within Barletta's own Democratic Revolutionary Party (PRD) and from outside its ranks. The outside opposition centered in the National Civil Coordinating Committee, which represented a cross section of middle-class professional groups increasingly concerned with the impact of government austerity programs. Discontent within the PRD was based on the perception that Barletta had abandoned Torrijos's reformist programs. Complaining loudly about the number of conservative technocrats holding cabinet positions, PRD populists, in May, forced Barletta to replace a majority of these individuals with PRD sympathizers.

Barletta's resignation in September, however, reportedly came at the insistence of General Manuel Antonio Noriega, head of the Defense Forces. Political analysts linked Noriega's move to the torture and decapitation of Hugo Spadafora, a leading critic of the armed forces, in mid-September. Barletta had hinted he might launch an official investigation of the killing, apparently carried out by the military. Noriega was widely seen as attempting to bury the growing scandal.

Panama had difficulties adjusting to the demands of international lending agencies that the government reduce spending and raise taxes. In February the National Assembly approved new tax legislation, placing the increased tax burden largely on the international banking community. A budget of $600 million was approved in March. Opposition to government austerity measures was highlighted in midyear by a wave of union protest marches. News of proposed changes in labor laws that would have adversely affected the working class sparked a two-day strike and demands for a 15-year moratorium on repayments of the country's foreign debt; the proposed changes were later dropped.

See STATISTICS OF THE WORLD.   S.R.

PAPUA NEW GUINEA. See STATISTICS OF THE WORLD. See also PACIFIC ISLANDS.

PARAGUAY. Infighting between "traditionalists" and "militants" within Paraguay's governing Colorado Party reached serious proportions in 1985, as a rare public debate was opened about the 1988 succession to the presidency. Traditionalist control of the party was increasingly challenged by the militants, led by President Alfredo Stroessner's private secretary, Mario Abdo Benítez. They were reported to support Stroessner's son, Colonel Gustavo Stroessner, as his father's successor. The traditionalists were in favor of the presidency's going to an alternative, possibly from within the Army.

Government relations with the Roman Catholic Church, the press, and human rights groups continued to be strained. A bishops' conference drew up a pastoral letter in support of peasants' rights to own land, while several church figures were outspoken in denouncing government corruption and violations of civil rights. The opposition coalition Acuerdo Nacional turned out up to 5,000 people at a May 14 Independence Day rally in Asunción, demanding a return to "true democracy." In June a demonstration of 2,000 students led to clashes with the police, the first of this kind in 25 years. In mid-July, 5,000 peasants met at Caaguazú to form a "Permanent Assembly of Landless Peasants."

In May, Paraguay's normally good relations with the United States were strained when President Ronald Reagan denounced the "entrenched dictatorships" of Paraguay, Chile, Cuba, and Nicaragua. In August the U.S. Congress made aid to Paraguay conditional on certification by Reagan that Stroessner's government had ended terror and abuse by military and security forces. Relations with West Germany also were shaky; a planned state visit to Bonn by General Stroessner was postponed in June, after West Germany's president and foreign minister arranged to be out of the country when Stroessner was to arrive.

A major cocaine smuggling operation was uncovered on the Brazilian border in July. High government and military figures were reportedly linked to the drug trade, including the commander of the 1st Army Corps.

See STATISTICS OF THE WORLD.   J.F., Jr.

PENNSYLVANIA. See STATISTICS OF THE WORLD.

303

People in the News

The year 1985 was dominated by the doings of the wealthy, the powerful, and the merely talented. Some celebrities inspired charity drives; others, scandalous headlines. News of rock stars and royalty, Hollywood stars and sports legends, lottery millionaires, deep-sea treasure-hunters, and an affluent Indian guru diverted people-watchers.

As usual, much of the public interest in personalities was focused on the White House. The first family settled into a second term with aplomb, after four days of glittering inauguration festivities, somewhat dimmed when cold forced cancellation of the traditional inaugural parade. The year was shadowed by the news that President **Ronald Reagan** had developed colon cancer. But the 74-year-old president responded well to surgery in July, and doctors were optimistic. Two later procedures to remove cancerous skin cells on his nose also left Reagan unfazed. "I can stand before you proudly and say 'My nose is clean,' " he quipped to the press.

The president was putting on a more serious face at the Geneva summit in November, when he met for the first time with Soviet leader **Mikhail Gorbachev.** By all accounts, the two hit it off on a personal level, although they hardly resolved their deep political differences. While their husbands conferred in private sessions, **Nancy Reagan** and **Raisa Gorbachev** made a string of public appearances and also shared some almond tea and pleasantries. President Reagan was not the only American politician to meet with Gorbachev close up; the Reverend **Jesse Jackson** succeeded in collaring the Soviet leader for an impromptu, 45-minute talk, in which Jackson broached the subjects of arms control and the plight of Soviet Jews.

Former President **Richard Nixon** further edged his way back toward public acceptance when he was made guest of honor at a Republican National Committee dinner—his first such engagement since Watergate. He also wrote a lead article on relations between the superpowers, which was published in the journal *Foreign Affairs* on the eve of the Geneva summit. He was even called upon to act as arbiter in a salary dispute between major league baseball umpires and team owners. "Baseball," Nixon declared, "can't survive without clean, honest umpires." Meanwhile, another former president, **Jimmy Carter,** was collaborating with his wife, **Rosalynn,** on a book for Random House, about making the most of later life. He was also kept busy watching over the planning, fund-raising, and construction of a $65 million presidential library complex in Atlanta, which will include a library, a museum, and a research and policy center to be used as a forum for debating and mediating major issues.

Senator Edward Kennedy (D, Mass.) surprised many viewers in December, when he announced in a taped broadcast over two Boston television stations that he would not make a try for the presidency in 1988. Kennedy, whose 1980 presidential campaign was dogged by questions about his personal life, cited family considerations as a factor in his announcement, as well as a desire to concentrate on public affairs without the distraction of a possible pending bid for the presidency. "I know this decision means that I may never be president," he said. "But the pursuit of the presidency is not my life." He also wanted to clear the political path for a new generation of Kennedys. Shortly before his announcement, **Joseph P. Kennedy 2d,** eldest son of the late Senator **Robert Kennedy,** said he would run for the Massachusetts congressional seat to be vacated by retiring House Speaker **Thomas P. ("Tip") O'Neill, Jr.** The young Kennedy promptly became front-runner in the 1986 race for a seat once held by his uncle, former President **John F. Kennedy.**

The Reverend Jesse Jackson and Mikhail Gorbachev held an impromptu discussion at the Soviet mission in Geneva during the Soviet leader's November summit talks with President Ronald Reagan. The two exchanged views on Soviet Jewry, South Africa, and nuclear issues.

John and Robert Kennedy were the object of some less welcome publicity. A new book by British author **Anthony Summers** and a British-produced television documentary revived the claim that both men had had affairs with the late actress **Marilyn Monroe.** These sources also contended that Robert had been with the star on the day she took a fatal overdose of barbiturates and that officials then cooperated in a cover-up to conceal his presence in Los Angeles. Such theories, along with speculation by some writers that the actress was actually murdered, led to a request by the Los Angeles Board of Supervisors to reopen an investigation into Monroe's death—but the request was rebuffed by a county grand jury in November.

Charles and **Diana,** the Prince and Princess of Wales, commanded most of the attention from fanciers of British royalty. The couple began the year with a 17-day tour of Italy, accompanied by four tons of luggage. Italian socialites and designers nonetheless criticized Diana for outfits they considered dowdy and even somewhat recycled; the uproar climaxed in Milan, when she attended a performance at La Scala garbed in a two-year-old pink chiffon dress last seen at a **Barry Manilow** concert in London. But Diana neatly floored her Italian detractors when she appeared in Florence in a widely admired flamenco-style outfit.

The youngest of the British royals got their share of publicity, especially when **Prince William,** Charles and Diana's eldest son, began nursery school. He and brother **Harry** also cavorted for the whole of Britain during a BBC television interview with Charles and Diana; the royal parents did the interview partly to counter a magazine article describing the future king as a reclusive eccentric and the princess as a self-absorbed clothes-a-holic. But unkind gossip did little to daunt public adulation of the prince and princess on their autumn trip to the United States, which took them from Washington, D.C., to Palm Beach, Fla. Competition for invitations to royal functions was intense, and celebrities were present in abundance. At a White House bash, Diana danced with **John Travolta** and **Clint Eastwood.** Amid the dinners and formal ceremonies, the royals visited a J. C. Penney store in suburban Virginia to promote a line of British merchandise. In Florida, Charles played polo and accompanied his wife to a charity ball.

Monaco's royalty was in the limelight as well. In January, **Princess Caroline** and husband **Stefano Casiraghi** set off from Paris in a 16-ton truck, on a road race that was to terminate in Dakar, Senegal. But just after they had reached the African continent, the truck turned over, and though the Casiraghis were unhurt, they retired early from the event. Caroline's sister **Stephanie,** 20, made news of her own by launching a modeling career. Her father, **Prince Rainier III,** was by no means publicity hungry. After Stephanie showed up on the island of Mauritius in a topless bikini, Rainier allegedly vowed to sue any publication that printed photographs of the uncovered princess.

Rock stars demonstrated concern for global problems. In January more than 40 singers banded together to help starving populations in Africa by recording the song "We Are the World," written by **Michael Jackson** and **Lionel**

Guru Bhagwan Shree Rajneesh returned to his native India as part of a plea bargain arrangement with the U.S. government, which had charged him with violations involving his commune in Oregon. He is shown here after being arrested in North Carolina as he allegedly tried to flee prosecution.

Richie. The record, which spawned an album, a video, and a home videotape on the making of the single, was inspired in part by **Harry Belafonte** as an answer to a similar British effort in late 1984 by a group of performers who dubbed themselves Band Aid. Not to be outdone, Irish rock singer **Bob Geldof,** who had organized Band Aid, helped put together an even bigger effort in the summer: the 16-hour Live Aid concert, broadcast from London and Philadelphia to an estimated 1.5 billion people around the world. Through the cooperation of such stars as **Mick Jagger, Tina Turner, the Who, Paul McCartney,** and **Bob Dylan,** over $65 million was raised.

A chance remark made by Dylan during the Live Aid show led to yet another fund-raising extravaganza, the Farm Aid concert. Headed by country singer **Willie Nelson** and rock singer **John Cougar Mellencamp,** the show featured an eclectic group of performers, including Dylan, **Neil Young, Lou Reed,** and the **Beach Boys.** Though the immediate proceeds were disappointing, organizers hoped the event would focus attention on farmers' woes. Undeterred by the possible overkill from such star turns, **Dionne Warwick, Stevie Wonder,** and others teamed up to record "That's What Friends Are For," for the benefit of AIDS research.

Outside the music world, comedian **Joan Rivers,** who said she was giving benefits for AIDS "before it was chic," led a one-night Broadway revue called *Comic Relief* that raised more than half a million dollars. Shortly after that event, it was disclosed that actor **Rock Hudson** had contracted the disease and that, unknown to most of his fans, the matinee idol was an active homosexual. Hudson's case drew increased attention to the plight of AIDS victims and led to a massive Hollywood AIDS benefit in September. Celebrities on the roster included **Elizabeth Taylor** (no longer engaged to entrepreneur **Dennis Stein**), **Burt Reynolds, Shirley MacLaine, Betty Ford,** and **Burt Lancaster,** who read a message from the ailing Hudson. "I am not happy that I have AIDS," the actor wrote. "But if that is helping others, I can at least know that my own misfortune has had some positive worth." Hudson died of the disease the following month.

Other well-known names were plagued by

legal troubles. **John DeLorean** was indicted in September for allegedly diverting nearly $9 million from his fledgling auto company for personal use. His divorce battle with **Cristina Ferrare** finally ended in December in a split decision; DeLorean failed to win custody of the two children, but the judge did uphold a prenuptial agreement preventing Ferrare from obtaining a major share of DeLorean's fortune, estimated at about $20 million.

Vanessa Redgrave suffered a legal reverse. The actress had won $100,000 in damages from the Boston Symphony Orchestra because it canceled her performance in a 1982 concert series allegedly on account of her vociferous support for the Palestine Liberation Organization. In February 1985 a Boston federal judge overturned the award, ruling that Redgrave was entitled only to the $27,500 performance fee specified in her contract with the orchestra. Redgrave appealed the decision.

Indian guru **Bhagwan Shree Rajneesh,** the controversial leader of an Oregon commune, was arrested in October on immigration charges, as he allegedly tried to flee the country to Bermuda. Prosecutors said Rajneesh had overstayed his 1981 temporary visa and had arranged sham marriages for his foreign disciples so that they could join him in the United States. Released on bail, the guru plea-bargained his way to a suspended sentence, paid a hefty $400,000 fine, and returned to his native India. The Bhagwan's 82 Rolls-Royces were sold for $5 million to a Texas dealer, and the rest of the commune's assets were put up for sale, as its residents departed, much to the delight of the handful of locals nearby, who had watched their town get taken over by the sect.

Some celebrities got good news in court. Danish-born socialite **Claus von Bülow** was acquitted on charges that he had twice tried to kill his wealthy wife, **Sunny,** with injections of insulin. (A 1982 conviction was overturned, leading to the 1985 retrial.) Although Sunny remained in a coma, von Bülow said it would be "bad taste" to divorce her to marry his current companion, **Andrea Reynolds.**

After years of leading a private, secluded life in Vermont, Soviet author and dissident **Aleksandr Solzhenitsyn** and his wife, **Natalya,** applied for U.S. citizenship in May. Also applying

Ukrainian-born Walter Polovchak celebrates his 18th birthday in October following a ceremony at which he became an American citizen. Polovchak had refused to return to the Soviet Union with his parents in 1980 and was granted political asylum.

for citizenship was teenage émigré **Walter Polovchak.** The young Ukrainian had originally been granted asylum by the federal government in 1980, after he refused to return to the Soviet Union with his parents. The courts in 1985 decided Polovchak's parents had been denied due process in the U.S. action, but the issue became moot when Walter reached his 18th birthday on October 3, 1985, and no longer was subject to their custody. Polovchak said he was certain that, despite the litigation, his parents were "real glad that I'm here."

Two rock stars' marriages made big headlines during the year. **Bruce Springsteen,** 35, married actress and model **Julianne Phillips,** 25, in

PEOPLE IN THE NEWS

May. "The Boss" had tried to keep the ceremony secret, but news leaked out and the media began descending on the bride's Oregon hometown well in advance of the announced wedding day. The couple responded by holding the ceremony two days early—just after midnight in a candlelit church. Said Springsteen, "I give my entire energy to the public and those who follow me. This is different. Things that are private should be kept private." Another "top-secret" event, the outdoor marriage of rock singer **Madonna,** 27, and actor **Sean Penn,** 24, in Malibu, Calif., became a public spectacle when it was invaded by helicopters laden with eager photographers.

Joan Collins, the seductive and venomous Alexis on television's Dynasty, *married businessman Peter Holm in Las Vegas.*

Canadian first lady Mila Mulroney, wife of Prime Minister Brian Mulroney, gave birth to the couple's third son, Daniel Nicolas Dimitri, in September.

Other celebrities tied the knot under less of a spotlight. Rock musician **Billy Joel,** 35, married model **Christie Brinkley,** 31, on a yacht in the middle of New York Harbor. Singer-songwriter **James Taylor,** 37, married actress **Kathryn Walker,** 42. *Dynasty* star **Joan Collins,** 52, wed businessman **Peter Holm,** 38, in a Las Vegas ceremony. And bodybuilder-turned-actor **Arnold Schwarzenegger,** 38, and **Maria Shriver,** 29, television personality and Kennedy clan member, made plans to marry in 1986.

Possibly the most conspicuous engagement of the year was that of sports commentator **Ahmad Rashad,** 36, and **Phylicia Ayers-Allen,** Bill Cosby's television wife; Rashad suddenly popped the question on nationwide TV, during NBC's coverage of Thanksgiving Day football. (Luckily for him, she accepted, and the couple were married in December in New York.)

Heading the list of proud parents were Canadian Prime Minister **Brian Mulroney,** 46, and first lady **Mila Mulroney,** 32, whose third son, **Daniel Nicolas Dimitri,** was born on September 4, exactly one year after his father's landslide victory in Canadian general elections; the new Mulroney weighed in at 7 pounds, 14 ounces. Rolling Stone **Mick Jagger,** 42, and live-in girlfriend **Jerry Hall,** 29, had a second child, **James Leroy Augustine,** in April. Other unwed couples to become parents during the year included filmmaker **Steven Spielberg,** 37, and actress **Amy Irving,** 31, who had a son in June (they later tied the knot in December); and Hollywood stars **Farrah Fawcett,** 37, and **Ryan O'Neal,** 43, who celebrated the birth of a baby boy in January. Later in the year, Ryan's daughter, **Tatum O'Neal,** was expecting a child; the father, tennis star **John McEnroe,** said a marriage was planned. Retired Swedish tennis star **Björn Borg,** 29, was presented with a son in September by his 19-year-old girlfriend, **Jannike Bjorling.**

The late Beatle **John Lennon** was honored when his widow, **Yoko Ono,** dedicated Strawberry Fields, a 2½-acre plot in New York City's Central Park, to his memory. About 100 countries donated a profusion of shrubs, flowers, and trees to beautify the "International Garden of Peace"; Ono herself gave about $1 million to refurbish the site. "It's our way of taking a sad song and making it better," said Ono. The late singer **Elvis Presley** was the subject of less reverent recollections, in a book by his former wife, **Priscilla.** In *Elvis and Me,* the 40-year-old *Dallas* star recounted details of their long, eccentric courtship and troubled marriage. She also discussed Presley's dependency on drugs, which she blamed on worry and insomnia.

One of the hottest new celebrities on the sports scene was a figure of unusual dimensions. When rookie defensive linebacker **William "The Refrigerator" Perry** entered the Chicago Bears' training camp, the only thing about him that impressed the Bears' coach was his weight—a whopping 330 pounds. But when the Bears put him in the offensive backfield against San Francisco, Chicago fans were thrilled by the way he bulldozed his adversaries. Football devotees across the country showed similar enthusiasm when, in a game against Green Bay, Perry cleared the way for two **Walter Payton** scores and then completed his own touchdown. Since then Perry has been in demand on TV talk shows and has been asked to endorse a wealth of products, including, of course, refrigerators. He also helped the Bears crush the Patriots in the 1986 Super Bowl.

If Perry seemed an unusual hero, so too were the 21 New York factory workers who, in August, collectively won a share of the largest lottery jackpot thus far offered in the United States—$41 million. The workers, most of them recent immigrants from countries such as Thailand, Trinidad, Hungary, Poland, and China, had each contributed to a pool set up just hours before New York Lottery officials announced the winning numbers. The "lucky 21," who stood to share a total of $13.6 million,

Nicknamed "The Refrigerator," rookie defensive lineman William Perry of the Chicago Bears weighs in at over 300 pounds, one of the most hulking presences in all of sport. His skills at defense—and offense as well—helped the Bears move on to take Super Bowl XX.

Celso Garcete from Paraguay, who chose the winning numbers for New York's August 21 Lotto drawing, gets a lift from his jubilant ticket sharers. The winning pool of 21 workers, most of them recent immigrants, shared part of the $41 million prize, the largest U.S. lottery payoff ever.

were touted nationwide as living symbols of the American dream. Another lucky lottery winner was furniture deliveryman **Jose Caballero,** who won $2 million in the California lottery. He also publicly admitted having entered the United States illegally from Mexico. Too much of a celebrity to evade the attention of the immigration authorities, the 24-year-old alien had to return to Mexico, but lottery officials said he was entitled to keep his winnings.

Perhaps the luckiest man of 1985 was **Mel Fisher,** who struck gold in July—lots of it. For 16 years, Fisher had led a dogged quest for the treasure of the Spanish galleon *Nuestra Señora de Atocha,* which sank off Key West, Fla., in 1622. His search had been marked by personal tragedy—his oldest son and daughter-in-law drowned while tracking down the wreck—and by financial woes. But Fisher and 700 investors in his expedition got good news when divers surfaced with word that the prize had been found. The well-preserved wreckage

contained one of the largest caches of sunken treasure ever discovered: as much as $400 million worth of gold, silver, and jewels. "It's fantabulous," Fisher said.   P.L.W.

BRADLEY, THOMAS (TOM)

Mayor of Los Angeles, born December 29, 1917, in Calvert, Texas. In April, Tom Bradley, already the first black mayor of Los Angeles, became the first person ever elected to a fourth term as the city's mayor. The liberal Democrat overwhelmed City Councilman John Ferraro, a conservative Democrat, taking more than two-thirds of the vote in a nonpartisan election. If he succeeds in an expected second bid for the governorship in 1986, he will be California's first black governor, as well as the first elected black governor in U.S. history. (In 1982, George Deukmejian had narrowly defeated Bradley for the governorship.)

In his 1985 mayoral campaign, Bradley adopted a newly assertive campaign style, which he applied to statewide issues as well. He strongly deplored the possible impact on local governments of President Ronald Reagan's tax reform plan and chided Deukmejian for not challenging the proposal. He also got various city pension funds to sell off their investments in firms doing business in South Africa.

Bradley continued to bask in the afterglow of 1984, when Los Angeles hosted the summer Olympics and the mayor was considered by Democratic presidential candidate Walter Mondale as a possible running mate. A statewide poll taken in 1985 showed that about 80 percent of the people surveyed had a favorable opinion of Bradley.

Thomas Bradley's family moved from Texas to Los Angeles when he was seven. A high school track star, he attended the University of California at Los Angeles on an athletic scholarship. In 1940 he joined the Los Angeles Police Department, retiring 21 years later as a lieutenant, after having attended law school in the evenings and passed the California bar examination in 1956. Between 1963 and 1973, he served on the Los Angeles City Council. In 1969, he lost his first bid for the mayoralty to

George Bush took on a new role on July 13 when he spent almost eight hours as the first official acting president in U.S. history. Ronald Reagan, before undergoing surgery, had signed a letter temporarily transferring the powers of the post to the vice-president.

Tom Bradley easily won a fourth term as mayor of Los Angeles in an April election. The son of Texas sharecroppers, Bradley displayed a new "action-oriented" political style as he appeared ready to seek the California governorship in 1986.

incumbent Sam Yorty, after a campaign with racist overtones. He defeated Yorty in 1973 and went on to win resounding reelection victories in 1977 and 1981, as well as in 1985.

BUSH, GEORGE H(ERBERT) W(ALKER)

U.S. vice-president, born June 12, 1924, in Milton, Mass. On July 13, George Bush became the first U.S. vice-president to be designated acting president by the incumbent. For a period of about eight hours, while President Ronald Reagan was undergoing surgery for removal of a cancerous growth in his colon, Bush was assigned the powers of the presidency, under the terms of an official letter issued by Reagan. Bush spent much of the time playing tennis at his Washington home and did not sign any laws or perform any important duties, but he was fulfilling a historic role. Such an official transfer of power had not been made when President Reagan was shot and temporarily incapacitated in 1981, nor had it been made by any previous president.

Bush's other activities during the year often went beyond the ceremonial functions vice-presidents traditionally perform. His travels

Tired of the poor quality of most television series, Bill Cosby elected to return to the small screen in The Cosby Show—*a true-to-life comedy about a New York City doctor, his lawyer wife, and their five children, which became one of the year's most popular shows.*

included a trip in March to drought-stricken areas of Africa, including Sudan, where he helped secure then-President Jafaar al-Nimeiry's consent to a CIA-sponsored airlift of refugee Ethiopian Jews to Israel. In Moscow later that month for Konstantin Chernenko's funeral, he met with the new Soviet leader, Mikhail Gorbachev, and extended Reagan's invitation to a summit meeting. Bush, who had represented the United States in China in the mid-1970's, visited there in October, signed a trade agreement, and was treated as an "old friend"— despite policy disagreements. In June, after the hijacking of TWA Flight 847, the president made him head of an administration task force investigating ways to combat terrorism.

Bush also took early steps toward organizing his own possible 1988 presidential campaign. He upgraded his staff and appointed highly regarded White House aide Craig L. Fuller as his new chief of staff. He allowed the formation of a political action committee in his name, which raised over $800,000 in its first two months of operation. In October the Bush organization announced the endorsement of

658 Republicans in Michigan, a state that was to begin selecting party convention delegates in August 1986.

COSBY, WILLIAM HENRY (BILL), JR.

Comedian and television actor, born July 12, 1937, in Philadelphia. Bill Cosby made a triumphant return to television during the 1984–1985 season with *The Cosby Show,* a gentle, true-to-life comedy that became the highest-rated new show of the season and won Emmy awards for best writing and direction. Cosby himself dominated the action on-screen, and his delivery, facial expressions, and perfect timing were perhaps as important to the comedy as the NBC program's scripts and themes— which Cosby also shaped as one of the show's producers.

In the show Cosby plays Heathcliff Huxtable, a genial New York City obstetrician. He and his wife, a legal aid attorney, are caught in a constant, exasperating battle with their son and four daughters, in circumstances modern parents can readily recognize. Cosby, who insisted that the show not rely on the contrived plots and gags of most situation comedies, even hired a Harvard University psychiatrist to check the scripts for psychological accuracy. The series also is the first American program to depict a middle-class black family without racial stereotypes or caricatures.

As the first black to star in a weekly network show, the adventure series *I Spy,* Cosby won Emmys in 1966, 1967, and 1968 for his role as a witty CIA agent in partnership with costar Robert Culp. Later, Cosby starred in *The Bill Cosby Show,* playing a high school physical education teacher, and in *Cos,* a short-lived variety show.

William Henry Cosby, Jr., dropped out halfway through high school, but later earned a high school equivalency diploma while serving in the Navy from 1956 to 1960. Subsequently, he dropped out of Temple University after two years because of his success performing as a comic in New York and Philadelphia clubs. (He eventually earned a bachelor's degree from Temple's School of Communications and Theater, plus a master's degree and a doctorate in education from the University of Massachusetts.)

Besides appearing on television and in night-clubs across the United States, he has put out over 20 comedy albums and received numerous Grammys. His film credits include *Uptown Saturday Night* (1974) and *California Suite* (1978). He and his wife, Camille Hanks, have four daughters and a son, just like the television family.

DOLE, ROBERT (JOSEPH)

U.S. Senate majority leader, born July 22, 1923, in Russell, Kan. Republican Robert Dole has always known how to twist the knife; he is humorous in a profession often considered humorless and biting in a way that often gets results, although his candor can be abrasive. After taking over as majority leader in January 1985, he began squabbling with numerous GOP leaders in government. Stressing the importance of budget deficit reduction, he fought constantly with Representative Jack F. Kemp of New York, who supported further tax cuts. The majority leader also publicly warned Donald Regan, then the White House chief of staff, to stay away from Capitol Hill, after Regan had criticized Congress—including the GOP-controlled Senate—for failing to act on the budget. After Dole led Republican senators out on a limb to vote for an administration-supported freeze on social security benefits, the White House backed off from the idea—and Dole was incensed. Unfortunately, Dole's complaint that the president was "surrendering to the budget" proved to be ill-timed: it came shortly before Reagan underwent cancer surgery.

Still, Dole and Regan eventually appeared to have settled their dispute, as they posed for the media with a symbolic peace pipe. Despite occasional acrimony, the independent-minded Dole received generally high marks from colleagues for his performance as majority leader, especially for his energetic efforts to promote deficit reduction.

Born into the family of a Kansas businessman, Dole enrolled as a pre-medical student at the University of Kansas before enlisting in the Army. After recovering from serious injuries sustained from machine-gun fire in World War II, he married in 1948 and went on to receive a B.A. in history and a law degree from Washburn Municipal University in Topeka. At 27, he was elected to the Kansas state legislature. He won a seat in the U.S. House of Representatives in 1960, and in 1968 he was elected to the Senate. Dole became chairman of the Republican National Committee in the early 1970's but was forced out by H. R. Haldeman and John Ehrlichman just in time to avoid the stigma of Watergate. In 1976, President Gerald Ford chose Dole as his running mate. After the GOP ticket lost, some observers blamed what they considered Dole's excessive rhetoric as "hatchet man" for the ticket. In any event, he has made little secret of his interest in a possible run for the 1988 Republican presidential nomination.

Dole and his first wife, who have a daughter, divorced in 1972. In 1975 he married Elizabeth Hanford, now U.S. transportation secretary.

EWING, PATRICK ALOYSIUS

Basketball player, born August 5, 1962, in Kingston, Jamaica. Patrick Ewing's formidable basketball skills began to attract attention in 1978 during his sophomore year at Rindge and Latin High School in Cambridge, Mass. A native of Jamaica who had never even seen a basketball before coming to the United States less

Although Senate Majority Leader Robert Dole was generally praised for his energetic performance in his post, the outspoken Kansas Republican found himself publicly at odds with others in his party, principally over the issue of budget deficit reduction.

than four years earlier, he led Rindge to the first of three straight Massachusetts state championships. By his junior year in high school, news of his shot-blocking and defensive skills had become so widespread that he was being hailed as the next Bill Russell, the spectacular Celtic center of the 1950's and 1960's. So it was only appropriate that the 7-foot Ewing chose to attend Georgetown University and play center for another former Celtic center, coach John Thompson.

During his four years at Georgetown (he graduated in May with a degree in fine arts), Ewing averaged more than 15 points a game, but of all his statistics, none is more indicative of his fierce, aggressive style of play than his 493 career blocked shots. With his intimidating, sphinxlike glare, amazing quickness for a big man, leaping ability, and intensity, Ewing led the Hoyas to a four-year record of 121 wins, 23 losses, the 1984 national championship, and two other trips to the NCAA final. He was a three-time all-American. Ewing's college career ended in April on a disappointing note, however, when the top-ranked Hoyas lost the 1985 NCAA championship game, 66-64, in an upset to Villanova.

On May 12 the National Basketball Association conducted its first-ever lottery to determine the first choices in the college draft. It was a foregone conclusion that the team to draw the right to make the first pick would choose Ewing. The New York Knicks won the "Ewing Lottery" and, in September, signed him to a complicated ten-year contract that guaranteed him $17 million for six years and could bring him $30 million.

While in college, Ewing had numerous opportunities to turn professional early and make millions right away. However, he fulfilled his promise to his mother, who died in 1983, to complete his education. Ewing has a son, Patrick, born in 1984 to his high school girlfriend.

GORBACHEV, MIKHAIL S(ERGEEVICH)

General secretary of the Soviet Communist Party, born March 2, 1931, in the village of Privolnoe, in Stavropol territory in southern Russia. After succeeding Konstantin Chernenko as Soviet leader on March 11, Mikhail Gorbachev moved quickly to consolidate his power.

The most powerful player in college basketball became the player most sought after by the NBA. Patrick Ewing, Georgetown's dominant 7-foot center, ultimately signed with the New York Knicks.

In April he added three members to the Politburo, the party's policy-making body, and in July he removed his chief rival. In December he retired a veteran Politburo member from his post as Moscow party leader. Promising economic reforms, Gorbachev took action against corruption, inefficiency, and sloth in the workplace, firing high officials, and clamping down on sales of alcohol.

In foreign affairs, Gorbachev succeeded in gaining favorable attention from many Westerners. He announced a unilateral moratorium on nuclear testing. In October he visited Paris and gave a press conference before Western reporters. He also gave a lengthy interview to *Time* magazine. And in late November he met with U.S. President Ronald Reagan in Geneva. Gorbachev did not succeed in budging Reagan from his plans to proceed with the U.S. missile defense system, popularly known as Star Wars, and the summit did not produce any major agreements. But it appeared to have established a working relationship between the two leaders, besides showing Gorbachev to be virtually as adept a media politician as Reagan.

The son of peasants, Gorbachev studied law at the elite Moscow State University, where he was active in the Young Communist League (Komsomol). Joining the party at 21, he became a party organizer in 1962 and in 1970 first secretary of the Stavropol territorial party committee. In 1978, Gorbachev was selected Central Committee secretary for agriculture of the Soviet Communist Party; the next year he was named a candidate (nonvoting) member of the Politburo, and in October 1980 a full member. At 49, he was 8 years younger than the next youngest member.

After Soviet leader Leonid Brezhnev's death in 1982, Gorbachev rose even faster. He became the Central Committee secretary for personnel (the traditional post of the heir apparent), secretary for planning, and—after the death of Brezhnev's successor, Yuri Andropov—secretary for ideology and relations with foreign Communists. He had such an enormous range of responsibilities—and levers of power—in his hands that he was a natural choice for general secretary when Chernenko (Andropov's successor) died.

Gorbachev was regarded as a strong leader

The Soviet Union got another new leader when Mikhail Gorbachev was named general secretary of the Communist Party in March. He brought a penchant for action, bold new proposals, and considerable personal charm and strength to his role.

and a skilled politician, both on the international scene and at home. However, some authorities believed his power at home was by no means absolute and that he had to contend with opposing factions resistant to his economic policies and his attempts to improve relations with the West.

IACOCCA, LEE (ANTHONY)
Business executive and author, born October 15, 1924, in Allentown, Pa. Lee Iacocca's success at bringing a moribund Chrysler Corporation back into the black has made him an almost legendary figure and given weight to his often blunt comments on business and economics. Chrysler was able to report profits of $2.38 billion for 1984; earlier, the company had lost some $3.5 billion in the near-failure

Chrysler Corporation chairman Lee Iacocca, hailed as a folk philosopher of the business world, became a best-selling author as his autobiography sold more copies than any other hardcover nonfiction book in recent memory.

Iacocca is credited with averting. His life story, *Iacocca: An Autobiography*, was equally successful; published in late 1984, it topped U.S. best-seller lists for several months and was ranked as one of the biggest hardcover best-sellers of all time.

Iacocca's rescue of Chrysler and his celebrity as an author and folk philosopher of the business world have led to talk that he should run for president. His sharp language, however, might pose a problem. Speaking to a group of Democratic politicians in March, for example, he made hypothetical remarks on trade policy to Japan's prime minister that some said were racist and that, in any event, were hardly diplomatic.

The son of Italian immigrants, Iacocca received a bachelor's degree in engineering from Lehigh University in 1945 and a master's from Princeton the next year. Later, after joining Ford as an executive trainee, he decided his real interest was in sales. Finding a job at the company's office in Chester, Pa., he remained

for about ten years. His enormously successful "56 for '56" sales campaign—offering a 1956 Ford for a down payment plus $56 a month for three years—brought him to the attention of Ford headquarters; he rose through the ranks to become president in 1970. Eight years later, Iacocca was fired by chairman Henry Ford II, who apparently saw him as a threat to his own power.

On the day Iacocca went to work for Chrysler in late 1978, the company reported record losses. With the help of drastic belt-tightening measures (including massive layoffs) and controversial federal loan guarantees, he turned things around. Meanwhile, Chrysler television commercials made his face familiar to millions.

Iacocca's wife died of complications of diabetes in 1983. As a tribute to her, he is supporting diabetes research through the Iacocca Foundation, run by his daughter Kathryn. His engagement to Peggy Johnson, an advertising executive, was announced early in 1985.

LANGE, DAVID (RUSSELL)

New Zealand prime minister, born August 4, 1942, in Otahuhu. New Zealand has always felt somewhat isolated from world events because of its geographical position. But under Labor Prime Minister David Lange (pronounced LONG-ee), the country has played an increasingly assertive—and conspicuous—role in world affairs. Since becoming prime minister in July 1984, Lange, a fervently committed Methodist lay preacher and former public defender, has taken on two of New Zealand's closest allies, the United States and France, in controversies involving nuclear weapons.

The problem with the United States came to a head in February, when Lange invoked an election promise and denied a request for a port visit by a U.S. Navy destroyer that might have been carrying nuclear weapons. Washington reacted angrily, but Lange held fast, supported at home by rallies and public opinion polls. He also defended his position during trips abroad—on one occasion debating the Reverend Jerry Falwell, the American fundamentalist, at Oxford University on the proposition that "nuclear weapons are morally indefensible." (Arguing for the affirmative, Lange won the debate by a vote of 298-250.)

The dispute with France grew out of the bombing in Auckland harbor in July of the *Rainbow Warrior,* a ship belonging to the environmental group Greenpeace, which was preparing a major protest against French nuclear testing in the Pacific. The French government at first denied but finally admitted its agents had been involved. When two French agents arrested in connection with the bombing were allowed to plead guilty to reduce charges and avoid a trial, Lange was accused of having made a deal with the French government, but he denied having done so.

Despite the popularity of his foreign policy and his image as a consensus-style leader, Lange had a hard time earning public support for his domestic austerity program. In a parliamentary by-election, Lange's party lost what had long been considered a safe Labor seat. The prime minister called for patience, stating that his government would stick to its basic economic course.

MADONNA

Rock star, born Madonna Louise Ciccone on August 16, 1958, in Bay City, Mich. In only two years, Madonna has had an enormous influence on fashion, has generated widespread controversy on the subject of her lifestyle, and has become practically ubiquitous on television screens and radios across North America and Europe. The queen of the pop music world, she embarked on her first full-fledged tour in the summer, playing to sellout crowds. She also appeared in the featured part of Susan, a funky East Village free spirit, in the movie *Desperately Seeking Susan.*

Madonna was the third child and oldest daughter in a large, religious family. Her mother died when she was six. Madonna attended the University of Michigan on a dance scholarship but left after three semesters for New York City, where she worked for a short time with the Alvin Ailey Dance Theater and with Pearl Lang's modern dance troupe. She also became involved with the burgeoning music scene in Manhattan and was signed to a contract with Sire Records. The record company regarded her as primarily a disco artist; her first record, "Lucky Star," was a mild disco hit. Her second single, "Borderline," picked up enough radio airplay to warrant an album; entitled *Madonna,*

the bouncy collection of dance tunes was released in 1983.

Like most disco stars, Madonna made several videos. These exploited her good looks and odd sense of fashion; she favored layers of junk jewelry, crucifixes, and rosaries worn over a mélange of thrift-shop dresses and lace lingerie. The videos helped make Madonna a runaway success, and her style of dress was copied by young girls across the United States.

Some controversy was ignited around the time *Like a Virgin,* her second album, came out late in 1984. *Rolling Stone* published an article implying that Madonna's success was due as much to her selection of lovers as to her talent. This image was reinforced by the lyrics of her hit single "Material Girl" and by a statement that she was not ashamed of nude

Madonna's album Like a Virgin *was one of the top-selling records of 1985. The flashy queen of the pop music scene enjoyed a sold-out concert tour, garnered enthusiastic reviews for her performance in the film* Desperately Seeking Susan, *and found time to marry actor Sean Penn in August.*

Brian Mulroney's Conservative Party held a formidable majority in the House of Commons, but all did not go well for the Canadian prime minister. Unemployment remained high, he was assailed for political patronage appointments, and his proposal to cut cost-of-living adjustments for pensioners raised a storm of protest.

photographs of her (taken years ago) that appeared in *Playboy* and *Penthouse* in 1985.

On August 16, her 27th birthday, Madonna married actor Sean Penn in Malibu, Calif.

MULRONEY, (MARTIN) BRIAN
Prime minister of Canada, born March 20, 1939, in Baie-Comeau, Québec. The first anniversary celebration of Prime Minister Brian Mulroney's landslide election victory took place September 4 at Ottawa General Hospital, where another cause for celebration—son Daniel Nicolas Dimitri Mulroney—came into the world with impeccable timing. But while Brian Mulroney and his wife, Mila, now had two reasons to commemorate the date, the luster of the prime minister's political success was beginning to dim.

Mulroney's government was assailed for patronage appointments and business deals with Conservative Party supporters, for failing to control Canada's high unemployment, and for proposing cutbacks in cost-of-living adjustments for pensioners—a proposal that he re-

tracted after it raised a storm of protest. The prime minister was embarrassed by revelations that his fisheries minister had authorized the sale of more than a million cans of tainted tuna to preserve jobs at a canning plant; questions were also raised about alleged campaign finance violations by his communications minister (both officials resigned, but the latter was reinstated after an investigation).

Things were calmer earlier in the year, when Mulroney and President Ronald Reagan got together in Québec on March 17–18 for a series of meetings and high-spirited media events soon dubbed the "shamrock summit." The two leaders, accompanied at public events by their wives, happily played up their Irish ancestry, in a warm display of U.S.-Canadian friendship that contrasted with the often icy U.S.-Canadian relationship under Mulroney's predecessor.

Whatever his troubles, Mulroney still had a formidable majority in the House of Commons, with four years to go before he would have to call another election. The economy was expanding. He had also begun making some difficult decisions his critics had accused him of avoiding. In response to Reagan's invitation to join in research for the controversial U.S. Strategic Defense Initiative ("Star Wars"), Mulroney announced that Canadian firms would be free to compete for contracts but that the government itself would not take part. Mulroney also took a controversial step when he decided to negotiate with the United States on more liberal trade agreements.

ORTEGA SAAVEDRA, DANIEL.
Nicaraguan president, born November 11, 1945, in La Libertad. On January 18, 1985, Daniel Ortega Saavedra was inaugurated as his country's president. Ortega had originally come to prominence as a leader in the leftist Sandinista revolution that overthrew dictator Anastasio Somoza Debayle in July 1979. Nominated for president by the ruling Sandinista National Liberation Front, he had faced no significant opposition in the November 1984 election.

Ortega promised to increase the distribution of land to peasants and allow freedom of the press. He also indicated a desire to improve relations with the U.S. government, which strongly opposed the Sandinista regime. The

Nicaraguan leader subsequently announced a moratorium on weapons acquisitions and a withdrawal of some Cuban advisers, but the United States regarded these steps as insignificant, and President Ronald Reagan announced a trade embargo in May. Ortega responded by traveling to Moscow in search of support, but this move angered Reagan administration critics in Congress; as a result, the administration won congressional support for a resumption of funding to antigovernment guerrillas in Nicaragua, though aid was restricted to "nonlethal" supplies.

By autumn, the Sandinista regime appeared somewhat hard pressed by rebel offensives, a deteriorating economy, and mounting internal opposition. Ortega announced a suspension of civil rights and of guarantees protecting those arrested by the government. He subsequently addressed the UN General Assembly, accusing the U.S. government of "state terrorism" in Nicaragua.

Daniel Ortega Saavedra was one of three sons of a merchant (his brother Humberto currently serves as Nicaragua's defense minister; his other brother was killed in a 1978 skirmish with Somoza forces). He became an activist during high school and was arrested at age 15 as an early recruit of an anti-Somoza youth movement. At Central American University, he led protests, was jailed again, and eventually dropped out. In 1967 he was imprisoned for taking part in a bank robbery in which a guard was killed; he was among those freed seven years later when comrades burst into a Managua Christmas party, took hostages, and negotiated a trade. The freed militants were flown to Cuba, where they received military training.

Ortega then turned his attention to urban revolution and gained support from many moderates opposed to Somoza. The Sandinista government originally included under its umbrella a wide range of anti-Somoza groups, but it became increasingly monolithic, while U.S. opposition increased sharply after the inauguration of Ronald Reagan.

PETERSON, DAVID ROBERT

Premier of Ontario, born December 29, 1943, in Toronto. Discounted early in 1985 for a somewhat lackluster political image, Peterson

Sandinista leader Daniel Ortega Saavedra was inaugurated president of Nicaragua in January. Ortega faced strong opposition from the United States and a continuing insurgency.

worked hard to build up his Liberal Party (then in opposition) and campaigned vigorously for the May elections to the Ontario legislature. The Liberals did surprisingly well, sharply cutting into Conservative strength, and by June, Peterson had become the province's first Liberal premier in 42 years.

In February, William Davis had stepped down as Ontario's Progressive Conservative premier after 13 years in power, to be succeeded by Frank Miller. The latter proved less effective than Davis as a campaigner, and his views represented the right wing of the Conservative party. The Conservative cause was further jolted when Anglican Archbishop Lewis Garnsworthy denounced the government's decision to extend, to the last three years of high school, government funding of Roman Catholic schools.

Peterson, meanwhile, successfully built up the Liberals' organization and, in the words of his campaign manager, Ross McGregor, "succeeded in putting an urban face on the party without abandoning the True Grit rural constituency." In the elections on May 2, the

Conservatives won 52 seats (a loss of 20), the Liberals 48, and the New Democratic Party 25. Peterson reached an informal "gentleman's agreement" with the NDP, and he defeated the government with a parliamentary no-confidence vote on June 4. The lieutenant governor then called on Peterson to form a new government, which he was able to do with NDP support.

Sworn in on June 26, Peterson promised to provide full funding of Roman Catholic secondary schools, and he vowed that he would begin negotiations to end extra-billing by doctors under the medicare system. He later made

David Peterson, the leader of Ontario's Liberal Party—shown savoring election night returns with his wife and son—became the province's first Liberal premier in 42 years.

headlines by opposing a Canadian free-trade arrangement with the United States that other provincial premiers supported.

Peterson obtained a bachelor's degree in philosophy and political science and a law degree, but he never practiced law. Instead, he took over his father's electronics firm in London, Ont. Elected to the provincial legislature in 1975 and again in 1977 and 1981, he was chosen as leader of Ontario's Liberals in 1982. He has described his marriage, to actress Shelley Matthews, as "unmitigated bliss"; the couple have three children.

REAGAN, NANCY (DAVIS)

U.S. first lady, wife of President Ronald Reagan, born Anne Francis Robbins on July 6 in 1923 (according to official sources) or 1921 (according to school records), in New York City. At the beginning of her husband's presidency, she was derided by some critics as "Fancy Nancy," preoccupied with a lavish wardrobe, new (and expensive) White House china, and social prominence. That began to change as she stepped up her antidrug campaign and also showed the Washington press corps she could laugh at herself. By 1985, Nancy Reagan's press was almost all positive. She sponsored an antidrug conference attended by wives of heads of state or government from around the world, and she represented the White House on a visit to Mexico City after the disastrous earthquake there. Press accounts described her influence on her husband as substantial, especially in personnel matters.

This year also had its difficulties. The president's surgery for colon cancer in July was a great worry. But during his hospitalization she showed strength by proceeding with her schedule of public appearances; she also took on the role of presidential gatekeeper, determining who could and who could not see the president.

Shortly after Nancy Reagan's birth, her mother, actress Edith Luckett, was divorced from her father, car salesman Kenneth Robbins, and for several years Nancy lived with her aunt and uncle while her mother toured in stage productions. In 1929, Edith married Loyal Davis, a prominent Chicago surgeon; Nancy took his last name at age 14 and thereafter considered him as her father. (He died in 1982.) His

Nancy Reagan, once criticized as being concerned only with a lavish wardrobe and high society, successfully shed her negative public image. The first lady worked diligently in fighting drug abuse and showed considerable strength during her husband's hospitalization for cancer surgery.

Donald Regan became President Ronald Reagan's top aide early this year when he left his post as treasury secretary to take the job of White House chief of staff. The second most powerful man in U.S. government was criticized by some for his high profile and tough, no-nonsense approach.

conservative political views are thought to have influenced her and, later, possibly her husband.

After graduating from Smith College, Nancy became an actress, first on Broadway, then in Hollywood. She made 11 movies but gave up her career for a family. She and Ronald Reagan, then divorced, met in 1951 and were married in March 1952, about 12 years before he launched his political career. The president and his wife have a daughter, Patricia, born in 1952, and a son, Ronald, born in 1958.

REGAN, DONALD THOMAS

White House chief of staff, born December 21, 1918, in Cambridge, Mass. A Marine hero, Wall Street millionaire, and treasury secretary in the first Reagan administration, Regan emerged in 1985 as probably the second most powerful individual in the U.S. government. After swapping jobs in January with White House Chief of Staff James Baker, who shifted to treasury secretary, Regan quickly solidified his control. A troika had dominated the White House staff in the first term, but Regan saw to it that all lines of authority flowed through him alone.

A tough, no-nonsense manager, Regan ran the staff the way he once ran the Wall Street firm Merrill Lynch. But his real authority stemmed from his close relationship with the president, with whom he met several times each working day. Instead of having the passion for anonymity that characterizes many advisers, the chief of staff delights in his power. When Reagan was hospitalized for surgery in July some believed that Regan, who set up an office at the hospital, assumed too high a profile.

Several members of Congress and some White House aides argued that the chief of staff was too much of a yes-man to the president and that his staff was better suited to the boardroom than to the politically sensitive White House. Regan received some blame for the president's controversial visit to a German military cemetery containing S.S. graves and for the decision to disown Republican lawmakers' efforts to freeze social security benefits. The departure of Secretary of Health and Human Services Margaret Heckler was attributed to a feud between her and Regan. For months rumors also persisted that Regan got along badly with Robert McFarlane, the president's national security adviser, and McFarlane also resigned.

321

The record books were rewritten on September 11 when Cincinnati Reds player-manager Pete Rose got the 4,192nd base hit of his career, becoming the most prolific hitter in baseball history. Rose broke the record of 4,191 hits held since 1928 by the legendary Ty Cobb.

prolific hitter in baseball history. In 1985, Rose—now the player/manager of the Cincinnati Reds—added new luster to an already brilliant career by breaking, at the age of 44, a record that had stood for more than half a century. On September 11 at Riverfront Stadium in Cincinnati, just 10 miles from where he had played sandlot baseball as a boy, Rose got the 4,192nd hit of his major league career, surpassing the mark of 4,191 set by Ty Cobb in 1928. It was the crowning moment of an illustrious career.

The fact that Cobb required significantly fewer games and at-bats to establish his hitting record (and had a lifetime batting average of .367 compared with Rose's .304) led some people to question the magnitude of Rose's accomplishment. But Rose holds 34 other major or National League records. He has the most seasons—ten—with 200 or more hits, and he has played in more games—and more winning games—than anyone else. In 1978 he hit safely in 44 straight games, the second-longest batting streak in baseball history and the longest in modern NL history. Rose has led the NL in hitting three times, and he was selected the NL's Most Valuable Player in 1973. He has also been on three World Series winners and has played in 16 All-Star games.

Rose came up to the majors in 1963, when he was named Rookie of the Year. He played with the Reds through 1978, then became a free agent and signed on with the Phillies. They let him go after the 1983 season. He joined the Montreal Expos, but in August 1984 they traded him back home to Cincinnati, where he took up the managerial reins as well. In 1985 he guided the Reds to a much-improved second-place finish in the NL West; he was rewarded with a $2.5 million, three-year contract. Rose, who was divorced in 1980, remarried in 1984.

The son of working-class parents, Regan graduated from Harvard and then served in the Marine Corps during World War II. Joining Merrill Lynch in 1946, he rose through the ranks to become chairman in 1971. A bold innovator, Regan, in one move, eliminated brokers' fixed-rate commissions on the sale of securities, as a means of stimulating competition. As treasury secretary from 1981, Regan was criticized for his optimistic economic projections—but many of them came true.

ROSE, PETE(R) (EDWARD)

Baseball player/manager, born April 14, 1941, in Cincinnati. Fans know Pete Rose as Charlie Hustle, the man who runs to first base after a walk and dives head first into bases even when there is no chance of his being tagged out. Opposing pitchers know him as one of the smartest, most capable players ever to wield a bat. And everyone knows him now as the most

THATCHER, MARGARET (HILDA ROBERTS)

Prime minister of Great Britain, born October 13, 1925, in Grantham, England. In 1985, Margaret Thatcher celebrated her tenth year as leader of the Conservative Party and her sixth as prime minister. According to public opinion polls, however, her personal approval rating, as well as that of the Conservative Party, had suffered some decline, largely because of Britain's continuing unemployment—over 3.3 million people, or 14 percent of the labor force. To help reverse the downward trend in the polls, Thatcher in September appointed Norman Tebbit, a close adviser, as chairman of the Conservative Party and Jeffrey Archer, a novelist, as vice-chairman. They had the task of refurbishing her government's image.

Early in the year the prime minister suffered an embarrassing rebuff when a panel of dons at her alma mater, Oxford University, angered by her steep budget cuts in education and research, voted to deny Thatcher an honorary degree. She reacted with aplomb: "If they do not wish to confer the honor," said she, "I am the last person who would wish to receive it."

The prime minister, however, could also point to several triumphs. At home, the country's longest and most violent labor dispute in recent years ended in March when the National Union of Mineworkers ordered those of its members still on strike to return to work, without having gained the concessions demanded from the government. In foreign affairs, Thatcher and Irish Prime Minister Garret FitzGerald in November signed a historic treaty on Northern Ireland that gave the Irish Republic a formal consultative role in that troubled province's affairs. The treaty was hailed by some as a framework for peace.

Earlier, in February, Thatcher visited the United States, where she addressed a joint session of Congress and took the opportunity to reinforce her close ties with President Ronald Reagan. In December, Great Britain became the first nation to sign an agreement with the United States on participation in the controversial U.S. Strategic Defense Initiative ("Star Wars").　　　　J.A., S.L.D., & S.M.G.

PERSIAN GULF STATES. The glut of oil on the world market in 1985 continued to depress the economies of the small oil-exporting states of the Persian Gulf region—Bahrain, Oman, Qatar, and the United Arab Emirates.

Oman suffered less than the other nations. The risk of attacks on tankers because of the Iran-Iraq war increased insurance rates for such vessels traveling into the Persian Gulf; the result was a significant savings for buyers purchasing from Oman's terminal, which is located outside the Persian Gulf, in the Gulf of Oman. Furthermore, Oman never became a member of the Organization of Petroleum Exporting Countries and thus was not constrained by OPEC production ceilings. The most pro-Western of the Gulf states, Oman continued to receive United States aid for the construction of military facilities. At the same time, Oman moved to establish diplomatic relations with the Soviet Union.

Qatar, which receives 90 percent of its revenues from oil exports, has seen its oil income halved since 1981. Qatar nevertheless continued to provide subsidies for its citizens for basic services and products. Bahrain was also experiencing a decline in oil income. In an attempt to offset a projected budget deficit of almost $17 million, the government announced in early April that ministries had been instructed to reduce operating expenditures by at least 5 percent.

The economy of the United Arab Emirates, like Qatar an OPEC member, suffered from oil price and production cuts. Nevertheless, two major projects were under way—construction of a liquefied natural gas plant and the creation of a grid to feed natural gas from the Sajaa field to the northern emirates.

See STATISTICS OF THE WORLD. *See also* KUWAIT.　　　　　　　　　　　L.A.K.

PERU. The election of Alan García Pérez as president in 1985 and his vigorous moves to deal with the country's problems brought an air of optimism to Peru. In balloting on April 14, García, candidate of the center-left American Popular Revolutionary Alliance (APRA), amassed 46 percent of the vote, far outstripping the three other major candidates. The next-closest candidate, representing a coalition of Marxist groups, won 21 percent and pulled out of a scheduled runoff election, which was then declared unnecessary. APRA also gained a substantial majority in elections for both chambers of Parliament.

García, in his July inaugural address, called for an end to the regional arms buildup, and he promptly instituted an emergency program to rescue Peru's battered economy. Controls on prices and imports, along with banking and currency reforms, brought a reduction in the inflation rate. García also halved an order for French-built fighter planes and placed a cap

323

on the salaries of government officials. His administration launched a reform of the corrupt judicial system, fired high police officials, and indicted several officials of the outgoing administration for drug trafficking, besides launching U.S.-financed raids on cocaine-processing centers. In December, Peru nationalized the U.S.-based Belco Petroleum Corporation following the company's refusal to accept new conditions for production and exploration. The government had also threatened to nationalize two other foreign-based operations but reached agreements with them instead.

García's initiatives raised morale in a country where living standards had plummeted and population growth continued to outpace any growth in industry and agriculture. About 60 percent of the nation's industrial capacity was idle, and well over half the labor force were unemployed or underemployed. To end strikes by the country's hard-pressed workers, the new government negotiated a "social truce" with organized labor. Most troublesome was the foreign debt of $14 billion, equivalent to a staggering 85 percent of gross national product.

With Peru in arrears even of interest payments on the debt, García announced his government would limit repayments to 10 percent of the nation's export earnings and would negotiate directly with creditors, ignoring earlier financial agreements with the International Monetary Fund.

The war between the government and the Maoist Sendero Luminoso (Shining Path) terrorists concluded its fifth year, having taken more than 6,000 lives. Sendero Luminoso greeted the new regime with a series of car bombings. García vowed to combat terrorism, but with safeguards to protect individual rights, and he created a Peace Commission to investigate possibilities for "dialogue" with the extreme left.

See STATISTICS OF THE WORLD.   D.W.

PETROLEUM AND NATURAL GAS. *See* ENERGY; ORGANIZATION OF PETROLEUM EXPORTING COUNTRIES.

PETS. According to figures released early in 1985, the cocker spaniel was pulling ahead of the poodle in popularity; they had been running almost neck and neck previously, as the two

Outspoken New Leader
Exuding self-confidence, 36-year-old Alan García Pérez assumed office on July 28 as president of Peru—becoming the youngest chief executive in Latin America. He gained prompt international attention when he announced that Peru would limit its debt repayment to 10 percent of its export earnings. At home, after only a short time in office, García was credited with pulling his nation out of a mood of despair engendered by a crippled economy, official corruption, widespread terrorism, and drug dealing. Besides taking first steps to deal with such problems, he adopted a populist style of governing and on many occasions made impromptu appearances on a balcony of the presidential palace, exchanging words with crowds below.

García was virtually born into the center-left American Popular Revolutionary Alliance (APRA). Both his parents were APRA activists, and after studying law and politics, he became a party functionary himself, rising to secretary-general in 1982 as part of a new generation of leadership in the party.

Alan García Pérez

Ch. Braeburn's Close Encounter, a Scottish terrier, was named Best in Show at the Westminster Kennel Club show in February in New York City.

breeds with the largest number of puppies registered with the American Kennel Club. The breeds that showed the greatest growth in popularity among the 25 most popular breeds were the Rottweiler, with a 30 percent increase in one year, and the chow chow, with an 18 percent increase. The Best in Show winner at the Westminster Kennel Club show in February was a Scottish terrier bitch, Ch. Braeburn's Close Encounter.

A New York State law effective in November made it illegal to sell pet birds that were not bred in captivity, regardless of whether the bird species being sold were endangered in the wild. The legislation has caused bitter conflicts between bird fanciers in the pet field and bird lovers among conservationists.

Reptile fanciers won one of the few legal skirmishes that have gone their way in recent years when a municipal judge in Tulsa, Okla., ruled in agreement with a snake owner that his king snakes and ball python were indeed pets, not "wild or dangerous" animals that Tulsa law proscribes within the city limits. Another reptile, however, was singled out for censure by the *Journal of the American Medical Association*, which reported that the millions of baby turtles shipped overseas from the United States each year as pets are all potential carriers of salmonellosis.

Helene Thiefenthaler of Billings, Mont., became $50,000 richer when her mixed-breed cat K.C. was chosen as possessor of the "Uni-versal Meow" in a contest sponsored by a cat food manufacturer. The panel of judges chose K.C.'s meow over those of other contestants partly because it possessed a "measure of intergalactic resonance"—a requirement for a cat chosen to communicate with the makers of "meow-like" sounds detected by the instruments of radio astronomy.

Still popular for its fur, the chinchilla also became much more widely available as a pet during 1985. The South American rodent is now available in a number of colors different from those of the wild stock first imported into the United States in 1923.   N.P.

WDOG-TV, The All-Dog Network

A dog's life has never been anything to boast about. But now, thanks to Kartes Video Communications Inc., of Indianapolis, your favorite pooch can while away a fulfilling half hour in front of the television set anytime you want. *Arf!*, a video for dogs, features all-canine actors and a soundtrack of barks, with English subtitles for the human eavesdropper, and sells for about $10. Programs include the *Duke Tough and the Newshound Update*, which reports on "our dog-eat-dog world"; *Recipes to Lick Your Chops Over*, starring Julia Chow; and *Fitness with Fifi*, who admonishes her charges to "roll over" and "get those tails in shape."

PHILIPPINES

PHILIPPINES. Political conflict dominated the news in the Philippines in 1985.

Under growing pressure from the United States, President Ferdinand Marcos announced in November that special presidential elections would be held in early 1986; Marcos's term is not up until 1987. His chief opponent was Corazón C. Aquino, widow of opposition leader Benigno S. Aquino, Jr., who was assassinated at Manila International Airport in August 1983; her running mate was her chief political rival, Salvador H. Laurel, a former senator. Their agreement on a unified ticket came after earlier attempts to avoid a splintered opposition had failed. Marcos named Arturo M. Tolentino as his vice-presidential candidate; Tolentino had been dismissed as foreign minister in March. In December the Philippines Supreme Court ruled that the election, scheduled for February 7, should be held even though there were doubts about whether it was constitutional;

Marcos, in announcing the election, had not officially yielded the office of president, as required by law.

On December 2, 1985, the trial of 25 military men and 1 civilian for involvement or complicity in Aquino's murder officially ended after more than nine months, with the announced acquittal of all 26 defendants. Among those tried was General Fabian C. Ver, armed forces chief of staff and a cousin and confidant of President Marcos. During the trial, two witnesses testified they had seen a soldier shoot Aquino as he left the plane returning him from self-imposed exile in the United States; this contradicted the government contention that Aquino had been murdered by Rolando Galman, a gunman allegedly hired by Communists, who himself was shot and killed at the scene. One of the witnesses later recanted his testimony. Some prospective witnesses for the prosecution disappeared, while others reported

Students marching on the palace of Philippine President Ferdinand Marcos on his 68th birthday were stopped by a barricade two blocks away; the protesters set fire to a coffin draped with a banner which read, "This is the students' gift to the dictator . . ."

threats from military personnel. The verdict, which was widely criticized, contradicted unanimous findings in 1984 by a commission headed by former court of appeals justice Corazón Agrava. Incriminating testimony before that commission was ruled inadmissible in the trial. After the verdict was announced, General Ver, on a leave of absence during the trial, was reinstated.

There were sporadic demonstrations against Marcos's rule. On September 20, eve of the 13th anniversary of his declaration of martial law, which was lifted in 1981, security forces in Escalante, Negros Island, opened fire on a protest march, with many fatalities. The next day, demonstrations in several cities attracted more than 80,000 protesters, and in October, 13 soldiers and militiamen were suspended from duty while an investigation into the Escalante incident continued.

The government appeared to be losing effective control of more of the countryside to the Communist-dominated New People's Army. The NPA gained increasing support because of alleged abuses by undisciplined military troops, local paramilitary forces, and right-wing death squads.

Low sugar prices in world markets and an anticipated continuing decline in the gross national product highlighted the Philippines' economic woes. A major financial rescue package was signed with foreign bank creditors on May 20; it included new loans and trade credits and steps to reschedule over $10 billion in debt. There were reports in the U.S. press that government officials had illegally diverted billions of dollars abroad. Although President Marcos and his wife, Imelda, were allegedly among those involved, the president appointed a commission to investigate. By its estimates, over $3 billion left the country illegally in 1983 and 1984.

Economic and political conditions in the Philippines remained a major concern to the United States, which has vital strategic posts there. A measure signed by President Ronald Reagan authorized $70 million in military aid to the Philippine government but restricted its use to nonlethal supplies. Economic aid was increased slightly, to $110 million.

See STATISTICS OF THE WORLD.   L.R.

André Kertész, who died in September at the age of 91, used his camera with wit and exuberance, as in "Satiric Dancer." A major retrospective of his work was shown in Chicago and New York.

PHOTOGRAPHY. The most ambitious program ever to be devoted to one single photographer was "The Work of Atget," a four-part series on Eugène Atget; it concluded at New York's Museum of Modern Art (MOMA) in March 1985 with Part III, "The Ancien Régime," and Part IV, "Modern Times." "The Ancien Régime" featured 120 park and chateaux pictures from Versailles, St. Cloud, and Sceaux—some of Atget's most lyrical and beautiful work. "Modern Times" included 117 photographs of such familiar facets of Atget's Paris as window displays, street scenes, prostitutes, and cafés.
Other Major Exhibits. "André Kertész: Of Paris and New York," the first in-depth critical examination of this major photographer's work, appeared at the Art Institute of Chicago in May and opened at the Metropolitan Museum of Art in New York in December. The show was a reconsideration of Kertész's years in Paris (1925–1936) and his first two decades in New York (1936–1954), including many images never seen publicly before. Kertész—who was one of the century's most original photogra-

PHOTOGRAPHY

phers and pioneered in the use of hand-held cameras—died in New York on September 27, at age 91.

"Bill Brandt: Behind the Camera, 1928–1983," a 140-work retrospective of the career of Great Britain's preeminent modern photographer, was organized by the Victoria and Albert Museum in London and came to the Philadelphia Museum of Art in late summer. The exhibition dramatically revised knowledge of Brandt's career. The original prints in this show revealed that the early social "documentary" pictures of the 1930's often had been retouched and were setups rather than candid shots; in this sense, the documentary images seemed almost as surreal as the nudes, landscapes, and portraits of his later career.

For its 50th anniversary, the San Francisco Museum of Modern Art created three exhibitions from its own collection: "Signs of the Times: Some Recurring Motifs in 20th-Century Photography," "Extending the Perimeters of 20th-Century Photography," and (scheduled for 1986 showing) "Facets of Modernism." Another important show was "Images of Ex-

cellence," a selection of photographs from the history of photography, drawn from the archives of the International Museum of Photography and exhibited at the IBM Gallery of Science and Art in New York City.

Major retrospectives of two photojournalists—Robert Capa and W. Eugene Smith—were mounted in the fall. The Capa exhibition, at the International Center of Photography in New York, confirmed his status as the preeminent war photographer of the mid-20th century. "W. Eugene Smith: Let Truth Be the Prejudice," at the Philadelphia Museum of Art, covered the full range of Smith's brilliant achievement, in 250 prints, including some of his most famous photographs from Life, Look, and Collier's.

"In the American West," at the Amon Carter Museum in Fort Worth, Texas, exhibited 109 portraits of ordinary people from 17 Western states, taken by fashion photographer Richard Avedon during five consecutive summers. "New Photography," at MOMA, displayed pictures by four little-known artists, each of whom worked in a different style representing one

Henry Peach Robinson's "Fading Away," a 19th-century photograph, was among the images featured in "Images of Excellence," a show culled from the renowned archives of the International Museum of Photography in Rochester. N.Y.

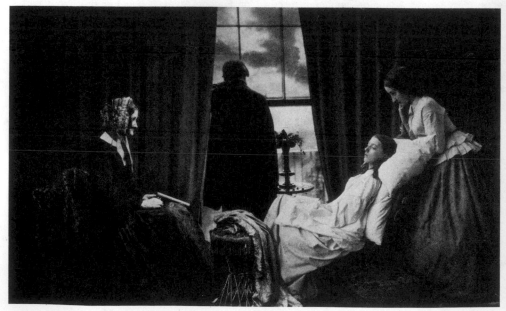

particular tendency in contemporary photography.

Eastman House Archives. Efforts to keep the renowned collections of the International Museum of Photography at Rochester's George Eastman House in New York State received a boost when the Eastman Kodak Company offered proceeds from the sale of an office building to endow the care and preservation of the archives if the trustees create a permanent home for them in Rochester by 1989. The museum had neared bankruptcy in 1984. The trustees voted to try to raise $10.5 million for construction of a new building to store the collection.

Art Market. New York's Pace-MacGill Gallery sold Paul Strand's *Wall Street* to the Canadian Center for Architecture for $170,000, a record for any photograph. This extraordinary platinum print, made by Strand for a childhood friend, is one of only two prints of his most important image. In another record-setting transaction, Malcolm Forbes, Jr., paid $104,500 at a Sotheby Parke Bernet auction for an 1864 photograph of Abraham Lincoln and his son Tad. The picture's mount bore an autograph by Lincoln, and there was debate as to whether the high price—the highest yet paid for an auctioned photograph—was for the photograph or the autograph.

Technology. Minolta introduced the Maxxum, the first production-line auto-focusing single-lens reflex camera with electronically operated interchangeable lenses. The standard Maxxum 7000 went on the market in March, with a professional-level model, the Maxxum 9000, following in October.   B.B.S.

PHYSICS. Much attention was focused in 1985 on a new theory that suggests a ten-dimensional universe. The year also saw the world's largest atom smasher go into operation.

Ten-Dimensional Universe? Physicists have long believed that the most elementary constituents of matter are "point" particles that do not occupy any volume in space. While such particles may have such properties as mass and electrical charge, they would not have a length, width, or height. Considerable discussion, however, surrounded a new theory that has increasingly captured the fancy of theoretical physicists. It conjectures that the most

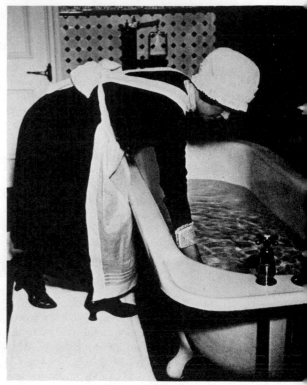

Photographer Bill Brandt, whose work was on exhibit this year in Philadelphia, used sharp contrasts to present his view of British life, as in "Parlormaid Preparing a Bath Before Dinner."

elementary particles—the quarks (which combine to make protons, neutrons, mesons, and the like) and the leptons (such as electrons and neutrinos)—are not points but entities having a single dimension, length. Not only do the particles become miniature strings in this theory, but the universe they inhabit is no longer the familiar four-dimensional one, but a ten-dimensional object.

How could something so contrary to everyday experience be true? Compactification is part of the answer. In this little-understood process, the six dimensions we do not experience get curled up to such a small size that they are not experimentally detectable. Although not a result of the compactification process, the length of a string representing an elementary particle is also very short, 10^{-32} centimeter, another undetectably small distance.

Bizarre as it all sounds, the superstring approach could evolve into a unified theory explaining all the forces of nature—a theory uniting in a single mathematical framework gravity, electromagnetism, and the two nuclear forces called strong and weak (which show up in the behavior of atomic nuclei and their components). Past attempts by physicists to construct such a unified quantum field theory were based on pointlike particles and were plagued with problems. So far, the superstring theory appears to be the best hope for overcoming these obstacles.

Local Lorentz Invariance. Physicists require that any physical law be independent of the velocity of the frame of reference in which measurements are done. This principle, called local Lorentz invariance, is part of the more general Einstein equivalence principle, which says that physical laws are the same at all times and everywhere. The validity of the equivalence principle cannot be proved, but it would be difficult to construct useful models of the universe, such as the superstring theory, without it. Scientists have been able to carry out experiments establishing limits on the magnitude of any possible violation of local Lorentz invariance. In 1985 experiments setting tighter limits than ever on how large the violations could be were reported by John Prestage and colleagues at the Boulder, Colo., laboratories of the U.S. National Bureau of Standards and by Frederick Raab, Blayne Heckel, and co-workers at the University of Washington.

Local Lorentz equivalence could be violated if not all frames of reference are equivalent—that is, if there exists some "preferred" frame of reference in the universe. The idea behind the NBS and Washington experiments was that if there is such a preferred frame of reference, the frequency (or wavelength) of light absorbed or emitted by an atom might depend on the orientation of the atom relative to its motion through that frame of reference. (Atoms of an element absorb or emit only light of certain frequencies.) If a change in frequency were observed, this would mean that the laws of electromagnetism that govern light depend on the motion of the atoms with respect to the preferred frame of reference—which would be a violation of local Lorentz invariance.

In any case, atoms can be oriented with respect to an applied magnetic field by the absorption of light from a laser or other high-intensity light source. Since the atoms are in a fixed orientation to the magnetic field, as the earth rotates (carrying the magnetic field and the collection of atoms with it), the orientation of the atoms with respect to the putative preferred frame of reference changes. The recent tests consisted in searching for changes in frequency over a 24-hour day. The NBS and Washington groups used somewhat different techniques in testing for frequency shifts, but the results were the same: no measurable shift was found.

Atom Smashers. The world's largest atom collider was activated in October at the Fermi National Laboratory in Batavia, Ill. Atom smashers, or particle accelerators, accelerate subatomic particles to a speed close to that of light and smash them together; the resulting debris helps scientists study the building blocks of nature. The new smasher, measuring 4 miles in circumference and using superconducting magnets, was also equipped with an antimatter beam, permitting the collision of matter and antimatter. Such collisions could prove useful in medicine, energy production, and the construction of powerful new bombs. Meanwhile, scientists were planning a still larger accelerator, to contain more than 6,000 superconducting magnets. The U.S. effort, dubbed the Superconducting Super Collider, if approved by Congress, would cost up to $6 billion, with completion anticipated in the 1990's. A.L.R.

POLAND. In 1985 the standard of living continued to decline in Poland, political rights remained unrecognized, and the Roman Catholic Church came under serious attack from the regime. Late in the year, General Wojciech Jaruzelski resigned as head of government but remained as party secretary.

New Prime Minister and Cabinet. In early November, General Jaruzelski stepped down as prime minister. He retained the more important post of first secretary of the ruling Polish United Workers (Communist) Party and remained head of state. Zbigniew Messner, an economics professor, was named as the new prime minister. According to observers, General Jaruzelski took the step in order to focus his attention on revitalizing the party, which had lost up to one-third of its membership during the rise of the independent (ultimately outlawed) Solidarity labor movement in 1980 and 1981. The new prime minister outlined a program directed at combating the country's economic ills—in particular, a high foreign debt, declining productivity, and an unbalanced internal market. Messner's cabinet contained a number of economists; at the same time, it retained generals in the most sensitive ministries, including those of defense and interior. A significant change was the removal of hard-liner Stefan Olszowski as foreign minister.

Church and State. The year was one of growing confrontation between the Catholic Church and the Communist Party. Communist authorities attacked the church for, in the words of the major party monthly, "letting its institutions be used as an organized base for activities by antisocialist forces." Pope John Paul II's social teachings were criticized in *Polityka*, the most important Polish political weekly.

Four state security policemen involved in the October 1984 murder of Father Jerzy Popieluszko (a popular supporter of Solidarity) were tried, found guilty, and sentenced in February to 14 to 25 years in prison. However, many Poles were disappointed because no senior officials had been implicated. During the unprecedented public trial the government sought to discredit Popieluszko and the church for having supported antigovernment activity.

Internal Affairs. Although "Underground Solidarity" continued to find it difficult to organize mass resistance against the government, major demonstrations were carried out in several cities on May 1 in opposition to official May Day celebrations. Meanwhile, the government stepped up its campaign of intimidation aimed at isolating Solidarity from the outside world; a number of Western visitors sympathetic to the opposition were harassed. Laws approved by the Sejm (Parliament) in May empowered the security forces to arrest anyone participating in independent gatherings or engaging in certain protest actions. And in July, despite national protests, the Sejm approved legislation to curtail academic freedoms won in 1981 and to bring Polish universities under stronger government control.

Economic Stagnation. Prices of consumer goods continued to rise more rapidly than real income; in March the government increased the cost of ten staple food items, including bread

The unprecedented open trial of four state security police (among them Grzegorz Piotrowski, shown here) accused of involvement in the 1984 murder of pro-Solidarity priest Father Jerzy Popieluszko was concluded in February. All four defendants were convicted and sentenced to long prison terms.

and cheese, by an average of more than 35 percent; on July 1 meat prices were raised an average of 10 percent. The housing situation, always desperate in Poland, was deteriorating steadily. A positive note in the economic picture was Poland's ability to renegotiate the terms of its debt. By late 1985 its total foreign debt, mostly to the West, stood at $28 billion. In January 1985 agreement was reached with 17 countries allowing Poland to spread its payments of principal and interest due between 1982 and 1984 over an 11-year period. A formal accord was signed in July.

Foreign Relations. Jaruzelski met with Mikhail Gorbachev, the new Soviet leader, in Warsaw in April, climaxing a month-long national celebration of Soviet culture. He also visited President François Mitterrand—the first such meeting in a Western capital with a Western head of state since martial law was imposed in 1981—and met with former West German Chancellor Willy Brandt in Warsaw. The French and German public voiced opposition to such meetings.

See STATISTICS OF THE WORLD.   R.E.K.

PORTUGAL. The Socialist Party of Prime Minister Mário Soares was defeated in October 1985 general elections in Portugal, and Anibal Cavaco Silva, leader of the Social Democrats, became the new prime minister. Earlier in the year, Portugal finally won agreement on a treaty providing for its admission into the European Community.

Elections. The Social Democratic Party (PSD) won a clear plurality, but far less than a majority, in the October 6 parliamentary elections. Led by Cavaco Silva, it received 30 percent of the vote, to about 20 percent for the Socialists. Soares had not led the Socialists in the campaign, since he planned to seek the presidency in 1986; António Almeida Santos was the Socialists' candidate for prime minister. The Democratic Renewal Party placed third with 18 percent of the vote; the Christian Democrats finished fourth. Following the election, Cavaco Silva, a professor of economics at Catholic University in Lisbon and a former finance minister, failed in his early efforts to form a coalition government. On November 6 he was sworn in as head of a minority government.

European Community Membership. On June 12, Portugal and Spain signed a treaty admitting them as the 11th and 12th members of the European Community, effective January 1, 1986. The event followed more than six years of negotiations, culminating in late March with an agreement on the terms of entry. The last roadblocks were overcome when Greece withdrew its threat to veto the treaty. The treaty was ratified by the parliaments of all existing EC members plus Spain and Portugal, as expected. On July 11, Portugal's Parliament approved entry by a wide margin, with Communist members dissenting. Adoption of the treaty was a personal triumph for Soares, who called it "one of the most significant events of contemporary Portuguese history."

Preelection Crisis. The day after the treaty was signed, the PSD formally withdrew from its two-year-old ruling coalition with the Socialists. Soares himself resigned in the wake of the PSD withdrawal, but he was induced to stay on until elections. The coalition had been divided by economic differences, with the PSD criticizing the Socialists for being too slow to make agrarian and labor reforms. Communist-led unions, at the same time, had organized national strikes protesting the government's austerity program and demanding its resignation. The Portuguese government was also plagued by a series of terrorist incidents, mostly directed against NATO activities, and in January a law was passed allowing for a declaration of a state of emergency under certain circumstances.

Foreign Relations. U.S. President Ronald Reagan visited Portugal in May and addressed the Parliament. During the speech 35 Communist members walked out in protest over U.S. foreign policy. Following the walkout, a member of the pacifist Green Party placed a caged white dove on his seat before leaving the chamber; the bird was removed when conservative members threatened to leave in protest against its presence.

President António Ramalho Eanes visited China in May and met with Premier Zhao Ziyang. Eanes said talks would begin in 1986 on return of the Portuguese-administered territory of Macao to Peking.

See also STATISTICS OF THE WORLD.   J.O.S.

PRESIDENT OF THE UNITED STATES. Ronald Wilson Reagan, 40th president of the United States, was born February 6, 1911, in Tampico, Ill. "In my 50 years in public life I've never seen a man more popular with the American people." This tribute to Reagan came from a political opponent, House Speaker Thomas P. ("Tip") O'Neill, Jr. (D, Mass.), on the eve of the president's inauguration to a second term in January 1985. Public opinion polls confirmed his continuing popularity, although he encountered controversy and was often impeded in Congress, sometimes by rebellious members of his own party. In July the 74-year-old president underwent apparently successful surgery for removal of a cancerous growth in his colon.

Economy. While inflation was running under 4 percent, growth in the gross national product was not nearly as great as in 1984, and the nation's mounting trade imbalance was cause for serious concern. Facing a projected trade deficit of close to $150 billion in 1985, the administration struggled to avert a major trade war, as hundreds of protectionist bills were introduced in Congress. One of them cleared Congress, to be vetoed to the president, who called protectionism a "one-way trip to economic disaster." Farm debt was also an acute problem. Reagan drew strong opposition from farmers, and from lawmakers of both parties in farm states, when he vetoed emergency aid legislation for farmers early in the year. In December he reluctantly signed an expensive farm aid bill, along with a measure to help bail out the Farm Credit System.

The soaring federal budget deficit was perhaps the biggest economic embarrassment. Late in the year, Reagan somewhat quietly signed a measure requiring specified annual deficit reductions leading to a balanced budget by 1991. The proposal gave the president authority to invoke automatic spending cuts if he and Congress could not agree on a plan to keep within the deficit ceilings set by the proposal. But it meant the president would probably have to accept tax increases or military spending cuts to keep the deficit down.

In May, Reagan proposed a sweeping overhaul of the tax code; he said his "second American revolution" would simplify the code and shift more of the tax burden from individ-

Ronald Reagan began his second term as president of the United States in January; here he enjoys a dance with wife Nancy at inaugural festivities in Washington, D.C.

uals to corporations, but despite frequent road trips to campaign for the plan, Reagan had difficulty maintaining momentum for it. Late in the year, the U.S. House approved a tax revision measure that differed significantly from the president's proposal. Reagan supported it in the hopes that its passage by the House would keep tax reform alive for Senate consideration, but House Republicans rebelled against the bill. Reagan had to go to Capitol Hill to plead with members of his own party in order to whip up enough GOP support to persuade House Speaker O'Neill to bring the matter to the floor for a vote. In the end he succeeded in getting 49 Republicans to back the bill in the House, which approved it late in the year.

Foreign Relations. In March, after a long walkout, the Soviets returned to arms limitation talks in Geneva, and the vigorous new Soviet leader, Mikhail Gorbachev, later agreed to meet with Reagan in Geneva. At the long-awaited summit, in mid-November, Reagan refused to scrap his Strategic Defense Initiative, or "Star Wars," program, a key sticking point, and no agreement on arms control was reached. However, the two leaders had the opportunity to exchange views and perceptions at great length. Reagan's statements against the San-dinista regime in Nicaragua raised eyebrows in 1985, but Congress ultimately approved $27 million in nonmilitary assistance to the anti-Sandinista rebels. The administration's policy of staying on friendly terms with the South African government in order to press for reforms in its system of apartheid foundered amid growing unrest there; to head off stronger congressional action, Reagan issued an exec-utive order imposing modest sanctions.

News of the president's May visit to Western Europe was dominated by his side trip, at the suggestion of West German Chancellor Helmut Kohl, to a military cemetery at Bitburg, West Germany. Too late the White House had learned that 49 soldiers of the SS, the elite Nazi guard, lay buried there. Jewish and veterans' groups had strongly opposed the visit, and, at a public White House ceremony, Holocaust survivor and author Elie Wiesel urged the president to cancel it. Reagan went ahead with his plans, believing relations with West Germany would be damaged if he did not go; he made a point of also visiting the site of the Bergen-Belsen concentration camp.

In June, Shiite Muslim terrorists seized a TWA airliner, killed an American on board, and put Reagan and the nation through a long ordeal, as American hostages were held in Lebanon. Reagan acknowledged that there was little he could do; ultimately, with the help of Syrian President Hafez al-Assad, the hijackers freed their hostages without public concession by the United States. In October, four terrorists seized the Italian cruise ship *Achille Lauro* and killed an American before surrendering the ship. In this case, the Reagan administration took direct action. U.S. Navy jet fighters forced an Egyptian plane carrying the terrorists to land in Sicily, where the hijackers were taken into custody. "They can run but they can't hide," Reagan observed triumphantly, although the Italians did free a fifth man on the plane who was believed to have masterminded the oper-ation.

Health Problems. In July the president went to the Bethesda Naval Medical Center for the removal of a noncancerous polyp in the lower colon and for examination of his entire colon. Doctors discovered and, in a separate opera-tion, removed a large growth in the upper colon. While Reagan was under anesthesia, the powers of the presidency were briefly assumed by Vice-President George Bush (see biography in PEOPLE IN THE NEWS.) After an analysis of the growth, Dr. Steven Rosenberg of the National Cancer Institute announced, "The president has cancer." Doctors stressed that they believed they had removed all of the malignancy, although a recurrence could not be ruled out. Subsequently, an unrelated skin cancer was detected on the president's nose. Twice he underwent procedures for removal of malignant skin tissue.

Cabinet of the United States

Vice-President George Bush

Secretary of State George Shultz
Secretary of the Treasury James Baker
Secretary of Defense Caspar Weinberger
Attorney General Edwin Meese III
Secretary of the Interior Donald Hodel
Secretary of Agriculture John Block
Secretary of Commerce Malcolm Baldrige
Secretary of Labor William Brock
**Secretary of Health and Human
  Services** Otis Bowen
**Secretary of Housing and Urban
  Development** Samuel Pierce, Jr.
Secretary of Transportation Elizabeth Dole
Secretary of Energy John Herrington
Secretary of Education William Bennett

**Director of the Office of Management and
  Budget** James Miller III
**Director of the Central Intelligence
  Agency** William Casey
**U.S. Representative to the United
  Nations** Vernon Walters
U.S. Trade Representative Clayton K.
  Yeutter

Although intended as a gesture of reconciliation, President Ronald Reagan's ceremonial visit to a German military cemetery in Bitburg stirred up a storm of protests. Here, Reagan walks through the cemetery with West German Chancellor Helmut Kohl (far left) and two retired American and German generals.

Personnel. There were numerous personnel changes during the year. Treasury Secretary Donald Regan (see biography in PEOPLE IN THE NEWS) and White House Chief of Staff James Baker swapped jobs in January. Meanwhile, longtime Reagan aide Michael Deaver returned to a career in public relations. In February, columnist Patrick Buchanan, an outspoken conservative, came to the White House as director of communications, while White House Counselor Edwin Meese III was confirmed by the Senate as attorney general, succeeding William French Smith. Meese's nomination had been held up for more than a year, as a special prosecutor considered and ultimately dismissed allegations of financial and ethical improprieties. In March, Labor Secretary Raymond Donovan resigned to face trial (scheduled for early 1986) on fraud charges; he was replaced by William Brock, formerly special U.S. trade representative.

Reagan's energetic, outspoken budget director, David Stockman, resigned in July to join a Wall Street investment firm and write his memoirs. He was replaced by James C. Miller III, formerly chairman of the Federal Trade Commission. Earlier in the year, Donald Hodel succeeded William Clark as secretary of the interior, John Herrington replaced Hodel at the Energy Department, and William Bennett replaced Terrel Bell as education secretary.

Two officials left late in the year, both reportedly after feuds with Donald Regan. Margaret Heckler resigned as secretary of health and human services, to be succeeded by former Governor Otis Bowen of Indiana; Heckler was "promoted"—in Reagan's phrasing—to ambassador to Ireland. Robert McFarlane, the national security adviser, also left; he was replaced by his deputy, Vice Admiral John Poindexter. Besides Regan, another figure said to be greatly influential in personnel matters in the administration was first lady Nancy Reagan (see biography in PEOPLE IN THE NEWS).

Late in the year, there was a controversy over a directive from President Reagan requir-

335

ing polygraph, or lie-detector, tests for officials with access to highly sensitive information. Secretary of State George Shultz said he had "grave reservations" about such tests and would resign if asked to take one; he was reportedly mollified after a meeting with Reagan on the subject.   J.A.

PRINCE EDWARD ISLAND. *See* STATISTICS OF THE WORLD.

PRIZES AND AWARDS The following is a selected listing of prizes awarded during 1985 and the names of the persons who received them. For some awards given in specific fields, see the appropriate subject entry, such as MOTION PICTURES.

NOBEL PRIZES

The majority of the 1985 Nobel Prize winners were from the United States. The awards, presented on December 10, carried with them approximately $225,000 in prize money for each category.

Chemistry. For their achievement in developing new techniques in crystallography, the study of molecular structures:

Herbert A. Hauptman (1917–), director of the Medical Foundation of Buffalo, N.Y. Born in The Bronx, N.Y., he graduated from the City College of New York, then earned a master's degree in mathematics from Columbia University and a Ph.D. from the University of Maryland. He became a professor of biophysics at the State University of New York at Buffalo in 1970. Since 1972 he has been director of research and vice-president of the privately run Medical Foundation.

Jerome Karle (1918–), of the Naval Research Laboratory in Washington. Born in Brooklyn, N.Y., he was a classmate of Hauptman's at City College. Karle went on to earn graduate degrees at Harvard University and the University of Michigan. He briefly worked on the Manhattan Project during the development of the atomic bomb. Later, he joined the Naval Research Laboratory, where he became chief scientist of a team studying the structure of matter.

Economics. For his development of theories on household economy and on financial market mechanisms:

Franco Modigliani (1918–), professor at the Massachusetts Institute of Technology. Born in

Franco Modigliani, an Italian-born professor of economics at the Massachusetts Institute of Technology, and his wife celebrate his being awarded the 1985 Nobel Prize for economics.

Rome, he earned a law degree at the University of Rome, then began to study economics after winning a prize for an essay in that field. Modigliani emigrated to the United States in 1940 and studied macroeconomics at the New School for Social Research in New York City. He became a naturalized U.S. citizen. After earning his doctorate, he taught at various schools before joining the faculty at MIT in 1962.

Literature. For "expressing a deepened awareness of time in the depiction of the human condition" and for "the poet's and painter's creativeness in his novels":

Claude Simon (1913–), French novelist and literary critic. Born on the island of Madagascar, he spent his boyhood in France's southern wine-producing region, where he still lives and supervises his own vineyards. As a young man, after brief periods at Oxford and Cambridge and a failed attempt at painting, he traveled extensively in Europe and fought on the Republican side during the Spanish Civil War before becoming disillusioned with the cause. During World War II, as a French cavalryman, he was captured by the Germans, escaped, and joined the French resistance. The first of

Simon's 15 works, *Le Tricheur* (The trickster), was written during the war and published in 1945.

Peace. For "spreading authoritative information and . . . creating an awareness of the catastrophic consequences of atomic warfare":

International Physicians for the Prevention of Nuclear War (IPPNW), founded by two physicians, one a U.S. citizen and one from the Soviet Union.

Yevgeny I. Chazov (1929–   ), director-general of the Moscow Cardiological Center. Born in Gorky, he graduated in 1953 from Kiev Medical Institute and then studied cardiology at the First Medical Institute in Moscow. Chazov later became chief of the Fourth Administration of the Ministry of Health, with responsibility for the healthcare of Soviet leaders. A leading cardiologist, he is also an energetic peace activist but not a critic of the Soviet government. He has been a Communist Party member since 1962 and became a member of its Central Committee in 1982. Chazov was one of 25 members of the Soviet Academy of Medical Science to sign a letter in 1973 denouncing Soviet dissident Andrei Sakharov for anti-Soviet activities. West German Chancellor Helmut Kohl and ten other Christian Democratic leaders in Europe cited this fact in a letter to the Nobel committee opposing the granting of the 1985 Peace Prize to Chazov. West Germany and the United States declined to send ambassadors to the awards ceremony.

Bernard Lown (1921–   ), professor at the Harvard University School of Public Health. Born in Lithuania, he emigrated to the United States in 1935, graduated from the University of Maine, and received a medical degree from the Johns Hopkins University in 1945. He served as a U.S. Army doctor during the Korean war. Concerned about the nuclear arms race, Lown and other physicians organized Physicians for Social Responsibility in 1961. Lown and Chazov met during the 1960's and conducted joint research; In 1980 they brought together Soviet and U.S. physicians to form the IPPNW, which by 1985 reportedly had about 135,000 members in different countries.

Physics. For demonstrating that electrical resistance occurs in precise and measurable units:

Klaus von Klitzing (1943–   ), of the Max Planck Institute for Solid State Physics in Stuttgart, West Germany. Born in Schroda, now part of Poland, he moved west with his family after World War II and took his doctorate in physics at Würzburg University in West Germany. After establishing a reputation as a computer expert, he made his breakthrough discovery about the nature of electrical resistance in 1980, while teaching at Würzburg. He later joined the Max Planck Institute.

Physiology or Medicine. For discoveries regarding cholesterol metabolism and cholesterol-related diseases:

Michael S. Brown (1941–   ), research fellow of Southwestern Medical School of the University of Texas in Dallas. Born in New York City, he earned his medical degree at the University of Pennsylvania in 1966. After com-

The two founders of International Physicians for the Prevention of Nuclear War, Bernard Lown (left) of the United States and Yevgeny I. Chazov of the Soviet Union, celebrate after learning that the organization had been awarded the 1985 Nobel Peace Prize.

pleting his internship and residency at Massachusetts General Hospital in Boston, he became a clinical associate in the Digestive and Hereditary Diseases Branch of the U.S. National Institutes of Health, doing research there on gastroenterology. In 1971 he became a research fellow at Southwestern Medical School. Joseph L. Goldstein (1940–   ), research fellow of Southwestern Medical School. Born in Sumter, S.C., he earned his medical degree at Southwestern Medical School in 1966 and went on to complete his internship at Massachusetts General Hospital, where he met Brown. Goldstein did genetic research at the Laboratory of Biomedical Genetics of the National Heart Institute and at the University of Washington in Seattle. When he returned to Dallas in 1972, he and Brown began to jointly study the genetic factors that cause some people to develop high blood-cholesterol levels.

PULITZER PRIZES

The 1985 Pulitzer Prizes were announced on April 24. Alison Lurie won the fiction award for her seventh novel, *Foreign Affairs*. The music prize went to Stephen Albert for his *Symphony, RiverRun*. Stephen Sondheim and James Lapine shared the drama award for the musical *Sunday in the Park With George*. In journalism, the public service award was earned by the Fort Worth *Star-Telegram*. Carolyn Kizer won the poetry prize for her *Yin* volume. The history award went to Thomas K. McCraw for *The Prophets of Regulation*.

Other Pulitzer Prizes in letters and journalism were:

Biography. Kenneth Silverman, for *The Life and Times of Cotton Mather*.

Commentary. Murray Kempton, columnist for *Newsday* (Long Island, N.Y.).

Criticism. Howard Rosenberg, Los Angeles *Times*.

Editorial Cartooning. Jeff MacNelly, Chicago *Tribune*.

Editorial Writing. Richard Aregood, Philadelphia *Daily News*.

Feature Writing. Alice Steinbach, Baltimore *Sun*.

General Nonfiction. Studs Terkel, *The Good War: An Oral History of World War II*.

Photography, Feature. Stan Grossfeld, Boston *Globe;* Larry C. Price, Philadelphia *Inquirer*.

Photography, Spot News. *The Register* (Santa Ana, Calif.).

Reporting, General News. Thomas Turcol, *Virginian-Pilot* and *Ledger-Star* (Norfolk, Va.).

Reporting, International. Josh Friedman, Dennis Bell, and Ozier Muhammad, *Newsday*.

Reporting, National. Thomas J. Knudson, Des Moines *Register*.

Reporting, Specialized. Randall Savage and Jackie Crosby, Macon (Ga.) *Telegraph and News*.

OTHER PRIZES AND AWARDS

Among other awards were the following:

Academy of American Poets. Fellowships to Amy Clampitt and Maxine Kumin; Walt Whitman Award to Christianne Balk.

Albert and Mary Lasker Foundation. $15,000 shared by Dr. Michael S. Brown and Dr. Joseph L. Goldstein for research in cholesterol metabolism. $15,000 to Dr. Bernard Fisher for breast cancer research. $15,000 each to columnist Ann Landers and to Lane Adams of the American Cancer Society.

American Academy of Arts and Letters. Gold Medals to Leonard Bernstein (music) and Robert Penn Warren (poetry). Award for Distinguished Service to the Arts to Senator Claiborne Pell. Special Citation for Service to the Arts to William Shawn. Charles Ives Fellowship in music ($10,000) to Thomas Oboe Lee. Goddard Lieberson Fellowships in music ($10, 000 each) to Todd Brief and Sheree Clement.

American Film Institute. Life Achievement Award to Gene Kelly.

Armand Hammer Prize Foundation. $100,000 award, for studies of adult T-cell leukemia, shared by Dr. Robert C. Gallo of the National Cancer Institute (half) and by Dr. Yorio Hanuma, Dr. Isao Miyoshi, and Dr. Kiyoshi Takatsuki, all researchers in Japan.

Association of American Publishers, American Book Awards. Awards of $10,000 each to Don DeLillo for *White Noise* (fiction), to J. Anthony Lukas for *Common Ground: A Turbulent Decade in the Lives of Three American Families* (nonfiction), to Bob Shacochis for *Easy in the Islands* (first work of fiction).

Bristol-Myers Award. $50,000 award for cancer research, shared by Dr. William S. Hayward (Memorial Sloan-Kettering) and Dr. Philip Leder (Harvard Medical School).

Medal of Freedom. Highest U.S. civilian honor, awarded to jazz musician Count Basie (posthumous), explorer Jacques-Yves Cousteau, educator Jerome Holland (posthumous), philosopher Sidney Hook, former U.S. representative to the UN Jeane Kirkpatrick, educator and NASA administrator George Low (posthumous), television news commentator Frank Reynolds (posthumous), former Smithsonian Institution secretary S. Dillon Ripley, entertainer Frank Sinatra, actor James Stewart, humanitarian Mother Teresa, World War II General Albert C. Wedemeyer, and retired Air Force General Charles Yeager.

Alexander Onassis Foundation. $100,000 awards to Dr. Hermann Gmeiner, founder of Children's Villages; to African poet and statesman Léopold Sédar Senghor; to the Erasmus Commission of the Royal Netherlands Academy of Arts and Sciences and to the secretary-general of the International Committee for Irrigation and Drainage (shared).

Samuel H. Scripps-American Dance Festival Award. $25,000 award to Alwin Nikolais.

Templeton Foundation. $185,000 Templeton Prize for Progress in Religion to Sir Alister Hardy, founding director of the Religious Experience Research Unit, Manchester College, Oxford.

Wolf Foundation. $100,000 each to Donald Steiner (medicine), Robert Burris (agriculture), Rudolf Marcus (chemistry), Conyers Herring and Philip Nozieres (physics; shared), Hans Lewy and Kuniho Kodairo (mathematics; shared), and sculptor Eduardo Chillida (arts).

R.F.

PUBLISHING. U.S. book sales, as well as newspaper and magazine revenues, grew in 1985, but more slowly than in 1984. Autobiographies were among the biggest best-sellers. The trend toward concentrated ownership of publishing operations by large media companies continued.

Books. According to figures from the Association of American Publishers for the first seven months of 1985, sales of adult trade hardbound books were up by 8 percent over the same period in 1984, and adult trade paperbacks by 12 percent. However, sales of mass market paperbacks, religious books, and juvenile paperbacks declined. Autobiographies were prominent best-sellers; Chrysler chairman Lee Iacocca's life story, published in late 1984, became one of the biggest nonfiction titles ever. Books by test pilot and Air Force General Chuck Yeager, tennis star Martina Navratilova, actress Shirley MacLaine, and Priscilla Presley (Elvis's ex-wife), among others, sold well.

An Overdue Place in the Sun
Elmore "Dutch" Leonard, author of a series of brilliant suspense novels and a string of superb Westerns, belatedly gained widespread national recognition in 1985 when his novel *Glitz* spent 18 weeks on the New York *Times* best-seller list and he made the cover of *Newsweek* magazine. A quiet professional who spends hours revising his work with a pencil, Leonard set to work on a screenplay for *Glitz*—the story of an off-duty Miami cop's search for a psychotic killer in Atlantic City—as well as a screenplay for his *LaBrava* (1983), which won the Edgar Allan Poe Award for best mystery novel. Before he switched to writing chilling suspense novels in the 1970's, Leonard produced *Hombre*, made into a celebrated Paul Newman movie in 1967, as well as other fine Westerns, which he wrote in the mornings before going to work at an ad agency.

Elmore Leonard

The New Yorker *magazine, an arbiter of literary taste and sophisticated humor for 60 years, became part of the publishing empire of Samuel I. Newhouse, Jr., in May. Newhouse promised that the New Yorker would keep its editorial independence. Right, the magazine's symbol, Eustace Tilley, who graces a cover every February.*

DRAWING BY RHEA IRVIN, © 1925, 1953 THE NEW YORKER MAGAZINE INC.

Frank Herbert returned to the best-seller lists with *Chapterhouse: Dune,* a continuation of his futuristic Dune series. The success of *The Hunt for Red October,* a first novel by Tom Clancy about the defection of a Soviet submarine crew, was aided by a prepublication endorsement from President Ronald Reagan. Danielle Steel scored another romantic triumph with *Family Album,* and Elmore Leonard established himself as a leader of the mystery genre with *Glitz.* In *Love and War,* John Jakes continued his popular series about the Civil War. Western writer Louis L'Amour scored high sales with *Jubal Sackett.* James Michener's latest saga, *Texas,* was also a best-seller. Stephen King did well with *The Talisman,* written with Peter Straub, and *Thinner,* authored under King's recently revealed pen name of Richard Bachman, as well as with his *Skeleton Crew* collection of horror tales.

Business books remained a popular category.

Thomas J. Peters, coauthor of *In Search of Excellence,* teamed up with Nancy K. Austin to produce *A Passion for Excellence,* one of many business books to draw heavy sales.

A record for a first novel by a "relatively unknown writer of fiction" was set in September, when Bantam agreed to pay over $1 million to the English author Sally Beauman for *Destiny,* set in Mississippi, London, and Paris and covering more than three decades. Washington figures also did well: for future books, former budget director David Stockman garnered $2 million, former UN Ambassador Jeanne Kirkpatrick $900,000, ABC correspondent Sam Donaldson $1 million, and former vice-presidential candidate Geraldine Ferraro $1 million. Writer Edmund Morris was to be paid a reported $3 million for a biography of President Ronald Reagan. As the computer market sagged and many publishers closed down their computer book and software operations, various publishers began marketing audiocassettes of book readings (by authors and actors) through book distribution channels.

In a decision that narrowed the definition of "fair use" under the Copyright Act, the U.S. Supreme Court ruled in May that the *Nation* magazine infringed the copyright of Harper & Row when it printed an article based on the memoirs of former President Gerald R. Ford, *A Time to Heal*, before the book's 1979 publication date. A June ruling by the Supreme Court, involving an erroneous credit rating of a construction firm by Dun & Bradstreet reduced the amount of protection publishers have against libel suits. The Court decided that a libel plaintiff was not required to prove "actual malice" to receive damages if the plaintiff was not a public figure and the libel did not involve a matter of "public concern."

Magazines. Growth in the magazine industry as a whole slowed down; total revenues were expected to increase about 4 percent, compared with 6 percent in 1984. Advertising volume was in a slump, and circulation grew modestly. Business magazines and many regional and city publications reported healthy gains, but sales of women's magazines declined. Single copy sales were a major weak spot.

In what was hailed as the biggest magazine deal ever, CBS Inc. agreed in February to pay $365 million for the Ziff-Davis Publishing Company's 12 consumer magazines, which, with a combined circulation of 4.7 million, were regarded by industry observers as the most successful group of special interest magazines in the United States. The deal increased the number of CBS magazines to 22, making CBS a giant in the consumer magazine field. In May, however, CBS complained to the Securities and Exchange Commission that Ziff-Davis had overstated the earnings of its consumer publications, possibly by as much as $3.9 million, and had failed to deduct certain expenses from its profit statement. The two companies were negotiating to resolve the dispute.

The takeover of the American Broadcasting Company by Capital Cities Communications, Inc., which already owned some important magazines, added *Los Angeles* magazine and a number of business, farm, leisure, and computer publications to the Capital Cities list. (The merger was approved in November by the Federal Communications Commission, and its completion was announced in early January 1986.) In May, Samuel Newhouse, Jr., added the sophisticated *New Yorker* to his magazine holdings; the profitable weekly had been independent since its founding 60 years ago.

Time Inc. began in September to test-market *Picture Week*, a newsweekly that would use photofeatures to highlight news events and personalities. Lower in price and photographic quality than *Life*, the new magazine was designed to compete with tabloids on the newsstands. The number of new magazines on motherhood grew to more than a dozen, as publishers sought to appeal to the many women reaching childbearing years. Newcomers included *Baby!*, *Motherhood*, *New Mother*, and *Stork*.

In the 20th annual National Magazine awards, *Life* was the first winner in the newly established category for photography. *American Heritage* received awards for general excellence among moderate-circulation magazines and for the best single-topic issue. *The Washingtonian* also was a double winner, for public service and for service to the individual.

Newspapers. The number of U.S. daily newspapers continued to drop, but total daily circulation was projected to increase by about 1 percent. Gains by morning newspapers more than offset losses in the evening field, and Sunday circulation continued to grow impressively. Newspaper advertising revenues were expected to exceed $26 billion for 1985, up about 10 percent from 1984. Higher ad rates were largely responsible; another factor was a further increase in volume of classified advertising. Newspaper profits were enhanced by price increases and less-than-anticipated increases in the cost of essential supplies, like newsprint. With profits up, spending for plant modernization and expansion was in excess of 1984's nearly $1 billion.

Acquisitions continued apace. Capital Cities, buyer of ABC and already a publishing and broadcasting giant, had newspaper holdings that included the Kansas City *Star and Times*, Fort Worth *Star-Telegram*, and *Women's Wear Daily*, and large book and magazine publishing operations as well. The Gannett Company made several major purchases. In January it bought the Des Moines *Register and Tribune,* ranked as one of the ten best U.S. newspapers, and the next month it purchased *Family Weekly* (renamed *USA Weekend* by Gannett), a weekend supplement carried by over 300 newspapers. In August, Gannett purchased the Evening News Association, owner of the Detroit *News*—the nation's sixth largest daily—as well as other newspapers and several radio and TV stations.

"Audio books" cater to a market of busy people who like to "read" while jogging, shaving, or doing the laundry. Some are narrated by the author, as with John Updike, below.

After *USA Today,* the Detroit *News* would be Gannett's largest paper.

Reuters, the British news agency, launched an international news picture service on January 1, based on its 1984 acquisition of United Press International's 24 foreign news picture bureaus. UPI meanwhile continued its struggle for survival. Luis Nogales was fired in March as the agency's president but was rehired a few days later under pressure from lenders. UPI filed for bankruptcy on April 28. By midyear, reforms and rate hikes had helped it achieve an operating profit, but the agency was still seeking buyers. In November, it was agreed to sell the agency to two bidders, for over $40 million in cash and pledges.

Former *Wall Street Journal* reporter R. Foster Winans and two associates were convicted in June on charges that they had profited from illegal stock trades based on advance knowledge of *Journal* articles. The verdict marked the first time a journalist had ever been found guilty of insider trading under the Securities Act of 1934.   J.M. & J.L.

PUERTO RICO. On January 2, 1985, Rafael Hernández Colón, leader of the Popular Democratic Party, was sworn in as governor of Puerto Rico. He had narrowly defeated incumbent Governor Carlos Romero Barceló in the November 1984 elections. Hernández Colón declared that the primary task of his administration would be to create jobs. (The unemployment rate at the beginning of the year was put officially at 21 percent, but unofficially it was estimated at closer to 40 percent.) A key goal was to attract more investment by U.S. industries, but such investment was jeopardized by President Ronald Reagan's federal tax reform plan, which called for the elimination of tax exemptions for Puerto Rican subsidiaries of U.S. corporations.

A major tropical front originating southeast of Puerto Rico moved slowly across the island in early October, dropping up to 15 inches of rain in some areas and causing widespread flooding as well as a series of landslides. The worst destruction occurred on October 7 near Ponce, on the southern coast, when a landslide swept away most of the hillside community of Mameyes; at least 200 people were killed, buried under more than 40 feet of mud and

Heavy rains lashed Puerto Rico in October, causing widespread flooding and landslides. The worst landslide destroyed much of the impoverished hillside community of Mameyes, shown here; at least 200 people were killed by the avalanche.

debris in the valley below. Rescue efforts proved almost impossible and were finally called off on October 19. Elsewhere, about 60 other people died; total property damage was estimated at $500 million.

In March, ten current and former police officers, indicted in 1984 on charges of lying to federal grand juries investigating the 1978 slayings of two young activists for Puerto Rican independence, were found guilty of perjury in a U.S. district court. By late in the year, one officer had been sentenced to 25 years in a psychiatric institution, and several others had received prison terms of up to 30 years. The officers also faced murder charges.

See STATISTICS OF THE WORLD.   T.G.S.

Q

QATAR. See STATISTICS OF THE WORLD. See also PERSIAN GULF STATES.

QUÉBEC. See STATISTICS OF THE WORLD. See also CANADA.

R

RADIO. See TELEVISION AND RADIO BROADCASTING.

RAILROADS. See TRANSPORTATION.
RECORDINGS. See MUSIC.

Religion

In 1985 the Roman Catholic Church looked back on the Second Vatican Council 20 years earlier, while Jews had occasion to remember the bitter events of the Holocaust. Protestant churches were involved with social issues and some sharp internal controversies.

Pope John Paul II, besides venturing on important foreign journeys, convened an extraordinary Synod of Bishops late in the year to reflect on the meaning and relevance of the Second Vatican Council. Protestant clergy and laity were in the forefront of those opposing apartheid in South Africa, and the "sanctuary movement" attracted growing attention. The National Council of Churches installed a new leader, as did the Episcopal Church and the Mormon Church. Bomb blasts severely damaged the historic Borobudur temple in Indonesia, as sectarian strife continued to be a serious problem in many parts of the world.

ROMAN CATHOLIC CHURCH

Pope John Paul II continued to maintain a high profile worldwide, as he ventured on trips to South America and Africa, as well as within Europe. An extraordinary session of the Synod of Bishops was convened in Rome late in the year.

Synod of Bishops. On January 25, in a major surprise, the pope announced that the Synod of Bishops would meet November 25 through December 8 to review the results of Vatican Council II (1962–1965). Some Catholics worried that the pope would use the event to roll back the Council's liberal reforms. However, at the end of the extraordinary session, exactly 20 years after the close of the Second Vatican Council, Vatican officials and both liberal and conservative bishops generally expressed satisfaction at the outcome. Conservatives were pleased by the call for a universal catechism to clarify and ratify church doctrine, while liberals noted that the importance of collegiality, as expressed in the work of national episcopal conferences, had been acknowledged.

The Synod of Bishops can offer advice to the pope but cannot make any binding decisions. The issue of the bishops' degree of pastoral autonomy in relation to Rome was a major focus of discussion, and the agreement by the pope to publish a detailed summary of the synod's proceedings was a departure from the policy followed at previous, ordinary synod sessions since 1974. Although such divisive issues as liberation theology were focused on in talks by individual bishops and in study groups, neither the final draft of the bishops' pastoral message nor the document summarizing their conclusions mentioned the term, or other controversial subjects such as church teachings on sexual relationships and reproduction. The two statements emphasized the Roman Catholic Church as a "mystery" rather than as an institution in the world.

Papal Trips. The pope visited 17 cities and mountain villages in Ecuador, Peru, and Venezuela early in the year. In his homilies, he repeatedly condemned ideologies "alien" to Catholic teaching; many thought he referred to liberation theology.

A ten-day May trip to the Benelux region confronted John Paul with some of Catholicism's most dissident elements. In the Netherlands he encountered protests over papal authority and Vatican teachings on women, sexuality, and birth control. In one demonstration, protesters hurled rocks and bottles at the pope's car. In Luxembourg and Belgium the pope was able to expatiate in a more cordial atmosphere on familiar themes relating to peace and social justice.

In August, John Paul embarked on a 12-day African journey to seven countries. During the trip, he presided at the 43rd Eucharistic Congress being held in Nairobi, Kenya, with the theme "The Eucharist and the Family," where he reiterated church teaching on marriage and birth control. He also called for dialogue between Christians and Muslims and spoke out against apartheid in South Africa.

On September 8, in the principality of Liechtenstein, the pope labeled abortion a "repulsive" crime and criticized Catholics who are "ashamed to stand up for those moral fundamentals" associated with their faith.

Conspiracy Trial. On May 27, Italian prosecutors brought eight defendants to trial, four of them in absentia, on charges that they had conspired to assassinate the pope in May 1981. The prosecution's principal witness was Mehmet Ali Agca, the Turkish terrorist serving a life sentence for the shooting. Agca had charged that accomplices had assisted him in the assassination attempt—which, he claimed, was plotted by the Bulgarian and Soviet security services, with the help of a right-wing Turkish group. In October, one of the defendants being tried in absentia died of a heart attack in Turkey. The hearing of evidence concluded in December, with summations scheduled for early 1986.

Other Activities. On May 25, John Paul consecrated 28 new cardinals in St. Peter's Basilica, bringing the total to 152. Three Americans were included: Archbishop John J. O'Connor of New York, Archbishop Bernard F. Law of Boston, and Archbishop Myroslav Ivan Lubachivsky, a naturalized U.S. citizen based in Rome as spiritual leader of the world's 6 million Ukrainian Catholics.

In July, John Paul issued his fourth encyclical, entitled *Slavorum Apostoli* (*Apostles of the Slavs*). It called for "solidarity" with the church's Slavic faithful, religious tolerance in Eastern Europe, and closer ties between Roman Catholics and followers of the Eastern Orthodox Church. In February, John Paul received Andrei A. Gromyko, then Soviet foreign minister, who reportedly urged him to oppose the Reagan administration's Strategic Defense Initiative, known as Star Wars.

United States. A report on the role of women in the church, issued by the National Conference of Catholic Bishops, urged the church to support the advancement of women in the church and in society, but it did not advocate the ordination of women. The report also called

The extraordinary Synod of Bishops ended on December 8 with a mass said by Pope John Paul II at St. Peter's in Rome. The bishops had gathered for the two-week session to assess the impact of Vatican Council II, concluded 20 years earlier.

In a historic overture to Islam, Pope John Paul II met with King Hassan II of Morocco in the king's palace in Casablanca. The occasion marked the first time that a pope had ever been officially invited to visit a Muslim country.

for greater efforts to reach blacks, Hispanics, and other minority groups.

Tension grew for a time between the Vatican and 24 American nuns who had signed a public statement in October 1984 saying that Roman Catholics hold a "diversity of opinions" on abortion and asking for open discussion on the topic. The Vatican ordered them to recant or face dismissal from their religious orders. Late in 1985 it was reported that the Vatican, apparently seeking to settle the issue quietly, had begun accepting unspecified private clarifications from some of the nuns.

Latin America. On January 29 the Vatican announced that it had ordered two Nicaraguan government officials—Father Ernesto Cardenal, minister of culture, and Maryknoll Father Miguel D'Escoto Brockman, foreign minister—to resign their posts in the Marxist-oriented Sandinista government or face suspension from exercising their priestly ministry. When the two failed to resign, they were suspended. In March the Vatican issued an 11-page criticism of Franciscan Father Leonardo Boff of Brazil, a leading proponent of liberation theology. Subsequently, Boff was ordered not to teach, publish, or give interviews for one year.

Europe and Asia. The Vatican asked in June that pilgrimages to Medjugorje, Yugoslavia, be discouraged. In 1981, six young people there contended that they were having daily visions of the Virgin Mary. Bishop Pavao Zanic of Mostar-Duvno later characterized the purported visions as "collective hallucination." Abortion became legal in Spain on August 3, over the strong opposition of the church there. The Spanish bishops pronounced excommunication upon any Catholic "who cooperates physically or morally" in an abortion.

Ties between Chinese Catholics and the Vatican continued to be prohibited by the Communist regime in Peking, but some Catholic churches were reopened in China under the auspices of the officially sanctioned Catholic Patriotic Association, which also welcomed Catholic visitors from abroad. On December 24 the historic Beitang Church in Peking, also known as the Church of the Savior, was reopened in an official ceremony, followed by midnight mass in Latin. (Because of its separation from Rome, Chinese Catholicism had no part in changes instituted by the Second Vatican Council.) The building, vandalized by militants during the Cultural Revolution, was renovated during 1985 with government funding and volunteer labor.

Ecumenism. In September, the Second Anglican-Roman Catholic International Commission, established in 1982 by the pope and the archbishop of Canterbury, announced that it had made progress on an agreement regarding the question of salvation. The 24 theologians reported having arrived at a compromise formula stating that while salvation depends on "the grace of God," virtuous personal conduct and good works are of assistance in attaining salvation. In April, Roman Catholic and Jewish leaders met in Rome to mark the 20th anniversary of *Nostra Aetate,* a Vatican Council document repudiating the view that the Jewish people were responsible for the death of Christ.   J.D.

PROTESTANT AND ORTHODOX CHURCHES
South Africa's apartheid policy, the so-called sanctuary movement, and continued strife

among southern Baptists were major Protestant concerns in 1985.

Antiapartheid Movement. Desmond Tutu was enthroned on February 3 as bishop of the Johannesburg diocese of the Anglican Church of South Africa. The 1984 Nobel Peace Prize laureate, Tutu was the first black to lead the diocese. He and another South African clergyman, the Reverend Allan Boesak—who was arrested and later released on bail after being charged with violating the country's security laws—took prominent roles in antiapartheid efforts, and their leadership influenced the thinking of U.S. Protestants on South Africa. The Reverend C. F. Beyers Naudé, another prominent foe of apartheid, succeeded Tutu as general secretary of the South Africa Council of Churches; Naudé, who is white, had recently been released from a seven-year "banning" order (the virtual equivalent of house arrest).

Church leaders in South Africa became bolder in challenging the authorities on theological grounds. Some 150 church leaders signed the historic "Kairos Statement" that condoned violence by oppressed people against an oppressor. The 1.5-million-member Nederduitse Gereformeerde Kerk (NGK), the most powerful white Dutch Reformed body in South Africa, suspended its membership in the Reformed Ecumenical Synod, an international grouping of conservative Calvinist churches, after the synod declared the NGK's theological justification of apartheid to be a heresy.

In the United States, a number of church bodies voted to sell their stock in any companies that failed to enforce the Sullivan Principles, a set of guidelines aimed at ensuring racial equality in American-owned businesses in South Africa. Others went so far as to vote for full divestiture of their South Africa-related stocks. Regular demonstrations by church groups in front of South Africa's embassy in Washington and consulates around the United States, which had begun in late 1984, continued and swelled in importance.

The Reverend Jerry Falwell, the conservative American television evangelist, was criticized by fellow Protestants when, following a brief tour of South Africa in August, he voiced support for State President P. W. Botha, called Bishop Tutu a "phony," and urged American Christians to buy South African gold coins.

Central America Issues. The clash between the U.S. government and the church-led sanctuary movement, which protects illegal Salvadoran and Guatemalan aliens in the United States who say they are political refugees fleeing violence in their home countries, came to a head in several trials of sanctuary workers. The Reverend John Fife, a Presbyterian minister considered a founder of the movement, and two United Methodist lay workers were among those charged, in a case in Arizona, with aiding and transporting illegal aliens.

Southern Baptist Acrimony. The six-year war between "moderates" and fundamentalist conservatives in the Southern Baptist Convention continued. A record 45,000 "messengers" (delegates) at the SBC's annual meeting in Dallas in June reelected the Reverend Charles Stanley, an Atlanta pastor and television personality, as president, continuing the fundamentalists' lock on that office. A conciliatory gesture came in the election of his moderate opponent, the Reverend Winfred Moore of Amarillo, Texas, to the second-ranking convention post.

Feminist Issues. The Church of England approved women deacons and appeared to be moving slowly toward the ordination of women priests, despite some opposition. Observers said the number of members leaving the Church of England for the Roman Catholic Church was increasing, partly because of the movement toward women's ordination and partly because of controversy over the theology of a leading cleric, Bishop David Jenkins of Durham, who had made statements casting doubt on the historical reality of the virgin birth and resurrection of Jesus.

National Council of Churches. The National Council of Churches, the major ecumenical umbrella group of U.S. Protestant and Orthodox churches, installed a new leader on January 1, the Reverend Arie Brouwer.

The council took a mediating role in a dispute involving migrant workers who have been seeking since 1978 to win collective bargaining rights on tomato and cucumber farms in western Ohio that supply the Campbell Soup Company. The NCC delayed joining a boycott of Campbell's products while mediation efforts continued. The NCC also issued a report from its study on sex and sexual violence in films, television programs, and videocassettes, which suggested that the Federal Communications Commission resume its regulatory role over the movie and TV industries.

Ecumenism. Leaders of Orthodox bodies from around the world gathered in Brookline, Mass., in June to begin their study of the landmark ecumenical document "Baptism, Eucharist, and Ministry," which they called the "most important statement ever produced by the World Council of Churches." Meanwhile, the International Lutheran-Orthodox ecumenical dialogue commission produced a joint statement, dealing with Scripture as an expression of divine revelation and the early church's experience.

Lutheran Dispute. In March the Reverend D. Douglas Roth was deposed from the ministry of the Lutheran Church in America for refusing to give up his pulpit after being dismissed; two other LCA pastors faced hearings on similar charges in 1986. The clergymen had generated controversy through their involvement in Denominational Ministry Strategy, a group of Protestant ministers allied with a labor organization, the Network to Save the Mon/Ohio Valley, that sought to draw attention to what it saw as the role of major corporations and banks in causing high unemployment in the Pittsburgh area's depressed steel industry. Charging that church authorities had sided with corporate interests, the network and DMS had used such confrontational tactics as disrupting church services where corporate and church officials worshiped and spraying "skunk oil" at churches and company facilities. The Lutheran pastors' use of sermons and church funds to support these activities led to conflict with their congregations, which petitioned the pastors' bishop for their removal. In a series of court hearings and confrontations with police during the winter and spring, the pastors and their supporters were forced to yield physical control of the churches and served jail terms for defying judicial orders.

Leadership Changes. The Episcopal Church prepared for a change in leadership, as Presiding Bishop John Allin neared the end of his 12-year term. Allin had opposed women's ordination, kept a low profile on social issues, and tried to be a reconciling figure following an era of divisiveness in the church. Bishop Edmond Browning of Hawaii, a liberal with overseas missionary experience, was elected to succeed Allin and was to be consecrated as presiding bishop in January 1986.

The Reverend William Schulz, 35, one of the youngest persons heading a major U.S. denomination, took the reins at the Unitarian Universalist Association and immediately challenged three fundamentalist leaders—Jerry Falwell, M. G. ("Pat") Robertson, and Hal Lindsey—to a debate. Schulz also criticized the Boy Scouts of America for denying a promotion in rank to a scout who said he did not believe in God. (The organization later changed its policy and approved the promotion.)   J.C.L.

MORMON CHURCH

On November 5, Spencer W. Kimball, president of the Mormon Church (officially, the Church of Jesus Christ of Latter-Day Saints) for the past 12 years, died at the age of 90. Kimball, who presided over a period of rapid growth in the church, was best known for his 1978 decree, striking down the church's 148-year-old policy of excluding blacks from full membership. He was succeeded by Ezra Taft Benson, 86, president of the church's Quorum of the Twelve Apostles and former U.S. secretary of agriculture under President Dwight Eisenhower.

Bomb explosions that killed two persons and injured a third in Salt Lake City in October exposed a web of shadowy deals for the purchase of documents possibly conflicting with the accepted Mormon account of the founding of their church. On October 16, Mark Hofmann, the document dealer, was hurt when a bomb, possibly one which he himself had been transporting, exploded in his car. The previous day, two people connected to the Mormon Church were killed in separate bomb blasts, including Steven Christensen, a church leader who in 1984 had purchased the so-called salamander letter from Hofmann. The letter in question, dated October 29, 1830, and purportedly written by an associate of Mormon founder Joseph Smith, says Smith claimed to have been led to the religion's golden tablets

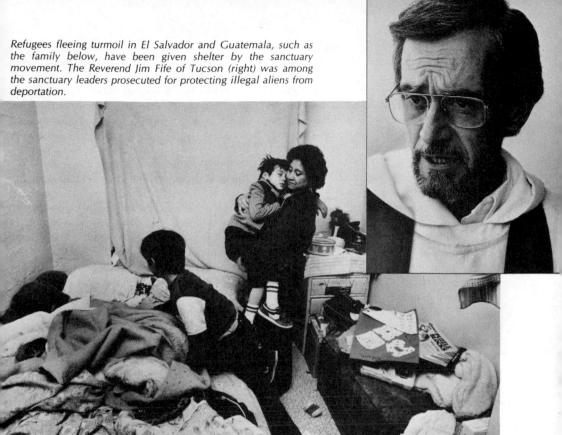

Refugees fleeing turmoil in El Salvador and Guatemala, such as the family below, have been given shelter by the sanctuary movement. The Reverend Jim Fife of Tucson (right) was among the sanctuary leaders prosecuted for protecting illegal aliens from deportation.

by a spirit that "transfigured himself from a white salamander." This version appeared to contradict the standard account that Smith was led to the tablets by an angel of God. Christensen had reportedly been negotiating to purchase further papers, possibly in order to prevent their being used to question church orthodoxy. One associate of Hofmann was arrested a few days after the blasts, and a police investigation was in progress.

JUDAISM

The March appointment of Mikhail Gorbachev as the new leader of the Soviet Union aroused hope that, along with a possible improvement in U.S.-Soviet relations, the situation of Jews in the Soviet Union would improve. But no immediate change occurred; by the end of October only about 900 Jews had been permitted to emigrate in 1985, and Soviet harassment of "refuseniks" (those denied exit visas) had not abated. The issue of Soviet Jewry was

quietly raised at November summit talks in Geneva between Gorbachev and President Ronald Reagan, who had met with Jewish leaders to discuss the upcoming summit. No agreement was reached to increase emigration, but U.S. Jewish organizations generally expressed optimism that the summit represented a beginning for U.S.-Soviet dialogue and possible negotiation on the issue. Prior to the summit, Moscow announced it would allow the emigration of several Russians with spouses or other family members in the United States. Shortly after the summit, a joint U.S.-Soviet research project in Judaic studies was approved as part of a cultural exchange agreement.

Early in the year, it was revealed that over 10,000 Ethiopian Jews—known in Amharic as Falashas ("strangers")—had been secretly airlifted to Israel from refugee camps in Sudan. For years they had been forbidden to emigrate and had been caught up in fighting between

349

the Marxist government and rebel forces. The Israeli government, which had been conducting small-scale rescue operations since the 1970's, stepped up efforts late in 1984 to evacuate Ethiopian Jews who had fled to camps in Sudan. Israel sought to maintain a news blackout on Operation Moses, code name of the rescue mission, fearing that publicity might lead Sudan to end its discreet cooperation and halt the airlift. When the news was leaked in January, the airlift was indeed halted, amid angry denunciations from Ethiopia. In March, however, the United States was allowed to evacuate the Ethiopian Jews remaining in Sudan to safety in Israel.

The long search for notorious Nazi prison camp doctor Josef Mengele ended with the revelation in June that he had died in a drowning accident in 1979 in Brazil, where he had apparently been living for many years. Information provided by West German investigations of Mengele's family and associates led Brazilian authorities to exhume the body of a man buried under the name Wolfgang Gerhard. It was discovered that the real Gerhard, an Austrian engineer, had before his death in 1978 given his identity card to Mengele. Brazilian forensic experts and an international team of

pathologists confirmed that the body "within a reasonable scientific certainty" was indeed that of Mengele.

Other bitter memories of Nazi Germany and the Holocaust were evoked by President Reagan's visit on May 5 to a German military cemetery—which contained the graves of 49 members of the SS, the elite Nazi guard—during a trip to Europe for an economic summit meeting. Although the president had hoped to stress his theme of reconciliation and friendship with West Germany, the plan to lay a wreath at the Bitburg cemetery, at the invitation of West German Chancellor Helmut Kohl, sparked widespread protests, which did not abate despite a subsequent announcement that Reagan would visit the Bergen-Belsen concentration camp the same day. Many members of Congress, other prominent Americans, and leading Jewish and non-Jewish organizations—including the U.S. Holocaust Memorial Council and its chairman, Elie Wiesel—publicly opposed the president's visit to Bitburg.

Eric Strom, an American boy from Connecticut, celebrated his bar mitzvah during September in Kraków, Poland, in the first such ceremony there in over 20 years. The event was arranged by the Federation of Jewish Phi-

An exhibit called "Anne Frank in the World, 1929–1945" opened simultaneously in Amsterdam, Frankfurt, and New York. Among its contents was a newly released snapshot of father Otto (center), Anne (third from right), and friends going to a 1941 wedding.

Bearing Witness
Throughout the controversy surrounding President Ronald Reagan's May visit to a West German military cemetery where 49 members of the Nazi SS were buried, no voice of protest was more anguished than that of writer, teacher, and concentration camp survivor Elie Wiesel, chairman of the U.S. Holocaust Memorial Council. The outcry over the Bitburg visit climaxed when, during ceremonies honoring Wiesel for his work in preserving the memory of the Holocaust, he implored the president "to do something else . . . to find another way, another site" to mark U.S.-German reconciliation. Despite the plea, Reagan went ahead with the visit. Elie Wiesel was born in 1928 in Romania; in 1944 he and the rest of his family were deported to Auschwitz, where most of them died. Wiesel settled in the United States in the 1950's and became a U.S. citizen in 1963. His writings—all infused with biblical imagery, talmudic legends, and mystical Hasidic symbolism—include *Night, Dawn,* and, in 1985, *The Fifth Son.*

Elie Wiesel

lanthropies to provide a bar mitzvah before Kraków's Jewish community, now consisting almost entirely of elderly people.

Early in the year, the Conservative Rabbinical Assembly adopted a resolution to admit upon ordination all members of the 1985 graduating class of the Jewish Theological Seminary, the Conservative movement's rabbinical school; the class included Amy Eilberg, who thus became the first woman ever ordained as a Conservative rabbi.   L.G.

BUDDHISM

Early in the year, bomb blasts severely damaged the 1,100-year-old Borobudur temple on the island of Java, Indonesia. The historic Buddhist monument, uncovered in the 19th century from beneath layers of volcanic ash, had been reopened in 1983 after an international restoration program. The objective of the bombing seemed to be the destruction of the statues of Buddha on the upper level of the temple. Although no group claimed responsibility, Indonesian authorities said they suspected Muslim fundamentalists. The temple is regarded as one of the supreme masterpieces of Indo-Buddhist architecture.

The ongoing conflict in Sri Lanka between the Sinhalese Buddhist majority and the separatist Tamil Hindu minority in the Jaffna region became increasingly violent. Talks aimed at negotiating a settlement were held in Bhutan under Indian auspices in July and August but collapsed when the Tamils withdrew, accusing government forces of violating a cease-fire. Another truce was negotiated in October.

HINDUISM

Stories of the persecution of untouchables—Harijans—by caste Hindus continued to appear in the Indian press. A village of 400 untouchables was forced to flee when attacked by non-Harijan Hindus at Karamchedu in Tamil Nadu State. In the state of Gujarat, violence erupted when concessions were granted to lower-caste Hindus in such matters as government job quotas and higher education.

In August the *Mahabharata,* an epic poem illustrating Hinduism's deepest religious values, was staged at the Avignon festival in France, in a French-language version. The performance was hailed as a theatrical triumph, and English-language translations were planned for India and the United States.

RELIGION

SIKHISM

Strife continued in North India between members of the Sikh religious sect and the Hindu majority, with terrorist incidents occurring through much of the year. The crash of an Air India 747 aircraft off the coast of Ireland in June, with the loss of 329 lives, may have been the result of a Sikh terrorist bomb. In July, Prime Minister Rajiv Gandhi and the president of Akali Dal, the major Sikh party in the state of Punjab, signed an accord to resolve the conflict between the Sikhs and the central government. This accord led to the assassination of the Akali Dal president, Sant Harchand Singh Longowal, on August 20 by Sikh extremists. State elections nevertheless went ahead in September, nearly on schedule, and the Akali Dal won a majority in the legislature.

ISLAM

The Egyptian Parliament voted nearly unanimously in July to give Muslim women the right to divorce their husband if he takes a second wife. Muslim law (*sharia*) allows a man to have four wives if he can support and care for each one equally; however, individual marriage contracts may specify that the husband cannot take a second wife without the first wife's permission. The new law allows a woman the absolute right to institute a divorce proceeding in the case of a husband's second marriage. This legislation was actually a reinstatement of reforms passed earlier but repealed in the spring under pressure from increasingly active Muslim fundamentalists.

April saw fighting erupt again between police and fanatics of the proscribed Maitatsine religious sect in the city of Gombe, Nigeria. The incident was the fourth outburst in five years involving the extremist Islamic sect, whose antimodernist beliefs were regarded as heretical by most Nigerian Muslims. The violence left more than 100 people dead.

OTHER FAITHS

In September followers of the Indian guru Bhagwan Shree Rajneesh, who lived in a religious commune of about 1,500 people near Antelope, Oregon, staged a public denunciation of former sect officer Ma Anand Sheela. Her religious robes were publicly burned, and Rajneesh declared that Sheela and others were guilty of various crimes. In October, Sheela and three associates, who had fled to West Germany, were arrested there on U.S. federal charges of conspiracy to violate immigration laws and on Oregon state charges of attempted murder. Rajneesh himself was arrested by federal authorities in October, as he allegedly tried to flee to Bermuda; he pleaded guilty to arranging sham marriages for Indian nationals and agreed to pay a $400,000 fine and leave the United States. Most sect members left the commune shortly after his departure.

C.S.J.W.

REPUBLICAN PARTY. The first year of President Ronald Reagan's second term also marked the start of the 1988 Republican presidential campaign. The GOP-controlled Senate showed a new independence of the White House, even as the announced retirement of three Republican senators dimmed the party's prospects for holding onto the Senate after 1986.

Running for 1988. Only a few months after a landslide election had swept Reagan into another four-year term, a handful of Republicans began to position themselves for the next presidential race. The party's Midwest Leadership Conference, held in Grand Rapids, Mich., in June, attracted not only Vice-President George Bush—the presumed front-runner—but also Senate Majority Leader Robert Dole (Kan.) and Representative Jack F. Kemp (N.Y.). Bush was expected to run in 1988 as a loyal supporter of Reagan's policies and as the president's most logical successor. Dole, at some risk, made deficit reduction his main issue. Kemp, a champion of supply-side theory, sought tax cuts and overhaul of the monetary system as means of reinvigorating the economy.

During the summer, Dole, generally regarded as a moderate, named a conservative, Donald J. Devine, as consulting director of his political action committee, Campaign America. Kemp, whom some polls showed to be an early favorite among party conservatives, raised more than $1 million at a $1,000-a-plate dinner in New York City in October. Howard H. Baker, Jr. (Tenn.), a former majority leader who declined to run for reelection to the Senate in 1984, also was actively assembling a 1988 campaign staff.

White House-Senate Feud. Looking nervously toward 1986, when 22 of the GOP's 53 Senate

Governor Thomas Kean of New Jersey greets second graders on election day, prior to his landslide reelection victory.

seats would be up for election, some Senate Republicans clashed with the White House over budget policy, protectionism, and civil rights. A prime reason for the Senate's new-found feistiness was Dole, an aggressive majority leader eager to show his independence of the Reagan-Bush administration. Reagan believed that economic growth would eliminate the record federal budget deficits, but Dole and many other Republicans argued that continuing deficits would cripple the economy. Concern over the trade deficit also drove many Republicans to call for quotas on imports of foreign-made goods. Worried about antagonizing blacks, several Republicans in Congress and the Republican National Committee also filed briefs in the Supreme Court opposing the administration in a voting-rights case in North Carolina.

Fueling Republican fears about the 1986 elections were announcements by John East (N.C.), Paul Laxalt (Nev.), and Charles Mathias, Jr. (Md.) that they would not seek reelection to the Senate. The decision by Laxalt, a close friend and political ally of Reagan, was an especially serious blow.

An Emerging Majority? Members of the American Political Science Association, meeting in New Orleans in late summer, agreed that Republicans during the 1980's had significantly narrowed the lead held by the Democrats among voters who identified with either major political party. A sweeping reelection victory in November by New Jersey Governor Thomas Kean, a moderate Republican, encouraged party leaders who had been urging the GOP to broaden its base of support. Kean successfully appealed to a broad spectrum of voters that normally vote Democratic, winning majorities not only among union members but also among blacks.

Notable among those who formally embraced the GOP in 1985 was Jeane Kirkpatrick, who while still a registered Democrat had been Reagan's chief delegate to the United Nations. Another recruit was William Lucas, Wayne County (Mich.) chief executive and a black, who was regarded as a possible contender for the Republican nomination for governor of Michigan in 1986. On May 7, Republican National Committee Chairman Frank Fahrenkopf, Jr., announced a 100-day drive to persuade 100,000 rank-and-file Democrats to switch parties. Although the drive fell nearly 46,000 voters short, the party claimed 40,636 "changes in progress"—by voters who had agreed to turn Republican but had not yet reregistered.

See ELECTIONS IN THE UNITED STATES. *See also* biographies of George Bush and Robert Dole in PEOPLE IN THE NEWS. G.M.H.

RHODE ISLAND. *See* STATISTICS OF THE WORLD.

353

RHODESIA. *See* ZIMBABWE.

ROMANIA. Speculation grew in 1985 that President Nicolae Ceauşescu was ill and that he was grooming his wife, Elena, the deputy prime minister, or son, Nicu, the minister of youth and sport, as a possible successor. The president, who was 67, disappeared from public view for about ten days during the summer and appeared to be in poor health thereafter. The birthdays of both Nicolae and Elena Ceauşescu have become official holidays. Meanwhile, a number of key changes took place within the leadership group, including the ouster of General Constantin Olteanu as defense minister.

U.S. Secretary of State George Shultz, visiting Romania in December, warned President Ceauşescu that Romania might lose its "most favored nation" trading status if it did not improve its treatment of various Christian sects. Ceauşescu denied that Christians were being persecuted.

Romania, which has been engaged since 1982 in a crash program to pay off its foreign debts, suffered seriously in 1985 from shortages of consumer goods and of energy. On September 4 the party leadership announced that, in enterprises not meeting their export or raw-materials extraction quota, all personnel would be penalized by losing part of their pay.

With energy supplies already insufficient, the unusually harsh winter of 1984–1985 had brought heavy snowfall and extreme cold, causing great hardship. Production at coal mines and natural gas fields fell. To conserve energy, the government banned the use of private cars from January to March 1985 and placed restrictions on lighting in private residences. Later in the year, anticipating another winter of severe shortages, President Ceauşescu dismissed ministers in charge of energy, electric power, and mining. During the winter of 1984–1985, the nation also suffered from a water shortage, as the Danube River sank to its lowest level in years. In an effort to keep hydroelectric energy production high, Romania allegedly utilized more than its share of water from a common reservoir also used by Yugoslavia, drawing strong criticism from the Yugoslav government.

See STATISTICS OF THE WORLD. R.A.P.

RUSSIA. *See* UNION OF SOVIET SOCIALIST REPUBLICS.

RWANDA. *See* STATISTICS OF THE WORLD.

S

SAHARA, WESTERN. *See* AFRICA; MOROCCO.

ST. KITTS-NEVIS (ST. CHRISTOPHER AND NEVIS). *See* STATISTICS OF THE WORLD. *See also* CARIBBEAN BASIN.

ST. LUCIA. *See* STATISTICS OF THE WORLD.

ST. VINCENT AND THE GRENADINES. *See* STATISTICS OF THE WORLD.

SAMOA, AMERICAN. *See* STATISTICS OF THE WORLD: *American Samoa.*

SAMOA, WESTERN. *See* STATISTICS OF THE WORLD: *Western Samoa.*

SAN MARINO. *See* STATISTICS OF THE WORLD.

SÃO TOMÉ and PRÍNCIPE. *See* STATISTICS OF THE WORLD.

SASKATCHEWAN. *See* STATISTICS OF THE WORLD.

SAUDI ARABIA. Saudi Arabia experienced economic strains in 1985, as worldwide demand for oil declined.

Petroleum. A world oil glut meant pricing and production problems for the Saudi petroleum industry, as the kingdom sought to support OPEC price and production levels. But widespread discounting and overproduction by some OPEC members, coupled with price reductions and increased output from certain non-OPEC states, made the Saudi effort difficult, and ultimately led to a significant change in OPEC strategy. The cartel decided at its December meeting in Geneva that it would no longer defend oil prices through cuts in production but instead would seek to preserve a "fair share" of the oil market by cutting prices as necessary. The new plan appeared to take pressure off Saudi Arabia, which had been acting as "swing producer"—varying its production to maintain the overall production and price levels supposedly agreed upon by OPEC.

Earlier in the year, in January, OPEC lowered the price of Saudi light, the industry marker, from $29 to $28 per barrel, maintaining an overall production quota of 16 million barrels per day (b/d). The Saudis accepted a reduced quota so as to allow other member states greater production levels. By June, however, Saudi production had dropped to 2.2 million b/d, far below its reduced quota of 4.35 million b/d. Saudi production rose in September, as the government began offering discounts of $2 per barrel on the official OPEC price.

Early in October, OPEC met in Vienna, but failed to reach an agreement on demands by six members for higher production quotas. Saudi Arabia indicated plans to increase its own production to an average of about 3.5 million b/d during the fourth quarter.

Economy. Reduced oil income and the continued bankrolling of Iraq in its war with Iran exacerbated a prolonged recession. Company failures were up significantly, and the government was forced to slow down, postpone, or eliminate some capital projects. Despite the cuts, the kingdom ended the 1984 fiscal year in March with a large budget deficit. A new five-year plan for 1985–1990 was budgeted at $277 billion; its goals included greater efficiency in use of resources; diversification in manufacturing, agriculture, and finance; and promotion of private-sector involvement in development.

Foreign Affairs. Relations with Iraq remained close, as the Saudis continued to pump 500,000 b/d of crude on Iraq's account and also completed construction of a 500,000-b/d pipeline spur from Iraqi oilfields to the Saudi east-west oil pipeline. Attempts were also made to improve relations with Iran, and, in May, Foreign Minister Saud al-Faisal became the first Saudi official to visit Tehran since the 1979 overthrow of the shah. Shortly after the visit, several bombs exploded in Riyadh, the Saudi capital. Iran blamed Iraq, saying it was an attempt to sabotage the reconciliation, although the pro-Iranian, Lebanese-based Islamic Holy War group reportedly claimed responsibility.

Saudi-American relations remained strained over the issue of arms sales. In late January the Reagan administration decided to postpone the sale of 40 F-15 fighter-bombers, along with other weapons, until a study of Saudi military requirements vis-à-vis regional stability was completed. In September the Saudis purchased more than $4 billion worth of fighter planes and other arms from Great Britain. It was the first time in roughly 20 years that Saudi Arabia had bought military aircraft from a country other than the United States.

Sultan Salman al-Saud of Saudi Arabia, a jet pilot, enjoys simulated weightlessness as he prepares to become the Arab world's first astronaut. During his flight aboard the U.S. space shuttle Discovery in June, the prince participated in experiments and observed the launching of a communications satellite for the Arab world.

The nation's most important social welfare program celebrated its golden anniversay this year; with Secretary of Labor Frances Perkins (center) and several senators as witnesses, the Social Security Act was signed into law by President Franklin D. Roosevelt in 1935.

In February, King Fahd made his first official state visit to Washington. Fahd and President Ronald Reagan reportedly got along well, but nothing of substance was said to have been accomplished.

See STATISTICS OF THE WORLD.   C.H.A.

SENEGAL. *See* STATISTICS OF THE WORLD.

SEYCHELLES. *See* STATISTICS OF THE WORLD.

SIERRA LEONE. *See* STATISTICS OF THE WORLD.

SINGAPORE. On January 2, 1985, 44-year-old Goh Chok Tong became Singapore's first deputy prime minister and heir-designate to Prime Minister Lee Kuan Yew. Lee, who has led the country since 1959, planned to relinquish the office of prime minister when he reaches age 65 in 1988. He was widely expected to be named to the thus far ceremonial office of president upon stepping down as prime minister.

In March the prime minister announced the resignation of incumbent President C. V. Devan Nair, stating that Nair was incapacitated because of a long-standing alcohol dependency. In August the head of state broadcasting, Wee Kim Wee, was named as the new president.

Government policies aimed at encouraging better educated parents to have more children by giving such children preference in admis-sion to the better schools were discontinued, after they had proved widely unpopular among all parents.

During the past decade, Singapore had led the world in economic growth, averaging about 8 percent per year. In 1984 that rate dropped sharply, and by mid-1985 the country faced a strong possibility of negative growth. Lagging recoveries in other countries helped damage Singapore's trade-dependent economy. A joint government-business study group also put blame on heavy labor costs—a result of government policies aimed at encouraging high technology and discouraging labor-intensive economic activity. To reverse the decline, unions agreed to forgo a midyear wage increase.

See STATISTICS OF THE WORLD.   K.M.

SOCIAL SECURITY. The U.S. Congress in 1985 debated whether, in the effort to cut federal budget deficits, social security benefits should be scrutinized in the same way as other federal programs. President Ronald Reagan had proposed doing so early in his administration, encountering a deluge of opposition. He promised during his 1984 reelection campaign to oppose cutbacks in social security, and the budget he transmitted to Congress in February kept that pledge. The Republican leadership in the Senate, however, felt that a deficit reduction package should require the elderly to bear some of the burden of budgetary restraint. Social security benefits had been automatically increased each year to reflect the annual rise in the federal Consumer Price Index. Republicans proposed to skip the January 1986 cost-of-living increase (COLA) for social security and all other programs which provided automatic benefit increases, except those (such as food stamps) that targeted benefits on low-income persons. The president endorsed the COLA freeze as part of an overall deficit reduction package, which the Senate approved in May by a vote of 50 to 49. Vice-President George Bush cast the deciding vote.

The budget plan approved by the House had, however, proposed full COLA's, and after protracted negotiations in conference committee the COLA's remained untouched. Reagan angered Senate Republicans by supporting the COLA's in early July, leaving the senators open to greater political risk for their stand.

In August the president suggested that social security revenues and expenditures not be counted in the federal budget. Congress subsequently approved legislation to remove both social security and medicare from the federal budget by 1993. In fact, after more than a decade of red ink, the social security trust funds in 1985 were taking in more in revenue than they were paying out. Medicare's long-term financial health was more precarious, because healthcare costs continued to rise more rapidly than prices generally. Both houses of Congress had pending legislation to control costs in medicare through freezes or limits on reimbursements to doctors and hospitals, as well as through extensions of the medicare component of the social security tax to employees not previously affected.

The Reagan administration announced in December that it would begin in January to review all 2.6 million persons on the social security disability rolls to determine their eligibility to continue receiving benefits. A similar review, halted in 1984, had provoked charges that thousands of persons were unjustly dropped from the disability rolls.   J.A.R.

SOLOMON ISLANDS. *See* STATISTICS OF THE WORLD.

SOMALIA. Famine and hostilities with Ethiopia continued to be the main problems facing Somalia in 1985. The severe drought that plagued much of Africa affected Somalia too. Some 3 million Somalis and hundreds of thousands of Ethiopian refugees were threatened by famine, and a cholera epidemic that broke out in March had killed over 2,000 people by midyear. Continued insurgency against government forces by the Democratic Front for the Salvation of Somalia, an Ethiopian-supported coalition of rebel groups, led to a clampdown on areas where the DFSS operates.

In April, President Muhammad Siad Barre restored political ties with Libya, broken in 1981 when Libyan leader Muammar al-Qaddafi had pledged $600 million to support DFSS insurgency. The Somali government also held talks with the new Sudanese regime following the overthrow of President Jaafar al-Nimeiry of Sudan, the closest Somali ally in the ongoing struggle with neighboring Ethiopia.

Relations with Ethiopia remained tense. An official Somali radio broadcast accused Ethiopian troops of attacking a Somali garrison on January 1, a charge the Ethiopians denied. In late October the Somali government reported that its troops had repulsed two attacks by Ethiopian forces in the north.

In January, Somalia took measures to revamp its weak economy; among them was a 29 percent currency devaluation. The International Monetary Fund later announced that it had awarded Somalia nearly $55 million in standby credits and currency adjustment loans.

See STATISTICS OF THE WORLD.   R.B.

SOUTH AFRICA. Violent clashes between government security forces and predominantly black antiapartheid protesters overshadowed other developments in South Africa in 1985. By year's end, the official death toll since widespread clashes first broke out in September 1984 was over 1,000. Unprecedented diplomatic and financial pressure on the South African government followed the July 21 imposition of a state of emergency—the first since 1960—in close to 40 riot-torn magisterial districts around Johannesburg, Port Elizabeth, and Cape Town.

Political and Social Unrest. President Pieter W. Botha initiated limited reforms early in the

Thousands of mourners gathered near Port Elizabeth, in South Africa, for the burial of black riot victims in April.

year that failed to still civil unrest. Sections of the 1957 Immorality Act and the entire 1949 Prohibition of Mixed Marriages Act (prohibiting sexual relations and marriages between races) were repealed, as was legislation that had restricted membership of a political party to one race. The reforms were described as insignificant by the major antiapartheid groups—the United Democratic Front, or UDF (a multiracial alliance of hundreds of trade unions and community, religious, and student organizations), and the outlawed African National Congress (the black nationalist group that seeks to overthrow the Pretoria government). In February, ANC leader Nelson Mandela, in prison for over 20 years under a life sentence for sabotage and subversion, refused an offer of freedom because it was conditional on his renouncing the use of violence. Mandela's wife, Winnie, was arrested twice in December for returning and for attempting to return to her home in Soweto, a center of black unrest, from which she had been banned.

By late 1985, South African Defense Force (SADF) troops had become a permanent feature in many townships. Black security force members and blacks seen as supporters of the government were targeted for attacks by other blacks.

Unrest spread from the large urban townships to remote towns and the tribal homelands set up by the government. On March 21, the 25th anniversary of the fatal shooting of 69 blacks by police at Sharpeville, police opened fire on a protest in the Eastern Cape, killing 20 people according to official reports. The incident had begun when several thousand blacks, in what the government called an illegal march, headed for a memorial service for blacks killed in recent rioting. Police said they ordered the crowd to disperse—an order demonstrators denied hearing—and then were forced to fire in self-defense. Because funerals had become a principal vehicle for protest demonstrations, new restrictions imposed in the emergency-decree areas in midyear banned open-air services, limited the number to be buried to one per service, and prohibited speakers from discussing government policies. Nevertheless, large funeral gatherings and incidents of violence continued. During a five-day period in late November, at least 36 blacks were killed in clashes with police near Pretoria.

Under the emergency provisions the government was also empowered to detain people without trial for (renewable) short periods, bar journalists from black townships, and impose curfews. There were widespread allegations that detainees were being assaulted and tortured by police.

In December, some foes of the government began to utilize violence more frequently. In one incident, on December 23, six whites were killed when a bomb went off at a shopping mall. Tribal violence also flared up. In the worst incident, on December 25, over 50 persons died in fighting between members of the Zulu and Pondo tribes.

In August, 38 UDF leaders were charged, in two trials in Pretoria and Natal, with the capital crime of treason. On the eve of the Natal trial, defense attorney and UDF activist Victoria Mxenge, a black, was assassinated by four black men at her Durban home. Mxenge's friends charged that her death was the work of a "death squad." Also in August, the Reverend Allan Boesak, a UDF leader and the head of the World Alliance of Reformed Churches, was detained after organizing a protest march. He was released the next month, pending a trial on subversion charges. On December 9, charges were dropped against 12 of the 16 UDF leaders on trial in Natal.

On August 15, faced with growing international isolation of his government, President Botha delivered a speech in Durban, to a meeting of his ruling National Party, that many had expected would propose extensive reforms. But Botha rejected outright the prospect of majority rule and committed himself only to negotiations with "duly elected" black leaders who renounced violence. On September 30, in a speech to a National Party congress, Botha outlined what he described as an agenda for racial reform. He said that political rights would be exercised within a system of complex structures so that "one group is not placed in a position where it can dominate other groups." Some weeks earlier, Botha had announced that black residents of the four independent homelands, who had lost their South African citizenship, would be granted a form of dual nationality.

On June 14 the SADF attacked South African refugees living in Gaborone, the capital of Botswana, killing at least 15 people. The raid—aimed at ANC insurgents—was unanimously condemned by the UN Security Council. The South African government was believed to be responsible for raids in December into Angola and Lesotho in which at least 15 South African dissidents and Namibian guerrillas were killed.

Foreign Affairs. South Africa found itself under broad diplomatic attack. In September, to forestall the imposition of strong economic sanctions by the U.S. Congress, President Ronald Reagan initiated less stringent sanctions by executive order. He placed a ban on the export of computers to police and security forces, on the export of nuclear technology, and on loans to the government except those that would further the welfare of all races. He also banned the sale of Krugerrands, the South African gold coins. In September the European Community also imposed sanctions, including an embargo on oil, arms, and law-enforcement equipment.

Economic Problems. Political unrest seriously eroded international investor confidence. In February, Citicorp, the largest U.S. bank, halted all new loans to South Africa. After the declaration of the state of emergency, many U.S. banks and other international lenders announced they would no longer roll over short-term loans or make new loans to the government or private borrowers. As a result, in late August the government froze all trading on the Johannesburg Stock Exchange for several days. On September 1 it suspended payments of principal on foreign loans and imposed restrictions on currency exchange and securities transactions in an effort to restrict foreign capital outflow.

See STATISTICS OF THE WORLD. See also SOUTH WEST AFRICA. J.F.

SOUTH CAROLINA. See STATISTICS OF THE WORLD.

SOUTH DAKOTA. See STATISTICS OF THE WORLD.

SOUTH WEST AFRICA, or NAMIBIA. In 1985, South Africa claimed that the war against guerrillas of the South West Africa People's Organization (Swapo) for control of South West Africa (Namibia) was almost won. However,

SOUTH WEST AFRICA

South Africa declared the territory's northern quarter out of bounds to all but security forces and local residents, saying it could not ensure the safety of others.

The government again stalled on the implementation of UN Resolution 435, which provides for Namibian independence and UN-supervised elections. Pretoria continued to insist on linking a Cuban troop withdrawal

The first all-military mission of the U.S. manned space program, reportedly the installation of an electronic spy satellite, was carried out on January 24–27 by the shuttle Discovery; here, Air Force instruments monitor the takeoff.

from Angola to the implementation of the UN resolution. Even the United States, which supports linkage, grew frustrated at the delay in implementing 435 and strongly criticized Pretoria's June establishment of a "transitional government of national unity" in the territory. However, the United States—and Britain—abstained when the Security Council voted to adopt a resolution condemning South Africa's policies in Namibia.

In April, South African forces completed their withdrawal from Angola, the base of Swapo forces, as called for in a 1984 agreement. In June, however, South Africa launched a new anti-Swapo operation in southern Angola. Another series of raids was launched in mid-September.   J.F.

SOVIET UNION. *See* UNION OF SOVIET SOCIALIST REPUBLICS.

SPACE EXPLORATION. While continuing to carry out scientific work and to launch and repair satellites, the U.S. space shuttle program performed its first classified military missions in 1985. The Soviet Union refurbished a Salyut space station that had been thought dead.

Space Shuttle. The first all-military shuttle mission—with coded communications, a classified payload, and even the launch time kept secret until minutes before ignition—was carried out by the shuttle *Discovery* on January 24–27. Despite the secrecy, reports surfaced from knowledgeable sources suggesting that the main payload was an electronic spy satellite, known as a ferret, with long roll-out dipole antennas for listening to Soviet communications. The *Discovery* flew again on April 12–19; the launching of two satellites, the main goal of this mission, was overshadowed by the presence among the seven crew members of "congressional observer" Jake Garn, Republican senator from Utah, who became the first politician to fly in space. The first satellite was launched without incident, but the second, a Hughes Aircraft communications satellite called Leasat 3 that was to be leased to the Defense Department, could not be activated.

An April 29–May 6 *Challenger* mission carried a crew of seven and, in the cargo bay, two satellites and the 15-ton, European-built Spacelab, with several materials-processing and life-sciences experiments. On board were 24

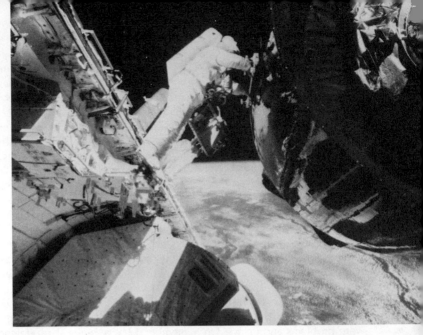

One of the most dramatic space flights of 1985 was the August 27 to September 3 trip of the Discovery, whose mission was to launch and repair satellites. Here, astronaut William Fisher prepares to redeploy the Leasat satellite after "hot-wiring" it during a space-walk.

rats and 2 squirrel monkeys, riding in a new holding pen that may need some design modification: the rats' food bars crumbled and floated loose in the lab module, as did some waste products. (Postflight examination of the rats showed a decrease in bone and muscle strength and in the release of growth hormone, both apparently the result of weightlessness.) TV and film cameras were used to take dazzling pictures of the auroras, the northern and southern lights, from above the atmosphere.

Another *Challenger* mission, flown by a crew of seven on July 29–August 6, carried an array of solar and stellar telescopes and completed the testing of the last major piece of Spacelab hardware, the instrument pointer. The mission was plagued by various technical troubles, but of more interest to many members of the public were the new space cans developed by Coca-Cola and Pepsi-Cola and tried out by the astronauts; they reported that neither brand yielded a tasty drink but that one Coke can at least delivered a genuine carbonated beverage rather than foam.

A flight by the *Discovery* on June 17–24 launched three communications satellites successfully, and a new kind of satellite, called Spartan, was flown with an X-ray telescope and then retrieved by the shuttle. The shuttle also carried a special mirror that was used in a target-tracking experiment, involving a laser beam fired from Hawaii—part of research for the Reagan administration's Strategic Defense Initiative, the "Star Wars" plan for defense against nuclear missiles.

The *Discovery* took off on August 27 with a crew of five to launch three satellites and to repair Leasat 3 by attaching new electronics so it could be controlled from the ground. Mission specialists James van Hoften and William Fisher performed the Leasat work during spacewalks over two days. On October 27 the satellite was launched toward its proper orbit by engineers controlling the craft from a Hughes Aircraft site in California.

The *Atlantis,* the fourth craft to join the U.S. shuttle fleet, made its first voyage on October 3–7 with a crew of five military officers and a classified cargo widely reported to be a pair of $100 million communications satellites for the advanced Defense Satellite Communications Systems (DSCS-3). These are hardened against the effects of nuclear explosions in space and incorporate features to protect against jamming. A Star Wars laser-tracking test was also believed to be part of the mission.

On October 30 the *Challenger* carried into orbit the largest space crew ever. The West German government paid NASA some $65 million for use of the shuttle. The eight-person crew, including two West Germans and one Dutch member, spent a week in orbit and conducted nearly 80 experiments.

Launched at night on November 26 into a moonlit sky, the *Atlantis* left a brilliant white trail as it began its successful second flight. Two members of its crew of seven "walked" in space for more than 12 hours as they assembled and took apart a 45-foot-long truss and a pyramid-shaped module.

Military Tests. The Air Force's antisatellite weapon (ASAT) scored its first hit on its first flight. The two-stage missile is fired from a rapidly climbing F-15 Eagle jet fighter, and infrared telescopes let it home in on the "body heat" of a satellite so it can destroy by direct impact rather than by using explosives. Originally the ASAT was to be tried against balloon targets launched by small rockets, but there were problems and delays. On September 13 the Department of Defense fired ASAT against what it described as a defunct satellite; it was later revealed, however, that the target was a solar studies satellite that had been returning useful data.

The Air Force contracted with Martin Marietta Aerospace to build ten single-use rockets to provide a backup for the shuttle system in times of national emergency or in case a shuttle is damaged. The program was started because of NASA's problems in maintaining its original ambitious launch schedules. On September 23 the Defense Department activated a unified space command, charged with overseeing all U.S. military programs in space.

Commercial Space. In July, NASA awarded five contracts as seed money for development of marketing plans and products ranging from available photos of the earth shot from space to protein crystals manufactured in orbit. Meanwhile, Space Services Inc. of Houston and the Celestis Group of Melbourne, Fla., announced that they soon would offer burials in space for cremated remains.

Soviet Activities. The Salyut 7 space station, launched in 1982, apparently suffered a major electrical system failure. The Soviet Union on June 6 launched a two-man crew in a Soyuz spacecraft to salvage the station. They spent several weeks reactivating it. On September 17 a spacecraft was launched with a crew of three to rendezvous with the Salyut. However, the crew returned to earth on November 21 after the commander became ill.

See also ASTRONOMY.   D.D.

SPAIN. On June 12, 1985, Spain and Portugal signed a treaty granting them entry, effective January 1, 1986, into the European Community (EC). In other events, the Spanish government of Prime Minister Felipe González Márquez sought to deal with internal terrorism and maintained a somewhat independent foreign policy vis à vis the United States.

EC Treaty. The last obstacle to the EC treaty was removed in March when Greece withdrew a threat to block Spanish and Portuguese entry. Greece had feared economic—particularly agricultural—competition from the Iberian states but was mollified by the EC's promise of a $1.5 billion subsidy. The only discordant note was a renewal of violence by Basque extremists. On the day Spain signed the treaty, the separatist group ETA (Basque Homeland and Liberty) claimed credit for assassinating an army colonel and his driver.

Terrorism. Containment of Basque terrorists continued to be a grave problem. There had been reason for optimism when, in late January, the Basque provincial government and Madrid forged an agreement they hoped would isolate the extremists. Much credit for the accord went to José Antonio Ardanza, a moderate who had been named head of the Basque Nationalist Party (PNV). An alliance between Socialists and the PNV in the regional parliament put greater pressure on the political wing of the ETA, Herri Batasuna (People's Unity). However, violent acts did not cease with the new alliance, which Herri Batasuna condemned.

The ETA subsequently claimed responsibility for the April 12 bombing of a restaurant near the joint U.S.-Spanish air base Torrejón de Ardoz, although officials believed Shiite Muslim extremists were responsible. No Americans were among the 20 persons killed.

Foreign Affairs. President Ronald Reagan visited Madrid in May, hoping he could strengthen González's resistance to internal pressure to revoke Spanish membership in NATO. Earlier in the year, in an awkward incident, Spain had expelled two U.S. diplomats for allegedly photographing the antennae on the roof of the presidential office complex in Madrid. To soften Spanish opposition to NATO, Reagan agreed to U.S.-Spanish talks on reduction of the U.S. troop force in Spain. A national referendum on NATO membership was scheduled for early 1986.

Politics. Two senior officials at the Spanish Foreign Ministry were asked to resign in early February when they were implicated in a scheme to channel secret funds to Switzerland. Their resignations came shortly after the arrest of the former Spanish consul general in Geneva; investigating officials obtained evidence implicating up to 80 Spaniards in the operation.

In July, González surprised many observers by overhauling his cabinet. The most significant result of the shakeup—which affected a half dozen ministerial posts—was the replacement of Foreign Minister Fernando Morán López by Francisco Fernandez Ordonez. Morán, reportedly bitter over his removal, had garnered much credit for Spain's successful negotiations with the EC.

Gibraltar. Sovereignty over the British crown colony of Gibraltar, at Spain's southern tip, continued to be a thorny problem. The border between Spain and Gibraltar was fully opened in February, in accord with a 1984 agreement with the British. In further Anglo-Spanish talks, Spain pushed for full sovereignty over the strategically located peninsula. At the same time, the Gibraltar Socialist Labor Party headed a petition drive opposing a transfer of sovereignty; nearly 10,000 signatures were collected among Gibraltar's 30,000 inhabitants, most of whom consider themselves British and oppose Spanish rule. Many Gibraltar residents expressed anxiety over an influx of Spanish workers into Gibraltar; some also voiced concerns that businesses might leave Gibraltar for Spain, where labor costs are lower.

See STATISTICS OF THE WORLD. J.O.S.

The border between Spain and the British crown colony of Gibraltar, which had been closed since 1969, was fully opened in February. An increase in tourism and in the number of Spaniards seeking work on the peninsula was expected.

Sports

In 1985, sports headlines sparkled with the names of veteran heroes like Pete Rose, Kareem Abdul-Jabbar, and Wayne Gretzky and rising stars such as Dwight Gooden, William ("The Refrigerator") Perry, and Boris Becker.

Upsets jolted the sports world in 1985. The lightly regarded Kansas City Royals defeated the St. Louis Cardinals in the first all-Missouri World Series. Villanova, an also-ran in the conference that included Georgetown, dethroned the Hoyas in an all-Big East finale for the college basketball championship. Michael Spinks handed Larry Holmes his first loss and became the first light heavyweight to win the heavyweight boxing title. Boris Becker, 17, became the youngest men's Wimbledon tennis

Champagne spurts for French auto racer Alain Prost (left), who won the 43rd Monaco Grand Prix on May 19; second place went to Italian Michele Alboreto (right).

champion. A tragic fire and a deadly riot marred the year in soccer.

AUTOMOBILE RACING

The Indianapolis 500 was won by Danny Sullivan, 35, a former New York City cabdriver from Louisville, Ky., who survived a 360-degree, 200-mile-per-hour spin in midrace to defeat veteran Mario Andretti by 2.47 seconds. Sullivan won 45 percent of a record $517,662 purse for his 3-hour, 16-minute ride in a March-Cosworth.

Andretti, 45, who had taken the 1984 Championship Auto Racing Teams (CART) title, won three of the first four 1985 races in the $11.2 million series, driving a Lola co-owned by actor Paul Newman and Chicago importer Carl Haas. In the Michigan 500, however, Andretti crashed and sustained injuries that forced him to miss a race for the first time in his 21-year career. Al Unser, Sr., took the series title by one point, over his son, Al Unser, Jr., in a duel that finished in the season's final race.

Bill Elliott set an all-time money-winning record for race drivers as he dominated the National Association for Stock Car Auto Racing (Nascar) season for late-model, American-built stock cars. He won more than $2 million. Nearly half of Elliott's total came in a bonus from the R. J. Reynolds Tobacco Company, after he had won all but the third of four races: the Daytona 500, Winston 500, World 500, and Southern 500. Despite winning 10 of the year's first 20 races, Elliott was passed by former champion Darrell Waltrip for the season championship. Waltrip had only 3 wins for the season, but he amassed points in short-track races where Elliott had trouble finishing.

After three years of winning more races than any other driver in the Formula One series,

Alain Prost of France gained enough points in 1985 to win the world championship title for the first time. McLaren took the constructors championship. Klaus Ludwig of West Germany won his third 24 Hours of Le Mans in June with the Joest/New Man Porsche team; the winning Porsche covered nearly 3,162 miles, a record. The factory Rothmans Porsche team took the World Endurance Championship later in the year. S.G.

BASEBALL

A season that saw Pete Rose break Ty Cobb's career base hit record, a two-day players' strike, and an image-deflating drug scandal was capped by the most remarkable series of postseason comebacks in baseball history. The Kansas City Royals rallied from 3-1 deficits in both the league championship playoffs (being played as a best-of-seven series for the first time) and the World Series, to become baseball's world champions.

Season Highlights. Rose led a big-name charge at the baseball record book, in which some of the game's greatest players firmly established their Hall of Fame credentials. On the same August day, Rod Carew of the California Angels, at age 39, became the 16th player in major league history to get 3,000 hits, while Tom Seaver of the Chicago White Sox, at age 40, became the 17th pitcher ever to notch 300 victories. Just three weeks earlier, Nolan Ryan of the Houston Astros, already the record-holder for career strikeouts, became the first pitcher in baseball history to strike out 4,000 batters. And on the last day of the season, Phil Niekro of the New York Yankees, an ageless wonder at 46, became the 18th pitcher to win 300 games.

But these achievements paled next to Rose's triumph. Ty Cobb had 4,191 hits, a record long thought unapproachable. But Rose, at age 44 a player-manager with the Cincinnati Reds, had spent over two decades chipping away at Cobb's mark. He lined a single on September 11 for hit number 4,192, to become the most prolific hitter in baseball history. (*See also* biography in PEOPLE IN THE NEWS.)

It wasn't only the old-timers who made the headlines. In his second season in the majors, 20-year-old Dwight Gooden of the New York Mets became the youngest pitcher ever to win

Zen Baseball

Sports Illustrated pulled off an April Fool's Day hoax with an article that generated even more interest than the annual swimsuit issue. In "The Curious Case of Sidd Finch," author George Plimpton unveiled the existence of an eccentric, mystical baseball prodigy who pitched 168 mile-per-hour fastballs and could not decide whether or not to join the New York Mets. Sidd (for "Siddhartha"), a Harvard dropout who plays the French horn, claimed to have learned "the art of the pitch" by throwing rocks in the Himalayas and meditating. Many *Sports Illustrated* readers swallowed Plimpton's masterful tall tale, and on an April 1 news broadcast, ABC-TV devoted three minutes of straight-faced coverage to the story before letting on that it was a spoof. Plimpton himself was soon working on a novel tracing Finch's fabulous career with the Mets.

20 games, on the way to a 24-4 mark, and the youngest ever to win a Cy Young Award; he was a unanimous selection as the National League's best pitcher. Vince Coleman of the St. Louis Cardinals stole 110 bases, setting a rookie record and becoming only the fourth player ever to steal 100 bases or more.

Don Mattingly of the Yankees was named the American League's Most Valuable Player on the basis of his .324 average, 35 homers, and a league-leading 145 runs batted in. Wade Boggs of the Boston Red Sox hit .368 with 240 hits, both league-leading figures. Darrell Evans of the Detroit Tigers led the American League in homers with 40. Twenty-one-year-old Bret Saberhagen of the Royals was the league's Cy Young Award winner with a 20-6 record and a 2.87 earned run average. Ron Guidry of the Yankees had the league's most wins, 22, and Dan Quisenberry of the Royals had the most saves, 37. Dave Stieb had the best earned run average among the league's starting pitchers, 2.48.

Willie McGee of the Cardinals was named the National League's Most Valuable Player; he led the league with a .353 batting average. Dale Murphy of the Atlanta Braves had the most home runs, 37, and Dave Parker of the Reds had the most RBI's, 125. Gooden not

The New York Mets' Dwight Gooden led all major league pitchers in victories (24), ERA (1.53), and strikeouts (268) and received the National League's Cy Young Award.

NATIONAL LEAGUE				
Eastern Division	**W**	**L**	**Pct.**	**GB**
St. Louis Cardinals	101	61	.623	—
New York Mets	98	64	.605	3
Montréal Expos	84	77	.522	16½
Chicago Cubs	77	84	.478	23½
Philadelphia Phillies	75	87	.463	26
Pittsburgh Pirates	57	104	.354	43½
Western Division				
Los Angeles Dodgers	95	67	.586	—
Cincinnati Reds	89	72	.553	5½
Houston Astros	83	79	.512	12
San Diego Padres	83	79	.512	12
Atlanta Braves	66	96	.407	29
San Francisco Giants	62	100	.383	33
AMERICAN LEAGUE				
Eastern Division	**W**	**L**	**Pct.**	**GB**
Toronto Blue Jays	99	62	.615	—
New York Yankees	97	64	.602	2
Detroit Tigers	84	77	.522	15
Baltimore Orioles	83	78	.516	16
Boston Red Sox	81	81	.500	18½
Milwaukee Brewers	71	90	.441	28
Cleveland Indians	60	102	.370	39½
Western Division				
Kansas City Royals	91	71	.562	—
California Angels	90	72	.556	1
Chicago White Sox	85	77	.525	6
Minnesota Twins	77	85	.475	14
Oakland Athletics	77	85	.475	14
Seattle Mariners	74	88	.457	17
Texas Rangers	62	99	.385	28½

PENNANT PLAYOFFS
National League—St. Louis defeated Los Angeles, 4 games to 2
American League—Kansas City defeated Toronto, 4 games to 3
WORLD SERIES—Kansas City defeated St. Louis, 4 games to 3

only led all pitchers in wins (24) but also in earned run average (1.53) and strikeouts (268). Jeff Reardon of the Montréal Expos led in saves with 41.

Playoffs. Kansas City and St. Louis both won pennants in their respective leagues and met in an all-Missouri World Series. The Royals had lost the first two games of the playoffs to the favored Toronto Blue Jays before recovering to win four of the last five. The Cardinals also lost their first two games to the Los Angeles Dodgers, then swept the last four, nailing down the pennant on a dramatic three-run, come-from-behind homer by Jack Clark.

World Series. The Royals bats were mostly silent as they lost the first game, 3-1. In the second game, Charlie Liebrandt took a two-hit shutout into the ninth inning, but the Cardinals exploded for four runs after two men were out to win, 4-2. After a 6-1 victory in the next game, the Royals were stopped, 3-0, on John Tudor's shutout and found themselves on the brink of elimination. Although Kansas City won the fifth game, 6-1, in the sixth they trailed, 1-0, going into the ninth inning against a team

that was 88-0 for the season in games in which they took a lead into the final inning. Once again the Royals defied the odds, pushing across two runs on three singles (one of them on an umpire's controversial call) and a passed ball. The deciding game was anticlimatic; the Royals destroyed the frustrated Cardinals, 11-0, as Saberhagen won his second Series game and the Most Valuable Player award.

Drug Scandal. Testimony about widespread drug use by major league baseball players tarnished the game's image. During one trial (of a man accused of selling cocaine to players), testimony in exchange for immunity from prosecution was given by seven current or former players—including Keith Hernandez of the Mets, Lonnie Smith of the Royals, and Dave Parker of the Reds. They told of their own drug use and mentioned other star players as users of cocaine and other drugs. Baseball commis-

Third baseman George Brett (above) and pitcher Bret Saberhagen (below) helped the Kansas City Royals take their first World Series title ever.

sioner Peter Ueberroth subsequently called on all major league players to submit voluntarily to testing for drug use. However, negotiations with the players' union failed to produce agreement on a testing program.

All-Star Game. The National League won for the 21st time in the last 23 All-Star games, beating the American League by a score of 6-1 in a game highlighted by the pitching of the Padres' LaMarr Hoyt and the Astros' Nolan Ryan. The 56th All-Star game was played in the Minneapolis Metrodome on July 16.

Players' Strike. A players' walkout on August 6 aroused fears that a repeat of 1981's 50-day strike was at hand, but the 1985 strike ended after just two days, with the players and owners signing a five-year agreement to replace one that had expired on December 31, 1984. The players agreed to increase the eligibility requirement for salary arbitration from two years of major league service to three (beginning in 1987). They also agreed to annual contributions to the benefit plan that were less than what they had sought—but still significantly higher than the prior level. The settlement also provided for an increase in the minimum player salary and removed limitations on free agency.   M.L.

BASKETBALL

Playing a near-perfect game, Villanova upset top-ranked Georgetown to win the National Collegiate Athletic Association championship. The Los Angeles Lakers achieved what they had been unable to accomplish in eight previous attempts—victory over the Boston Celtics in a National Basketball Association championship series.

College. In one of the most stunning upsets in the 47-year history of the NCAA tournament, Villanova won its first title ever on April 1 in Lexington, Ky., snapping Georgetown's 17-game winning streak. The final score was 66-64.

Georgetown was seeking to become the first team since 1973 to repeat as the NCAA champion. During the regular season they lost only three games, while the Wildcats lost ten times, twice to the Hoyas. In upsetting Georgetown, the Wildcats came very close to perfection, hitting 22 of 28 shots from the field and 22 of 27 from the free-throw line. During the regular season, defensive-minded Georgetown, led by 7-foot center Patrick Ewing, had limited its opponents to an average of 39 percent shooting from the field, the lowest in the nation.

Jacksonville (Ala.) State took NCAA Division II honors, and North Park (Ill.) won its fourth Division III championship in eight years. In women's play, Old Dominion defeated Georgia, 70-65, for the NCAA Division I championship, the third national title for the Lady Monarchs but their first under the auspices of the NCAA. California Poly-Pomona won the Division II championship and Scranton (Pa.) the Division III title. In other championship play, Fort Hays (Kans.) won its second straight

Ed Pinckney, Villanova star center, played a prominent part in the Wildcats' thrilling 66-64 upset victory over top-ranked Georgetown, in the NCAA title game.

NATIONAL BASKETBALL ASSOCIATION
1984–1985 Regular Season

EASTERN CONFERENCE

Atlantic Division	W	L	Pct.	GB
Boston Celtics	63	19	.768	—
Philadelphia 76ers	58	24	.707	5
New Jersey Nets	42	40	.512	21
Washington Bullets	40	42	.488	23
New York Knicks	24	58	.293	39

Central Division	W	L	Pct.	GB
Milwaukee Bucks	59	23	.720	—
Detroit Pistons	46	36	.561	13
Chicago Bulls	38	44	.463	21
Cleveland Cavaliers	36	46	.439	23
Atlanta Hawks	34	48	.415	25
Indiana Pacers	22	60	.268	37

WESTERN CONFERENCE

Midwest Division	W	L	Pct.	GB
Denver Nuggets	52	30	.634	—
Houston Rockets	48	34	.585	4
Dallas Mavericks	44	38	.537	8
San Antonio Spurs	41	41	.500	11
Utah Jazz	41	41	.500	11
Kansas City Kings	31	51	.378	21

Pacific Division	W	L	Pct.	GB
Los Angeles Lakers	62	20	.756	—
Portland Trail Blazers	42	40	.512	20
Phoenix Suns	36	46	.439	26
Los Angeles Clippers	31	51	.378	31
Seattle SuperSonics	31	51	.378	31
Golden State Warriors	22	60	.268	40

PLAYOFFS

First Round
Boston defeated Cleveland, 3 games to 1
Philadelphia defeated Washington, 3 games to 1
Milwaukee defeated Chicago, 3 games to 1
Detroit defeated New Jersey, 3 games to 0
Los Angeles defeated Phoenix, 3 games to 0
Denver defeated San Antonio, 3 games to 2
Utah defeated Houston, 3 games to 2
Portland defeated Dallas, 3 games to 1

Second Round
Boston defeated Detroit, 4 games to 2
Philadelphia defeated Milwaukee, 4 games to 0
Los Angeles defeated Portland, 4 games to 1
Denver defeated Utah, 4 games to 1

Conference Finals
Boston defeated Philadelphia, 4 games to 1
Los Angeles defeated Denver, 4 games to 1

Championship Finals
Los Angeles defeated Boston, 4 games to 2

National Association of Intercollegiate Athletics men's championship, and undefeated Southwestern Oklahoma won its third NAIA women's title in four years. UCLA won the National Invitation Tournament.

Xavier McDaniel of Wichita State became the first Division I NCAA player to win both the national scoring and rebounding titles. The 6'8" senior forward averaged 27.2 points and 14.8 rebounds a game.

Three Tulane basketball players were among eight persons indicted by a New Orleans grand jury on April 4 on charges of taking part in a point shaving scheme. Because of the scandal, Tulane suspended its men's basketball program; the coach, Ned Fowler, who admitted making illegal cash payments to players, and Tulane's athletic director, Hindman Wall, both resigned. Several of those indicted pleaded guilty, but a mistrial was declared in the case of John Williams, the team's star.

A new rule adopted for the 1985–86 season by the NCAA, NAIA, junior colleges, and armed service teams established a 45-second shot clock, requiring the team with the ball to attempt a field goal within 45 seconds or lose possession. Another rule change entitled a team against whom a foul judged intentional had been committed to two free throws plus automatic possession of the ball.

Professional. Playing on their opponents' home court, the Los Angeles Lakers defeated the Boston Celtics, 111-100, on June 9 to win the NBA championship series, four games to two, and halt the Celtics' bid to become the first team since 1969 to win successive championships. The Lakers' overpowering 7'2" center, Kareem Abdul-Jabbar, playing in his 16th pro season at the age of 38, was unanimously selected the Most Valuable Player of the series.

In contrast to the mauling, brawling playing style of the Celtics, the Lakers counted heavily on their running game and pressure offense to overwhelm opponents, averaging 118.2 points a game during the regular season. They set new season records for field goal percentage and assists. After a mediocre start, they won 36 of their final 42 games and finished with a 62-20 mark. They compiled an 11-2 record against the Phoenix Suns, Portland Trail Blazers, and Denver Nuggets in advancing to the championship round. The Celtics successively defeated the Cleveland Cavaliers, Detroit Pistons, and Philadelphia 76ers.

Bernard King of the New York Knicks won the league scoring title, averaging 32.9 points per game before undergoing knee surgery following a late-season injury. The 1,123 assists amassed by Isiah Thomas of Detroit broke the league record. Mark Eaton and Darrell Griffith of the Utah Jazz established league records in

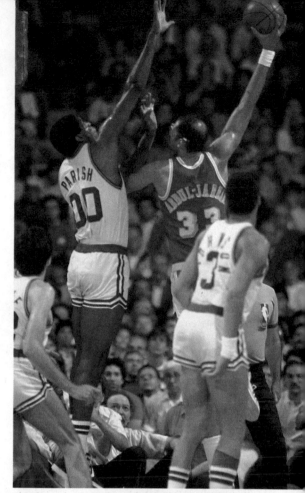

The legendary Kareem Abdul-Jabbar, the highest scorer in NBA history, led the Los Angeles Lakers to their first victory over the Boston Celtics in a championship series.

winning their respective categories for a second straight season. Eaton, the 7'4" center selected as the league's best defensive player, finished with 456 blocked shots, while Griffith collected 92 three-point field goals, breaking his own record. Michael Ray Richardson, the New Jersey Nets guard named the Comeback Player of the Year, was the leader in steals with 2.96 per game. Moses Malone of the 76ers took a fifth straight rebounding title (13.1 a game). Larry Bird of the Celtics, who averaged 20 points and 10 rebounds a game, was named the league's Most Valuable Player for the second straight season. Michael Jordan, the exciting Chicago Bulls guard, was named Rookie of the Year.

369

In the NBA's first-ever draft lottery, held on May 12, the Knicks won the top prize: the draft rights to Patrick Ewing (see biography in PEOPLE IN THE NEWS). The draft lottery, which determined the first seven draft choices for the teams that failed to make the playoffs, replaced the previous system whereby a coin toss between the teams that finished with the worst records in each conference determined the first pick. Ewing signed a complex contract with the Knicks that could bring him as much as $30 million over a period of ten years. He was expected to earn $1.7 million for his first year, making him the highest paid rookie in NBA history.

In other news, the 35th annual NBA All-Star game, played on February 10 at the Hoosier Dome in Indianapolis, was won by the West, which defeated the East, 140-129. The league set a new season attendance record, and television ratings were up. The Kansas City Kings sought and received approval to relocate in Sacramento, Calif., for the 1985–86 season.

S.M.G.

BOWLING

The 1985 Professional Bowlers Association tour's 35 national and 120 regional tournaments offered $6.25 million in prize money. Mike Aulby, a 25-year-old left-hander from Indianapolis, won 5 PBA tournaments, including the $235,000 PBA championship. In the final, Aulby routed his brother-in-law, Steve Cook of Roseville, Calif., 253-211. Aulby won $201,200 during the season, surpassing Earl Anthony's 1981 single-season record of $164,735. Marshall Holman of Jacksonville, Ore., became the first bowler to win the United States Open twice. He earned $200,000 by defeating Wayne Webb of Indianapolis, 233-205, in the final.

On the Ladies Professional Bowlers Tour, Pat Mercatanti of Yardley, Pa., beat Nikki Gianulias of Vallejo, Calif., 214-178, in the United States Open final. Patty Costello of Scranton, Pa., won her 24th career victory, a women's record. Aleta Sill of Cocoa, Fla., led the women's tour in earnings, with $52,655, and in season average, with 211.10.   F.L.

BOXING

Larry Holmes's reign as world heavyweight champion ended in 1985 when Michael Spinks became the first light heavyweight ever to dethrone a heavyweight champion. Holmes went into the fight with a 48-0 professional record (including 20 title defenses), hoping to tie the 49-0 career record set by the late Rocky Marciano. Spinks was also undefeated, at 27-0, and had defended his light-heavyweight title

---

Living Up to His Name

Marvin Hagler changed his name legally to Marvelous Marvin Hagler in 1982, but despite the name and a record of 60 wins (50 by knockouts) against only 2 losses and 2 draws, his claim to greatness was disputed by many. Then on April 15, 1985, Hagler silenced his detractors by knocking out Thomas "Hit Man" Hearns—an imposing boxer with a 40-1 record—in just three rounds. The victory, in what was later described as one of the fiercest title bouts in history, was Hagler's 11th defense of the undisputed world middleweight title he captured in 1980, just 3 short of Carlos Monzon's record of 14. Marvin Hagler, born in Newark, N.J. in 1954, started his boxing career as a teenager. With his muscled physique, shaved head, fierce scowl, and sheer fighting skill, Hagler is a menacing figure in the ring, so daunting, in fact, that no one has beaten him since 1976.

Marvelous Marvin Hagler

ten times. The fight was held September 21 in Las Vegas; Spinks won a unanimous decision in a close, well-fought bout. Spinks was officially recognized as heavyweight champion by the International Boxing Federation and by most fans; in October he was stripped of his light-heavyweight title because of a World Boxing Council (WBC) rule prohibiting champions from simultaneously holding titles in more than one division.

Pinklon Thomas won his first WBC heavyweight title defense on June 15 by knocking out Mike Weaver in eight rounds. Greg Page lost his World Boxing Association (WBA) heavyweight title on April 19 to Tony Tubbs on a 15-round decision.

The only champion recognized by all three major governing bodies (aside from Spinks as light heavyweight champ) was Marvelous Marvin Hagler, the middleweight champion since 1980. He retained the title with a third-round knockout of Thomas Hearns on April 15.

Livingstone Bramble kept his WBA lightweight title by outpointing Ray ("Boom Boom") Mancini on February 16. Though a post-fight specimen showed traces of a banned stimulant in Bramble's urine, he was not stripped of his title. Mancini later retired from boxing to become an actor.

Eusebio Pedroza of Panama defended the WBA featherweight title—which he had held since 1978—for the 19th time by outpointing Jorge Lujan of Panama on February 2 in Panama City. But on June 8 in London, Pedroza lost the decision and the title to Barry McGuigan of Northern Ireland. McGuigan successfully defended the title against Bernard Taylor in a September 28 bout in Belfast. F.L.

FOOTBALL

The highest-ranking defenses in the 1985 season belonged to the Chicago Bears among the National Football League's 28 teams and to the University of Oklahoma among the major colleges. After the NFL regular season and the college bowl games, they were also the highest-ranked teams overall.

The Bears allowed only 258.4 yards per game en route to a 15-1 record, by far the best in the NFL. They went on to triumph in the Super Bowl. Oklahoma allowed only 193.5 yards per game in compiling a 10-1 record

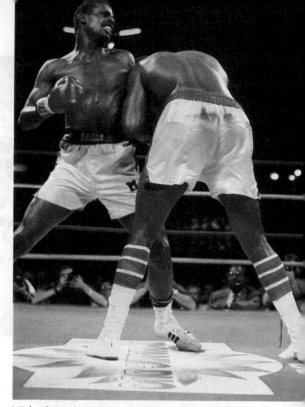

Michael Spinks (left) hammers away at defending heavyweight champion Larry Holmes during their September title bout in Las Vegas. Spinks defeated Holmes in a unanimous 15-round decision.

during the regular season, then defeated top-ranking Penn State in the Orange Bowl on January 1, 1986. A day later, Oklahoma was named national champion by the Associated Press, United Press International, the National Football Foundation and Hall of Fame, and the Football Writers Association of America.

U.S. Pro Football. Except for the running of Walter Payton, the NFL's career rushing leader, the Bears' offense was ordinary during their sensational regular season. Their defense was solid and aggressive, led by such Pro Bowl players as Richard Dent at end, Dan Hampton at tackle, Mike Singletary at middle linebacker, and Otis Wilson at outside linebacker. The best-known defender was William ("The Refrigerator") Perry, a 308-pound rookie tackle who became a folk hero when he was used successfully as a ballcarrier, blocker, and pass receiver near the opposition goal line.

The six division winners were the Bears, Miami Dolphins (12-4), Los Angeles Raiders

University of Oklahoma quarterback Jamelle Holieway looks for an open man during the Sooners' Orange Bowl game against unbeaten Penn State on January 1, 1986. Oklahoma won, 25-10, and was subsequently named the nation's best collegiate team.

(12-4), Los Angeles Rams (11-5), Dallas Cowboys (10-6), and Cleveland Browns (8-8). They qualified for the playoffs along with the four "wild-card" teams—the New England Patriots (11-5), New York Jets (11-5), New York Giants (10-6), and San Francisco 49ers (10-6).

The 49ers, who had defeated Miami, 38-16, to win Super Bowl XIX on January 20, 1985, were eliminated the next season in their first playoff game by the Giants, 17-3. In the other wild-card game, New England defeated the Jets, 26-14. In conference semifinals, the results were: Rams 20, Dallas 0; Chicago 21, Giants 0; Miami 24, Cleveland 21; and New England 27, Raiders 20. In conference finals, on January 12, 1986, the Bears shut out the Rams, 24-0, and the Patriots upset the Dolphins, 31-14. Then Chicago went on to demolish New England, 46-10, in the Super Bowl on January 26.

In all, the NFL enjoyed a successful year. Attendance was an average of 59,568 per game, the fourth-highest ever. Television ratings climbed. The Hall of Fame induction class was distinguished—Joe Namath, Roger Staubach, O. J. Simpson, Frank Gatski, and Pete Rozelle, who by 1985 had served as NFL commissioner for 25 years.

The United States Football League planned to move to the fall in 1986 and compete directly with the NFL for attendance, television exposure, and media and public attention. The USFL expected to have 9 or 10 teams at that time, down from 18 in spring 1984. Its 1985 season was a struggle; franchises moved and merged, and payrolls often were not met. Television income, television ratings, and attendance (24,452 per game) were a fraction of the NFL's, and the new league reported three-year losses of $150 million. Even the Baltimore Stars, who won the championship by defeating the Oakland Invaders, 28-24, on July 14 in East Rutherford, N.J., lost money. In another disappointment, Doug Flutie, who had been named the best college football player in 1984, made only a so-so pro debut as a quarterback for the New Jersey Generals. Commissioner Chet Simmons resigned under pressure in January 1985, because he could not deliver a 1986 television contract with a major network. He was replaced by Harry Usher, who had been executive vice-president and general manager of the Los Angeles Olympic Organizing Committee, but Usher also failed to arrange such a contract. The USFL (whose games were shown on ABC in 1985) contended that the NFL violated antitrust laws because its games were shown on all three major networks. Its suit against the NFL, for $1.32 billion, was scheduled for trial in March 1986.

Canadian Football. The British Columbia Lions defeated the Hamilton Tiger-Cats, 37-24, November 24 in Montréal, in the Grey Cup championship game of the Canadian Football League. Ned Armour of the Lions, a former San Diego State track star who never played college football, caught touchdown passes of 84 and 59 yards from Roy Dewalt.

College Football. During the regular season, Oklahoma lost only to Miami of Florida, 27-14. Miami lost its opening game to Florida, then won its last 10. Iowa won 10 of 11, losing only to Ohio State. Penn State won all 11 games. Penn State, Oklahoma, Miami, and Iowa dominated the final regular-season polls of the major wire services, with Penn State ranked first; all four had opportunities to become the national champion.

Penn State needed only a victory over Oklahoma in the Orange Bowl, but instead, Oklahoma stopped Penn State's running game, forced it to pass, and intercepted four passes. A 71-yard touchdown pass from freshman quarterback Jamelle Holieway to Keith Jackson put Oklahoma ahead en route to its 25-10 victory. Meanwhile, Miami was upset by Tennessee, 35-7, in the Sugar Bowl; Vinny Testaverde, Miami's bright young quarterback, was sacked eight times and fumbled away the ball

three times. Iowa was beaten by UCLA, 45-28, in the Rose Bowl. UCLA freshman Eric Ball scored four touchdowns and ran for 227 yards; Ronnie Harmon of Iowa lost four fumbles, negating the passing success of quarterback Chuck Long, who had finished second to Bo Jackson, the Auburn tailback, in voting for the Heisman Trophy as the nation's outstanding college player. Jackson also had a bad day as Texas A&M defeated Auburn, 36-16, in the Cotton Bowl.

Gerry Faust, the embattled coach at Notre Dame, resigned just before the end of the season. Minnesota coach Lou Holtz succeeded Faust at Notre Dame.

College football was shaken by scandals at several schools, notably in the Southwest Conference. They largely involved illegal payments to athletes by so-called boosters, who were alumni or friends of the athletic program. Southern Methodist received one of the harshest penalties ever assessed by the National Collegiate Athletic Association. In addition to television and bowl bans, Southern Methodist was stripped of all 30 new football scholarships for the 1986 season and 15 for the following year. Texas Christian suspended seven players who admitted accepting cash payments from boosters.   F.L.

Robinson Into the Record Books

Grambling coach Eddie Robinson set two impressive records during the 1985 college football season. First, Grambling's 27-7 defeat of Prairie View A&M on October 5 gave him 324 career victories, breaking the college record set by Alabama's Paul "Bear" Bryant. Then, just two weeks later, Grambling's 31-21 win over Mississippi Valley gave Robinson his 326th career victory, one more than the professional record held by George Halas of the Chicago Bears. Robinson, 66, has coached Grambling—a small, predominantly black college in northern Louisiana—since 1941. He has recruited some 200 future NFL players, more than any other school has had. As he told his players after winning No. 324: "I've never tackled anyone. I've never thrown a pass. . . . I just feel like the luckiest man in the world to have been able to coach people like you."

Eddie Robinson

Scotland's Sandy Lyle became the first British winner of the British Open in 16 years.

GOLF

In 1985, Tom Watson, one of the best golf players ever, did not win a tournament. Jack Nicklaus, maybe the best ever, did not make the cut in either the U.S. or the British Open—events he had won a total of six times. Ben Crenshaw, the 1984 Masters winner, tied for 57th place this time (and missed the cut in 12 other tournaments). West Germany's Bernhard Langer won the Masters, while Scotland's Sandy Lyle became the first British winner in 16 years in the British Open, at Royal St. George's in Sandwich, England. U.S. golfer Curtis Strange set a season record with $542,321 in earnings, breaking Watson's mark of $530,808, set in 1980. An amateur—Scott Verplank of Oklahoma State University—won a Professional Golfers' Association tour event for the first time since 1956. The European Ryder Cup team beat the U.S. team for the first time since 1957.

There were 11 first-time PGA tournament winners, including Langer, who followed up his Masters victory with a win at the Sea Pines

Heritage Classic the next week. Besides Langer, Roger Maltbie, Mark O'Meara, Calvin Peete, Joey Sindelar, Curtis Strange, Hal Sutton, Jim Thorpe, and Lanny Wadkins each won more than one tournament during the season.

Nancy Lopez won five tournaments, including the Ladies Professional Golf Association Championship and the Hall of Fame Championship, and set an LPGA record by shooting 20 under par in winning the Henredon Classic (by ten strokes). Kathy Baker was the surprise winner of the Women's U.S. Open, by three strokes over Judy Clark. Other than Lopez, multiple winners were Alice Miller (4); Amy Alcott and Pat Bradley (3); JoAnne Carner, Betsy King, and Patty Sheehan (2).   T.McC.

GYMNASTICS

The Soviet Union won the men's and women's team and all-around titles at the 1985 world championships in Montréal. Yuri Korolev was the men's all-around champion for a second time, narrowly defeating teammate Vladimir Artemov. Two Soviet gymnasts—Oksana Omeliantchik, 15, the Soviet champion, and Elena Shoushounova, 16, the European champion—scored a perfect 10 in floor exercises and earned a total of 78.663 points, sharing the women's all-around championship. The Soviet team won 15 medals (11 gold) during the competition. Dmitri Bilozerchev of the Soviet Union won seven gold medals at the European championships in Helsinki and six at the World University Games in Japan, but missed the world championships because he had broken a leg in a car accident.

Mary Lou Retton, a leading U.S. star of the 1984 Olympics, did not compete in the world championships, but won the women's all-around championship in the American Cup competition. Tim Daggett was the men's all-around winner. The 15-year-old Sabrina Mar dominated the U.S. championships, which Retton did not enter. Mar won the senior all-around title, taking two gold and two silver medals in the four individual women's events. Brian Babcock, 24, was the U.S. men's champion.   F.L.

HARNESS RACING

Prakas won the 60th Hambletonian at the Meadowlands in New Jersey with a combined two-heat time of 3:49⅘, a record for trotting's premier event. Four weeks later, he easily won the World Trotting Derby at Du Quoin, Ill., in straight heats. His combined two-heat time was a record 3:48⅘, and Prakas's 1:53⅖ second-heat time established a record for a trotter in a race. His 1985 earnings at that point were a record $1,223,546 for annual winnings, and his career earnings reached an all-time high of $1,568,994.

In the $250,000 International Invitational Trot at Roosevelt Raceway in Westbury, N.Y., France's Lutin d'Isigny defeated Sandy Bowl of the United States by 2¾ lengths in 2:31. A week later, he took the $100,000 1½-mile Challenge Cup in 3:03⅕, becoming the only horse ever to win both races in the same year.

Owner Lou Guida swept pacing's Triple Crown with three colts: Pershing Square, Chairmanoftheboard, and Nihilator. W.L.

HORSE RACING

Early in 1985, ten-year-old John Henry was named Horse of the Year for 1984, having won six of his nine starts and earned over $2 million. He was retired later in 1985 with $6,597,947 in career earnings, a world record for any breed of horse.

For the sixth year in a row, the Kentucky Derby favorite failed to win, as Chief's Crown finished third to Spend a Buck, with Stephan's Odyssey second. Spend a Buck jumped to the front at the start of the 1¼-mile race and stayed there. His 5¼-length win, with the third-fastest time of 2:00⅕ and the biggest victory margin since 1946, earned him $406,800. Following the Derby, Spend a Buck's owners decided to skip the Preakness Stakes and run him instead nine days later in the $1 million Jersey Derby at Garden State Park. At the Preakness, Chief's Crown was again made the favorite, but he was caught in the final yards by Tank's Prospect, who took in $423,000 for his victory.

Any horse that won the Garden State's two prep races—the Cherry Hill Mile Handicap and the Garden State Stakes—as Spend a Buck had, plus the Kentucky Derby could earn a $2 million bonus by also winning the Jersey Derby. On May 27, Spend a Buck did. None of the first three Preakness finishers turned out to challenge him in the Jersey Derby for the winner's share of $600,000. Although Creme Fraiche led at the top of the stretch, the son of Buckaroo and Belle de Jour won by a head, in 2:02⅗ for the 1¼ miles. Jockey Angel Cordero, Jr., who had ridden Spend a Buck in

Spend a Buck, ridden by jockey Laffit Pincay, Jr., won the 1985 Kentucky Derby by the biggest margin in nearly 40 years.

the Cherry Hill, Garden State Stakes, and Kentucky Derby, was kept off the colt in the Jersey Derby by a previous commitment. Victorious rider Laffit Pincay, Jr., picked up 10 percent of the purse and bonus money, or $260,000.

When the Belmont Stakes was run on June 8, Spend a Buck was resting in New Jersey, but the 1½-mile "Test of the Champion" in New York lured Tank's Prospect, Stephan's Odyssey, Creme Fraiche, and Chief's Crown. Creme Fraiche won by a half-length over Stephan's Odyssey in 2:27, becoming the first gelding to win the Belmont.

On September 14, Spend a Buck was retired from racing because of an ankle injury. By that time, the horse had earned over $4.2 million for his owners, who bought him for $12,500.

Mom's Command, owned by Peter Fuller and ridden by his 26-year-old daughter, Abigail, became the sixth horse ever to win New York's Triple Crown for fillies. Lady's Secret,

Wayne Gretzky, named the NHL's Most Valuable Player for an unprecedented sixth time, led the Edmonton Oilers to their second consecutive Stanley Cup championship.

a daughter of Secretariat, won eight consecutive stakes late in the season. On November 2, in the $3 million Breeder's Cup Classic, Proud Truth came from last place to beat Gate Dancer by a head. Chief's Crown, favored to win as he had been in all three Triple Crown races, was fourth.   W.L.

ICE HOCKEY

Ice hockey in 1985 remained the only major sport without network television coverage in the United States, where 14 of 21 National Hockey League (NHL) franchises are based. This did not seem to affect the game's popularity; attendance figures continued to rise.

The Edmonton Oilers snared their second consecutive Stanley Cup with a well-balanced team that featured solid defense and goalkeeping, as well as spectacular scoring. The Oilers triumphed by defeating the Philadelphia Flyers, four games to one, in the best-of-seven Stanley Cup final series. After dropping the first game, 4-1, the Oilers played well consistently, clinching their triumph with an 8-3 rout of the injury-battered Flyers on May 30. "We've got to be rated as good as any team that ever won two Cups in a row," said Wayne Gretzky, the superstar center whom many experts consider the greatest hockey player ever. "We'd like to win a couple more, too." The Oilers had advanced to the finals with relatively few problems. Gretzky, who amassed a record of 47 points during the playoffs, was the prime mover in their success story.

The Flyers—like the Oilers a hardworking, young team—surprised some observers by accumulating 113 points during their 80-game schedule in the Patrick Division. The Oilers started briskly, with a 12-0-3 record for their first 15 games. Although they finished 13 points ahead of Winnipeg, the Oilers did falter toward season's end, winding up with 109 points. The St. Louis Blues won the Norris Division by three points over Chicago, and the Montréal Canadiens nudged the Québec Nordiques by the same margin to finish at the top of the Adams Division.

Gretzky, playing every game for the Oilers, scored 73 goals and added 135 assists for 208 points in the regular season. Mario Lemieux of the Pittsburgh Penguins led all rookie scorers with 100 points. Gretzky, who became the

NATIONAL HOCKEY LEAGUE 1984–1985 Regular Season				
PRINCE OF WALES CONFERENCE				
Patrick Division	**W**	**L**	**T**	**Pts.**
Philadelphia Flyers.............	53	20	7	113
Washington Capitals	46	25	9	101
New York Islanders	40	34	6	86
New York Rangers	26	44	10	62
New Jersey Devils	22	48	10	54
Pittsburgh Penguins...........	24	51	5	53
Adams Division				
Montréal Canadiens...........	41	27	12	94
Québec Nordiques	41	30	9	91
Buffalo Sabres	38	28	14	90
Boston Bruins	36	34	10	82
Hartford Whalers	30	41	9	69
CAMPBELL CONFERENCE				
Norris Division	**W**	**L**	**T**	**Pts.**
St. Louis Blues	37	31	12	86
Chicago Black Hawks	38	35	7	83
Detroit Red Wings	27	41	12	66
Toronto Maple Leafs	20	52	8	48
Minnesota North Stars	25	43	12	62
Smythe Division				
Edmonton Oilers..............	49	20	11	109
Winnipeg Jets	43	27	10	96
Calgary Flames	41	27	12	94
Los Angeles Kings	34	32	14	82
Vancouver Canucks...........	25	46	9	59

STANLEY CUP PLAYOFFS

Division Semifinals
Philadelphia defeated N.Y. Rangers, 3 games to 0.
N.Y. Islanders defeated Washington, 3 games to 2.
Montréal defeated Boston, 3 games to 2.
Québec defeated Buffalo, 3 games to 2.
Minnesota defeated St. Louis, 3 games to 0.
Chicago defeated Detroit, 3 games to 0.
Edmonton defeated Los Angeles, 3 games to 0.
Winnipeg defeated Calgary, 3 games to 1.

Division Finals
Philadelphia defeated N.Y. Islanders, 4 games to 1.
Québec defeated Montréal, 4 games to 3.
Chicago defeated Minnesota, 4 games to 2.
Edmonton defeated Winnipeg, 4 games to 0.

Conference Finals
Philadelphia defeated Québec, 4 games to 2.
Edmonton defeated Chicago, 4 games to 2.

Championship Finals
Edmonton defeated Philadelphia, 4 games to 1.

East Germany's Katarina Witt combined grace and skill to win her second straight World Figure Skating Championship.

18th and by far the youngest member of the NHL's 1,000-career-points club, won the Hart Trophy as Most Valuable Player for an unprecedented sixth time. Paul Coffey of the Oilers won the Norris Trophy as best defenseman. The Oilers' Jari Kurri received the Lady Byng Trophy for combining talent with sportsmanship. Lemieux was voted the Calder Trophy for best rookie.   B.V.

ICE SKATING

In the 75th World Figure Skating Championships, held in Tokyo on March 6–9, 1985, the young Soviet skater Alexander Fadeev posted a decisive victory. Canada's Brian Orser, with a strong free skating program, edged out the new U.S. champion Brian Boitano for second place. Reigning women's champion Katarina Witt of East Germany staged a characteristic comeback in the free skating to win the women's title. Her perennial Soviet rival Kira Ivanova finished second, just ahead of California's Tiffany Chin. Yelena Valova and Oleg Vasiliev of the Soviet Union won the pairs title, while their compatriots Natalya Bestemyanova and Andrey Bukin won the ice dancing competition.

In the men's World Speed Skating Competition, held February 16–17 in Hamar, Norway, Hein Vergeer of the Netherlands won the world championship narrowly over the 1984 champion, Oleg Bogiev of the Soviet Union. Andrea Schöne of East Germany dominated the women's competition, held in Sarajevo, Yugoslavia, winning all four races and breaking her own world record in the 5,000-m race. Her teammates Gabie Schönbrunn and Sabine Brehm took second and third place.   I.A.A.

SKIING

At the men's Alpine World Championships, Pirmin Zurbriggen of Switzerland, recovering from an injury, took gold medals in both the regular downhill race and the combined, plus a silver medal in the giant slalom. The giant slalom was won by West Germany's Markus Wasmaier and the slalom by Sweden's Jonas Nilsson. In the women's races, Switzerland's Michela Figini captured the downhill gold as expected, while U.S. teenagers Diann Roffe and Eva Twardokens unexpectedly took the gold and the bronze in the giant slalom. Perrine Pelen of France won the gold in the slalom. The combined champion was Switzerland's Erika Hess.

In the Nordic World Championships, Sweden's Gunde Svan won golds in the 30-kilometer and 50-km events. Kari Haerkonen of Finland took the 15-km. Annette Boe of Norway won both the 5-km and 10-km events, while Norway's Grete Nykkelmo took the 20-km. The Soviet Union won the women's 20-km relay; the men's 40-km went to Norway.

Marc Girardelli and Zurbriggen finished one-two in the 1984-1985 World Cup overall standings. Girardelli, an Austrian skiing for Luxembourg, scored the maximum points possible in the slalom and also won the giant slalom. He won all 11 races he completed. The overall women's champion was Michela Figini, who also took the downhill crown. Svan and Boe captured, respectively, the men's and women's Nordic overall World Cup honors. Matti Nykänen of Finland won the jumping title.   S.C.

SOCCER

Tragedy and violence struck the soccer world in 1985. On May 11, in Bradford, England, 56 people were killed and scores injured when the main grandstand caught fire during a game. On May 29, Liverpool (England) supporters attacked fans of the Italian club Juventus before the start of the European Cup final in Brussels; in the ensuing panic, 38 people were killed. The Belgian hosts, fearful of worse trouble if the game were canceled, started it late. Juventus won, 1–0, while bodies of dead fans were being removed from the stadium. Belgian authorities were heavily criticized for positioning Juventus and Liverpool fans next to each other, but it was clear that the Brussels tragedy was an ugly climax to years of hooliganism and violence by English soccer fans visiting Europe. The Union of European Football Associations (UEFA) reacted by banning all English club teams from playing in Europe.

The 1984 South American club championship was won by Independiente of Buenos Aires, which went on to beat the 1984 European champions, Liverpool of England, 1–0, to become unofficial world club champion. The European Cup Winners' Cup went to Everton of England, which defeated Rapid-Vienna of Austria. Real Madrid of Spain won the UEFA cup over Videoton of Hungary.

Early qualifiers for the 1986 World Cup competition included Uruguay, Argentina, Brazil, and Hungary, with Brazil and Argentina the early favorites to win the title. Also qualifying were Spain, Bulgaria, West Germany, Poland, Canada (for the first time), Portugal, England, Mexico (as host nation), Italy (as holder of the trophy), the Soviet Union, Algeria, Morocco, Northern Ireland, South Korea, Denmark, Paraguay, France, Belgium, Iraq, and Scotland.

Full-time professional soccer ended in the United States with the collapse of the North American Soccer League (NASL). Overexpansion, inflated player salaries, lack of a television contract, and the rise of a professional indoor league, the Major Indoor Soccer League (MISL), were contributing factors. The San Diego Sockers won the MISL championship title by beating the Baltimore Blast four games to one in a best-of-seven series. The U.S. national team's attempt to qualify for the 1986 World Cup ended in failure for the ninth consecutive time since 1950.   P.G.

SWIMMING

Michael Gross of West Germany (6 feet 7½ inches) and Matt Biondi of Moraga, Calif. (6 feet 6 inches), were two of the most successful world-class swimmers of 1985. Gross won the 400-m freestyle in a world-record 3 minutes, 47.80 seconds in June at the West German championships. In August, in the European championships, he lowered his own butterfly record to 1:56.65. Gross ended the season holding four world records, including two he had set in the 1984 Olympics; previously, only Mark Spitz ever held four individual world swimming records simultaneously.

At U.S. long-course championships in August at Mission Viejo, Calif., Biondi won the final of the glamorous 100-m freestyle in a world-record 48.95 seconds. On this and other occasions, he surpassed world and U.S. records held by Rowdy Gaines, now retired. Biondi also anchored U.S. teams that broke two world records at the Pan Pacific meet, during August in Tokyo.

The only other man who broke a world record was Igor Polyansky of the Soviet Union, in the 200-m backstroke. The only woman was Silke Hoerner of East Germany, in the 200-m breaststroke. U.S. competitors won 24 of 32 events in the Pan Pacific Games. The most significant dual meet of the year involved East Germany and the Soviet Union in March at Erfurt, West Germany. The East Germans won, taking all 15 events for women and 5 of the 15 for men.   F.L.

TENNIS

The players who captured the attention of the tennis world in 1985 were a 17-year-old West German, Boris Becker, and two Czechs, Hana Mandlikova and Ivan Lendl. The confident and composed Becker defied odds-makers by be-

Michel Platini (in stripes) of Italy's Juventus club rushes in on the ball at the European Cup final; with Platini's penalty kick, Juventus beat Liverpool, 1-0, in a game that was played despite a deadly riot in the stands beforehand.

coming the youngest male player ever to triumph in singles at Wimbledon. He was also the first unseeded player to win the men's singles title, and the first German men's champion. Mandlikova and Lendl knocked off Martina Navratilova and John McEnroe, respectively, in the singles finals of the U.S. Open.

Women. Navratilova and Chris Evert Lloyd continued to dominate the women's tour. Evert Lloyd beat Navratilova in the French Open, 6-3, 6-7, 7-5, wresting away the No. 1 world ranking that Navratilova had held since June 1982 and becoming the winningest woman ever at the French—with six singles crowns—since the tournament went international in 1925. Navratilova exacted revenge at Wimbledon by downing Evert Lloyd, 4-6, 6-3, 6-2; the title was her sixth at the All-England Club and her fourth straight. Navratilova also defeated Evert Lloyd in the finals of the Australian Open in December. In the U.S. Open in September, however, neither player proved good enough to beat Mandlikova. The 23-year-old had defeated both Evert Lloyd and Navratilova earlier—Evert Lloyd in the finals at the Virginia Slims of California, and Navratilova in the semifinals of an event in Princeton, N.J. (she took the final as well)—but had long been regarded as lacking the mental toughness to win big matches. At the U.S. Open she broke through that psychological barrier, stunning Evert Lloyd in the semifinals, 4-6, 6-2, 6-3, and subduing Navratilova in the finals, 7-6, 1-6, 7-6.

Men. Becker's serve-and-volley game was the equal of any veteran's. With thundering serves and slashing, diving volleys, he defeated Kevin Curren in the Wimbledon finals, 6-3, 6-7, 7-6, 6-4. Becker's remarkable display overshadowed Curren's feat in reaching the finals: Curren was the first player to beat both McEnroe (in the quarterfinals) and Jimmy Connors (in the semifinals) in the same Grand Slam event. Meanwhile, Lendl, like Mandlikova, had a reputation for being unable to win the big events; indeed, he had lost to Sweden's Mats Wilander in the French Open final, 3-6, 6-4, 6-2, 6-2, even after taking the first set in a fleet 43 minutes, and had lost all three previous U.S. Open finals. But Lendl finally won a U.S. Open, devastating McEnroe, the defending

Czechoslovakia's Hana Mandlikova (above) captured the women's singles title at the U.S. Open, upsetting Martina Navratilova in a closely fought finals match. Boris Becker of West Germany (below) became, at the age of 17, the youngest men's singles winner in Wimbledon history, with a victory over Kevin Curren in the finals.

Britain's Steve Cram hits the finish line to break the world record in the 1,500 meters on July 16. Close behind is Morocco's Said Aouita, who set a new world record in that event the following month.

champion, 7-6, 6-3, 6-4. Following his win, Lendl gained the No. 1 world ranking. He subsequently won several events, including November's European Champions' Championship of Tennis Tournament, played in Antwerp, Belgium. Lendl received a special trophy—a $700,000 life-size racket studded with diamonds—for winning the event three times in a five-year span. In the Australian Open, defending champ Wilander was upset by fellow Swede Stefan Edberg, 6-4, 6-3, 6-3. Later in December, Edberg won the final singles match against Michael Westphal of West Germany, 3-6, 7-5, 6-4, 6-3, to give Sweden its second consecutive Davis Cup title. R.J.L.

TRACK AND FIELD

Successful athletes in 1985 included Britain's Steve Cram, Morocco's Said Aouita, the Soviet Union's Sergei Bubka, and Mary Decker Slaney of Eugene, Ore. Cram began a winning streak on July 16 in Nice, where he set a world record of 3:29.67 for 1,500 meters. On July 27 in Oslo, he lowered the world record for the mile to 3:46.31, and on August 4 in Budapest, he shaved the world record for 2,000 m by one-hundredth of a second, to 4:51.39. Cram's 1,500-m mark was shattered August 23 in West Berlin by Aouita, with a time of 3:29.45. Aouita had broken the world record for the 5,000 m in Oslo, when he finished in 13:00.40.

Slaney, at age 27, ran 14 outdoor races

during the year and won them all. She broke the women's world record for the mile on August 21 in Zurich, with 4:16.71, and set five U.S. records. Zola Budd, the South African-born runner who had become a British citizen to compete in the 1984 Olympics, set a women's world record of 14:48.07 for 5,000 m in London on August 26.

In Paris on July 13, Bubka slept at pitside while other pole vaulters competed, then cleared 18 feet 8¼ inches in his first try. He had the bar raised to 19'8¼" (exactly 6 m) and cleared it on his third and final attempt, breaking his own world record. In the high jump, Igor Paklin of the Soviet Union raised the world record to 7'10¾" in Kobe, Japan, in September, after his countryman Rudolf Povarnitsin had moved it to 7'10½" in August. Triple jumper Willie Banks of Los Angeles broke a ten-year-old record in his event when he achieved a 58'11½" total on June 16 in Indianapolis. World records were set in the marathon by Ingrid Kristiansen of Norway, who forged a women's record of 2 hours, 21 minutes, 6 seconds in London, and by 1984 Olympic champion Carlos Lopes of Portugal, who won in 2:07.11 in Rotterdam.

At the European Cup, held August 17–18 in Moscow, the Soviet men beat the East Germans by one point; the women's results were the reverse. At the World Cup in Canberra, Australia, October 4–6, the East German women

Tacking in tandem, United States (right) and Swedish teams compete in the Liberty Cup match-racing series in New York harbor. The American team beat entries from seven other nations.

won while their male compatriots came in third, behind the United States and the Soviet Union.   F.L.

YACHTING

In a generally disappointing year for Americans, a highly touted team could manage no better than ninth in the Admiral's Cup competition off the coast of England. Collisions, demastings, and other accidents befell U.S. boats, while West German, British, and New Zealand teams took the top three positions. In the International Catamaran Challenge, or Little America's Cup, the Australian team took the trophy home for the first time since 1976.

The ending was happier for Americans in the Liberty Cup series held in New York Harbor. Gary Jobson of Annapolis, Md., topped an international field of hopefuls expecting to skipper 12-meter yachts in the 1986 America's Cup challengers' trials off Australia.

D.M.P.

SRI LANKA. Violent conflict between Sri Lanka's Buddhist Sinhalese majority and the Hindu Tamil minority intensified in 1985. By midyear, by conservative estimates, close to 1,000 Sri Lankans had died since November 1984. Among other incidents, separatist Tamil guerrillas blew up a train on January 19, killing at least 38 people, and kidnapped and murdered the government agent of the Mullaittivu district, a Tamil, on February 22.

In April, clashes erupted between Tamils and Muslims in the Eastern Province, following Tamil attempts to force Muslims, Sri Lanka's other large minority group, to support their demands for Tamil autonomy in northern and eastern Sri Lanka. On May 14, Tamil guerrillas raided the predominantly Sinhalese North-Central Province; unofficial estimates of the death toll ranged from 35 to 150. In reprisal, Sinhalese mobs and security forces attacked and set on fire more than a dozen Tamil villages in eastern Sri Lanka, killing at least 80 civilians and leaving more than 6,000 homeless. However, in general, the government apparently succeeded in greatly reducing attacks on Tamil civilians in Sinhalese areas.

On June 18, under pressure from India, the government and the separatists agreed to a "cessation of violence" as a prelude to negotiations. In July and August, Indian Prime Minister Rajiv Gandhi brought together representatives of the Sri Lankan government and of six major Tamil groups. The talks ended without success on August 17. In October, India announced it had negotiated a new cease-fire between the government and one of the guerrilla groups; however, incidents of violence continued.

Sri Lanka's relations with India, whose southern Tamil Nadu state has been used as a base of operations by the Sri Lankan Tamil guerrillas, improved somewhat. Gandhi invited President Junius Jayewardene to New Delhi for talks in June that led to negotiations involving the Sri Lankan government and Tamil groups. Later in the year, India deported several Tamil leaders and arrested participants in a massive civil disobedience campaign protesting the deportations.

See STATISTICS OF THE WORLD.   T.F.

STAMPS, POSTAGE. Anniversaries, political events, and worldwide problems of health and ecology were among themes most noted on postage stamps in 1985.

United States Issues. The U.S. Postal Service issued 30 commemorative and special stamps during 1985. Persons honored included composer Jerome Kern, black educator Mary McLeod Bethune, former first lady Abigail Adams, and Statue of Liberty sculptor Frédéric Auguste Bartholdi. Stamps were issued to commemorate or honor the Winter Special Olympics, AMERIPEX '86 (the International Philatelic Exhibition to be held in Chicago in 1986), the 50th anniversary of the Rural Electrification Administration, Korean war veterans, World War I veterans, the 50th anniversary of the Social Security Act, and Public Education in America, as well as to highlight the need to "Help End Hunger." Three special blocks of four se tenant commemoratives (stamps attached together but of different individual designs) featured the themes of duck decoys and American horses and gave recognition to International Youth Year. The Youth Year commemorative honored YMCA/Youth Camping, Boy Scouts of America, Big Brothers/Big Sisters, and Camp Fire Inc. Special annual issues included a new "Love" stamp and two Christmas stamps.

A nondenominated "D" stamp was released in February for the new 22 cent letter rate, to serve until adequate supplies of regular stamps

A train blown off the rails by a bomb planted by Tamil separatist guerrillas is guarded by Sri Lankan government soldiers. At least 38 people were killed in the blast.

would be available. Changes in domestic and international postal rates made necessary the issuing of new definitive stamps in the following denominations: 3.4¢, 4.9¢, 6¢, 7¢, 8¢, 8.3¢, 9¢, 10.1¢, 11¢, 12.5¢, 14¢, 18¢, 21.1¢, 22¢, 39¢, and 50¢. A special booklet of 22¢ stamps was issued containing five different seashell designs arranged in two panes of ten stamps each. A $10.75 express mail stamp released in April was the highest-denomination U.S. postage stamp ever issued.

Airmail stamps required to meet new international rates were issued in denominations of 33¢, 39¢, and 44¢. Penalty Mail (formerly called Official Mail) stamps were issued in 14¢ and 22¢ denominations, for use by government officials, and a 17¢ value was added to the postage-due series.

Worldwide Issues. A theme reflected worldwide was observance of International Youth Year. Other major events noted included the 40th anniversary of the United Nations, the 85th birthday of Britain's Queen Mother Elizabeth, European Music Year, conclusion of the Decade for Women, the 40th anniversary of the end of World War II, the annual Europa issues by members of the European Communities (CEPT), and the tricentennial of the births of composers Johann Sebastian Bach, George Frideric Handel, and (Giuseppe) Domenico Scarlatti.

United Nations Issues. The UN Postal Administration (UNPA) released commemorative issues in recognition of the 40th anniversary of

Opposite page: Some outstanding stamps of 1985. Top row (left to right): Europa commemorative from Belgium; Great Britain notes the 500th anniversary of the publication of Le Morte Darthur; Kenya stresses the theme of energy conservation. Second row: the United States publicizes an international philatelic exhibition to be held in 1986 in Chicago, commemorates International Youth Year, and recognizes public education. Third row: Ireland participates in European Music Year; Belize celebrates the British queen mother's 85th birthday; Cameroon honors the visit of Pope John Paul. Fourth row: Australia observes International Youth Year; the Marshall Islands marks the UN Decade for Women; Canada notes the 75th anniversary of the Girl Guides. Fifth row: the United Nations commemorates its 40th anniversary, adds the flag of Mexico to its continuing flag series, and gives special recognition to the Turin Center of the International Labor Organization.

the signing of the UN Charter, the Turin Center of the International Labor Organization, the United Nations University, and Child Survival. These stamps were issued simultaneously in New York, Geneva, and Vienna in the currency of the respective country.

The sixth annual group of 16 flag stamps was released in September. These were 22 cent denominations and were issued only in New York. The member countries included were Chad, Dominican Republic, Finland, German Federal Republic, Ghana, Grenada, India, Liberia, Mauritius, Mexico, Oman, Saudi Arabia, São Tomé and Príncipe, Sierra Leone, Uganda, and Union of Soviet Socialist Republics.

J.W.K.

STATE GOVERNMENT REVIEW. All state legislatures met in regular or special session in 1985. State governments took a cautious approach to taxing and spending, looked for ways to help the distressed farm community, continued efforts to upgrade education, and struggled with the continuing problems of prison overcrowding and environmental pollution.

Taxes and Budgets. A dozen states cut income taxes in 1985, with New York making the largest cut in absolute terms. The overall taxload was raised in 25 states and decreased in 20 others, for a net tax reduction of over $1 billion. However, most states were still recovering from budget cuts made in 1983. Although only one state, Vermont, experienced a deficit for the 1985 fiscal year, ending balances were marginal in most states. Nearly half had balances below the 5 percent regarded as fiscally prudent.

Oklahoma raised its sales tax rate from 2 percent to 3.25 percent. Oregon voters defeated a legislative proposal for a sales tax. Other tax activity included higher motor fuel taxes in about 15 states (mostly earmarked for road improvement), higher cigarette taxes in nearly half the states, and higher alcoholic beverage taxes in several states.

Legal lotteries were started in 3 states—California, Iowa, and Oregon—while Missouri and West Virginia expected theirs to get under way in 1986. The 5 new entries bring the total of lottery states to 22.

State Economies. The major economic news for many states was the decision by General

Motors to locate its new Saturn automobile plant in Spring Hill, Tenn. Thirty-eight states had competed for the $5 billion facility.

Financial services and bank regulation remained a major state concern. States were given the go-ahead by courts to regulate so-called nonbank banks (in order to ban securities firms and retail chains from offering bank services) and to limit banking across state lines to specified states in a region. More than half the states allow interstate banking; about a dozen states enacted legislation on the matter in 1985.

Midwestern states dealt with the farm credit crisis by providing operating loans for farmers. Iowa ordered a stop to farm mortgage foreclosures. The collapse of privately insured thrift institutions in Ohio and Maryland generated legislation and state investigations. States were expected to benefit from a federal law amending the U.S. Supreme Court's *Garcia* decision, which had held that minimum wage and overtime provisions of the Fair Labor Standards Act applied to state and local government employees; the new law allowed states and localities to continue to offer compensatory time off in lieu of overtime pay to employees.

Education. Most states increased their spending on education at a faster rate than for any other budget item. Hawaii spent $40 million on repair and maintenance of facilities—more than ever before. More than half the states boosted teachers' salaries, and at least four raised minimum pay levels for teachers. About half of the states now provided career-ladder programs for teachers, providing rewards for performance and subject knowledge. All but five states tested new or prospective teachers, and a growing number were evaluating the performance of current teachers. In 1985, Illinois and Nevada mandated teacher evaluations, and Arkansas teachers were required to take a state competency test in March.

Children. States continued to improve their child protective services by passing new or updated laws designed to curb or prevent child abuse, child pornography, and child abduction. To spare child victims further trauma, many states now allow them to testify on videotape rather than in the courtroom. Other new state measures were intended to improve investigation of suspected child abuse and to screen employees of child-care facilities. Trust funds for child protective services have been established in more than 30 states, financed by state income tax checkoffs and surcharges on birth certificate and marriage license fees. Many states have also established centers or improved laws to speed searches for missing children.

States also strengthened their efforts to enforce child support payments so as to comply with new federal standards. New legislation included measures making it easier to withhold income tax refunds or attach wages from parents who have fallen too far behind in their payments. Wisconsin went so far as to make grandparents responsible for the support of the offspring of their own underage children.

Law and Public Safety. Prodded into action by a federal rule that will mandate air bags and automatic seat belts in new cars unless states representing two-thirds of the U.S. population enact mandatory belt use laws, 16 states had approved such laws by late October. In addition, all but 15 states have acted to raise their drinking age to 21; those that fail to do so by October 2, 1986, will lose a portion of their federal highway funds.

Prison overcrowding became the topic of a special session of the Tennessee legislature in late 1985, as various states experimented with early-release and intensive-supervision programs to relieve overcrowded conditions. Ken-

---

A Locked Room Mystery

The director of sanitation for Fayetteville, N.C., made a disturbing discovery when he checked over the daily telephone records for his department. More than 100 telephone calls had been placed in one night from two extensions in a tightly locked office. There were no signs of a break-in by garrulous pranksters. When the culprits were finally identified, they turned out to be two Coca-Cola machines programmed to phone the local distributor with automatic requests for a refill. For some reason, the distributor had given them the cold circuit, so they just kept phoning . . . and phoning.

tucky, Florida, Oklahoma, and several other states placed prisoners under "house arrest" at their homes, using intensive human or electronic supervision. Tennessee, Alaska, and Kentucky, among other states, considered proposals to turn prisons over to private operators. Texas agreed to settle a class-action suit brought by prisoners against the state, ending a 13-year dispute. The settlement required the state to build new prisons, upgrade existing ones, hire more guards, and make other improvements costing hundreds of millions of dollars.

Health and Welfare. To contain healthcare costs, states set hospital rates, promoted competition in healthcare, and adopted diagnostic-based payment systems for medicare patients and state controls on the building of new health facilities. New York, Florida, Illinois, Nevada, and other states enacted legislation to hold down medical malpractice insurance rates. Action was taken by 13 states in 1985 on right-to-die, or living will, legislation; patients in 36 states now have the right to refuse in advance extraordinary technical lifesaving measures.

Environment. Emergency response to toxic leaks also became an issue in August when the Union Carbide plant in Institute, W. Va., accidentally released chemicals into the air that injured 6 workers and about 135 nearby residents. States enacted community and worker right-to-know laws on toxic substances in the workplace which for the most part conformed with new federal standards. Protecting groundwater from toxic substances, especially from leaking underground storage tanks, was also an increasing concern.

Other Issues. Plans for a world's fair in Chicago in 1992 fell through after the Illinois legislature deemed the enterprise too costly. Divestment of South Africa-related securities was approved by several states as part of a growing protest worldwide against South Africa's racial policies.

Governors Under the Gun. An attempt to impeach Alaska Governor William J. Sheffield (D) failed when the state Senate ruled in August that there was insufficient evidence of any wrongdoing. Impeachment hearings had started in July after a grand jury said Sheffield and an aide had abused their offices by awarding a lease for state office space to a building partly

The racketeering trial of Louisiana Governor Edwin W. Edwards (above) was declared a mistrial in December. A move to impeach Alaska Governor William J. Sheffield (below) ended in August when a state Senate committee found insufficient evidence of wrongdoing.

owned by one of the governor's political supporters. Sheffield denied all of the charges in the grand jury's report.

In September, Louisiana Governor Edwin W. Edwards (D) went on trial with seven others, including his brother and nephew, for racketeering and wire and mail fraud. A grand jury had charged the group with using the influence of the governor's office to make millions of dollars by manipulating the way in which state permits were granted for hospital construction. Charges against three of the defendants were dismissed in early December. On December 18 a mistrial was declared in the cases of Edwards and the other four defendants when the jury could not agree on a verdict after six days of deliberation. After the ruling Edwards, noting that the jury had leaned heavily toward acquittal, declared the outcome "a complete vindication" and announced he would seek a fourth term in 1987.   E.S.K.

SUDAN. On April 6, 1985, while Sudan's President Jaafar al-Nimeiry was out of the country, his regime was overthrown in a military coup led by General Abdul Rahman Swar al-Dahab, who had recently been appointed defense minister and commander-in-chief of the People's Armed Forces. Dahab established a Transitional Military Council and then a provisional cabinet to run the country. The new rulers promised parliamentary elections within a year, eventually scheduling them for April 1–12, 1986.

Several political moves by Nimeiry apparently had served as catalysts for the coup. Imposition in 1983 of strict Islamic law had given rise to discontent, particularly in the largely non-Muslim south. In March 1985, Nimeiry had denounced the influential fundamentalist Muslim Brotherhood and dismissed several members from key government positions. Nimeiry further upset his opponents by doubling government wages while austerity measures—to satisfy International Monetary Fund loan conditions—were in effect.

After the coup, Colonel John Garang, leader of the Sudanese People's Liberation Army, continued to fight in the south. Garang, aided by Libya and Ethiopia, posed a serious threat to the Sudanese economy, particularly because of attacks on oil production facilities. In August his forces moved north, threatening government control within 300 miles of Khartoum. In October, Garang agreed to a cease-fire, pledging that his forces would not attack government garrisons; however, rebels continued to attack troops if they moved from their bases.

With millions suffering from famine brought on by a five-year drought, July rains were a further disaster for Sudan. Floods washed out bridges and railroad tracks essential to food distribution, and much topsoil necessary for a good harvest was destroyed. A new wave of Ethiopian refugees appeared to be flowing into Sudan late in the year, after another poor harvest there, and the needs of destitute Ethiopians and Sudanese competed. There were estimates in midsummer that at least 20,000 children were dying monthly in Sudan.

The Sudanese economy, essentially dependent on international aid, remained in miserable condition throughout the year. The coup against Nimeiry, if anything, made the situation worse by frightening off private U.S. and Saudi interests. In June the new leadership announced that Sudan's international debt had reached $9 billion.

In the postcoup period, Dahab's Transitional Military Council declared an international policy of nonalignment. Egypt, which traditionally had provided refuge for deposed Arab leaders, refused a request to send Nimeiry back to stand trial on a range of charges. Sudan and Libya resumed diplomatic relations in April and signed a defense pact in July, but Sudan denied that it was aligning itself with Libyan leader Muammar al-Qaddafi. Late in the year, the regime ordered the expulsion of three refugee resettlement agencies reportedly involved in an airlift of Ethiopian Jews from Sudan to Israel, and former Vice-President Omar al-Tayeb was on trial for treason, on charges that he had played a role in the resettlement.

See STATISTICS OF THE WORLD.   R.B.

SUPREME COURT OF THE UNITED STATES. No landmark cases appeared on the U.S. Supreme Court's calendar in 1985. Justice Lewis F. Powell, Jr., was absent for nearly three months because of illness, leading to a number of tie decisions, which automatically affirm lower court rulings but have no value as precedents. (*See also* BLACKS IN THE UNITED

SUPREME COURT OF THE UNITED STATES

States; Civil Liberties and Civil Rights; and Women.)

Prominent Precedents. Some cases did set significant precedents. In *Wayte v. United States* the Court found, 7-2, that the government was not guilty of selective prosecution in focusing its pursuit of people refusing to register for a possible draft on those who most defiantly opposed military registration. Powell's majority decision reasoned that even if the government's policy had a discriminatory effect, there was insufficient evidence to prove that the effect was officially intended. In another 7-2 decision, the Court in *Federal Election Commission v. National Conservative Political Action Committee* struck down, as a violation of free speech, a federal statute which limited to $1,000 the amount a presidential candidate accepting federal campaign funding could receive from any private political action committee.

In *Tennessee v. Garner* the justices ruled, 6-3, that a police officer could not use deadly force to stop an escaping suspect, unless such force was necessary to prevent flight and the officer had probable cause to believe that the suspect was likely to kill or seriously injure someone. Writing for the majority, Justice Byron White emphasized the suspect's "fundamental" right to life.

Detention of Suspects. Speaking through Justice Sandra Day O'Connor, the Court decided unanimously in *United States v. Hensley* that police personnel could briefly detain a person suspected of committing a past crime, as opposed to a recent or ongoing crime, even if the information on which they relied was sketchy or drawn from another agency's "flyer." In *United States v. Sharpe* the majority emphasized the importance of brevity in such stops, in upholding a 20-minute detention of a truck and its driver.

Search and Seizure. The Court ruled, 6-3, in *New Jersey v. T.L.O.*, that although the search and seizure limitations of the Fourth Amendment did govern searches of students by school officials, no warrant was required so long as the intrusion by the officials was "reasonable." And in *United States v. Johns* the Court found that law enforcement officials could search, without a warrant, packages taken from motor

vehicles several days earlier. The majority's reasoning was carried a step further in *California v. Carney*; there, the Court voted, 6-3, to affirm the warrantless search of a parked, but mobile, motor home. The majority stressed the mobile aspect of the vehicle, while the dissent, written by Justice John Paul Stevens, argued for treating it more as a residence.

Other Criminal Cases. In *Wainwright v. Witt* the Court ruled, 7-2, that a judge could exclude a juror from service in a death penalty case if qualms about capital punishment would "prevent or substantially impair the performance of his duties as a juror." In a decision more favorable to defendants (*Ake v. Oklahoma*), the Court held, 8-1, that an indigent defendant was entitled to the assistance of a psychiatrist at state expense if the defendant's sanity would be a central issue in the trial.

In *United States v. Bagley*, the Court held that a defendant was not automatically entitled to a reversal of a conviction because the government had failed to disclose to the defense certain monetary inducements granted to key government witnesses. On the other hand, the Court ruled unanimously in *Luce v. United States* that a defendant reluctant to testify because prior convictions might be revealed, and thus damage the credibility of the testimony, must testify or else forfeit the right to raise on appeal the question of inadmissibility of the prior convictions as evidence.

In *Heath v. Alabama*, the Court upheld a restrictive interpretation of double jeopardy. The defendant had been convicted of hiring two men to kidnap his wife in Alabama and kill her; her body was later found in Georgia. The husband pleaded guilty in Georgia and received a life sentence, after which Alabama convicted him of murder and sentenced him to death. In her majority opinion, O'Connor held that each state was sovereign and that the defendant had committed a separate offense against the laws of each.

In *Maine v. Moulton* the Court, 5-4, threw out a theft conviction, finding that police had acted unconstitutionally in planting a recording device on an alleged accomplice prior to a meeting between him and the second indicted defendant. At the meeting the "wired" man elicited incriminating statements from the sec-

Setting an important precedent, the U.S. Supreme Court ruled in March that the government's prosecution of only those draft resisters who publicize their refusal to register for the draft does not constitute selective enforcement of the law. The case had been brought by draft resister David Alan Wayte, shown here with his wife, Jackie.

ond defendant concerning the crime for which both had been indicted.

Wetlands Protection. The Court held unanimously in *United States* v. *Riverside Bayview Homes, Inc.* that all wetlands, including marshes, swamps, and bogs adjacent to navigable bodies of water, are "waters" and therefore protected by the Clean Water Act. The decision meant that anyone seeking to develop wetlands would need a permit from the Army Corps of Engineers.

Freedom of Press and Speech. In *Harper & Row Publishers* v. *Nation Enterprises*, the Court voted, 6-3, that a magazine that printed without permission a 300-word excerpt of former President Gerald R. Ford's memoirs infringed the copyright of the book publisher. The dissent argued that the inherent news value of a former chief executive's autobiography rendered the excerpt an example of "fair use."

In *Dun & Bradstreet, Inc.* v. *Greenmoss Builders, Inc.*, a case involving an erroneous credit report, a three-justice plurality and two concurring justices held that a plaintiff who is not a public figure need not prove "actual malice" by a credit reporting service in order to win a libel judgment against the service, so long as the subject matter at hand was not one of "public concern." In *McDonald* v. *Smith* the justices unanimously denied that the First Amendment's clause giving people the right to "petition the Goverment" provides absolute immunity from libel for anything that is said in letters to the president of the United States criticizing a candidate for federal office.

Constitutional Debate. Attorney General Edwin Meese criticized the Court, during the summer, for a series of rulings since 1925 holding the states, as well as the federal government, responsible for upholding the liberties guaranteed by the Constitution. Meese suggested that the framers of the Constitution would consider "bizarre" the Court's decisions requiring neutrality between religion and irreligion. In October, Justice Stevens rebutted Meese's argument point by point; it was the first time in memory that a member of the Court had criticized a sitting attorney general by name. Stevens asserted that Meese's stress on the framers' original intention overlooked the importance of subsequent events in the development of the law. Also in October, Justice William Brennan, Jr., without mentioning Meese by name, branded the attorney general's view of the Constitution as "little more than arrogance cloaked as humility." J.F.H., III

SURINAME. *See* STATISTICS OF THE WORLD.

SWAZILAND. *See* STATISTICS OF THE WORLD.

SWEDEN. In a fairly close race, Sweden's governing Social Democrats narrowly defeated the country's three nonsocialist parties in parliamentary elections on September 15, 1985. Prime Minister Olof Palme and his cabinet thereby secured a mandate to maintain Sweden's mixed economy and comprehensive welfare services for another three-year term.

Despite a loss of 7 seats, the Social Democrats easily remained Sweden's largest political party, with 45 percent of the popular vote and 159 seats in the new Riksdag (Parliament). The indirect support of 19 Communist deputies gave the Social Democrats a de facto majority of 178 seats, compared with 171 for the three nonsocialist parties—the Liberal Party, the (conservative) Moderate Unity Party, and the Center Party. The Social Democrats had governed Sweden for 47 of the past 53 years. They lost the elections of 1976 and 1979 to the nonsocialists but regained power in 1982 after the latter proved incapable of governing as a cohesive three-party coalition, especially in the face of an economic slowdown.

Once back in office, the Social Democrats, who have erected one of the world's most comprehensive welfare systems, embarked on a mixed set of policies that included devaluation of the Swedish krona to stimulate exports, increased state aid to combat unemployment, fiscal restraint, and introduction of a controversial system of "wage-earner funds"— union-controlled funds drawn from corporate and payroll taxes and used to buy shares of stock in Swedish corporations. After 1982, industrial production and profits rose, exports surged, the government's budgetary deficit was marginally reduced, and the unemployment level fell to 2.6 percent. On the negative side, inflation remained relatively high (rising to 8 percent by August, 1985). Moreover, to finance the nation's elaborate welfare services, the government had to borrow more than $8.7 billion abroad.

The country experienced additional economic problems in midspring, when air traffic controllers and customs officials staged a 17-day strike for wage increases that had been promised under a 1984 accord between the government and state employees. Their actions temporarily closed airports and halted most foreign trade. Prime Minister Palme personally intervened to facilitate a settlement on terms favorable to the government. In an effort to dampen inflationary pressure, as well as stem a flight of capital abroad, the cabinet in May imposed economic austerity measures that in-

cluded interest rate increases and restrictions on the use of credit cards.

A foreign policy squabble developed in January, when Defense Minister Anders Thunborg threatened to resign after Foreign Minister Lennart Bodström asserted that he did not believe Soviet submarines were continuing to violate Swedish territorial waters. Bodström later explained he meant there was no certainty as to the national origin of submarines that have been reported at various times off the eastern

Holding roses for socialism, Swedish Prime Minister Olof Palme and his wife, Lisbeth, celebrate the outcome of September 15 elections; his party, the Social Democrats, retained a working majority in the Riksdag (Parliament), giving Palme a second consecutive three-year term in office.

coast. Nonsocialist leaders introduced a vote of no confidence against Bodström in the Riksdag in February, but the Social Democratic majority easily defeated the motion.

On June 21, Tage Erlander, Sweden's prime minister from 1946 to 1969 and one of the chief developers of the country's social welfare programs, died near Stockholm at the age of 84.

See STATISTICS OF THE WORLD.   M.D.H.

SWITZERLAND. Developments related to banking and finance were much in the news in 1985. After years of controversy, the Federal Council, Switzerland's highest executive authority, took a major step when it approved giving the U.S. Securities and Exchange Commission confidential bank records relating to the case of the Santa Fe International Corporation, a U.S. firm sold to Kuwait Petroleum Corporation in 1981. The case involved insider trading in Santa Fe stocks and options by investors who allegedly made $5 million in profits. In other financial news, unusually large cash transfers between the First National Bank of Boston and three Swiss banks alerted U.S. Treasury officials to an apparent money-laundering operation involving funds obtained by organized crime from drug trafficking. The Boston bank pleaded guilty to failure to report the transactions and was fined $500,000. Also, Robert Leclerc, a Swiss banker, was sentenced to five years in prison after being found guilty of diverting $18 million from clients' accounts in his former Geneva-based private bank, Leclerc and Company.

Swiss watch exports showed improvement early in the year over 1984 levels. The Swatch, a trendy, relatively inexpensive timepiece, paced the industry's recover. Until recently, the Swiss had made only costly precision mechanical watches.

In June, Swiss voters rejected a ballot proposal to severely limit abortions and ban some forms of contraception. The electorate also approved a law granting women rights within marriage on an equal basis with men; previously, husbands had enjoyed the legal right to prevent wives from working, to manage family finances unilaterally, and to determine the family's place of residence. In December,

A Swiss soldier stands guard at Geneva's Cointrin airport, as part of the large security contingent deployed for the November summit meeting between President Ronald Reagan and Soviet leader Mikhail Gorbachev.

voters rejected a referendum proposal to ban most experiments using animals.

A portrait of Spain's King Philip IV by the Flemish painter Peter Paul Rubens, valued at $2 million, was burned beyond repair on June 13, when a West German visitor to Zurich's Kunsthaus museum set it on fire to protest environmental pollution.

Geneva was the site of a headline-making summit meeting between U.S. President Ronald Reagan and Soviet leader Mikhail Gorbachev in November. Security was tight, as government officials from both countries and some 3,500 journalists from around the world gathered for the events (see also UNION OF SOVIET SOCIALIST REPUBLICS; UNITED STATES OF AMERICA).

See STATISTICS OF THE WORLD. J.F.S.

SYRIA. Syria appeared to solidify its role as the paramount power in Lebanon during 1985. Relations with the United States were slightly improved as a result of Syria's role in resolving the TWA hijacking crisis.

Relations With Palestinians and Jordan. The Syrian regime continued its efforts to undermine Yasir Arafat, chairman of the Palestine Liberation Organization, and appeared anxious to prevent any strengthening of ties between moderate Palestinians and Jordan. After Arafat and Jordan's King Hussein reached agreement on February 11 on a joint approach to Mideast peace negotiations, Syrian-backed dissident PLO factions established the Palestine National Salvation Front in order to fight the accord.

The Syrian regime's war against Arafat and his followers was also evident in Lebanon. On April 17, the Shiite Amal militia, with Druze backing, inflicted a crushing defeat on the Sunni Murabitun militia, with which pro-Arafat Palestinians were allied, and took complete control of West Beirut. Syria was widely believed to have played a role in the showdown. Even heavier fighting broke out between the Amal militia and Palestinians on May 19 over control of the refugee camps around Beirut. Once again, Syrian involvement was suspected. Much to Syria's consternation, however, the protracted "war of the camps," which left several hundred dead on both sides, brought pro- and anti-Arafat Palestinian factors together against Amal and exposed the Damascus government to criticism within the Arab world.

The possibility of a realignment within the Syria-Jordan-Palestinian triangle was raised when King Hussein visited Syrian President Hafez al-Assad in Damascus in late December. However, no communiqué was issued at the end of the two-day meeting, their first in six years.

Involvement in Lebanon. After Israel completed the withdrawal of its combat forces from Lebanon in June, Syria found itself as the only foreign power with important influence in the country. Anxiety about Syria's influence provoked a serious revolt against Lebanese President Amin Gemayel on March 12, from within his own Christian Phalangist party. When fighting broke out in Sidon among the rebels, loyalist Phalangists, and Muslim groups, Assad reportedly threatened Syrian military intervention if the revolt was not put down. Christian leaders then issued a statement blaming Israel for the revolt and reiterating the importance of Lebanon's ties with Syria. The rebellion crumbled soon after.

Syrian efforts to broker a permanent peace among Lebanon's warring ethnic groups collapsed in August amid renewed violence in Beirut. In October a conference in Damascus was reported to have produced an agreement between Shiite, Christian, and Druze leaders on a new power-sharing arrangement, but signing of the pact was delayed because of objections from some Christians. Meanwhile, fierce fighting had engulfed Tripoli, where Syrian-backed militas were trying to wrest control of the city from Sunni fundamentalists. More than 500 people were reported killed and over 1,000 wounded before a Syrian-brokered truce went into effect. In late December, a new accord between Shiite, Christian, and Druze leaders, mediated by Syria, was signed in Damascus; its prospects for success were uncertain.

Hostage Release Efforts. Syria used its influence in Lebanon to help win the freedom of 39 Americans held hostage by Shiite Muslims seeking the release of more than 700 prisoners (most of them Shiites) held in Israel. The 39 were among 153 people on board a TWA jet hijacked shortly after leaving Athens on June 14. The hostages were released on June 30 and driven to Damascus before being flown to West Germany.

Four Soviet diplomats were kidnapped on September 30 in West Beirut by Muslim fundamentalists protesting Syria's involvement in the Tripoli fighting; one of the diplomats was shot to death two days later. Because Syria is the Soviet Union's main client in the Middle East, the kidnappers evidently sought Soviet pressure on Syria to end the siege. Over two weeks after a truce had been achieved in Tripoli, the remaining three hostages were freed, reportedly through Syrian efforts.

Confrontation With Israel. After Israeli fighter planes shot down two Syrian MIG jet fighters near the Syrian-Lebanese border on November 19, Syria reportedly installed SAM-6 and SAM-8 antiaircraft missiles near the Syrian border inside Lebanon. These mobile missiles were apparently withdrawn in early December, then reintroduced later in the month. Early in 1986, the mobile missiles were reportedly withdrawn to the Syrian side of the border.

See STATISTICS OF THE WORLD.   A.D.

T

TAIWAN. During 1985 the Taiwan government was shaken by scandals. In January the Government Information Office announced that three top officials of the Intelligence Bureau of the Ministry of National Defense—including the bureau's director, Vice-Admiral Wong Hsi-ling—had been arrested in connection with the 1984 murder in California of Henry Liu, a Chinese-American critical of the Taiwan government. Wong was convicted and sentenced by a military court to life imprisonment in April; his codefendants each received 2½-year prison terms. Three crime syndicate members accused of carrying out the shooting, among them gang leader Chen Chi-li, were tried for murder in a Taipei district court and given life sentences earlier in the month. The Kuomintang (KMT) government, however, refused to extradite the convicted men to the United States.

A serious financial scandal came to light in February, with bank runs at Taipei Tenth Credit Cooperative, Taiwan's largest savings and loan institution, and the Cathay Investment and Trust Company, another quasi-bank. It later emerged that government officials had not only tolerated $197 million in illegal loans to sister companies within the Cathay group but also had loaned more than $2.2 billion to the failing cooperative. The scandal led to the resignation of Hsu Lih-teh, minister of economic affairs. The finance minister, Loh Jen-kang, was forced to step down, and other high officials also resigned or were fired. Shortly before the financial

crisis became public, the KMT secretary-general, Tsiang Yen-shih, was abruptly removed, apparently because of his rumored involvement in the Cathay scandal. Tsiang's KMT post went to 76-year-old Mah Soo-lay, Taiwan's unofficial ambassador in Japan.

President Chiang Ching-kuo, 75, continued to suffer from health problems. Late in the year, he told Parliament that no member of his family would succeed him as president and promised that the next president would be elected by the National Assembly, as provided in the constitution.

In financial developments, Taiwan was experiencing an economic slowdown during the year with growth running at around 4 percent in the second and third quarters.

See STATISTICS OF THE WORLD.   P.H.C.

TANZANIA. Julius K. Nyerere, one of the Third World's leading spokesmen and ideologists and Tanzania's leader since independence in 1961, officially stepped down as president on November 5, 1985. Ali Hassan Mwinyi, president of Zanzibar and vice-president of Tanzania, succeeded him, after October elections in which Mwinyi was the sole candidate. Nyerere's influence was expected to remain substantial, since he was to continue as chairman of the ruling Chama Cha Mapinduzi (CCM) Party until 1987. Mwinyi, a Muslim, was expected to maintain close unity between Zanzibar and the mainland and establish a clear recognition of Islam by the union government.

In February, Tanzania and Kenya continued

their reconciliation by reopening rail links for the first time since 1977. Steamer service for the transshipment of goods on Lake Victoria between the two countries was planned. Tanzania also reached agreement with Uganda on Uganda's use of Tanzanian routes and ships for exports and imports. In May, Tanzania and Malawi announced that they intended to establish diplomatic relations.

Tanzania continued to suffer from massive external debt and chronic budget deficits, inflation was estimated at about 30–35 percent, and factories were running at just 25 percent of capacity. The food crop was expected to be excellent, for the first time in many years, but shortages of fuel, equipment, and storage facilities—caused by a shortage of foreign exchange—threatened to forestall economic recovery. Among the few positive signs were the discoveries of gold, uranium, and precious metals. Although the private sector was reportedly being enlarged, the fiscal 1986 budget, introduced in June, projected a 22 percent rise in public spending.

On December 28, eight army officers and one civilian were sentenced to life in prison on charges of conspiring to assassinate the president in 1982; six other defendants were acquitted.

See STATISTICS OF THE WORLD.   Γ.C.

TECHNOLOGY. Technological achievements reported in 1985 included the development of experimental weapons for use in outer space, record-breaking optical fibers, microtools for biomedicine, and new ways to manage or destroy dioxin.

Star Wars. While political and military analysts debated the wisdom and practicality of devising "Star Wars"-type weapons to shoot down incoming strategic nuclear missiles, researchers took very preliminary steps toward establishing the feasibility of such defensive weaponry.

Particle beams have been called the ultimate weapons. Not only can they do more damage than lasers, but they also inflict that damage almost instantaneously. In April scientists at Sandia National Laboratories in Albuquerque, N.M., announced that an intense electron particle beam had been guided into a straight-line course through a gas. Charged-particle beams, like the one involved in this test, were

being developed for use as potent defensive weapons against missiles, planes, and other weapons in the earth's atmosphere. In such experiments, the large electric current in an electron beam moving through the atmosphere sets up a strong magnetic field that pinches the beam's electrons into a tightly focused stream. Although that keeps the beam from spreading into a diffuse and harmless spray, it does not keep the beam from arcing and

Engineers are working on the "latest" in aerospace technology—propellers. The new propellers, called prop-fans, have eight or more thin, sharply curved blades that can produce the speed of a jet while cutting down fuel consumption by an estimated 20 to 30 percent.

TECHNOLOGY

snaking unpredictably as it passes through a gas such as earth's atmosphere; so the Sandia scientists used a low-power laser. An annular laser beam (one whose light, in cross section, forms a circle) was briefly directed along the straight-line path the electron beam was to follow. Energy deposited by the laser's light stripped electrons off any gas atoms it contacted, creating a conducting plasma tunnel. When the particle beam was then pulsed down the core of this channel, a magnetic current was set up inside the tunnel's walls that evenly repelled the beam from all sides and thereby confined it to the straight-line path.

In the Sandia test, a single pulse of electrons traveled 5 feet along a straight path. Subsequently, researchers at Los Alamos (N.M.) National Laboratory, working with multiple, back-to-back pulses of electrons, extended the straight-line beam transmission record to 11 feet.

A more spectacular test of the ability to knock down enemy targets took place. On September 13, when a two-stage solid-fueled rocket, launched from an F-15 jet fighter, tracked and destroyed an orbiting satellite. It was the first operational test of an antisatellite (ASAT) weapon by the United States. The satellite was identified by its heat emissions. Miniature telescopes on the heat-seeking warhead focused on the satellite as a computer-assisted guidance system homed the warhead in for its kill. The satellite was destroyed when the warhead collided with it.

The ASAT's target was to have been an instrumented space balloon, but last-minute problems with it caused ASAT planners to seek an alternative target. The six-year-old satellite chosen for destruction happened to be one that carried highly useful, functioning instruments to photograph the sun's outer atmosphere.

In December a major underground nuclear weapons test was conducted in Nevada. Details were secret, but it was believed to involve a nuclear X-ray laser, powered by a hydrogen bomb and intended to destroy enemy missiles in space.

Optical Fiber Feats. At one time, all telephone and other data communications signals were sent down copper wires, encoded as electrical signals. But optical fibers—tiny glass fibers—are now becoming the conduit for messages that are encoded as pulses of light. In February, records were announced for the distance that information was transmitted through optical fibers—without a repeater to boost the signal—and the number of bits of information transmitted per second.

Scientists often multiply the distance that data travel by the number of bits of information transmitted to get a measure of accomplishment known as bit-kilometers per second (bit-km/s). AT&T Bell Laboratories achieved a record 1.37 trillion bit-km/s by sending a signal of 20 billion bits per second over a fiber 68.3 km long. Roughly equivalent to carrying 300,000 simultaneous telephone calls, that is a tenfold improvement over previous data transmission rates. To achieve the feat, engineers combined ten different signals of 2 billion bits per second each within a single fiber. Each signal was delivered by a separate laser tuned to a slightly different wavelength.

Spheres From Space. On July 17, billions of tiny plastic spheres that had been manufactured aboard the maiden voyage of the space shuttle *Challenger* were offered for sale by the National Bureau of Standards. Each a near-perfect 10 micrometers in diameter (there are about 25,000 micrometers to the inch), these polystyrene beads became the first commercial product ever made in space. As reference standards, they serve roughly the same function as do yardsticks; they provide a base against which other microscopic ground-powder spheres can be measured—whether the spheres are grains of face powder or the silver used in photographic emulsions.

Although 18,000 spheres would fit on the head of a pin, it is not how small they are but rather how relatively large they are that makes their manufacture impossible on earth. Developed from a gooey lighter-than-water chemical, the tiny beads tend to clump together during several manufacturing phases. Stirring alleviates the sticking in beads smaller than a micrometer, but the degree of stirring that would be necessary for these larger beads would cause them to bind together into cottage cheese-like curds. In zero gravity, however, the beads could be manufactured with a minimum of stirring and clumping.

Microtools. The world's smallest heater—a mere 1/25 the diameter of a human hair—was developed by biophysicist Frederick Sachs at the State University of New York in Buffalo. To record minute temperature changes in human cells heated with the device, Sachs developed a companion tool, the world's smallest thermometer. Only half the diameter of the heater, the thermometer was able to discern temperature changes as small as 1/100,000th of a degree Celsius.

The heater consists of an open-tipped cylindrical glass pipette—filled with a low-melting point alloy—that is 2 micrometers in diameter at its tip. A thin layer of gold that coats the outside of the pipette makes an electrically conducting contact between the outside and the inner metal. When the heater is hooked to a power source, current driven inside the device heats the metal. The thermometer started as an even smaller cylindrical glass micropipette having a closed bottom tip. A partition running down its length creates two internal chambers that are filled with saltwater. The speed at which the ions move within its salty water offers a gauge of temperature.

Although Sachs developed these tools to probe ion channels (the electrically conducting structures in individual cells), the devices may also have various medical applications, from measuring blood flow in capillaries to studying airflow rates in air sacs of the lung.

Dioxin Cleanup. New methods for sequestering or destroying dangerous chemicals at hazardous waste sites were reported. One technique, developed at the University of Michigan, modifies naturally occurring clay so that it binds with organic chemicals—especially TCDD, the most toxic species of dioxin; it can extract 3 milligrams of dioxin from 20 million gallons of water. Also, in four trial burns, an experimental incinerator developed by the Environmental Protection Agency was found to destroy 99.9999 percent of both liquid and solid wastes contaminated with TCDD. The system can reportedly decontaminate wastes containing various organic chemicals, but it is too expensive to be useful for large areas.

The "Hexapod." In June the Defense Department unveiled its new mechanical "horse"—a computerized, flexible, six-legged vehicle

Downtown Shopping

A series of radio ads for Plummet Mall, "the world's first underground vertical mall," galvanized the citizens of Cincinnati early this year, proving to some the power of advertising and to others the public's gullibility—and greed. Stirred by the slogan "the best value in town is a hole in the ground," business people scrambled to negotiate leases in this inverted skyscraper with its spiral escalators; aboveground retailers fretted about the buried competition. Most, if not all, listeners had caught on to the joke by the final ad, which sadly announced that the ground beneath the city had shifted, moving the phantom mall westward, "somewhere between Cincinnati and Lincoln, Neb."

able to carry heavy loads while maneuvering through terrain too rough for jeeps and trucks. The "hexapod," officially known as the Adaptive Suspension Vehicle, stands 17 feet long and 8 feet tall and is designed to walk 5 to 8 miles an hour, carrying loads up to 500 pounds. Outdoor testing was planned for 1986.   J.R.

TELEVISION AND RADIO BROADCASTING. Television in 1985 was characterized by changes in viewing habits, the burgeoning sales of VCR's and dish antennas, and the growth of stereo television. The trend in radio leaned more toward talk and less toward music. The ratings wars on both television and radio were as fierce as ever.

Viewing Decline. For the first time in the history of U.S. television, the three major commercial networks lost their majority hold on the nation's prime-time viewing habits. According to an A. C. Nielsen survey covering the 30-week 1984–1985 season, the networks' combined prime-time rating dipped below 50 percent, meaning that more than half of the potential television audience had decided not to watch network fare.

This decline, which began in 1979 was not generally interpreted as an indication that Americans were watching less television; rather, they were said to be turning more and more toward the various nonnetwork alternatives, such as cable television and home video.

397

Hot New Star
A key ingredient in a spicy mélange of sex, violence, rock music, and designer clothing, actor Don Johnson became one of the year's television sensations as a stubble-faced, street-smart Florida detective on NBC's popular police series, *Miami Vice*. Johnson, 35, blond and handsome, played Sonny Crockett, partner to Philip Michael Thomas's Ricardo Tubbs; the pair epitomized the visual style that marked the show. Johnson's new success belied a troubled past; behind him was a string of flop movies, failed television pilots, broken marriages, and bouts with drugs and alcohol. Since becoming a celebrity, the Missouri-born Johnson also won praise for his performances in a remade-for-television movie, *The Long Hot Summer,* and in *Cease Fire,* a film made earlier but not released until 1985.

Don Johnson

The Ratings Game. One network did register a dramatic gain in ratings for the 1984–1985 season. NBC, which had consistently finished in third place since the 1974–1975 season, came in second behind CBS, which scored its sixth straight seasonal triumph. The final ratings were as follows: CBS, 16.9; NBC, 16.2; ABC, 15.4. (Each rating point represents 1 percent of the 84.9 million U.S. television households.)

An important reason for NBC's rise was the extraordinary success of *The Cosby Show,* the family comedy series starring Bill Cosby (see biography at PEOPLE IN THE NEWS). Ironically, *The Cosby Show* had been rejected by ABC, which was once known for this sort of program, only to land on NBC's fall 1984 schedule and become the biggest new hit series since *Mork and Mindy* in 1978. *The Cosby Show*—featuring Bill Cosby as a successful doctor, Phylicia Ayers-Allen as his attorney-wife, and five children—upset the conventional wisdom among television executives that situation comedies were becoming a relic of the past. It also attracted millions of white viewers to a show with an entirely black cast, another surprise for network programmers.

The program finished as the season's third-rated series, behind two prime-time soap operas—*Dynasty* on ABC and *Dallas* on CBS. The remainder of the top ten programs, in order of popularity, were *60 Minutes,* CBS; *Family Ties,* NBC; *The A-Team,* NBC; *Simon & Simon,* CBS; *Knots Landing,* CBS; and *Murder, She Wrote,* CBS; with *Falcon Crest* and *Crazy Like a Fox,* both CBS, tied for tenth place. *Murder, She Wrote* and *Crazy Like a Fox* were both new shows in the 1984–1985 season. Among new shows in the top 20 was *Highway to Heaven* (NBC), conceived by and starring Michael Landon. *Miami Vice,* a new police series on NBC, finished in 44th position during its first season but received considerable attention for its slick production values and use of rock music. It started the 1985–1986 season as one of television's top-rated shows.

Viewers demonstrated resistance to the long miniseries, reversing a previous pattern. One example was *Space,* based on the James Michener book, which ran for 13 hours but was a major disappointment for CBS, achieving only a 16.8 rating and a meager 27 share. *Space,* in fact, finished in 14th place among the year's miniseries. The leaders were *Fatal Vision,* NBC; *Hollywood Wives,* ABC; *Evergreen,* NBC; *Ellis Island,* CBS; and *The Atlanta Child Murders,* CBS. The top made-for-TV movies were *The Burning Bed,* NBC; *Ewok Adventure,* ABC; and *The Dirty Dozen: The Next Mission,* NBC.

The 1985–1986 Season. The networks went into the new season with schedules offering 25 percent new programming. Most of the changes were concentrated in the prime 8 P.M. to 9 P.M. hour; the fewest occurred at 10 P.M. The dominant prime-time genre continued to be the action-adventure show, which accounted for 25 hours (38 percent) of the networks' prime-time scheduling. Despite the popularity of *The Cosby Show*, as well as *Family Ties* and *Cheers*, comedy comprised only 17 percent of the prime-time programming. Amid the forest of action-adventure shows, one that attracted particular notice was ABC's *Moonlighting*, starring Cybill Shepherd and Bruce Willis as a pair of sleuths; the show debuted in March and was going strong in the new 1985–1986 season.

The anthology format, long considered dormant, came back to life at the season's start. CBS put out a revival of *The Twilight Zone*, Rod Serling's 1960's hit series, and also brought back Mary Tyler Moore late in the year, as an older and wiser divorcée working on a seedy newspaper, in the comedy series *Mary*. NBC looked to the past with a revival of *Alfred Hitchcock Presents*, and to the future too, with an anthology series called *Amazing Stories* that marked the television debut of movie producer Steven Spielberg. Among other shows, those given a good chance for survival included *The Golden Girls*, starring Bea Arthur, Betty White, Rue McClanahan, and Estelle Getty, on NBC; *Dynasty II: The Colbys* and *Our Family Honor* on ABC; and CBS's *The Equalizer*, starring Edward Woodward in the title role. ABC was pinning a good deal of its hopes for resurgence on *North and South*, a miniseries based on the John Jakes Civil War novel. However, it was something of a popular (as well as a critical) disappointment.

Special programming made an impressive showing early in the 1985–1986 season. ABC televised an extraordinary three-hour look at the 40 years following the end of World War II in *45/85*, produced by Av Westin and narrated by Peter Jennings and Ted Koppel. CBS presented a blockbuster adaptation of Arthur Miller's 1949 Pulitzer Prize-winning drama, *Death of a Salesman;* the television production, a reprise of the 1984 Broadway revival of the play, starred Dustin Hoffman as the tragic, suffering salesman, with Kate Reid, John Malkovich, Charles Durning, and Stephen Lang.

PBS began the season with its customary array of timely public-affairs programs. Among them were *War: A Commentary by Gwynne Dyer*, a history of human conflict from the Napoleonic wars to the Middle East crisis; *The Skin Horse*, a documentary on the emotional and sexual needs of the severely handicapped; and *The Statue of Liberty*, a history of the monument from its initial design and construction in Paris to the refurbishing under way in advance of its centennial in 1986. PBS had stirred controversy in June when it decided to air an hour-long rebuttal to its own award-winning 13-part series, *Vietnam: A Television History*. The rebuttal, entitled *Television's Vietnam: The Real Story* and narrated by actor Charlton Heston, was prepared by Accuracy in Media, a conservative group that charged the original series with distortions.

Dramatic offerings on PBS included *The Last Place on Earth*, a miniseries on the race between Captain Robert Scott and Roald Amundsen to reach the South Pole; an eight-part adaptation of Dickens's *Bleak House*, starting in December; and performances of *The Importance of Being Earnest* and *"Master Harold"* . . . *and the Boys*.

Wrestling. One of the more surprising developments was the professional wrestling craze. At one point the "sport"—long considered something of a farce because of its preordained outcomes and outlandish antics—accounted for four of the ten highest-rated cable programs. One extravagantly publicized March event in New York City, dubbed "WrestleMania," attracted an estimated 1 million viewers at 200 closed circuit outlets in 27 countries. The seemingly sudden popularity of wrestling heroes and villains such as Hulk Hogan and Rowdy Roddy Piper was attributed to heavy promotion, attention given to it by ringside celebrities like Andy Warhol and, probably most significantly, high exposure on MTV, especially in the videos of pop singer Cyndi Lauper.

Awards. The Peabody Awards, considered the most prestigious in broadcasting, were presented in New York City in May. Among the networks, ABC won three while CBS and NBC received one each. The Showtime Cable Network and the Turner Broadcasting System,

owned by maverick Ted Turner, took one award each, and the public television station WNET in New York won two. Among those honored were Roone Arledge as news and sports director for ABC, Bill Moyers for *A Walk Through the 20th Century With Bill Moyers,* Britain's Granada Television for *The Jewel in the Crown,* Roger Rosenblatt for his essays on the *MacNeil/Lehrer Newshour,* Ted Koppel for his *Nightline,* and the NBC hospital drama *St. Elsewhere.*

At the 37th annual Emmy Awards ceremonies, in September, *Cagney and Lacey,* starring Sharon Gless and Tyne Daly as detectives, was named top dramatic series. *The Cosby Show* was chosen the best comedy series, and *The Jewel in the Crown,* public television's widely praised dramatic series about the period of

British rule in India, was named best limited series. Richard Crenna won as the best actor in a limited series for the drama *The Rape of Richard Beck.* Joanne Woodward received the award for best actress in a limited series for *Do You Remember Love?,* a drama about a woman afflicted with Alzheimer's disease. William Daniels of *St. Elsewhere* was named best lead actor in a drama series. Five-time nominee Betty Thomas won the prize as best supporting actress in a drama series for her role as Officer Lucy Bates in *Hill Street Blues.* Acting awards in comedy series were spread among four different shows: Robert Guillaume was named best lead actor for his *Benson* title role, Jane Curtin was tapped as best leading actress for *Kate and Allie,* Rhea Perlman of *Cheers* repeated as best supporting actress, and John

Larroquette of *Night Court* was named best supporting actor.

Westmoreland Libel Suit. General William C. Westmoreland dropped a $120 million libel suit against CBS in exchange for a joint statement in which CBS said it respected the general's "long and faithful service to his country" and Westmoreland praised CBS's "distinguished journalistic tradition." The charge stemmed from a 1982 documentary entitled "The Uncounted Enemy: A Vietnam Deception," which accused him of engaging in a conspiracy to understate enemy troop strength during his tenure as commander of U.S. forces in Vietnam from 1964 to 1968. Westmoreland claimed the statement was an apology, but CBS issued a separate statement saying it stood by its story.

Bottom Line. Significant transactions attempted in the broadcasting business included a bid by Ted Turner, chairman of the Turner Broadcasting System Inc. of Atlanta, to take over CBS. In April, Turner offered to trade stock and securities valued at $175 for each CBS share. The CBS management foiled the bid, in part by repurchasing 21 percent of its own stock at $150 a share in cash and securities. Agreements between CBS and its creditor banks limited the amount of debt CBS could assume and thus blocked a takeover by Turner, which would have increased the debt greatly. In October the Loews Corporation, a conglomerate headed by Laurence A. Tisch, said it planned to increase its holdings of CBS stock to as much as 25 percent. CBS, in turn, offered Tisch a seat on the CBS board of directors. The move was widely seen as an attempt by CBS to further bolster itself against any unfriendly takeover threat that might develop.

In March, ABC was acquired by Capital Cities Communications Inc. for a reported $3.43 billion in cash and long-term stock options, marking the first time a television network's ownership would change hands. The Federal Communications Commission approved the transaction in November. The FCC also approved the purchase by Rupert Murdoch, the Australian overseer of a worldwide communications empire (which includes the *Times* of London and the New York *Post* newspapers), of seven U.S. television stations

from Metro-Media Inc. for more than $2 billion. Since FCC law limits noncitizens to 25 percent ownership of any U.S. broadcast station, Murdoch obtained his U.S. citizenship papers in September. FCC law also bars an individual from owning a newspaper and a broadcast facility in the same market. Murdoch, who owned papers in two of the cities—New York and Chicago—involved in the transaction, received a two-year exemption from the ban from the FCC. Murdoch indicated that he planned to consolidate the six stations with another of his holdings, the 20th-Century Fox Film Corporation, which he also purchased in 1985, to form the Fox Television Network.

VCR's, the Dish, and Stereo. The sales of videocassette recorders continued to increase, causing analysts to claim that the VCR had

Professional wrestling, often considered pure theatrics, soared in popularity on cable TV during 1985, largely through the antics of such stars as Hulk Hogan, shown here applying a headlock to his hapless opponent.

brought about the most fundamental change in the way Americans enjoy filmed entertainment since commercial television's postwar expansion. New units were selling at a rate of over 20,000 per day; film rentals were booming as well.

The rate of growth of the VCR's was exceeded by an even more futuristic video item—the big dish satellite antenna. By late 1985 roughly 400,000 such backyard space stations were operating in the United States, and sales were growing at an annual rate of 300 percent. The dish operates by pulling in signals directly from satellite relays, which hover in the sky 22,000 miles above the earth; more than 70 channels are thus made available. Most of the dishes are to be found in rural areas, where reception is poor, but the dish also appeals to city-dwellers whose television reception is impeded by tall buildings; satellite dish reception is unaffected by such obstructions. The cost of the dish ranges from $2,000 to $10,000.

The year also brought rapid growth in the trend toward stereo television broadcasts, a technology introduced in 1984. By summer 1985 there were 100 stations around the country broadcasting in stereo, and by year's end more than half of all U.S. households were expected to be within range of at least one stereo broadcast signal.

William Daniels (center) won a 1985 Emmy award as best actor in a dramatic series for his role as Dr. Craig in the NBC hospital drama St. Elsewhere.

Radio. The biggest new star in radio, Garrison Keillor, continued to attract nationwide audiences with his *A Prairie Home Companion,* broadcast Saturdays on public radio from St. Paul, Minn. The most popular feature of the broadcast was Keillor's comic portrait of the mythical Minnesota small town Lake Wobegon. Expanding on his theme, Keillor wrote a book entitled *Lake Wobegon Days,* which became an immediate best-seller.

The trend in commercial radio leaned away from music, long a broadcasting staple, and toward talk—most of it intended to be humorous. Although radio has enjoyed renewed success it faced the problem of heightened competition because of a glut of new stations. The key to a successful radio station continued to be the ability to specialize in a format that reached a specific audience, thus enabling the advertiser to target that precise audience; this is in contrast to television stations, which reach much more diverse audiences, potentially diluting the efficacy of certain kinds of advertising. What radio had in common with television, particularly in large cities, was the ratings war; radio stations waged a continuing and expensive battle for listeners' loyalty. In Los Angeles, one station, KIIS, spent an estimated $2 million during the year for prizes that ranged from rock-concert tickets to a new car. D.F.

TENNESSEE. See STATISTICS OF THE WORLD.

TEXAS. See STATISTICS OF THE WORLD.

THAILAND. An attempt by elements of Thailand's military to overthrow the government of Prime Minister Prem Tinsulanonda failed on September 9, 1985. The plotters, who had also failed in a 1981 attempt, mustered only 400 to 500 soldiers this time. A total of 5 people were killed, including 2 Western journalists, and 59 were wounded. The rebels struck while Prem and the armed forces commander, General Arthit Kamlangek, were out of the country. Armored and cavalry units entered Bangkok before dawn, and the rebels seized control of the radio station. Rebel tanks and machine guns also fired at an army building in order to knock out a rival radio transmitter. By midafternoon, however, the outnumbered insurgents gave up the fight. The leader of the coup was allowed to leave the country, but in October,

40 Thais were charged with sedition, including former Prime Minister Kriangsak Chamanand.

Prem extended General Arthit's tenure as supreme commander of the armed forces and commander in chief of the army after Arthit's supporters lobbied hard for his retention beyond the official retirement age of 60. This strengthened Arthit's position as a possible successor to Prem, who enhanced his own position by naming 76 new senators, mostly military men loyal to himself.

Dry-season fighting between Vietnamese occupation forces in Cambodia and Cambodian resistance groups spilled over into Thailand early in the year, and over 200,000 Cambodians fled into Thailand from border camps destroyed by the Vietnamese offensive. In July foreign ministers of the Association of South East Asian Nations (Asean) proposed indirect negotiations to end the fighting in Cambodia, but Vietnam rejected the idea. The Asean governments unsuccessfully pressed the Soviet Union to reduce its military aid to Vietnam and to support a political solution to the conflict in Cambodia.

The United States agreed in March to sell Thailand 12 F-16 fighter-bombers—the first to be stationed in Southeast Asia. In March, Chinese President Li Xiannian visited Thailand and stressed Peking's support for Thailand's security.

Thailand's government attempted to reduce trade deficits, maintain price stability, and cut government deficits. Progress was made in the first two efforts, but the government had less success with its own budget. The main difficulty was revenue shortfalls brought on by sluggish economic growth. Existing and planned austerity measures brought strong complaints from the business community, which faced high interest rates and low prices for farm products.

See STATISTICS OF THE WORLD. A.R.

THEATER. New York, the theater capital of the United States, reached a low ebb in 1985. According to the League of American Theaters and Producers, only 33 shows had opened on Broadway by the end of the 1984–1985 season—the smallest number in this century. Box office receipts dipped sharply, and theater attendance was the lowest in almost a decade.

Big River: The Adventures of Huckleberry Finn *was an exuberant new version of the classic Mark Twain tale, featuring Ron Richardson (left) as Jim and Daniel H. Jenkins as Huck.*

Broadway. Early 1985 omens for Broadway musicals were far from promising. The misses began with *Harrigan 'n' Hart*, which tried unsuccessfully to celebrate a legendary 19th-century vaudeville team. *Leader of the Pack*, recapturing the girl-group sound of the early 1960's, failed to attract audiences, as did *Grind*, featuring the exuberant Ben Vereen and staging by Harold Prince. Then *Big River: The Adventures of Huckleberry Finn* came along in April. It lifted sagging spirits and proved to be the show audiences had been waiting for. Composed by Roger Miller, the new version of the Mark Twain classic arrived in New York via the American Repertory Theater of Cambridge, Mass. and California's La Jolla Playhouse. Another apparent audience pleaser—oddly enough—was *Singin' in the Rain*, adapted from the 1952 MGM musical. Despite a deluge of bad notices, the show kept running, bolstered by an effective ad campaign and audience

word of mouth. Among the year's final musicals was *Song and Dance*, the Broadway version of the London hit by composer Andrew Lloyd Webber and lyricist Don Black. Reviews were mixed, but critics praised its star, Bernadette Peters. *The Mystery of Edwin Drood*, based on Charles Dickens's last, unfinished novel, opened in December.

Broadway was enriched in the fall by Eugene O'Neill's *The Iceman Cometh*, marching in from the American National Theater in Washington, D.C. The production reunited Jason Robards, Jr. and director José Quintero, whose 1956 collaboration was a landmark in the midcentury O'Neill renaissance. Earlier in 1985, Rod Serling's TV drama *Requiem for a Heavyweight*, starring John Lithgow, came to Broadway from the Long Wharf Theater in New Haven, Conn.

The British again made worthwhile contributions. Hugh Whitemore's *Pack of Lies*, with Rosemary Harris, dramatized the dilemma of a British family that discovers its Canadian neighbors and best friends are Communist spies. A predominantly British cast headed by Glenda Jackson provided fresh insight into Eugene O'Neill's classic *Strange Interlude*. In light-hearted contrast, Rex Harrison and Claudette Colbert took a nostalgic trip to 1920's Britain in Frederick Lonsdale's *Aren't We All?*

The Circle in the Square presented a modernized version of Beaumarchais's 18th-century comedy *The Marriage of Figaro*, directed by Andrei Serban and starring Anthony Heald. The company's revival of George Bernard Shaw's *Arms and the Man* was marked by major contributions from John Malkovich as director and his wife, Glenne Headly, as costar; also starring were Kevin Kline and Raul Julia.

New Broadway plays were scarce. Glenn Close and Sam Waterston appeared in Michael Frayn's *Benefactors*, which traced the dissolution of marriages, principles, and faith in the future. Jane Wagner's one-woman play *The Search for Signs of Intelligent Life in the Universe*, starring Lily Tomlin, was a deserved comedy hit. But it was Neil Simon who did the most to keep comedy alive. In his *Biloxi Blues*, Eugene Morris Jerome (Matthew Broderick) of the earlier *Brighton Beach Memoirs* survived World War II basic training and learned the facts of life. Also noteworthy was a revised version of *The Odd Couple*, with Rita Moreno and Sally Struthers starring.

Off Broadway. Off Broadway had something for almost every taste. Joseph Papp's Public Theater was a powerhouse of activity. One of its most admired offerings was *Tracers*, a riveting collaborative creation by the Vietnam Veterans Ensemble Group, conceived and directed by John Di Fusco. For contrast, there were Albert Innaurato's bizarre semi-memoir, *Coming of Age in Soho*, and Christopher Durang's blistering satire *The Marriage of Bette and Boo*, in which Durang also appeared. In addition, the Public Theater offered several plays from Britain, some of them in collaboration with London's Royal Court Theatre. They included Michael Hastings's *Tom and Viv*, which explored the deterioration of the first marriage of T. S. Eliot (Edward Herrmann); Ron Hutchinson's searing *A Rat in the Skull*, in which a brutal London police interrogation of a suspected Irish terrorist epitomized centuries of Anglo-Irish conflict; and *Aunt Dan and Lemon*, a bizarre, well-received comedy by American playwright Wallace Shawn. In *Salonika*, Jessica Tandy, as an octogenarian widow, and Elizabeth Wilson, as her elderly daughter, found the past haunting the present during their visit to the Greek gravesite of the widow's husband. *A Map of the World*, by David Hare, dealt sardonically with a group of international characters during a United Nations poverty conference. Of new American works the ones most relevant to current issues included William M. Hoffman's touching *As Is* and Larry Kramer's angry *The Normal Heart*, both of which dealt with AIDS. At the end of its Off Broadway run, *As Is* moved to Broadway. Another play that moved to Broadway was Herb Gardner's new comedy *I'm Not Rappaport*. The play, about two aged men—one Jewish and one black—starred Judd Hirsch and Cleavon Little. The Circle Repertory Company paired Lanford Wilson's *Talley and Son*, the third installment of the Talley family trilogy, in repertory with *Tomorrow's Monday*, a 1934 play by Paul Osborn. Sam Shepard was represented by a revival of *The Curse of the Starving Class*, about an embattled family; his new work dealing with tortuous family relationships, *A Lie of the Mind*, opened in December.

Joseph Papp's New York Shakespeare Festival staged a musical version of Charles Dickens's last, unfinished novel, The Mystery of Edwin Drood. *Here George Rose, as the master of ceremonies, asks the audience to vote on an ending for the murder mystery.*

Neil Simon's comedy Biloxi Blues, the sequel to the autobiograph-ical Brighton Beach Memoirs, took Eugene (older but still an aspiring writer) to basic training in the 1943 wartime army. Matthew Broderick starred.

Off Broadway revivals ranged from ancient Greek to contemporary French, American, and British. The City Stage Company mounted Christopher Martin's modern arrangement of Aeschylus's *Oresteia*, and Craig Kinzer's staging of Ibsen's *Brand*. The Mirror Company shone brightly in Jean Giraudoux's *The Madwoman of Chaillot* and Robert Bolt's *Vivat! Vivat Regina!* Roy Dotrice animated Dr. Stockmann, Ibsen's stubborn idealist, in the Roundabout Theater Company's revival of *An Enemy of the People*. The Roundabout's production of Peter Nichols's *A Day in the Death of Joe Egg*, starring Jim Dale and Stockard Channing, was so successful it moved to Broadway.

Off Broadway musicals were varied and abundant. They included *Mayor*—a cheerfully satiric revue by Charles Strouse and Warren Leigh, which poked fun at New York City's first citizen—and *Yours, Anne*, an adaptation from *The Diary of Anne Frank*, put together by Enid Putterman and Michael Cohen.

Regional Theater. New York's recognition of the regional theater was reflected in the appointment of Gregory Mosher, longtime artistic director of Chicago's Goodman Theater, as director of the Vivian Beaumont Theater at Lincoln Center. And in its first season, New York's American Theater Exchange presented

three plays: Heather McDonald's whimsical *Faulkner's Bicycle* (which originated at the Yale Repertory Theater), Alan Ayckbourn's comedy *Season's Greetings* (Houston's Alley Theater), and *In the Belly of the Beast*, the Adrian Hall-Robert Woodruff adaptation of Jack Henry Abbott's prison letters (Los Angeles's Mark Taper Forum).

Among the most newsworthy developments outside New York was the first production of the newly created American National Theater at the Kennedy Center in Washington, D.C., under the artistic direction of Peter Sellars. The inaugural play, Shakespeare's *Henry IV, Part I*, directed by Timothy S. Mayer, flopped, but Mayer recovered somewhat with his eccentric production of Alexandre Dumas's *The Count of Monte Cristo*. The new company triumphed with its well-received revival of O'Neill's *The Iceman Cometh*.

The Yale Repertory Theater's opening play of the fall season—a revival of *The Blood Knot* by the South African writer Athol Fugard—masterfully examined the apartheid dilemma. This production starred the original cast: Fugard, who also directed the play, and Zakes Mokae. It moved to Broadway late in the year. The Acting Company, a national touring troupe specializing in classical repertory theater, premiered *Orchards*, which consisted of dramatizations of seven Chekhov short stories by, among others, John Guare, David Mamet, and Wendy Wasserstein.

Awards and Honors. The 1985 Antoinette Perry (Tony) awards were marked by a first: no awards were given in three categories—leading actor and actress in a musical and choreography. *Big River* was chosen as best musical and honored for its book, score, featured actor (Ron Richardson), scenic design, lighting design, and direction by Des McAnuff. Gene Saks won the Tony for best director of a play (*Biloxi Blues*) and Leilani Jones for best featured actress in a musical (*Grind*). The award for best actress in a play went to Stockard Channing in Peter Nichols's *A Day in the Death of Joe Egg*. Derek Jacobi won the Tony for best actor in a drama for his portrayal of Benedick in the Royal Shakespeare Company's production of *Much Ado About Nothing*. And Neil Simon won his first regular Tony for *Biloxi Blues*, named best play. Special Tony awards were given to Edwin Lester, founder and general director of the Los Angeles Light Opera, and to actor Yul Brynner, who died of cancer later in the year; on June 30 he had given his 4,625th and final performance as the King in Rodgers and Hammerstein's *The King and I.*

The 1985 Pulitzer Prize for drama went to Stephen Sondheim and James Lapine for their musical *Sunday in the Park With George*. The New York Drama Critics Circle chose August Wilson's *Ma Rainey's Black Bottom* as best play of the 1984–1985 season but voted not to honor a musical.   J.B.

TOGO. *See* STATISTICS OF THE WORLD.

TONGA. *See* STATISTICS OF THE WORLD.

TRANSPORTATION. Business dropped off somewhat for many transportation companies in the United States in 1985 after the preceding banner year. Some companies, however, benefited by handling the imports that flooded the country because of the strength of the dollar. Passenger aviation traffic was up significantly. While it proceeded with deregulation efforts in various areas, the federal government was still trying to close the sale of the freight carrier Conrail. The rail and trucking industries were both preoccupied with controlling labor costs. New mass transit systems opened or saw development go forward.

Trailblazer in Musicals
Over the past 15 years, composer/lyricist Stephen Sondheim has almost singlehandedly transformed the musical theater and its traditions. In 1985, Sondheim was rewarded with the Pulitzer Prize in drama for *Sunday in the Park With George*, his most innovative work to date. It was the most recent in a string of successes that began in 1957, when he wrote the lyrics to Leonard Bernstein's music for *West Side Story*. *A Funny Thing Happened on the Way to the Forum*—for which Sondheim wrote both lyrics and music—followed a few years later, and in the early 1970's he won three Tonys in quick succession for the scores of *Company*, *Follies*, and *A Little Night Music*. *Sweeney Todd*, a 1979 operatic work focusing on a murderous barber, garnered a fourth. Like *Sunday*, which was inspired by the painter Georges Seurat, it was hardly a typical Broadway musical, but Sondheim disclaims any intention of being a pathbreaker. His innovations, he says come from "a feeling of not wanting to cover the same material twice or to bore yourself."

Stephen Sondheim

TRANSPORTATION

AVIATION

In the first nine months of the year, U.S. passenger miles were 12 percent above the same period in 1984. Net profits for the first six months were up sharply, primarily because of reduced taxes and interest costs. Many airlines gained from declining fuel costs, but profitable operating results probably owed more to improving economic conditions, airline cost controls, and success with promotional fares. Nearly 2,000 persons died in airplane crashes around the world in 1985, the most tragic year in commercial aviation history (see ACCIDENTS AND DISASTERS).

Acquisitions. U A L, Inc., the parent of United Air Lines and the nation's biggest airline, bought Hertz, the nation's biggest car-rental company. The deal appeared to give U A L an interesting niche in the travel industry business. U A L also agreed to buy the Pacific Ocean operations of Pan American; the acquisition meant the end of Pan Am's trans-Pacific operations, which had begun in 1935.

Trans World Airlines was the target of a high-stakes bidding war waged between financier Carl Icahn and Texas Air Corporation, parent of Continental Air Lines. After Icahn made his initial move to take over the troubled carrier,

Texas Air appeared as a "white knight" with a special interest in TWA's profitable international routes. Frank Lorenzo, Texas Air's president, offered $925 million for TWA, which agreed to be acquired by Texas Air. But TWA's unions were apparently worried about events at Continental, which was allegedly forced into bankruptcy by Lorenzo in order to dissolve expensive labor contracts. With union encouragement, Icahn took the initiative during the summer, boosting his share of TWA stock from 32 percent to 52 percent. In September, Texas Air agreed to withdraw from its merger pact, thereby clearing the way for Icahn to officially take control. Despite obstacles late in the year, he succeeded, becoming TWA's chairman in January 1986.

In other acquisitions news, People Express bought Frontier Airlines and agreed to acquire Britt Airways, which serves 29 Midwestern cities. Chrysler bought Gulfstream Aerospace, and General Dynamics agreed to purchase Cessna. A leading produce of corporate planes, Lear Fan, declared bankruptcy.

Labor Settlements. United Air Lines pilots struck on May 17 to protest management's proposal for a two-tier wage system between salaries for current pilots and those for newly hired ones.

Transportation Secretary Elizabeth Dole presents a toy train car to Robert Claytor, chairman of the Norfolk Southern Corporation, the railroad company that offered $1.2 billion for the government-owned Conrail freight carrier. Congress still had to approve the deal; opponents vowed to fight the sale.

Only 14 percent of United's 1,500 daily flights, carrying 120,000 passengers, were able to continue. An agreement reached on June 12 provided for the two-tiered pay scale for five years, after which the issue would be submitted to binding arbitration.

In April, two unions decided to call off a strike against Continental that began in 1983. The carrier had continued operations, employing new hires and union members who crossed picket lines. A third union remained on strike until October, when it was ordered by the courts to accept a settlement. (See LABOR UNIONS).

Terrorism and Security. On June 14 a TWA jetliner was hijacked by Shiite Muslim terrorists shortly after its departure from the Athens airport; one U.S. passenger was killed and 39 were held hostage in Lebanon. These and other incidents (see MIDDLE EAST) increased concern over the vulnerability of airline travelers to terrorism. For a time, the U.S. government cautioned travelers about lax security at the Athens airport. The advisory was withdrawn after security appeared to improve, but concerns heightened after the November 23 hijacking of an Egyptian airliner that had taken off from the Athens airport. (Sixty people were killed in the incident). On November 27, U.S. Transportation Secretary Elizabeth Dole ordered a review of security levels at Mideast airports. Terrorist attacks in December at airports in Rome and Vienna, in which 20 persons (including four terrorists) were killed, underscored the gravity of the security problem in the airline industry.

BUS INDUSTRY

The bus industry's problems continued, according to statistics from the Interstate Commerce Commission (ICC), as ridership declined 5 percent in 1984 from 1983 levels and the nation's 20 biggest carriers suffered a net operating loss of $3.4 million. The largest bus company, Greyhound Lines, laid off 2,000 workers in 1985 and planned to close some of its 127 terminals and end service on money-losing routes.

MASS TRANSIT

Miami saw the first phase of its elevated passenger rail system completed, bringing the system to 20 stations on 21 miles. A 10.5-mile light rail transit system, partially underground, neared completion in Pittsburgh at a cost of $550 million. In San Diego construction began on the first 4.3 miles of a planned 17.3-mile trolley line. In the Washington, D.C. area, 6.9 more miles of the Metro (subway) system were opened, lengthening the system to about 60 of a planned 101 miles. Larger projects got under way in Sacramento, Calif., which plans to build an 18.3-mile light rail system, and in Dallas, where a $10 billion program involving both expressway expansion and a new 143-mile subway and surface rail system is contemplated. Buffalo opened most of its $526 million subway system but initially attracted a small ridership; the 6.4 mile line was scheduled to be completed in 1986.

RAILROADS

Freight traffic totaled 921.5 billion ton-miles in 1984, an 11 percent increase over 1983 and just above the previous record of 919 billion ton-miles in 1980, according to the Association of American Railroads. The rise in traffic reportedly translated into a jump of almost 50 percent in earnings for major carriers.

Conrail. The federal government's effort to sell the Consolidated Rail Corporation, or Conrail, to the private sector was the most significant railroad story of the year. The fate of the freight carrier, in which the government had an 85 percent share, was a major issue both because the government poured more than $7 billion in subsidies into the railroad before it became profitable in the 1980's and because Conrail provides vital transportation service to industries in the Northeast and Midwest. After paring down a list of 15 bidders for the carrier to three, Transportation Secretary Elizabeth Dole, on February 8, recommended acceptance of a $1.2 billion offer by the Norfolk Southern Corporation, the southern railroad giant. The combination of Conrail with Norfolk would create the country's largest railroad system.

Conrail's management, which guided the carrier to estimated 1985 profits of $500 million, was against the Norfolk proposal. So was the U.S. Department of Justice, which concluded that Norfolk-Conrail could monopolize traffic in some markets and drive regional carriers out of business. Conrail mustered considerable political opposition to the Norfolk purchase, and its investment adviser, Morgan Stanley & Company, organized a consortium of investors that tendered a $1.2 billion counteroffer in May. Legislation was introduced to implement both the Norfolk and Morgan Stanley purchase proposals, but neither house of Congress took final action in 1985.

Alaska Railroad. While it was unable to make a quick deal on Conrail, the Department of Transportation completed the sale of another government-owned carrier, the Alaska Railroad. The carrier which operates 525 miles of track between Fairbanks and Seward, was sold to the state of Alaska for $22.3 million on January 5.

Amtrak. The government-owned National Railroad Passenger Corporation, or Amtrak, faced deep budget cuts for fiscal year 1986 (beginning on October 2, 1985). The Reagan administration proposed to eliminate funding altogether for the railroad, which had drawn $684 million from the government in fiscal year 1985. Congress, however, refused to approve the administration's plan and eventually agreed to provide $616 million in funding.

Labor Negotiations. Negotiations between carriers and the 13 major labor unions representing railroad workers began in July 1984 and continued in 1985. In October the largest labor group, the United Transportation Union, ratified a pact calling for a 10.5 percent wage increase over 40 months in exchange for the gradual elimination through normal attrition of 8,000 jobs deemed obsolete. The Brotherhood of Locomotive Engineers reached a tentative pact in December providing a similar increase. Negotiations with most of the other unions were in the hands of a mediation board early in 1986.

Milwaukee Road. A federal bankruptcy judge on February 8 approved a $571 million offer by the Soo Line Railroad to purchase the Chicago, Milwaukee, St. Paul & Pacific Railroad, or Milwaukee Railroad, a midwestern carrier that went bankrupt in 1977. The new railroad is known as the Soo/Milwaukee System, operating over about 7,500 miles of track in the Midwest and plains states. The judge's decision closed, perhaps forever, the era of rail bankruptcies that in the 1970's cost the

federal government billions of dollars in various forms of subsidies.

SHIPPING

Business for shipping companies serving the United States was good, particularly for those hauling imports. The flood of imported consumer goods, most of which move in containers that increase handling efficiency, spurred steamship companies to use a new form of service, the double-stack train, that may revolutionize both international and domestic transportation. Used for cargo destined to inland points, double-stack trains are made up solely of specially designed rail cars with wells scooped out of the bottom so they may carry containers stacked two-high. Compared with conventional container trains, double-stacks can cut transportation costs by as much as 40 percent and dramatically reduce transit time between a port and an inland rail unloading facility.

Barges. The major development affecting barge companies that serve the nation's rivers was the official dedication of the Tennessee-Tombigbee Waterway in Alabama and Mississippi. Opened for business in January, two years ahead of schedule, the $2 billion, 234-mile waterway links the Tennessee and Tombigbee rivers. More earth was excavated for it than for the Panama Canal.

Welland Canal. The Welland Canal, a 26-mile-long passage between Lake Erie and Lake Ontario that serves as a vital link in the St. Lawrence Seaway, became blocked on October 14 when a concrete wall in one of the canal's eight locks collapsed, trapping a freighter and effectively closing the seaway at the height of its busy season. Traffic, primarily grain and iron ore shipments from western Great Lakes ports, was halted for more than three weeks, as work crews struggled to make repairs, completed in early November. The shipping season, which normally ends in mid-December, was extended by seaway officials in order to accommodate the backlog of traffic.

TRUCKING.

Final ICC statistics for 1984 revealed that the trucking industry's fortunes improved somewhat from 1983, but there were indications in 1985 that business was dropping off as the economic recovery lost steam.

The Sea-Land Corporation was one of several U.S. steamship lines and railroads that began cost-cutting "double-stack" operations during 1985; special scooped-out trains carry stacked containers from port to inland facilities.

Teamsters. The 1.9-million member Teamsters union agreed to a new, three-year national labor contract following expiration of the previous pact on March 31. The old contract provided average wages of $13.26 per hour. The new contract calls for pay hikes of 10.9 percent over three years and allows trucking companies to pay new employees 30 percent less than in previous contracts.

Roadway and United Parcel Service. The nation's largest general freight carrier, Roadway Express, created a new subsidiary called Roadway Package System Inc. designed to compete directly with United Parcel Service for shipments weighing less than 100 pounds. RPS proved initially successful and by October had expanded to serve 48 cities in 24 states. Meanwhile, UPS, which handles about a quarter-million shipments daily, expanded its own services. It doubled its geographic coverage and started new next-day air package delivery and letter service.

See also AUTOMOBILE INDUSTRY.

R.J.K. & R.E.B.

TRINIDAD AND TOBAGO. *See* STATISTICS OF THE WORLD.

TUNISIA. In 1985, Tunisia held municipal elections and experienced strains in relations with Libya, the United States, and Egypt.

Municipal elections were held throughout Tunisia in May. Opposition party officials called for an election boycott, claiming that control of the election machinery by the ruling Destour Socialist Party (DSP) made a landslide victory for DSP candidates all but inevitable. DSP candidates, in fact, faced only token opposition, and the boycott appeared ineffectual, with voter turnout reported at 92 percent.

Libya provided many foreign policy headaches. In January, seven Libyans were arrested after having illegally crossed the Tunisian border; they were suspected of seeking to incite a rebellion. In August, Libya expelled 29,000 Tunisian emigrant workers, supposedly for economic reasons; Tunisia in turn expelled nearly

Peaceful Footnote

In the 2nd century B.C., the Romans razed the city of Carthage, sold the survivors as slaves, and sowed the soil with salt, thus solidifying their awesome power over the western Mediterranean. But empires and enmities eventually fade, and after 2,000 years, the mayors of modern Rome and contemporary Carthage—now a wealthy suburb of Tunisia's capital city—have vowed to let bygones be bygones. On February 5, 1985, they met in Tunis to sign a peace treaty and a symbolic pact of friendship and cooperation. The Third Punic War, which led to the destruction of ancient Carthage in 146 B.C., was now officially ended.

300 alleged Libyan spies. In early September, Tunisia announced that it was recalling its 60,000 remaining workers from Libya and severing trade relations. Later, Tunisia expelled four Libyan diplomats, accused of mailing letter bombs to Tunisian journalists, and broke off diplomatic relations with Libya.

Relations with the United States were strained in early October over U.S. reaction to Israel's raid on Palestine Liberation Organization headquarters located just south of Tunis, the country's capital. Israel said the attack was in retaliation for the murders of three Israelis in Cyprus. Tunisia called the attack, in which about 70 Palestinians and Tunisians were killed, an act of "state terrorism." The United States initially backed Israel but subsequently toned down its support. Tunisian President Habib Bourguiba sponsored a United Nations resolution condemning the raid, which was adopted by the Security Council on October 4 by a vote of 14–0, with the United States abstaining.

Further complicating relations with the United States was the hijacking, soon afterward of the Italian cruise ship *Achille Lauro* by four Palestinian gunmen. After surrendering to Egyptian authorities in exchange for a promise of safe passage out of Egypt, the gunmen were placed on an Egyptian airplane and flown out of the country. But the plane was intercepted by U.S. Navy jet fighters and, having been denied permission to land in Tunis (and Athens), was forced to land in Italy, where the hijackers were taken into custody. Tunisia's refusal to let the plane land sparked Egyptian charges— denied by Tunisia—that Tunisia had colluded with the United States. There were also calls from some Tunisians to lessen ties with the United States.

See STATISTICS OF THE WORLD.   K.J.B.

TURKEY. In April 1985, Prime Minister Turgut Özal's right-wing Motherland Party, holding 212 of the 400 seats in Turkey's Grand National Assembly, convened its first congress since its 1983 election victory. Özal easily won reelection to the party's leadership, and his most loyal supporters were voted onto key committees. He thus prevailed over the embarrassment caused him in previous months when corruption charges were brought against three cabinet ministers (all of whom subsequently resigned).

Turkish authorities periodically announced the arrest of small groups described as terrorists, Marxist-Leninists, or separatists. Martial law, which the military government imposed on all 67 provinces in 1980, was, however, eased further. By late 1985 it remained only in nine provinces, all in Kurdish areas. Meanwhile, the government passed a controversial bill that granted police wider powers of search, arrest, and detention, plus the authority to deal with "moral" matters.

In the east, Turkish military forces continued to battle Kurdish separatists, some of whom had infiltrated from neighboring Iran, Iraq, and Syria.

Numerous court trials involving large numbers of people—most of them charged with offenses committed before or just after the 1980 coup—were concluded in 1985. In January, 28 members of the militant Dev-Yol (Revolutionary Path) organization were convicted of terrorist crimes and received prison terms ranging from three years to life.Two long trials in Diyarbakir, involving close to 1,000 Kurds accused of crimes including the attempted establishment of a separate state, robbery, and murder, ended in January and February. Death sentences were handed down to 25 defendants, hundreds received prison terms, and 176 were acquitted. Another trial of Dev-Yol members ended with the sentencing of 373 defendants— 11 of them to death—in November. In December, a military court acquitted 10 defendants on charges of helping Mehmet Ali Agca in the 1979 killing of a Turkish newspaper editor; an 11th defendant received three years in prison for harboring Agca after his escape from prison that year.

A visit by Özal to the United States in April— the first by a Turkish premier in 14 years— achieved generally good results. U.S. President Ronald Reagan assured Özal that his administration would support continuing substantial military and economic aid.

As part of its effort to transform Turkey's economy into an export-oriented, free-market system, the government offered tax incentives to exporters and attempted to sell off some of its economic enterprises.

See STATISTICS OF THE WORLD.   P.J.M.

TUVALU. *See* STATISTICS OF THE WORLD.

U

UGANDA. On July 27, 1985, the troubled, four-year-old government of President Milton Obote was overthrown in a coup headed by Brigadier General Basilio Olaro Okello, commander of the army's northern brigade. Throngs of people crowded the streets to celebrate. The coup marked the second time Obote—who also served as president from 1967 to 1971—had been forced from office. Plagued by continuing attacks from guerrilla factions, his regime had, in addition, been widely criticized for alleged human rights abuses. However, the major cause of the coup seemed to be Obote's alleged policy of favoring soldiers from his own Langi tribe over Acholi soldiers for military promotions. When fighting broke out between the two groups in July, disaffected Acholi officers fled to the north, where they gained a measure of control before heading south to take the capital, Kampala.

On July 29, Lieutenant-General Tito Okello—commander of the armed forces and no relation to Basilio Okello—was sworn in as Uganda's chief of state. A military council was appointed to govern until elections, which the regime later promised within a year's time. There were reports of widespread looting, gunfire, and general chaos in Kampala only hours after the takeover announcement, and on July 31, troops loyal to Obote went on a rampage in the deposed president's hometown of Lira. In August, Uganda's major guerrilla force, the National Resistance Army, launched a series of attacks. The NRA claimed it had laid the groundwork for the coup and deserved a share in power.

The government announced in early October that it had offered the NRA six seats on the military council; there were reports that, by then, NRA guerrillas had gained control of the western part of the country. By late October gunfire was heard in the outskirts of Kampala; meanwhile, talks between the two sides proceeded in Kenya, leading to an accord in mid-December. As part of the agreement, the rebel leader, Yoweri Museveni, was reportedly named deputy chairman of the ruling Military Council.

However, the accord was never implemented, and fighting later resumed.

Obote's government had succeeded in bringing about a degree of economic recovery. The economy, however, suffered from political instability, poor fiscal management, and a loss of confidence on the part of the international community. Independent sources pegged the rate of inflation at 100 percent or more.

See STATISTICS OF THE WORLD. F.C.

UNION OF SOVIET SOCIALIST REPUBLICS. For the third time in 2½ years the Soviet Union had a new Communist Party general secretary in 1985. This time, however, the man selected, Mikhail S. Gorbachev (see biography in PEOPLE IN THE NEWS), was only 54 years old, and it appeared likely that the transition would be the last for some time. The year saw a resumption of Soviet-U.S. arms control talks and a flurry of arms limitation proposals from both sides. Gorbachev and President Ronald Reagan held a summit meeting in Geneva on November 19–20.

End of an Era. The death on March 10 of Konstantin U. Chernenko, who was both party general secretary and chief of state, marked the end of an era. Chernenko, born in 1911, was the last of the Soviet Union's leaders who began their careers in the party before World War II. During his one year in office, Chernenko, who suffered from emphysema, heart trouble, and other ailments, carried on the policies of his longtime mentor, Leonid I. Brezhnev, and he halted any movement toward economic reform that had been initiated by his predecessor and Brezhnev's successor, Yuri V. Andropov.

New Leader. By all appearances, the selection of Gorbachev as general secretary was almost a foregone conclusion at the time of Chernenko's death. Given a broad range of responsibilities during the previous two years, he had been treated as the heir apparent. Gorbachev assumed power under favorable conditions: the country had had ten years of ailing leadership and was yearning for a strong person at the helm.

Mourners fill Red Square in Moscow for the funeral of Soviet leader Konstantin U. Chernenko. He had been Communist Party general secretary for only 13 months at his death on March 10; he was succeeded by Mikhail Gorbachev.

Gorbachev moved rapidly to change the membership of the Politburo, which serves as the country's cabinet. On April 23 he added Viktor Chebrikov (chairman of the KGB, or secret police), Yegor Ligachev (the second secretary of the Central Committee), and Nikolai Ryzhkov (then the secretary of the Central Committee for economics). In July he removed his chief rival, Grigori Romanov, from the Politburo and had the new foreign minister, Eduard Shevardnadze, elected to membership. On September 27 the 80-year-old chairman of the Council of Ministers (prime minister), Nikolai Tikhonov, resigned, and on October 15 he was removed from the Politburo. Ryzhkov was named chairman of the Council of Ministers. In December, Viktor Grishin, another veteran Politburo member, was retired as head of the Communist Party in Moscow. During 1985, Gorbachev also acted to remove many other older governmental and party officials who might oppose him and replaced them with his own supporters, who would be elected to the Central Committee in years to come.

Economic Policy. Whereas Chernenko had defended the economic status quo, Gorbachev promised a radical change in the functioning of the economic system, a 4.5 percent annual growth in national income through the end of the century, a maintenance of oil production at its present level, and a raising of Soviet technology to world levels. The difficulty of achieving these goals was suggested by the economic performance of the first half of 1985. Compared with the first half of 1984, industrial production was up only 3.1 percent, although it was up 4.2 percent on a working-day basis. Petroleum production fell below the 1984 level, but the 1985 grain harvest appeared to be good.

The first manifestations of Gorbachev's policy appeared quickly. A strong attack on alcoholism was launched, and in April the Politburo rejected the outlines of the five-year plan based on Chernenko's directives and ordered an increase in the rate of growth. A sharp increase in the rate of production of consumer goods was also promised. In the administrative sphere Gorbachev began to attack the government ministries, and he made it clear that he would make them the scapegoat for the country's economic ills. He began removing ministers, and he set up a commission to consider ways to restructure the ministries and reduce ministerial staffs.

Political Controls and Human Rights. Official policy toward dissidents remained harsh, and Jewish emigration remained at very low levels. However, Moscow continued to give some recognition to the principle of emigration to reunite families. Just before the Gorbachev-Reagan summit, the Soviet Union announced that a number of Soviet citizens married to Americans would be allowed to emigrate to join their spouses.

Yelena Bonner, the wife of Soviet dissident and nuclear physicist Andrei Sakharov, received permission late in the year to go abroad for medical treatment. Sakharov, winner of the 1975 Nobel Peace Prize for his efforts in behalf of human rights, had engaged in hunger strikes to protest the denial of a visa to Bonner and was reportedly force-fed by authorities. After a few days in Italy, Bonner arrived in the United States in December.

Restrictions on debates in the Soviet press were loosened in 1985, especially on matters relating to economic reform. In November the Soviet press published an interview, after deleting certain passages, that President Reagan had given earlier to a group of Soviet journalists in Washington.

Foreign Policy. Andrei Gromyko, foreign minister since 1957, was replaced on July 2 by Shevardnadze, first secretary of the party central committee in the republic of Georgia. (Gromyko, in his mid-70's, was given the ceremonial post of president.) Shevardnadze, who had known Gorbachev since the late 1950's, had no foreign policy experience, other than travel abroad on several delegations.

Perhaps the most noticeable difference in foreign policy, however, was in style. Gorbachev submitted to interviews, in Moscow, with *Time* magazine and with French television journalists, and he held press conferences during his visits to Paris and Geneva. He seemed at ease with the modern media of communications.

Arms Control. The Soviet Union took some arms control initiatives. A first step was its return in March to the negotiating table at Geneva, which the Soviets had left in late 1983 in protest against the deployment of new U.S. missiles in Europe. When the talks resumed, the Soviet Union focused criticism on President Reagan's Strategic Defense Initiative (nicknamed Star Wars)—the plan to develop a ground-based and space-based defensive shield against attacking nuclear missiles and warheads. Soviet officials said in October they would develop their own missile defense system if the United States proceeded with Star Wars. (A Soviet research effort in this area has been under way for some time.)

A series of Soviet proposals and initiatives, most of which were shot down by the United States almost as quickly as they were launched, were unveiled in the months preceding the November Reagan-Gorbachev summit. Gor-

Vitaly Yurchenko, left, a senior KGB official who had defected to the West during the summer, announced at a November news conference in Washington, D.C., that he was returning to the Soviet Union. U.S. officials were unsure whether Yurchenko had been a double agent all along or whether he had simply changed his mind.

bachev announced in April that the Soviet Union would cease to deploy intermediate-range nuclear missiles in Europe until November. The White House said the United States would not reciprocate because the Soviet Union had a great numerical advantage in missiles deployed in Europe. In August, on the 40th anniversary of the dropping of the first atomic bomb, the Soviet Union began a moratorium on atomic testing, scheduled to last until January 1, 1986. (In December the Soviets offered to extend the moratorium and to allow some on-site inspection of testing areas if the United States would join the halt, but the Americans refused.) Meeting with Reagan in the White House on September 27, Foreign Minister Shevardnadze proposed a 50 percent reduction in the two sides' offensive nuclear arsenals—contingent on U.S. abandonment of Star Wars—and this was put on the table at Geneva on September 30. Washington opposed the Star Wars provision and the Soviets' definition of which types of weapons were to be cut; Reagan nevertheless said he welcomed the Soviet initiative, and the United States made a counterproposal on November 1.

While in France in October, Gorbachev offered to make a separate agreement on arms control with France and Britain, which maintain their own nuclear arsenals; the Soviets had previously insisted that these missiles be included in any overall settlement. Britain and France, rejected any such agreement until after a superpower missile settlement was reached.

Gorbachev had portrayed arms control as the central issue at his summit with Reagan in Geneva, but the meeting produced little concrete evidence of progress. After the summit's conclusion, Gorbachev said his talks with Reagan had been "frank, sharp, sometimes very sharp," and both admitted they had not been able to change the other's position on Star Wars. However, agreements were reached to accelerate arms negotiations, to hold regular high-level meetings on other issues, and to renew cultural and other exchanges; also approved was a major agreement on cooperative environmental protection projects. In addition, Gorbachev agreed to visit the United States in 1986, and Reagan agreed to go to Moscow in 1987.

Defector's "Redefection." Two weeks before the summit, a well-publicized spy case took an astounding turn. During the summer a senior KGB official, Vitaly Yurchenko, defected to the West while in Italy. Yurchenko reportedly became annoyed at the publicity given in the press to his disclosures about Soviet espionage activities, and on November 4 he appeared at a news conference at the Soviet embassy in Washington and announced that he was returning to the Soviet Union. He charged that he had been kidnapped in Rome by American authorities, drugged, taken to the United States, and held prisoner by the CIA. U.S. officials dismissed his story, and there was some speculation that he may have been a double agent.

Other Foreign Policy. Gorbachev visited President François Miterrand in France before he met with Reagan. In the Third World, the Soviet Union increased its aid to Nicaragua, but it also made efforts to woo countries not having leftist regimes.

On September 30 four members of the Soviet embassy staff in Beirut were seized by a fundamentalist Muslim faction, which demanded that the Soviet Union pressure its ally Syria to end the fighting in Tripoli, Lebanon, between fundamentalists and Syrian-backed militias. The body of one of the captives, Arkady Katkov, a consular attaché, was found in Beirut on Oc-

Operation Belukha

Soviet authorities faced an intriguing problem early in 1985, when they learned that thousands of white beluga whales (belukhas in Russian) were trapped by thick ice in the frigid Senyavin Strait and faced suffocation or starvation. The icebreaker Moskva was sent to the rescue, but a seemingly insurmountable difficulty soon emerged—how could the whales be enticed to follow the ship to safety before the ice closed up behind it? Finally, somebody remembered that the animals had an ear for music. Strains of all kinds were piped out from shipboard, and the culturally discriminating creatures soon warmed to the music, reportedly showing a pronounced preference for the classics. Frolicking and happy, they followed the Moskva out to sea, and "Operation Belukha" was successfully completed.

Four Soviet embassy officials were abducted by Muslim fundamentalists in Beirut on September 30; pictures (right) were released by the captors, who demanded that the Soviet Union intervene to stop fighting between fundamentalists and Syrian-backed militias in Tripoli. Arkady Katkov (top row, right) was executed; above, a Soviet diplomat escorted by Druze militiamen, goes to identify his body. The three other hostages were later released unharmed.

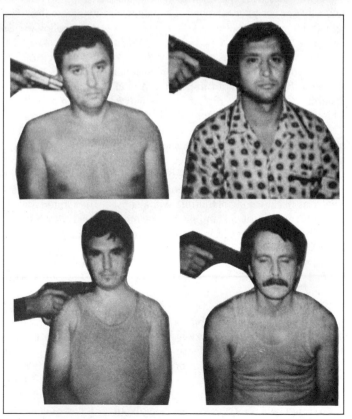

tober 2. Subsequent negotiations led to the release of the three remaining hostages on October 30.

See STATISTICS OF THE WORLD. See also AFGHANISTAN; MILITARY AND NAVAL AFFAIRS; SPACE SCIENCE AND EXPLORATION.   J.F.H.

UNITED ARAB EMIRATES. See STATISTICS OF THE WORLD. See also PERSIAN GULF STATES.

UNITED NATIONS, THE. The 40th anniversary of the United Nations was commemorated from October 14 to October 24, 1985. More than 60 heads of state or government attended, including U.S. President Ronald Reagan and Prime Ministers Yasuhiro Nakasone of Japan, Margaret Thatcher of Britain, and Brian Mulroney of Canada. Whether such widespread rededication to the organization's purposes and principles would be reflected in the often immobilized Security Council remained to be seen. The role of peacemaker fell by default during 1985 to the secretary-general, Javier Pérez de Cuéllar, but success proved elusive in the Iran-Iraq war, the Cyprus dispute and such other issues as the Soviet occupation of Afghanistan and the Vietnamese occupation of Cambodia. The UN's disappointing record in resolving conflict contrasted with its success in stimulating and coordinating famine relief efforts for the countries of sub-Saharan Africa.

Namibia. At first, U.S. diplomatic initiatives linking UN-supervised independence for Namibia (South West Africa) to the withdrawal of Cuban troops from neighboring Angola showed promise of producing a negotiated solution— despite disapproval of such linkage by the South West Africa People's Organization (Swapo), which has been waging a guerrilla war against South African control of Namibia, and by other southern African states. On April 15, South Africa said that it would withdraw the rest of its troops from Angola under a 1984 agreement in which Angola undertook to restrain Swapo guerrillas from entering Namibia. But on April 18, South Africa announced plans for an interim government for Namibia. The territory would become semi-independent with South Africa retaining control of defense and foreign policy and a veto over internal policy. Power would be shared among appointed representatives of several parties, not including Swapo, which is thought to represent a majority of

Namibia's inhabitants. The plan came under immediate fire from the United States, Swapo, and the Organization of African Unity.

In May, two South African soldiers were killed and one was captured in Angola, apparently while preparing to sabotage a partly American-owned oil facility. Angola refused to negotiate further with South Africa. The Security Council on June 19, with the United States and Britain abstaining, condemned the interim Namibian government, which had been installed two days earlier. In late June, South African troops attacked Swapo guerrillas across the Angolan border. Angola suspended talks with the United States on July 13 to protest repeal by the U.S. Congress of the Clark Amendment, which had prohibited U.S. aid to the Angolan insurgency under Jonas Savimbi. South Africa revealed for the first time that it was actively supporting the Savimbi insurgency. The Security Council on September 20 unanimously condemned a second South African raid and called for the unconditional withdrawal of South African forces from Angola. Following South African air attacks that killed at least 65 people on Angolan territory, the council on October 7 again called unanimously for South African withdrawal.

South Africa. In March the Security Council condemned the South African security forces' harsh response to racial unrest. In July, after the government had declared a state of emergency in 36 magisterial districts, the council urged governments to suspend new investments in South Africa and take other steps to force South Africa to dismantle its apartheid policy. The United States and Britain abstained. In an August statement the council condemned South Africa for killings, mass arrests, and the state of emergency.

Arab-Israeli Dispute. Talks sponsored by the UN peacekeeping force Unifil between Lebanon and Israel on an Israeli troop withdrawal from Lebanon were broken off by Israel in January. Israel then announced plans for a three-stage unilateral withdrawal, after which a narrow strip of Lebanon between Israel's border and Unifil positions would be secured by the South Lebanon Army (SLA), an Israel-financed, predominantly Christian militia. The United States vetoed a council resolution condemning alleged Israeli mistreatment of civilians in southern Lebanon. Israeli units completed their withdrawal in June, but some personnel and equipment were left to help the SLA prevent Palestinian incursions.

On June 7 the SLA seized 24 Finnish Unifil troops and held 21 of them for eight days, charging that Finnish soldiers had turned over 11 SLA members to a Shiite Amal militia. The Finns were freed after the International Committee of the Red Cross gave assurances that the 11 had not been forced to go against their will. A UN Board of Inquiry concluded that the Finns had agreed to stage a mock battle to permit the SLA members to defect to Amal while avoiding retribution against their families.

In retaliation, it said, for terrorist acts committed by the Palestine Liberation Organization in Cyprus, Israel on October 1 bombed PLO headquarters in Tunisia, killing about 70 Palestinians and Tunisians. The Council condemned the raid, 14-0, with the United States abstaining. The council also condemned the hijacking by Palestinian terrorists of the Italian cruise ship *Achille Lauro*.

Terrorism. In December the General Assembly, for the first time, passed a comprehensive resolution condemning all terrorist acts as "criminal." The vote was unanimous after Cuba, which had cast the sole dissenting vote in the legal committee, changed its position. The Security Council, also voting unanimously, condemned "all acts of hostage-taking and abduction" and called for the freeing of all hostages and abducted people.

Iran-Iraq War. UN investigators reported in February that both sides in the Iran-Iraq war were treating prisoners badly. In March both sides asked UN help in exchanging prisoners. Nothing had come of that request by late in the year, but some informal exchanges were taking place. The moratorium on bombing and missile attacks on civilians, negotiated in 1984 by Secretary-General Pérez de Cúellar, broke down in early 1985. Pérez de Cúellar visited Tehran and Baghdad in April to promote renewal of the moratorium and settlement of the war, but found the gap between the two countries "as wide as ever." Iraq later agreed to renew the moratorium on strikes against civilians if Iran would go along; Iran would not.

The United Nations celebrated its 40th anniversary in October with a session attended by more than 60 heads of state or government. The Secretariat building in New York City was specially lit to mark the occasion.

Cyprus. In 1984 the secretary-general began indirect, or "proximity," talks between President Spyros Kyprianou of Cyprus, representing the Greek Cypriots, and Rauf Denktash, leader of the Turkish Cypriots. A UN peacekeeping force has been on the island since 1964, seeking to keep the hostile factions apart. The secretary-general arranged a direct meeting between the two leaders in January, and, in major concessions, the Turkish Cypriot side agreed to give up all but 29 percent of Cyprus and to permit a Greek Cypriot president, rather than a rotating presidency, heading a unified federal republic in which both communities would have considerable autonomy. Kyprianou, however, wanted further negotiations before accepting any agreement. After the Turkish Cypriots approved a constitution for their new republic (proclaimed in 1984) and elected a president (Denktash), the proximity talks resumed.

Nicaragua. Oral arguments began in September in Nicaragua's suit before the World Court accusing the United States of violating international law by supporting military attacks against Nicaragua. In January the United States had said it would refuse to participate further in the case and had charged the court with misusing its powers; in October the Reagan administration terminated U.S. acceptance of the court's compulsory jurisdiction, which had been in effect since 1946. The United States retained the option of seeking court rulings in certain instances, such as in routine commercial or border disputes.

Arms Control and Disarmament. A meeting of the UN's 40-nation Conference of the Committee on Disarmament early in the year roughly coincided with the resumption of U.S.-Soviet arms control talks, after a 15-month hiatus. The conference established a subcommittee to press for resumption of negotiations for a comprehensive nuclear test ban. During the year, for the first time, the Soviet Union agreed to on-site inspection by the International Atomic Energy Agency of two nuclear power reactors (to verify that they were not being used for military purposes).

African Famine. Lingering drought continued to cause famine in sub-Saharan Africa. The UN Office for Emergency Operations in Africa, which began operations in January, coordinated relief efforts of all UN agencies responsible for relief, development, and refugees. At a donors' conference in Geneva, the office estimated that 30 million people were then affected, and it appealed for $1.5 billion in immediate aid. By April officials were confident of meeting the immediate needs of the hungry. By August the drought had broken in most areas, but food stocks remained dangerously low where transportation was primitive or in areas of civil strife.

Decade for Women. The UN Decade for Women ended with a conference in Nairobi, Kenya, during July. Representatives of over 150 countries attended the conference, while thousands of others attended a simultaneous forum on women arranged by nongovernmental organizations. Studies made for the conference indicated gains for women: in a majority of countries men and women had legal equality, and the education gap had begun to close. A gap remained between men's and women's wages, and women's political participation did not increase. The final document, entitled "Forward-Looking Strategies," was adopted unanimously. Though nonbinding, it had symbolic value as a mandate for change and an agenda for a potentially powerful international women's movement.

Unesco. The United States withdrew from the UN Educational, Scientific, and Cultural Organization on December 31, 1984, to protest what it saw as Unesco's lack of fiscal responsibility, hostility to a free press and free markets, and misplaced emphasis on political issues. (On February 17, 1985, the United States was granted observer status by Unesco's executive board.) Britain and Singapore withdrew at the end of 1985. Unesco's financial bind, with the loss of the 25 percent of its budget the United States has paid, was ameliorated somewhat by gifts from other countries. However, Director-General Amadou Mahtar M'Bow remained on a collision course with his critics because of his plan to spend funds earmarked as inflation insurance rather than pare controversial programs. The shrunken budget led to a plan to cut 600 of the organization's 2,000 employees. At the biennial Unesco conference in Sofia, Bulgaria, in the autumn, Algeria and other Third World nations, along with the Soviet Union, sought to have 130 U.S. nationals on the staff be the first to lose their jobs. The move was rejected by a resolution adopted on October 25.   I.C.B.

United States of America

In a year marked by changes in top-level personnel, the Reagan administration battled with Congress over the federal budget, national defense, tax reform, the farm crisis, and other issues. In foreign affairs, a U.S.-Soviet summit conference shared attention with a series of terrorist episodes involving Americans abroad.

As federal spending continued to rise, the national debt passed the $2 trillion mark. President Ronald Reagan reluctantly signed a bill that would force a balanced budget by 1991; he also carried on a campaign for a major overhaul of the nation's tax structure. Despite his tangles with Congress, Reagan remained popular, aided late in the year by a decisive action against terrorism and by his meeting, in Geneva, with a Soviet leader for the first time in his presidency. Nicaragua and South Africa were among trouble spots abroad that caused controversy at home.

DOMESTIC AFFAIRS

President Ronald Reagan's personal triumphs and traumas dominated U.S. politics in 1985. On January 20 he was inaugurated for a second term, becoming at age 73 the oldest president ever to take the oath of office. Six months later, on July 13, Reagan lay on an operating table, as surgeons removed a large cancerous tumor from the muscle of his bowel wall. He appeared healthy and fit during his November "fireside summit" conference with Soviet leader Mikhail Gorbachev—a meeting that, despite few substantive accomplishments, lifted Reagan's domestic popularity to new heights.

Second Term, Second Team. Perhaps the most significant of the many changes in Reagan's cabinet and staff in 1985 involved James Baker III and Donald Regan; Baker succeeded Regan as treasury secretary, while Regan took Baker's old job as White House chief of staff. The move made Baker the chief salesman for the administration's tax reform bill, which was rewritten before being passed by the Demo-cratic-controlled House of Representatives in December; it faced an uncertain future in the Senate. Regan, meanwhile, became the chief White House power broker. In other cabinet changes announced in January, Energy Secretary Donald Hodel succeeded William Clark as secretary of the interior; John Herrington, the White House personnel director, was appointed to the Energy post; and William J. Bennett was named secretary of education.

In February, Vernon Walters, a retired Army general and former deputy director of the CIA, was named chief U.S. delegate to the United Nations, replacing Jeane Kirkpatrick, who left the administration reportedly after her bid for a higher-level foreign policy post was turned down. In March, Labor Secretary Raymond Donovan resigned after being ordered to stand trial on fraud and larceny charges stemming from his prior service as vice-president of a construction company. Donovan, who had taken a leave of absence after pleading not guilty in October 1984, was replaced by U.S. Trade Representative Bill Brock.

In July, David Stockman, controversial director of the Office of Management and Budget, announced he was leaving the administration to join a Wall Street investment firm; his replacement was James Miller III, chairman of the Federal Trade Commission. With obvious reluctance, Margaret Heckler announced in October that she would step down as secretary of health and human services to become ambassador to Ireland; she was reported to have been the victim of a feud with Regan. Otis Bowen, a former Indiana governor and family

421

doctor, was named to succeed her. National Security Adviser Robert McFarlane, another reported loser in a power struggle with Regan, stepped down in December; his successor was his assistant, Vice Admiral John Poindexter. Other appointments included those of Beryl Sprinkel as chairman of the Council of Economic Advisers and Admiral William Crowe, Jr., as chairman of the Joint Chiefs of Staff.

The Economy. Big numbers dominated the national economy. In his annual budget message, submitted in February, Reagan projected outlays for the 1986 fiscal year at $973.7 billion and revenues at $793.7 billion, for a deficit of $180 billion. The budget resolution passed by Congress in August cut outlays to $967.6 billion and the projected deficit to about $172 billion.

For the 1985 calendar year the administration forecast an increase in the gross national product (after inflation) of 3.9 percent; in the end, real growth came to only 2.3 percent. After-tax profits—up 5.3 percent in the third quarter—were strong, however, and the Dow Jones industrial average soared from about 1,200 in January to over 1,500 late in the year. Inflation was under 4 percent.

Deficits. The United States became a debtor nation in 1985. For the first time since World War I, foreign claims on U.S. assets exceeded American ownership of assets abroad. A record trade deficit, expected to approach $150 billion, led some members of Congress and leaders of labor and industry to intensify their push

for protectionist measures, especially against Japan. In December, however, Reagan vetoed a bill that would limit imports of textiles and other products.

As the nation experienced its 24th budget deficit in 25 years, Congress took steps to stem the tide of federal red ink. Legislation enacted in December established a series of annual deficit ceilings that would drop to zero by 1991; in any year that Congress failed to meet the deficit target, the president would be required to make the appropriate spending cuts, with half of the cuts to come from the military budget and half from nondefense spending. Although the bill, proposed by Senators Phil Gramm (R, Texas), Warren Rudman (R, N.H.), and Ernest Hollings (D, S.C.), enjoyed considerable bipartisan support, it was also criticized variously for abdicating congressional responsibility to the White House, jeopardizing social programs, and backtracking on the president's opposition to cuts in defense. Reagan signed it reluctantly. Congress adjourned without passing another measure, intended to reduce budget deficits by $74 million over three years.

National Defense. In Reagan's federal budget proposal for 1986, defense was the fastest-rising expenditure category. Congress, however, chipped away at defense spending. It continued funding the MX missile system and the space-based Strategic Defense Initiative, or "Star Wars," but at levels below what Reagan wanted. In the end, the increase in total appropriations for defense did not cover the rate of inflation. Defense Secretary Caspar Weinberger canceled a major weapons program, the multibillion-dollar Sergeant York antiaircraft gun, because of its failure to meet performance specifications. The year also brought the arrest of a large number of suspected spies; they were variously accused of passing defense information to the Soviet Union, China, Ghana, and Israel.

Trouble on the Farm. Reagan's budget for fiscal 1986 envisioned a 37 percent reduction in farm aid programs, but it soon became clear that this cut was economically, and politically, unrealistic. Rising farm debt, declining farmland values, a weakening export market, and low commodity prices drove some farmers to the brink of bankruptcy and threatened the stability of the farm credit system. Citing budgetary problems, President Reagan vetoed emergency farm credit legislation in March. In December, however, he signed a bill to rescue the farm credit system, as well as a major five-year farm aid package, even though the aid was more extensive than he had wished.

Legal Matters. By striking down an Alabama school-prayer law, a Connecticut statute giving employees an unlimited right not to work on their chosen Sabbath, and two local ordinances providing public aid for parochial schools, the U.S. Supreme Court reaffirmed a strong concept of the constitutional separation of church and state. All four cases found the Reagan administration on the losing side. Attorney General Edwin Meese III, confirmed by the Senate in February after a 13-month delay because of questions about his ethical conduct, repeatedly complained that the Court had diverged from the intent of the Constitution's framers. In a rare counterattack, Justice John Paul Stevens made a detailed rebuttal in which he criticized Meese by name.

Mega-Mergers and Scandals. Mergers and takeovers continued to change the face of corporate America. Among the major takeovers announced or consummated during 1985 were those of General Foods by Philip Morris, Nabisco by R. J. Reynolds, and Hughes Aircraft by General Motors. The major media were especially prized: RCA (including NBC) agreed to be acquired by General Electric and ABC

by Capital Cities Communications. CBS was courted unsuccessfully by several suitors.

More than a few firms had black eyes by year's end. Major defense contractors cited by the armed services for illegal and unethical practices included General Electric and General Dynamics. Union Carbide, still reeling from the disastrous leak of toxic gas at its plant in India in 1984, suffered a chemical leak in West Virginia in August, experienced severe financial losses, and became the unwilling target of a takeover bid by GAF. The brokerage firm of E. F. Hutton was fined $2 million for an elaborate bank-overdraft scheme. In August the Manville Corporation, besieged by asbestos-related claims, offered to pay $2.5 billion in compensation—the heftiest health-related settlement ever offered by a U.S. firm. The largest civil damage award in U.S. history, a judgment of more than $10.5 billion plus interest, was handed down in November against Texaco, for injuries suffered by Pennzoil when Texaco acquired Getty Oil after Getty had agreed in principle to be acquired by Pennzoil.

Americana. Coca-Cola officials were red-faced when public complaints about a much-vaunted "new Coke" formula forced the company to bring back "old Coke" under the name Coca-Cola Classic. By fall, the "real thing" was outselling the new formula nationwide.

In baseball, the national pastime, pitchers Tom Seaver and Phil Niekro notched their 300th victories, Rod Carew stroked his 3,000th hit, Nolan Ryan whiffed his 4,000th strikeout victim, and Pete Rose surpassed Ty Cobb's lifetime 4,191-hit total. On the down side, the sport was rocked by revelations of widespread cocaine use. In another national pastime, popular music, performers staged concerts and released songs to benefit African famine victims, American farmers, the antiapartheid movement in South Africa, and victims of acquired immune deficiency syndrome (AIDS). G.M.H.

FOREIGN AFFAIRS

A U.S.-Soviet summit conference helped ease superpower tensions in 1985. Relations with Nicaragua were bitter, and little progress was made toward peace in the Middle East.

Soviet Union. The long buildup to the summit influenced U.S.-Soviet relations in 1985. Secretary of State George Shultz and Soviet Foreign Minister Andrei Gromyko, meeting in Geneva in January, paved the way for talks that began there in March, on strategic arms (Start), on intermediate-range nuclear forces (INF), and on space-based and defensive weapons. Start and INF talks had broken down in 1983 after NATO countries began deploying U.S. missiles in Western Europe. The new round of talks made little headway. The Soviets insisted that the United States stop work on its Strategic Defense Initiative, the president's controversial "Star Wars" program, intended to develop the technology to destroy attacking missiles before they could reach their targets. The United States refused to link work on SDI with other arms control issues.

Soviet leader Konstantin Chernenko died in March and was succeeded by Mikhail Gorbachev. When Schulz and Vice-President George Bush visited Moscow for Chernenko's funeral, Gorbachev was given an invitation to a summit meeting. He was noncommittal, but the two sides eventually agreed to meet in Geneva on November 19–20, in the first top-level U.S.-Soviet meeting since 1979.

In late summer and fall both capitals waged a propaganda war, each side apparently trying to convince world opinion that it was the more serious about arms control. Gorbachev, a master of public relations, denounced SDI in an interview with *Time* Magazine editors, but Reagan said it was not negotiable. The new Soviet foreign minister, Eduard Shevardnadze, met with Reagan, and the Soviets made a proposal to cut both strategic nuclear arsenals by 50 percent and end research on SDI. In a UN speech on October 24, Reagan called for a "fresh start" in U.S.-Soviet relations and urged Moscow to help resolve regional conflicts in Aghanistan and elsewhere. On November 1 in Geneva, the United States proposed a ban on mobile long-range missiles and future "heavy" missiles. Meanwhile, Reagan was interviewed by four Soviet journalists—the first such Soviet questioning of a president since 1961.

At the summit, no dramatic breakthroughs occurred on arms control, regional conflicts, or other key issues, and no concessions were made on SDI. Instead, the two leaders estab-

lished frank, direct relations. They also reached agreement on a number of points, including accelerating the arms control talks in Geneva, renewing academic and cultural exchanges, setting up new consulates in Kiev and New York, and holding regular high-level meetings. Also approved was a broad environmental accord providing for cooperation and exchange of information in a wide range of areas.

Nicaragua. The United States maintained its support for the counterrevolutionaries, or contras, fighting to overthrow the leftist Sandinista government of Nicaragua. The United States said in January that it would not participate further in the World Court case brought in 1984 by Nicaragua, which charged that Washington was violating Nicaraguan sovereignty by backing the contras. In October the United States announced that it would no longer automatically comply with World Court decisions in the type of case filed by Nicaragua.

Reagan said in February that the U.S. aim was to "remove" the "present structure" of the Nicaraguan government. Congress had rejected aid to the contras in 1984, and the House did so again in April 1985. But after Nicaraguan President Daniel Ortega Saavedra visited Moscow to receive assurances of more economic and military aid, the House voted to provide $27 million in nonmilitary aid to the contras, though barring the dispensing of the aid by the CIA or the Defense Department. The aid was approved in this form by the whole Congress.

Relations With Allies. The annual economic summit conference of the seven major non-Communist industrial nations was held in Bonn, West Germany, in May. While in Europe, President Reagan participated in several events marking the 40th anniversary of the end of World War II. One of these proved to be an embarrassment. He had agreed to a request from West German Chancellor Helmut Kohl to visit a cemetery containing the graves of German war dead, as a gesture of reconciliation. When the cemetery chosen at Bitburg was found to contain the graves of 49 members of the SS, the elite Nazi guard, American Jews and veterans denounced the idea. Unwilling to risk insulting Kohl, a staunch ally, Reagan went to Bitburg, but spent only eight minutes at the cemetery. He added a visit to the site of the Bergen-Belsen concentration camp.

At the economic summit, U.S. allies complained about the overvalued U.S. dollar and high U.S. interest rates. No important agreement was reached, and French President François Mitterrand blocked Reagan's effort to set a date for talks on eliminating free trade. (Late in the year, a 1986 date was set). During September, top economic officials of five major nations agreed on a concerted effort to depress the dollar's value.

New Zealand. The alliance of Australia, New Zealand, and the United States—known as Anzus—was threatened when New Zealand turned down a U.S. request for a port visit by a Navy destroyer because of New Zealand's new policy to ban nuclear-powered and nuclear-armed ships from its waters. In response the United States canceled Anzus maneuvers and stopped exchanging intelligence information with New Zealand.

South Africa. Throughout the year, thousands of Americans participated in demonstrations against the apartheid policies of the South African government and the harsh measures it used to suppress black protest. Universities, local governments, and unions began to sell off holdings in firms doing business with South Africa. By July, when South Africa imposed a state of emergency in some areas, it had become apparent that the Reagan administration's policy of "constructive engagement"— an attempt to change the system of racial separation by diplomatic means—was not succeeding. In August the U.S. House passed a bill imposing stiff economic sanctions on South Africa. To head off Senate action and retain control of policy himself, the president issued an executive order in September, imposing some of the sanctions in the bill. He banned shipments of some high-tech equipment and forbade loans that did not benefit all races. He also proposed a ban, later made final, on the sale of South African gold coins.

Middle East. U.S. Assistant Secretary of State Richard Murphy, Jr., met with Israel's Prime Minister Shimon Peres in April and suggested

President Ronald Reagan and Soviet leader Mikhail S. Gorbachev meet for talks at Fleur d'Eau, a villa on the shores of Lake Geneva; their November summit was the first between Soviet and American leaders in six years.

The hijacking of TWA flight 847 by Lebanese Shiite Muslims was a major crisis for the United States. Above, Shiite gunmen guard the hijacked jet on a runway at Beirut airport. The plane was commandeered after taking off from Athens with 153 people aboard; of these, one American seaman was killed and 40 others, all American men, were kept as hostages. Left, at a chaotic press conference arranged by the captors, several hijack victims urged the United States to refrain from a military rescue operation.

that Israel take part in a peace process agreed on by King Hussein of Jordan and Palestine Liberation Organization leader Yasir Arafat. Their plan called for the return of Israel-occupied land in exchange for peace. The composition of the joint Palestinian-Jordanian delegation to future talks became a sore point. Peres wanted no avowed PLO members on the delegation, and in November he and Hussein reportedly reached an agreement on this issue.

The Reagan administration sought to sell advanced arms to Jordan but, under a provision of the fiscal 1986 foreign aid authorization bill, could not do so unless it certified that Jordan was committed to achieving peace with Israel. The administration pointed to Hussein's peace initiative and—stressing that Jordan faced a threat from Syria—informed Congress that it intended to sell Jordan $1.5 billion in arms, including aircraft. In October, faced with rejection of the arms deal by Congress, Reagan endorsed a congressional resolution barring the sale at least until March 1986 unless Jordan and Israel began negotiating before then.

Terrorism. On June 14, two Lebanese Shiite Muslims commandeered TWA flight 847 after it took off from Athens. In the next 48 hours the terrorists took the jet on a mad dash across the Middle East before finally coming to rest at the Beirut airport. They shot to death a U.S. seaman, Robert Stethem, but released most of their 153 hostages in a few days. They held the remaining 40 American men in Lebanon (releasing one of them for medical reasons). The Shiites demanded that the United States force Israel to free over 700 prisoners it had seized while occupying Lebanon. The United States said it would not negotiate with hijackers; Israel said it would release the prisoners earlier than scheduled only if the United States publicly asked it to do so. The United States did not.

The United States sought a diplomatic solution, relying on the mediation of Syria's President Hafez al-Assad and Nabih Berri, leader of the relatively moderate Amal group, who had stepped in to take control of most hostages and expressed sympathy with the hijackers demands. After protracted negotiations, the hostages were released in Syria's custody on June 30 and then flown to West Germany. Israel, continuing an ongoing process, freed its prisoners over the next three months. The United States had little success in gaining the release of seven other Americans who had been kidnapped in Lebanon between March 1984 and June 1985. One, the Reverend Benjamin Weir, was freed in September, but terrorists claimed to have killed another, diplomat William Buckley.

On October 7, four heavily armed men hijacked the Italian cruise ship *Achille Lauro* in the Mediterranean Sea with more than 400 people aboard, and demanded that Israel free 50 jailed Palestinians. After negotiations with Egyptian and Italian officials, the hijackers surrendered the ship to Egypt on October 9, having been guaranteed safe-conduct apparently on condition that all hostages were safe. It was then discovered that they had killed one captive—Leon Klinghoffer, a wheelchair-bound

New York City resident—and thrown his body overboard. The United States asked Egypt to prosecute the gunmen, but they were put on an Egyptian airliner and allowed to leave the country. U.S. Navy jets then intercepted the plane and forced it to land in Italy, where authorities seized the hijackers and charged them with murder and kidnapping. Egyptian President Hosni Mubarak denounced the U.S. action as "piracy."

Two Palestinian officals were also on the plane; one, Muhammad Abbas, was suspected of being the mastermind for the terrorists. Angering Washington, Italy allowed the two to leave the country after the United States had issued an arrest warrant for Abbas. He traveled to Yugoslavia, which refused to detain or extradite him, and soon afterward apparently returned to the Middle East.   R.D.S.

UPPER VOLTA. *See* STATISTICS OF THE WORLD.

URUGUAY. The inauguration of President Julio Maria Sanguinetti, of the centrist Colorado Party, on March 1, 1985, completed the country's long-awaited transition to democratic rule. Early March witnessed the lifting of censorship of news sent abroad, the legalization of trade unions and strikes, and the release of all of the more than 250 political prisoners still being held.

Prior to taking office, Sanguinetti advocated the establishment of a government of national unity. Although the moderately left-of-center National Party (Blancos) and the leftist Broad Front declined offers of cabinet posts in such a government, they agreed to cooperate in other areas and not to obstruct the Colorados in Congress. But in early June the Broad Front walked out of a congressional session, when it was not consulted on nominations to the electoral court and the comptroller's office.

The country's biggest problems were economic. Inflation was running at 37 percent in the first six months of the year. Unemployment ranged between 12 and 15 percent. At over $5 billion, Uruguay's debt was one of Latin America's highest per capita. In June the International Monetary Fund gave preliminary approval to the government's economic plan, opening the way to a $120 million loan from the fund and another $150 million from private banks. A general strike was averted in April,

A ticker tape parade hailed the inauguration of President Julio Maria Sanguinetti of Uruguay (left), riding with Vice-President Enrique Tarigo, on March 1. Sanguinetti's presidency marked the end of 12 years of military rule in Uruguay.

when joint labor-business salary councils reached agreements on wage increases of 25–33 percent in many sectors of the economy. Aid to 150,000 people living below the poverty line came in the form of a $20 million emergency relief plan called Winter 1985.

Venezuela established diplomatic relations with Uruguay on March 1; they had been cut in 1976 when Uruguayan troops stormed into Venezuela's Montevideo embassy to arrest a woman seeking asylum. And in October, Uruguay announced that it was resuming diplomatic relations with Cuba, which had been broken since 1964.

See STATISTICS OF THE WORLD.   J.F., Jr.

UTAH. See STATISTICS OF THE WORLD.

V

VANUATU. See STATISTICS OF THE WORLD.

VENEZUELA. A campaign against corruption was begun in 1985 by President Jaime Lusinchi's administration. It was well received by a public grown skeptical about the effectiveness of the nation's democratic and legal institutions. However, opposition leaders criticized the government for allegedly shielding the armed forces from investigation. The president had been given two reports in March calling for stronger sanctions against corruption and proposing a battery of reforms.

Venezuela's economic and financial problems have weakened its banking system, leaving even some of the larger institutions in serious trouble. The government took over the privately owned Banco de Comercio, one of Venezuela's ten largest banks, on June 3.

An agreement rescheduling Venezuela's $21 billion public-sector debt to some 450 international banks was reached during the year, without a requirement that Venezuela submit itself to an International Monetary Fund adjustment program. A balance-of-payments deficit of $1 billion was forecast for 1985, reflecting a shortfall in petroleum revenues. An accord negotiated in Washington in June stipulated that Venezuela would reduce its annual steel exports to the United States to less than half the 1984 level.

Bilateral discussions with Colombia, held in Bogotá during February, resulted in a new commercial agreement with Colombia. Also in February, Venezuela and Guyana agreed to exchange information and technology on ocean fishing, agriculture, and healthcare. In January, Pope John Paul II made the first visit to Venezuela by a reigning pontiff, at the start of his 12-day tour of South America.

See also STATISTICS OF THE WORLD.   L.L.P.

VERMONT. See STATISTICS OF THE WORLD.

VICE-PRESIDENT OF THE UNITED STATES. See PEOPLE IN THE NEWS: GEORGE BUSH.

VIETNAM. In 1985, Vietnam's aging leadership quickened the pace of economic liberalization. Le Duc Tho, long an influential Politburo member, was highly visible, fueling speculation that he was the likely successor to the ailing Le Duan as head of the Communist Party. Nguyen Van Linh, party chief of Ho Chi Minh City (formerly Saigon), was brought back into the Politburo after a three-year absence, tipping the balance in favor of liberalization, which was resisted by elements in the military.

On the advice of international financial institutions, Vietnam devalued its currency by more than 850 percent. Then, on September 13, the Vietnamese issued a new dong, equivalent to ten old dong, hoping to weaken the black market and help control inflation. The eighth plenum of the Fifth Party Congress, held in June, reaffirmed commitment to the overall economic liberalization program—which includes incentives to workers, provision for profit-making by merchants, and some decentralization of economic decision-making. The policy of forcing factories to become profitable or shut down was continued. Authorities in the south tightened their policing of merchants expected to bring in foreign exchange, while encouraging industries to increase exports.

For the first time in its six-year occupation of Cambodia, Vietnam launched full-scale attacks on the Cambodian resistance bases near the Thai border. In a four-month offensive beginning in December 1984, Vietnamese forces overran the main base camps of the three resistance groups who oppose the Vietnamese-installed Cambodian regime of Heng Samrin, and the resistance forces were forced to rely entirely on guerrilla warfare. However, a decisive victory proved elusive to the Vietnamese. Nor was the stalemate broken by diplomatic

initiatives, which included an effort by the UN secretary-general. The Vietnamese government refused to make concessions that could lead to a peaceful withdrawal of its troops from Cambodia.

In August the Vietnamese, in an apparent effort to forge better relations with the United States, returned 26 sets of remains believed to be those of U.S. servicemen missing in action from the Vietnam War. In October, Hanoi agreed to a joint U.S.-Vietnamese search of a B-52 crash site for the first time, and excavations were completed in December.

The Vietnamese commemorated the tenth anniversary of their victory over the U.S.-backed regime in South Vietnam on April 30. The centerpiece of the anniversary celebration

Celebrations were held in Vietnam on April 30 to mark the tenth anniversary of the fall of Saigon; as part of the festivities, young Vietnamese paraded through the streets carrying a portrait of revolutionary leader Ho Chi Minh.

was a procession of workers, students, and soldiers in Ho Chi Minh City.

The United Nations began a Rescue at Sea Resettlement Offers (RASRO) program in May, to encourage ships to pick up Vietnamese refugees, who continued to emigrate illegally in small, often barely seaworthy, boats. The program guaranteed to place the refugees promptly and to reimburse shipowners for costs involved in rescuing them. Pirate attacks continued; in a major atrocity in December, 50 Vietnamese were killed and 10 women raped on a boat in the South China Sea.

See STATISTICS OF THE WORLD. E.H.B.

VIRGINIA. See STATISTICS OF THE WORLD.

VIRGIN ISLANDS. See STATISTICS OF THE WORLD.

WARSAW TREATY ORGANIZATION. See COMMUNIST WORLD.

WASHINGTON. See STATISTICS OF THE WORLD.

WESTERN SAHARA. See AFRICA; MOROCCO.

WESTERN SAMOA. See STATISTICS OF THE WORLD.

WEST VIRGINIA. See STATISTICS OF THE WORLD.

WISCONSIN. See STATISTICS OF THE WORLD.

WOMEN. Controversies over alleged sex discrimination and "comparable worth" persisted in 1985. The Reagan administration's opposition to hiring quotas affected women as well as minorities (see BLACKS IN THE UNITED STATES). Two international women's conferences were held in Kenya, and the National Organization for Women elected a new president.

Title IX. Civil rights activists energetically sought to reverse Grove City College v. Bell (1984), in which the Supreme Court held that Title IX of the Education Act Amendments of 1972, prohibiting sex discrimination in programs receiving federal aid, applied only to the specific program receiving aid and not to the entire institution. After this ruling, enforcement of Title IX and provisions in three other laws relating to discrimination had virtually stopped. In May two U.S. House committees agreed to a bill that would apply to all four statutes and clarify that entire institutions are covered when federal aid goes to any component. The bill failed to gain passage, however.

Comparable Worth. The comparable worth concept holds that jobs held mainly by women (such as clerical positions) should be valued and paid as highly as male-dominated jobs (such as truck driving) requiring comparable training or responsibility. In April the U.S. Civil Rights Commission voted to reject the concept as "profoundly and irretrievably flawed," saying that different jobs could not be compared and that adequate protection was already available to women through the Equal Pay Act of 1963 and the Civil Rights Act of 1964. In August the Justice Department supported the state of Illinois in a suit filed against it by the American Nurses Association, arguing that judges should not be determining how people ought to be compensated for different jobs.

In September a federal appeals court panel overturned a district court ruling that had

The concept of comparable worth was widely debated in 1985. Congress, state legislatures, and the courts considered whether to try to remedy what many felt was an unjustified "wage gap."

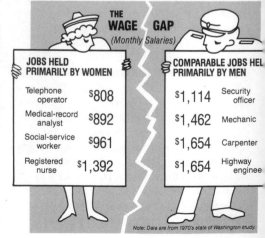

THE **WAGE GAP**
(Monthly Salaries)

JOBS HELD PRIMARILY BY WOMEN		COMPARABLE JOBS HELD PRIMARILY BY MEN	
Telephone operator	$808	$1,114	Security officer
Medical-record analyst	$892	$1,462	Mechanic
Social-service worker	$961	$1,654	Carpenter
Registered nurse	$1,392	$1,654	Highway engineer

Note: Data are from 1970's state of Washington study.

Veteran American feminist Betty Friedan (right) holds a seminar at the University of Nairobi campus during Forum '85, a series of workshops on international women's issues that ran concurrently with the UN Decade for Women conference in Kenya during July.

required comparable pay for all state employees in Washington state. Citing free market considerations, the court ruled that the state need not comply with the 1983 decision which found it had improperly set lower pay scales for female-dominated jobs. However, on January 1, 1986, the state reached a tentative settlement with employee unions providing for phasing in of a pay equity plan over seven years. Meanwhile, the city of Los Angeles in May agreed on a comparable-pay plan for female-dominated positions.

Nairobi Conferences. In Nairobi, Kenya, during July, some 15,000 women from nearly 160 countries attended two conferences that closed the United Nations Decade for Women. The UN-sponsored conference drew 2,000 delegates, and the rest attended Forum '85, a parallel conference involving about 150 non-governmental organizations. Maureen Reagan, daughter of the President Ronald Reagan and leader of the U.S. delegation to the UN conference, successfully opposed efforts to commit that conference to positions on general political issues. She said she would have led a U.S. walkout if delegates had approved a resolution equating Zionism with racism.

Birth control was a controversial issue, as delegates from some Western nations traded charges with many representatives of developing countries who argued that limiting family size was essential to economic development. The International Planned Parenthood Federation was a primary target of conservatives, who opposed artificial contraception and criticized the federation's sex education program as encouraging children to be sexually active.

The Nairobi conferences took cheer from the fact that during the past decade, literacy rates, life expectancy, and the level of schooling for women had increased worldwide. The number of countries with equal-pay laws had risen from 20 to 98 in number in seven years. Nonetheless, UN data showed that women still received less than three-fourths the pay men earned for similar jobs. After a series of compromises, the UN conference arrived at and unanimously adopted a nonpolitical final document providing for "forward-looking strategies," outlining a blueprint for action on women's issues up to the year 2000.

Organization Elections. Eleanor Smeal, who had served as president of the National Organization for Women from 1977 to 1982, unseated the incumbent president, Judy Goldsmith, in a hard-fought election in July. In the election campaign Goldsmith advocated advancing NOW's objectives through lobbying, while Smeal argued that "it's time to go back into the streets." Her main objectives were an abortion rights march in Washington, D.C., in 1986 and legislation to reverse *Grove City College* v. *Bell*.

Promising to wage a "high-stakes, in-the-trenches" fight for women seeking elective office, Irene Natividad, a New York educator, was elected president of the National Women's Political Caucus in June. She asserted that the

431

biggest challenge facing feminism was a conservative tide sweeping the country.

First Ladies and Drugs. In Washington and Atlanta in April, and in New York City during the UN's 40th anniversary observation in October, Nancy Reagan was hostess at meetings for wives of world leaders, devoted to the topic of drug abuse. Noting that they were a nonpolitical group that could not actually change the laws, Reagan urged the others to fight drugs on a "mother-to-mother basis." In an impromptu remark as the October meeting was disbanding, the wife of the prime minister of Sri Lanka said that drugs were a calamity for developing countries and called for convening a new conference somewhere in the Third World.   M.Gr. & D.Y.

WYOMING. *See* STATISTICS OF THE WORLD.

Y

YEMEN, PEOPLE'S DEMOCRATIC REPUBLIC OF. On February 14, President Ali Nasser Muhammad relinquished the prime minister's post, which he had held for 14 years, to Haidar Bakr al-Attas, an engineer and former construction minister. Muhammad, considered a moderate, remained head of state of the People's Democratic Republic of Yemen (South Yemen), as well as secretary-general of the Yemen Socialist Party (YSP), South Yemen's sole political party, and chairman of the presidium of the Supreme People's Council (Parliament).

In July the National Security Ministry announced the discovery of an espionage network. Twelve South Yemeni men and one woman were charged with having spied for a foreign power beginning in 1980. Charges against the woman were later dropped; the men were convicted in November, and three received death sentences.

Relations with Oman, established in 1982, continued to improve. In late February and early March, Muhammad visited Syria, Algeria, and Libya; those countries, along with South Yemen and Lebanon, boycotted the Arab League summit conference held later in Casablanca.

East Germany contracted to build roads, bridges, and tunnels around Aden, and a French firm was awarded the contract for the $85 million Batais cement plant. A new pact provided for Soviet aid in agriculture, transportation, energy, and geological research, and a Soviet group made new mineral discoveries in Hadramut province, east of Aden.

See STATISTICS OF THE WORLD.   C.H.A.

YEMEN ARAB REPUBLIC. A 1984 oil discovery by Yemen Hunt Oil Company, at its Ma'rib concession area in northeast Yemen, continued to generate optimism in 1985. (Yemen Hunt is a joint venture by the national oil company and Dallas-based Hunt Oil Company.) The oilfield was judged to have a possible yield of 300,000 barrels per day, with oil exports expected to begin in 1987. Exploration efforts continued with the awarding in June of an oil and minerals concession in the central highlands to Exxon Corporation. Yemen Hunt and the British Petroleum Company were also searching for new deposits.

In February a council on oil and gas development was formed, to supervise applications for oil exploration and to encourage investment in the oil sector. Later in the year, a petroleum and mineral resources ministry was established. A contract for a 10,000-barrels-a-day refinery to be built near Ma'rib was awarded to Yemen Hunt; the facility, to be a modular unit manufactured in Texas, was expected to start operations in early 1986.

The 1985 budget estimated expenditures at $1.51 billion, with revenues of only $1.06 billion. The Constituent Peoples' Assembly called for a reduction of expenditures on imports, particularly of luxury goods. Water resources and agriculture remained primary concerns.

See STATISTICS OF THE WORLD.   C.H.A.

YUGOSLAVIA. Yugoslavia remained troubled by chronic economic problems. Servicing costs of nearly $6 billion were projected for 1985 on the country's foreign debt, which stood at around $19 billion. In April the International Monetary Fund gave final approval to a $300 million loan and a debt rescheduling program. A rescheduling agreement with commercial lenders was reached in September.

An inflation rate of 75 percent as of late 1985, high unemployment, and a continuing movement of workers to jobs abroad were daily reminders of the ailing economy. Productivity remained low; economists estimated that 1984's public sector output was less than half what it should have been.

In February, after a three-month trial, three Belgrade intellectuals who had been accused in 1984 of counterrevolution and "antistate activities" were convicted on charges of "spreading propaganda hostile to the state." Each was sentenced to one to two years in prison, relatively mild penalties by Yugoslav standards. One man later had his conviction overturned on appeal, and the other two had their sentences reduced. In a separate proceeding early in the year, another dissident intellectual was sentenced to 18 months in prison for allegedly having contacted Croatian émigrés in Paris.

In March a U.S. federal magistrate in Los Angeles ordered Andrija Artuković, 85, extradited to Yugoslavia to be tried on charges relating to his alleged involvement in mass murders during World War II, when he was interior minister of the government of Croatia. At the end of May, Prime Minister Milka Planinc journeyed to Washington for talks with President Ronald Reagan and Secretary of State George Shultz, which were described as "friendly and helpful." In October, however, relations with the United States were strained by Yugoslavia's refusal to detain Muhammad

The Yugoslav-built Yugo, offered as a two-door hatchback minicompact, was launched in the U.S. market in 1985. Price: a low $3,990.

Abbas, the Palestinian thought to have masterminded the hijacking of the Italian cruise ship *Achille Lauro*, during which an elderly American tourist was murdered. During a December visit to Belgrade, Shultz pounded a table in anger when the Yugoslav foreign minister told a reporter that while Yugoslavia condemned terrorism, "one must also view the causes that lead to it."

Apparently fearing the impact of a religious revival, the League of Communists halted construction of a "grand mosque" that was to have been opened in Zagreb. Authorities also held up permission for construction of Serbian Orthodox cathedrals in Belgrade and in the Dalmatian town of Split.

See STATISTICS OF THE WORLD.   R.A.P.

YUKON TERRITORY. *See* STATISTICS OF THE WORLD.

Z

ZAIRE. In 1985, President Mobutu Sese Seko celebrated the 20th anniversary of his taking power in Zaire. Internal security remained tense, as localized rebellions were quelled by force in Eastern Kasai, in South Kivu, and, for the second time in less than a year, in the town of Moba in Shaba province. A six-day strike of transport workers in January over the amount of their pay hike was also interpreted as an act of rebellion and was met by threat of force.

Since strikes, as well as all other forms of dissent and protest, were illegal, internal opposition continued to be diffuse and unorganized; nevertheless, surveillance increased.

The 11-member Paris Club of creditor governments agreed to reschedule over ten years Zaire's foreign debt repayments due in 1985 and 1986 and also to allow a five-year grace period. The agreement was to be formally approved after Zaire successfully passed a review by the International Monetary Fund.

Despite its debt problems, Zaire's economy had shown a 2.8 percent upturn in overall performance in 1984, the first after a decade of decline. Prices for the key exports of copper and cobalt rose slightly, and oil output increased markedly, as did diamond sales through official channels. Domestic sales of agricultural produce rose in response to decontrol of food crop prices. Official figures put 1984 inflation at less than 20 percent, a marked drop from the more than 100 percent registered in 1983.

New private investment remained in doubt in 1985 despite the improved economic climate, but the government did obtain new loans, including its first major commercial loan in five years. However, living standards of the majority, already among the lowest in Africa, continued to decline. The daily minimum wage in agriculture was only 6 zaires—about 15 cents, and government austerity measures eliminated 80,000 jobs.

New defense and security accords were announced between Zaire and Angola; the accords prohibited either country from allowing its territory to be used for attacks on the other. However, rebels of the National Union for the Total Independence of Angola (Unita) were still reported to be using an airfield and supply bases in Zaire for attacks on northern Angola. Refugees from areas burned out by the South Africa-supported rebels sought food and security in southwestern Shaba camps organized by the United Nations.

See STATISTICS OF THE WORLD.   B.S.

ZAMBIA. A weak economy and debt problems continued to dominate events in Zambia in 1985. However, for the first time since the mid-1970's, Zambia was expected to produce enough maize and other food crops to virtually feed itself. Improved output for export crops continued for a second year.

The need for additional financial resources and for relief from debt payments coming due remained urgent. Creditor governments agreed to cooperate in a major international rescue effort, but at a heavy political price to President Kenneth Kaunda's government. No new development projects could begin unless they would have a sizable and immediate positive effect on the country's foreign exchange reserves.

In May, with the Bank of Zambia still in arrears to the International Monetary Fund, the IMF suspended Zambia's use of its special drawing rights account until arrears were paid. The IMF pressed for a devaluation of the kwacha by at least 50 percent or the adoption of a limited auction system to distribute to industries or others the country's limited amounts of foreign exchange, which could be used to buy imports. In October the first foreign exchange auction—of $5 million—was held. The number of kwacha bid for these dollars meant that in effect the currency was devalued by 56 percent.

Austerity measures contributed to considerable public dissatisfaction and to a running battle between trade unions and the government. In January, Kaunda reacted to a wave of strikes and work stoppages at major hospitals by workers demanding pay raises. By presidential decree—a rarely used device—he banned such strikes. In March the Zambian Congress of Trade Unions canceled a two-day nationwide strike by workers in banks and several public sector corporations after Kaunda again took emergency action to ban such strikes. A wildcat work stoppage in the copper belt in June over a pension plan led to the dismissal of 4,364 miners by the Zambia Consolidated Copper Mines.

See STATISTICS OF THE WORLD.   K.W.G.

ZIMBABWE. In the country's first national elections since independence in 1980, Prime Minister Robert Mugabe's Zimbabwe African National Union-Patriotic Front (Zanu-PF) won a landslide victory, taking 63 (up from 57) of the 79 seats reserved for blacks in Parliament. Joshua Nkomo's Zimbabwe African People's Union (Zapu) collected 15 seats, while the

Young citizens in Harare join festivities celebrating the fifth anniversary of Zimbabwe's independence from Great Britain.

Reverend Ndabaningi Sithole won his party's sole seat. In an earlier stage of the elections, Ian Smith's party won 15 of the 20 seats reserved for whites. After the elections, Mugabe hinted strongly that he would soon move to repeal constitutional clauses guaranteeing disproportionate white representation in Parliament. He also moved closer to his goal of one-party rule when, in October, it was announced that he and Nkomo had made a tentative agreement to merge their two parties. Earlier, after the election victory, Mugabe announced a new cabinet, dropping the popular white agriculture minister, Dennis Norman.

The Zanu-PF landslide triggered widespread violence against opposition party supporters. In some areas, mobs of Zanu-PF youths and women looted homes of people listed as not being party members. At least ten deaths resulted. Pre-election violence, too, had been common. Zanu-PF fanatics, especially youths, broke up opposition rallies, harassed and abducted opposition supporters, raided party offices, and were apparently responsible for gunning down five members of Bishop Abel Muzorewa's United African National Council. Early in March, more than 4,000 police and soldiers sealed off black townships around Bulawayo and arrested about 1,300 "political agitators, criminals, and dissidents" in house-to-house searches. In mid-March, Nkomo complained that 300 of his followers had vanished. The government seemed unable or unwilling to curb the excesses of its supporters, but it denied a November charge by the human rights group Amnesty International that there had been a sharp rise in cases of arrest and torture of political opponents.

The political unrest came at a time of economic progress. At a time when many African nations were unable to feed themselves, Zimbabwe had achieved a 30 percent increase in farm production by the end of 1984, despite a three-year drought. The 1985 harvest was expected to be even better, and total economic output was increasing.

An electrified fence erected by South Africa along its border with Zimbabwe was completed in March. In the spring, Zimbabwe announced that it would donate 25,000 tons of maize to famine-wracked Ethiopia—a pledge believed to be the first of its kind from an African nation since the famine began. In August, Zimbabwean soldiers supported Mozambican forces in a major offensive against guerrilla headquarters inside Mozambique. They also worked to repair an oil pipeline that had been blown up by insurgents.

In December, Mugabe, on his first official visit to Moscow, signed an accord aimed at improving relations with the Soviet Union.

See STATISTICS OF THE WORLD.   K.W.G.

THE COUNTRIES OF THE WORLD

Nation Capital	Population	Area of Country (sq mi/ sq km)	Type of Government	Heads of State and Government	Currency: Value in U.S. Dollars	GNP (000,000): GNP Per Capita
AFGHANISTAN Kabul	14,700,000 1,800,000	250,000 647,497	People's republic	President, Revolutionary Council: Babrak Karmal Prime Minister: Sultan Ali Keshtmand	Afghani 0.02	$ NA NA
ALBANIA Tiranë	3,000,000 220,000	11,100 28,748	People's socialist republic	Chairman, Presidium of the People's Assembly: Ramiz Alia Chairman, Council of Ministers (Premier): Adil Çarçani	Lek 0.146	1,930[1] 645[1]
ALGERIA Algiers	22,200,000 2,000,000	919,595 2,381,741	Republic	President: Col. Chadli Benjedid Premier: Abdelhamid Brahimi	Dinar 0.21	49,450 2,227
ANGOLA Luanda	7,900,000 1,200,000	481,353 1,246,700	People's republic	President: José Eduardo dos Santos	Kwanza 0.03	3,320 420
ANTIGUA AND BARBUDA St. Johns	100,000 25,000	171 442	Parliamentary state (C)	Governor-General: Sir Wilfred E. Jacobs Prime Minister: Vere C. Bird, Sr.	East Caribbean dollar 0.37	140 1,400
ARGENTINA Buenos Aires	30,600,000 2,922,800	1,068,301 2,766,889	Federal republic	President: Raúl Alfonsín	Austral 1.27	58,560 1,913
AUSTRALIA Canberra	15,800,000 264,400	2,967,907 7,686,848	Federal parliamentary state (C)	Governor-General: Sir Ninian M. Stephen Prime Minister: Robert Hawke	Dollar 0.69	116,230 7,356
AUSTRIA Vienna	7,500,000 1,531,300	32,374 83,849	Federal republic	President: Rudolf Kirchschläger Chancellor: Fred Sinowatz	Schilling 0.057	69,830 9,311
BAHAMAS Nassau	228,000 135,400	5,380 13,935	Parliamentary state (C)	Governor-General: Sir Gerald C. Cash Prime Minister: Lynden O. Pindling	Dollar 1.005	900 3,947
BAHRAIN Manama	409,000 122,000	240 622	Emirate	Emir: Isa bin Sulman al-Khalifah Prime Minister: Muhammed Khalifa bin Sulman al-Khalifa	Dinar 2.655	4,120 10,073
BANGLADESH Dacca	101,500,000 3,605,000	55,598 143,998	Republic (C)	President: H. M. Ershad Prime Minister: Atuar Rahman Khan	Taka 0.04	12,530 123
BARBADOS Bridgetown	252,000 7,500	166 431	Parliamentary state (C)	Governor-General: Hugh Springer Prime Minister: H. Bernard St. John	Dollar 0.50	1,020 4,047
BELGIUM Brussels	9,900,000 982,400	11,781 30,513	Constitutional monarchy	King: Baudouin Prime Minister: Wilfried Martens	Franc 0.02	90,540 9,136

The section on countries presents the latest information available. All monetary figures are expressed in United States dollars. The symbol (C) signifies that the country belongs to the Commonwealth of Nations. NA means that the data were not available. * indicates that the category does not apply to the country under discussion. Footnotes at the end of the section contain more specialized information.

Imports Exports	Revenue Expenditure	Elementary Schools: Teachers Students	Secondary Schools: Teachers Students	Colleges and Universities: Teachers Students
$ 695,000,000	$ 675,576,000	37,537	7,532	1,212
704,000,000	988,832,000	1,198,286	136,898	13,611
246,000,000[2]	1,140,000,000	26,440	5,000	1,240
267,000,000[2]	1,130,000,000	532,300	86,700	17,500
11,505,000,000	13,838,593,000	100,288	47,771	9,778
14,056,000,000	13,733,848,000	3,241,924	1,154,709	78,027
1,640,000,000	3,974,000,000	NA	4,280	374
1,744,000,000	3,974,000,000	1,178,467	141,672	2,666
137,000,000	28,609,230	300	358	NA
33,000,000	16,984,797	9,557	6,927	NA
10,017,000,000	26,600,000,000	206,535	178,681	33,322
7,905,000,000	29,400,000,000	4,197,372	1,296,839	411,113
30,639,000,000	55,168,000,000	NA	86,364	19,377
30,026,000,000	59,398,000,000	1,659,734	1,110,319	337,953
21,034,000,000	43,000,000,000	27,731	66,756	9,414
15,841,000,000	44,500,000,000	367,691	705,441	134,621
3,085,000,000	278,000,000	1,555	1,316	NA
2,465,000,000	278,000,000	32,664	NA	NA
4,386,000,000	1,320,414,500	2,577	1,184	70
3,541,000,000	1,256,489,200	48,451	26,528	227
2,542,000,000	1,630,000,000	NA	111,927	2,484
791,000,000	1,000,000,000	8,450,000	2,362,906	39,699
617,000,000	239,700,000	1,492	1,209	140
338,000,000	263,700,000	30,337	27,640	1,606
62,067,000,000[3]	26,100,000,000	NA	NA	NA
55,615,000,000[3]	38,000,000,000	780,408	818,611	96,795

Nation Capital	Population	Area of Country (sq mi/ sq km)	Type of Government	Heads of State and Government	Currency: Value in U.S. Dollars	GNP (000,000): GNP Per Capita
BELIZE .... Belmopan	157,700.... 2,900	8,867.... 22,965	Parliamentary state (C)	Governor-General:........... Minita Gordon Prime Minister: Manuel Esquivel	Dollar....... 0.50	$ 170 1,077
BENIN .... Porto-Novo	4,000,000.... 144,000	43,484.... 112,622	People's republic	President: Ahmed Kérékou	CFA franc[4]... 0.0026	1,110 277
BHUTAN .... Thimbu	1,400,000.... 16,500	18,147.... 47,000	Monarchy	King: Jigme Singye Wangchuk	Ngultrum 0.08	110 78
BOLIVIA .... Sucre La Paz	6,200,000.... 80,000 881,400	424,164.... 1,098,581	Republic	President: Víctor Paz Estenssoro	Peso 0.000001	3,070 495
BOTSWANA .... Gaborone	1,100,000.... 59,700	231,805.... 600,372	Republic (C)	President: Quett K. J. Masire	Pula 0.50	920 836
BRAZIL .... Brasília	138,400,000.... 1,176,900	3,286,487.... 8,511,965	Federal republic	President: .... José Sarney	Cruzeiro 0.0001	245,590 1,774
BRUNEI .... Bandar Seri Begawan	200,000.... 49,900	2,226.... 5,765	Constitutional monarchy (C)	Sultan: .... Muda Hassanal Bolkiah	Dollar 0.468	4,420 22,100
BULGARIA .... Sofia	8,900,000.... 1,070,400	42,823.... 110,912	People's republic	Chairman, Council of State: ...... Todor Zhivkov Chairman, Council of Ministers (Premier): Grisha Filipov	Lev 1.002	37,390[1] 4,201[1]
BURMA .... Rangoon	36,900,000.... 2,400,000	261,218.... 676,552	Socialist republic	President: .... U San Yu Prime Minister: U Maung Maung Kha	Kyat.......... 0.13	6,500 176
BURUNDI .... Bujumbura	4,600,000.... 151,000	10,747.... 27,834	Republic	President: Col. Jean-Baptiste Bagaza	Franc 0.009	1,050 228
CAMBODIA .... **(PEOPLE'S REPUBLIC OF KAMPUCHEA)** Phnom Penh	6,200,000.... 600,000	69,898.... 181,035	People's republic	President, Council of State:..... Heng Samrin Chairman, Council of Ministers (Premier): Hun Sen	New riel ..... NA	NA NA
CAMEROON .... Yaoundé	9,700,000.... 485,200[5]	183,569.... 475,442	Republic	President: .... Paul Biya Prime Minister: Etecki Nbomou	CFA franc[4] 0.0026	7,640 787
CANADA .... Ottawa	25,400,000.... 300,000	3,851,809.... 9,976,139	Federal parliamentary state (C)	Governor-General:........... Jeanne Sauvé Prime Minister: Brian Mulroney	Dollar 0.72	300,400 11,826
CAPE VERDE .... Praia	300,000.... 39,000	1,557.... 4,033	Republic	President: .... Aristides M. Pereira Premier: Pedro Rodrigues Pires	Escudo 0.0112	110 366
CENTRAL AFRICAN .. **REPUBLIC** Bangui	2,700,000.... 500,000	240,535.... 622,984	Republic	Chairman, Military Committee..... for National Recovery (President): Gen. André Kolinga	CFA franc[4]... 0.0026	690 255
CHAD .... N'Djamena	5,200,000.... 303,000	495,755.... 1,284,000	Republic	President: Hissène Habré	CFA franc[4]... 0.0026	490 94
CHILE .... Santiago	12,000,000.... 4,132,300	292,258.... 756,945	Republic	President: .... Gen. Augusto Pinochet Ugarte	Peso 0.0057	21,890 1,824
CHINA, PEOPLE'S.... **REPUBLIC OF** Peking	1,042,000,000.... 9,230,700[5]	3,705,406.... 9,596,961	People's republic	Chairman, Standing Committee of the National People's Congress: Peng Zhen Premier: Zhao Ziyang	Yuan 0.34	301,840 289
COLOMBIA .... Bogotá	29,400,000.... 4,584,000	439,737.... 1,138,914	Republic	President:.............. Belisario Betancur Cuartas	Peso 0.01	38,830 1,320
COMOROS.......... Moroni	500,000.... 16,000	838.... 2,171	Federal Islamic republic	President: Ahmed Abdallah Abderemane	CFA franc[4]... 0.0026	110 220

Imports Exports	Revenue Expenditure	Elementary Schools: Teachers Students	Secondary Schools: Teachers Students	Colleges and Universities: Teachers Students
$ 162,000,000 ....$	40,300,000	1,463	NA	NA
94,000,000	44,500,000	35,113	6,308	NA
320,000,000	381,841,120	11,339	NA	196
46,000,000	381,841,120	428,185	NA	749
NA	39,731,720	1,167	394	15
NA	46,158,910	41,372	5,298	180
514,000,000	301,300,000	45,024	NA	3,480
789,000,000	2,030,000,000	1,022,624	166,325	56,632
834,000,000	387,600,000	5,628	1,437	144
573,000,000	384,700,000	178,107	22,962	1,022
22,995,000,000	25,700,000,000	NA	180,782	109,788
19,732,000,000	25,700,000,000	23,657,618	2,537,949	1,377,286
703,000,000	869,190,000	1,800	1,538	51
3,565,000,000	499,050,000	31,677	17,869	436
11,527,000,000	15,000,000,000	60,168	25,102	13,254
11,428,000,000	14,980,000,000	1,052,925	305,577	85,824
791,000,000	951,471,000	82,543	32,430	2,260
515,000,000	1,009,364,400	3,968,000	996,200	27,830
165,000,000	167,400,000	5,252	NA	231
71,000,000	234,000,000	206,408	18,544	1,784
NA	NA	NA	NA	NA
NA	NA	NA	NA	NA
1,760,000,000	1,353,000,000	26,763	NA	447
1,862,000,000	1,353,000,000	1,379,205	234,090	10,185
69,795,000,000	47,200,000,000	180,763	139,100	33,900
72,627,000,000	73,600,000,000	2,271,784	2,388,308	692,775
75,000,000	24,300,000	1,436	144	NA
4,000,000	27,000,000	57,587	3,073	NA
88,000,000	101,100,000	4,284	NA	239
136,000,000	132,570,000	259,525	50,345	1,904
137,000,000	10,800,000,000	2,610	NA	62
141,000,000	24,000,000,000	210,882	19,580	758
2,754,000,000	9,040,000,000	62,746	27,207	10,372
3,840,000,000	9,400,000,000	2,092,597	536,428	121,138
22,340,000,000	56,800,000,000	5,504,600	2,870,500	286,908
20,900,000,000	58,300,000,000	139,720,400	47,027,900	1,175,238
4,813,000,000	4,240,000,000	131,745	90,171	33,210
3,103,000,000	4,510,000,000	4,076,200	1,816,628	296,030
30,000,000	6,270,000	1,292	449	NA
13,000,000	10,590,000	59,709	13,798	NA

439

Nation Capital	Population	Area of Country (sq mi/ sq km)	Type of Government	Heads of State and Government	Currency: Value in U.S. Dollars	GNP (000,000): GNP Per Capita
CONGO Brazzaville	1,700,000 400,000	132,047 342,000	People's republic	President: Col. Denis Sassou-Nguesso Premier: Ange Edouard Poungui	CFA franc[4] 0.0026	$ 2,180 1,282
COSTA RICA San José	2,600,000 265,400	19,575 50,700	Republic	President: Luis Alberto Monge Alvarez	Colón 0.02	2,420 930
CUBA Havana	10,100,000 2,003,600	44,218 114,524	Socialist republic	President of the Councils of State and Ministers: Fidel Castro Ruz	Peso 1.07	12,330 1,220
CYPRUS Nicosia	640,200 183,400	3,572 9,251	Republic (C)	President:[6] Spyros Kyprianou	Pound[6] 1.84	4,860[6] 7,591[6]
CZECHOSLOVAKIA Prague	15,500,000 1,185,700	49,370 127,869	Federal socialist republic	President: Gustáv Husák Premier: Lubomir Štrougal	Koruna 0.15	89,260 5,758
DENMARK[7] Copenhagen	5,110,000 638,200	16,629 43,069	Constitutional monarchy	Queen: Margrethe II Prime Minister: Poul Schlüter	Krone 0.11	58,850 11,516
DJIBOUTI Djibouti	300,000 200,000	8,494 22,000	Republic	President: Hassan Gouled Aptidon Premier: Barkad Gourad Hamadou	Djibouti franc 0.0067	180 600
DOMINICA Roseau	75,000 8,350	290 751	Republic (C)	President: Clarence A. Seignoret Prime Minister: (Mary) Eugenia Charles	East Caribbean dollar 0.37	80 1,066
DOMINICAN REPUBLIC Santo Domingo	6,200,000 1,300,000	18,816 48,734	Republic	President: Salvador Jorge Blanco	Peso 0.34	8,170 1,317
ECUADOR Quito	8,900,000 1,110,050	109,483 283,561	Republic	President: Léon Febrés Cordero Rivadeneira	Sucre 0.01	11,690 1,313
EGYPT Cairo	48,300,000 10,000,000[5]	386,661 1,001,449	Republic	President: Hosni Mubarak Prime Minister: Ali Lotfi	Pound 1.23	31,880 660
EL SALVADOR San Salvador	5,100,000 445,000	8,124 21,041	Republic	President: José Napoleón Duarte	Colón 0.40	3,690 723
EQUATORIAL GUINEA Malabo	300,000 37,240	10,831 28,051	Republic	President, Supreme Military Council: Lt. Col. Teodoro Obiang Nguema Mbasogo	Ekuele 0.0026	60 200
ETHIOPIA Addis Ababa	36,000,000 1,277,200	471,778 1,221,900	Socialist state	Head of State, Chairman, Provisional Military Administrative Council and Council of Ministers: Mengistu Haile Mariam	Birr 0.49	4,860 135
FIJI Suva	700,000 71,300	7,056 18,274	Parliamentary state (C)	Governor-General: Penaia Ganilau Prime Minister: Kamisese Mara	Dollar 0.91	1,190 1,700
FINLAND Helsinki	4,900,000 484,500	130,129 337,032	Republic	President: Mauno Koivisto Prime Minister: Kalevi Sorsa	Markka 0.18	50,730 10,353
FRANCE Paris	55,000,000 2,330,000	211,208 547,026	Republic	President: François Mitterrand Premier: Laurent Fabius	Franc 0.13	568,700 10,340
GABON Libreville	1,370,000 250,000	103,347 267,667	Republic	President: Omar Bongo Premier: Léon Mébiame	CFA franc[4] 0.0026	2,950 2,153

Imports / Exports	Revenue / Expenditure	Elementary Schools: Teachers / Students	Secondary Schools: Teachers / Students	Colleges and Universities: Teachers / Students
$ 791,000,000	$ 651,794,000	6,997	4,899	292
1,040,000,000	651,794,000	406,835	190,668	7,255
1,198,000,000	858,700,000	10,784	6,540	4,343
968,000,000	1,210,000,000	342,373	165,374	54,334
6,293,000,000	12,744,340,000	83,358	88,199	12,222
5,536,000,000	12,739,789,000	1,363,078	1,017,556	173,403
NA	540,000,000[6]	2,221[6]	3,093[6]	255[6]
NA	737,000,000[6]	46,198[6]	48,527[6]	1,804[6]
15,800,000,000	48,701,465,000	90,702	32,852	21,863
16,507,000,000	48,677,130,000	1,956,634	390,051	192,397
17,565,000,000	24,378,000,000	NA	NA	NA
16,027,000,000	34,744,000,000	420,064	498,462	85,145
139,000,000	107,500,000	496	334	NA
77,000,000	161,500,000	21,847	6,331	NA
47,000,000	24,814,790	NA	NA	59
24,000,000	22,740,718	14,803	6,779	284
1,601,000,000	745,600,000	23,578	NA	NA
1,174,000,000	973,900,000	1,092,838	379,377	42,412
2,332,000,000	1,420,000,000	45,225	45,539	11,679
2,562,000,000	2,030,000,000	1,610,722	672,603	258,054
9,078,000,000	6,650,000,000	141,562	120,958	25,503
3,120,000,000	8,400,000,000	4,748,414	2,919,364	567,128
962,000,000	436,200,000	17,441	3,080	802
794,000,000	677,800,000	709,567	73,030	18,434
58,000,000	9,726,700	NA	165	68
26,000,000	13,186,500	NA	4,523	1,140
842,000,000	797,100,000	37,844	NA	1,001
431,000,000	1,400,000,000	2,374,362	NA	10,512
551,000,000	301,300,000	4,150	2,442	NA
313,000,000	343,200,000	116,318	45,843	2,299
14,174,000,000	12,000,000,000	24,752	37,098	6,618
14,011,000,000	11,900,000,000	365,965	432,761	87,488
120,951,000,000	125,800,000,000	NA	288,621	NA
106,425,000,000	131,800,000,000	3,914,450	5,050,028	927,230
956,000,000	1,310,584,000	3,526	1,583	NA
2,196,000,000	1,310,584,000	160,349	30,222	1,058

Nation Capital	Population	Area of Country (sq mi/ sq km)	Type of Government	Heads of State and Government	Currency: Value in U.S. Dollars	GNP (000,000): GNP Per Capita
GAMBIA, THE Banjul	800,000 49,200	4,361 11,295	Republic (C)	President: Sir Dawda K. Jawara	Dalasi 0.29	$ 200 250
GERMAN DEMOCRATIC REPUBLIC East Berlin	16,700,000 1,185,500	41,768 108,178	Socialist republic	Chairman, Council of State: Erich Honecker Chairman, Council of Ministers (Premier): Willi Stoph	Mark 0.38	120,940 7,241
GERMANY, FEDERAL REPUBLIC OF Bonn	61,500,000 292,900	95,976 248,577	Federal republic	President: Richard von Weizsäcker Chancellor: Helmut Kohl	Deutsche mark 0.398	702,440 11,421
GHANA Accra	14,300,000 840,000	92,100 238,537	Republic (C)	Chairman, Provisional National Defense Council (Head of State): Jerry J. Rawlings	Cedi 0.02	3,980 278
GREAT BRITAIN[8] London	56,400,000 6,754,500	94,227 244,046	Limited monarchy (C)	Queen: Elizabeth II Prime Minister: Margaret Thatcher	Pound 1.49	505,610 8,964
GREECE Athens	10,100,000 885,100	50,944 131,944	Republic	President: Christos Sartzetakis Prime Minister: Andreas Papandreou	Drachma 0.01	39,210 3,882
GRENADA St. George's	115,000 10,000	133 344	Parliamentary state (C)	Governor-General: Sir Paul Scoon Prime Minister: Herbert A. Blaize	East Caribbean dollar 0.37	110 956
GUATEMALA Guatemala City	8,161,400 754,200	42,042 108,889	Republic	President: Oscar Humberto Mejía Victores	Quetzal 1.00	8,890 1,089
GUINEA Conakry	6,100,000 763,000	94,926 245,857	Republic	President: Lansana Conté Premier: Diarra Traoré	Syli 0.06	1,740 285
GUINEA-BISSAU Bissau	900,000 109,500	13,948 36,125	Republic	President, Council of the Revolution: Cmdr. João Bernardo Vieira	Peso 0.01	150 166
GUYANA Georgetown	800,000 187,600	83,000 214,969	Republic (C)	President: Desmond Hoyte Prime Minister: Hamilton Green	Dollar 0.24	410 512
HAITI Port-au-Prince	5,800,000 719,700	10,714 27,750	Republic	President: Jean-Claude Duvalier	Gourde 0.20	1,700 293
HONDURAS Tegucigalpa	4,400,000 509,000	43,277 112,088	Republic	President: Roberto Suazo Córdova	Lempira 0.50	2,740 622
HUNGARY Budapest	10,700,000 2,064,300	35,919 93,030	People's republic	Chairman, Presidential Council: Pál Losonczi Chairman, Council of Ministers (Premier): György Lázár	Forint 0.02	23,050[1] 2,154[1]
ICELAND Reykjavík	200,000 88,500	39,769 103,000	Republic	President: Vigdís Finnbogadóttir Prime Minister: Steingrímur Hermannsson	New króna 0.02	2,430 12,150
INDIA New Delhi	762,200,000 2,500,000	1,269,345 3,287,590	Federal republic (C)	President: Zail Singh Prime Minister: Rajiv Gandhi	Rupee 0.085	190,710 250
INDONESIA Jakarta	168,400,000 6,503,400	782,662 2,027,087	Republic	President: Suharto	Rupiah 0.001	87,120 517
IRAN Tehran	45,100,000 5,433,700	636,296 1,648,000	Islamic republic	President: Hojatolislam Sayed Ali Khamenei Prime Minister: Mir Hussein Moussavi	Rial 0.01	69,170 1,533

Imports Exports	Revenue Expenditure	Elementary Schools: Teachers Students	Secondary Schools: Teachers Students	Colleges and Universities: Teachers Students
$ 115,000,000 48,000,000	$ 56,340,000 59,930,000	2,347 53,774	774 12,424	NA NA
21,524,000,000 23,793,000,000	164,500,000,000 164,430,000,000	171,381 2,024,220	NA 476,334	29,460 139,699
163,911,000,000 176,086,000,000	91,700,000,000 106,700,000,000	267,417 4,500,991	307,179 4,254,046	130,743 1,198,330
1,184,000,000 878,000,000	2,078,000,000 3,610,000,000	51,109 1,574,719	35,045 772,471	623 5,011
99,461,000,000 102,715,000,000	196,200,000,000 207,900,000,000	250,510 4,688,572	NA 5,329,275	39,377 414,508
9,632,000,000 4,459,000,000	8,500,000,000 11,000,000,000	37,315 900,641	39,571 740,058	6,129 83,485
54,000,000 14,000,000	12,460,000 38,000,000	760 17,331	NA NA	71 926
1,690,000,000 1,393,000,000	749,100,000 1,110,000,000	25,862 930,130	11,828 167,724	NA 47,433
351,000,000 428,000,000	473,625,000 473,625,000	7,165 257,547	NA 101,113	614 3,750
52,000,000 15,000,000	10,493,100 17,378,400	3,363 74,359	465 6,294	NA NA
416,000,000 422,000,000	399,900,000 147,963,000	3,909 130,832	NA 71,327	322 1,681
587,000,000 333,000,000	176,300,000 366,500,000	14,927 658,102	4,392 99,894	559 4,099
986,000,000 846,000,000	1,185,050,000 1,242,250,000	17,930 671,786	5,227 147,528	1,760 29,195
9,159,000,000 8,726,000,000	13,200,000,000 13,600,000,000	80,798 1,244,094	NA 395,976	10,610 60,168
1,024,000,000 895,000,000	455,000,000 451,000,000	NA 25,018	NA 26,627	527 2,789
15,169,000,000 7,844,000,000	19,130,000,000 21,400,000,000	1,345,376 72,687,840	NA 25,831,558	277,468 5,345,580
13,520,000,000 22,101,000,000	16,600,000,000 18,400,000,000	971,893 27,990,275	403,422 6,320,013	NA 570,392
12,634,000,000 10,169,000,000	25,100,000,000 29,900,000,000	280,649 5,592,808	188,064 2,693,540	8,823 107,896

STATISTICS OF THE WORLD

Nation Capital	Population	Area of Country (sq mi/ sq km)	Type of Government	Heads of State and Government	Currency: Value in U.S. Dollars	GNP (000,000): GNP / GNP Per Capita
IRAQ Baghdad	15,500,000 3,236,000	167,925 434,924	Republic	President and Chairman, Revolutionary Command Council: Saddam Hussein al-Takriti	Dinar 3.23	$ 39,500 2,548
IRELAND, REPUBLIC OF Dublin	3,600,000 526,000	27,136 70,283	Republic	President: Patrick J. Hillery Prime Minister: Garret FitzGerald	Pound 1.23	16,960 4,711
ISRAEL Jerusalem	4,200,000 420,000	8,019 20,770	Republic	President: Chaim Herzog Prime Minister: Shimon Peres	Shekel 0.001	21,990 5,235
ITALY Rome	57,400,000 2,827,700	116,304 301,225	Republic	President: Francesco Cossiga Prime Minister: Bettino Craxi	Lira 0.0006	357,570 6,229
IVORY COAST Abidjan	10,100,000 1,800,000	124,504 322,463	Republic	President: Félix Houphouët-Boigny	CFA franc[4] 0.0026	6,730 666
JAMAICA Kingston	2,300,000 132,500	4,244 10,991	Parliamentary state (C)	Governor-General: Florizel A. Glasspole Prime Minister: Edward P. G. Seaga	Dollar 0.18	2,940 1,278
JAPAN Tokyo	120,800,000 8,170,400	143,751 372,313	Constitutional monarchy	Emperor: Hirohito Prime Minister: Yasuhiro Nakasone	Yen 0.005	1,204,270 9,969
JORDAN Amman	3,600,000 1,300,000	37,738 97,740	Constitutional monarchy	King: Hussein I Prime Minister: Zaid al-Rifai	Dinar 2.81	4,400 1,222
KENYA Nairobi	20,200,000 906,400	224,961 582,646	Republic (C)	President: Daniel arap Moi	Shilling 0.07	6,450 319
KIRIBATI (GILBERT ISLANDS) Tarawa	60,000 17,900	332 861	Republic (C)	President: Ieremia T. Tabai	Dollar 0.67	30 500
KOREA, DEMOCRATIC PEOPLE'S REPUBLIC OF P'yŏngyang	20,100,000 1,800,000	46,540 120,538	People's republic	President: Marshal Kim Il Sung Premier: Kang Song San	Won 1.06	17,040 847
KOREA, REPUBLIC OF Seoul	42,700,000 9,204,300[5]	38,025 98,484	Republic	President: Chun Doo Hwan Prime Minister: Lho Shin Yong	Won 0.0012	80,310 1,880
KUWAIT Kuwait	1,900,000 60,500	6,880 17,818	Constitutional emirate	Emir: Sheikh Jabir al-Ahmad al-Sabah Prime Minister: Sheikh Saad al-Abdullah al-Salem al-Sabah	Dinar 3.46	30,290 15,942
LAOS Vientiane	3,584,800 377,400	91,429 236,800	People's republic	President: Prince Souphanouvong Premier: Kaysone Phomvihan	New kip 0.029	290 80
LEBANON Beirut	2,600,000 1,000,000	4,015 10,400	Republic	President: Amin Gemayel Prime Minister: Rashid Karami	Pound 0.057	NA NA
LESOTHO Maseru	1,500,000 45,000	11,720 30,355	Constitutional monarchy (C)	King: Moshoeshoe II Prime Minister: Chief Leabua Jonathan	Loti 0.37	670 446
LIBERIA Monrovia	2,200,000 208,600	43,000 111,369	Republic	Head of State and Chairman, People's Redemption Council: Gen. Samuel K. Doe	Dollar 1.00	990 450

Imports Exports	Revenue Expenditure	Elementary Schools: Teachers Students	Secondary Schools: Teachers Students	Colleges and Universities: Teachers Students
$ 18,907,000,000 9,372,000,000	$ 61,915,700,000 61,915,700,000	107,479 2,620,883	38,678 1,065,588	4,624 85,573
10,596,000,000 7,789,000,000	7,340,000,000 10,200,000,000	14,829 420,871	19,705 295,592	2,897 33,982
9,501,000,000 5,381,000,000	27,000,000,000 29,690,000,000	42,395 667,207	NA 219,670	NA 72,481
91,102,000,000 75,284,000,000	16,600,000,000 21,600,000,000	NA 4,215,841	526,431 5,290,862	47,936 1,083,403
2,434,000,000 2,586,000,000	1,730,000,000 1,730,000,000	24,441 954,190	NA 214,298	666 12,541
1,518,000,000 738,000,000	477,855,000 749,070,000	8,676 359,488	NA 248,001	397 4,548
142,868,000,000 151,500,000,000	211,300,000,000 211,300,000,000	475,000 11,901,000	553,684 10,011,340	178,097 1,916,792
3,907,000,000 682,000,000	2,060,000,000 2,080,000,000	14,873 473,027	14,126 295,989	1,011 22,305
2,121,000,000 1,216,000,000	1,860,000,000 2,410,000,000	115,042 4,120,145	17,809 477,317	NA 9,312
36,000,000 3,000,000	13,609,382 14,539,770	453 13,612	130 1,901	NA NA
899,000,000 843,000,000	27,872,346,000 27,872,346,000	NA 2,561,674	NA NA	NA NA
26,192,000,000 24,445,000,000	12,600,000,000 11,800,000,000	126,163 5,257,164	128,967 4,571,459	23,040 839,748
8,042,000,000 16,561,000,000	11,100,000,000 10,000,000,000	8,346 160,188	17,155 209,592	735 12,085
85,000,000 9,000,000	119,000,000 215,200,000	16,109 479,291	4,605 90,435	140 1,408
374,000,000 122,000,000	NA NA	22,810 398,977	NA 287,310	NA 70,314
NA NA	181,335,000 181,912,500	5,295 277,945	1,495 28,717	NA 847
1,942,000,000 1,141,000,000	399,600,000 420,100,000	9,099 227,431	NA 54,623	NA 3,702

Nation Capital	Population	Area of Country (sq mi/ sq km)	Type of Government	Heads of State and Government	Currency: Value in U.S. Dollars	GNP (000,000): GNP Per Capita
LIBYA Tripoli	4,000,000 1,223,000	679,362 1,759,540	Socialist republic	Revolutionary Leader (Head of State): Col. Muammar al-Qaddafi Secretary-General, General People's Congress: Muhammad al-Zarrouk Rajab	Dinar 3.38	$ 25,100 6,275
LIECHTENSTEIN Vaduz	26,400 4,900	61 157	Constitutional monarchy	Sovereign: Prince Francis Joseph II Chief of Government: Hans Brunhart	Swiss franc 0.48	NA NA
LUXEMBOURG Luxembourg	400,000 79,000	998 2,586	Constitutional monarchy	Grand Duke: Jean President: Jacques Santer	Franc 0.02	4,470 11,175
MADAGASCAR Antananarivo	10,000,000 773,000	226,658 587,041	Socialist republic	President: Cmdr. Didier Ratsiraka Prime Minister: Lt. Col. Désiré Rakotoarijaona	Franc 0.002	2,730 273
MALAWI Lilongwe	7,100,000 98,700	45,747 118,484	Republic (C)	President: Hastings Kamuzu Banda	Kwacha 0.59	1,390 195
MALAYSIA Kuala Lumpur	15,700,000 937,900	127,317 329,749	Federal constitutional monarchy (C)	Supreme Head of State: Sultan Mahmood Iskandar Prime Minister: Datuk Seri Mahathir bin Mohamad	Dollar 0.41	27,760 1,768
MALDIVES Male	200,000 29,500	115 298	Republic	President: Maumoon Abdul Gayoom	Rufiyaa 0.14	40 200
MALI Bamako	7,700,000 399,900	478,766 1,240,000	Republic	President: Brig. Gen. Moussa Traoré	Franc 0.0013	1,110 144
MALTA Valletta	329,200 14,100	122 316	Republic (C)	President: Agatha Barbara Prime Minister: Carmelo Mifsud-Bonnici	Pound 2.37	1,310 3,979
MAURITANIA Nouakchott	1,900,000 135,000[5]	397,955 1,030,700	Islamic republic	President and Chairman, Military Committee for National Salvation: Maouya Ould Sidi Ahmed Taya	Ouguiya 0.01	720 378
MAURITIUS Port Louis	1,000,000 147,600	790 2,045	Parliamentary state (C)	Governor-General: Seewoosagur Ramgoolam Prime Minister: Anerood Jugnauth	Rupee 0.07	1,250 1,250
MEXICO Mexico City	79,700,000 10,500,000	761,604 1,972,547	Federal republic	President: Miguel de la Madrid Hurtado	Peso 0.002	168,070 2,108
MONACO Monaco	27,000 4,000	0.58 1.49	Constitutional monarchy	Prince: Rainier III Minister of State: Jean Ausseil	French franc 0.13	NA NA
MONGOLIAN PEOPLE'S REPUBLIC Ulan Bator	1,900,000 470,500	604,250 1,565,000	People's republic	Presidium Chairman: Jambyn Batmönh Premier: Dumaagiyn Sodnom	Tugrik 0.30	1,100 578
MOROCCO Rabat	24,300,000 566,900	172,414 446,550	Constitutional monarchy	King: Hassan II Prime Minister: Muhammad Karim Lamrani	Dirham 0.10	15,620 642
MOZAMBIQUE Maputo	13,900,000 785,500	309,496 801,590	People's republic	President: Samora M. Machel	Metical 0.02	2,800 201
NAURU Yaren	8,400 NA	8 21	Republic (C)	President: Hammer DeRoburt	Australian dollar 0.67	NA NA

Imports Exports	Revenue Expenditure	Elementary Schools: Teachers Students	Secondary Schools: Teachers Students	Colleges and Universities: Teachers Students
$ 15,414,000,000 16,391,000,000	$ NA 13,019,106,000	42,696 721,701	30,673 340,703	NA 15,267
NA NA	123,960,000 123,780,000	95 1,899	92 1,831	NA NA
NA NA	1,350,000,000 1,410,000,000	1,685 22,826	2,020 24,341	236 699
494,000,000 335,000,000	685,400,000 685,400,000	23,937 1,311,000	NA NA	NA 32,599
360,000,000 380,000,000	218,600,000 306,800,000	12,540 809,862	976 20,407	301 1,829
13,987,000,000 13,917,000,000	7,070,000,000 9,510,000,000	81,664[9] 2,120,050[9]	54,787[9] 1,173,202[9]	3,064 33,030
36,000,000 9,000,000	25,292,330 36,488,130	NA 34,090	NA NA	NA NA
370,000,000 154,000,000	237,000,000 266,000,000	7,214 298,831	NA NA	321 1,631
873,000,000 444,000,000	561,000,000 562,000,000	1,617 33,187	2,180 26,700	146 1,010
571,000,000 325,000,000	204,000,000 240,000,000	2,100 90,530	NA 22,102	NA NA
543,000,000 283,000,000	390,800,000 491,600,000	6,420 131,594	2,177 65,113	96 490
8,136,000,000 21,399,000,000	93,300,000,000 93,300,000,000	418,982 15,353,251	301,939 5,332,131	79,934 879,240
NA NA	166,309,000 199,803,400	NA 1,354	NA 3,132	NA NA
566,000,000 416,000,000	1,490,000,000 1,480,000,000	4,700 150,100	10,215 237,190	1,300 18,700
4,487,000,000 2,160,000,000	6,000,000,000 6,600,000,000	67,682 2,442,726	43,455 895,743	3,284 96,953
773,000,000 457,000,000	514,000,000 594,000,000	20,769 1,162,617	3,519 121,033	327 1,110
NA NA	83,416,742 95,426,887	129[10] 400[10]	129[10] 400[10]	* *

447

Nation Capital	Population	Area of Country (sq mi/ sq km)	Type of Government	Heads of State and Government	Currency: Value in U.S. Dollars	GNP (000,000): GNP Per Capita
NEPAL Kathmandu	17,000,000 393,500	54,362 140,797	Constitutional monarchy	King: Birendra Bir Bikram Shah Deva Prime Minister: Lokendra Bahadur Chand	Rupee 0.055	$ 2,660 156
NETHERLANDS, THE Amsterdam	14,500,000 676,400	15,770 40,844	Constitutional monarchy	Queen: Beatrix Prime Minister: Ruud Lubbers	Guilder 0.35	142,420 9,822
NEW ZEALAND Wellington	3,300,000 342,000	103,736 368,676	Parliamentary state (C)	Governor-General: Paul Reeves Prime Minister: David Lange	Dollar 0.57	24,000 7,272
NICARAGUA Managua	3,000,000 902,000	50,193 130,000	Republic	President: Daniel Ortega Saavedra	Córdoba 0.10	2,690 896
NIGER Niamey	6,500,000 343,600	489,191 1,267,000	Republic	President, Supreme Military Council: Col. Seyni Kountché Prime Minister: Hamid Algabid	CFA franc[4] 0.0026	1,460 224
NIGERIA Lagos	91,200,000 4,200,000	356,669 923,768	Federal republic (C)	President: Ibrahim Babangida	Naira 1.08	71,030 778
NORWAY Oslo	4,200,000 487,300	125,182 324,219	Constitutional monarchy	King: Olav V Prime Minister: Kaare Willoch	Krone 0.13	57,090 13,592
OMAN Masqat	1,200,000 6,000	82,030 212,457	Sultanate	Sultan and Prime Minister: Qabus bin Sa'id	Rial 2.89	7,070 5,891
PAKISTAN Islamabad	99,200,000 388,000	310,404 803,943	Federal republic	President and Chief Martial Law Administrator: Gen. Muhammad Zia ul-Haq Prime Minister: Muhammad Khan Junejo	Rupee 0.06	35,000 352
PANAMA Panamá	2,000,000 655,000	29,762 77,082	Republic	President: Eric Arturo Delvalle	Balboa 1.00	4,070 2,035
PAPUA NEW GUINEA Port Moresby	3,300,000 140,000	178,260 461,691	Parliamentary state (C)	Governor-General: Kingsford Dibela Prime Minister: Paias Wingti	Kina 0.9875	2,510 760
PARAGUAY Asunción	3,600,000 474,100	157,048 406,752	Republic	President: Gen. Alfredo Stroessner	Guarani 0.004	4,540 1,261
PERU Lima	19,500,000 4,164,600	496,224 1,285,216	Republic	President: Alan García Pérez Prime Minister: Luís Alva Castro	Sol 0.0001	18,650 956
PHILIPPINES Manila	56,800,000 1,630,500	115,831 300,000	Republic	President: Ferdinand E. Marcos Prime Minister: César Virata	Peso 0.05	39,420 694
POLAND Warsaw	37,300,000 1,641,300	120,725 312,677	People's republic	Head of State: Gen. Wojciech W. Jaruzelski Premier: Zbigniew Messner	Zloty 0.007	139,780[1] 3,747[1]
PORTUGAL Lisbon	10,300,000 812,400	35,553 92,082	Republic	President: Gen. António Ramalho Eanes Prime Minister: Anibal Cavaco Silva	Escudo 0.006	22,490 2,183
QATAR Doha	300,000 190,000	4,247 11,000	Constitutional emirate	Emir and Prime Minister: Sheikh Khalifa bin Hamad al-Thani	Riyal 0.28	5,960 19,866
ROMANIA Bucharest	22,800,000 1,861,000	91,699 237,500	Socialist republic	Head of State and President, State Council: Nicolae Ceauşescu Chairman, Council of Ministers (Premier): Constantin Dăscălescu	Leu 0.25	57,030[1] 2,501[1]

Imports Exports	Revenue Expenditure	Elementary Schools: Teachers Students	Secondary Schools: Teachers Students	Colleges and Universities: Teachers Students
$ 765,000,000	$ 202,000,000	32,259	16,454	2,918
271,000,000	404,800,000	1,474,698	370,082	38,450
67,298,000,000	47,200,000,000	60,434	NA	NA
68,746,000,000	55,300,000,000	1,201,512	1,440,242	155,025
5,739,000,000	6,892,339,200	22,277	NA	4,727
5,607,000,000	7,750,974,400	367,986	351,034	45,311
731,000,000	624,900,000	14,711	4,103	1,423
529,000,000	771,800,000	534,996	139,957	31,537
449,000,000	187,026,400	5,475	961	289
297,000,000	187,026,400	233,441	27,196	1,853
18,776,000,000	13,960,000,000	NA	NA	7,759
18,727,000,000	15,982,000,000	12,556,881	1,826,629	83,357
15,637,000,000	24,238,968,000	47,802	NA	4,001
17,988,000,000	20,622,613,000	383,599	368,624	39,827
2,221,000,000	4,800,000,000	4,649	2,298	NA
4,416,000,000	4,800,000,000	117,295	27,041	NA
5,410,000,000	3,864,996,000	159,062	128,467	7,042
3,075,000,000	4,482,756,000	5,741,490	2,253,298	156,558
2,880,000,000	1,060,000,000	12,853	8,924	3,378
317,000,000	1,400,000,000	336,740	174,791	50,186
1,224,000,000	506,100,000	10,236	2,289	589
860,000,000	873,000,000	326,021	49,334	3,458
600,000,000	492,000,000	20,746	NA	1,945
296,000,000	67,000,000	539,889	164,464	20,496
4,200,000,000	3,510,000,000	89,370	NA	16,913
3,649,000,000	3,200,000,000	3,343,631	1,203,116	305,390
8,864,000,000	6,520,000,000	272,134	90,266	NA
5,756,000,000	7,740,000,000	8,591,267	3,092,128	1,201,872
9,931,000,000	41,540,000,000	253,037	140,046	58,933
10,951,000,000	48,928,000,000	4,377,472	1,542,344	396,629
9,762,000,000	3,570,380,800	NA	NA	6,906
4,145,000,000	4,731,596,800	1,223,127	438,474	67,652
1,571,000,000	3,690,000,000	2,508	2,139	215
3,978,000,000	3,470,000,000	34,805	18,864	4,015
11,542,000,000	18,500,000,000	152,228	49,159	13,931
10,235,000,000	17,200,000,000	3,140,101	1,347,169	181,081

Nation Capital	Population	Area of Country (sq mi/ sq km)	Type of Government	Heads of State and Government	Currency: Value in U.S. Dollars	GNP (000,000): GNP Per Capita
RWANDA Kigali	6,300,000 176,700	10,169 26,338	Republic	President: Maj. Gen. Juvénal Habyarimana	Franc 0.01	$ 1,540 244
SAINT KITTS– NEVIS Basseterre	40,000 14,700	104 269	Parliamentary state (C)	Governor-General: Sir Clement Arrindell Prime Minister: Kennedy Simmonds	East Caribbean dollar 0.37	40 1,000
SAINT LUCIA Castries	100,000 45,000	238 616	Parliamentary state (C)	Governor-General: Allen Lewis Prime Minister: John G. M. Compton	East Caribbean dollar 0.37	130 1,300
SAINT VINCENT AND THE GRENADINES Kingstown	138,000 22,800	150 388	Parliamentary state (C)	Governor-General: Sir Sydney Douglas Gun-Munro Prime Minister: James Mitchell	East Caribbean dollar 0.37	90 652
SAN MARINO San Marino	21,200 4,400	24 61	Republic	Co-Regents: Renzo Renzi Germano De Biagi	Italian lira 0.0005	NA NA
SÃO TOMÉ AND PRÍNCIPE São Tomé	100,000 25,000	372 964	Republic	President and Prime Minister: Manuel Pinto da Costa	Dobra 0.02	30 300
SAUDI ARABIA Riyadh	11,200,000 1,100,000	830,000 2,149,690	Monarchy	King and Prime Minister: Fahd ibn Abdul-Aziz	Riyal 0.275	127,080 11,346
SENEGAL Dakar	6,700,000 978,600	75,750 196,192	Republic	President: Abdou Diouf Premier: Habib Thiam	CFA franc[4] 0.0026	2,730 407
SEYCHELLES Victoria	66,000 23,300	108 280	Republic (C)	President: France Albert René	Rupee 0.15	160 2,424
SIERRA LEONE Freetown	3,600,000 214,400	27,699 71,740	Republic (C)	President: Joseph Momoh	Leone 0.17	1,230 341
SINGAPORE Singapore	2,600,000 2,531,000	224 581	Republic (C)	President: Luce Kim Wee Prime Minister: Lee Kuan Yew	Dollar 0.48	16,560 6,369
SOLOMON ISLANDS Honiara	263,000 20,800	10,983 28,446	Parliamentary state (C)	Governor-General: Sir Baddeley Devesi Prime Minister: Peter Kenilorea	Dollar 0.64	160 608
SOMALIA Mogadisho	6,500,000 400,000	246,201 637,657	Republic	President and Chairman, Council of Ministers: Maj. Gen. Muhammad Siad Barre	Somali 0.03	1,140 175
SOUTH AFRICA,[11] REPUBLIC OF Cape Town Pretoria	32,500,000 790,900 528,400	471,445 1,221,037	Republic	President: Pieter Willem Botha	Rand 0.37	76,890 2,365
SPAIN Madrid	38,500,000 3,188,300	194,897 504,782	Constitutional monarchy	King: Juan Carlos I Prime Minister: Felipe González Márquez	Peseta 0.006	182,760 4,747
SRI LANKA (CEYLON) Colombo	16,400,000 602,000	25,332 65,610	Republic (C)	President: Junius R. Jayewardene Prime Minister: Ranasinghe Premadasa	Rupee 0.04	5,140 313
SUDAN Khartoum	21,800,000 476,200	967,499 2,505,813	Republic	President, Transitional Military Council: Abdul Rahman Swar al-Dahab	Pound 0.40	8,420 386
SURINAME Paramaribo	370,000 200,000	63,037 163,265	Republic	President: Dési Bouterse Prime Minister: Wim Udenhout	Guilder 0.57	1,280 3,459
SWAZILAND Mbabane	600,000 38,600	6,704 17,363	Monarchy (C)	Queen: Ntombi Prime Minister: Prince Bhekimpi Dlamini	Emala 0.37	610 1,016

Imports Exports	Revenue Expenditure	Elementary Schools: Teachers Students	Secondary Schools: Teachers Students	Colleges and Universities: Teachers Students
$ 191,000,000 147,000,000	$ 174,000,000 193,000,000	13,590 747,172	1,037 14,230	290 1,212
45,000,000 19,000,000	24,370,346 20,222,202	331 8,320	NA NA	8 40
46,000,000 15,000,000	43,036,994 56,370,314	1,102 31,199	336 5,148	85 546
61,000,000 32,000,000	17,000,000 20,300,000	1,184 21,497	NA 8,058	41 259
NA NA	87,370,000 87,370,000	164 1,493	170 1,317	NA NA
26,000,000 13,000,000	6,740,000 17,700,000	628 16,132	NA 6,303	NA NA
35,268,000,000 113,328,000,000	60,776,000,000 73,840,000,000	55,836 994,901	29,573 379,575	6,943 64,290
1,035,000,000 416,000,000	690,600,000 690,600,000	10,586 452,679	4,834 103,821	580 11,754
88,000,000 20,000,000	65,800,000 65,800,000	656 14,361	213 3,168	28 144
238,000,000 277,000,000	185,000,000 161,000,000	9,472 263,724	NA 63,157	270 1,809
28,153,000,000 21,833,000,000	5,100,000,000 8,100,000,000	10,286 289,092	10,231 187,148	1,737 12,424
87,000,000 68,000,000	26,279,916 46,291,921	1,199 30,246	257 4,030	NA NA
405,000,000 133,000,000	219,100,000 219,100,000	8,122 271,704	2,089 43,841	NA 2,899
23,118,000,000 22,670,000,000	14,600,000,000 16,100,000,000	190,846 6,002,609	NA NA	NA 159,403
32,153,000,000 20,335,000,000	25,800,000,000 35,500,000,000	214,391 3,633,713	NA 4,039,580	32,040 517,215
1,938,000,000 1,020,000,000	873,000,000 1,800,000,000	133,658 2,153,595	NA 1,088,089	1,913 30,164
1,942,000,000 820,000,000	2,510,000,000 3,570,000,000	46,437 1,524,381	18,689 426,932	6,081 25,151
511,000,000 429,000,000	289,400,000 441,500,000	3,476 80,844	2,326 35,742	165 951
NA NA	211,110,000 325,550,000	3,769 125,303	NA 23,655	113 1,064

Nation Capital	Population	Area of Country (sq mi/ sq km)	Type of Government	Heads of State and Government	Currency: Value in U.S. Dollars	GNP (000,000): GNP / GNP Per Capita
SWEDEN Stockholm	8,300,000 650,900	173,732 449,964	Constitutional monarchy	King: Carl XVI Gustaf Prime Minister: Olof Palme	Krona 0.13	$ 103,240 12,438
SWITZERLAND Bern	6,500,000 143,900	15,941 41,288	Federal republic	President: Kurt Furgler	Franc 0.48	105,060 16,163
SYRIA Damascus	10,600,000 2,083,000	71,498 185,180	Socialist republic	President: Hafez al-Assad Prime Minister Abdel al-Raouf al-Kassem	Pound 0.255	16,510 1,557
TAIWAN or FORMOSA (REPUBLIC OF CHINA) Taipei	19,200,000 2,400,000	13,892 35,981	Republic	President: Chiang Ching-kuo Premier: Yu Kuo-hua	New Taiwan dollar 0.03	38,200 1,989
TANZANIA Dar es-Salaam	21,700,000 279,800	364,900 945,087	Republic (C)	President: Ali Hassan Mwinyi Prime Minister: Salim Ahmed Salim	Shilling 0.06	4,880 224
THAILAND Bangkok	52,700,000 5,500,000	198,456 514,000	Constitutional monarchy	King: Bhumibol Adulyadej Prime Minister: Gen. Prem Tinsulanonda	Baht 0.04	40,380 766
TOGO Lomé	3,000,000 275,000	21,925 56,785	Republic	President: Gen. Gnassingbé Eyadéma	CFA franc[4] 0.0026	790 263
TONGA Nukualofa	99,000 20,560	270 699	Constitutional monarchy	King: Taufa'ahau Tupou IV Prime Minister: Prince Fatafehi Tu'ipelehake	Australian dollar 0.69	80 808
TRINIDAD AND TOBAGO Port of Spain	1,200,000 61,200	1,981 5,130	Republic (C)	President: Sir Ellis E. I. Clarke Prime Minister: George M. Chambers	Dollar 0.43	7,870 6,558
TUNISIA Tunis	7,200,000 1,000,000	63,170 163,610	Republic	President: Habib Bourguiba Prime Minister: Muhammad M'zali	Dinar 1.28	8,860 1,230
TURKEY Ankara	52,100,000 1,877,800	301,382 780,576	Republic	President: Gen. Kenan Evren Prime Minister: Turgut Özal	Lira 0.002	58,260 1,118
TUVALU (ELLICE ISLANDS) Funafuti	7,300 NA	10 26	Parliamentary state (C)	Governor-General: Sir Penitala Fiatau Teo Prime Minister: Tomasi Puapua	Australian dollar 0.69	5 714
UGANDA Kampala	14,700,000 458,000	91,134 236,036	Republic (C)	Chairman, Ruling Military Council: Tito Okello	Shilling 0.001	3,090 210
UNION OF SOVIET SOCIALIST REPUBLICS Moscow	274,000,000 8,396,000	8,649,534 22,402,200	Federal socialist state	Chairman, Presidium of the Supreme Soviet: Andrei Gromyko Chairman, Council of Ministers (Premier): Nikolai Rhyzkov	Ruble 1.32	1,212,000[1] 4,423[1]
UNITED ARAB EMIRATES Abu Dhabi	1,300,000 516,000	32,278 83,600	Federal state	President: Sheikh Zayed bin Sultan al-Nahayan Prime Minister: Sheikh Rashid bin Saeed al-Maktoum	Dirham 0.27	25,770 19,823
UNITED STATES OF AMERICA Washington, D.C.	238,740,000 623,000	3,618,770 9,372,569	Federal republic	President: Ronald W. Reagan Vice-President: George Bush	Dollar *	3,292,340 13,781

Imports Exports	Revenue Expenditure	Elementary Schools: Teachers Students	Secondary Schools: Teachers Students	Colleges and Universities: Teachers Students
$ 28,842,000,000	$ 28,900,000,000	40,800	51,397	NA
28,566,000,000	42,900,000,000	658,127	607,199	113,348
30,688,000,000	9,290,000,000	NA	NA	5,882
27,037,000,000	8,870,000,000	415,478	450,372	66,206
4,603,000,000	3,510,000,000	62,959	40,119	NA
2,205,000,000	4,720,000,000	1,716,795	687,435	113,507
18,888,000,000	7,990,000,000	70,648	74,873	19,166
22,204,000,000	8,870,000,000	2,242,641	1,682,364	395,153
1,136,000,000	1,070,000,000	81,659	4,006	893
553,000,000	1,410,000,000	3,538,183	77,398	3,662
10,330,000,000	5,050,000,000	333,351	NA	16,245
6,784,000,000	6,820,000,000	7,449,219	1,990,866	795,970
597,000,000	227,420,000	10,214	NA	346
344,000,000	227,420,000	492,329	119,106	3,833
47,000,000	14,897,347	793	NA	13
5,000,000	14,883,627	16,701	17,085	79
2,869,000,000	2,689,848,000	NA	NA	NA
3,570,000,000	2,895,322,500	167,950	90,363	2,503
3,923,000,000	2,790,000,000	30,411	18,521	4,105
2,209,000,000	2,790,000,000	1,150,580	355,101	34,077
9,348,000,000	15,990,000,000	212,795	129,268	16,272
5,694,000,000	14,880,000,000	5,859,711	2,393,477	158,130
4,000,000	NA	NA	NA	NA
2,000,000	3,001,250	1,338	236	NA
395,000,000	507,300,000	44,426	7,022	369
317,000,000	537,300,000	1,616,791	145,389	4,854
80,267,000,000	459,300,000,000	2,338,000	NA	375,600
91,331,000,000	459,000,000,000	22,660,000	19,669,000	5,315,200
9,549,000,000	6,120,000,000	5,290	NA	279
20,939,000,000	5,080,000,000	115,211	45,957	4,227
273,351,000,000	734,000,000,000	2,390,000	2,390,000	305,982
233,738,000,000	945,900,000,000	27,794,000	14,643,000	7,572,657

STATISTICS OF THE WORLD

Nation Capital	Population	Area of Country (sq mi/ sq km)	Type of Government	Heads of State and Government	Currency: Value in U.S. Dollars	GNP (000,000): GNP Per Capita
UPPER VOLTA (BURKINA FASO) Ouagadougou	6,900,000 247,900	105,869 274,200	Republic	Head of State and Government: Thomas Sankara	CFA franc[4]...$ 0.0026	1,210 175
URUGUAY Montevideo	3,000,000 1,500,000	68,037 176,215	Republic	President: Julio María Sanguinetti	New peso 0.009	7,390 2,463
VANUATU (NEW HEBRIDES) Vila	100,000 15,000	5,700 14,763	Republic (C)	President: Ati George Sokomanu Prime Minister: Rev. Walter H. Lini	Vatu 0.01	40 400
VENEZUELA Caracas	17,300,000 2,664,200	352,144 912,050	Federal republic	President: Jaime Lusinchi	Bolivar 0.07	70,820 4,093
VIETNAM Hanoi	60,500,000 3,000,000	127,242 329,556	Socialist republic	Chairman, Council of State (President): Truong Chinh Chairman, Council of Ministers (Premier): Pham Van Dong	New dong 0.0107	7,750 128
WESTERN SAMOA Apia	200,000 33,200	1,097 2,842	Constitutional monarchy (C)	Head of State: Malietoa Tanumafili II Prime Minister: Va'ai Kolone	Talà 0.47	NA NA
YEMEN, PEOPLE'S DEMOCRATIC REPUBLIC OF Aden	2,100,000 272,000	128,560 332,968	People's republic	President: Chairman of the Presidium of the Supreme People's Council: Ali Nasser Muhammad al-Hasani Prime Minister: Haidar Bakr al-Attas	Dinar 2.92	1,020 485
YEMEN ARAB REPUBLIC Sana	6,100,000 278,000	75,290 195,000	Republic	President: Col. Ali Abdullah Saleh Prime Minister: Abdel Aziz Abdel Ghani	Rial 0.13	3,930 644
YUGOSLAVIA Belgrade	23,100,000 1,470,100	98,766 255,804	Federal socialist republic	President: Radovan Vlajković President, Federal Executive Council (Prime Minister): Milka Planinc	Dinar 0.003	58,520[1] 2,533[1]
ZAIRE Kinshasa	33,100,000 1,700,000	905,567 2,345,409	Republic	President: Mobutu Sese Seko First State Commissioner (Prime Minister): Kengo wa Dondo	Zaire 0.02	5,050 152
ZAMBIA Lusaka	6,800,000 538,500	290,586 752,614	Republic (C)	President: Kenneth D. Kaunda Prime Minister: Kebby Musokotwane	Kwacha 0.18	3,630 533
ZIMBABWE (RHODESIA) Harare	8,600,000 656,000	150,804 390,580	Republic (C)	President: Rev. Canaan S. Banana Prime Minister: Robert G. Mugabe	Dollar 0.61	6,400 744

1. Figure is for gross domestic product.
2. Figure excludes trade with members of the Soviet bloc.
3. Figure includes trade for Luxembourg.
4. "CFA" stands for Communauté Financière Africaine.
5. Figure includes the whole metropolitan area.
6. Information pertains to the Greek sector only. The president of the Turkish sector (Turkish Republic of Northern Cyprus) is Rauf Denktash. The sector's budget in 1982–1983 was balanced at $51,785,900.

Imports Exports	Revenue Expenditure	Elementary Schools: Teachers Students	Secondary Schools: Teachers Students	Colleges and Universities: Teachers Students
$ 323,000,000 ....$ 133,000,000	142,200,000 159,900,000	4,410 250,628	NA 31,398	289 3,086
647,000,000 1,015,000,000	2,670,000,000 8,870,000,000	16,821 363,179	NA 187,190	4,149 36,706
64,000,000 31,000,000	3,724,000,000 3,724,000,000	934 22,244	188 2,480	NA NA
12,758,000,000 19,634,000,000	22,700,000,000 19,300,000,000	97,045 2,591,051	45,888 820,660	24,186 298,483
838,000,000 430,000,000	1,002,309,000 1,002,309,000	204,104 7,887,439	115,348 2,987,997	17,242 114,701
64,000,000 17,000,000	16,030,860 12,555,051	NA .... NA	NA 21,643	NA NA
1,527,000,000 779,000,000	651,093,100 959,121,450	10,832 270,167	2,016 31,705	403 3,645
1,758,000,000 47,000,000	1,510,000,000 1,060,000,000	13,165 602,212	3,826 60,683	157 4,519
15,817,000,000 10,929,000,000	9,510,000,000 9,730,000,000	61,432 1,456,916	134,360 2,381,969	20,718 303,392
480,000,000 569,000,000	1,156,000,000 1,331,000,000	NA 3,919,395	NA 704,332	NA NA
915,000,000 1,170,000,000	510,000,000 750,000,000	21,455 1,041,938	4,431 97,529	329 3,646
1,430,000,000 1,273,000,000	1,600,000,000 2,940,000,000	NA 2,044,029	8,549 227,613	325 3,091

7. Entries include data for Greenland and the Faeroe Islands.
8. Figures include data for Northern Ireland.
9. Figures are for peninsular Malaysia only.
10. These are combined figures for elementary and secondary education.
11. Data generally exclude the homelands that have been granted independence. Estimated population of the homelands, including homeland citizens residing in South Africa, in 1984 was: Bophuthatswana, 1,417,000; Ciskei, 706,000; Transkei, 2,517,000; Venda, 396,000. Presidents of the homelands were: Bophuthatswana, Lucas Mangope; Ciskei, Lennox Sebe; Transkei, Kaiser Matanzima; Venda, Patrick Mphephu.

THE STATES AND OUTLYING AREAS OF THE UNITED STATES

State Capital	Population	Area (sq mi/ sq km)	Per Capita Personal Income	Governor Lieutenant-Governor	Revenue Expenditure	Public Roads (Miles)
ALABAMA Montgomery	4,021,000 182,400	51,705 133,915	$ 9,992	George Wallace (D) William Baxley (D)	$ 5,250,000,000 5,220,000,000	87,598
ALASKA Juneau	521,000 22,000	591,004 1,530,693	17,487	William J. Sheffield (D) Stephen McAlpine (D)	5,247,000,000 3,836,000,000	8,772
ARIZONA Phoenix	3,187,000 866,700	114,000 295,259	11,841	Bruce E. Babbitt (D) *	3,969,000,000 3,589,000,000	76,334
ARKANSAS Little Rock	2,359,000 178,100	53,187 137,753	9,805	Bill Clinton (D) Winston Bryant (D)	2,739,000,000 2,488,000,000	77,053
CALIFORNIA Sacramento	26,635,000 309,400	158,706 411,047	14,487	George Deukmejian (R) Leo T. McCarthy (D)	43,768,000,000 42,493,000,000	174,033
COLORADO Denver	3,231,000 506,700	104,091 269,594	13,847	Richard D. Lamm (D) Nancy Dick (D)	4,203,000,000 4,062,000,000	75,423
CONNECTICUT Hartford	3,174,000 135,700	5,018 12,997	16,556	William A. O'Neill (D) Joseph L. Fauliso (D)	4,707,000,000 4,427,000,000	19,534
DELAWARE Dover	622,000 23,500	2,044 5,295	13,685	Michael N. Castle (R) S. B. Woo (D)	1,315,000,000 1,072,000,000	5,280
DISTRICT OF COLUMBIA *	626,000	69 178	17,113	Mayor: Marion S. Barry, Jr. (D)		1,102
FLORIDA Tallahassee	11,366,000 116,200	58,664 151,938	12,763	D. Robert Graham (D) Wayne Mixson (D)	10,569,000,000 9,874,000,000	93,074
GEORGIA Atlanta	5,976,000 426,100	58,910 152,575	11,551	Joe Frank Harris (D) Zell B. Miller (D)	6,992,000,000 6,563,000,000	104,955
HAWAII Honolulu	1,054,000 380,000	6,471 16,759	13,042	George R. Ariyoshi (D) John Waihee (D)	2,308,000,000 2,178,000,000	4,297
IDAHO Boise	1,005,000 107,200	83,564 216,431	10,092	John V. Evans (D) David Leroy (R)	1,349,000,000 1,245,000,000	68,447
ILLINOIS Springfield	11,535,000 99,600	56,345 145,933	13,802	James R. Thompson, Jr. (R) George H. Ryan (R)	15,120,000,000 15,004,000,000	134,599
INDIANA Indianapolis	5,499,000 710,300	36,185 93,720	11,717	Robert D. Orr (R) John M. Mutz (R)	6,166,000,000 5,843,000,000	91,736
IOWA Des Moines	2,884,000 191,000	56,275 145,752	12,160	Terry E. Branstad (R) Robert Anderson (D)	4,106,000,000 4,157,000,000	112,289
KANSAS Topeka	2,450,000 118,900	82,277 213,097	13,248	John W. Carlin (D) Tom Docking (D)	2,990,000,000 2,864,000,000	132,265
KENTUCKY Frankfort	3,726,000 26,000	40,409 104,660	10,300	Martha Layne Collins (D) Steven Beshear (D)	5,364,000,000 5,165,000,000	69,150

The material in the following tables is the latest available. As before, it should be noted that the symbol * indicates that the category is not applicable to the area mentioned, and that NA means that the data were not available. The Office of Territorial Affairs was helpful in supplying some data for the table on Outlying Areas.

Railways (Miles)	Aircraft Departures	English-language Daily Newspapers	Public Elementary Schools (K–8): Teachers Students	Public Secondary Schools (9–12): Teachers Students	Colleges and Universities: Institutions Students
4,185	40,751	29	18,534 510,814	14,865 211,087	60 171,381
526	109,945	7	3,400 65,998	2,059 26,920	15 26,045
1,785	98,666	20	18,877 350,961	7,391 152,267	29 213,437
2,724	9,167	31	11,385 304,975	11,856 127,145	35 76,702
6,464	444,409	130	102,865 2,813,524	71,425 1,275,493	273 1,730,847
3,458	160,149	29	16,051 376,775	12,370 165,421	47 172,650
484	25,949	23	11,490 328,574	15,987 149,011	47 164,344
220	231	3	2,461 61,181	2,968 30,225	8 31,945
47	112,853	2	2,053 63,297	2,206 25,546	18 80,367
3,335	348,203	49	40,574 1,044,107	34,966 451,436	85 443,436
4,928	258,195	32	29,564 738,258	19,578 312,601	80 201,453
0	91,442	5	3,809 110,419	2,981 51,822	12 52,065
2,381	17,436	11	4,618 148,363	4,352 57,989	9 42,911
8,971	271,186	87	56,697 1,271,525	29,846 581,791	160 673,084
5,329	56,476	71	22,324 670,440	23,643 313,944	74 256,470
4,699	25,095	37	14,977 333,198	16,156 164,089	60 152,968
7,688	38,485	47	12,911 282,389	10,602 122,833	53 141,709
3,347	31,912	23	21,061 454,931	11,397 192,483	57 146,503

State Capital	Population	Area (sq mi/ sq km)	Per Capita Personal Income	Governor Lieutenant-Governor	Revenue Expenditure	Public Roads (Miles)
LOUISIANA Baton Rouge	4,481,000 246,500	47,752 123,676	$10,808	Edwin W. Edwards (D) Robert L. Freeman (D)	$ 6,947,000,000 7,431,000,000	58,010
MAINE Augusta	1,164,000 22,000	33,265 86,156	10,813	Joseph E. Brennan (D) *	1,685,000,000 1,671,000,000	21,953
MARYLAND Annapolis	4,392,000 31,700	10,460 27,092	14,464	Harry R. Hughes (D) J. Joseph Curran (D)	6,598,000,000 6,921,000,000	27,425
MASSACHUSETTS Boston	5,822,000 570,700	8,284 21,456	14,784	Michael Dukakis (D) *	9,383,000,000 9,332,000,000	33,796
MICHIGAN Lansing	9,088,000 128,000	58,527 151,585	12,607	James J. Blanchard (D) Martha W. Griffiths (D)	16,097,000,000 14,789,000,000	117,467
MINNESOTA St. Paul	4,193,000 267,800	84,402 218,600	13,247	Rudy Perpich (DFL) Marlene Johnson (DFL)	8,074,000,000 6,496,000,000	131,475
MISSISSIPPI Jackson	2,613,000 209,000	47,689 123,515	8,777	Bill Allain (D) Brad Dye (D)	3,346,000,000 3,132,000,000	71,075
MISSOURI Jefferson City	5,029,000 34,600	69,697 180,515	12,151	John Ashcroft (R) Harriet Woods (D)	5,319,000,000 4,780,000,000	118,713
MONTANA Helena	826,000 24,000	147,046 380,846	10,546	Ted Schwinden (D) George Turman (D)	1,376,000,000 1,263,000,000	71,553
NEBRASKA Lincoln	1,606,000 180,400	77,355 200,349	12,430	Robert Kerrey (D) Don McGinley (D)	1,881,000,000 1,807,000,000	91,961
NEVADA Carson City	936,000 32,000	110,561 286,351	13,320	Richard Bryan (D) Robert Cashell (R)	1,696,000,000 1,570,000,000	43,806
NEW HAMPSHIRE Concord	998,000 30,900	9,279 24,031	13,192	John Sununu (R) *	1,167,000,000 1,109,000,000	14,545
NEW JERSEY Trenton	7,562,000 92,300	7,787 20,169	15,440	Thomas H. Kean (R) *	12,604,000,000 11,764,000,000	33,871
NEW MEXICO Santa Fe	1,450,000 55,000	121,593 314,923	10,262	Toney Anaya (D) Mike Runnels (D)	3,343,000,000 2,692,000,000	54,127
NEW YORK Albany	17,783,000 100,000	49,108 127,189	14,318	Mario M. Cuomo (D) *	35,851,000,000 31,921,000,000	109,837
NORTH CAROLINA Raleigh	6,255,000 184,100	52,669 136,412	10,850	James G. Martin (R) Robert P. Jordan 3rd (D)	7,662,000,000 7,232,000,000	92,404
NORTH DAKOTA Bismarck	685,000 44,500	70,702 183,118	12,352	George Sinner (D) Ruth Meiers (D)	1,330,000,000 1,302,000,000	85,811
OHIO Columbus	10,744,000 566,100	41,330 107,043	12,355	Richard F. Celeste (D) *	17,682,000,000 15,901,000,000	112,252
OKLAHOMA Oklahoma City	3,301,000 443,200	69,956 181,185	11,655	George Nigh (D) Spencer Bernard (D)	4,805,000,000 4,772,000,000	110,072
OREGON Salem	2,687,000 92,700	97,073 251,417	11,611	Victor G. Atiyeh (R) *	4,696,000,000 4,356,000,000	133,469
PENNSYLVANIA Harrisburg	11,853,000 53,300	45,308 117,347	12,314	Richard L. Thornburgh (R) William W. Scranton 3rd (R)	17,776,000,000 16,733,000,000	115,601
RHODE ISLAND Providence	968,000 154,100	1,212 3,140	12,820	Edward D. Di Prete (R) Richard Licht (D)	1,835,000,000 1,708,000,000	6,289
SOUTH CAROLINA Columbia	3,347,000 105,000	31,113 80,582	10,116	Richard W. Riley (D) Michael S. Daniel (D)	4,598,000,000 4,229,000,000	63,264
SOUTH DAKOTA Pierre	708,000 12,000	77,116 199,729	11,069	William J. Janklow (R) Lowell C. Hansen 2nd (R)	961,000,000 859,000,000	73,375

Railways (Miles)	Aircraft Departures	English-language Daily Newspapers	Public Elementary Schools (K–8): Teachers Students	Public Secondary Schools (9–12): Teachers Students	Colleges and Universities: Institutions Students
3,127	69,535	26	27,168 561,181	15,011 221,253	32 179,647
2,249	7,879	8	7,554 145,814	5,880 63,939	29 53,347
909	41,371	16	15,071 451,716	19,156 231,775	57 239,232
1,098	90,012	47	17,856 578,306	32,703 300,538	117 423,348
3,600	128,722	48	42,515 1,132,701	18,778 603,180	92 515,760
6,088	99,517	27	18,635 466,579	20,757 238,663	67 214,219
2,574	21,587	22	13,528 327,509	11,427 140,235	42 109,728
5,631	197,250	45	23,371 546,155	22,847 249,298	92 248,329
3,486	26,535	10	6,419 108,268	3,060 45,378	16 37,877
4,755	32,509	19	9,321 185,941	8,227 81,057	28 95,162
1,492	85,449	7	3,375 102,358	3,134 48,084	8 43,768
419	2,847	8	4,796 106,303	5,025 52,727	27 53,143
1,410	98,549	28	37,038 761,194	29,099 386,377	60 314,468
2,061	39,295	18	6,152 191,824	6,349 77,877	20 66,094
3,873	300,785	81	64,836 1,735,517	60,573 909,001	296 1,022,521
2,799	134,524	55	34,981 761,053	19,352 328,553	128 301,675
4,756	14,593	10	4,474 82,321	2,593 34,892	18 37,591
6,854	152,783	91	51,517 1,240,344	45,410 586,956	139 535,592
3,853	50,072	46	15,980 420,913	15,528 170,476	45 174,171
2,940	43,382	20	13,112 307,121	10,510 139,988	45 141,172
6,453	161,679	97	43,897 1,130,767	48,313 607,185	202 545,112
146	6,860	7	3,867 87,789	3,953 48,391	13 70,811
2,524	26,613	17	20,461 423,016	11,862 181,537	62 134,532
2,037	18,109	12	5,667 86,324	2,668 36,736	20 35,015

State Capital	Population	Area (sq mi/ sq km)	Per Capita Personal Income	Governor Lieutenant-Governor	Revenue Expenditure	Public Roads (Miles)
TENNESSEE Nashville	4,762,000 462,500	42,144 109,151	$10,419	Lamar Alexander (R) John S. Wilder (D)	$ 4,783,000,000 4,578,000,000	83,789
TEXAS Austin	16,370,000 436,000	266,807 691,026	12,572	Mark White (D) William P. Hobby (D)	17,400,000,000 15,796,000,000	275,784
UTAH Salt Lake City	1,645,000 164,900	84,899 219,888	9,733	Norman H. Bangerter (R) W. Val Oveson (R)	2,442,000,000 2,304,000,000	46,078
VERMONT Montpelier	535,000 8,300	9,614 24,900	10,802	Madeleine Kunin (D) Peter Smith (R)	900,000,000 890,000,000	13,994
VIRGINIA Richmond	5,706,000 219,100	40,767 105,585	13,254	Charles S. Robb (D) Richard J. Davis (D)	7,540,000,000 6,747,000,000	65,102
WASHINGTON Olympia	4,409,000 28,600	68,139 176,478	12,792	Booth Gardner (D) John A. Cherberg (D)	8,353,000,000 7,908,000,000	85,731
WEST VIRGINIA Charleston	1,936,000 64,000	24,231 62,759	9,728	Arch A. Moore, Jr. (R) *	3,202,000,000 3,046,000,000	34,673
WISCONSIN Madison	4,775,000 174,800	56,153 145,435	12,474	Anthony S. Earl (D) James T. Flynn (D)	8,545,000,000 7,633,000,000	108,225
WYOMING Cheyenne	509,000 47,300	97,809 253,325	12,224	Ed Herschler (D) *	1,597,000,000 1,263,000,000	38,170

OUTLYING AREAS OF THE UNITED STATES

Area Capital	Population	Area (sq mi/ sq km)	Status	Governor Lieutenant-Governor	Revenue Expenditure	Roads (Miles)
AMERICAN SAMOA Pago Pago	35,300 2,732	77 199	Unorganized, unincorporated territory	A. P. Lutali Eni Hunkin	$ 38,410,412 48,464,661	95
GUAM Agaña	119,800 896	209 541	Unincorporated territory	Ricardo J. Bordallo Edward D. Reyes	185,800,000 NA	419
PUERTO RICO San Juan	3,279,000 435,000	3,515 9,103	Commonwealth	Rafael Hernández Colón *	3,895,000,000 3,819,000,000	8,520
TRUST TERRITORY OF THE PACIFIC ISLANDS[1] Capitol Hill, on Saipan Island	155,933 NA	708 1,834	UN trust territory[1]	High Commissioner: Janet J. McCoy[1]	114,100,000 NA	362
VIRGIN ISLANDS Charlotte Amalie	107,500 11,756	133 344	Unincorporated territory	Juan Luis Julio Brady	267,719,000 NA	641

1. The Northern Mariana Islands in 1985 were an internally self-governing part of the Trust Territory of the Pacific Islands. The government of the Northern Marianas was headed by Gov. Pedro P. Tenorio. The capital was Susupe, on Saipan Island. Figures used in the table include the Northern Marianas.

Railways (Miles)	Aircraft Departures	English-language Daily Newspapers	Public Elementary Schools (K–8): Teachers Students	Public Secondary Schools (9–12): Teachers Students	Colleges and Universities: Institutions Students
2,785	99,619	27	24,713 / 587,014	14,696 / 235,043	80 / 207,777
12,917	456,499	107	75,431 / 2,155,012	75,996 / 834,784	157 / 795,741
1,651	62,763	5	8,313 / 281,649	5,558 / 97,416	14 / 103,324
102	5,091	9	2,794 / 63,452	3,378 / 26,964	22 / 31,306
3,596	49,594	38	31,745 / 674,016	24,200 / 292,094	69 / 288,588
4,225	80,300	25	17,098 / 503,551	15,353 / 232,688	50 / 229,639
3,387	8,212	23	10,965 / 263,254	8,445 / 107,997	29 / 83,202
3,850	66,171	35	21,140 / 500,778	18,470 / 273,868	63 / 277,751
2,081	9,055	9	4,100 / 73,861	2,085 / 27,104	8 / 23,844

Railways (Miles)	Aircraft Departures	Daily Newspapers	Public Elementary and Secondary School Teachers	Public School Students: Elementary Secondary	Higher Education: Institutions Students
0	3,728	0	543	6,216 / 2,805	1 / 758
0	5,662	1	1,334	19,331 / 6,918	2 / 3,436
0	11,626	4	32,247	582,564 / 182,782	39 / 155,276
0	2,400	0	2,281	34,105 / 5,518	2 / 736
0	3,647	2	1,665	19,298 / 6,828	1 / 2,602

THE PROVINCES AND TERRITORIES OF CANADA

Province Capital	Population	Area (sq mi/ sq km)	Per Capita Personal Income	Premier Lieutenant-Governor
ALBERTA	2,360,300	255,285	$14,652	Donald Getty
Edmonton	551,300	661,185		Helen Hunley
BRITISH COLUMBIA	2,865,100	366,255	14,339	William R. Bennett
Victoria	66,100	948,596		Robert Gordon Rogers
MANITOBA	1,051,500	251,000	12,063	Howard R. Pawley
Winnipeg	602,000	650,087		Pearl McGonigal
NEW BRUNSWICK	719,200	28,354	10,040	Richard B. Hatfield
Fredericton	66,800	73,436		George F. G. Stanley
NEWFOUNDLAND	580,000	156,185	9,179	Brian Peckford
St. John's	88,000	404,517		William A. Paddon
NORTHWEST TERRITORIES	50,500	1,304,903	14,282[1]	Commissioner:
Yellowknife	12,500	3,379,684		John H. Parker
NOVA SCOTIA	850,000	21,425	10,889	John M. Buchanan
Halifax	114,600	55,491		Alan R. Abraham
ONTARIO	8,700,000	412,582	14,784	David Peterson
Toronto	600,000	1,068,582		John Black Aird
PRINCE EDWARD ISLAND	126.800	2,184	10,056	James M. Lee
Charlottetown	15,600	5,657		Robert Lloyd George MacPhail
QUÉBEC	6,600,000	594,860	12,531	Robert Bourassa
Québec	176,600	1,540,680		Gilles Lamontag
SASKATCHEWAN	1,020,000	251,700	12,686	Grant Devine
Regina	174,500	651,900		Frederick Johnston
YUKON TERRITORY	24,000	186,300	14,282[1]	Commissioner:
Whitehorse	14,800	482,515		Douglas Bell

1. Figure is the combined average for the Northwest Territories and Yukon Territory.

462

The material in this table has been prepared with the assistance of Statistics Canada. It should be noted that all dollar figures are in Canadian dollars.

Revenue Expenditure	Motor Vehicle Registrations	Railways (Miles)	Radio and Television Stations	Daily Newspapers	Elementary and Secondary Schools: Teachers Enrollment	Postsecondary Education: Institutions Enrollment
$ 9,765,000,000 10,000,000,000	1,796,454	2,165	87 14	10	25,300 467,680	23 67,170
8,166,000,000 9,056,000,000	2,083,659	3,512	126 12	18	26,475 524,210	25 57,470
3,122,500,000 3,618,700,000	688,950	2,374	31 6	6	12,120 218,850	15 24,810
2,856,000,000 2,923,000,000	389,458	2,799	33 5	4	7,345 142,810	13 16,830
2,029,500,000 2,102,300,000	199,465	279	49 7	3	8,160 143,080	11 12,500
614,500,000 615,700,000	22,229	0	9 2	0	670 13,410	1 120
2,517,900,000 2,702,500,000	549,639	441	36 6	6	10,500 177,380	23 25,950
25,915,900,000 27,883,200,000	5,181,954	9,280	186 35	47	95,740 1,850,660	52 282,100
431,100,000 435,800,000	71,006	0	5 1	3	1,275 25,070	3 2,640
22,465,000,000 25,640,000,000	2,924,351	2,799	142 45	11	71,240 1,164,740	91 268,500
3,175,000,000 3,467,000,000	694,372	2,496	33 10	5	11,210 215,240	8 22,980
206,000,000 256,000,000	19,111	0	2 1	0	270 4,790	1 200

KEY TO SIGNED ARTICLES

Here is a list of contributors to this Yearbook. The initials at the end of an article are those of the author, or authors, of that article.

A.D., ALASDAIR DRYSDALE, PH.D.
Assistant Professor, University of New Hampshire.

A.L.R., ARTHUR L. ROBINSON, PH.D.
Senior Writer, Research News Section, *Science* Magazine.

A.M., ANN MARTIN, A.B.
Freelance Writer and Editor. Author, *Me and Katie the Pest, Inside Out, Stage Fright.*

A.R., ANSIL RAMSAY, A.B., PH.D.
Professor of Government, St. Lawrence University. Editorial Board Member, *Asian Survey.*

B.B., BRUCE BOWER, B.A., M.A.
Staff Writer, *Science News.*

B.B.S., BONNIE BARRETT STRETCH, A.B., M.S.
Contributing Editor, *Art & Auction;* Columnist, *American Photographer.*

B.G.V., BRUCE G. VANDENBERGH, A.B., M.S., PH.D.
Acting Chairman, Department of Advertising, Michigan State University.

B.J., BRUCE JUDDERY, A.B.
Canberra Correspondent, *Australian Business.*

B.R., BEA RIEMSCHNEIDER, A.B., M.A.
Editor in Chief, *Archaeology.* Associate Trustee, American Schools of Oriental Research.

B.S., BROOKE GRUNDFEST SCHOEPF, PH.D.
Anthropologist and Development Consultant. Former Fulbright Senior Research Scholar, Zimbabwe.

B.V., BOB VERDI, A.B.
Columnist, Chicago *Tribune.*

C.B., CHRISTIE BARTER, A.B.
Music Editor, *Stereo Review.*

C.F., CHARLOTTE FAHN, B.A.
Yearbook Staff Editor.

C.H.A., CALVIN H. ALLEN, JR., A.B., M.A., PH.D.
Associate Professor of History, School of the Ozarks, Mo.

C.S.J.W., CHARLES S. J. WHITE, B.A., M.A., PH.D.
Professor and Chairman, Department of Philosophy and Religion, The American University; former Director of the Center for Asian Studies.

D.B., DON BOHNING, A.B.
Latin American Editor, Miami *Herald.*

D.D., DAVID DOOLING
Research Associate, Essex Corporation; former Science Editor, Huntsville *Times.* Coauthor, *Space Travel—A History.*

D.D.B., DARALICE D. BOLES, A.B., M.ARCH.
Senior Editor, *Progressive Architecture.*

D.E.S., DONALD E. SCHULZ, B.A., PH.D.
Assistant Professor of Political Science, University of Tampa.

D.F., DON FREEMAN
Television Editor and Columnist, San Diego *Union* and Copley News Service.

D.F.A., DONALD F. ANTHROP, PH.D.
Professor of Environmental Studies, San Jose State University. Author, *Noise Pollution.*

D.G., DIANE GRANAT, B.S.J.
Reporter, *Congressional Quarterly Weekly Report.*

D.G.S., DAVID G. SAVAGE, A.B., M.S.
Education Writer, Los Angeles *Times.*

D.L.L., DAVID L. LEWIS, B.S., M.S., M.A., PH.D.
Professor of Business History, Graduate School of Business Administration, University of Michigan.

D.M.P., DAVID M. PHILIPS, A.B.
Sports Writer, Providence *Journal.*

D.P., DON PERETZ, A.B., M.A., PH.D.
Professor of Political Science, State University of New York at Binghamton. Author, *Middle East Today.*

D.R.W., DONALD R. WHITAKER, A.B. Economist, Office of Industry Services, National Marine Fisheries Service. Contributor, *Fishing Gazette.*

D.S., DAVID STAINES, A.B., A.M., PH.D. Professor of English, University of Ottawa. Author, *Tennyson's Camelot: The Idylls of the King and Its Medieval Sources.*

D.S.M., DONALD S. MACDONALD, PH.D. Research Professor of Korean Studies, School of Foreign Service, Georgetown University. Former State Department Foreign Service Officer.

D.W., DAVID P. WERLICH, A.B., A.M., PH.D. Professor of History, Southern Illinois University. Author, *Peru: A Short History.*

D.Y., DONALD YOUNG, B.A., M.A. Yearbook Staff Editor.

E.C.R., EDWARD C. ROCHETTE, B.S. Executive Vice-President, American Numismatic Association.

E.H.B., ELIZABETH H. BECKER, A.B. Free-lance Writer. Former Indochina Correspondent, Washington *Post.*

E.J.F., ERIK J. FRIIS, B.S., M.A. Editor and Publisher, *The Scandinavian–American Bulletin.*

E.J.G., ELLEN J. GREENFIELD, A.B., M.A. Free-lance Writer. Former Textiles Editor, *Women's Wear Daily.*

E.S.K., ELAINE S. KNAPP, B.A. Editor, Council of State Governments

E.W., ED WARD Free-lance Writer, Rolling Stone Press.

F.C., FRANK M. CHITEJI, B.A., M.A., PH.D. Professor of History and Director, African and African-American Studies, Ohio State University. Author, *The Development and Socio-Economic Impact of Transportation in Tanzania from 1884 to Present.*

F.D.S., FREDERICK D. SCHNEIDER, PH.D. Professor of History, Vanderbilt University.

F.L., FRANK LITSKY, B.S. Sports Writer, New York *Times.*

G.D.W., G. DAVID WALLACE, B.A. Money and Banking Editor, *Business Week.* Author, *Money Basics.*

G.F., GREG FRY, B.COMM., M.A. Postdoctoral Fellow, Strategic and Defense Studies Center, Research School of Pacific Studies, Australian National University.

G.H., GARY HANSEN, B.S., M.S., PH.D. Professor of Economics, Utah State University. Director, Utah Center for Productivity and Quality of Working Life.

G.L., GEORGE LAMSON, PH.D. Professor of Economics, Carleton College, Northfield, Minn.

G.M.H., GEOFFREY M. HORN, A.B., M.A. Free-lance Writer. Coauthor, *Bible Stories for Children.*

H.C.H., HAROLD C. HINTON, PH.D. Professor of Political Science and International Affairs, George Washington University. Editor, *The People's Republic of China, 1949–1979: A Documentary Survey.*

H.W.H., HARRY W. HENDERSON, A.B. Free-lance Writer. Former Writer-Economist, U.S. Department of Agriculture.

I.A.A., IAN A. ANDERSON, A.B. Publications Director, U.S. Figure Skating Association.

I.C.B., IRIRANGI COATES BLOOMFIELD, A.B., M.A., PH.D. Lecturer and Writer. Former United Nations Delegate.

I.K., INDULIS KEPARS, B.A. Chief Reference Librarian, Australian Studies, National Library of Australia.

J.A., JONATHAN ALTER, A.B. General Editor, *Newsweek* Magazine.

J.A.P., JOHN A. PETROPULOS, PH.D. Professor of History, Amherst College. Author, *Politics and Statecraft in the Kingdom of Greece.*

J.A.R., JAMES A. ROTHERHAM, A.B., M.A., M.A.L.D., PH.D. Senior Specialist for Human Resource Programs, Committee on the Budget, U.S. House of Representatives.

J.B., JOHN BEAUFORT Contributing Drama Critic, *Christian Science Monitor.*

J.C., JAMES CARPER, B.S. Managing Editor, *Professional Builder.*

J.C.L., JEAN CAFFEY LYLES, A.B. Protestant Editor, *The Christian Century.* Contributing Editor, *The Wittenberg Door.*

J.D., JOHN IJAMIS, PH.D. Professor of Political Science, Portland State University. Consultant, U.S. Department of State.

J.F., JULIE FREDERIKSE, A.B. Southern Africa Correspondent, National Public Radio.

J.F., Jr. JOHN FORAN, JR., A.B., M.A. Teaching Assistant and Doctoral Candidate in Sociology, University of California, Berkeley.

J.F.H., JERRY F. HOUGH, PH.D. Professor of Political Science, Duke University. Staff Member, Brookings Institution. Author, *Soviet Leadership in Transition.*

J.F.H., III, JEREMIAH F. HEALY, III, A.B., J.D. Professor, New England School of Law, Boston. Free-lance Writer.

J.F.J., JAMES F. JEKEL, M.D., M.P.H. Professor of Epidemiology and Public Health, Yale University Medical School.

J.F.S., JOANNE F. SCHNEIDER, A.B., M.A., PH.D. Assistant Professor of History, Wheaton College.

J.G.D., JOHN G. DEEDY, A.B., M.A. Former Managing Editor, *Commonweal.* Contributor, New York *Times.* Author, *The New Nuns: Serving Where the Spirit Leads.*

J.H., JOHN HAY, A.B. Editorial Board Member, Ottawa *Citizen.*

J.H.B., JAMES H. BUDD Free-lance Writer Based in Mexico. Correspondent, Murdoch Magazines and Gemini News Service.

J.J.Z., JOSEPH J. ZASLOFF, A.B., M.A., PH.D. Professor of Political Science, University of Pittsburgh. Specialist in Southeast Asian Affairs.

J.L., JOHN LUTER, A.B. Professor and Chairman, Journalism Department, University of Hawaii.

J.M., JOHN MUTTER, B.A. Associate News Editor, *Publishers Weekly.*

J.O.S., JAMES O. SAFFORD III, A.B., M.A., PH.D. Instructor of History, The Shipley School, Bryn Mawr, Pa.

J.R., JANET RALOFF, B.S.J., M.S.J. Policy and Technology Editor, *Science News.*

J.S.I., JACQUELINE S. ISMAEL, B.A., M.A., PH.D. Associate Professor of Social Welfare, University of Calgary; Author, *Kuwait: Social Change in Historical Perspective.*

J.T.S., JAMES T. SHERWIN, A.B., LL.B. Former New York State, Intercollegiate, and U.S. Speed Chess Champion and International Master.

J.W.K., JOHN W. KAMPA, B.S. Former Editorial Board Member, *Minkus World-Wide Stamp Catalog* and *New American Stamp Catalog.*

K.C., KATHY CASEY, B.A., M.L.S. Yearbook Staff Editor.

K.F.R., KARL F. REULING Managing Editor, *Ballet News.*

K.J.B., KIRK J. BEATTIE, A.B., M.A. Assistant Professor of Government, Simmons College.

K.M., KENT MULLINER, B.S., M.A. Assistant to the Director, Ohio University Libraries.

K.W.G., KENNETH W. GRUNDY, A.B., M.A., PH.D. Professor of Political Science, Case Western Reserve University.

L.A.K., LAWRENCE A. KLETTER, A.B., M.A., J.D. Certificate in Middle Eastern Studies, Columbia University. Associate, Nutter, McClennen & Fish.

L.D., LARRY DIAMOND, B.A., M.A., PH.D. Senior Research Fellow, Hoover Institution.

L.G., LOIS GOTTESMAN, A.B., M.A. Free-lance Writer; Former Research Analyst, American Jewish Committee.

465

L.J.R., LEIF J. ROBINSON
Editor, *Sky & Telescope.*

L.L.P., LARRY L. PIPPIN, A.B., M.A., PH.D.
Professor of Political Science, Elbert Covell College, University of the Pacific.

L.R., LINDA RICHTER, A.B., M.A., PH.D.
Assistant Professor of Political Science, Kansas State University. Author, *Land Reform and Tourism Development: Policy-Making in the Philippines.*

L.R.H., LINDLEY R. HIGGINS, P.E., A.B., M.S.
Consulting Engineer. President, Piedmont Publications. Author, *Handbook of Construction Equipment Maintenance and Maintenance Engineering Handbook.*

L.S.G., LOVETT S. GRAY, A.B.
Free-lance Writer and Consultant. Former Editor, National Council on Crime and Delinquency.

L.W.G., LOWELL W. GUDMUNDSON, A.B., M.A., PH.D.
Assistant Professor of History, University of Oklahoma.

L.Z., LAWRENCE ZIRING, B.S., M.I.A., PH.D.
Director, Institute of Government and Politics, Professor of Political Science, Western Michigan University. Author, *Pakistan: The Enigma of Political Development* and *The Asian Political Dictionary.*

M.C.H., MICHAEL C. HUDSON, A.B., M.A., PH.D.
Professor of International Relations and Government; Director, Center for Contemporary Arab Studies, Georgetown University. Author, *Arab Politics: The Search for Legitimacy.*

M.D., MICHAEL DIRDA, A.B., M.A., PH.D.
Staff Editor, *The Washington Post Book World.*

M.D.H., M. DONALD HANCOCK, PH.D.
Professor of Political Science, Vanderbilt University.

M.G., MURIEL GRINDROD, A.B.
Author, *Italy, Rebuilding of Italy.*

M.Gr., MILTON GREENBERG, A.B., M.A., PH.D.
Provost, The American University. Coauthor, *The American Political Dictionary, Political Science Dictionary.*

M.G.G., M. GRANT GROSS, A.B., M.S., PH.D.
Director, Division of Ocean Sciences, National Science Foundation. Author, *Oceanography: A View of the Earth.*

M.L., MIKE LITTWIN
Sports Writer, Los Angeles *Times.*

M.S.B., MICHAEL S. BAKER, A.B., M.A.
Certificate in East Asian Studies, Columbia University.

M.W., MARGARET WILLY, F.R.S.L.
Lecturer, City Literary Institute, London. Lecturer, Morley College, London. Poetry Collected in *The Invisible Sun, Every Star a Tongue.*

N.J.P., NEALE J. PEARSON, B.S., M.S., PH.D.
Professor of Political Science, Texas Tech University.

N.M.R., NATHAN M. REISS, PH.D.
Associate Professor of Meteorology, Cook College, Rutgers University.

N.P., NEAL PRONEK, B.B.A.
Managing Editor, *Tropical Fish Hobbyist.*

N.P.N., NANCY PEABODY NEWELL, A.B.
Coauthor, *The Struggle for Afghanistan.*

P.G., PAUL GARDNER
Free-lance Writer. Author, *The Simplest Game, Nice Guys Finish Last.* Commentator, NBC Soccer Telecasts.

P.H.C., PARRIS H. CHANG, PH.D.
Professor of Political Science, Chairman of Asian Area Studies, Pennsylvania State University. Author, *Power and Policy in China.*

P.J.M., PAUL J. MAGNARELLA, A.M., PH.D.
Professor of Anthropology, University of Florida. Author, *Tradition and Change in a Turkish Town, The Peasant Venture.*

P.L.W., PENELOPE L. WANG, A.B., M.A.
Senior Editorial Assistant, *Newsweek.*

P.S., PATRICIA STAMP, B.A., M.L.S.
Associate Professor, York University; Free-lance Writer.

P.W., PETER WINN, A.B., PH.D.
Associate Professor of History, Tufts University. Senior Research Fellow, Research Institute on International Change, Columbia University.

R.A.M., ROBERT A. MORTIMER, A.B., M.A., PH.D.
Professor of Political Science, Haverford College. Author, *The Third World Coalition in International Politics.*

R.A.P., RICHARD A. PIERCE, PH.D.
Professor Emeritus of History, Queen's University, Ontario. Author, *Eastward to Empire: Exploration and Conquest on the Russian Open Frontier to 1750.*

R.B., RICHARD E. BISSELL, A.B., M.A., PH.D.
Executive Editor, *Washington Quarterly.* Adjunct Professor of Government, Georgetown University.

R.C., ROBERT I. CRANE, B.A., M.A., PH.D.
Ford-Maxwell Professor of South Asian History, Syracuse University. Coauthor, *Self-study Guide on Urban Problems and Urbanism in South Asia.* Contributor, *Journal of Asian Studies, South Asia in Review.*

R.D.S., ROBERT D. SCHULZINGER, B.A., M. PHIL., PH.D.
Professor of History, University of Colorado. Author, *The Wise Men of Foreign Affairs: The History of the Council on Foreign Relations, American Diplomacy in the Twentieth Century.*

R.E.B., ROGER E. BILSTEIN, B.A., M.A., PH.D.
Professor of History, University of Houston at Clear Lake City. Author, *Stages to Saturn: A Technological History of the Apollo/Saturn Launch Vehicles* and *Flight in America, 1900–1983.*

R.E.K., ROGER E. KANET, PH.B., A.B., M.A., A.M., PH.D.
Professor and Head of Political Science Department, University of Illinois at Urbana-Champaign. Editor, *Background to Crisis: Policies and Politics in Gierek's Poland.*

R.F., ROSALIE FADEM, B.A.
Yearbook Staff Editor.

R.J.K., ROBERT J. KURSAR, A.B.
Associate Editor, *Traffic World* Magazine.

R.J.L., ROBERT J. LaMARCHE, A.B.
Senior Editor, *TENNIS* Magazine.

R.J.W., RICHARD J. WILLEY, A.B., M.A., PH.D.
Professor of Political Science, Vassar College. Author, *Democracy in the West German Trade Unions.* Contributor, New York *Times.*

R.L.B., RICHARD L. BUTWELL, A.B., M.A., D. PHIL.
President and Professor of Political Science, California State University, Dominguez Hills. Author, *Southeast Asia, A Political Introduction; U Nu of Burma.*

R.L.K., ROBERT L. KOVACH, M.A., PH.D.
Professor of Geophysics, School of Earth Sciences, Stanford University.

R.M., R. J. MAY, M.E.C., D. PHIL.
Senior Fellow, Research School of Pacific Studies, Australian National University. Former Director, Institute of Applied Social and Economic Research, Papua New Guinea.

R.O.F., ROBERT O. FREEDMAN, PH.D.
Dean and Professor of Political Science, School of Graduate Studies, Baltimore Hebrew College. Editor, *Israel in the Begin Era.*

R.S., ROBERT SCHWARZ, A.B., M.A., PH.D.
Professor of Philosophy, Florida Atlantic University. Contributor, *Socialism and Anti-Semitism in Austria.*

S.A., SUSAN AVALLONE, B.A., M.S.
Editorial Coordinator, *Library Journal.* Editor, Columbia University *Library School News.*

S.A.W., STANLEY A. WOLPERT, A.B., A.M., PH.D.
Professor of History, University of California, Los Angeles, Author, *A New History of India.*

S.C., STEVE COHEN, B.A.
Executive Editor, *Ski* Magazine.

S.E., SANFORD ELWITT, PH.D.
Professor of History, University of Rochester. Author, *The Making of the Third Republic, The Republic Defended.* Contributor, *Journal of Modern History, French Historical Studies.*

S.F., SHIRLEY FLEMING, A.B., M.A.
Editor, *Musical America.*

S.G., SHAV GLICK, A.B.
Motor Racing Writer, Los Angeles *Times.*

S.L.D., SPENCER L. DAVIDSON
Associate Editor, *Time* Magazine.

S.M., SIEGFRIED MANDEL, A.B., M.A., PH.D.
Professor of English and Comparative Literature, University of Colorado. Author, *Contemporary European Novelists.*

S.M.G., SAM M. GOLDAPER.
Sports Reporter, New York *Times.* New York Area Chairman, Pro Basketball Writers Association.

S.M.H. STEPHEN M. HEAD, M.A., PH.D.
Lecturer in Zoology, University of the West Indies, Jamaica.

S.R., STEVE C. ROPP, PH.D.
Professor of Political Science, University of Wyoming. Author, *Panamanian Politics: From Guarded Nation to National Guard.*

S.W., SUSAN WALTON, A.B., M.A.
Free-lance Science and Education Writer.

T.D., THOMAS DEFRANK, B.A., M.A.
Deputy Bureau Chief and White House Correspondent, *Newsweek* Magazine.

T.F., TISSA FERNANDO, A.B., D. PHIL.
Associate Professor of Sociology, University of British Columbia. Co-editor, *Modern Sri Lanka.*

T.G.S., THEODORE G. STAVROU
Yearbook Staff Editor.

T.H.M., THOMAS H. MAUGH, II, PH.D.
Science Writer, Los Angeles *Times.* Coauthor, *Energy and the Future, Seeds of Destruction: The Science Report on Cancer Research.*

T.I., TAREQ Y. ISMAEL, A.B., M.A., PH.D.
Professor of Political Science, University of Calgary. Author, *The Middle East in World Politics: A Study in Contemporary International Relations.*

T.J.O.H., T.J.O. HICKEY
Member, Editorial Staff, *The Times* of London.

T.McC., TOM McCOLLISTER, A.B.
Sports Writer, Atlanta *Constitution.*

V.L., VINCE LOVETT
Public Information Specialist, Bureau of Indian Affairs, U.S. Department of the Interior.

W.C.C., WILLIAM C. CROMWELL, A.B., M.A., PH.D.
Professor of International Relations, American University. Author, *The Eurogroup and NATO.*

W.D.M., WILLIAM D. MARBACH, B.A., M.A.
General Editor, *Newsweek* Magazine.

W.F., WILLIAM FREDERICK, PH.D.
Assistant Professor of History, Ohio University.

W.L., WILLIAM LEGGETT, A.B.
Senior Writer, *Sports Illustrated.*

W.M., WILLIAM MINTER, PH.D.
Staff Writer, Africa News Service. Author, *King Solomon's Mines Revisited: Western Interests, Images, and Policies in Southern Africa.*

W.N., WILLIAM NEIKIRK, A.B.
Economics Correspondent, Washington Bureau, Chicago *Tribune.*

W.W., WILLIAM WOLF, A.B.
Film Critic, Gannett News Service. Lecturer, New York University and St. John's University. Author, *Landmark Films, The Marx Brothers.*

PICTURE CREDITS

9 Shostal Associates **10** Click/Chicago **11** Illustrations by Martin Eichtersheimer **12** Canapress Photo **13** *Top:* James P. Rowan/Click/Chicago; *Bottom:* Gary *Post Tribune* **14** F. Prazak/Miller Services **15** *Top:* Library of Congress; *Bottom:* Doris De Witt/Click/Chicago **16** Miller Services **17** *Top:* Wide World; *Bottom:* Joe Traver **18** Robert Frerck/Click/Chicago **19** Cathlyn Melloan/Click/Chicago **20** Dick Pietrzyk/Click/Chicago **22** William Thompson **24** © Bill Grimes/*Time* Magazine **25** David Madison/Duomo **27** *All:* Carl Boenish/Photochuting Enterprises **28** Lanny Johnson/Woodfin Camp **29** Jean Keppler/Rainbow **30** J. Irwin/Black Star **31** Sandy Macys/Focus on Sports **32** Focus on Sports **33** Bill Kwok/UPI/Bettmann Newsphotos **34** Marka/Focus on Sports **38** Randy Taylor/Sygma **39** Skyline Features **40** Vic Delucia/The New York *Times* **41** Hank Morgan/Rainbow **42** *Both:* J. Ross Baughman/Visions **43** *Top:* Culver Pictures; *Bottom:* E. R. Degginger/Bruce Coleman Inc. **44** John Bowden/© *Discover* Magazine **45** NASA **46** Newsday **47** Wide World **48** *Both:* NOAA **50** UPI/Bettmann Newsphotos **51** Photo News/Gamma-Liaison **52** Tannenbaum/Sygma **53** *Both:* UPI/Bettmann Newsphotos **54** Reuters/Bettmann Newsphotos **55** Pablo Bartholomew/Gamma-Liaison **56** Reuters/Bettmann Newsphotos **58** Roger Ressmeyer/Wheeler Pictures **61** Sebastiao Salgado/Magnum **62** Reuters/Bettmann Newsphotos **64** Ron Jaap/Midland *Reporter-Telegram* **65** *Left:* J. P. Laffont/Sygma; *Right:* UPI/Bettmann Newsphotos **70** Wide World **71** George Becker **72** PA Consulting Services, Inc. **73** Kohn Pedersen Fox Associates **74** John Nye/Photo Trends **76** National Gallery of Art **77** Giancarlo Botti/Sygma **78** The Museum of Modern Art **79** Kim Steele/*Time* Magazine **80** *Top:* Science Photo Library/Photo Researchers; *Inset:* Jacques Chenet/*Newsweek* **83** Pete Souza/The White House **84** Jean Guichard/Sygma **86** UPI/Bettmann Newsphotos **89** Reprinted with permission from the Minneapolis *Star & Tribune* **90** *Left:* Mary Hagler/Black Star; *Right:* Pamela Price/Picture Group **93** Wide World **95** Photo News/Gamma-Liaison **96** UPI/Bettmann Newsphotos **97** Jeff Rotman **99** *Top:* Alain Keler/Sygma; *Right:* Claudio Edinger/Gamma-Liaison **101** Alain Nogues/Sygma **103–104** Canapress Photo **105** Brian Willer **106** K. Lozoway/Gamma-Liaison **109** Don Renner **111** Tass from Sovfoto **112** Carlos Carrion/Sygma **115** *Top:* J. Ross Baughman/Visions; *Bottom:* Dagmar Fabricius **116** Wide World **118** Mary Ann Carter/*Time* magazine **120** El Espectador/Sygma **121** Gamma-Liaison **124** Michael Nichols/Magnum **127** Timothy A. Murphy/*U.S. News & World Report* **128** George Tames/The New York *Times* **133** *Left:* Ralph Fitzgerald/Picture Group; *Right:* Wide World **134–135** UPI/Bettmann Newsphotos **137** Wide World **140** Martha Swope **141** © Linda Vartoogian **144–145** Reuters/Bettmann Newsphotos **146** *Top:* The Bettmann Archive; *Right:* Woods Hole Oceanographic Institution **148** Zigy Kaluzny/Gamma-Liaison **149** Dirck Halstead/*Time* Magazine **150** *Bottom:* Marty Katz; *Inset:* Cynthia Johnson/*Time* Magazine **154** Boston Latin School **155** *Top:* A. Tannenbaum/Sygma; *Bottom:* UPI/Bettmann Newsphotos **157** Reuters/Bettmann Newsphotos **160** Agence France-Presse **162–164** UPI/Bettmann Newsphotos **166** Frank Murray **169** W. Campbell/Sygma **171** T. Westenberger/Sygma **172** *Left:* P. Vauthey/Sygma; *Right:* Daniel Simon/Gamma-Liaison **175** *Top:* Habans/Philippot/Sygma; *Bottom:* Tristan Siegmann/Gamma-Liaison **176** Eric Preau/Sygma **177** Eastfoto **180** Ghislaine Morel/Gamma-Liaison **182** John Voos/Times Newspapers Ltd. **183** Syndication International/Photo Trends **184–185** Wide World **187** Sygma **188** *Left:* Jim Pozarik/Gamma-Liaison; *Right:* Paul Harris/Outline **191** UPI/Bettmann Newsphotos **192** Wide World **195** Cindy Karp/*Time* Magazine **198** Sandro Tucci/Gamma-Liaison **201** Dan Budnik/The New York *Times* **203** The New York *Times* **205** Ali Laghaee/Gamma-Liaison **207** Jacques Pavlovsky/Sygma **208** Reuters/Bettmann Newsphotos **209** Milner/Sygma **211** Wide World **212** Giansanti/Sygma **213** Thierry Rannou/Gamma-Liaison **215** Robin Moyer/*Time* Magazine **216** Reuters/Bettmann Newsphotos **218** *Left:* Robert Maass/Photoreporters; *Right:* James Colburn/Photoreporters **220** Wide World **223** UPI/Bettmann Newsphotos **225** Alain Nogues/Sygma **226** Frank Vieljeux/Sygma **228** American Library Association **231** James D. Wilson/*Newsweek* **234** Dr. Ronald H. Cohn/The Gorilla Foundation **235** *Both:* Larry Burr/Gamma-Liaison **236** Jim Brandenberg **238** Dean Abramson/The New York *Times* **239** Roger Garwood **240** J. Williamson/First Light **241** Sydney Goldstein **243** Ruby Washington/The New York *Times* **244** Dominique Nabokov/Gamma-Liaison **245** From *Saint George and the Dragon*, retold by Margaret Hodges and illustrated by Trina Schart Hyman; illustration © 1984 by Trina Schart Hyman, by permission of Little, Brown & Company. **249** Nancy Pierce **251** Sergio Dorantes/Sygma **253** Reuters/Bettmann Newsphotos **254** *Both:* Boccon Gibod/Black Star **256** Wide World **257** courtesy University of California, Lawrence Livermore National Laboratory **259** Cynthia Johnson/*Time* Magazine **261** Peter Jordan/Gamma-Liaison **262** © Peters; 1985 Dayton *Daily News*/United Features Syndicate **264** Eddie Adams/Gamma-Liaison **265** Documents/Gamma-Liaison **266** Nancy Moran/Sygma **267** J. Bryson/Sygma **268** Nancy Ellison/Sygma **270** Neal Preston/Camera 5 **271** *Top:* N. Benson/Gamma-Liaison; *Bottom:* Anthony Suau/Black Star **272** Trebitz/Gamma-Liaison **273** Morris/Camera Press/Photo Trends **274** J. Heffernan **275** *Left:* Staatsbibliothek Berlin Bildarchiv (Handke); *Right:* courtesy National Portrait Gallery **278** Gianni Giansanti/Sygma **281** Claudio Urraca/Sygma **285** Fred R. Conrad/The New York *Times* **286** Henry Grossman **287** Barden/Ballantine Books **288** George Tames/The New York *Times* **289–290** Phototeque **292** UPI/Bettmann Newsphotos **293** The New York *Times* **294** *Top:* UPI/Bettmann Newsphotos; *Bottom:* Phototeque **295** Jacques Prayer/Gamma-Liaison **296** Movie Star News **297** Wide World **298** *Top:* Phototeque; *Bottom:* The New York *Times* **301** Jacques Langevin/Sygma **305** Reuters/Bettmann Newsphotos **306–307** UPI/Bettmann Newsphotos **308** *Left:* C. Schachmes/Sygma; *Right:* Andrew Clark/Office of the Prime Minister (Canada) **309** Wide World **310** Hemsey/Gamma-Liaison **311** *Left:* UPI/Bettmann Newsphotos; *Right:* Daniel Simon/Gamma-Liaison **312** Phototeque **313–314** UPI/Bettmann Newsphotos **315** Georges De Keerle/Gamma-Liaison **316** Ted Thai/*Time* Magazine **317** Ross-Marino/Sygma **318** © Jim Merrithew/Picture Group **319** Jason Bleibtreu/Gamma-Liaison **320** Gail Harvey **321** *Top:* Reuters/Bettmann Newsphotos; *Bottom:* Judy Sloan/Gamma-Liaison **322** Focus on Sports **324** Carrion/Sygma **325** UPI/Bettmann Newsphotos **326** Reuters/Bettmann Newsphotos **327** © 1985 Estate of Andre Kertész **328** International Museum of Photography **329** © Estate of Bill Brandt **331** Sygma/Interpress **333** UPI/Bettmann Newsphotos **335** Reuters/Bettmann Newsphotos **336** Wide World **337** Alain Morvan/Gamma-Liaison **339** Andrew Sacks/Black Star **340** *Left:* Wide World **342** Nicholas Latimer **343** UPI/Bettmann Newsphotos **345–346** Gianni Giansanti/Sygma **349** *Both:* Barry Staver/*People Weekly*/© 1985 Time, Inc. **350** © Anne Frank Center **351** Neal Boenzi/The New York *Times* **353** William E. Sauro/The New York *Times* **355** Edward/Gamma-Liaison **356** The Bettmann Archive **358** A. Tannenbaum/Sygma **360–361** UPI/Bettmann Newsphotos **363** Gamma-Liaison **364** Reuters/Bettmann Newsphotos **366–367** Focus on Sports **370** UPI/Bettmann Newsphotos **371** Focus on Sports **372** Wide World **373** Steven E. Sutton/Duomo **374** Dave Cannon/Duomo **375–377** Focus on Sports **378–379** Dave Cannon/Duomo **380** *Top:* Trevor Jones/Duomo; *Bottom:* Adam J. Stoltman/Duomo **381** Gerard Vandystadt/*Sports Illustrated* **382** Barton Silverman/The New York *Times* **383** Sandro Tucci/Gamma-Liaison **384** John W. Kampa **387** *Top:* UPI/Bettmann Newsphotos; *Bottom:* Wide World **390** UPI/Bettmann Newsphotos **391** Tomi Sica/Gamma-Liaison **392** Gamma-Liaison **395** John Rossino/courtesy Lockheed Georgia Company **398** Nancy Ellison/Sygma **400** © 1985 National Broadcasting Company, Inc. **401** Rick Browne/Picture Group **402** © 1985 National Broadcasting Company, Inc. **404–405** © 1985 Martha Swope **406** Wide World **407** Sara Krulwich/The New York *Times* **408** Wide World **411** courtesy Sea-Land Corporation **414** Tass from Sovfoto **415** Jose R. Lopez/The New York *Times* **417** *Both:* Reuters/Bettmann Newsphotos **419** Adam Stottman/Duomo **422** Penny Ann Dolin/The New York *Times* **425** Sygma **426** *Top:* Alain Nogues/Sygma; *Bottom:* Reuters/Bettmann Newsphotos **428** Wollman/Gamma-Liaison **429** E. Adams/Gamma-Liaison **430** chart by Corinne Abbazia/Hekker Graphics **431** Wide World **433** UPI/Bettmann Newsphotos **435** A. Tannenbaum/Sygma

INDEX TO THE
1986 YEARBOOK
EVENTS OF 1985

INTRODUCTION

This index is a comprehensive listing of persons, organizations, and events that are discussed in the 1986 Yearbook. Entries in **boldface** letters indicate subjects on which the Yearbook has an individual article. Entries in lightface type indicate individual references within articles. In either type of entry, the letters a and b refer, respectively, to the left and right column of the page cited. If no letter follows a page number, the reference is to text that is printed across the full width of a page. Only the first significant mention of a subject in a given article has been included in the index.

In a main entry such as **Australia:** 85a, the first number refers to the page on which the article begins. The succeeding lightface page numbers refer to other text discussions in the volume. The first number in lightface entries, when not in numerical order, will similarly provide the most extensive information on the subject. Subtitles following major entries refer to further references on the main subject, as in **Congress of the United States:** 125a; Elections, 159a. In the case of comprehensive articles such as the **United States of America,** reference is made to the page location of the beginning of the article. The discussion of foreign relations of the United States in that article may be augmented by reference to separate articles on the countries and international organizations concerned.

When an entry is followed by the abbreviation **illus.,** the reference is to a caption and picture on the page mentioned. When a text mention and an illustration of the same subject fall within the same article, only the text location is included in the Index.

LIST OF ABBREVIATIONS USED IN THE INDEX

NATO   North Atlantic Treaty Organization
OPEC   Organization of Petroleum Exporting Countries
PLO   Palestine Liberation Organization
U.N.   United Nations
U.S.   United States
U.S.S.R.   Union of Soviet Socialist Republics

473